ESSENTIALS OF ECONOMICS

ESSENTIALS OF ECONOMICS

Seventh edition

John Sloman
The Economics Network, University of Bristol
Visiting Professor, University of the West of England

Dean Garratt
Nottingham Business School

PEARSON

Harlow, England • London • New York • Boston • San Francisco • Toronto • Sydney
Auckland • Singapore • Hong Kong • Tokyo • Seoul • Taipei • New Delhi
Cape Town • São Paulo • Mexico City • Madrid • Amsterdam • Munich • Paris • Milan

Pearson Education Limited
Edinburgh Gate
Harlow CM20 2JE
United Kingdom
Tel: +44 (0)1279 623623
Web: www.pearson.com/uk

First edition published 1998 (print)
Second edition published 2001 (print)
Third edition published 2004 (print)
Fourth edition published 2007 (print)
Fifth edition published 2010 (print)
Sixth edition published 2013 (print and electronic)
Seventh edition published 2016 (print and electronic)

ISBN: 978-1-292-08224-0 (print)
       978-1-292-08231-8 (PDF)
       978-1-292-08225-7 (eText)
       978-1-292-08232-5 (ePub)

British Library Cataloguing-in-Publication Data
A catalogue record for this book is available from the British Library

Library of Congress Cataloguing-in-Publication Data
A catalogue record for this book is available from the Library of Congress

10 9 8 7 6 5 4 3 2 1
19 18 17 16

Front cover images © John Sloman
Typeset in Stone Serif ITC Pro 8/12 by Lumina Datamatics
Printed and bound by L.E.G.O. S.p.A., Italy

NOTE THAT ANY PAGE CROSS REFERENCES REFER TO THE PRINT EDITION

About the authors

John Sloman is Visiting Fellow at the University of Bristol and Associate of the Economics Network (www.economicsnetwork.ac.uk) a UK-wide organisation, where, until his retirement in 2012, he was Director. The Economics Network is based at the University of Bristol and provides a range of services designed to promote and share good practice in learning and teaching economics. The Network is supported by grants from the Royal Economic Society, the Scottish Economic Society and university economic departments and units from across the UK.

John is also visiting professor at the University of the West of England, Bristol, where, from 1992 to 1999, he was Head of School of Economics. He taught at UWE until 2007.

John has taught a range of courses, including economic principles on social science and business studies degrees, development economics, comparative economic systems, intermediate macroeconomics and managerial economics. He has also taught economics on various professional courses.

He is also the co-author with Alison Wride and Dean Garratt of *Economics* (Pearson Education, 9th edition 2015),

with Dean Garratt, Jon Guest and Elizabeth Jones of *Economics for Business* (Pearson Education, 7th edition 2016) and with Elizabeth Jones of *Essential Economics for Business* (4th edition 2014). Translations or editions of the various books are available for a number of different countries with the help of co-authors around the world.

John is very interested in promoting new methods of teaching economics, including group exercises, experiments, role playing, computer-aided learning and use of audience response systems and podcasting in teaching. He has organised and spoken at conferences for both lecturers and students of economics throughout the UK and in many other countries.

As part of his work with the Economics Network he has contributed to its two sites for students and prospective students of economics: Studying Economics (www.studyingeconomics.ac.uk) and Why Study Economics? (www.whystudyeconomics.ac.uk)

From March to June 1997, John was a visiting lecturer at the University of Western Australia. In July and August 2000, he was again a visiting lecturer at the University of Western Australia and also at Murdoch University in Perth.

In 2007, John received a Lifetime Achievement Award as 'outstanding teacher and ambassador of economics' presented jointly by the Higher Education Academy, the Government Economic Service and the Scottish Economic Society.

Dean Garratt is a Principal Lecturer in Economics at Nottingham Business School (NBS), Assistant Head of Economics and the course leader for the School's MSc Economics programme. In 2014/15 Dean worked as a Principal Teaching Fellow in Economics at the University of Warwick having previously been at NBS from 2001, including a period as course leader for the undergraduate economics courses.

Dean teaches economics at a variety of levels to students both on economics courses and non-economics courses. He is passionate about encouraging students to communicate economics more intuitively, to deepen their interest in economics and to apply economics to a range of issues.

Earlier in his career Dean worked as an economic assistant at both HM Treasury and at the Council of Mortgage Lenders. While at these institutions Dean was researching

and briefing on a variety of issues relating to the household sector and to the housing and mortgage markets.

Dean is a Senior Fellow of the Higher Education Academy and an Associate of the Economics Network helping to promote high-quality teaching practice. Dean has been involved in several projects promoting a problem-based approach in the teaching of economics.

In 2006 Dean was awarded the Outstanding Teaching Prize by the Economics Network. The award recognises exemplary teaching practice that deepens and inspires interest in economics. In 2013, Dean won the student-nominated Nottingham Business School teacher of the year award.

Dean is an academic assessor for the Government Economic Service (GES). In this role he helps to assess potential recruits to the GES with particular focus on the ability of candidates to articulate their understanding of economics and its applications.

Outside of work, Dean is an avid watcher of most sports. Having been born in Leicester, he is a season ticket holder at both Leicester City Football Club and Leicestershire County Cricket Club.

Brief contents

Detailed contents

Part C MACROECONOMICS

Part D **INTERNATIONAL ECONOMICS**

Custom publishing

Custom publishing allows academics to pick and choose content from one or more textbooks for their course and combine it into a definitive course text.

Here are some common examples of custom solutions which have helped over 1000 courses across Europe:

■ different chapters from across our publishing imprints combined into one book;
■ lecturer's own material combined together with textbook chapters or published in a separate booklet;
■ third-party cases and articles that you are keen for your students to read as part of the course;
■ any combination of the above.

The Pearson Education custom text published for your course is professionally produced and bound – just as you would expect from any Pearson Education text. Since many of our titles have online resources accompanying them we can even build a Custom website that matches your course text.

If you are teaching a first year Economics course you may have a large teaching team with different lecturers teaching the micro and macroeconomics sections. Do you find that it can be difficult to agree on one textbook? If you do, you might find combining the macro and micro halves from different Pearson textbooks a useful solution. You may teach a mixed ability class and would like to be able to provide some advanced material from Sloman's larger economics text or perhaps you take more of a business focus where chapters from Sloman's *Economics for Business* might be useful.

Custom publishing has enabled adopters of this text to employ these different solutions.

If, once you have had time to review this title, you feel Custom publishing might benefit you and your course, please do get in contact. However minor, or major the change – we can help you out.

For more details on how to make your chapter selection for your course please go to www.pearsoned.co.uk/sloman and select the custom publishing link.

You can contact us at: **www.pearsoncustom.co.uk** or via your local representative at: **www.pearsoned.co.uk/replocator**.

Student Resources

General Resources (open access)

- News Blog site
  - Current News Articles with Questions
  - Archive Searchable by Chap or Month
  - Hotlinks to over 200 sites
  - Animated Models with Audio (demo)

MyEconLab (access using pincode in book)

Homework Quizzes and Tests

- Study Plan (exercises)
- Calendar for Homework and Tests
- Assigned Homework
  - Results
- Practice and Assigned Tests
  - Results

Chapter Resources

- Glossary Flashcards
- Animated Models with Audio (iPod)
- Case Studies
- Web Appendices
- Multiple-choice Questions and Answers
- Answers to Questions in Book
  - Odd-numbered End-of-chapter Questions
  - Pause for Thought Questions

Other Resources for Book

- Glossary
- Ebook to View Any Chapter Online
- Threshold Concepts and Key Ideas
- Grapher to Make Your Own Graphs
- MyEconLab Help

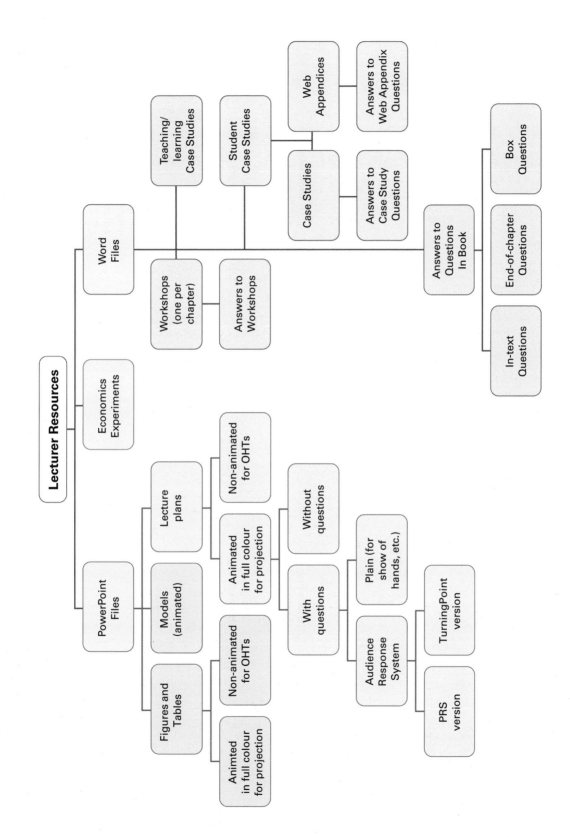

Preface

Welcome to this introduction to economics. Whether you are planning to study economics beyond this level, or whether this will be your only exposure to this fascinating subject, we hope that you will find the book enjoyable and that it will give you some insight into the economy in which you live and the economic forces that shape all our lives.

Although you have probably never studied the subject before, you will almost certainly know quite a lot of economics already. After all, you make economic decisions virtually every day of your life. Every time you go shopping, you are acting as an 'economist': deciding what to buy with your limited amount of money. And it is not just with decisions about buying that we act as economists. How much to work (something that students are increasingly forced to do nowadays), how much to study, even how much time to devote to various activities during the course of the day, are all, in a way, *economic* choices.

To satisfy us as consumers, goods and services have to be produced. We will therefore study the behaviour of firms and what governs the decisions that they make. How will the decisions of big businesses differ from those of small firms? How will the degree of competition affect the extent to which we gain or lose from the activities of firms?

In analysing economic choices we look at some of the big economic issues that face us all as members of society in the twenty-first century. Despite huge advances in technology, and despite the comfortable lives led by many people in the industrialised world, we continue to suffer from volatile economic growth, industrial change and unemployment and all the insecurity that these bring. We continue to witness poverty and inequality, and in many countries the gap between rich and poor has actually grown wider; our environment is polluted; our growing affluence as consumers is increasingly bought at the expense of longer hours at work and growing levels of stress.

We live in a highly interdependent world where actions have implications elsewhere. The banking crisis of the late 2000s and the subsequent effect on economies and the financial well-being of people, businesses and governments illustrates starkly how individual choices can have not only national but global effects.

So what can be done about these problems? This book seeks not only to analyse these problems but also to examine the sorts of policies that governments might pursue in their attempt to address them.

The book is designed with one overriding aim: to make this exciting and highly relevant subject as clear to understand as possible. To this end, the book has a number of important features:

- A direct and straightforward written style; short paragraphs to aid rapid comprehension. The aim all the time is to provide maximum clarity.
- A careful use of colour to guide you through the text and make the structure easy to follow.
- Key ideas highlighted and explained where they first appear. These ideas are key elements in the economist's 'toolkit'. Whenever they recur later in the book, an icon appears in the margin and you are referred back to the page where they are defined and explained. All the key ideas are gathered together at the beginning of the Glossary.
- Some of the key ideas are particularly important in affecting the way we see the world: they help us think like economists. We call these 'threshold concepts' and there are 15 of these.
- Clear chapter-opening pages, which set the scene for the chapter. They also highlight the issues that will be covered in the chapter and can thus be seen as 'learning objectives'.
- Summaries at the end of each section (rather than each chapter). These provide a very useful means of revising and checking your understanding as you progress.
- Definitions of all technical terms given at the foot of the page where the term is first used. The term itself is highlighted in the text.
- 'Pause for thought' questions integrated in the text. These are designed to help you reflect on what you have just read and to check on your understanding. Answers to all 'pause for thought' questions are given in MyEconLab.
- A comprehensive index, including reference to all defined terms. This enables you to look up a definition as required and to see it used in context.
- An alphabetical glossary at the end of the book. This gathers together all the defined terms.

- Plentiful use of up-to-date examples to illustrate the arguments. This helps to bring the subject alive and puts it in context.
- Review questions at the end of each chapter for either individual or class use.
- Answers to all odd-numbered questions are given in MyEconLab. These questions will be helpful for self-testing, while the even-numbered ones can be used for class testing.
- Many boxes (typically four to six per chapter) providing case studies, news items, applications, or elaborations of the text. The boxes are of two types: Case Studies and Applications; and Exploring Economics.
- A comprehensive set of web references at the end of each of the four parts of the book. Each reference is numbered to match those in the Web Appendix at the end of the book.

You can easily access any of these sites from this book's own website (at http://www.pearsoned.co.uk/sloman). When you enter the site, click on **Hot Links**. You will find all the sites from the Web Appendix listed. Click on the one you want and the 'hot link' will take you straight to it.

- Appendices for most chapters appear in MyEconLab. These Web Appendices take the argument further than in the text and look at some more advanced theories. Whilst none of these is necessary for studying this book, and many courses will not refer to them, they provide the necessary additional material for more advanced courses that still require a short textbook.

Good luck with your studies, and have fun. Perhaps this will be just the beginning for you of a lifelong interest in economic issues and the economy.

TO LECTURERS AND TUTORS

This seventh edition of *Essentials of Economics* is an abridged version of *Economics,* 9th edition (John Sloman, Alison Wride and Dean Garratt). Some passages have been directly transcribed, while others have been extensively rewritten in order to provide a consistent coverage of the 'essentials' of economics. Like *Economics*, 9th edition, the book attempts to address the concerns expressed by many people since the financial crisis that the economics we teach to our students should reflect the real world and meet the needs of employers.

The book is designed specifically for one-semester courses in introductory economics. There are 14 chapters (1 introductory, 6 micro, 5 macro and 2 international), each providing about a week's worth of reading. The book is also ideal for year-long courses that are designed for those not going on to specialise in economics, or where economics is only a subsidiary component at level 2.

Naturally, in a one-semester course, or in courses for non-specialists, tutors cannot hope to cover all the principles of economics. Thus some things have had to go. The book does not cover indifference curves or isoquants. The analysis of costs is developed with only an informal reference to production functions. Distribution theory is confined to the determination of wage rates. In macroeconomics, *IS/LM* analysis has been left out, as have some of the more advanced debates in monetary and exchange rate theory. In addition, many passages have been simplified to reflect the nature of courses on which the book is likely to be used. The result is a book that is approximately half the length of *Economics*, 9th edition.

Suggestions for longer or more advanced courses

If you want to use this book on more rigorous courses, most chapters have one or more Web Appendices. These introduce students to more advanced models, such as indifference

analysis, isoquant analysis, general equilibrium in both a closed and an open economy, *IS/LM* and *IS/MP* analysis, the full money multiplier, and trade creation and diversion. You can use any or all of them to fit your course.

The book is also ideal for the new economics A-level syllabuses of the various boards.

The book as also highly suitable for courses, such as HND, where the economic environment component is part of a larger module.

Extensive revision

In bringing economics alive and applying economic ideas and principles to the real word, the seventh edition of *Essentials of Economics* contains a great deal of applied material. Consequently, there have been considerable revisions from the previous editions to reflect contemporary issues, debates and policy interventions. In particular, this has meant further extensive updating of the macroeconomic chapters. However, the exciting debates around the discipline and the teaching of economics have meant a reworking of the microeconomic chapters too. Specifically, you will find that:

- Many of the boxes are new or extensively revised.
- There are many new examples given in the text.
- All tables and charts have been updated, as have factual references in the text.
- Economic analysis and debate has been strengthened and revised at various points in the book in light of economic events and developments in economic thinking.
- There is further discussion around behavioural economics and the insights that it offers across both the micro and macro chapters.
- We have extended the analysis throughout the book on the significance of financial well-being and balance sheets on economic choices and outcomes.

- The sections on money and banking, and fiscal and monetary policies have been further strengthened given the continuing issues around financial institutions and the state of governments' finances.
- We have significantly extended the analysis on the euro and its future.
- All policy sections have been thoroughly revised to reflect the changes that have taken place since the last edition allowing us to consider the array of challenges that national and global policy-makers face in the 2010s.
- Most importantly, every part of the book has been carefully considered, and if necessary redrafted, to ensure both maximum clarity and contemporary relevance.

The book also contains 36 'key ideas' and these are highlighted and explained when they first appear. These fundamental concepts provide a 'toolkit' for students. Students can see them recurring throughout the book, and an icon appears in the margin to refer back to the page where the idea first appears. Showing how these ideas can be used in a variety of contexts helps students to relate the different parts of the subject to each other. Fifteen of these concepts are given the special status of 'Threshold Concepts'. Understanding and being able to use these concepts, such as opportunity cost, help students to 'think like an economist'. Each of these concepts is explained in detail in MyEconLab.

We hope that your students will find this an exciting and interesting text that is relevant to today's issues.

SUPPLEMENTS

MyEconLab for students

MyEconLab provides a comprehensive set of online resources. If you have purchased this text as part of a pack, then you can gain access to MyEconLab by following the instructions to register the access code included on the enclosed access card. If you've purchased this text on its own, then you can purchase access online at www.myeconlab .com. See Getting Started with MyEconLab in the 'Guided Tour' area of this text for more details.

MyEconLab provides a variety of tools to enable you to assess your own learning. A personalised Study Plan identifies areas to concentrate on to improve grades, and specific tools are provided to enable you to direct your studies in a more efficient way.

In addition, there are many other resources in MyEcon-Lab to support your learning. These include:

- Detailed descriptions of each of the fifteen threshold concepts and just why understanding and using each concept helps to transform the way you can approach the analysis of economic issues.
- Animations of key models with audio explanations. These 'talk you through' the models in an attractive way. You can stop, start and replay the animations to make notes and aid your understanding.
- Sloman Economics News: a news blog with news items added several times each month, with introductions, links to newspaper and other articles and to relevant data, questions for use in class or for private study, and references to chapters in the book. You can search the extensive archive by chapter or keyword.
- More than 200 case studies with questions for self-study, ordered chapter by chapter and referred to in the text.
- 25 Web Appendices. As explained above, these take the theoretical arguments further than in the text and are suitable for more advanced courses.

- Updated list of over 250 hot links to sites of use for economics, with references at the end of each Part of the book to specific sites.
- Glossary flashcards. These help you to learn and test your knowledge of all the defined terms in the book.
- Answers to all in-chapter questions.
- Answers to odd-numbered, end-of-chapter questions.
- An ebook, which enables you to access the book anywhere with an internet connection.

Note that Sloman Economics News and hotlinks can also be accessed directly from http://pearsonblog.campaignserver. co.uk/. See the Guided Tour for more details.

MyEconLab for lecturers and tutors

MyEconLab can be set up by you as a complete virtual learning environment for your course or embedded into Blackboard, WebCT or Moodle. You can customise its look and feel and its availability to students. You can use it to provide support to your students in the following ways:

- My EconLab's gradebook automatically records each student's time spent and performance on the tests and Study Plan. It also generates reports you can use to monitor your students' progress.
- You can use MyEconLab to build your own tests, quizzes and homework assignments from the question base provided.
- Questions are generated algorithmically so they use different values each time they are used.
- You can create your own exercises by using the econ exercise builder.

Contact your local Pearson representative to gain access.

Additional resources for lecturers and tutors

There are many additional resources for lecturers and tutors that can be downloaded from the lecturer site of MyEcon-Lab. These have been thoroughly revised for the seventh edition. These include:

- PowerPoint® slide shows in full colour for use with a data projector in lectures and classes. These can also be made available to students by loading them on to a local network. There are several types of slideshows:
  - *All figures from the book and most of the tables*. Each figure is built up in a logical sequence, thereby allowing tutors to show them in lectures in an animated form.
  - *A range of models*. Each one builds up in around 20 to 80 screens.
  - *Customisable lecture plans*. These are a series of bullet-point lecture plans. There is one for each chapter of the book. Each one can be easily edited, with points added, deleted or moved, so as to suit particular lectures. A consistent use of colour is made to show how the points tie together. They come in various versions:
    - Lecture plans with integrated diagrams. These lecture plans include animated diagrams, charts and tables at the appropriate points.
    - Lecture plans with integrated diagrams and questions. These are like the above but also include multiple-choice questions, allowing lectures to become more interactive. They can be used with or without an audience response system (ARS).

ARS versions are available for InterWrite PRS® and TurningPoint® (in two TurningPoint versions) and are ready to use with appropriate 'clickers' or students' own internet-enabled devices, such as smartphones, laptops or tablets.

- Lecture plans without the diagrams. These allow you to construct your own on the blackboard or whiteboard, or using a visualiser or OHP.

  Note that these lecture plans are organised by chapter for ease of use. It is not intended that the whole PowerPoint is shown in a single lecture.

- Case studies. These, also available in the student part of MyEconLab, can be reproduced and used for classroom exercises or for student assignments. Answers are also provided (not available on the student site).
- Workshops. There are 14 of these – one for each chapter. They are in Word® and can be reproduced for use with large groups (up to 200 students) in a lecture theatre or large classroom. In A-level classes, they can be used as worksheets, either for use in class or for homework. Suggestions for use are given in an accompanying file. Answers to all workshops are given in separate Word® files.
- Teaching/learning case studies. There are 20 of these. They examine various approaches to teaching introductory economics and ways to improve student learning.
- Answers to all end-of-chapter questions, pause for thought questions, questions in boxes, questions in Web Cases and Web Appendices and to the 14 workshops. As these are in Word files, you can print them off for students or post them on your VLE or intranet.

ACKNOWLEDGEMENTS

As with previous editions, we owe a debt to various people. A special thanks to Peter Smith from the University of Southampton for authoring the MyEconLab questions and tests. Thanks to the team at Pearson Education, and especially to Kate Brewin, who has been a tremendous help and support at every stage of revising the book. Thanks also to Tim Parker, Louise Hammond and Zoe Smith for all the work they have put in to producing the book and its supplements. Thanks too to the many users of the book who have given us feedback. We always value their comments.

John: I continue to owe a huge debt to my family, and especially my wife and soulmate Alison, whose love and support have made this and previous editions possible. She is remarkably patient and tolerant of my long hours at the computer. And many thanks once again to Dean, whose ideas and enthusiasm have been fantastic. It's been great to work together.

Dean: A special thank you must go to Patricia, my very special Warwickshire bear! She is an absolute rock and remains incredibly supportive to this Leicestershire fox. I would like to thank my parents for all their love and support, particularly in supporting me through university. Finally, thanks to John for again inviting me to be involved on this project and sharing with me a desire that we communicate the relevance and applicability of economics.

Publisher's acknowledgements

We are grateful to the following for permission to reproduce copyright material:

Figures

Figure 8.A2 UK GDP: 2013, Annual Abstract of Statistics, 2013 (National Statistics (2014), Office for National Statistics licensed under the Open Government Licence v.3.0, www.ons.gov.uk.

Tables

Table on page 45 after IMF Primary Commodity Prices (IMF) and World Economic Outlook Database (IMF), April 2015; Tables 3.1, 3.2 from *Intermediate Microeconomics*, 11th ed., South Western College Publishing, a division of Cengage Learning (Nicholson, W. and Snyder, C. 2011); Table on page 78 from *World Population Prospects:* The 2012 Revision (United Nations, Department of Economic and Social Affairs), http://esa.un.org/unpd/wpp/, reprinted with the permission of the United Nations; Tables on pages 152 and 153 from Annual Survey of Hours and Earnings (National Statistics 2014) Office for National Statistics licensed under the Open Government Licence v.3.0, www. ons.gov.uk; Table 6.1 The effects of taxes and benefits on household income, 2014/15 – Reference Tables, Table 26 (National Statistics, 2015), adapted from data from the Office for National Statistics licensed under the Open Government Licence v. 3.0, www.ons.gov.uk; Table 6.2 from Family Spending, Tables A39 and A44 (National Statistics, 2014), Office for National Statistics licensed under the Open Government Licence v.3.0, www.ons.gov.uk; Table 6.3 from Wealth and Assets Survey (National Statistics, 2014), Office for National Statistics licensed under the Open Government Licence v.3.0, www.ons.gov.uk; Table 8.1 from National Accounts Estimates of Main Aggregates (United Nations Statistics Division), © (2015) United Nations. Reprinted with the permission of the United Nations, http://unstats.un.org; Tables 8.A1 and 8.A2 from United Kingdom National Accounts (National Statistics), Office for National Statistics licensed under the Open Government Licence v.3.0, www.ons.gov.uk, accessed 2015; Table 10.5 from Statistical Interactive Database (Bank of England), www.bankofengland.co.uk/boeapps/iadb/, accessed 2 March 2015; Tables on page 371 from International Trade Statistics, 2014, © World Trade Organization (WTO), www. wto.org; Table 14.1 from Balance of Payments, Quarter 4 and Annual 2014 (Office for National Statistics, 2015), Office for National Statistics licensed under the Open Government Licence v.3.0, www.ons.gov.uk; Table 14.5 from HIPC At-A-Glance Guide (International Monetary Fund, Autumn 2014), www.imf.org.

Introduction

Economic issues

You may never have studied economics before, and yet traditional and social media are full of stories relating to the economy and to particular economic issues. Consequently, we are continually being made aware of local, national and international economic issues: whether it be price increases (or sometimes decreases), new products on the market, the effects of globalisation, interest rate changes, fluctuations in exchange rates, unemployment, economic recessions, the stability of the banking system or the state of the government's finances.

An important reason for the interest in economics is that as individuals we are continually faced with economic problems and decisions of our own. What should I buy in the supermarket? Should I save up for a summer holiday, or spend more on day-to-day living? Should I go to university, or should I try to find a job now?

Yet while these and other economic issues are relevant to so much that affects our daily lives, the events following the financial and economic crisis of the late 2000s have undoubtedly increased the interest in economics and the views of economists. The magnitude of this crisis and its subsequent effects mean that anybody studying economics is doing so in incredibly interesting, if not turbulent, times. It also means that there is considerable debate among economists about the discipline, including questions around the way economists study economic issues and around the economics curriculum in schools, colleges and universities.

So just what is economics about? In this introduction we will attempt to answer this question and to give you some insights into the subject you will be studying by using this book.

We will also see how the subject is divided up, and in particular we will distinguish between the two major branches of economics: microeconomics and macroeconomics.

After studying this chapter, you should be able to answer the following questions:

- What is economics about?
- What is the central economic problem faced by all individuals and societies?
- How can people set about making the best of their limited resources?
- What is meant by 'opportunity cost'? How is it relevant when people make economic choices?
- What is the difference between microeconomics and macroeconomics?
- How can you represent simply economic relationships in a graph?
- How do different economic systems tackle the problem of scarcity?

We conclude by considering alternative ways in which economies are run. How would they work if all decisions were taken by the government or, at the other extreme, if they relied totally on the decisions of households and firms? How, in practice, are individual decisions influenced by the government?

At this point it's worth drawing your attention to the Economics News site that accompanies this book. You can access it directly at http://pearsonblog.campaignserver.co.uk/ or from MyEconLab's home page, or simply Google 'Sloman Economics news site'. The site shows how items in the news are related to the economic issues you will be studying in this book. There are links to newspaper articles, videos, data sources and reports. There are questions for you to consider and a powerful search feature that lets you browse earlier articles by chapter of the book, month and keywords.

1.1 ENGAGING WITH ECONOMICS

Is economics relevant to me?

Economics provides us with important insights into addressing not only some of the most important questions societies face but also much 'smaller' questions: ones that affect all of us. To help illustrate the sorts of questions that economists analyse we begin with a flight of fancy.

An island economy

Assume that we wake up tomorrow charged with running an island economy. Once we get over the initial excitement, we might begin to appreciate it's not going to be all palm trees and days by the pool. An economy has people who need to eat, be housed and will need access to healthcare. It may have other islands, nearby, who are friendly and want to trade – or who are not friendly and may want to invade.

Being in charge suddenly seems to involve quite a few decisions. We have choices to make. What is this island going to produce so that people can live? Is it going to be self-sufficient, or to 'swap' goods with other countries? How are people going to know what to produce? How will the products be shared out? Will they be allocated to everyone, even those who do not work? What will we do if some people are too old to work and haven't got savings or families? What should we do if the island bank runs out of money? How can we be sure that we will have enough resources to support the people next year, as well as this?

Of course, we are never actually going to be parachuted in to be in charge of an island, although some of you reading this book may aspire to go into politics. But the questions we have posed above are a reflection of the real challenges countries face. Important choices have to be made. We will look at the role of government throughout this book: decisions that need to be taken, different approaches to solving economic problems, and what happens when governments need to work together.

Economic puzzles and issues

From our discussion of the island economy you will have got a sense that economists study choices which, in one way or another, are related to consumption and production – a theme we will develop further in this chapter. Consequently, economists look at a wide variety of economic puzzles and issues. Let's take a look at some specific examples which you might find interesting.

A pay rise

Do you work? By which we mean, do you work for money? If so, note down your hourly pay and how many hours you work per week.

Let's assume you are earning £7.50 per hour. Would you like a pay-rise to £15 per hour? You would? And what will you do with the extra money you earn? You might go on holiday, or save more, or perhaps you'll simply go out for an extra evening per week, or buy nicer food when you go shopping.

But before we start talking about that, we need to go back to that note of yours. If your rate of pay doubled, how many hours would you work now? You might work the same number of hours; you might think it's worth working more hours; or, you might decide that you can work fewer hours and have more time for other things. It's an interesting puzzle for you to think about. You could ask your friends how they might react in this situation. Perhaps you, or some of your friends, aren't working at the moment, but might do so if higher rates of pay were on offer.

We've thought about this from *your* point of view. Who else might be interested in the puzzle? Employers are obviously involved. If they want people to do more work, they might consider whether offering higher hourly rates will achieve that. Imagine how annoying it would be if, instead, people want to work fewer hours, not more. We will see in Chapter 6 that governments might be interested too.

Information and decision making

One thing that economists spend a lot of time talking and thinking about is information. We will see in the rest of this book how important it is when making decisions. And as you've already seen, most of economics is about looking at decisions. In deciding whether to take a particular job and how many hours to work, you will need to have all sorts of information: rates of pay, what hours are offered, what the job is actually like, what you'll have to wear. You can probably think of at least three or four other things just on this decision. If you are going to make a 'good' decision you need 'good' information.

Of course, having information is going to affect your decision making: that's the whole point. So let's imagine you are choosing whether or not to see a film that has just been released. You can get information about the plot, the actors, the special effects, the rating, etc. You can also read opinions of critics and reviewers on the quality of the film. Hopefully all this information will help you decide whether to spend money and time going to see it. Similarly, you can get information about many of the other goods and services you might want to buy, by talking to friends or family, researching on the Internet or browsing in shops.

What about a bigger piece of information? Suppose someone could tell you exactly how long you will live? Would that be a useful piece of information? How would it change your decisions every day? Would you behave differently right away? Does your answer depend on who gives the information? You might be more inclined to believe a doctor or scientist than an astrologer!

In practice, no one is going to be able to tell you your exact life expectancy (to the day). Accidents can happen and medicine moves on. So the best you could currently expect is an informed prediction based, usually, on statistical probability. But such informed predictions about life expectancy are crucial for insurance companies deciding on premiums.

Information is all around us – in fact, we are said to live in the information age. So the problem is often not one of a lack of information, but one of too much and what information is reliable. We hope, by reading this book, you will be better able to assess information and its usefulness for making economic decisions.

We need to save more. We need to spend more

Puzzles like the two above are concerned with individual decisions and these are probably the easiest type to identify. But there are some which apply to a whole economy or country. The second half of this book, Chapters 8 onwards,

looks at 'whole economy' economics, so let's identify an issue in that area.

How much do you save? The answer will depend on your income, your spending habits and probably on something that's hard to pin down, but really is about how 'good' you are at saving.

There are all sorts of reasons why saving is a 'good thing'. We are living longer and, unless we save more, we may not have enough to be comfortable in our old age. When we save, we have a buffer against emergencies. When we save, we receive interest, which gives us additional income.

All of these reasons can be scaled up to the whole economy. You have probably heard politicians say that the country needs to save for the future, especially if we all are going to live longer. The nation, they argue, needs to reduce its debts so that we can reduce the interest we have to pay, leaving more left over for the things people want, such as a better health service and better education. And if emergencies arise (the financial crisis of 2007/8 is a really good example) the country will be in a better position if banks have plenty of money. It's also true that saving by individuals provides a source of funds for businesses that want and need to borrow for investment.

You might be wondering why this is a puzzle, since it seems pretty straightforward.

So now let's imagine the opposite situation where, instead of saving only a little bit, you saved a great deal of your income, much more than you do now. Imagine that you only bought the barest of necessities, grew your own food, wore the same clothes for years and didn't buy any new technology, or even have an occasional night out. You might have a pretty miserable life.

Now scale this up to the whole economy again. If no one is spending much, what will happen? Businesses will very quickly be in trouble. The banks will be full of our savings, but no one will be borrowing. Spending will therefore be low and firms won't be able to make profits. We will have lots of security in the form of future spending, but an economy that is in recession and very soon could be in crisis.

Of course this is an exaggerated example. But you can see the puzzle: saving is good, but so is spending. What should we do? What should the government encourage us to do?

1.2 THE ECONOMIC PROBLEM

What is economics all about?

From reading Section 1.1 you should have got a sense that economics involves an analysis of decision making by individuals, businesses, governments and countries. These are decisions concerned with the following:

- The **production** of goods and services: how much the economy produces; what particular combination of goods and services; how much each firm produces; what techniques of production it uses; how many people it employs.

- The **consumption** of goods and services: how much the population as a whole spends (and how much it saves); what the pattern of consumption is in the economy; how much people buy of particular items; what particular individuals choose to buy; how people's consumption is affected by prices, advertising, fashion and other factors.

But we still have not quite got to the bottom of what economics is about. What is the crucial ingredient that makes a problem an *economic* one? The answer is that there is one central problem faced by all individuals and all societies. From this one problem stem all the other economic problems we shall be looking at throughout this book.

This central economic problem is *scarcity*. This applies not only in poor countries, but also in the UK, the USA, Japan, France and throughout the world. For an economist, scarcity has a very specific definition. Let's examine that definition.

The problem of scarcity

Ask people if they would like more money, and the vast majority would answer 'yes'. They want more money so that they can buy more goods and services; and this applies not only to poor people but also to most wealthy people too. The point is that human wants are virtually unlimited.

Yet the means of fulfilling human wants are limited. At any one time the world can produce only a limited amount of goods and services. This is because the world has only a limited amount of resources. These resources, or *factors of production* as they are often called, are of three broad types:

- Human resources: **labour**. The labour force is limited both in number and in skills.
- Natural resources: **land and raw materials**. The world's land area is limited, as are its raw materials.
- Manufactured resources: **capital**. Capital consists of all those inputs that have themselves been produced in the first place. The world has a limited stock of capital: a limited supply of factories, machines, transportation and other equipment. The productivity of capital is limited by the state of technology.

So here is the reason for scarcity: human wants are virtually unlimited, whereas the resources available to satisfy these wants are limited. We can thus define **scarcity** as shown in the box.

> **KEY IDEA 1**
> *Scarcity* is the excess of human wants over what can actually be produced. Because of scarcity, various choices have to be made between alternatives.

Of course, we do not all face the problem of scarcity to the same degree. A poor person unable to afford enough to eat or a decent place to live will hardly see it as a 'problem' that a rich person cannot afford a second Ferrari. But economists do not claim that we all face an *equal* problem of scarcity. In fact, this is one of the major issues economists study: how resources and products are *distributed*, whether between different individuals, different regions of a country or different countries of the world.

Pause for thought

If we would all like more money, why doesn't the government simply print a lot more?

But given that people, both rich and poor, want more than they can have, this makes them *behave* in certain ways. Economics studies that behaviour. It studies people at work, producing the goods that people want. It studies people as consumers buying the goods they themselves want. It studies governments influencing the level and pattern of production and consumption. In short, it studies anything to do with the process of satisfying human wants.

Demand and supply

We said that economics is concerned with consumption and production. Another way of looking at this is in terms of *demand* and *supply*. In fact, demand and supply and the relationship between them lie at the very centre of economics. But what do we mean by the terms, and what is their relationship with the problem of scarcity?

Demand is related to wants. If goods and services were free, people would simply demand whatever they wanted. Such wants are virtually boundless, perhaps limited only by people's imagination. *Supply*, on the other hand, is limited. It is related to resources. The amount firms can supply depends on the resources and technology available.

Given the problem of scarcity, given that human wants exceed what can actually be produced, *potential* demands will exceed *potential* supplies. Society therefore has to find some way of dealing with this problem. Somehow it has to try to match demand and supply. This applies at the level of the economy overall: total spending in the economy must balance total production. It also applies at the level of individual goods and services. The demand and supply of cabbages must balance, and so must the demand and supply of smartphones, cars, houses and package holidays.

KI 1 p 5

Definitions

Production The transformation of inputs into outputs by firms in order to earn profit (or meet some other objective).

Consumption The act of using goods and services to satisfy wants. This will normally involve purchasing the goods and services.

Factors of production (or resources) The inputs into the production of goods and services: labour, land and raw materials, and capital.

Labour All forms of human input, both physical and mental, into current production.

Land (and raw materials) Inputs into production that are provided by nature: e.g. unimproved land and mineral deposits in the ground.

Capital All inputs into production that have themselves been produced: e.g. factories, machines and tools.

Scarcity The excess of human wants over what can actually be produced to fulfil these wants.

But if potential demand exceeds potential supply, how are *actual* demand and supply to be made equal? Either demand has to be curtailed, or supply has to be increased, or a combination of the two. Economics studies this process. It studies how demand adjusts to available supplies, and how supply adjusts to consumer demands.

Recap

1. The central economic problem is that of scarcity.
2. Given that there is a limited supply of factors of production (labour, land and capital), it is impossible to provide everybody with everything they want.
3. Potential demands exceed potential supplies.

1.3 DIVIDING UP THE SUBJECT

What's meant by 'macroeconomics' and 'microeconomics'?

Economics is traditionally divided into two main branches – *macroeconomics and microeconomics*, where 'macro' means big, and 'micro' means small.

Macroeconomics is concerned with the economy as a whole. It is thus concerned with **aggregate demand** and **aggregate supply**. By 'aggregate demand' we mean the total amount of spending in the economy, whether by consumers, by customers outside the country for our exports, by the government, or by firms when they buy capital equipment or stock up on raw materials. By 'aggregate supply' we mean the total national output of goods and services.

Microeconomics is concerned with the individual parts of the economy. It is concerned with the demand and supply of *particular* goods and services and resources: cars, butter, clothes and haircuts; electricians, shop assistants, blast furnaces, computer chips and oil.

Macroeconomics

KI 1
p 5
Because things are scarce, societies are concerned that their resources should be used as *fully as possible,* and that over time their national output should *grow*.

The achievement of growth and the full use of resources is not easy, however, as demonstrated by the periods of high unemployment and stagnation that have occurred from time to time throughout the world – for example, in the 1930s, the early 1980s, the early 1990s and the late 2000s. Furthermore, attempts by government to stimulate growth and employment have often resulted in inflation and a large rise in imports. Even when societies do achieve growth, it can be short-lived. Economies are inherently unstable and display what are known as business cycles: periods of high growth followed by periods of low or even negative growth.

Macroeconomics, then, studies the determination of national output and its growth over time. It also studies the problems of recession, unemployment, inflation, the balance of international payments and cyclical instability,

and the policies adopted by governments to deal with these problems.

Macroeconomic problems are closely related to the balance between aggregate demand and aggregate supply.

If aggregate demand is *too high* relative to aggregate supply, inflation and balance of trade deficits are likely to result.

- **Inflation** refers to a general rise in the level of prices throughout the economy. If aggregate demand rises substantially, firms are likely to respond by raising their prices. After all, if demand is high they can probably still sell as much as before (if not more) even at the higher prices, and thus make more profit. If firms in general put up their prices, inflation results.
- **Balance of trade deficits** are the excess of imports over exports. If aggregate demand rises, people are likely

---

Definitions

Macroeconomics The branch of economics that studies economic aggregates (grand totals): e.g. the overall level of prices, output and employment in the economy.

Aggregate demand The total level of spending in the economy.

Aggregate supply The total amount of output in the economy.

Microeconomics The branch of economics that studies individual units: e.g. households, firms and industries. It studies the interrelationships between these units in determining the pattern of production and distribution of goods and services.

Rate of inflation The percentage increase in the level of prices over a 12-month period.

Balance of trade Exports of goods and services minus imports of goods and services. If exports exceed imports, there is a 'balance of trade surplus' (a positive figure). If imports exceed exports, there is a 'balance of trade deficit' (a negative figure).

to buy more imports. In other words, part of the extra expenditure will go on Japanese electrical goods, German cars, Chilean wine, and so on. Also if inflation is high, home-produced goods will become uncompetitive with foreign goods. We are likely, therefore, to buy more foreign imports, and people abroad are likely to buy fewer of our exports.

If aggregate demand is *too low* relative to aggregate supply, unemployment and recession may well result.

- **Recession** is defined as a decline in the output of an economy (negative growth) for two or more consecutive quarters. A recent example was the decline in UK output for five consecutive quarters from the second quarter of 2008. During this period the UK economy shrank by 6 per cent. Recessions are associated with low levels of consumer spending, perhaps because of a reduction in the amount of credit advanced by financial institutions to consumers, as was the case following the financial crisis of the late 2000s, or because of worries about job security. If people spend less, shops are likely to find themselves with unsold stocks. As a result they will buy less from the manufacturers, which in turn will cut down on production.
- **Unemployment** is likely to result from cutbacks in production. If firms are producing less, they will need to employ fewer people.

Government macroeconomic *policy*, therefore, tends to focus on the balance of aggregate demand and aggregate supply. It can be **demand-side policy**, which seeks to influence the level of spending in the economy. This in turn will affect the level of production, prices and employment. Or it can be **supply-side policy**. This is designed to influence the level of production directly: for example, by trying to create more incentives for firms to innovate.

Microeconomics

Microeconomics and choice

KI 1
p 5 Because resources are scarce, *choices* have to be made. There are three main categories of choice that must be made in any society.

- *What* goods and services are going to be produced and in what quantities? How many cars, how much wheat, how much insurance, how many rock concerts, etc. will be produced?
- *How* are things going to be produced? What resources are going to be used and in what quantities? What techniques of production are going to be adopted? Will cars be produced by robots or by assembly-line workers? Will electricity be produced from coal, oil, gas, nuclear fission, renewable resources or a mixture of these?
- *For whom* are things going to be produced? In other words, how will the nation's income be distributed?

After all, the higher your income, the more you can consume of the nation's output. What will be the wages of farm workers, printers, cleaners and accountants? How much will chief executives of large companies receive? How much will pensioners receive? How much of the nation's income will go to shareholders or landowners?

All societies have to make these choices, whether they be made by individuals, by groups or by the government. These choices can be seen as *micro*economic choices, since they are concerned not with the *total* amount of national output, but with the *individual* goods and services that make it up: what they are, how they are made, and who gets the incomes to buy them.

Choice and opportunity cost

Choice involves sacrifice. The more food you choose to buy, the less money you will have to spend on other goods. The more food a nation produces, the less resources there will be for producing other goods. In other words, the production or consumption of one thing involves the sacrifice of alternatives. This sacrifice of alternatives in the production (or consumption) of a good is known as its **opportunity cost**.

 The opportunity cost of something is what you give up to get it/do it.

If the workers on a farm can produce either 1000 tonnes of wheat or 2000 tonnes of barley, then the opportunity cost of producing 1 tonne of wheat is the 2 tonnes of barley forgone. The opportunity cost of buying a textbook is the new pair of jeans you also wanted that you have had to go without. The opportunity cost of working overtime is the leisure you have sacrificed.

Definitions

Recession A period where national output falls for two quarters or more.

Unemployment The number of people who are actively looking for work but are currently without a job. (Note that there is much debate as to who should officially be counted as unemployed.)

Demand-side policy Government policy designed to alter the level of aggregate demand, and thereby the level of output, employment and prices.

Supply-side policy Government policy that attempts to alter the level of aggregate supply directly.

Opportunity cost The cost of any activity measured in terms of the best alternative forgone.

BOX 1.1   MACROECONOMIC ISSUES

An historical perspective

Macroeconomics is often characterised by lively debates. These debates reflect differences among economists over how economies work and how the *transmission mechanisms* of economic policy operate. Transmission mechanisms describe how policy changes, such as those to interest rates or government spending, impact on economic outcomes, such as output and inflation.

Understandably, the focus of macroeconomic debates is affected by the macroeconomic issues of the time. It is not surprising that many of the debates and advancement of ideas have arisen because existing theories appeared unable to explain the prevailing macroeconomic conditions. Sometimes this has resulted in relatively small incremental changes to theory and to policy, but on other occasions very different views of how economies work have come to the fore and, as a result, policy has been radically reshaped.

In short, a historical perspective helps us to understand both the focus and development of macroeconomic debates. The chart shows the path of a selection of key macroeconomic indicators for the UK since 1900.

Macroeconomics in the 1920s and 30s

Macroeconomics as a separate branch of economics had its birth with the mass unemployment experienced in the 1920s and 1930s. The old 'classical theories' of the time essentially said that free markets, i.e. economies with little government intervention (see Section 1.4), would provide a healthy economy with *full* employment. But such analysis seemed totally at odds with the facts.

A new analysis of the economy – one that *did* offer solutions to mass unemployment – was put forward by the economist John Maynard Keynes. His book *The General Theory of Employment, Interest and Money,* published in 1936, saw the dawn of 'Keynesian economics'. Keynes advocated active intervention by governments, in particular through changes in government spending and taxation to affect aggregate demand (total spending). This type of policy response is known as *fiscal policy.* By carefully managing the total demand for goods and services in the economy, the government could prevent mass unemployment on the one hand, or an 'overheated' economy with unsustainable growth and high inflation on the other.

The development of macroeconomics after the Second World War

After the Second World War, governments around the world adopted Keynesian demand-management policies; and they seemed to be successful. The 1950s and 1960s were a period of low inflation, low unemployment and relatively high economic growth. Macroeconomists were largely concerned with refining Keynesian economics.

In the 1970s, however, the macroeconomic consensus broke down. As we can see from the chart, unemployment rose while the rate of inflation rose and growth slowed down. Macroeconomic debates became increasingly lively with different 'schools of thought' having their own explanations of what was going wrong, and each had its own solutions to the problems.

Then, as the macroeconomic environment generally improved in the 1990s, so increasingly common ground began to emerge with a fusion of ideas.

Macroeconomics since the financial crisis of 2007/8

Then, with the financial crisis of the late 2000s and the subsequent global economic downturn and deterioration of government finances (see Box 1.4), debates among economists again intensified. These were mirrored by the debates among politicians and policy makers.

In many ways, the debates of the late 2000s and early 2010s were a microcosm of much of the preceding 100 years. Consequently, many familiar questions were once again being asked, not least those concerning the role that governments should play in modern, developed economies. Are macroeconomic problems the result of too much or too little government intervention?

Some disagreement among economists is probably inevitable given the seriousness of the issues being debated. However, there exist some areas of broad

---

Opportunity cost as the basis for choice is a key idea. But it is more than that. It is also the first of our 'Threshold Concepts' (click on the Threshold Concepts link in MyEconLab for a detailed explanation of each one). There are 15 of these threshold concepts, which we shall be exploring throughout the book. Each of them keeps recurring in a variety of different contexts.

Once you have grasped these concepts and seen their significance, they will affect the way that you understand and analyse economic problems. They help you to 'think like an economist'.

Rational choices

When trying to understand behaviour economists typically start by assuming 'rational decision-making'.

Consequently, they often refer to **rational choices.** This simply means the weighing-up of the *costs* and *benefits* of any activity, whether it be firms choosing what and how much to produce, workers choosing whether to take a particular job or to work extra hours, or consumers choosing what to buy.

Definition

Rational choices Choices that involve weighing up the benefit of any activity against its opportunity cost.

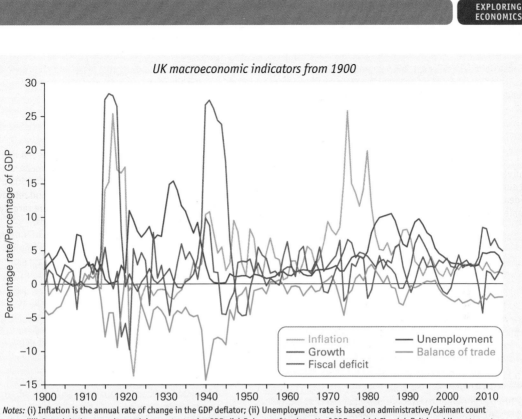

UK macroeconomic indicators from 1900

Notes: (i) Inflation is the annual rate of change in the GDP deflator; (ii) Unemployment rate is based on administrative/claimant count rates; (iii) Growth is the annual growth in constant-price GDP; (iv) Balance of trade as % of GDP; and (v) Fiscal deficit is public sector net borrowing as a % of GDP

Source: Based on data from Bank of England available at http://www.bankofengland.co.uk/research/Pages/onebank/threecenturies.aspx and National Statistics (Various)

agreement among many macroeconomists over the causes of macroeconomic problems and the appropriate policies to deal with them.

Therefore, particularly through the second half of the book, we will be identifying areas not only where disagreement remains, but where there is more agreement.

Use the chart to compose a short report on the patterns observed in these key macroeconomic indicators in the UK since 1900.

Definitions

Transmission mechanism The process by which a change in a policy instrument (such as interest rates or taxation) affects economic outcomes (such as inflation or unemployment).

Fiscal policy Changes made to government spending and/or taxation in order to affect total spending and thereby the level of economic activity.

Imagine you are doing your shopping in a supermarket and you want to buy a bottle of wine. Do you spend a lot of money and buy a top-quality French wine, or do you buy a cheap Eastern European one instead? To make a rational (i.e. sensible) decision, you will need to weigh up the costs and benefits of each alternative. The top-quality wine may give you a lot of enjoyment, but it has a high opportunity cost: because it is expensive, you will need to sacrifice quite a lot of consumption of other goods if you decide to buy it. If you buy the cheap bottle, however, although you will not enjoy it so much, you will have more money left over to buy other things: it has a lower opportunity cost.

Thus rational decision making, as far as consumers are concerned, involves choosing those items that give you the best value for money: i.e. the *greatest benefit relative to cost*.

The same principles apply to firms when deciding what to produce. For example, should a car manufacturer open up another production line? A rational decision will again involve weighing up the benefits and costs. The benefits are the revenues that the firm will earn from selling the extra cars. The costs will include the extra labour costs, raw material costs, costs of component parts, etc. It will be profitable to open up the new production line only if the revenues earned exceed the costs entailed: in other words, if it adds to profit.

BOX 1.2 THE OPPORTUNITY COSTS OF STUDYING ECONOMICS

CASE STUDIES & APPLICATIONS

What are you sacrificing?

TC 1 p 7

You may not have realised it, but you probably consider opportunity costs many times a day. The reason is that we are constantly making choices: what to buy, what to eat, what to wear, whether to go out, how much to study, and so on. Each time we make such a choice, we are in effect rejecting some alternative. This alternative forgone is the opportunity cost of the action we chose.

Sometimes the opportunity costs of our actions are the direct monetary costs we incur. Sometimes it is more complicated.

Take the opportunity costs of your choices as a student of economics.

Buying a textbook costing £49.99

This choice involves a direct money payment. What you have to consider is the alternatives you could have bought with the £49.99. You then have to weigh up the benefit from the best alternative against the benefit of the textbook.

 1. What might prevent you from making the best decision?

Coming to classes

Even though students (or their parents) now pay fees for their degrees in many countries, there is no extra (marginal) monetary cost in coming to classes once the fees have been paid. You will not get a refund by skipping classes!

So are the opportunity costs zero? No: by coming to classes you are *not* working in the library; you are *not* having an extra hour in bed; you are *not* sitting drinking coffee with friends, and so on. If you are making a rational decision to come to classes, then you will consider such possible alternatives.

2. If there are several other things you could have done, is the opportunity cost the sum of all of them?

Choosing to study at university or college

What are the opportunity costs of being a student in higher education? At first it might seem that the costs would include the following:

- Tuition fees.
- Books, stationery, etc.
- Accommodation expenses.
- Transport.
- Food, entertainment and other living expenses.

But adding these up does *not* give the *opportunity* cost. The opportunity cost is the *sacrifice* entailed by going to university or college *rather* than doing something else. Let's assume that the alternative is to take a job that has been offered. The correct list of opportunity costs of higher education would include:

- Tuition fees paid by you (as opposed to your parents or anyone else).
- Books, stationery, etc.
- Additional accommodation and transport expenses over what would have been incurred by taking the job (this figure could be negative).
- Wages that would have been earned in the job, less any income received as a student.

3. Why is the cost of food not included?
4. Make a list of the benefits of higher education.
5. Is the opportunity cost to the individual of attending higher education different from the opportunity costs to society as a whole?

Marginal costs and benefits

TC 2 p 11

In economics we argue that rational choices involve weighing up **marginal costs** and **marginal benefits**. These are the costs and benefits of doing a little bit more or a little bit less of a specific activity. They can be contrasted with the *total* costs and benefits of the activity.

Take a familiar example. What time will you set the alarm clock to go off tomorrow morning? Let us say that you have to leave home at 8.30. Perhaps you will set the alarm for 7.00. That will give you plenty of time to get up and get ready, but it will mean a relatively short night's sleep. Perhaps then you will decide to set it for 7.30 or even

8.00. That will give you a longer night's sleep, but much more of a rush in the morning to get ready.

So how do you make a rational decision about when the alarm should go off? What you have to do is to weigh up the costs and benefits of *additional* sleep. Each extra minute in bed gives you more sleep (the marginal benefit) but gives you more of a rush when you get up (the marginal cost). The decision is therefore based on the costs and benefits of *extra* sleep, not on the *total* costs and benefits of a whole night's sleep.

This same principle applies to rational decisions made by consumers, workers and firms. For example, the car

---

Definitions

Marginal costs The additional costs of doing a little bit more (or *1 unit* more if a unit can be measured) of an activity.

Marginal benefits The additional benefits of doing a little bit more (or *1 unit* more if a unit can be measured) of an activity.

firm we were considering just now will weigh up the marginal costs and benefits of producing cars: in other words, it will compare the costs and revenue of producing *additional* cars. If additional cars add more to the firm's revenue than to its costs, it will be profitable to produce them.

> **KEY IDEA 3**
> **TC 2**
> *Rational decision making* involves weighing up the marginal benefit and marginal cost of any activity. If the marginal benefit exceeds the marginal cost, it is rational to do the activity (or to do more of it). If the marginal cost exceeds the marginal benefit, it is rational not to do it (or to do less of it).

Decision making based on marginal costs and benefits is the second of our threshold concepts, explored on the book's website.

The social implications of choice

Microeconomics does not just study how choices are made. It also looks at their consequences. Under certain conditions the consequences may be an efficient use of the nation's resources.

> **Pause for thought**
>
> *Imagine that, as a student, you are short of money and that you are offered employment working in the student union shop. You can choose the number of hours each week that you work. How would you make a 'rational' decision about the number of hours to work in any given week?*

However, a whole series of possible problems can arise from the choices that people make, whether they are made by individuals, by firms or by the government. These problems include such things as inefficiency, waste, inequality and pollution.

Take the case of pollution. It might be profitable for a firm to tip toxic waste into a river. But what is profitable for the firm will not necessarily be 'profitable' for society. There may be serious environmental consequences of the firm's actions.

Throughout the book we will be considering how well the economy meets various economic and social objectives: whether micro or macro. We will examine why problems occur and what can be done about them.

> ## Recap
>
> 1. The subject of economics is usually divided into two main branches, macroeconomics and microeconomics.
> 2. Macroeconomics deals with aggregates' such as the overall levels of unemployment, output, growth and prices in the economy.
> 3. Microeconomics deals with the activities of individual units within the economy: firms, industries, consumers, workers, etc. Because resources are scarce, people have to make choices. Society has to choose by some means or other what goods and services to produce, how to produce them and for whom to produce them. Microeconomics studies these choices.
> 4. Rational choices involve weighing up the marginal benefits of each activity against its marginal opportunity costs. If the marginal benefits exceed the marginal costs, it is rational to choose to do more of that activity.

1.4 MODELLING ECONOMIC RELATIONSHIPS

How can diagrams be used to illustrate economic issues?

Economics books and articles frequently contain diagrams. The reason is that diagrams are very useful for illustrating economic relationships. Ideas and arguments that might take a long time to explain in words can often be expressed clearly and simply in a diagram.

Such diagrams are an example of an **economic model**. Models are a simplification of reality in order to show clearly how things are related. For example, a model could show how the demand for a product is related to price. It would show how demand changed as price changed. We would expect that as the price of a product rose, so the quantity demanded would fall. If you glance forward to Figure 2.1, you will see a diagram relating the demand for potatoes to the price of potatoes.

To examine such relationships, we have to assume that other things that might affect the outcome do not change. For example, if we were modelling how the demand for

Cheddar cheese was affected by changes in its price, we would have to assume that the price of other products, including other types of cheese, were held constant. This is known as the '*ceteris paribus*' assumption. *Ceteris paribus*

> ## Definitions
>
> **Economic model** The representation, graphically, mathematically or in words, of the relationship between two or more variables. A model is a simplification of reality designed to explain just part of a complex process of economic relationships. It is thus based on various simplifying assumptions.
>
> *Ceteris paribus* Latin for 'other things being equal'. This assumption has to be made when constructing and using models.

is Latin for 'other things being equal'. If the price of other products *did* change, we would then have to re-specify our model.

Modelling in economics is the third of our threshold concepts.

> **KEY IDEA 4**
> **TC 3**
>
> *Modelling in economics* involves specifying how one variable (the 'dependent variable') depends on one or more other variables ('independent variables'). It involves 'holding constant' all other variables that might influence the outcome (the *ceteris paribus* assumption). A model can be expressed in words, as a graph, or mathematically in terms of one or more equations. In this book we use mainly verbal descriptions and graphs.

Two of the most common types of diagram used in economics are graphs and flow diagrams. In the next two sections we will look at one example of each. These examples are chosen to illustrate the distinction between microeconomic and macroeconomic issues.

The production possibility curve

TC 3
p 12
We start by having a look at a **production possibility curve**. This diagram is a graph. Like many diagrams in economics it shows a simplified picture of reality – a picture stripped of all details that are unnecessary to illustrate the points being made. A production possibility curve is shown in Figure 1.1. The graph is based on the data shown in Table 1.1.

Assume that some imaginary nation devotes all its resources – land, labour and capital – to producing just two goods, food and clothing. Various possible combinations that could be produced over a given period of time (e.g. a year) are shown in the table. Thus the country, by devoting all its resources to producing food, could produce 8 million units of food but no clothing. Alternatively, by producing, say, 7 million units of food it could release enough resources – land, labour and capital – to produce 2.2 million units of clothing. At the other extreme, it could produce 7 million units of clothing, with no resources at all being used to produce food.

The information in the table can be transferred to a graph (Figure 1.1). We measure units of food on one axis (in this case the vertical axis) and units of clothing on the other. The curve shows all the combinations of the two goods that can be produced with all the nation's resources

Definition

Production possibility curve A curve showing all the possible combinations of two goods that a country can produce within a specified time period with all its resources fully and efficiently employed.

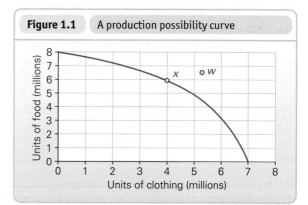

Figure 1.1 A production possibility curve

Table 1.1	Maximum possible combinations of food and clothing that can be produced in a given time period

Units of food (millions)	Units of clothing (millions)
8.0	0.0
7.0	2.2
6.0	4.0
5.0	5.0
4.0	5.6
3.0	6.0
2.0	6.4
1.0	6.7
0.0	7.0

fully and efficiently employed. For example, production could take place at point *x*, with 6 million units of food and 4 million units of clothing being produced. Production cannot take place beyond the curve. For example, production is not possible at point *w*: the nation does not have enough resources to do this.

Note that there are two simplifying assumptions in this diagram. First, it is assumed that there are just two types **TC 3 p 12** of good that can be produced. It is necessary to make this assumption since we only have two axes on our graph.

The other assumption is that there is only one type of food and one type of clothing. This is implied by measuring their output in particular units (e.g. tonnes).

These two assumptions are obviously enormous simplifications when we consider the modern complex economies of the real world. But despite this, the diagram still allows important principles to be illustrated, and illustrated simply.

Microeconomics and the production possibility curve

A production possibility curve illustrates the microeconomic issues of *choice* and *opportunity cost*.

If the country chose to produce more clothing, it would **KI 1 p 5** have to sacrifice the production of some food. This sacrifice of food is the opportunity cost of the extra clothing.

The fact that to produce more of one good involves producing less of the other is illustrated by the downward-sloping nature of the curve. For example, the country could move from point *x* to point *y* in Figure 1.2. In doing so it would be producing an extra 1 million units of clothing, but 1 million fewer units of food. Thus the opportunity cost of the 1 million extra units of clothing would be the 1 million units of food forgone.

It also illustrates the phenomenon of **increasing opportunity costs**. By this we mean that as a country produces more of one good it has to sacrifice ever-*increasing* amounts of the other. The reason for this is that different factors of production have different properties. People have different skills. Land differs in different parts of the country. Raw materials differ one from another; and so on. Thus as the nation concentrates more and more on the production of one good, it has to start using resources that are less and less suitable – resources that would have been better suited to producing other goods. In our example, then, the production of more and more clothing will involve a growing *marginal cost*: ever-increasing amounts of food have to be sacrificed for each additional unit of clothing produced.

It is because opportunity costs increase that the production possibility curve is bowed outward rather than being a straight line. Thus in Figure 1.2 as production moves from point *x* to *y* to *z*, so the amount of food sacrificed rises for each additional unit of clothing produced. The opportunity cost of the fifth million units of clothing is 1 million units of food. The opportunity cost of the sixth million units of clothing is 2 million units of food.

Macroeconomics and the production possibility curve
There is no guarantee that resources will be fully employed, or that they will be used in the most efficient way possible.

The nation may thus be producing at a point inside the curve: for example, point *v* in Figure 1.3.

What we are saying here is that the economy is producing less of both goods than it could possibly produce, either because some resources are not being used (for instance, workers may be unemployed), or because it is not using the most efficient methods of production possible, or a combination of the two. By using its resources to the full, however, the nation could move out onto the curve: to point *x* or *y*, for example. It could thus produce more clothing *and* more food.

Here we are not concerned with the combination of goods produced (a microeconomic issue), but with whether the total amount produced is as much as it could be (a macroeconomic issue).

As we move closer to an economy's full-capacity output and resources become increasingly scarce it is likely that inflationary pressures will increase. Therefore, it is unlikely that an economy could sustain working at full capacity beyond the short term. But, over time, the production possibilities of a nation are likely to increase. **Investment** in new plant and machinery will increase the stock of capital; new raw materials may be discovered; technological advances are likely to take place; through education and training, labour is likely to become more productive. This growth in full-capacity output is illustrated by an outward shift in the production possibility curve.

Figure 1.2 Increasing opportunity costs

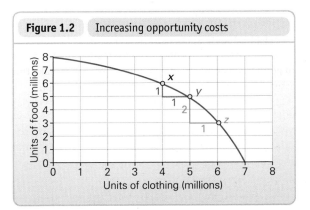

Figure 1.3 Making a fuller use of resources

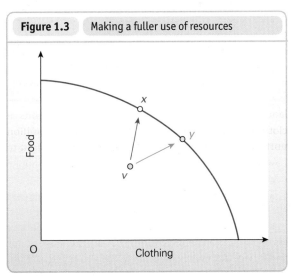

Definitions

Increasing opportunity costs When additional production of one good involves ever-increasing sacrifices of another.

Investment The production of items that are not for immediate consumption.

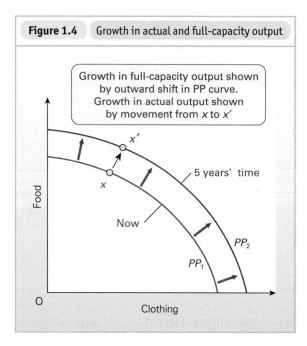

Figure 1.4 Growth in actual and full-capacity output

Growth in full-capacity output shown by outward shift in PP curve. Growth in actual output shown by movement from *x* to *x'*

This will then allow actual output to increase: for example, from point *x* to point *x'* in Figure 1.4.

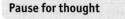

Pause for thought

Will economic growth necessarily involve a parallel outward shift in the production possibility curve? Explain.

The circular flow of goods and incomes

The process of satisfying human wants involves producers and consumers. The relationship between them is two-sided and can be represented in a flow diagram (see Figure 1.5).

The consumers of goods and services are labelled 'households'. Some members of households, of course, are also workers, and in some cases are the owners of other factors of production too, such as land. The producers of goods and services are labelled 'firms'.

Firms and households are in a twin 'demand and supply' relationship with each other.

First, in the top half of the diagram, households demand goods and services, and firms supply goods and services. In the process, exchange takes place. In a money economy (as opposed to a **barter economy**), firms exchange goods and services for money. In other words, money flows from households to firms in the form of consumer expenditure, while goods and services flow the other way – from firms to households.

This coming together of buyers and sellers is known as a **market** – whether it be a street market, a shop, the Internet, an auction, a mail-order system or whatever. Thus we talk about the market for apples, the market for oil, for cars, for houses, for televisions, and so on.

Secondly, firms and households come together in the market for *factors of production*. This is illustrated in the bottom half of the diagram. This time, the demand and supply roles are reversed. Firms demand the use of factors of production owned by households – labour, land and capital. Households supply them. Thus the services of labour and other factors flow from households to firms, and in exchange firms pay households money – namely, wages, rent, dividends and interest. Just as we referred to particular goods markets, so we can also refer to particular factor markets – the market for bricklayers, for secretaries, for hairdressers, for land, and so on.

There is thus a circular flow of incomes. Households earn incomes from firms, and firms earn incomes from households. The money circulates. There is also a circular flow of goods and services, but in the opposite direction. Households supply factor services to firms, which then use them to supply goods and services to households.

The flow diagram in Figure 1.5, like the production possibility curve, can help us to distinguish between micro- and macroeconomics.

Microeconomics is concerned with the composition of the circular flow: *what* combinations of goods make up the goods flow; *how* the various factors of production are combined to produce these goods; *for whom* the wages, dividends, rent and interest are paid out.

Macroeconomics is concerned with the total size of the flow and what causes it to expand and contract.

Techniques of analysis

If you glance through the book, you will see that there are many diagrams and tables and some equations. But this does not mean that there are many mathematical techniques that you will have to master in order to study this book. In fact, there are relatively few techniques – and simple ones at that! But they are ones which we use many times in many different contexts. You will find that if you are new to the subject, you will very quickly become familiar with these techniques. To help you check your understanding of them, you should visit Web Appendix 1.1 in the Chapter 1 resources of MyEconLab (www.myeconlab.com).

This book does not use calculus. If, however, your course does, you will find some optional Web appendices in MyEconLab, some of which use differentiation to explore some of the theories we cover. The rules of differentiation and their use to find maximum and minimum points are given in Web Appendix 1.2.

Definitions

Barter economy An economy where people exchange goods and services directly with one another without any payment of money. Workers would be paid with bundles of goods.

Market The interaction between buyers and sellers.

Figure 1.5 Circular flow of goods and incomes

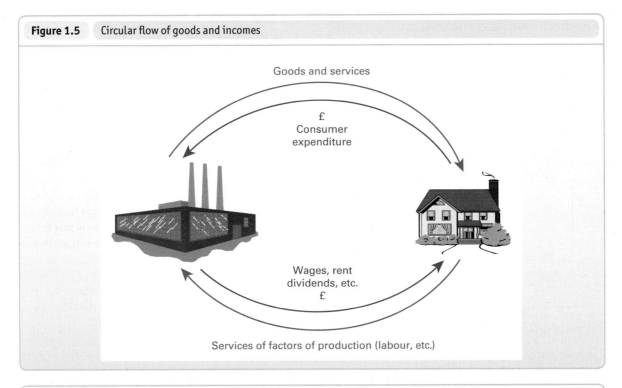

Goods and services

£
Consumer
expenditure

Wages, rent
dividends, etc.
£

Services of factors of production (labour, etc.)

Recap

1. The production possibility curve shows the possible combinations of two goods that a country can produce in a given period of time. Assuming that the country is already producing on the curve, the production of more of one good will involve producing less of the other. This opportunity cost is illustrated by the slope of the curve.

2. If the economy is producing within the production possibility curve as a result of idle resources or inefficiency, it can produce more of both goods by taking up this slack. In the longer term it can only produce more of both by shifting the curve outwards through investment, technological progress, etc.

3. The circular flow of goods and incomes shows the interrelationships between firms and households in a money economy. Firms and households come together in markets. In goods markets, firms supply goods and households demand goods. In the process, money flows from households to firms in return for the goods and services that the firms supply. In factor markets, firms demand factors of production and households supply them. In the process, money flows from firms to households in return for the services of the factors that households supply.

1.5 ECONOMIC SYSTEMS

How do countries differ in the way their economies are organised?

KI 1
p 5

All societies are faced with the problem of scarcity. They differ considerably, however, in the way they tackle the problem. One important difference between societies is in the degree of government control of the economy.

At the one extreme lies the completely **planned or command economy**, where all the economic decisions are taken by the government.

At the other extreme lies the completely **free-market economy**. In this type of economy there is no government intervention at all. All decisions are taken by individuals and firms. Households decide how much labour and other factors to supply, and what goods to consume. Firms decide what goods to produce and what factors to employ. The pattern of production and consumption that results

Definitions

Centrally planned or command economy An economy where all economic decisions are taken by the central authorities.

Free-market economy An economy where all economic decisions are taken by individual households and firms, with no government intervention.

| Figure 1.6 | Classifying economic systems |

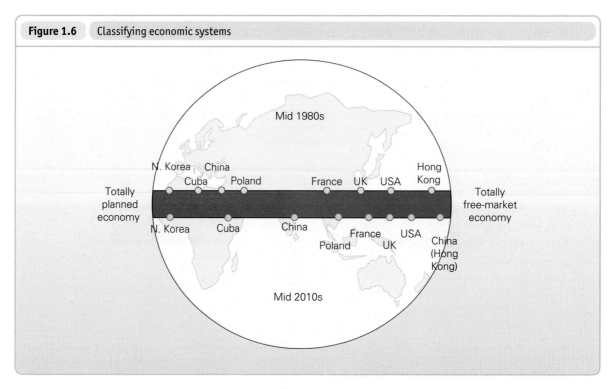

depends on the interactions of all these individual demand and supply decisions.

In practice, all economies are a mixture of the two. It is therefore the *degree* of government intervention that distinguishes different economic systems. The government plays a large role in China, whereas in the USA, the government plays a much smaller role.

It is nevertheless useful to analyse the extremes in order to put the different **mixed economies** of the real world into perspective. The mixture of government and the market can be shown by the use of a spectrum diagram such as Figure 1.6. It shows where particular economies of the real world lie along the spectrum between the two extremes.

> **Pause for thought**
>
> *How do you think the positions of these eight countries will change over the next decade?*

We start by having a brief look at the command economy. Then we will see how a free-market economy operates. We conclude by considering some general reasons for government intervention in market economies. In subsequent chapters we will examine in more detail the various ways in

which governments intervene in market economies: and so at the various forms of **mixed market economy**.

The command economy

The command economy is usually associated with a socialist or communist economic system, where land and capital are collectively owned. The state plans the allocation of resources at three important levels:

- It plans the allocation of resources between current consumption and investment for the future. By sacrificing some present consumption and diverting resources into investment, it could increase the economy's growth rate. The amount of resources it chooses to devote to investment will depend on its broad macroeconomic strategy: the importance it attaches to growth as opposed to current consumption.
- At a microeconomic level it plans the output of each industry and firm, the techniques that will be used and the labour and other resources required by each industry and firm.
- In order to ensure that the required inputs are available, the state would probably conduct some form of **input–output analysis**. All industries are seen as users of

TC 3
p 12

> **Definitions**
>
> **Mixed economy** An economy where economic decisions are made partly by the government and partly through the market.
> **Mixed market economy** A market economy where there is some government intervention.
>
> **Input–output analysis** This involves dividing the economy into sectors where each sector is a user of inputs from and a supplier of outputs to other sectors. The technique examines how these inputs and outputs can be matched to the total resources available in the economy.

inputs from other industries and as producers of output for consumers or other industries. For example, the steel industry uses inputs from the coal and iron-ore industries and produces output for the vehicle and construction industries. Input–output analysis shows, for each industry, the sources of all its inputs and the destination of all its output. The state then attempts to match up the inputs and outputs of each industry so that the planned demand for each industry's product is equal to its planned supply.

■ It plans the distribution of output between consumers. This will depend on the government's aims. It may distribute goods according to its judgement of people's *needs*; or it may give more to those who produce more, thereby providing an *incentive* for people to work harder.

It may distribute goods and services directly (e.g., by a system of rationing); or it may decide the distribution of money incomes and allow individuals to decide how to spend them. If it does the latter, it may still seek to influence the pattern of expenditure by setting appropriate prices: low prices to encourage consumption, and high prices to discourage consumption.

Assessment of the command economy

With central planning, the government could take an overall view of the economy. It could direct the nation's resources in accordance with specific national goals.

High growth rates could be achieved if the government directed large amounts of resources into investment. Unemployment could be largely avoided if the government carefully planned the allocation of labour in accordance with production requirements and labour skills. National income could be distributed more equally or in accordance with needs. The social repercussions of production and consumption (e.g. the effects on the environment) could be taken into account, provided the government was able to predict these effects and chose to take them into account.

In practice, a command economy could achieve these goals only at considerable social and economic cost. The reasons are as follows:

■ The larger and more complex the economy, the greater the task of collecting and analysing the information essential to planning, and the more complex the plan. Complicated plans are likely to be costly to administer and involve cumbersome bureaucracy.

■ If there is no system of prices, or if prices are set arbitrarily by the state, planning is likely to involve the inefficient use of resources. It is difficult to assess the relative efficiency of two alternative techniques that use different inputs if there is no way in which the value of those inputs can be ascertained. For example, how can a rational decision be made between an oil-fired and a coal-fired furnace if the prices of oil and coal do not reflect their relative scarcity?

■ It is difficult to devise appropriate incentives to encourage workers and managers to be more productive without a reduction in quality. For example, if bonuses are given according to the quantity of output produced, a factory might produce shoddy goods, since it can probably produce a larger quantity of goods by cutting quality. To avoid this problem, a large number of officials may have to be employed to check quality.

■ Complete state control over resource allocation would involve a considerable loss of individual liberty. Workers would have no choice where to work; consumers would have no choice what to buy.

■ The government might enforce its plans even if they were unpopular.

■ If production is planned, but consumers are free to spend money incomes as they wish, then there will be a problem if the consumer wishes change. Shortages will occur if consumers decide to buy more, and surpluses will occur if they decide to buy less.

Most of these problems were experienced in the former Soviet Union and the other Eastern bloc countries, and were part of the reason for the overthrow of their communist regimes (see Box 1.3). These problems are still experienced today in the remaining centrally planned economies, such as North Korea and Cuba.

Pause for thought

Queues were a common feature of the former Soviet Union. Why do you think they were so commonplace? Is a system of queuing a fair way of allocating scarce goods and resources?

The free-market economy

Free decision making by individuals

The free-market economy is usually associated with a pure capitalist system, where land and capital are privately owned. All economic decisions are made by households and firms, which are assumed to act in their own self-interest. The following assumptions are usually made:

■ Firms seek to maximise profits.
■ Consumers seek to get the best value for money from their purchases.
■ Workers seek to maximise their wages relative to the human cost of working in a particular job.

It is also assumed that individuals are free to make their own economic choices: consumers are free to decide what to buy with their incomes; workers are free to choose where and how much to work; firms are free to choose what to sell and what production methods to use.

The resulting supply and demand decisions of firms and households are transmitted to each other through their effect on *prices*.

BOX 1.3 **COMMAND ECONOMIES**

Rise and fall of planning

Russia

The Bolsheviks under the leadership of Lenin came to power in Russia with the October Revolution of 1917. Communism was introduced and the market economy abolished. Industries were nationalised; workers were told what jobs to do; food was taken from peasants to feed the towns; workers were allocated goods from distribution depots.

With the ending of the civil war in 1921, the economy was in bad shape and Lenin embarked on the New Economic Policy. This involved a return to the use of markets. Smaller businesses were returned to private hands and peasants were able to sell their crops. The economy began to recover; however, Lenin died in 1924 and Stalin came to power.

The Russian economy underwent a radical transformation from 1928 onwards. The key features of the Stalinist approach were collectivisation, industrialisation and central planning. Peasant farms were abolished and replaced by large-scale collective farms where land was collectively owned and worked, and by state farms, owned by the state and run by managers. This caused disruption and famine, with peasants slaughtering their animals rather than giving them up. However, in the longer term more food was produced. Both collective and state farms were given quotas of output that they were supposed to deliver, for which the state would pay a fixed price.

Alongside the agricultural reforms a drive to industrialisation took place and a vast planning apparatus was developed. At the top was *Gosplan*, the central planning agency. This prepared five-year plans, which specified the general direction in which the economy was to move, and annual plans, which gave details of what was to be produced and with what resources for some 200 or so key products. The system operated without either the price mechanism or the profit motive, although incentives existed with bonuses paid to managers and workers if targets were achieved.

Stalin died in 1953, but the planning system remained largely unchanged throughout the Soviet Union until the late 1980s. Initially, high growth rates had been achieved, though at a cost of low efficiency. Poor flows of information led to inconsistencies in the plans. Targets were often unrealistic, and as a result there were frequent shortages and sometimes surpluses. There was little product innovation and

goods were frequently of poor quality. A large 'underground economy' flourished in which goods were sold on the illegal market and in which people did second 'unofficial' jobs.

Moves to the market

By the time Gorbachev came to power in 1985 many people were pressing for economic reform. Gorbachev responded with his policy of *perestroika* (economic reconstruction), which involved managers preparing their own plans and managers and workers being rewarded for becoming more efficient. Under the new system, one-person businesses and larger co-operatives were allowed, while the price mechanism was re-introduced with the state raising prices if there were substantial shortages.

These reforms, however, did not halt the economic decline. Managers resented the extra responsibilities and people were unclear as to what to expect from the state. Queues lengthened in the shops and people became disillusioned with *perestroika*.

Communism fell apart in 1989 and both the Soviet Union and the system of central planning came to an end. Russia embarked upon a radical programme of market reforms in which competition and enterprise were intended to replace state central planning (see Case Study 1.7 in MyEconLab).

Initially, the disruption of the move to the market led to a sharp decline in the Russian economy. GDP fell by an average of 5.5 per cent per annum between 1993 and 1998. However, this was followed by a period of rapid economic growth, which averaged 7 per cent from 2000 to 2008.

But the economy declined by nearly 8 per cent in the 2009 recession. However, recovery followed, with growth averaging 4.4 per cent per annum for 2010–12. However, with a fall in oil prices, growth slowed in 2013 and then, with the crisis in Ukraine and the imposition of sanctions on Russia by western countries, growth slowed further. This was compounded by a further dramatic fall in oil prices, which between June 2014 and January 2015 had fallen from around $114 to $50 per barrel. Economic growth was a mere 0.5 per cent in 2014 and was forecast to plummet to –3.5 per cent in 2015. Further ahead, growth is expected to average a mere 1.5 per cent for the second part of the 2010s. Macroeconomic data for Russia are available in the IMF's *World Economic Outlook*.

The price mechanism

The **price mechanism** works as follows. Prices respond to *shortages* and *surpluses*. Shortages cause prices to rise. Surpluses cause prices to fall.

If consumers decide they want more of a good (or if producers decide to cut back supply), demand will exceed supply. The resulting *shortage* will encourage sellers to *raise* the price of the good. This will act as an incentive to producers to supply more, since production will now be more profitable. At the same time, it will discourage consumers from buying so much. *The price will continue rising until the shortage has thereby been eliminated.*

If, on the other hand, consumers decide they want less of a good (or if producers decide to produce more), supply

will exceed demand. The resulting *surplus* will encourage sellers to *reduce* the price of the good. This will act as a disincentive to producers, who will supply less, since production will now be less profitable. It will encourage consumers to buy more. *The price will continue falling until the surplus has thereby been eliminated.*

Definitions

Price mechanism The system in a market economy whereby price changes that occur in response to changes in demand and supply have the effect of making demand equal to supply.

Many commentators point to decades of underinvestment in industry and in road and rail infrastructure, corruption, disillusionment and continuing political uncertainty as root causes of this sluggish growth rate.

China

In contrast to the Soviet Union, China's move towards a more market-based economy has been carefully managed by the ruling Communist Party. From the 1940s to the 1970s central planning, combined with the removal of all property rights, resulted in low productivity, a creaking infrastructure and famine.

But after the death of Party Chairman Mao Zedong in 1976, a new breed of Chinese leaders came to power, and they were increasingly pragmatic. There was a focus on making use of aspects of capitalism alongside government control of the economy. Productivity was valued equally with political stability, while consumer welfare was considered as important as the elimination of unemployment.

Economic zones were set up, where foreign investment was encouraged, and laws on patents and other intellectual property encouraged innovation. This approach was developed further over the following decades and from 1992 to 2010 China averaged growth of 10.5 per cent per annum, compared to global growth of 3.7 per cent per annum.

Although growth has slowed during the 2010s to around 7 per cent, China is now the world's largest economy, albeit with much lower output *per head* than many rich countries (see Box 13.6). Yet its human rights record remains a concern to many around the world; economic liberalisation and growth have not been accompanied by political freedom. Furthermore it is experiencing some of the problems of capitalism: pollution, income inequality and potential instability of the financial system. It remains unclear how long the combination of capitalist economics alongside tight political control can continue to deliver.

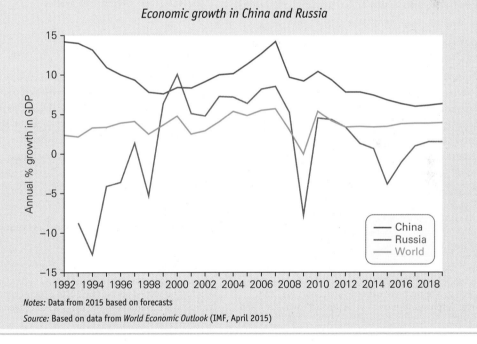

Economic growth in China and Russia

Notes: Data from 2015 based on forecasts

Source: Based on data from *World Economic Outlook* (IMF, April 2015)

TC 3
p 12 This price, where demand equals supply, is called the **equilibrium price**. By **equilibrium** we mean a point of balance or a point of rest: in other words, a point towards which there is a tendency to move.

Definition

Equilibrium price The price where the quantity demanded equals the quantity supplied: the price where there is no shortage or surplus.

Equilibrium A position of balance. A position from which there is no inherent tendency to move away.

The same analysis can be applied to factor markets. If the demand for a particular type of labour exceeds its supply, the resulting shortage will drive up the wage rate (i.e. the price of labour) as employers compete with each other for labour. The rise in the wage rate will have the effect of curbing firms' demand for that type of labour and encouraging more workers to take up that type of job. Wages will continue rising until demand equals supply: until the shortage is eliminated.

Likewise if there is a surplus of a particular type of labour, the wage will fall until demand equals supply. As with price, the wage rate where the demand for labour equals the supply is known as the *equilibrium* wage rate.

The response of demand and supply to changes in price illustrates a very important feature of how economies work:

KEY IDEA 5 *People respond to incentives.* It is important, therefore, that incentives are appropriate and have the desired effect. This is another of our threshold concepts. For details, see MyEconLab.

TC 4

people respond to incentives. It is important, therefore, that incentives are appropriate and have the desired effect. This is our fourth threshold concept.

The effect of changes in demand and supply

How will the price mechanism respond to changes in consumer demand or producer supply? After all, the pattern of consumer demand changes. For example, people may decide they want more mountain bikes and fewer racers. Likewise the pattern of supply also changes. For example, changes in technology may allow the mass production of microchips at lower cost, while the production of hand-built furniture becomes relatively expensive.

In all cases of changes in demand and supply, the resulting changes in *price* act as both *signals* and *incentives*.

TC 4
p 20 *A change in demand.* A rise in demand is signalled by a rise in price. This then acts as an incentive for firms to produce more of the good: the quantity supplied rises. Firms divert resources from goods with lower prices relative to costs (and hence lower profits) to those goods that are more profitable.

A fall in demand is signalled by a fall in price. This then acts as an incentive for firms to produce less: such goods are now less profitable to produce. Thus the quantity supplied falls.

KEY IDEA 6 *Changes in demand or supply cause markets to adjust.* Whenever such changes occur, the resulting 'disequilibrium' will bring an automatic change in prices, thereby restoring equilibrium (i.e. a balance of demand and supply).

A change in supply. A rise in supply is signalled by a fall in price. This then acts as an incentive for consumers to buy more: the quantity demanded rises. A fall in supply is signalled by a rise in price. This then acts as an incentive for consumers to buy less: the quantity demanded falls.

The interdependence of markets

The interdependence of goods and factor markets. A rise in demand for a good will raise its price and profitability. Firms will respond by supplying more. But to do this they will need more inputs. Thus the demand for the inputs will rise, which in turn will raise the price of the inputs. The suppliers of inputs will respond to this incentive by supplying more. This can be summarised as follows: **TC 4** **p 20**

1. Goods market
    -   Demand for the good rises.
    -   This creates a shortage.
    -   This causes the price of the good to rise.
    -   This eliminates the shortage by choking off some of the demand and encouraging firms to produce more.
2. Factor market **KI 6** **p 20**
    -   The increased supply of the good causes an increase in the demand for factors of production (i.e. inputs) used in making it.
    -   This causes a shortage of those inputs.
    -   This causes their prices to rise.
    -   This eliminates their shortage by choking off some of the demand and encouraging the suppliers of inputs to supply more.

Goods markets thus affect factor markets.

It is common in economics to summarise an argument like this by using symbols. It is a form of shorthand. Figure 1.7 summarises this particular sequence of events.

Interdependence exists in the other direction too: factor markets affect goods markets. For example, the discovery

> **Pause for thought**
>
> *Summarise this last paragraph using symbols like those in Figure 1.7.*

of raw materials will lower their price. This will lower the production costs of firms using these raw materials and increase the supply of the finished good. The resulting surplus will lower the price of the good, which will encourage consumers to buy more.

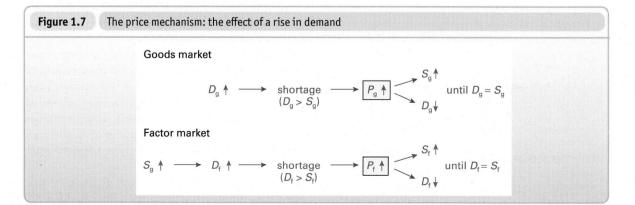

| **Figure 1.7** | The price mechanism: the effect of a rise in demand |

Goods market

$$D_g \uparrow \longrightarrow \text{shortage} \atop (D_g > S_g) \longrightarrow \boxed{P_g \uparrow} \begin{smallmatrix} \nearrow S_g \uparrow \\ \searrow D_g \downarrow \end{smallmatrix} \text{until } D_g = S_g$$

Factor market

$$S_g \uparrow \longrightarrow D_f \uparrow \longrightarrow \text{shortage} \atop (D_f > S_f) \longrightarrow \boxed{P_f \uparrow} \begin{smallmatrix} \nearrow S_f \uparrow \\ \searrow D_f \downarrow \end{smallmatrix} \text{until } D_f = S_f$$

The interdependence of different goods markets. A rise in the price of one good will encourage consumers to buy alternatives. This will drive up the price of alternatives. This in turn will encourage producers to supply more of the alternatives.

Interdependence and the public interest. Even though all individuals are merely looking to their own self-interest in the free-market economy, they are in fact being encouraged to respond to the wishes of others through the incentive of the price mechanism. For example, if consumers want more of a product, firms will supply more – not out of the goodness of their hearts, but because it is profitable to do so. It is often claimed that this is a major advantage of a free-market economy. We will be examining this claim in subsequent chapters.

Competitive markets

In the next chapter we will examine the working of the price mechanism in more detail. We will look first at demand, then at supply, and then we will put the two together to look at the determination of price.

The markets we will be examining are highly competitive markets, with many firms competing against each other. In economics we call this **perfect competition**. This is where consumers and producers are too numerous to have any control over prices: they are **price takers.**

In the case of consumers, this means that they have to accept the prices as given for the things that they buy. On most occasions this is true. For example, when you get to the supermarket checkout you cannot start haggling with the checkout operator over the price of a can of beans or a bar of chocolate.

In the case of firms, perfect competition means that producers are too small and face too much competition from other firms to be able to raise prices. Take the case of farmers selling wheat. They have to sell it at the current market price. If individually they try to sell at a higher price, no one will buy, since purchasers of wheat (e.g. flour millers) can get all the wheat they want at the market price.

Of course, many firms *do* have the power to choose their prices. This does not mean that they can simply charge whatever they like. They will still have to take account of overall consumer demand and their competitors' prices. Ford, when setting the price of its Focus cars, will have to ensure that they remain competitive with Astras, Golfs, 308s, etc. Nevertheless, most firms have some flexibility in setting their prices: they have a degree of 'market power'.

If this is the case, then why do we study *perfect* markets, where firms are price takers? One reason is that they provide a useful approximation to the real world and give us many insights into how a market economy works. Many markets do function very similarly to the markets we shall be describing.

Another is that perfect markets provide an ideal against which to compare the real world. It is often argued that perfect markets benefit the consumer, whereas markets dominated by big business may operate against the consumer's interests. For example, the consumer may end up paying higher prices in a market dominated by just a few firms than in one operating under perfect competition.

The mixed market economy

A 'mixed system' is one containing elements of markets and government control. Most economies today can be described as 'mixed market economies', where markets are the predominant means by which a society's scarce resources are allocated, but where there is some government intervention. However, both the *degree* to which governments intervene and the *types* of intervention vary from country to country and from government to government within countries.

Government intervention creates considerable debate among not only economists, but also policy makers and the wider public too. Such debates intensified in the wake of the financial crisis of the late 2000s, the subsequent economic downturn and the sovereign (government) debt crisis of the early 2010s. This is considered in Box 1.4.

Subsequent chapters will consider government intervention in market economies. But we conclude this chapter by outlining four broad *economic* reasons for intervention. These can, in turn, be used as a framework to help analyse the effects of government interventions.

First, a government may choose to intervene to affect the allocation of resources: an **allocative role**. More specifically, it can attempt to affect levels of consumption and/or production. For instance, it may choose to provide compulsory primary and secondary education in the belief that in not doing so too little would be provided and/or too little would be consumed. On the other hand, it may choose to levy taxes on certain products, such as cigarettes and alcohol, to raise their price and thereby discourage their consumption.

Secondly, the government may choose to affect the distribution of resources and/or the resulting distribution of income, wealth and welfare: a **distributive role**. The income tax system, for instance, can be designed to create a more equal distribution of income, while the subsidising

---

Definitions

Perfect competition (preliminary definition) A situation where the consumers and producers of a product are price takers. (There are other features of a perfectly competitive market; these are examined in Chapter 5.)

Price taker A person or firm with no power to be able to influence the market price.

Allocative role Interventions by government to affect the allocation of resources in consumption and/or production.

Distributive role Interventions by government to affect the distribution of resources such as the distribution of incomes.

BOX 1.4 AFFORDING THE MIXED ECONOMY

The sovereign debt crisis of the early 2010s

Financial crisis and the public finances

The role that governments play in a mixed market economy is a source of considerable debate among both economists and non-economists. The events following the financial crisis of the late 2000s further inflamed this already lively debate.

As we shall see in the second half of this book, governments around the world were proactive in attempting to stabilise their financial systems. This involved injecting capital into banks, nationalising ailing financial institutions (taking private institutions into public ownership) or providing guarantees for those transacting with financial institutions. But they were also proactive in stimulating economic activity. Governments looked to boost their spending and reduce taxation to raise aggregate demand.

The interventions that began in the late 2000s impacted on countries' public finances. Part (a) of the table shows the average budget balance – the difference between

government receipts and expenditures – for a sample of countries in the European Union across three sub-periods from 2003. The figures relate to local and central government, known collectively as *general government*. They are expressed as a percentage of GDP, where GDP stands for 'gross domestic product', which measures a country's national income – in other words, the value of what a country produces.

Positive budget balance figures indicate budget surpluses, while negative figures indicate budget deficits (borrowing). We can see that the budgetary positions deteriorated from 2008, with the exception of Germany. In the cases of Ireland and Greece, borrowing averaged over 10 per cent of GDP.

Increased levels of government borrowing have implications for the stock of government debt (also known as either 'sovereign debt' or 'national debt'). Part (b) shows how government debt stocks rose in many countries from 2008; in Ireland the debt-to-GDP ratio almost trippled.

General government fiscal indicators, percentage of GDP

	(a) Budget balance			(b) Debt		
	2003–07	2008–11	2012–16	2003–07	2008–11	2012–16
Cyprus	−2.2	−4.2	−4.2	67.2	60.1	112.8
France	−3.1	−5.6	−4.3	63.8	77.6	94.5
Germany	−2.5	−2.0	0.2	66.5	76.0	75.4
Greece	−6.4	−11.6	−2.9	102.4	140.3	167.6
Ireland	1.3	−15.5	−4.6	26.5	72.8	112.1
Italy	−3.3	−4.0	−2.5	104.6	115.6	133.3
Latvia	−0.7	−6.5	−0.7	11.7	31.8	35.4
Netherlands	−0.9	−3.3	−2.5	47.0	57.8	68.6
Portugal	−4.2	−7.0	−4.1	61.6	89.4	127.9
Romania	−2.1	−5.7	−2.2	38.6	44.9	44.3
Spain	1.1	−8.7	−6.4	42.8	56.6	96.3
UK	−3.2	−8.5	−5.2	41.4	70.4	91.5

Note: 2012–16 averages are based on projected figures for 2015–16
Source: World Economic Outlook Database, International Monetary Fund, April 2015

or provision of services, such as libraries and parks, is a means of granting more equal access to society's scarce resources.

Thirdly, the government can choose to regulate the actions of consumers and producers: a **regulatory role**. By the implementation of legally enforceable rules, such as on the correct labelling of products or prohibiting collusion between powerful firms, this role can help government achieve its allocative and distributive aims. This role too recognises the importance to economic activity in a market-based economy of a legal framework of rights and protections.

Finally, the government may choose to intervene so as to reduce the volatility of the macroeconomy and/or to help promote the long-term growth of the economy: a

Definitions

Regulatory role Interventions by government to regulate economic activity through legally enforceable rules or actions.

Macroeconomic role Interventions by government either to stabilise the economy in the short term or to promote longer-term economic growth.

macroeconomic role. This role, particularly the stabilisation function, is keenly debated by economists. However, many economists recognise the role that governments can play in helping to advance longer-term growth by

Government bonds

When governments run deficits, these must be financed by borrowing. The main form of borrowing is government bonds. To persuade people (mainly private-sector institutions, such as pension funds) to buy these bonds, an interest rate must be offered. Bonds are issued for a fixed period of time and at maturity are paid back at face value to the holders. Thus new bonds are issued not just to cover current deficits but also to replace bonds that are maturing. The shorter the average term on existing government bonds, the greater the amount of bonds that will need to be replaced in any one year.

In normal times, bonds are seen as a totally safe asset to hold. On maturity, the government would buy back the bond from the current holder at the full face value. In normal times, interest rates on new bonds reflect market interest rates with no added risk premium. The interest rate (or 'coupon') on a bond is fixed with respect to its face value for the life of the bond. In other words, a bond with a face value of £100 and an annual payment to the holder of £6 would be paying an interest rate of 6 per cent on the face value.

As far as existing bonds are concerned, these can be sold on the secondary market (i.e. to other people, rather than back to the government) and the price at which they are sold reflects current interest rates. If, for example, the current interest rate falls to 3 per cent, then the market price of a £100 bond with a 6 per cent coupon will rise to £200, since £6 per year on £200 is 3 per cent – the current market rate of interest. The annual return on the *current* market price is known as the 'yield' (3 per cent in our example). Normally, the yield will reflect current market rates of interest.

The early 2010s, however, were not 'normal' times. Bonds issued by many countries were no longer seen as a totally safe form of investment. Worries grew about the sustainability of the debts of many eurozone countries. As a result, bond yields began to rise, even in countries such as Germany and Austria, which had been previously seen as totally safe. And the effect is self-reinforcing. As the interest rates on new bonds are driven up by the market, so this is taken as a sign of the countries' weakness and hence investors require even higher rates to persuade them to buy more bonds, further undermining confidence and further driving up rates.

How quickly to cut?

The eurozone sovereign debt crisis resulted in bailouts, funded by the International Monetary Fund and the European Union, being granted to the governments of Greece, Ireland, Portugal and Cyprus. In return they were required to adopt tough austerity measures in order to reduce their budget deficits and hence reduce the growth in their borrowing.

But this stoked a debate about the pace of fiscal tightening. It was a debate that extended to many advanced economies, including the UK, since the financial well-being of many governments had severely deteriorated following the financial crisis. Would attempts to improve the public finances by rapid cuts in government expenditure and/or higher taxes be counter-productive? After all, the effects of such policies is to reduce aggregate demand in the economy. This then negatively impacts on the public finances by raising income-related government spending, such as benefits to the unemployed, and by reducing tax receipts as income and consumption falls. In other words, by being thrifty, a government could actually find its financial position deteriorates!

The counter-argument is that by 'tightening their belts' governments reassure the markets and interest rates begin falling. Lower interest rates may stimulate private-sector investment and raise demand in the economy. In effect, private-sector spending would begin to replace public-sector spending and, in the longer term, the rebalancing towards the private sector would help to raise economic growth. This was the thrust of the argument of the UK's Conservative–Liberal Democrat Coalition government that held power from 2010 to 2015.

1. *Does the global power of bond markets prevent countries (including non-eurozone ones, such as the UK and USA) from using fiscal policy to avert sliding into recession?*
2. *What do you think is meant when economists refer to government borrowing as a 'flow' concept, but to government debt as a 'stock' concept (see Key Idea 21 on page 148)?*

---

providing, for instance, infrastructure and education and training.

The fact that government intervention can, at least in principle, correct market failures is the fifth of our fifteen threshold concepts.

Government intervention may be able to rectify various failings of the market. Government intervention in the market can be used to achieve various economic objectives that may not be best achieved by the market. Governments are not perfect, however, and their actions may bring adverse as well as beneficial consequences.

Pause for thought

Why do governments on the political right tend to intervene less in markets than governments on the political left? Does this mean that whether something is an economic 'problem' depends on your perspective?

Recap

1. The economic systems of different countries vary according to the extent to which they rely on the market or the government to allocate resources.

2. At the one extreme, in a command economy, the state makes all the economic decisions. It plans how many resources to allocate for present consumption and how many for investment for future output. It plans the output of each industry, the methods of production it will use and the amount of resources it will be allocated. It plans the distribution of output between consumers.

3. A command economy has the advantage of being able to address directly various national economic goals, such as rapid growth and the avoidance of unemployment and inequality. A command economy, however, is likely to be inefficient: a large bureaucracy will be needed to collect and process information; prices and the choice of production methods are likely to be arbitrary; incentives may be inappropriate; shortages and surpluses may result.

4. At the other extreme is the free-market economy. In this economy, decisions are made by the interaction of demand and supply. Price changes act as the mechanism whereby demand and supply are balanced. If there is a shortage of a product, its price will rise until the shortage is eliminated. If there is a surplus, its price will fall until that is eliminated.

5. Perfect markets are markets where both producers and consumers are price takers.

6. A mixed market economy is a predominantly market-based economic system with some government intervention. We can identify four broad roles for government intervention: allocative, distributive, regulatory and macroeconomic.

QUESTIONS

1. Imagine that you won millions of pounds on the National Lottery. Would your 'economic problem' be solved?

2. Would redistributing incomes from the rich to the poor reduce the overall problem of scarcity?

3. In what way does specialisation reduce the problem of scarcity?

4. Which of the following are macroeconomic issues, which are microeconomic ones and which could be either depending on the context?
   a. Inflation.
   b. Low wages in certain service industries.
   c. The rate of exchange between the pound and the euro.
   d. Why the price of cabbages fluctuates more than that of cars.
   e. The rate of economic growth this year compared with last year.
   f. The decline of traditional manufacturing industries.
   g. A decline in house prices.
   h. A reduction in the supply of credit by financial institutions.

5. Assume that in a household one parent currently works full time and the other stays at home to look after the family. How would you set about identifying and calculating the opportunity costs of the second parent now taking a full-time job? How would such calculations be relevant in deciding whether it is worth taking that job?

6. When you made the decision to study economics, was it a 'rational' decision (albeit based on the limited information you had available at the time)? What additional information would you like to have had in order to ensure that your decision was the right one?

7. Assume you are looking for a job and are offered two. One is more unpleasant to do, but pays more. How would you make a rational choice of which of the two jobs to accept?

8. Imagine that a country can produce just two things: goods and services. Assume that over a given time period it could produce any of the following combinations:

Units of goods	0	10	20	30	40	50	60	70	80	90	100
Units of services	80	79	77	74	70	65	58	48	35	19	0

   a. Draw the country's production possibility curve.
   b. Assuming that the country is currently producing 40 units of goods and 70 units of services, what is the opportunity cost of producing another 10 units of goods?
   c. Explain how the figures illustrate the principle of increasing opportunity cost.
   d. Now assume that technical progress leads to a 10 per cent increase in the output of goods for any given amount of resources. Draw the new production possibility curve. How has the opportunity cost of producing extra units of services altered?

9. Under what circumstances would the production possibility curve be (a) a straight line, (b) bowed in towards the origin? Are these circumstances ever likely?

10. Using a chart similar to that in Figure 1.7, trace through the following effects: (a) a fall in demand for a good; (b) an increased supply of a factor of production. (In the case of (b) you will need to consider the factor market first, and then the goods market.)

11. Draw up a list of policy measures that may help government to affect: (i) the allocation of resources; (ii) the distribution of resources. Is it possible that the policies you have identified in each case could conflict with each other?

MyEconLab

This book can be supported by MyEconLab, which contains a range of additional resources, including an online homework and tutorial system designed to test and build your understanding.

You need both an access card and a course ID to access MyEconLab:

1. Is your lecturer using MyEconLab? Ask your lecturer for your course ID.

2. Has an access card been included with the book at a reduced cost? Check the inside back cover of the book.

3. If you have a course ID but no access card, go to: http://www.myeconlab.com/ to buy access to this interactive study programme.

ADDITIONAL CASE STUDIES IN THE *ESSENTIALS OF ECONOMICS* MyEconLab (www.pearsoned.co.uk/sloman)

1.1 **Scarcity and abundance.** If scarcity is the central economic problem, is anything truly abundant?

1.2 **Global economics.** This examines how macroeconomics and microeconomics apply at the global level and identifies some key issues.

1.3 **Buddhist economics.** A different perspective on economic problems and economic activity.

1.4 **Green economics.** This examines some of the environmental costs that society faces today. It also looks at the role of economics in analysing these costs and how the problems can be tackled.

1.5 **Positive and normative statements.** A crucial distinction when considering matters of economic policy.

1.6 **Adam Smith (1723–90).** Smith, the founder of modern economics, argued that markets act like an invisible hand guiding production and consumption.

1.7 **Free-market medicine in Russia.** This examines the operation of the fledgling market economy in Russia and the successes and difficulties in moving from a planned to a market economy.

WEBSITES RELEVANT TO PART A

Numbers and sections refer to websites listed in the Web appendix and hotlinked from this book's website at **www.pearsoned.co.uk/sloman**.

■ For news articles relevant to this Introduction, see the *Economics News Articles* link from the book's website.

■ For a tutorial on finding the best economics websites see site C8 (The *Internet Economist*).

■ For general economics news sources, see websites in section A of the Web Appendix at the end of the book, and particularly A1–5, 7–9, 35, 36. See also A38, 39, 42, 43, 44 for links to newspapers worldwide.

■ For sources of economic data, see sites in section B and particularly B1, 3, 21, 29, 33, 34 and 47.

■ For general sites for students of economics, see sites in section C and particularly C1–7.

■ For sites giving links to relevant economics websites, organised by topic, see sites I8, 11, 12, 17, 18.

■ For news on the Russian economy (Box 1.3), see sites A14, 15.

WEB APPENDICES

1.1 **Some techniques of economic analysis.** This appendix explains how economists use graphs, tables and simple equations to represent economic data.

1.2 **Elementary differentiation.** This gives the rules for simple differentiation. Although this book does not use calculus (of which differentiation is part), the techniques are widely used by economists and you will need to use calculus if you progress to more advanced economic courses.

Microeconomics

Markets, demand and supply

In this section of the book we focus on *microeconomics*. Despite being 'small economics' – in other words, the economics of the individual parts of the economy, rather than the economy as a whole – it is still concerned with many of the big issues of today.

We will study why the pattern of production and consumption changes over time; why some people are rich and others poor; why our lives seem to be dominated by market forces beyond our control. We will look at the world of big business at one extreme and highly competitive markets at the other. We will look at many of the seemingly intractable problems we face: from the growing problem of pollution, to our limited power as consumers, to the widening inequality of incomes in society.

We will look at how markets work. We will examine what determines how much of any product gets produced and sold, and why some goods rise in price, whereas others fall. In the process we will be looking at one of the most important theories in the whole of economics: the theory of supply and demand.

After studying this chapter, you should be able to answer the following questions:

- How do markets operate?
- What determines the amount that consumers buy of a product?
- What determines how much producers supply of a product?
- How are market prices determined and when are they likely to rise or fall?
- How do markets respond to changes in demand or supply?
- What are the major strengths and weaknesses of a free-market economy?
- How do people in practice make decisions about buying and selling, when information is lacking and people can be influenced by emotion, impulse and habit?

2.1 DEMAND

How much will people buy of any item?

The relationship between demand and price

The headlines announce, 'Major crop failures in Brazil and East Africa: coffee prices soar'. Shortly afterwards you find that coffee prices have doubled in the shops. What do you do? Presumably you will cut back on the amount of coffee you drink. Perhaps you will reduce it from, say, six cups per day to two. Perhaps you will give up drinking coffee altogether.

This is simply an illustration of the general relationship between price and consumption: *when the price of a good rises, the quantity demanded will fall*. This relationship is known as the **law of demand**. There are two reasons for this law:

- People will feel poorer. They will not be able to afford to buy so much of the good with their money. The purchasing power of their income (their real income[1]) has fallen. This is called the **income effect** of a price rise.
- The good will now be dearer relative to other goods. People will thus switch to alternative or 'substitute' goods. This is called the **substitution effect** of a price rise.

Similarly, when the price of a good falls, the quantity demanded will rise. People can afford to buy more (the income effect), and some will switch to consuming this good from alternative goods (the substitution effect).

Therefore, returning to our example of the increase in the price of coffee, we will not be able to afford to buy as much as before, and we will probably drink more tea, cocoa, fruit juices or even water instead.

A word of warning: be careful about the meaning of the words **quantity demanded**. They refer to the amount consumers are willing and able to purchase at a given price over a given period (e.g. a week, or a month, or a year). They do *not* refer to what people would simply *like* to consume. You might like to own a luxury yacht, but your demand for luxury yachts will almost certainly be zero at the current price.

The demand curve

Consider the hypothetical data in Table 2.1. The table shows how many kilos of potatoes per month would be purchased at various prices.

Columns (2) and (3) show the **demand schedules** for two individuals, Dean and John. Column (4), by contrast, shows the total **market demand schedule**. This is the total demand by all consumers. To obtain the market demand schedule for potatoes, we simply add up the quantities demanded at each price by *all* consumers: i.e. Dean, John and everyone else who demands potatoes. Notice that we are talking about demand *over a period of time* (not at a *point* in time). Thus we would talk about daily demand, or weekly demand, or annual demand or whatever.

The demand schedule can be represented graphically as a **demand curve**. Figure 2.1 shows the market demand curve for potatoes corresponding to the schedule in

Table 2.1	The demand for potatoes (monthly)		
Price (pence per kilo) (1)	Dean's demand (kilos) (2)	John's demand (kilos) (3)	Total market demand (tonnes: 000s) (4)
A	20	28	16	700
B	40	15	11	500
C	60	5	9	350
D	80	1	7	200
E	100	0	6	100

Definitions

Law of demand The quantity of a good demanded per period of time will fall as price rises and will rise as price falls, other things being equal.

Income effect The **effect of** a change in price on quantity demanded arising from the consumer becoming better or worse off as a result of the price change.

Substitution effect The effect of a change in price on quantity demanded arising from the consumer switching to or from alternative (substitute) products.

Quantity demanded The amount of a good that a consumer is willing and able to buy at a given price over a given period of time.

Demand schedule for an individual A table showing the different quantities of a good that a person is willing and able to buy at various prices over a given period of time.

Market demand schedule A table showing the different total quantities of a good that consumers are willing and able to buy at various prices over a given period of time.

Demand curve A graph showing the relationship between the price of a good and the quantity of the good demanded over a given time period. Price is measured on the vertical axis; quantity demanded is measured on the horizontal axis. A demand curve can be for an individual consumer or group of consumers, or more usually for the whole market.

---

[1]'Real income' is income measured in terms of its purchasing power: i.e. after taking price changes into account. Thus if prices doubled and your money income stayed the same, your real income would have halved. In other words, you would only be able to buy half as much as before with your income.

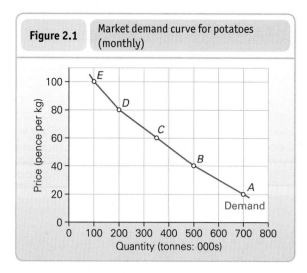

Figure 2.1 Market demand curve for potatoes (monthly)

Table 2.1. The price of potatoes is plotted on the vertical axis. The quantity demanded is plotted on the horizontal axis.

Point *E* shows that at a price of 100p per kilo, 100 000 tonnes of potatoes are demanded each month. When the price falls to 80p we move down the curve to point *D*. This shows that the quantity demanded has now risen to 200 000 tonnes per month. Similarly, if the price falls to 60p we move down the curve again to point *C*: 350 000 tonnes are now demanded. The five points on the graph (*A–E*) correspond to the figures in columns (1) and (4) of Table 2.1. The graph also enables us to read off the likely quantities demanded at prices other than those in the table.

A demand curve could also be drawn for an individual consumer. Like market demand curves, individuals' demand curves generally slope downwards from left to right: the lower the price of a product, the more a person is likely to buy.

Two points should be noted at this stage:

■ In textbooks, demand curves (and other curves too) are only occasionally used to plot specific data. More frequently they are used to illustrate general theoretical arguments. In such cases, the axes will simply be price and quantity, with the units unspecified.

■ The term demand 'curve' is used even when the graph is a straight line! In fact, when using demand curves to illustrate arguments we frequently draw them as straight lines – it's easier.

Other determinants of demand

Price is not the only factor that determines how much of a good people will buy. Demand is also affected by the following:

Tastes. The more desirable people find the good, the more they will demand. Tastes are affected by advertising, by fashion, by observing other consumers, by considerations of health and by the experiences from consuming the good on previous occasions.

The number and price of substitute goods (i.e. competitive goods). The higher the price of **substitute goods**, the higher will be the demand for this good as people switch from the substitutes. For example, the demand for coffee will depend on the price of tea. If tea goes up in price, the demand for coffee will rise.

The number and price of complementary goods. **Complementary goods** are those that are consumed together: cars and petrol, shoes and polish, fish and chips. The higher the price of complementary goods, the fewer of them will be bought and hence the less will be the demand for this good. For example, the demand for electricity will depend on the price of electrical goods. If the price of electrical goods goes up, so that fewer are bought, the demand for electricity will fall.

Income. As people's incomes rise, their demand for most goods will rise. Such goods are called **normal goods**. There are exceptions to this general rule, however. As people get richer, they spend less on **inferior goods**, such as supermarkets' 'value lines', and switch to better-quality goods.

Distribution of income. If national income were redistributed from the poor to the rich, the demand for luxury goods would rise. At the same time, as the poor got poorer they might have to turn to buying inferior goods, whose demand would thus rise too.

Expectations of future price changes. If people think that prices are going to rise in the future, they are likely to buy more now before the price does go up.

Movements along and shifts in the demand curve

A demand curve is constructed on the assumption that 'other things remain equal' (sometimes known by the Latin term *ceteris paribus*). In other words, it is assumed that

TC 3
p 12

Definitions

Substitute goods A pair of goods that are considered by consumers to be alternatives to each other. As the price of one goes up, the demand for the other rises.

Complementary goods A pair of goods consumed together. As the price of one goes up, the demand for both goods will fall.

Normal good A good whose demand rises as people's incomes rise.

Inferior good A good whose demand falls as people's incomes rise.

Ceteris paribus Latin for 'other things being equal'. This assumption has to be made when making deductions from theories.

none of the determinants of demand, other than price, changes.[2] The effect of a change in price is then simply illustrated by a movement along the demand curve–for example, from point *B* to point *D* in Figure 2.1 when the price of potatoes rises from 40p to 80p per kilo.

What happens, then, when one of these other determinants does change? The answer is that we have to construct a whole new demand curve: the curve shifts. If a change in one of the other determinants causes demand to rise – say, income rises – the whole curve will shift to the right. This shows that at each price, more will be demanded than before. Thus in Figure 2.2 at a price of *P*, a quantity of Q_0 was originally demanded. But now, after the increase in demand, Q_1 is demanded. (Note that D_1 is not necessarily parallel to D_0.)

If a change in a determinant other than price causes demand to fall, the whole curve will shift to the left.

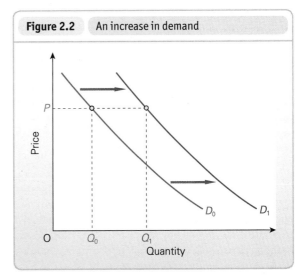

Figure 2.2   An increase in demand

To distinguish between shifts in and movements along demand curves, we refer to a shift in demand as a **change in demand**, and a movement along the demand curve as a result of a change in price as a **change in the quantity demanded**.

Utility and the demand curve

Consumption and utility

When you buy something, it's normally because you want it. You want it because you expect to get pleasure, satisfaction or some other sort of benefit from it. This applies to everything from cups of coffee, to train journeys, to music downloads, to jeans, to insurance. Economists use the term 'utility' to refer to the benefit we get from consumption.

Clearly, the nature and amount of utility that people get varies from one product to another, and from one person to another. But there is a simple rule that applies to virtually all people and all products. As you consume more of a product, and thus become more satisfied, so your desire for additional units of it will decline.

Economists call this rule the **principle of diminishing marginal utility**.

KEY IDEA 8   ***The principle of diminishing marginal utility.*** **The more of a product a person consumes over a given period of time, the less will be the additional utility gained from one more unit.**

Pause for thought

The price of cinema tickets rises and yet it is observed that cinema attendance increases. Does this means that the demand curve for cinema tickets is upward sloping?

For example, the second cup of tea in the morning gives you less additional satisfaction than the first cup. The third cup gives less still. We call the additional utility you get from consuming an extra unit of a product the **marginal utility (*MU*)**. So the rule says that the marginal utility will fall as we consume more of a product over a given period of time.

Pause for thought

How will your marginal utility from the consumption of butter depend on the amount of margarine you consume?

There is a problem, however, with the concept of marginal utility. How can it be measured? After all, we cannot get inside each other's heads to find out just how much pleasure we are getting from consuming a product!

One way round the problem is to measure marginal utility in *money terms*: in other words, the amount that a person would be prepared to pay for one more unit of a product.

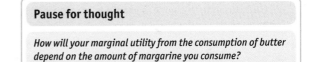
Definitions

Change in demand   The term used for a shift in the demand curve. It occurs when a determinant of demand other than price changes.

Change in the quantity demanded   The term used for a movement along the demand curve to a new point. It occurs when there is a change in price.

Principle of diminishing marginal utility   As more units of a good are consumed, additional units will provide less additional satisfaction than previous units.

Marginal utility (*MU*)   The extra satisfaction gained from consuming one extra unit of a good within a given time period.

---

[2]We make this assumption to keep the analysis simple at the outset. We can then drop the assumption by changing things one at a time and seeing what happens.

Thus if you were prepared to pay 50p for an extra packet of crisps per week, then we would say that your marginal utility from consuming it is 50p. As long as you are prepared to pay more than or the same as the actual price, you will buy an extra packet. If you are not prepared to pay that price, you will not.

Utility and the individual's demand curve

We can now see how utility relates to a downward-sloping demand curve. We will focus first on an individual consumer's demand and then on the whole market demand.

Let us assume that consumers are **rational**, in the sense that they try to get as much value from their money as possible. This means that if a good is worth more to you than it costs ($MU > P$), you will buy more of it. If it is worth less to you than it costs ($MU < P$), you will not buy it or, if you are already buying some, you will buy less.

Let us take the case where the price of a good exactly equals marginal utility ($MU = P$). Assume that the price now falls. As it does so, it will be worth buying extra units. You will buy more because the price will now be below the amount you are prepared to pay: i.e. price is less than your marginal utility.

But as you buy more, your marginal utility from consuming each extra unit will get less and less. How many extra units do you buy? You will stop when the marginal utility has fallen to the new lower price of the good: when $MU = P$.

We can illustrate these ideas graphically. Figure 2.3, shows the marginal utility curve for a particular person and a particular good. If the price of the good were P_1, the person would consume Q_1, where $MU = P_1$. Thus point a would be

one point on that person's demand curve. If the price fell to P_2, consumption would rise to Q_2, since this is where $MU = P_2$. Thus point b is a second point on the demand curve. Likewise if price fell to P_3, Q_3 would be consumed. Point c is a third point on the demand curve.

Because rational individuals consume where $P = MU$, their demand curve will be along the same line as their marginal utility curve.

The market demand curve

The market demand curve is simply the *horizontal* sum of all individuals' demand curves and hence MU curves.

Its shape will reflect the rate at which MU diminishes. If there are close substitutes for a good then its MU will diminish slowly as its consumption increases. The reason is that increased consumption of this product will be accompanied by decreased consumption of the alternative products. People will have substituted this product for the alternatives. Since total consumption of this product plus the alternatives has increased only slightly (if at all), the marginal utility will fall only slowly.

Definitions

Rational consumer behaviour The attempt to get as much value as possible from your money when purchasing a good. If $MU > P$, you will buy more; if $MU < P$, you will buy less (or not buy at all); if $MU = P$, you will maintain your current level of consumption.

Figure 2.3   Deriving an individual's demand curve

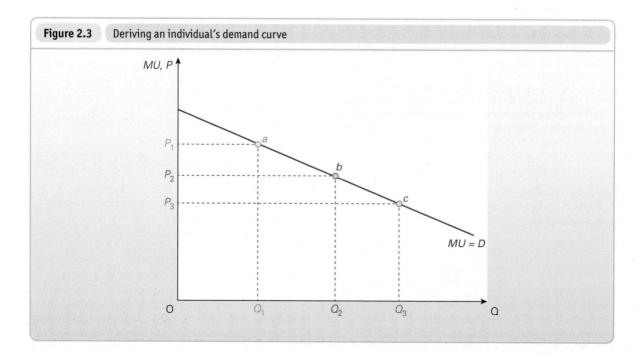

| BOX 2.1 | SATISFACTION AND THE RATIONAL CONSUMER | EXPLORING ECONOMICS |

Consumer surplus and 'benefit drivers'

In the act of consuming goods and services we look to derive some form of benefit or satisfaction. As explained in the text, each extra unit of a product consumed is likely to give you less additional utility (satisfaction) than previous units. This is the idea *of diminishing marginal utility*. Rational consumers will continue to consume more of a product so long as the price they are prepared to pay exceeds the price they are charged (*P*). Since the additional amount they are prepared to pay reflects their marginal utility (*MU*), people will continue to purchase additional units as long as $MU > P$.

Consumer surplus and the rational consumer

Additional insight into the behaviour of rational consumers can be gained by introducing the concept of *consumer surplus*.

Marginal consumer surplus (*MCS*) is the difference between what you are willing to pay for one more unit of a good and what you are actually charged. If Dean is willing to pay £3.00 for another regular cup of cappuccino in his favourite coffee shop but it actually costs him £2.25, he would be getting a marginal consumer surplus of 75p. Hence $MCS = MU - P$.

Total consumer surplus (*TCS*) is the sum of all the marginal consumer surpluses that you have obtained from all the units of a good you have consumed over a specified time period (e.g. a day, a month or a year). It is the difference between the total utility from all the units and your expenditure on them. If Dean consumes two regular cups of cappuccino in a day, and if he would have been prepared to spend £5.00 on them and only had to spend £4.50, then his total consumer surplus is 50p. Hence, $TCS = TU - TE$, where *TU* is total utility and *TE* is total expenditure ($P \times Q$).

So we can define *rational consumer behaviour* as the attempt to maximise consumer surplus. In doing so, people will go on purchasing additional units as long as they gain *additional* consumer surplus: i.e. as long as $MU > P$.

Because of diminishing marginal utility, people are prepared to pay less for each additional unit they consume. They will cease to consume additional units when no further consumer surplus can be gained. As they purchase more, their marginal utility will go on falling until $MU = P$. At this point, there is no extra (marginal) consumer surplus that can be gained and hence their *total* consumer surplus is maximised. In other words, their optimum level of consumption has been reached. If they continued to purchase beyond this point, *MU* would be less than *P*, and thus they would be paying more for the last units than they were worth to them; their total consumer surplus would fall.

Preparedness to pay and product attributes

Consumers obtain consumer surplus when the price they are being charged is less than what they are prepared to pay. Since utility affects preparedness to pay, the key to understanding the potential for consumer surplus is to understand how consumers derive their utility. Kelvin Lancaster[3] popularised the idea that individuals derive their utility from the *characteristics* or *attributes* of goods and services.

Let's think how this helps us to understand Dean's preparedness to pay for cappuccinos. It might be that the utility Dean derives from a cappuccino may come from outputs such as 'the quenching of thirst' and 'flavour'. But, if it is consuming it in a particular coffee shop, then, in fact, his utility is influenced not only by the characteristics of the coffee itself but by the characteristics of the environment in which he is consuming the drink.

The characteristics of products, therefore, affect the preparedness to pay of consumers. They can be the source of consumer surplus. Sometimes these characteristics are known as 'benefit drivers'.

In complex products, such as housing, there can be a multitude of benefit drivers which appeal differently to different consumers. For instance, some groups of buyers might be prepared to pay more for a property whose location has good transport connections, while others might be attracted by the proximity to particular schools.

The characteristics approach to consumer choice is analysed in Case Study 2.9 in MyEconLab.

1. Make a list of possible 'benefit drivers' when purchasing: (i) housing; (ii) season tickets to watch live sport; (iii) kilo bags of sugar.
2. Why would we expect firms to be interested in 'benefit drivers'?

---

[3]K. Lancaster, 'A new approach to consumer theory', *The Journal of Political Economy*, 74 (1966), 122–57.

Definitions

Consumer surplus The excess of what a person would have been prepared to pay for a good (i.e. the utility) over what that person actually pays.

Marginal consumer surplus The excess of utility from the consumption of one more unit of a good (*MU*) over the price paid: $MCS = MU - P$.

Total consumer surplus The excess of a person's total utility from the consumption of a good (*TU*) over the total amount that person spends on it (*TE*): $TCS = TU - TE$.

Rational consumer behaviour (alternative definition) The attempt to maximise total consumer surplus.

If the price of an *alternative* product in consumption was to change, then the *MU* schedule for a particular product will shift. For example, consider the marginal utility of (and hence demand for) margarine following a rise in the price of butter. The higher price of butter would cause less butter to be consumed. This would increase the marginal utility of margarine, since if people are using less butter, their desire for margarine is higher. The *MU* curve (and hence the demand curve) for margarine thus shifts to the right.

Recap

1. When the price of a good rises, the quantity demanded per period of time will fall. This is known as the 'law of demand'. It applies both to individuals' demand and to the whole market demand.

2. The law of demand is explained by the income and substitution effects of a price change.

3. The relationship between price and quantity demanded per period of time can be shown in a table (or 'schedule') or as a graph. On the graph, price is plotted on the vertical axis and quantity demanded per period of time on the horizontal axis. The resulting demand curve is downward sloping (negatively sloped).

4. Other determinants of demand include tastes, the number and price of substitute goods, the number and price of complementary goods, income, the distribution of income and expectations of future price changes.

5. If price changes, the effect is shown by a movement along the demand curve. We call this effect 'a change in the quantity demanded'.

6. If any other determinant of demand changes, the whole curve will shift. We call this effect 'a change in demand'. A rightward shift represents an increase in demand; a leftward shift represents a decrease in demand.

7. Consumers will attempt to get the best value from their money when buying goods. They will do this by consuming more of a good as long as its marginal utility to them (measured in terms of the price they are prepared to pay for it) exceeds its price. But as they buy more, marginal utility will diminish. They will stop buying additional amounts once *MU* has fallen to equal the price.

8. An individual's demand curve lies along the same line as the individual's marginal utility curve. The market demand curve is the sum of all individuals' marginal utility curves.

2.2 SUPPLY

How much of any item will firms want to produce?

Supply and price

Imagine you are a farmer deciding what to do with your land. Part of your land is in a fertile valley. Part is on a hillside where the soil is poor. Perhaps, then, you will consider growing vegetables in the valley and keeping sheep on the hillside.

Your decision will largely depend on the price that various vegetables will fetch in the market and likewise the price you can expect to get from sheep and wool. As far as the valley is concerned, you will plant the vegetables that give the best return. If, for example, the price of potatoes is high, you will probably use a lot of the valley for growing potatoes. If the price gets higher, you may well use the whole of the valley, perhaps being prepared to run the risk of potato disease. If the price is very high indeed, you may even consider growing potatoes on the hillside, even though the yield per hectare is much lower there. In other words, the higher the price of a particular crop, the more you are likely to grow in preference to other crops.

This illustrates the general relationship between supply and price: *when the price of a good rises, the quantity supplied will also rise.* There are three reasons for this:

■ As firms supply more, they are likely to find that beyond a certain level of output costs rise more and more rapidly. Only if price rises will it be worth producing more and incurring these higher costs.

In the case of the farm we have just considered, once potatoes have to be grown on the hillside the costs of producing them will increase. Also, if the land has to be used more intensively, say by the use of more and more fertilisers, again the costs of producing extra potatoes are likely to rise

quite rapidly. It is the same for manufacturers. Beyond a certain level of output, costs are likely to rise rapidly as workers have to be paid overtime and as machines approach capacity working. If higher output involves higher costs of production, producers will need to get a higher price if they are to be persuaded to produce extra output.

■ The higher the price of the good, the more profitable it becomes to produce. Firms will thus be encouraged to produce more of it by switching from the production of less profitable goods.

■ Given time, if the price of a good remains high, new producers will be encouraged to set up in production. Total market supply thus rises.

The first two determinants affect supply in the short run. The third affects supply in the long run. We distinguish between short-run and long-run supply in Chapter 3 (page 59).

The supply curve

The amount that producers would like to supply at various prices can be shown in a **supply schedule**. Table 2.2 shows

Definitions

Supply schedule A table showing the different quantities of a good that producers are willing and able to supply at various prices over a given time period. A supply schedule can be for an individual producer or group of producers, or for all producers (the market supply schedule).

Table 2.2	The supply of potatoes (monthly)		
	Price of potatoes (pence per kilo)	Farmer X's supply (tonnes)	Total market supply (tonnes: 000s)
A	20	50	100
B	40	70	200
C	60	100	350
D	80	120	530
E	100	130	700

a monthly supply schedule for potatoes, both for an individual farmer (farmer X) and for all farmers together (the whole market).

The supply schedule can be represented graphically as a **supply curve**. A supply curve may be an individual firm's supply curve or a market curve (i.e. that of the whole industry).

Figure 2.4 shows the *market* supply curve of potatoes. As with demand curves, price is plotted on the vertical axis and quantity on the horizontal axis. Each of the points *a–e* corresponds to a figure in Table 2.2. For example, a price rise from 60p per kilo to 80p per kilo will cause a movement along the supply curve from point *c* to point *d*: total market supply will rise from 350 000 tonnes per month to 530 000 tonnes per month.

Not all supply curves will be upward sloping (positively sloped). Sometimes they will be vertical, or horizontal, or even downward sloping. This will depend largely on the time period over which firms' response to price changes is considered. This question is examined in Chapter 3 in the section on the elasticity of supply (Section 3.3) and in more detail in Chapters 4 and 5.

Other determinants of supply

Like demand, supply is not simply determined by price. The other determinants of supply are as follows:

The costs of production. The higher the costs of production, the less profit will be made at any price. As costs rise, firms will cut back on production, probably switching to alternative products whose costs have not risen so much.

The main reasons for a change in costs are:

- Change in input prices: costs of production will rise if wages, raw material prices, rents, interest rates or any other input prices rise.
- Change in technology: technological advances can fundamentally alter the costs of production. Consider, for example, how the microchip revolution has changed production methods and information handling in virtually every industry in the world.
- Organisational changes: various cost savings can be made in many firms by reorganising production.
- Government policy: costs will be lowered by government subsidies and raised by various taxes.

The profitability of alternative products (substitutes in supply). If some alternative product (a **substitute in supply**) becomes more profitable to supply than before, producers are likely to switch from the first good to this alternative. Supply of the first good falls. Other goods are likely to become more profitable if their prices rise or their costs of production fall. For example, if the price of carrots goes up, or the cost of producing carrots comes down, farmers may decide to produce more carrots. The supply of potatoes is therefore likely to fall.

The profitability of goods in joint supply. Sometimes when one good is produced, another good is also produced at the same time. These are said to be **goods in joint supply**. An example is the refining of crude oil to produce petrol. Other grade fuels will be produced as well, such as diesel and paraffin. If more petrol is produced, due to a rise in demand, then the supply of these other fuels will rise too.

Nature, 'random shocks' and other unpredictable events. In this category we would include the weather and diseases

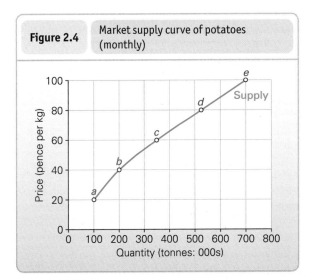

Figure 2.4	Market supply curve of potatoes (monthly)

affecting farm output, wars affecting the supply of imported raw materials, and the breakdown of machinery, industrial disputes, earthquakes, floods and fire, and so on affecting a whole range of production.

The aims of producers. A profit-maximising firm will supply a different quantity from a firm that has a different aim, such as maximising sales. For most of the time we shall assume that firms are profit maximisers.

Expectations of future price changes. If price is expected to rise, producers may temporarily reduce the amount they sell. Instead they are likely to build up their stocks and release them on to the market only when the price does rise. At the same time they may plan to produce more, by installing new machines, or taking on more labour, so that they can be ready to supply more when the price has risen.

The number of suppliers. If new firms enter the market, supply is likely to rise.

Pause for thought

By reference to each of the above determinants of supply, identify what would cause (a) the supply of potatoes to fall and (b) the supply of leather to rise.

Movements along and shifts in the supply curve

The principle here is the same as with demand curves. The effect of a change in price is illustrated by a movement along the supply curve–for example, from point *d* to point *e* in Figure 2.4 when price rises from 80p to 100p. Quantity supplied rises from 530 000 to 700 000 tonnes per month.

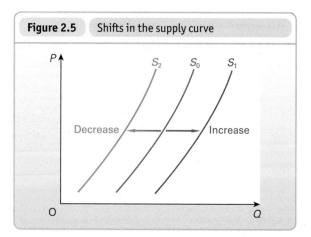

Figure 2.5 Shifts in the supply curve

If any other determinant of supply changes, the whole supply curve will shift. A rightward shift illustrates an increase in supply. A leftward shift illustrates a decrease in supply. Thus in Figure 2.5, if the original curve is S_0, the curve S_1 represents an increase in supply (more is supplied at each price), whereas the curve S_2 represents a decrease in supply (less is supplied at each price).

A movement along a supply curve is often referred to as a **change in the quantity supplied**, whereas a shift in the supply curve is simply referred to as a **change in supply**.

Definitions

Change in the quantity supplied The term used for a movement along the supply curve to a new point. It occurs when there is a change in price.

Change in supply The term used for a shift in the supply curve. It occurs when a determinant other than price changes.

Recap

1. When the price of a good rises, the quantity supplied per period of time will usually also rise. This applies both to individual producers' supply and to the whole market supply.

2. There are two reasons in the short run why a higher price encourages producers to supply more: (a) they are now willing to incur higher costs per unit associated with producing more; (b) they will switch to producing this product instead of now less profitable ones. In the long run there is a third reason: new producers will be attracted into the market.

3. The relationship between price and quantity supplied per period of time can be shown in a table (or schedule) or as a graph. As with a demand curve, price is plotted on the vertical axis and quantity per period of time on the horizontal axis. The resulting supply curve is upward sloping (positively sloped).

4. Other determinants of supply include the costs of production, the profitability of alternative products, the profitability of goods in joint supply, random shocks and expectations of future price changes.

5. If price changes, the effect is shown by a movement along the supply curve. We call this effect 'a change in the quantity supplied'.

6. If any determinant other than price *changes*, the effect is shown by a shift in the whole supply curve. We call this effect 'a change in supply'. A rightward shift represents an increase in supply; a leftward shift represents a decrease in supply.

2.3 THE DETERMINATION OF PRICE

How much of any item will actually be bought and sold and at what price?

Equilibrium price and output

We can now combine our analysis of demand and supply. This will show how the actual price of a product and the actual quantity bought and sold are determined in a free and competitive market.

Let's return to the example of the market demand and market supply of potatoes, and use the data from Tables 2.1 and 2.2. These figures are given again in Table 2.3.

What will be the price and output that actually prevail? If the price started at 20p per kilo, demand would exceed supply by 600 000 tonnes ($A - a$). Consumers would be unable to obtain all they wanted and would thus be willing to pay a higher price. Producers, unable or unwilling to supply enough to meet the demand, will be only too happy to accept a higher price. The effect of the shortage, then, will be to drive up the price. The same would happen at a price of 40p per kilo. There would still be a shortage; price would still rise. But as the price rises, the quantity demanded falls and the quantity supplied rises. The shortage is progressively eliminated.

What would happen if the price started at a much higher level: say at 100p per kilo? In this case supply would exceed demand by 600 000 tonnes ($e - E$). The effect of this surplus would be to drive the price down as farmers competed against each other to sell their excess supplies. The same would happen at a price of 80p per kilo. There would still be a surplus; price would still fall.

In fact, only one price is sustainable. This is the price where demand equals supply: namely 60p per kilo, where both demand and supply are 350 000 tonnes. When supply matches demand the market is said to **clear**. There is no shortage and no surplus.

As we saw earlier (page 19), the price where demand equals supply is called the *equilibrium price*. In Table 2.3, if the price starts at other than 60p per kilo there will be a

tendency for it to move towards 60p. The equilibrium price is the only price at which producers' and consumers' wishes are mutually reconciled: where the producers' plans to supply exactly match the consumers' plans to buy.

> **KEY IDEA 9**
>
> **TC 6**
>
> *Equilibrium is the point where conflicting interests are balanced.* Only at this point is the amount that demanders are willing to purchase the same as the amount that suppliers are willing to supply. It is a point which will be automatically reached in a free market through the operation of the price mechanism. This is another of our threshold concepts. For details, visit MyEconLab.

Demand and supply curves

The determination of equilibrium price and output can be shown using demand and supply curves. Equilibrium is where the two curves intersect.

Figure 2.6 shows the demand and supply curves of potatoes corresponding to the data in Table 2.3. Equilibrium price is P_e (60p) and equilibrium quantity is Q_e (350 000 tonnes).

At any price above 60p, there would be a surplus. Thus at 80p there is a surplus of 330 000 tonnes ($d - D$). More is supplied than consumers are willing and able to purchase at that price. Thus a price of 80p fails to clear the market. Price will fall to the equilibrium price of 60p. As it does so, there will be a movement along the demand curve from point D to point C, and a movement along the supply curve from point d to point c.

At any price below 60p, there would be a shortage. Thus at 40p there is a shortage of 300 000 tonnes ($B - b$). Price will rise to 60p. This will cause a movement along the supply curve from point b to point c and along the demand curve from point B to point C.

Point Cc is the equilibrium: where demand equals supply.

Movement to a new equilibrium

The equilibrium price will remain unchanged only so long as the demand and supply curves remain unchanged. If either of the curves shifts, a new equilibrium will be formed.

Table 2.3	The market demand and supply of potatoes (monthly)	
Price of potatoes (pence per kilo)	Total market demand (tonnes: 000s)	Total market supply (tonnes: 000s)
20	700 (*A*)	100 (*a*)
40	500 (*B*)	200 (*b*)
60	350 (*C*)	350 (*c*)
80	200 (*D*)	530 (*d*)
100	100 (*E*)	700 (*e*)

Definition

Market clearing A market clears when supply matches demand, leaving no shortage or surplus.

Figure 2.6 The determination of market equilibrium (potatoes: monthly)

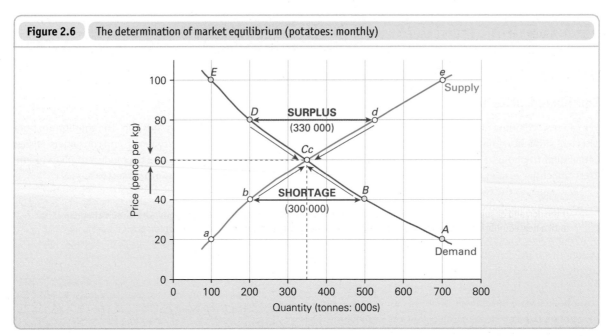

A change in demand

If one of the determinants of demand changes (other than price), the whole demand curve will shift. This will lead to a movement along the supply curve to the new intersection point.

For example, in Figure 2.7, if a rise in consumer incomes led to the demand curve shifting to D_2, there would be a shortage of $h - g$ at the original price P_{e1}. This would cause price to rise to the new equilibrium P_{e2}. As it did so, there would be a movement along the supply curve from point g to point i, and along the new demand curve (D_2) from point h to point i. Equilibrium quantity would rise from Q_{e1} to Q_{e2}.

The effect of the shift in demand, therefore, has been a movement along the supply curve from the old equilibrium to the new: from point g to point i.

A change in supply

Likewise, if one of the determinants of supply changes (other than price), the whole supply curve will shift. This will lead to a movement *along* the *demand* curve to the new intersection point.

For example, in Figure 2.8, if costs of production rose, the supply curve would shift to the left: to S_2. There would be a shortage of $g - j$ at the old price of P_{e1}. Price would rise from P_{e1} to P_{e3}. Quantity would fall from Q_{e1} to Q_{e3}. In other words, there would be a movement along the demand curve from point g to point k, and along the new supply curve (S_2) from point j to point k.

Pause for thought

Is the following statement true? 'An increase in demand will cause an increase in price. This increase in price will cause a reduction in demand, until demand is reduced back to its original level.' Explain your answer and try using a demand and supply diagram to illustrate what is going on.

Figure 2.7 Effect of a shift in the demand curve

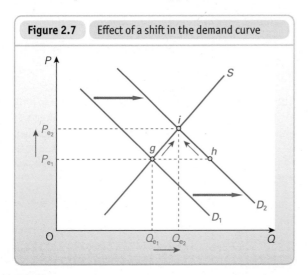

Figure 2.8 Effect of a shift in the supply curve

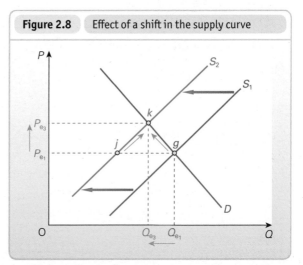

To summarise: a shift in one curve leads to a movement along the other curve to the new intersection point. Sometimes a number of determinants might change. This may lead to a shift in *both* curves. When this happens, equilibrium simply moves from the point where the old curves intersected to the point where the new ones intersect.

Recap

1. If the demand for a good exceeds the supply, there will be a shortage. This will lead to a rise in the price of the good.

2. If the supply of a good exceeds the demand, there will be a surplus. This will lead to a fall in the price.

3. Price will settle at the equilibrium. The equilibrium price is the one that clears the market: the price where demand equals supply.

4. If the demand or supply curve shifts, this will lead either to a shortage or to a surplus. Price will therefore either rise or fall until a new equilibrium is reached at the position where the supply and demand curves now intersect.

| BOX 2.2 | UK HOUSE PRICES | CASE STUDIES & APPLICATIONS |

From raising the roof to falling through the floor

Housing is one of the most important markets in many economies. One reason is that housing is a significant component of the household sector's wealth, or what economists call its 'net worth' (see Box 8.1). This is calculated as the sum of their financial and non-financial wealth *less* their financial liabilities.

At the end of 2014, the value of residential buildings owned by the UK household sector was estimated at £4.8 trillion – just over half of households' net worth of £9.4 trillion. Yet, because housing is nearly always purchased with a mortgage, it constitutes a significant financial liability too. UK households had amassed a stock of outstanding mortgage debt of close to £1.3 trillion by the end of 2014. Such debt needs to be serviced too: each month the household sector is devoting income to capital repayments and to interest payments. It is easy to see why housing will be of interest to macroeconomists. We will return to this in Chapter 8.

But here we take a microeconomic perspective and consider what causes house prices to rise or fall. UK house prices display two notable patterns. First, they rise over the long term, but secondly, they are highly volatile.

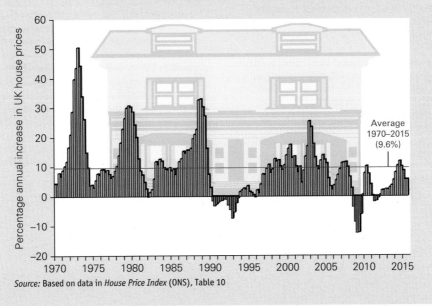

UK house price inflation (all houses, all buyers)

Source: Based on data in *House Price Index* (ONS), Table 10

| BOX 2.2 | UK HOUSE PRICES *(continued)* |

These patterns can be observed in the chart. On average since 1970 UK house prices have increased by 9.7 per cent per year. Over the same period, the annual rate of increase in consumer prices has averaged only 6.3 per cent. The fact that actual (or 'nominal') UK house prices have increased more quickly than consumer prices means that there has been an increase in the real price of housing. In other words, the price of housing has increased *relative* to the average price of a basket of consumer goods and services.

However, the chart also shows the considerable variability in the annual rate of house price inflation. There were marked increases in house prices in the early 1970s, with annual house price inflation rates exceeding 50 per cent, and again in the early 1980s when rates exceeded 30 per cent. On both occasions, house price inflation rates soon moderated, but the level of house prices continued to increase. We see further very strong growth in house prices in the late 1980s, but this time it was followed by a period of protracted house price falls.

By the end of the 1990s house price inflation picked up again and the UK then experienced a protracted period of robust house price growth. But from 2008, as the UK economy entered recession, UK house prices began to decline again; 2009 was to see rapid rates of decline. The early 2010s saw the average UK house price intially recover, then stutter once more before rising strongly in 2013 and 2014, buoyed by strong growth in London and south-east England.

The determinants of house prices

House prices are determined by demand and supply. If demand rises (i.e. shifts to the right) or if supply falls (i.e. shifts to the left), the equilibrium price of houses will rise. Similarly, if demand falls or supply rises, the equilibrium price will fall.

So why have UK house prices increased over the long term and at a rate in excess of that of consumer prices? The answer is that demand has grown faster than supply.

A key factor affecting supply has been the amount of new build–that is, the volume of residential property construction. Annual levels of new build have generally trended downwards over the past 40 to 50 years. In the 1970s the average level of new build was over 320 000 per year. In the 2000s the figure had dipped under 200 000. As levels of new build have trended downwards, the average real house price has trended upwards.

And why have we seen such volatility in house prices? The answer here lies in *fluctuations* in demand combined with a stock of housing that changes only slowly.

Let us examine the various factors that affected the demand for houses.

Incomes (actual and anticipated). The second half of the 1980s, 1996 to 2007 and 2013 onwards saw rising incomes. This was on the back of an economy experiencing robust growth or, from 2013, a recovery following the financial crisis. Stronger income growth encouraged people to devote some of their extra income to housing: either buying a house for the first time, or moving to a better one. Crucially, many people thought that their incomes would continue to grow, and were thus prepared to stretch themselves financially in the short term by buying a more expensive house, confident that their mortgage payments would become more and more affordable over time.

The early 1990s and late 2000s/early 2010s, by contrast, were periods of low or negative economic growth, with rising unemployment and falling incomes. Consequently, people had much less confidence about their ability to afford large mortgages. Further, many existing homeowners deferred plans to trade up to larger properties, while potential first-time buyers looked to the rental sector to satisfy their housing needs.

The number of households. Social and demographic changes have resulted in a sharp increase in the number of households over the past 30 years. In 1981 there were 20 million households in the UK; by 2014 this had increased to 26.7 million. Reasons include more lone parents, increased life expectancy and flows of workers from EU countries. Average household size is lower but, even so, the overall impact has been an increase in demand for housing.

The cost of mortgages. Interest rates affect the cost of servicing a mortgage: i.e. interest payments and the repayment of capital. When interest rates fall, the costs of servicing debt fall. This helps to fuel the demand for housing.

During the second half of the 1980s, mortgage interest rates were generally falling, enabling households to afford larger mortgages and thus afford to buy more expensive houses. In 1989, however, this trend was reversed. Mortgage interest rates went up sharply and this deterred buyers from entering the market or from buying a larger property. This helps explains the sharp fall in demand seen in 1989 and 1990. During the period from 1997 mortgage rates were historically low, helping to fuel the demand for houses once more. Even when mortgage rates rose gradually over 2006 to 2007 they did not come close to the rates reached in the early 1990s.

KI 6
p 20

From 2008 to 2015 interest rates remained low. Until 2013, this did not induce an increase in housing demand due to the continued economic uncertainty created by the financial crisis and banks being cautious over their lending. But the recovery in housing demand from around 2013, although driven partly by the recovery of the economy, was helped by continuing low interest rates.

The availability of mortgages. In the two housing boom periods of the late 1980s and from 1997 to 2007, mortgages were readily available. With house prices rising, banks and building societies were prepared to accept smaller deposits on houses, and to lend a larger multiple of people's income. After all, if borrowers were to default, lenders would still have a very good chance of getting all their money back.

In the early 1990s, however, and again from the late 2000s, banks and building societies became more cautious about granting mortgages. They were aware that with falling house prices, rising unemployment and the growing problem of negative equity (people owing more than their house was worth), there was an increased danger that borrowers would default on payments. However, the problem in the late 2000s was compounded by the financial crisis, which meant that banks had less money to lend. Credit criteria remained tight into the early 2010s so that purchasers had to find historically large deposits. Inevitably, this significantly reduced the number of first-time buyers.

The deposit requirement eased a little through 2013 and 2014 and government-backed 'Help to Buy' schemes were introduced to help borrowers get a mortgage with a 5 per cent deposit. This was another factor that contributed towards the acceleration of the average UK house price.

Speculation. A belief that house prices will continue to move in a particular direction can exacerbate house price movements. In other words, speculation tends to increase house price volatility. For instance, both in the late 1980s and during much of the 2000s there was a belief that house prices would continue to rise. This encouraged people to buy as soon as possible, and to take out the biggest mortgage possible, before prices went up any further. There was also an effect on supply. Those with houses to sell held back until the last possible moment in the hope of getting a higher price. The net effect was for a rightward shift in the demand curve for houses and a leftward shift in the supply curve. The effect of this speculation, therefore, was to help bring about the very effect that people were predicting (see Section 3.5).

In the early 1990s, and again from 2008, the opposite occurred. With house prices falling, those thinking of buying houses held back, hoping to buy at a lower price. People with houses to sell tried to sell as quickly as possible before prices fell any further. Again the effect of this speculation was to aggravate the change in prices – this time a fall in prices.

A global dimension to falling house prices

The fall in UK house prices in 2008 had global origins. The dramatic growth in mortgage lending in the UK was also a feature of many other industrialised countries at this time, most notably the USA, where there had been similar dramatic rises in house prices.

Banks and other mortgage lenders bundled up these large mortgage debts into 'financial instruments' and sold them on to other global financial institutions so that they could meet their everyday liquidity requirements of paying bills and meeting customers' demands for cash. This worked well while there was economic prosperity and people could pay their mortgages. However, it became apparent in 2007 that many of the mortgages sold, notably in the USA, were to people who could not meet their repayments.

As the number of mortgage defaults increased, the value of the mortgage-laden financial instruments sold on to other financial institutions fell. As banks found it increasingly difficult to meet their liquidity requirements, they reduced the number of mortgages to potential home-owners.

Although housing markets in many countries have recovered as more housing finance has become available and as confidence has returned, the world economy has continued to become more interdependent. This means that the state of the global economy has become an increasingly important determinant of house prices.

1. *Draw supply and demand diagrams to illustrate what happened to UK house prices (a) in the second half of the 1980s and the period from 1997 to 2007; (b) in the early 1990s and the period from 2008; (c) in London and the south-east of England in 2014.*
2. *What similarities exist between the causes of the house price bust of the early 1990s and that in the late 2000s?*
3. *If actual (nominal) house prices are rising can real house prices fall? Explain your answer.*

BOX 2.3   STOCK MARKET PRICES

Demand and supply in action

Firms that are quoted on the stock market (see Case Study 4.1 in MyEconLab) can raise money by issuing shares. These are sold on the 'primary stock market'. People who own the shares receive a 'dividend' on them, normally paid six-monthly. This varies with the profitability of the company.

People or institutions that buy these shares, however, may not wish to hold on to them for ever. This is where the 'secondary stock market' comes in. It is where existing shares are bought and sold. There are stock markets, primary and secondary, in all the major countries of the world.

At the end of March 2015, there were 2426 companies whose shares are listed on the London Stock Exchange. Shares are traded each Monday to Friday (excluding bank holidays).

The prices of shares depend on demand and supply. For example, if the demand for Tesco shares at any one time exceeds the supply on offer, the price will rise until demand and supply are equal. Share prices fluctuate throughout the trading day and sometimes price changes can be substantial.

To give an overall impression of share price movements, stock exchanges publish share price indices. The best-known example in the UK is the FTSE 100, which stands for the 'Financial Times Stock Exchange' index of the 100 largest companies' shares. The index was first calculated on 3 January 1984 with a base level of 1000 points. The chart shows the opening monthly value of the FTSE 100 since January 1985. The chart also shows the retail price index (RPI), re-based so that it too was equal to 1000 in January 1984. The RPI shows weighted average prices of all goods and ser-vices. (See Web Appendix 1.1 in MyEconLab for details on the construction and use of price indices.)

From its start in 1984 to April 2015, the FTSE 100 increased by an average of 7.0 per cent per year. However, this figure masks some significant variations in the prices of shares. The index reached a peak of 6930 points on 30 December 1999 and fell to 3287 on 12 March 2003; it then rose again, reaching a high of 6730 on 12 October 2007. In the midst of the financial crisis the index fell to a low of 3781 on 21 November 2008,

but by early 2010 it had partially recovered, passing 6000 for a brief period, before levelling out and fluctuating around an average of 5500 to mid-2012, only to rise above 6000 again at the start of 2013. Between 2013 and early 2015 (when writing), it remained above 6500, rising above 7000 in April 2015.

When you compare the FTSE 100 with the RPI, you can see that share prices rose faster than prices generally (the RPI rose by an annual average of 3.6 per cent from 1984 to 2015). In other words, *real* share prices rose. Also share prices fluc-tuated much more than the general level of prices.

The long-run upwards trend in real share prices coupled with their volatility is something we also see in UK house prices (see Box 2.2).

But what causes share prices to change? Why were they so high in 1999, but only just over half that value just three years later, and why did this trend repeat itself in the late 2000s? The answer lies in the determinants of the demand and supply of shares.

Demand

There are five main factors that affect the demand for shares.

The dividend yield. This is the dividend on a share as a percentage of its price. The higher the dividend yields on shares, the more attractive they are as a form of saving. One of the main explanations of rising stock market prices from 2003 to 2007 was high profits and resulting high dividends. Similarly, the slowdown in the world economy after 2007 led to falling profits and falling dividends.

The price of and/or return on substitutes. The main substitutes for shares in specific companies are other shares. Thus if, in comparison with other shares, Tesco shares are expected to pay high dividends relative to the share price, people will buy Tesco shares. As far as shares in general are concerned, the main substitutes are other forms of saving. Thus if the interest rate on savings accounts in banks and building societies fell, people with such accounts would be tempted to take their money out and buy shares instead.

KI 6
p 20

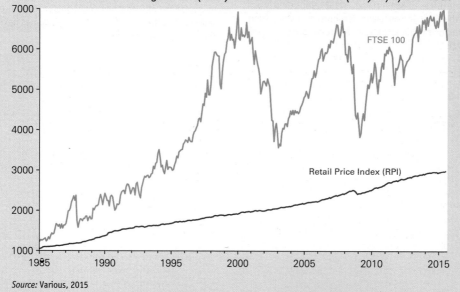

Financial Times Stock Exchange Index (FTSE) and Retail Price Index (RPI): 3/1/84= 1000

Source: Various, 2015

Another major substitute is property. If house prices rise rapidly, as they did at the start of the 2000s (see Box 2.2), this will reduce the demand for shares as many people switch to buying property in anticipation of even higher prices. If house price growth weakens, as it did during 2005–6, it makes shares relatively more attractive as an investment and can boost the demand for them.

Of course, other factors may affect *both* house prices *and* shares in the same way. Thus the 'credit crunch' of 2007–8, when finance became both harder and more expensive to obtain, resulted in both falling house prices *and* falling share prices as the economy slowed down and profits fell. Instead, investors looked towards other, safer, investments such as gold, government debt (Treasury bills and gilts) or even holding cash.

But then with interest rates, including those on savings accounts, being dramatically cut as a result of Bank of England measures to stimulate the economy in 2009, many people saw shares as an attractive alternative to bank and building society accounts. The stock market began rising again.

Incomes. If the economy is growing rapidly and people's incomes are thus rising rapidly, they are likely to buy more shares. For instance, between 1996 and 2000, real household sector disposable income grew by an average of 4 per cent per year. This period saw share prices rise rapidly (see chart). As growth rates fell in the early 2000s, so share prices fell. Similarly, as income growth improved in the middle of the decade, shares prices increased. However, they fell back with the global financial crisis in 2007–8 and the onset of recession and declining real incomes from 2008. They were to rise again as the recovery took hold from around 2013.

Wealth. 'Wealth' is people's accumulated savings and property. Wealth rose in the second half of the 1990s and people used it to buy shares. It was a similar picture in the mid-2000s. Much of the wealth worldwide was in relatively 'liquid' form and, hence, in a form that could easily be turned into cash and used to buy shares. The growth in wealth was halted in the late 2000s by the financial crisis. In looking to consolidate their financial positions some looked to 'cash in' their shares, so depressing share prices and actually causing a further deterioration of financial well-being.

Expectations. In both the mid-to-late 1980s and 1990s, people expected share prices to go on rising. In the 1980s there was a sense that the UK economy had undergone a transformation enabling permanently higher rates of economic growth. In the case of the late 1990s, reforms to policy making, including central bank independence (see Chapter 12), again suggested better economic times lay ahead and an end to 'boom and bust'. These positive sentiments encouraged people to buy shares and pushed prices up even more, which then further fuelled speculation and further share buying.

In the early 2000s, by contrast, confidence was shaken. Most countries experienced a slowing down in economic growth, or even a recession (a fall in national output). This, combined with other negative factors, such as the 11 September 2001 attack on the World Trade Center and various corporate scandals such as the accounting fraud concerning the giant US company Enron, caused share prices to plummet. As people anticipated further price falls, so they held back from buying, thereby pushing prices even lower.

Conversely, as share prices began rising again from 2003 onwards, so this boosted the demand for shares, thereby fuelling the surge in share prices.

Then with the credit crunch and falling profits from 2007, share prices fell, with the falls resulting in further selling and further falls as confidence waned. Things reached crisis point in October 2008, as people feared banking collapses and the onset of recession. On 10 October, the FTSE fell as low as 3874, 31 per cent down on early September and 42 per cent down from October of the previous year. However, with bank rescue plans announced by governments around the world, expectations became more positive and the FTSE rose by 17 per cent in just two days.

As recession deepened and as more news about banks' bad debts emerged, so share prices remained volatile. Gradually, a rising trend emerged as the worst of the downturn appeared over and investor confidence returned.

The rise and fall in share prices associated with expectations mirror those seen in the housing market and discussed in Box 2.2.

Supply

The factors affecting supply are largely the same as those affecting demand, but in the opposite direction.

If the return on alternative forms of saving falls, people with shares are likely to hold on to them, as they represent a better form of saving. The supply of shares to the market will fall. Similarly, if incomes or wealth rise, people are likely to want to hold on to their shares.

As far as expectations are concerned, if people believe that share prices will rise, they will hold on to the shares they have. Supply to the market will fall, thereby pushing up prices. If, however, they believe that prices will fall, as they did in 2008, they will sell their shares now before prices do fall. Supply will increase, driving down the price.

Share prices and business

Companies are crucially affected by their share price. If a company's share price falls, this is taken as a sign that 'the market' is losing confidence in the company. This will make it more difficult to raise finance, not only by issuing additional shares in the primary market, but also from banks.

It will also make the company more vulnerable to a takeover bid. This is where one company seeks to buy out another by offering to buy all its shares. A takeover will succeed if the owners of more than half of the company's shares vote to accept the offered price. Shareholders are more likely to agree to the takeover if the company's shares have not been doing very well recently.

Can you buck the market?

Many individuals like to play the market, thinking that they can make easy profits. However, beware! The 'efficient markets hypothesis' predicts that historical share price information, such as that shown in the chart or in the pages of today's financial press, provides no help whatsoever in determining future share prices. Why? Because the current share price *already* reflects what people anticipate will happen. Future share price movements will occur only as *new* (unanticipated) information arrives – and it's pure chance if you can predict the unanticipated! In this purist view, the market for shares is said to be a perfectly efficient market

1. *If the rate of economic growth in the economy is 3 per cent in a particular year, can we expect share prices to rise by 3 per cent that year? Explain your answer.*
2. *Why would you expect the return on shares to be greater than that offered by a banks savings account?*

BOX 2.4 COMMODITY PRICES

Riding the commodities Big Dipper?

The term 'commodity' in the context of commodity prices refers to the prices of *foodstuffs* (e.g. cereals, fruits, meat and cooking oils), *beverages* (e.g. coffee, tea and cocoa), *agricultural raw materials* (e.g. cotton, rubber, wool and logs), *metals* (e.g. copper, aluminium and tin), and *fuels* (e.g. crude oil, diesel, coal and natural gas).

As we can see in the chart, the global economy witnessed periods of soaring commodity prices in the period from the mid-2000s, and again in the early 2010s. The overall world commodity price index rose by 135 per cent between May 2005 and July 2008. With the financial crisis, prices then fell back, so that by February 2009 the overall commodity price index was 55 per cent lower. Then a rebound took place as the global economy began to recover; overall commodity prices rose by 114 per cent up to April 2011. But with recovery faltering, prices eased a little in 2012, with the overall index at the end of the year 13 per cent lower than compared with the April 2011 peak. Commodity prices then generally flat-lined up until summer 2014 when a significant decline commenced. By January 2015 the overall index was 38 per cent lower, with the price of fuels 51 per cent lower.

Changes in commodity prices result in macroeconomic issues and we will explore these in the second half of the text. However, we now consider some of the factors that lead to shifts in the demand and supply of commodities. These shifts then result in changes to commodity prices.

Income

Economic growth through its impact on incomes is a crucial determinant of the demand for certain commodities. The demand for commodities is acutely sensitive to changes in incomes. The rate of economic growth in developing countries has been especially important in affecting the demand for commodities. The table allows us to compare rates of economic growth and of commodity price inflation.

The rapid rate of growth of developing countries during the 2000s, including the nations collectively knows as the BRICS (Brazil, Russia, India, China and South Africa), helped to fuel the demand for raw materials. The global economic downturn in 2009, particularly in advanced economies, contributed to a weakening in demand which caused commodity prices to decline.

Economic growth resumed in many advanced economies later in 2009. In fact, a large number of developing countries had continued to experience growth throughout the global downturn, albeit growth rates were generally weaker. As the table shows, economic growth in China and India remained relatively robust in 2009 and in the case of India it was actually higher.

However, economic growth remained fragile in the first half of the 2010s, particularly as many governments were looking to consolidate their financial positions in response to burgeoning budget deficits (see Box 1.4). This helped to surpass the general demand for commodities.

Speculation

Many financial institutions, companies and individuals speculate in commodities, hoping to make money by buying at a low price and selling at a high price. When successful, speculators can make large percentage gains in a short period of time. However, they can also lose by getting their predictions wrong.

In uncertain times, speculation can be destabilising, exaggerating price rises and falls as speculators 'jump on the bandwagon', seeing price changes as signifying a trend. In more stable times, speculation can even reduce price fluctuations as speculators buy when prices are temporarily low and sell when they are temporarily high. (We examine speculation in more detail in Section 3.5.)

During particularly uncertain times, such as those in the late 2000s and early 2010s, confidence and, hence, commodity prices, fluctuated significantly. Therefore, on days of good

KI 6
p 20

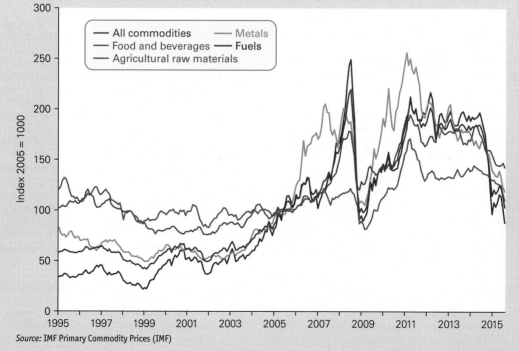

Commodity prices (2005 = 100)

Source: IMF Primary Commodity Prices (IMF)

Annual rates of change in commodity prices and real GDP (%)

	2000–7	2008	2009	2010	2011–13	2014
Commodity price growth						
All	14.4	30.4	−24.5	27.8	7.5	−6.2
Metals	18.1	−8.1	−12.8	52.0	−3.9	−10.1
Foodstuffs	6.0	25.8	−11.4	12.2	3.7	−2.2
Fuels	21.8	45.6	−29.6	28.8	6.1	−7.3
Agricultural raw materials	2.9	−0.6	−15.9	33.7	3.9	2.0
Economic growth						
World	4.5	3.0	0.0	5.4	3.6	3.3
Advanced economies	2.6	0.1	−3.4	3.1	1.7	1.2
UK	3.2	−0.8	−5.2	1.7	1.0	3.2
USA	2.7	−0.3	−2.8	2.5	2.0	2.2
Eurozone	2.2	0.4	−4.5	2.0	0.2	0.8
Emerging & developing economies	6.6	5.8	3.1	7.5	0.6	1.4
Brazil	3.5	5.2	−0.3	7.5	2.1	0.3
Russia	7.2	5.2	−7.8	4.5	3.0	0.2
India	7.1	3.9	8.5	10.3	5.5	5.6
China	10.5	9.6	9.2	10.4	8.2	7.4
South Africa	4.3	3.6	−1.5	3.1	2.7	1.4

Source: After IMF Primary Commodity Prices (IMF) and World Economic Outlook Database (IMF), April 2015

economic news demand for commodities would tend to rise as people believe that a growing world economy will drive up the demand for commodities and hence their prices. On days of bad economic news the price of commodities would tend to fall as the demand for commodities fell.

Tastes

Changing tastes and trends can also affect prices. The growth of the 'coffee-shop culture' and the fashion for speciality coffees has moved beyond advanced economies and into developing countries. Countries such as China, India and Brazil have seen large increases in consumption. The demand for coffee makes it the second most traded commodity after oil.

Natural events

The supply of commodities is susceptible to natural events, ranging from droughts or floods to earthquakes. For example, during 2009 wholesale tea prices reached record highs when supply fell following droughts in several tea-exporting nations, including parts of India and Kenya. In December 2009, tea prices were over 60 per cent higher than they had been in December 2008.

Poor harvests, partly the result of inclement weather, but also coffee plant diseases and pests, also helped to push up the price of coffee beans markedly during 2009. The price of cocoa beans in November 2009 was up by 65 per cent on the previous November. It is argued, by some, that the increased susceptibility of coffee harvests in this period to pests and diseases arose from producers finding it more difficult to access the finance needed to purchase pesticides and fertilisers. The problems with the supply of coffee beans were intensified by our seemingly insatiable demand for coffee.

Alternative land uses

In some cases, the land used to provide particular commodities has alternative uses. Increases in energy prices, concerns over greenhouse gas emissions and incentives from governments have seen the conversion of agricultural land to the production of biofuels. Ethanol, for instance, can be produced by fermenting the sugars from crops such as wheat and sugar canes and can then be used to power petrol engines (see Case Study 2.8 in MyEconLab for an examination of the demand for ethanol in Brazil).

New sources of supply

The fall in the price of fuels from summer 2014 was partly the result of faltering global demand but mainly the result of increased supply from shale oil deposits, particularly in the USA. The increased supply of shale oil was not offset by a reduction in other production. Indeed OPEC (the Organization of Petroleum Exporting Countries), which as of 2015 represents 15 oil producing nations, declared that it would not cut back production even if the price of oil were to fall to $20 per barrel. The average price of a barrel in the first quarter of 2015 was $52 per barrel. By maintaining lower prices it made shale oil production increasingly less profitable and, as a result, it was hoped, would discourage further shale exploration and investment.

1. *What might explain why the price of some commodity types rose less during the period of economic growth from 2000 to 2007?*
2. *Explain how speculation can contribute to the volatility of commodity prices.*
3. *Would you expect commodity prices to fluctuate more than house prices?*

2.4 THE FREE-MARKET ECONOMY

How well does it serve us?

Advantages of a free-market economy

The fact that a free-market economy functions automatically is one of its major advantages. There is no need for costly and complex bureaucracies to co-ordinate economic decisions. The economy can respond quickly to changing demand and supply conditions.

When markets are highly competitive, no one has great power. Competition between firms keeps prices down and acts as an incentive to firms to become more efficient. The more firms there are competing, the more responsive they will be to consumer wishes.

The more efficiently firms can combine their factors of production, the more profit they will make. The more efficiently workers work, the more secure will be their jobs and the higher their wages. The more carefully consumers decide what to buy, the greater the value for money they will receive.

TC 6
p 37

Thus people pursuing their own self-interest through buying and selling in competitive markets helps to minimise the central economic problem of scarcity, by encouraging the efficient use of the nation's resources in line with consumer wishes. From this type of argument, the following conclusion is often drawn by defenders of the free market: 'The pursuit of private gain results in the social good.' This is obviously a highly significant claim and has profound moral implications (see Threshold Concepts 6 and 7).

> **KEY IDEA 10**
> **TC 7**
>
> *People gain from voluntary interaction.* When people buy from or sell to other people, or when they are employed by or employ other people, both parties will gain from the interaction. This is the seventh of our threshold concepts.

Problems with a free-market economy

In practice, however, markets do not achieve maximum efficiency in the allocation of scarce resources, and governments feel it necessary to intervene to rectify this. This is the allocative role for government that we identified in Section 1.5 along with other potential roles for government (see page 21). The problems of a free market include the following:

- Competition between firms is often limited. A few *TC 4 / p 20* giant firms may dominate an industry. In these cases they may charge high prices and make large profits. Rather than merely responding to consumer wishes, they may attempt to persuade consumers by advertising. Consumers are particularly susceptible to advertisements for products that are unfamiliar to them.
- Lack of competition and high profits may remove the incentive for firms to be efficient.
- Power and property may be unequally distributed. Those who have power and/or property (e.g. big business, unions, landlords) will gain at the expense of those without power and property.
- The practices of some firms may be socially undesirable or have adverse environmental consequences. For example, a chemical works may pollute the environment.
- Some socially desirable goods would simply not be produced by private enterprise. What firm would build and operate a lighthouse, unless it were paid for by the government?
- A free-market economy may lead to macroeconomic instability. There may be periods of recession with high unemployment and falling output, and other periods of rising prices.
- Finally, there is the ethical objection that a free-market *TC 4 / p 20* economy, by rewarding self-interested behaviour, may encourage selfishness, greed, materialism and the acquisition or pursuit of power.

We shall be examining these various problems in more detail in later chapters and the ways governments intervene to tackle them.

> **Pause for thought**
>
> *Go through the potential problems of a free market listed here and identify which of the roles for government (outlined on pages 21–3) each is consistent with.*

Recap

1. A free-market economy functions automatically, and if there is plenty of competition between producers, this can help to protect consumers' interests.
2. In practice, however, competition may be limited: there may be great inequality; there may be adverse social and environmental consequences; there may be macroeconomic instability. Consequently, governments intervene in market economies in various ways in order to correct the failings of the free market.

2.5 BEHAVIOURAL ECONOMICS

Do people always behave 'rationally'?

What is behavioural economics?

Much of what we have talked about so far relates to choices: after all, scarcity necessitates choices. The traditional economic approach is to assume that people behave rationally. It is not an unreasonable starting point. However, a moment's thought leads to examples of behaviour that does not appear 'rational'. For example, have you ever bought something simply because a lot of other people were buying it? The answer is probably 'yes'! 'Behavioural economics' relaxes the rationality assumption of traditional economics and looks at the way people *actually* behave.

Behavioural economics recognises that people are subject to emotions and impulses, which can result in 'errors' and biases in their decision making. It is argued that by recognising this we can gain a greater understanding of economic systems and of individuals' behaviour. The growth in behavioural economics is another demonstration of how economics embraces different and sometimes competing ideas.

In what follows we consider some of the reasons why *consumers* appear to behave irrationally. In Section 4.5 we consider why producers might not behave rationally.

Explaining 'irrational' consumer choices

Of course, identifying that consumers do not always behave in a rational manner is only part of the task facing behavioural economists. They also need to explain *why* people behave the way they do. This is the subject of a rich and growing literature; but some of the main ideas are described below.

How options are framed

In traditional models of consumer choice, individuals aim to maximise their utility (see Box 2.1) when choosing between goods, or bundles of goods. The context in which the choices are offered is not considered.

Yet, in real life, we see that context is important; people will often make different choices when they are presented, or framed, in different ways. For example, people will buy more of a good when it is flagged up as a special offer than they do if there is no mention of an offer, even though the price is the same. This principle has led to the development of 'nudge' theory, which underpins many marketing techniques. We look at it in more detail in Box 2.5 below.

Too much choice

Choice is generally thought to be a good thing. But can we have too much choice? Choice should allow us to maximise our utility by making 'better' decisions. Yet this does not always seem to be the case. Experiments have been conducted which appear to show that, in certain circumstances, consumers are more likely to buy when presented with less choice. Too much choice can be confusing and hinder decision making, thereby reducing consumers' utility.

Bounded rationality

A person might want to maximise utility, but faces complex choices and imperfect information. Sometimes it *would* be possible to obtain better information, but the person decides it is not worth the time and effort, and perhaps expense, of getting more information. Their ability to be 'rational' is thus limited or **bounded** by the situation in which they find themselves. So they may resort to making the best guess, or to drawing on past experiences of similar choices that turned out to be good or bad. Behavioural economists seek to understand the different assumptions people make and their different responses in situations of bounded rationality.

This use of past experience, or rules of thumb or trial and error, is known as **heuristics**. The decision is not guaranteed to be optimal, but it might be the best bet given the limited information or time available.

> **Pause for thought**
>
> *Why might different people respond differently from each other in otherwise similar circumstances?*

Relativity matters

If I am making a choice about buying a car, traditional economics says my demand will derive from a number of factors: my income; my tastes for driving and for particular cars; the prices of the car I am considering and of the alternatives; and the associated costs of motoring. Yet I might also be highly influenced by the car my sister drives; if she chooses an Audi, perhaps I would like a more expensive car – a Mercedes possibly. If she switches to a Jaguar, then perhaps I will opt for a Porsche. I want a better (or faster or more expensive) car than my sister; I am concerned not only with my choice of car but with my *relative* choice.

This does not disprove that our choices depend on our perceived utility. But it does demonstrate that our satisfaction often depends on our consumption *relative* to that of

> **Definitions**
>
> **Bounded rationality** When the ability to make rational decisions is limited by lack of information or the time necessary to obtain such information.
>
> **Heuristics** People's use of strategies that draw on simple lessons from past experience when they are faced with similar, although not identical, choices.

other people, such as our peers. This is something that the advertising industry is only too well aware of. Adverts often try to encourage you to buy a product by showing that *other* people are buying it.

Herding and 'groupthink'

Being influenced by what other people buy, and thus making relative choices, can lead to herd behaviour. A fashion might catch on; people might grab an item in a sale because other people seem to be grabbing it as well; people might buy a particular share on the stock market because other people are buying it.

Now part of this may simply be bounded rationality. Sometimes it may be a good rule of thumb to buy something that other people want, as they might know more about it than you do. But there is a danger in such behaviour: other people may also be buying it because other people are buying it, and this builds a momentum. Sales may soar and the price may be driven well above a level that reflects the utility that people will end up gaining.

Sunk costs

Think back to our definition of rational decision making: consumers will weigh up the *marginal* costs and benefits of any action. This must imply that costs already incurred in the past are irrelevant. These are called sunk costs. Yet when we look at how people actually behave, they do seem to be influenced by sunk costs. An example of this arises if you find yourself reading a novel, but not enjoying it. What should you do? The answer is that, unless you believe that you will start enjoying the story soon, you should stop reading it. Many people would argue that they have paid for the book and so should carry on to the end. But this is not rational. It doesn't matter whether the book cost £5 or £50, the decision to read on should only take the future (opportunity) costs and future benefits into account.

Relevance to economic policy

Governments, in designing policy, will normally attempt to change people's behaviour – both consumers and

---

| BOX 2.5 | NUDGING PEOPLE | EXPLORING ECONOMICS |

How to change behaviour

One observation of behavioural economists is that people make many decisions out of habit. They use simple rules, such as: 'I'll buy the more expensive item because it's bound to be better'; or 'I'll buy this item because it's on offer'; or 'I'm happy with Brand X, so why should I change brands?'; or 'Other people are buying this, so it must be worth having'.

Given that people behave like this, how might they be persuaded to change their behaviour? Governments might want to know this. What policies will encourage people to stop smoking, or save energy, or take more exercise or eat more healthy food? Firms too will want to know how to sell more of their products or to motivate their workforce.

According to Richard Thaler and Cass Sunstein,[4] people can be 'nudged' to change their behaviour. For example, healthy food can be placed in a prominent position in a supermarket or healthy snacks at the checkout. Often it is the junk foods that are displayed prominently and unhealthy, but tasty, snacks are found by the checkout. If fashion houses ceased to use ultra-thin models, it could reduce the incentive for many girls to under-eat. If kids at school are given stars or smiley faces for turning off lights or picking up litter, they might be more inclined to do so.

Another example concerns 'opting in' versus 'opting out'. With organ donor cards, or many company pension schemes or charitable giving, people have to opt in. In other words, they have to make the decision to take part. Many as a result do not, partly because they never seem to find the time to do so, even though they might quite like to. With the busy lives people lead, it's too easy to think, 'Yes, I'll do that some time', but never actually get round to doing it.

With an 'opt-out' system, people are automatically signed up to the scheme, but can freely choose to opt out. Thus it would be assumed that organs from people killed in an accident who had not opted out could be used for transplants. If you did not want your organs to be used, you would have to join a register. It could be the same with charitable giving. Some firms add a small charitable contribution to the price of their products (e.g. airline tickets or utility bills), unless people opt out. Similarly, firms could automatically deduct pension contributions from employees' wages unless they opted out of the scheme.

Opt-in schemes have participation rates of around 60 per cent, while otherwise identical opt-out funds retain between 90 and 95 per cent of employees. It is no wonder that Adair Turner, in his report on pensions, urged legislation to push pension schemes to an opt-out default position and that policy is moving in this direction.[5]

Understanding people's behaviour and then adjusting incentives, often only very slightly, can nudge people to behave differently. Politicians are increasingly looking at ways of nudging people to behave in ways that they perceive as better, whether socially, environmentally or simply personally.

In the UK, the Coalition government formed in 2010 set up a dedicated 'nudge' unit, officially known as the Behavioural Insights Team, for this purpose. Subsequently, it became independent of the UK government, operating as a social purpose company to help organisations to apply behavioural insights in support of 'social purpose goals'.

Some examples of the way the team has influenced policy certainly appear impressive. A trial with HMRC was carried out, informing people who failed to pay their tax that most other people had already paid. This increased payment rates by over 5 percentage points!

1. *How would you nudge members of a student household to be more economical in the use of electricity?*
2. *How could the government nudge people to stop dropping litter?*
3. *In the 2011 Budget, George Osborne announced that charitable giving in wills would be exempt from inheritance tax. Do you think this will be an effective way of encouraging more charitable donations?*

---

[4] Richard H. Thaler and Cass R. Sunstein, *Nudge: Improving Decisions about Health, Wealth, and Happiness* (Yale University Press, 2008).
[5] Richard Reeves, 'Why a nudge from the state beats a slap', *Observer* (20 July 2008).

producers. They might want to encourage people to choose to work harder, to save more, to recycle rubbish, to use their cars less, to eat more healthily, and so on. If the policy is to be successful, it is vital for the policy measures to contain appropriate incentives: whether it be a tax rise, a grant or subsidy, a new law or regulation, an advertising campaign or direct help.

But whether the incentives are appropriate depends on how people will respond to them, and, to know that, the policy makers will need to understand people's behaviour. This is where behavioural economics comes in. People might respond as rational maximisers; but they may not. It is thus important to understand how context affects behaviour and adjust policy incentives appropriately.

Recap

1. Traditional economics is based on the premise that consumers act rationally, weighing up the costs and benefits of the choices open to them. Behavioural economics acknowledges that real-world decisions do not always appear rational; it seeks to understand and explain what economic agents actually do.

2. A number of effects can explain why rational decision making may fail to predict actual behaviour. These include: the roles of framing and relativity; individuals failing to disregard sunk costs and being confused by too many choices. Research undertaken by behavioural economists is bringing together aspects of psychology and economics, in order to understand fully how we behave.

QUESTIONS

1. Why do the prices of fresh vegetables fall when they are in season? Could an individual farmer prevent the price falling?

2. If you were the owner of a clothes shop, how would you set about deciding what prices to charge for each garment at the end-of-season sale?

3. How would marginal utility and market demand be affected by a rise in the price of a complementary good?

4. The number of owners of mobile phones has grown rapidly and hence the demand for mobile phones has also grown rapidly. Yet the prices of mobile phones have fallen. Why?

5. Assume that oil begins to run out and that extraction becomes more expensive. Trace through the effects of this on the market for oil and the market for other fuels.

6. This question is concerned with the supply of oil for central heating. In each case consider whether there is a movement along the supply curve (and in which direction) or a shift in it (and whether left or right).
   a. New oil fields start up in production.
   b. The demand for central heating rises.
   c. The price of gas falls.
   d. Oil companies anticipate an upsurge in demand for central heating oil.
   e. The demand for petrol rises.
   f. New technology decreases the costs of oil refining.
   g. All oil products become more expensive.

7. The weekly demand and supply schedules for t-shirts (in millions) in a free market are as follows:

Price (£)	8	7	6	5	4	3	2	1
Quantity demanded	6	8	10	12	14	16	18	20
Quantity supplied	18	16	14	12	10	8	6	4

   a. What is the equilibrium price and quantity?
   b. Assume that changes in fashion cause the demand for t-shirts to rise by 4 million at each price. What will be the new equilibrium price and quantity? Has equilibrium quantity risen as much as the rise in demand? Explain why or why not.
   c. Now plot the data in the table on a graph and mark the equilibrium. Also plot the new data corresponding to (b) and mark the new equilibrium.

8. On separate demand and supply diagrams for bread, sketch the effects of the following: (a) a rise in the price of wheat; (b) a rise in the price of butter and margarine; (c) a rise in the price of rice, pasta and potatoes. In each case, state your assumptions.

9. For what reasons might the price of foreign holidays rise? In each case identify whether these are reasons affecting demand or supply (or both).

10. If both demand and supply change, and if we know in which direction they have shifted but not how much, why is it that we will be able to predict the direction in which either price *or* quantity will change, but not both? (Clue: consider the four possible combinations and sketch them if necessary: (a) *D* left, *S* left; (b) *D* right, *S* right; (c) *D* left, *S* right; (d) *D* right, *S* left.)

11. What will happen to the equilibrium price and quantity of butter in each of the following cases? You should state whether demand or supply (or both) have shifted and in which direction. (In each case assume *ceteris paribus*.)
   a. A rise in the price of non-dairy spreads.
   b. A rise in the demand for yoghurt.
   c. A rise in the price of bread.
   d. A rise in the demand for bread.
   e. An expected rise in the price of butter in the near future.
   f. A tax on butter production.
   g. The invention of a new, but expensive, process for removing all cholesterol from butter, plus the passing of a law which states that all butter producers must use this process.

12. How does economics predict rational consumers will treat spending on credit cards compared with spending cash? Do you think that there are likely to be differences in the way people spend by each? If so, can you explain why?

13. Many European countries operate organ donor schemes, some with schemes requiring that potential donors opt in, others with a system of opting out, or presumed consent. Explain why a system of presumed consent is likely to result in much higher numbers of donors. Does your answer suggest that we should move to presumed consent for organ donors in the UK?

MyEconLab

This book can be supported by MyEconLab, which contains a range of additional resources, including an online homework and tutorial system designed to test and build your understanding.

You need both an access card and a course ID to access MyEconLab:

1. Is your lecturer using MyEconLab? Ask your lecturer for your course ID.

2. Has an access card been included with the book at a reduced cost? Check the inside back cover of the book.

3. If you have a course ID but no access card, go to: http://www.myeconlab.com/ to buy access to this interactive study programme.

ADDITIONAL CASE STUDIES IN THE *ESSENTIALS OF ECONOMICS* MyEconLab (www.pearsoned.co.uk/sloman)

2.1 **The interdependence of markets.** A case study in the operation of markets, examining the effects on a local economy of the discovery of a large coal deposit.

2.2 **Bentham and the philosophy of utilitarianism.** This looks at the historical and philosophical underpinning of the ideas of utility maximisation.

2.3 **Stocks and flows.** This examines one of the most important distinctions in economics and one that we shall come across on several occasions.

2.4 **Adjusting to oil price shocks.** A case study showing how demand and supply analysis can be used to examine the price changes in the oil market since 1973.

2.5 **Rationing.** A case study in the use of rationing as an alternative to the price mechanism. In particular, it looks at the use of rationing in the UK during the Second World War.

2.6 **Coffee prices.** An examination of the coffee market and the implications of fluctuations in the coffee harvest for growers and coffee drinkers.

2.7 **Is economics the study of selfish behaviour?** To what extent do we take other people's interests into account when we make economic choices?

2.8 **Response to changes in petrol and ethanol prices in Brazil.** This case examines how drivers with 'Flex-fuel' cars responded to changes in the relative prices of two fuels: petrol and ethanol (made from cane sugar).

2.9 **The characteristics approach to analysing consumer demand.** An overview of the theory that people demand goods not for their own sake, but for the characteristics they possess.

WEB APPENDICES

2.1 **Marginal utility theory.** This develops the analysis of section 2.1 and Box 2.1 and considers the relationship between marginal utility and demand, not just for an individual product but for the choice between products.

2.2 **Indifference analysis.** This examines the choices consumers make between products and shows how these choices are affected by the prices of the products.

Markets in action

In this chapter we explore the working of markets in more detail. We start by examining one of the most important concepts in the whole of economics – that of elasticity (Sections 3.1–3.4).

A bumper harvest may seem like good news for farmers: after all, they will be able to sell more. But is it good news? Although they will sell more, the effect of the increased supply will be to drive down the price – and that's bad news for farmers! So will the increased sales (the good news) be enough to compensate for the reduction in price (the bad news)? Will farmers end up earning more or less from their bumper harvest? It all depends on just how much the price falls, and this depends on the *price elasticity of demand* for their produce. This is a measure of how *responsive* demand is to a change in price.

It is not just the responsiveness of *demand* that is important in determining the functioning of markets. It is also the responsiveness of *supply*. Why do some firms respond to a rise in price by producing a lot more, whereas others produce only a little more? Is it simply because of different technologies? We will discover just what influences the price elasticity of supply in Section 3.3.

In Section 3.5 we compare across time the adjustment paths of markets to changes in demand or supply. We see how important elasticities are in affecting the nature of this adjustment as well as the role played by expectations. In some markets expectations can help to fuel volatility, while in others they dampen volatility. This leads us to a discussion in Section 3.6 about the impact of uncertainty and risk in economic decision making and why people are prepared to pay to insure against certain eventualities.

The chapter closes by looking at what happens if governments set about *controlling* prices. Why will shortages occur if the government sets the price too low, or surpluses if it sets it too high? When might governments feel that it is a good idea to fix prices?

After studying this chapter, you should be able to answer the following questions:

- How responsive is consumer demand to changes in prices and changes in incomes?
- How responsive is firms' output to a change in price?
- How does this responsiveness (or 'elasticity') of demand and supply affect the working of markets?
- Why are markets likely to be more responsive in the long run than the short run to changes in demand or supply?
- How will people respond if they anticipate a change in price?
- Why are people prepared to pay for insurance?
- What will happen if the government sets a price either above or below the market equilibrium?

3.1 PRICE ELASTICITY OF DEMAND

How responsive is demand to a change in price?

KI 6
p 20

When the price of a good rises, the quantity demanded will fall. That much is fairly obvious. But in most cases we will want to know more than this. We will want to know just *how much* the quantity demanded will fall. In other words, we will want to know how *responsive* demand is to a rise in price.

Take the case of two products: oil and carrots. In the case of oil, a rise in price is likely to result in only a slight fall in the quantity demanded. If people want to continue driving, they have to pay the higher prices for fuel. A few may turn to riding bicycles, and some people may try to make fewer journeys, but for most people, a rise in the price of petrol and diesel will make little difference to how much they use their cars.

In the case of carrots, however, a rise in price may lead to a substantial fall in the quantity demanded. The reason is that there are alternative vegetables that people can buy. Many people, when buying vegetables, are very conscious of their prices and will buy whatever is reasonably priced.

TC 3
p 12

We call the responsiveness of demand to a change in price the **price elasticity of demand.** If we know the price elasticity of demand for a product, we can predict the effect on price and quantity of a shift in the *supply* curve for that product. For example, we can predict the effect of the bumper harvest that we considered at the beginning of the chapter.

Figure 3.1 shows the effect of a shift in supply with two quite different demand curves (*D* and *D′*). Curve *D′* is more elastic than curve *D* over any given price range. In other words, for any given change in price, there will be a larger change in quantity demanded along curve *D′* than along curve *D*.

Assume that initially the supply curve is S_1, and that it intersects with both demand curves at point *a*, at a price of P_1 and a quantity of Q_1. Now supply shifts to S_2. What will happen to price and quantity? In the case of the less elastic demand curve *D*, there is a relatively large rise in price (to P_2) and a relatively small fall in quantity (to Q_2): equilibrium is at point *b*. In the case of the more elastic demand curve *D′*, however, there is only a relatively small rise in price (to P_3) but a relatively large fall in quantity (to Q_3): equilibrium is at point *c*.

Measuring the price elasticity of demand

What we want to compare is the size of the change in quantity demanded with the size of the change in price. But since price and quantity are measured in different units, the only sensible way we can do this is to use percentage or proportionate changes. This gives us the following **formula for the price elasticity of demand ($P\varepsilon_D$)** for a product: percentage (or proportionate) change in quantity demanded divided by the percentage (or proportionate) change in price. Putting this in symbols gives:

$$P\varepsilon_D = \frac{\%\Delta Q_D}{\%\Delta P}$$

where ε (the Greek epsilon) is the symbol we use for elasticity, and Δ (the capital Greek delta) is the symbol we use for a 'change in'.

Thus if a 50 per cent rise in the price of oil caused the quantity demanded to fall by a mere 10 per cent, the price elasticity of oil over this range would be:

$$-10\%/50\% = -0.2$$

On the other hand, if a 5 per cent fall in the price of carrots caused a 20 per cent rise in the quantity demanded, the price elasticity of demand for carrots over this range would be:

$$20\%/-5\% = -4$$

Carrots have a more elastic demand than oil, and this is shown by the figures. But just what do these two figures show? What is the significance of minus 0.2 and minus 4?

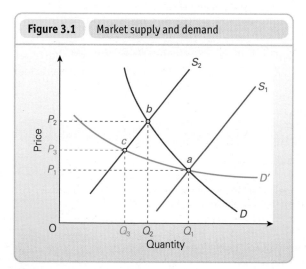

| Figure 3.1 | Market supply and demand |

Definitions

Price elasticity of demand The responsiveness of quantity demanded to a change in price.

Formula for price elasticity of demand ($P\varepsilon_D$) The percentage (or proportionate) change in quantity demanded divided by the percentage (or proportionate) change in price: $\%\Delta Q_D \div \%\Delta P$.

Interpreting the figure for elasticity

The use of proportionate or percentage measures

Elasticity is measured in proportionate or percentage terms for the following reasons:

- It allows comparison of changes in two qualitatively different things, and thus which are measured in two different types of unit: i.e. it allows comparison of *quantity* changes with *monetary* changes.
- It is the only sensible way of deciding *how big a* change in price or quantity is. Take a simple example. An item goes up in price by £1. Is this a big increase or a small increase? We can answer this only if we know what the original price was. If a can of beans goes up in price by £1, that is a huge price increase. If, however, the price of a house goes up by £1, that is a tiny price increase. In other words, it is the percentage or proportionate increase in price that we look at in deciding how big a price rise it is.

The sign (positive or negative)

Demand curves are generally downward sloping. This means that price and quantity change in opposite directions. A *rise* in price (a positive figure) will cause a *fall* in the quantity demanded (a negative figure). Similarly a *fall* in price will cause a *rise* in the quantity demanded. Thus when working out price elasticity of demand we either divide a negative figure by a positive figure, or a positive figure by a negative. Either way, we end up with a negative figure.

The value (greater or less than 1)

If we now ignore the negative sign and just concentrate on the value of the figure, this tells us whether demand is elastic or inelastic.

- **Elastic demand** ($\varepsilon > 1$). This is where a change in price causes a proportionately larger change in the quantity demanded. In this case the value of elasticity will be greater than 1, since we are dividing a larger figure by a smaller figure.
- **Inelastic demand** ($\varepsilon < 1$). This is where a change in price causes a proportionately smaller change in the quantity demanded. In this case elasticity will be less than 1, since we are dividing a smaller figure by a larger figure.
- **Unit elastic demand** ($\varepsilon = 1$). This is where price and quantity demanded change by the same proportion. This will give an elasticity equal to 1, since we are dividing a figure by itself.

Determinants of price elasticity of demand

The price elasticity of demand varies enormously from one product to another. Table 3.1 gives some examples. But why do some products have a highly elastic demand, whereas others have a highly *in*elastic demand? What determines price elasticity of demand?

Table 3.1	Estimates of price elasticity of demand for the USA
Product	**Price elasticity of demand**
Food	−0.21
Medical services	−0.18
Housing	
Rental	−0.18
Owner-occupied	−1.20
Electricity	−1.14
Cars	−1.20
Petrol	−0.55
Beer	−0.26
Wine	−0.88
Cigarettes	−0.35
Transatlantic air travel	−1.30
Imports	−0.58

Source: W. Nicholson and C. Snyder, *Intermediate Microeconomics*, 11th edition (Cengage Learning, 2011)

The number and closeness of substitute goods. This is the most important determinant. The more substitutes there are for a good, and the closer they are, the more will people switch to these alternatives when the price of the good rises: the greater, therefore, will be the price elasticity of demand.

Pause for thought

Why will the price elasticity of demand for a particular brand of a product (e.g. Texaco) be greater than that for the product in general (e.g. petrol)? Is this difference the result of a difference in the size of the income effect or the substitution effect?

Returning to our examples of oil and carrots, there is no close substitute for oil and thus demand is relatively inelastic. There are plenty of alternatives to carrots, however, and thus demand is relatively elastic.

The proportion of income spent on the good. The higher the proportion of our income we spend on a good, the more we

---

Definitions

Elastic demand Where quantity demanded changes by a larger percentage than price. Ignoring the negative sign, it will have a value greater than 1.

Inelastic demand Where quantity demanded changes by a smaller percentage than price. Ignoring the negative sign, it will have a value less than 1.

Unit elastic demand Where quantity demanded changes by the same percentage as price. Ignoring the negative sign, it will have a value equal to 1.

will be forced to cut consumption when its price rises: the bigger will be the income effect (see page 29) and the more elastic will be the demand.

Thus salt has a very low price elasticity of demand. We spend such a tiny fraction of our income on salt that we would find little difficulty in paying a relatively large percentage increase in its price: the income effect of a price rise would be very small. By contrast, there will be a much bigger income effect when a major item of expenditure rises in price. For example, if mortgage interest rates rise (the 'price' of loans for house purchase), people may have to cut down substantially on their demand for housing, being forced to buy somewhere smaller and cheaper, or to live in rented accommodation.

The time period. When price rises, people may take time to adjust their consumption patterns and find alternatives.

The longer the time period after a price change, then the more elastic is the demand likely to be.

To illustrate this, let us return to our example of oil. Between December 1973 and June 1974 the price of crude oil quadrupled, which led to similar increases in the prices of petrol and other oil products (such as central heating oil). Over the next few months, there was only a very small fall in the consumption of oil products. Demand was highly inelastic. The reason was that people still wanted to drive their cars and heat their houses.

Over time, however, as the higher oil prices persisted, new fuel-efficient cars were developed and many people switched to smaller cars or moved closer to their work. Similarly, people switched to gas or solid fuel central heating, and spent more money insulating their houses to save on fuel bills. Demand was thus much more elastic in the long run.

Recap

1. Price elasticity of demand is a measure of the responsiveness of demand to a change in price.

2. It is defined as the proportionate (or percentage) change in quantity demanded divided by the proportionate (or percentage) change in price. Given that demand curves are downward sloping, price elasticity of demand will have a negative value.

3. If quantity changes proportionately more than price, the figure for elasticity will be greater than 1 (ignoring the sign): demand is elastic. If the quantity changes proportionately less than price, the figure for elasticity will be less than 1 (again, ignoring the sign): demand is inelastic. If quantity and price change by the same proportion, the elasticity has a value of (minus) 1: demand is unit elastic.

4. Demand will be more elastic the greater the number and closeness of substitute goods, the higher the proportion of income spent on the good and the longer the time period that elapses after the change in price.

3.2 PRICE ELASTICITY OF DEMAND AND CONSUMER EXPENDITURE

How much do we spend on a good at a given price?

One of the most important applications of price elasticity of demand concerns its relationship with the total amount of money that consumers spend on a product. **Total consumer expenditure (*TE*)** is simply price times quantity purchased:

$$TE = P \times Q$$

For example, if consumers buy 3 million units (*Q*) at a price of £2 per unit (*P*), they will spend a total of £6 million (*TE*). Note that total consumer expenditure will be the same as the **total revenue (*TR*)** received by firms from the sale of the product (before any taxes or other deductions).

What will happen to consumer expenditure (and hence firms' revenue) if there is a change in price? The answer depends on the price elasticity of demand.

Elastic demand

As price rises so quantity demanded falls, and vice versa. When demand is elastic, quantity demanded changes proportionately more than price. Thus the change in quantity has a bigger effect on total consumer expenditure than does the change in price. For example, when the price rises, there will be such a large fall in consumer demand that less will be spent than before. This can be summarised as follows:

Definitions

Total consumer expenditure on a product (*TE*) (per period of time) The price of the product multiplied by the quantity purchased: $TE = P \times Q$.

Total revenue (*TR*) (per period) The total amount received by firms from the sale of a product, before the deduction of taxes or any other costs. The price multiplied by the quantity sold: $TR = P \times Q$.

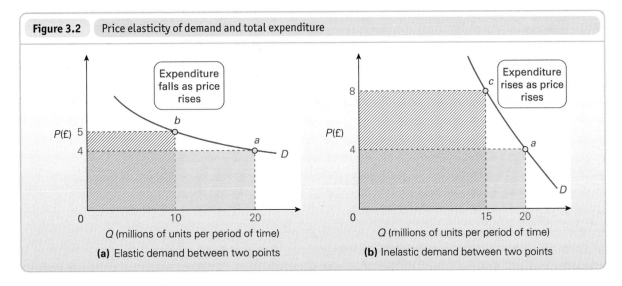

Figure 3.2   Price elasticity of demand and total expenditure

(a) Elastic demand between two points

(b) Inelastic demand between two points

■ *P* rises; *Q* falls proportionately more: therefore *TE* falls.
■ *P* falls; *Q* rises proportionately more: therefore *TE* rises.

In other words, total expenditure changes in the same direction as *quantity*.

This is illustrated in Figure 3.2(a). The areas of the rectangles in the diagram represent total expenditure. But why? The area of a rectangle is its height multiplied by its length. In this case, this is price multiplied by quantity purchased, which, as we have seen, gives total expenditure.

Demand is elastic between points *a* and *b*. A rise in price from £4 to £5 causes a proportionately larger fall in quantity demanded: from 20 million to 10 million. Total expenditure *falls* from £80 million (the striped area) to £50 million (the lilac shaded area).

When demand is elastic, then a rise in price will cause a fall in total consumer expenditure and thus a fall in the total revenue that firms selling the product receive. A reduction in price, however, will result in consumers spending more, and hence firms earning more.

Pause for thought

If a firm faces an elastic demand curve, why will it not necessarily be in the firm's interests to produce more? (Clue: you will need to distinguish between revenue and profit. We will explore this relationship in the next chapter.)

Inelastic demand

When demand is inelastic, it is the other way around. Price changes proportionately more than quantity. Thus the change in price has a bigger effect on total consumer expenditure than does the change in quantity. To summarise the effects:

■ *P* rises; *Q* falls proportionately less: therefore *TE* rises.
■ *P* falls; *Q* rises proportionately less: therefore *TE* falls.

In other words, total consumer expenditure changes in the same direction as *price*.

This is illustrated in Figure 3.2(b). Demand is inelastic between points *a* and *c*. A rise in price from £4 to £8 causes a proportionately smaller fall in quantity demanded: from 20 million to 15 million. Total expenditure *rises* from £80 million (the striped area) to £120 million (the lilac shaded area).

In this case, firms' revenue will increase if there is a rise in price, and fall if there is a fall in price.

Special cases

Figure 3.3 shows three special cases: (a) a totally inelastic demand ($P\varepsilon_D = 0$); (b) an infinitely elastic demand ($P\varepsilon_D = -\infty$); and (c) a unit elastic demand ($P\varepsilon_D = -1$).

Totally inelastic demand. This is shown by a vertical straight line. No matter what happens to price, quantity demanded remains the same. It is obvious that the more the price rises, the bigger will be the level of consumer expenditure. Thus in Figure 3.3(a) consumer expenditure will be higher at P_2 than at P_1.

Infinitely elastic demand. This is shown by a horizontal straight line. At any price above P_1 in Figure 3.3(b) demand is zero. But at P_1 (or any price below) demand is 'infinitely' large.

This seemingly unlikely demand curve is in fact relatively common for an *individual producer*. In a perfect market, as we have seen, firms are small relative to the whole market (like the small-scale grain farmer). They have to accept the price as given by supply and demand in the *whole market*, but at that price they can sell as much as they produce. (Demand is not *literally* infinite, but as far as the firm is concerned it is.) In this case, the more the individual farmer produces, the more revenue will be earned. In Figure 3.3(b), more revenue is earned at Q_2 than at Q_1.

BOX 3.1 **THE MEASUREMENT OF ELASTICITY**

We have defined price elasticity as the percentage or proportionate change in quantity demanded divided by the percentage or proportionate change in price. But how, in practice, do we measure these changes for a specific demand curve?

A common mistake that students make is to think that you can talk about the elasticity of a whole *curve*. The mistake here is that in most cases the elasticity will vary along the length of the curve.

Take the case of the demand curve illustrated in Figure (a). Between points *a* and *b*, total expenditure rises ($P_2Q_2 > P_1Q_1$): demand is thus elastic between these two points. Between points *b* and *c*, however, total revenue falls ($P_3Q_3 < P_2Q_2$). Demand here is inelastic.

Normally, then, we can refer to the elasticity only of a *portion* of the demand curve, not of the *whole* curve.

There is, however, an exception to this rule. This is when the elasticity just so happens to be the same all the way along a curve, as in the three special cases illustrated in Figure 3.3.

Although we cannot normally talk about the elasticity of a whole curve, we can nevertheless talk about the elasticity between any two points on it. Remember the formula we used was:

$$\frac{\% \text{ or proportionate } \Delta Q}{\% \text{ or proportionate } \Delta P} \text{ (where } \Delta \text{ means change in)}$$

The way we measure a *proportionate* change in quantity is to divide that change by the level of Q: i.e. $\Delta Q/Q$. Similarly, we measure a proportionate change in price by dividing that change by the level of P: i.e. $\Delta P/Q$. Price elasticity of demand can thus now be rewritten as:

$$\frac{\Delta Q}{Q} \div \frac{\Delta P}{P}$$

(a) Different elasticities along different portions of a demand curve

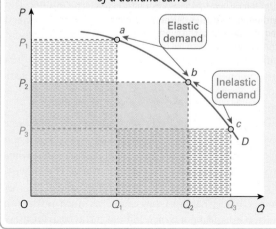

(b) Measuring elasticity using the arc method

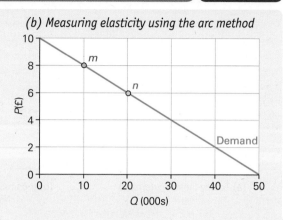

But just what value do we give to P and Q? Consider the demand curve in Figure (b). What is the elasticity of demand between points *m* and *n*? Price has fallen by £2 (from £8 to £6), but what is the proportionate change? Is it 2/8 or 2/6? The convention is to express the change as a proportion of the average of the two prices, £8 and £6: in other words to take the mid-point price, £7. Thus the proportionate change is 2/7.

Similarly the proportionate change in quantity between points *m* and *n* is 10/15, since 15 is mid-way between 10 and 20.

Thus using the ***average (or 'mid-point') formula***, elasticity between *m* and *n* is given by:

$$\frac{\Delta Q}{\text{average } Q} \div \frac{\Delta P}{\text{average } P} = \frac{10}{15} \div \frac{-2}{7} = -2.33$$

Since 2.33 is greater than 1, demand is elastic between *m* and *n*.

 Referring again to Figure (b), what is the price elasticity of demand between a price of (a) £6 and £4; (b) £4 and £2? What do you conclude about the elasticity of a straight-line demand curve as you move down it?

In this box we have looked at the measurement of elasticity over a segment of the demand curve. This gives what is known as 'arc elasticity'. An alternative is to measure elasticity at a single point on the demand curve. This gives, not surprisingly, what is known as 'point elasticity'. This method is examined in Web Appendix 3.1.

Definitions

Average (or 'mid-point') formula for price elasticity of demand $\Delta Q_D/\text{average } Q_D \div \Delta P/\text{average } P$.

Figure 3.3 Elasticity of demand: special cases

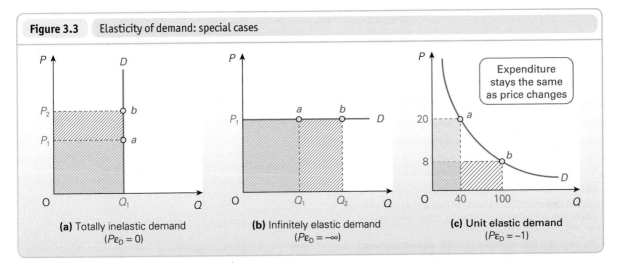

(a) Totally inelastic demand
$(P\varepsilon_D = 0)$

(b) Infinitely elastic demand
$(P\varepsilon_D = -\infty)$

(c) Unit elastic demand
$(P\varepsilon_D = -1)$

BOX 3.2   ADVERTISING AND ITS EFFECT ON DEMAND CURVES

CASE STUDIES & APPLICATIONS

How to increase sales and price

When we are told that brand X will make us more beautiful, enrich our lives, wash our clothes whiter, help us attract more friends, give us a new taste sensation or allow us to save the planet, just what are the advertisers up to? 'Trying to sell the product', you may reply. In fact there is a bit more to it than this. Advertisers are trying to do two things:

■ Shift the product's demand curve to the right.
■ Make it less price elastic.

This is illustrated in the diagram.

D_1 shows the original demand curve with price at P_1 and sales at Q_1. D_2 shows the curve after an advertising campaign. The rightward shift allows an increased quantity (Q_2) to be sold at the original price. If the demand is also made highly inelastic, the firm can also raise its price and still have a substantial increase in sales. Thus in the diagram, price can be raised to P_2 and sales will be Q_3, still substantially above Q_1. The total gain in revenue is shown by the shaded area.

How can advertising bring about this new demand curve?

Effect of advertising on the demand curve

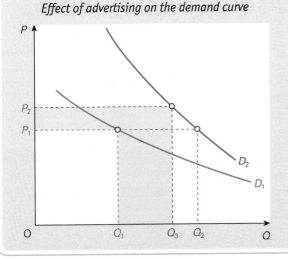

Shifting the demand curve to the right

This can occur in two ways. First, if the advertising brings the product to more people's attention, then the market for the good grows and the demand curve shifts to the right. Secondly, if the advertising increases people's desire for the characteristics or attributes of a product, they will be prepared to pay a higher price for each unit purchased.

Making the demand curve less elastic

This will occur if the advertising creates a greater attachment to a product, a range of products or indeed to an organisation (brand loyalty). In other words, advertising can be used to affect perceptions of the characteristics of products and even those of firms.

If advertising is successful in generating a sense of uniqueness amongst consumers for a product it allows a firm to raise the price of the product without a significant fall in sales. If it is successful in differentiating its brand, then the firm can raise prices across its range of products, again without hitting sales. Successful advertising therefore reduces the size of the substitution effect (see page 29) since consumers have been led to believe that there are few, if any, close substitutes.

1. *Think of some recent advertising campaigns and identify what 'characteristics' the advertising was attempting to highlight.*
2. *Imagine that 'Sunshine' sunflower margarine, a well-known brand, is advertised with the slogan, 'It helps you live longer'. What do you think would happen to the demand curve for a supermarket's own brand of sunflower margarine? Consider both the direction of shift and the effect on elasticity. Will the elasticity differ markedly at different prices? How will this affect the pricing policy and sales of the supermarket's own brand? What do you think might be the response of government to the slogan?*

Unit elastic demand. This is where price and quantity change in exactly the same proportion. Any rise in price will be exactly offset by a fall in quantity, leaving total revenue unchanged. In Figure 3.3(c) the striped area is exactly equal to the lilac shaded area: in both cases total expenditure is £800.

You might have thought that a demand curve with unit elasticity would be a straight line at 45° to the axes. Instead it is a curve. The reason for its particular shape is that the proportionate *rise* in quantity must equal the proportionate *fall* in price (and vice versa). As we move down the demand curve, in order for the *proportionate* change in both price and quantity to remain constant there must be a bigger and bigger *absolute* rise in quantity and a smaller and smaller

absolute fall in price. For example, a rise in quantity from 200 to 400 is the same proportionate change as a rise from 100 to 200, but its absolute size is double. A fall in price from £5 to £2.50 is the same percentage as a fall from £10 to £5, but its absolute size is only half.

> ### Pause for thought
>
> *Two customers go to the fish counter at a supermarket to buy some cod. Neither looks at the price. Customer A orders 1 kilo of cod. Customer B orders £3 worth of cod. What is the price elasticity of demand of each of the two customers?*

Recap

1. The total expenditure on a product is found by multiplying the quantity sold by the price of the product.
2. When demand is price elastic, a rise in price will lead to a reduction in total expenditure on the good and hence a reduction in the total revenue of producers.
3. When demand is price inelastic, a rise in price will lead to an increase in total expenditure on the good and hence an increase in the total revenue of producers.

3.3 PRICE ELASTICITY OF SUPPLY ($P\varepsilon_S$)

How responsive is supply to a change in price?

When price changes, there will be not only a change in the quantity demanded, but also a change in the quantity *supplied*. Frequently we will want to know just how responsive quantity supplied is to a change in price. The measure we use is the **price elasticity of supply**.

Figure 3.4 shows two supply curves. Curve S_2 is more elastic between any two prices than curve S_1. Thus, when price rises from P_1 to P_2 there is a larger increase in quantity supplied with S_2 (namely, Q_1 to Q_3) than there is with S_1

(namely, Q_1 to Q_2). For any shift in the demand curve there will be a larger change in quantity supplied and a smaller change in price with curve S_2 than with curve S_1. Thus the effect on price and quantity of a shift in the demand curve will depend on the price elasticity of supply.

The **formula for the price elasticity of supply ($P\varepsilon_S$)** is: the percentage (or proportionate) change in quantity supplied divided by the percentage (or proportionate) change in price. Putting this in symbols gives:

$$P\varepsilon_S = \frac{\%\Delta Q_s}{\%\Delta P}$$

In other words, the formula is identical to that for the price elasticity of demand, except that quantity in this case is quantity *supplied*. Thus if a 10 per cent rise in price caused a 20 per cent rise in the quantity supplied, the price elasticity of supply would be:

$$20\%/10\% = 2$$

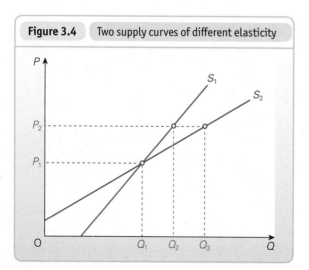

Figure 3.4 Two supply curves of different elasticity

> ### Definitions
>
> **Price elasticity of supply** The responsiveness of quantity supplied to a change in price.
>
> **Formula for price elasticity of supply (arc method)** ΔQ_s/average $Q_s \div \Delta P$/average P.

and if a 10 per cent rise in price caused only a 5 per cent rise in the quantity, the price elasticity of supply would be:

5%/10% = 0.5

In the first case, supply is elastic ($P\varepsilon_s > 1$); in the second it is inelastic ($P\varepsilon_s < 1$). Notice that, unlike the price elasticity of demand, the figure is positive (assuming that the supply curve is upward sloping). This is because price and quantity supplied change in the *same* direction.

The determinants of price elasticity of supply

The amount that costs rise as output rises. The less the additional costs of producing additional output, the more will firms be encouraged to produce for a given price rise: the more elastic will supply be.

Supply is thus likely to be elastic if firms have plenty of spare capacity, if they can readily get extra supplies of raw materials, if they can easily switch away from producing alternative products and if they can avoid having to introduce overtime working (at higher rates of pay). If all these conditions hold, costs will be little affected by a rise in output and supply will be relatively elastic. The less these conditions apply, the less elastic will supply be.

Time period

- Immediate time period. Firms are unlikely to be able to increase supply by much immediately. Supply is virtually fixed, or can vary only according to available stocks. Supply is highly inelastic.
- Short run. If a slightly longer time period is allowed to elapse, some inputs can be increased (e.g. raw materials) while others will remain fixed (e.g. heavy machinery). Supply can increase somewhat.
- Long run. In the long run, there will be sufficient time for all inputs to be increased and for new firms to enter the industry. Supply, therefore, is likely to be highly elastic. In some circumstances the long-run supply curve may even slope downwards (see Section 4.2).

Recap

1. Price elasticity of supply measures the responsiveness of supply to a change in price. It has a positive value.
2. Supply will be more elastic the less costs per unit rise as output rises and the longer the time period.

3.4 OTHER ELASTICITIES

How does demand respond to changes in income and to changes in the price of other goods?

Income elasticity of demand

So far we have looked at the responsiveness of demand and supply to a change in price. But price is just one of the determinants of demand and supply. In theory, we could look at the responsiveness of demand or supply to a change in *any* one of their determinants. We could have a whole range of different types of elasticity of demand and supply.

> **KEY IDEA 11**
> **TC 8**
>
> *Elasticity.* The responsiveness of one variable (e.g. demand) to a change in another (e.g. price). This concept is fundamental to understanding how markets work and is thus one of our threshold concepts (no. 8). The more elastic variables are, the more responsive is the market to changing circumstances.

In practice there are just two other elasticities that are particularly useful to us, and both are demand elasticities.

The first is the **income elasticity of demand** ($Y\varepsilon_D$). This measures the responsiveness of demand to a change in consumer incomes (Y).[1] It enables us to predict how much the demand curve will shift for a given change in income. The **formula for income elasticity of demand** is: the percentage (or proportionate) change in demand divided by the percentage (or proportionate) change in income. Putting this in symbols gives:

$$Y\varepsilon_D = \frac{\%\Delta Q_D}{\%\Delta Y}$$

> ### Definitions
>
> **Income elasticity of demand ($Y\varepsilon_D$)** The responsiveness of demand to a change in consumer incomes.
>
> **Formula for income elasticity of demand** The percentage (or proportionate) change in demand divided by the percentage (or proportionate) change in income: $\%\Delta Q_D \div \%\Delta Y$.

---

[1] Note that we use the letter Y rather than the letter I to stand for 'income'. This is normal practice in economics. The reason is that the letter I is used for 'investment'.

In other words, the formula is identical to that for the price elasticity of demand, except that we are dividing the change in demand by the change in *income* that caused it rather than by a change in price. Thus if a 2 per cent rise in income caused an 8 per cent rise in a product's demand, then its income elasticity of demand would be:

$$8\%/2\% = 4$$

Pause for thought

Assume that you decide to spend a quarter of your income on clothes. What is (a) your income elasticity of demand; (b) your price elasticity of demand?

The major determinant of income elasticity of demand is the degree of 'necessity' of the good. In a developed country, the demand for luxury goods expands rapidly as people's incomes rise, whereas the demand for basic goods, such as bread, rises only a little. Thus items such as designer clothes and foreign holidays have a high income elasticity of demand, whereas items such as potatoes and bus journeys have a low income elasticity of demand (see Table 3.2).

Table 3.2	Estimates of income elasticity of demand for the USA

Product	Income elasticity of demand
Food	+0.28
Medical services	+0.22
Housing	
Rental	+1.00
Owner-occupied	+1.20
Electricity	+0.61
Cars	+3.00
Petrol	+1.60
Beer	+0.38
Wine	+0.97
Cigarettes	+0.50
Transatlantic air travel	+1.40
Imports	+2.73

Source: W. Nicholson and C. Snyder, *Intermediate Microeconomics*, 11th edition (Cengage Learning, 2011)

The demand for some goods actually decreases as income rises. These are *inferior goods* such as many of the supermarkets' value lines. As people earn more, so they switch to regular lines or even 'finest' products. Unlike **normal goods**, which have a positive income elasticity of demand, **inferior goods** have a negative income elasticity of demand.

Income elasticity of demand is an important concept to firms considering the future size of the market for their product. If the product has a high income elasticity of demand, sales are likely to expand rapidly as national income rises, but may also fall significantly if the economy moves into recession. (See Case Study 3.3, Income elasticity of demand and the balance of payments, in MyEconLab. This shows how the concept of income elasticity of demand can help us understand why so many developing countries suffered from chronic balance of trade problems in the past, but why many have seen an improvement in recent years.)

Cross-price elasticity of demand

This is often known by its less cumbersome title of **cross elasticity of demand**. It is a measure of the responsiveness of demand for one product to a change in the price of another (either a substitute or a complement). It enables us to predict how much the demand curve for the first product will shift when the price of the second product changes. For example, knowledge of the cross elasticity of demand for Coca-Cola to the price of Pepsi would allow Coca-Cola to predict the effect on its own sales if the price of Pepsi were to change.

The **formula for the cross-price elasticity of demand** ($C\varepsilon_{Dab}$) is: the percentage (or proportionate) change in demand for good a divided by the percentage (or proportionate) change in price of good b. Putting this in symbols gives:

$$C\varepsilon_{Dab} = \frac{\%\Delta Q_{Da}}{\%\Delta P_b}$$

If good b is a *substitute* for good a, a's demand will *rise* as b's price rises. In this case, cross elasticity will be a positive figure. For example, if the demand for butter rose by 2 per cent when the price of non-dairy spreads (a substitute) rose by 8 per cent, then the cross elasticity of demand for butter with respect to non-dairy spreads would be:

$$2\%/8\% = 0.25$$

Definitions

Normal goods Goods whose demand increases as consumer incomes increase. They have a positive income elasticity of demand. Luxury goods will have a higher income elasticity of demand than more basic goods.

Inferior goods Goods whose demand decreases as consumer incomes increase. Such goods have a negative income elasticity of demand.

Cross-price elasticity of demand The responsiveness of demand for one good to a change in the price of another.

Formula for cross-price elasticity of demand ($C\varepsilon_{Dab}$) The percentage (or proportionate) change in demand for good a divided by the percentage (or proportionate) change in price of good b: $\%\Delta Q_{Da} \div \%\Delta P_b$.

If good b is *complementary* to good a, however, a's demand will *fall* as b's price rises and thus as the quantity of b demanded falls. In this case, cross elasticity of demand will be a negative figure. For example, if a 4 per cent rise in the price of bread led to a 3 per cent fall in demand for butter, the cross elasticity of demand for butter with respect to bread would be:

$$-3\%/4\% = -0.75$$

The major determinant of cross elasticity of demand is the closeness of the substitute or complement. The closer it is, the bigger will be the effect on the first good of a change in the price of the substitute or complement, and hence the greater the cross elasticity – either positive or negative.

Firms will wish to know the cross elasticity of demand for their product when considering the effect on the demand for their product of a change in the price of a rival's product or of a complementary product. These are vital pieces of information for firms when making their production plans.

Another example of the usefulness of the concept of cross elasticity of demand is in the field of international trade and the balance of payments. A government will wish to know how a change in domestic prices will affect the demand for imports. If there is a high cross elasticity of demand for imports (because they are close substitutes for home-produced goods), and if prices at home rise due to inflation, the demand for imports will rise substantially, thus worsening the balance of trade.

> ### Recap
>
> 1. Income elasticity of demand measures the responsiveness of demand to a change in income. For normal goods it has a positive value; for inferior goods it has a negative value.
> 2. Demand will be more income elastic the more luxurious the good and the less rapidly demand is satisfied as consumption increases.
> 3. Cross-price elasticity of demand measures the responsiveness of demand for one good to a change in the price of another. For substitute goods the value will be positive; for complements it will be negative.
> 4. The cross-price elasticity will be more elastic the closer the two goods are as substitutes or complements.

3.5 MARKETS AND ADJUSTMENT OVER TIME

How do markets respond over the longer term to a change in demand or supply?

The full adjustment of price, demand and supply to a situation of disequilibrium will not be instantaneous. It is necessary, therefore, to analyse the time path which supply takes in responding to changes in demand, and which demand takes in responding to changes in supply.

Short-run and long-run adjustment

As we have already seen, the price elasticities of demand and supply vary with the time period under consideration. The reason is that producers and consumers take time to respond to a change in price. The longer the time period, the bigger the response, and thus the greater the elasticity of demand and supply.

This is illustrated in Figures 3.5 and 3.6. In both cases, as equilibrium moves from points *a* to *b* to *c*, there is a large short-run price change (P_1 to P_2) and a small short-run quantity change (Q_1 to Q_2), but a small long-run price change (P_1 to P_3) and a large long-run quantity change (Q_1 to Q_3).

Price expectations and speculation

In a world of shifting demand and supply curves, prices do not stay the same. Sometimes they go up; sometimes they come down. If prices are likely to change in the foreseeable future, this will affect the behaviour of buyers and sellers *now*. If, for example, it is now December and you are thinking of buying a new winter coat, you might decide to wait until the January sales, and in the meantime make do with your old coat. If, on the other hand, when January comes you see a new summer jacket in the sales, you might well

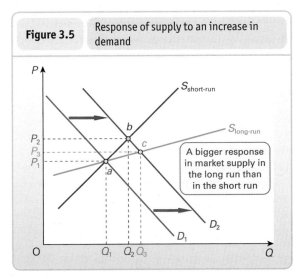

Figure 3.5 Response of supply to an increase in demand

A bigger response in market supply in the long run than in the short run

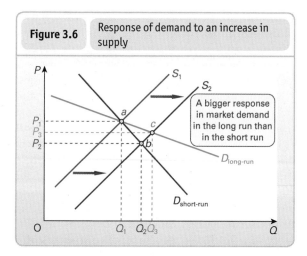

Figure 3.6 Response of demand to an increase in supply

buy it now and not wait until the summer for fear that the price will have gone up by then. Thus a belief that prices will go up will cause people to buy now; a belief that prices will come down will cause them to wait.

The reverse applies to sellers. If you are thinking of selling your house and prices are falling, you will want to sell it as quickly as possible. If, on the other hand, prices are rising sharply, you will wait as long as possible so as to get the highest price. Thus a belief that prices will come down will cause people to sell now; a belief that prices will go up will cause them to wait.

> **KEY IDEA 12**
>
> **TC 9**
>
> **People's actions are influenced by their expectations.** People respond not just to what is happening now (such as a change in price), but to what they anticipate will happen in the future. Understanding the crucial role that expectations play in determining economic behaviour makes this a threshold concept – the ninth of our fifteen.

This behaviour of looking into the future and making buying and selling decisions based on your predictions is called **speculation**. Speculation is often based on current trends in price behaviour. If prices are currently rising, people may then try to decide whether they are about to peak and go back down again, or whether they are likely to go on rising. Having made their prediction, they will then act on it. This speculation will thus affect demand and supply, which in turn will affect price. Speculation is commonplace in many markets: the stock exchange, the foreign exchange market and the housing market are three examples.

Speculation tends to be **self-fulfilling**. In other words, the actions of speculators tend to bring about the very effect on prices that speculators had anticipated. For example, if speculators believe that the price of BP shares is about to

rise, they will buy more of them. But by doing this they will ensure that the price *will* rise. The prophecy has become self-fulfilling.

Speculation can either help to reduce price fluctuations or aggravate them: it can be stabilising or destabilising.

Stabilising speculation

Speculation will tend to have a **stabilising** effect on price fluctuations when suppliers and/or demanders believe that a change in price is only *temporary*.

Assume, for example, that there has recently been a rise in price, caused, say, by an increase in demand. In Figure 3.7(a) demand has shifted from D_1 to D_2. Equilibrium has moved from point a to point b, and price has risen from P_1 to P_2. How do people react to this rise in price? **TC 3** **p 12**

Given that they believe this rise in price to be only temporary, suppliers bring their goods to market now, before price falls again. Supply shifts from S_1 to S_2. Demanders, however, hold back until price does fall. Demand shifts from D_2 to D_3. The equilibrium moves to point c, with price falling back towards P_1.

A good example of stabilising speculation occurs in agricultural commodity markets. Take the case of wheat. When it is harvested in the autumn there will be a plentiful supply. If all this wheat were to be put on the market, the price would fall to a very low level. Later in the year, when most of the wheat would have been sold, the price would then rise to a very high level. This is all easily predictable.

So what do farmers do? The answer is that they speculate. When the wheat is harvested they know the price will tend to fall, and so instead of bringing it all to market they put a lot of it into store. The more the price falls, the more they will put into store *anticipating that the price will later rise*. But this holding back of supplies prevents prices from falling. In other words, it stabilises prices.

Later in the year, when the price begins to rise, they will gradually release grain on to the market from the stores. The more the price rises, the more they will release on to the market *anticipating that the price will fall again by the time of the next harvest*. But this releasing of supplies will again stabilise prices by preventing them rising so much.

> ### Definitions
>
> **Speculation** Where people make buying or selling decisions based on their anticipations of future prices.
>
> **Self-fulfilling speculation** The actions of speculators tend to cause the very effect that they had anticipated.
>
> **Stabilising speculation** Where the actions of speculators tend to reduce price fluctuations.

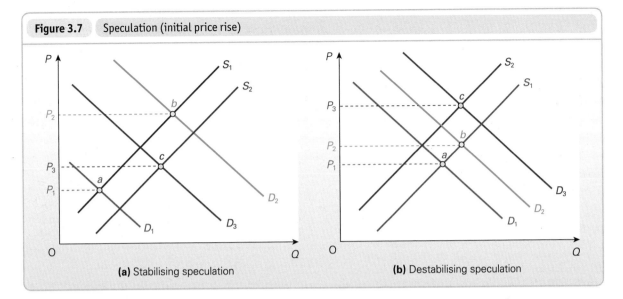

Figure 3.7 Speculation (initial price rise)

(a) Stabilising speculation

(b) Destabilising speculation

Rather than the farmers doing the speculation, it could be done by grain merchants. When there is a glut of wheat in the autumn, and prices are relatively low, they buy wheat on the grain market and put it into store. When there is a shortage in the spring and summer they sell wheat from their stores. In this way they stabilise prices just as the farmers did when they were the ones that operated the stores.

Destabilising speculation

Speculation will tend to have a **destabilising** effect on price fluctuations when suppliers and/or buyers believe that a change in price heralds similar changes to come.

Assume again that there has recently been a rise in price, caused by an increase in demand. In Figure 3.7(b), demand has shifted from D_1 to D_2 and price has risen from P_1 to P_2. This time, believing that the rise in price heralds further rises to come, suppliers wait until the price rises further. Supply shifts from S_1 to S_2. Demanders buy now before any further rise in price. Demand shifts from D_2 to D_3. As a result, the price continues to rise: to P_3.

Box 2.2 examined the housing market. In this market, speculation is frequently destabilising. Assume that people see house prices beginning to move upwards. This might be the result of increased demand brought about by a cut in mortgage interest rates or by growth in the economy. People may well believe that the rise in house prices signals a boom in the housing market: that prices will go on rising. Potential buyers will thus try to buy as soon as possible before prices rise any further. This increased demand (as in Figure 3.7(b)) will thus lead to even bigger price rises. This is precisely what happened in the UK housing market in 1999–2007 and, to some extent, from mid-2013 in southern Britain. Conversely, in early 2008 prices started to fall; potential buyers believed that they would fall further and thus held off entering the market, leading to even bigger price falls.

Pause for thought

Draw two diagrams like Figures 3.7(a) and (b), only this time assume an initial fall in demand and hence price. The first diagram should show the effects of stabilising speculation and the second the effect of destabilising speculation.

Conclusion

In some circumstances, then, the action of speculators can help keep price fluctuations to a minimum (stabilising speculation). This is most likely when markets are relatively stable in the first place, with only moderate underlying shifts in demand and supply.

In other circumstances, however, speculation can make price fluctuations much worse. This is most likely in times of uncertainty, when there are significant changes in the determinants of demand and supply. Given this uncertainty, people may see price changes as signifying some trend. They then 'jump on the bandwagon' and do what the rest are doing, further fuelling the rise or fall in price.

Definition

Destabilising speculation Where the actions of speculators tend to make price movements larger.

| BOX 3.3 | SHORT SELLING | EXPLORING ECONOMICS |

Gambling on a fall in share prices

Short selling is a form of speculation that can be very damaging to stock markets. It involves people take advantage of anticipated falls in share prices by borrowing shares, selling them, then buying them back later before finally returning them to the lender of the shares. Let's consider a hypothetical example to illustrate how this process might work.

Assume that a share price is currently £10 per share and traders on the stock market believe that the price is about to fall. They want to take advantage of this but don't possess any. What they do is borrow shares from dealers who do own some and agree to return them on a specified date. They pay a fee for doing this. In the meantime they sell the shares on the market at the current price of £10 and wait for it to fall. They are now 'short' of the shares (i.e. they don't possess them but still owe them).

Assume that just before the agreed time comes for returning the shares the price has fallen to £8. The trader then buys the shares, returns them to the dealer who had lent them and pockets the difference of £2 (minus the fee).

Although anyone can short sell shares, it is largely traders from various financial institutions who engage in this practice. Huge bonuses can be earned from their employers if the short selling is profitable. This encourages an atmosphere of risk taking and looking to short-term gains rather than providing long-term capital to firms.

Short selling in the banking crisis of 2008

The practice of short selling had become rife in recent years and added to the instability of markets, driving share prices down that were anticipated to fall. This was a particular problem in 2008, when worries about bad debts and losses in the banking sector led many traders to short sell the shares of banks and other financial institutions felt to be most at risk.

The short selling of Halifax Bank of Scotland (HBOS) shares in September 2008 was a major contributing factor to the collapse in its share price. HBOS, the UK's largest mortgage lender, had been suffering losses as a result of falling house prices and

the difficulties of many house owners in keeping up with their monthly mortgage payments. The share price plummeted by over 70 per cent in the space of a few days. The fall was driven on by speculation, much of it short selling. On 17 September it was announced that HBOS would be taken over by Lloyds TSB.

Concerns about the practice of short selling driving instability in financial markets have led a number of governments – or agencies acting on their behalf – to ban the practice. In September 2008 the Financial Services Authority, the UK industry's regulator at the time, announced a four-month ban on the practice. At the same time, the US financial regulator, the Securities and Exchange Commission, announced a similar move. Both these bans were imposed for a matter of months, but Denmark held a similar policy for more than two years.

In May 2010 the German government put in place a ban on short selling all EU government debt and bank shares. Then in 2012 the European Union passed legislation which gives it the power to ban short selling in emergency situations.

The European Union has banned the practice of 'naked short selling'. This occurs if a speculator agrees to sell securities, such as shares and sovereign debt, that have not yet been borrowed. If the speculator is unable to borrow the security then the transaction will 'fail to deliver', but in the short term will have depressed prices by temporarily 'creating' a supply.

Is short selling always profitable?

Short selling, as with other forms of speculation, is a form of gambling. If you gamble on a price fall and the price does fall, your gamble pays off and you make a profit. If you get it wrong, however, and the price rises, you will make a loss. In the case of short selling, you would have to buy the shares (to give back to the lender) at a higher price than you sold them.

This is just what happened in September 2008. With central banks around the world supporting markets, with the US government announcing that it would take over the bad debts of banks and with future short selling temporarily banned, share prices rapidly increased. The FTSE rose by a record 8.8 per cent on 19 September. Those with 'short positions' – i.e. those who had sold shares they had borrowed – then had to buy them back at a much higher price. Losses of hundreds of millions of pounds were made by short sellers. But they gained little sympathy from the general public, who blamed their 'greed' for much of the falls in share prices of the previous weeks.

Definition

Short selling (or shorting) Where investors borrow an asset, such as shares or foreign currency; sell the asset, hoping the price will soon fall; then buy it back later and return it to the lender. Assuming the price has fallen, the short seller will make a profit of the difference (minus any fees).

? *Why would owners of shares, such as pension funds, lend them to short sellers rather than selling the shares themselves and then buying them back later?*

Recap

1. A complete understanding of markets must take into account the time dimension.

2. Given that producers and consumers take a time to respond fully to price changes, we can identify different equilibria after the lapse of different lengths of time. Generally, short-run supply and demand tend to be less price elastic than long-run supply and demand. As a result, any shifts in demand *or supply curves* tend to have a relatively bigger effect on price in the short run and a relatively bigger effect on quantity in the long run.

3. People often anticipate price changes and this will affect the amount they demand or supply. This speculation will tend to stabilise prices (i.e. reduce fluctuations) if people believe that the price changes are only temporary. However, speculation will tend to destabilise prices (i.e. make price changes larger) if people believe that prices are likely to continue to move in the same direction as at present – at least for some time.

What to do when you can't be certain of outcomes

When analysing demand and supply decisions, it is important to recognise that people often have *imperfect information* when making choices. Consider a consumer. In many cases it is reasonable to assume that when people buy goods and services, they know exactly what price they will pay and how much utility they will gain. When you buy a bar of chocolate, you clearly do know how much you are paying for it and have a very good idea how much you will like it.

But what about a mobile phone, or a tablet, or a car, or a washing machine, or any other consumer durable? In each of these cases you are buying something that will last you a long time, and the further into the future you look, the less certain you will be of its costs and benefits to you. When you buy it, therefore, you are taking a bit of a gamble.

Consider now the problem facing buyers and sellers over future prices. They will try to anticipate price changes, but unfortunately on many occasions they cannot be certain just what these price changes will be.

Take the case of stocks and shares. If you anticipate that the price of, say, HSBC shares is likely to go up substantially in the near future, you may well decide to buy some now and then sell them later after the price has risen. But you cannot be *certain* that they will go up in price; they may fall instead. Again, therefore, decision making involves taking a gamble.

Responding to risk and uncertainty

So how does a lack of certainty affect people's behaviour and the choices they make? The answer is that it depends on their attitudes towards taking a gamble. To examine these attitudes let us assume that a person does at least know their *chances* when taking a gamble (i.e. the *probabilities involved* in doing so). In other words, the person is operating under conditions of **risk** rather than **uncertainty**. Under uncertainty, *the probability of an outcome is not known*.

Imagine that as a student you only have £105 left out of your student loan to spend. You are thinking of buying an instant lottery ticket/scratch card. The lottery ticket costs £5 and there is a 1 in 4 (i.e. 25 per cent) chance that it will be a winning ticket. A winning ticket pays a prize of £20. Would you buy the lottery ticket? This will depend on your attitude towards risk.

In order to explain people's attitude towards risk it is important to understand the concept of expected value. The **expected value** of a gamble is the amount the person would earn on average if the gamble were repeated many times. To calculate the expected value of a gamble you simply multiply each possible outcome by the probability that it will occur. These values are then added together.

In this example the gamble has only two possible outcomes – you purchase a winning ticket or a losing ticket.

There is a 25 per cent chance it is a winning ticket, which will give you a total of £120 to spend (£100 left out of your loan plus a £20 prize). There is a 75 per cent chance it is a losing ticket, in which case you will only have £100 left to spend out of your student loan. Therefore the expected value (EV) of this gamble is £105:

$$EV = 0.25(120) + 0.75(100) = 105$$

If you had not taken the gamble you would have £105 to spend for sure.

Attitudes towards risk

We can identify three possible categories of attitude towards risk.

- **Risk neutral.** If people are risk neutral they will always choose the option with the highest expected value. Therefore a student who is risk neutral would be indifferent between buying or not buying the instant lottery ticket, as each outcome has the same expected value of £105.

- **Risk averse.** If people are risk averse they will never choose a gamble if it has the same expected value as the pay-off from not taking a gamble. Therefore a student who is risk averse would definitely not buy the instant lottery ticket.

It is too simplistic, however, to say that a risk-averse person will never take risks. Such a person may choose a gamble if it has a greater expected value than the pay-off from not taking the gamble. However, whether or not risk-averse people do take a gamble depends on the strength of their aversion to risk, which will vary from one individual to another. The greater people's level of risk

---

Definitions

Risk When an outcome may or may not occur, but its probability of occurring is known. It is a measure of the variability of that outcome.

Uncertainty When an outcome may or may not occur and its probability of occurring is not known.

Expected value The predicted or average value of an outcome over a number of occurrences, calculated by taking each of the possible outcomes and multiplying it by its probability of occurrence and then adding each of these values.

Risk neutral When a person is indifferent between a certain outcome and a gamble with the same expected value.

Risk averse Where you would require a gamble to have a higher expected value than a certain outcome before being willing to take the gamble. The more risk averse you are, the higher the expected value you would require (i.e. the better would have to be the odds).

aversion, the greater the expected value of a gamble they are willing to give up in order to have a certain pay-off.

■ *Risk loving*. If people are risk loving they would always choose a gamble if it had the same expected value as the pay-off from not taking the gamble. Therefore a risk-loving student would definitely purchase the instant lottery ticket.

Once again, it is too simplistic to say that risk-loving people will always choose a gamble. It would depend on the extent to which that person enjoyed taking risks. The more risk loving people are, the greater the return from a certain pay-off they are willing to sacrifice in order to take a gamble.

> **KEY IDEA 13** *People's actions are influenced by their attitudes towards risk. Many decisions are taken under conditions of risk or uncertainty. Generally, the lower the probability of (or the more uncertain) the desired outcome of an action, the less likely will people be to undertake the action.*

Diminishing marginal utility of income and attitudes towards risk taking

Most people, for most of the time, are risk averse. We prefer to avoid insecurity. This is because risk-averse behaviour accords with the principle of *diminishing marginal utility*. In the case of each individual good, the more we consume, the less satisfaction we gain from each additional unit: the marginal utility falls. But the same principle applies if we look at our *total* consumption. The higher our level of total consumption, the less additional satisfaction will be gained from each additional £1 spent. What we are saying here is that there is a **diminishing marginal utility of income**. The more you earn, the lower will be the utility from each *extra* £1.

Because of the diminishing marginal utility of income, the gain in utility to people from an extra £100 is less than the loss of utility from forgoing £100. Thus if people are offered the gamble of a 50:50 chance of winning or losing £100, they will probably decline the gamble. This means that risk aversion is part of rational utility-maximising behaviour.

Decision making under uncertainty

On most occasions we will not know the probabilities of taking a gamble or have only a rough sense of what they may be. Gambling on the stock exchange is like this. You may have a good idea that a share will go up in price, but is it a 90 per cent chance, an 80 per cent chance or what? In other words, we will be operating under conditions of *uncertainty*. This could make us very cautious indeed. The more pessimistic we are, the more cautious we will be.

Risk, and particularly uncertainty, pervade the whole of economic life and decisions are constantly having to be made whose outcome cannot be known for certain (see Web Appendix 3.2 in MyEconLab for more analysis of risk and uncertainty).

Reducing the problem of uncertainty

Futures or forward markets. A futures market involves buyers and sellers agreeing prices today for the future delivery of commodities or financial instruments. For example, our wheat farmer could be quoted a price today for the delivery of a quantity of wheat in six months' time. This price is known as a **future price**. No matter what happens to the **spot price** (i.e. the current market price) in the meantime, the selling price has been agreed. Of course, the farmer will lose out if the spot price turns out to be greater than the agreed future price.

Prices in futures markets are determined in the same way as in other markets: by demand and supply. Such markets will naturally attract speculators, largely financial institutions, who never actually handle the commodities themselves.

Buffer stocks. Suppliers can reduce the problem of uncertainty by holding stocks. For instance, wheat farmers uncertain as to what the price of wheat will be when they take it to market can make use of storage facilities and wait until the price is 'right'. They can put the wheat into store if the price is low and then wait until it goes up. Alternatively, if the price of wheat is high at harvest time, they can sell it straight away.

> **Pause for thought**
>
> *The demand for pears is more price elastic than the demand for bread and yet the price of pears fluctuates more than that of bread. Why should this be so? If pears could be stored as long and as cheaply as flour, would this affect the relative price fluctuations? If so, how?*

Consumers too can hold buffer stocks of products. But, here the concept of buffer stocks is most commonly used in the context of saving. When households save they postpone an amount of current consumption but increase their potential future consumption. Crucially, by building up a stock of wealth that they can draw on, people can reduce the impact of any future falls in income.

> ## Definitions
>
> **Risk loving** Where you would be willing to take a gamble even if its expected value was lower than that of certain outcomes. The more risk-loving you are, the lower the expected value you would be prepared to accept (i.e. the worse the odds would need to be).
>
> **Diminishing marginal utility of income** Where each additional unit of income earned yields less additional utility than the previous unit.
>
> **Future price** A price agreed today at which an item (e.g. commodities) will be exchanged at some set date in the future.
>
> **Spot price** The current market price.

BOX 3.4   PROBLEMS WITH INSURANCE MARKETS

Adverse selection and moral hazard

Two problems encountered by insurance companies in setting insurance premiums (the price of insurance) are termed *adverse selection* and *moral hazard*. Both these problems arise as a consequence of *asymmetric information*, when the insurance company knows less about the individual seeking insurance than the person himself or herself does.

Adverse selection

This is where the people who take out insurance are likely to be those who have the highest risk.

For example, suppose that a company offers health-care insurance. It surveys the population and works out that the average person requires £200 of treatment per year. The company thus sets the premium at £250 (the extra £50 to cover its costs and provide a profit). But it is probable that the people most likely to take out the insurance are those most likely to fall sick: those who have been ill before, those whose families have a history of illness, those in jobs that are hazardous to health, etc. These people on average may require £500 of treatment per year. The insurance company would soon make a loss.

But could not the company then simply raise premiums to £550 or £600? It could, but it would thereby be depriving the person of average health of reasonably priced insurance and reducing the potential to sell insurance to people who value it.

The answer is for the company to obtain information that will allow it to identify the risk different people face. This process is known as 'screening'. There are several methods that the company can adopt. It can ask for personal information; for example, if you are applying for health-care insurance, you may have to fill out a questionnaire giving details of your lifestyle and family history or undergo a medical so that the company can have an expert opinion on your level of risk and set an appropriate premium.

The second form of screening occurs when an insurance company makes use of market data to assess risk. For example, companies offering life insurance can make use of information on life expectancy.

Moral hazard

This occurs when having insurance makes you less careful and thus increases your risk to the company. For example, if your bicycle is insured against theft, you may be less concerned to

go through the hassle of chaining it up each time you leave it. Again this is an example of asymmetric information, because the insurance company cannot determine for any individual whether taking out insurance will make him or her more careless.

If insurance companies work out risks by looking at the total number of bicycle thefts, these figures will understate the risks to the company because they will include thefts from *uninsured* people who are likely to be more careful. One solution is for insurance companies to write contracts that allow them to reduce the incidence of moral hazard. For example, they could require the insured person to pay the first so much of any claim (an 'excess').

The problem of moral hazard occurs in many other walks of life. A good example is that of debt. If someone else is willing to pay your debts (e.g. your parents), it is likely to make you less careful in your spending! A similar issue arose for policy makers around the world during the financial crisis of 2007/8. How could support be given to banks in trouble, and thereby prevent the financial system from collapsing, without encouraging banks to behave recklessly in the future? Of course, some argue that because financial institutions believed all along they would not be allowed to fail, they were already behaving recklessly – and hence the need to be bailed out in the first place.

If the problems of adverse selection and moral hazard cannot be overcome by screening and carefully written contracts then this is not a problem for insurance companies alone. Most people in society are risk averse and are willing to pay others to reduce the risk that they face. Insurance markets have grown up in response to this. If insurance markets fail, then society suffers as a consequence.

1. *What details does an insurance company require to know before it will insure a person to drive a car?*
2. *How will the following reduce moral hazard?*
   a. *A no-claims bonus.*
   b. *An excess, which means that the claimant has to pay the first part of any claim.*
   c. *Offering lower premiums to those less likely to claim (e.g. lower house contents premiums for those with burglar alarms).*

KI 13
p 66

We would expect greater economic uncertainty to increase the buffer stock of saving that people would wish to hold. This accords with the evidence from after the financial crisis of the late 2000s when across households in the UK the proportion of income saved rose sharply. Households were effectively insuring themselves against the heightened uncertainty around future incomes.

Insurance. Insurance is the opposite of gambling. It removes the risk. If, for example, you risk losing your job if you are injured, you can remove the risk of loss of income by taking out an appropriate insurance policy.

Given that many people are risk averse, they may be prepared to pay the premiums even though it will leave

them with less than the expected value from taking the gamble.

Definitions

Adverse selection The tendency of those at greatest risk to take out insurance.

Moral hazard The temptation to take more risk when you know that other people (e.g. insurers) will cover the risks.

Asymmetric information Where one party in an economic relationship has more or better information than another.

The total premiums paid to an insurance company will be *more* than the amount it pays out: that is how such companies make a profit. An insurance company is prepared to shoulder the risks that its customers are not because it is able to **pool its risks**.

Because an insurance company will be insuring many customers, for example against property burning down, it will be able to collect more than enough to cover its payments. The more clients it insures, the smaller will be the variation in the proportion of claims it will need to pay out on each year. This is an application of the **law of large numbers**. In other words, the more people the insurance company insures, the more predictable is the total outcome.

The pooling of risks does not just require a large number of policies; it also requires the risks to be **independent**. If an insurance company insured properties *all in the same neighbourhood*, and then there were a fire in the area, the claims would be enormous; the risks of fire were not independent. If, however, it provides fire insurance for houses scattered all over the country, the risks *are* independent.

But, why are people prepared to take out insurance products against specific events when the cost of premiums exceeds the expected financial loss? The answer is that people are generally risk averse and are paying to avoid a particular gamble.

Recap

1. Many economic decisions are taken under conditions of risk or uncertainty. If we know the probabilities, we are said to be operating under conditions of *risk*. If we do not know the probabilities, we are said to be operating under conditions of *uncertainty*.

2. People can be divided into risk lovers, risk averters and those who are risk neutral. Because of the diminishing marginal utility of income it is rational for people to be risk averters (unless gambling is itself pleasurable).

3. Uncertainty over future prices can be tackled by holding stocks or through transactions in futures markets. Consumers may hold a buffer stock of saving because of the uncertainty around future incomes.

4. Insurance markets provide a way of eliminating risk. If people are risk averse they are prepared to pay premiums to obtain insurance. Insurance companies are able to pool risk by selling a large number of policies, but require that the risks are independent.

3.7 MARKETS WHERE PRICES ARE CONTROLLED

What happens if the government fixes prices?

TC 5
p 23

At the equilibrium price, there will be no shortage or surplus. The equilibrium price, however, may not be the most *desirable* price. The government, therefore, may prefer to keep prices above or below the equilibrium price.

Setting a minimum (high) price

If the government sets a **minimum price** above the equilibrium (a price floor), there will be a surplus: $Q_s - Q_d$ in

Figure 3.8. Price will not be allowed to fall to eliminate this surplus. The government may do this for various reasons:

■ To protect producers' incomes. If the industry is subject to supply fluctuations (e.g. crops, due to fluctuations in weather) and if industry demand is price inelastic, prices are likely to fluctuate severely. Minimum prices

---

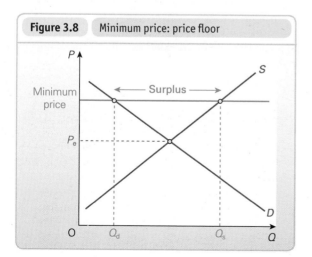

Figure 3.8 Minimum price: price floor

Definitions

Pooling risks (for an insurance company) The more policies an insurance company issues and the more independent the risks from these policies are, the more predictable will be the number of claims.

Law of large numbers The larger the number of events of a particular type, the more predictable will be their average outcome.

Independent risks Where two risky events are unconnected. The occurrence of one will not affect the occurrence of the other.

Minimum price A price floor set by the government or some other agency. The price is not allowed to fall below this level (although it is allowed to rise above it).

will prevent the fall in producers' incomes that would accompany periods of low prices.

■ To create a surplus (e.g. of grains), particularly in periods of plenty, which can be stored in preparation for possible future shortages.

■ In the case of wages (the price of labour), minimum wages legislation can be used to prevent workers' wage rates from falling below a certain level (see Box 6.4).

There are various methods the government can use to deal with the surpluses associated with minimum prices:

■ The government could buy the surplus and store it, destroy it or sell it abroad in other markets.

■ Supply could be artificially lowered by restricting producers to particular quotas. In Figure 3.8, supply could therefore be reduced to Q_d.

■ Demand could be raised by advertising, by finding alternative uses for the good, or by reducing consumption of substitute goods (e.g. by imposing taxes or quotas on substitutes, such as imports).

One of the problems with minimum prices is that firms with surplus on their hands may try to evade the price control and cut their prices.

Another problem is that high prices may cushion inefficiency. Firms may feel less need to find more efficient methods of production and cut their costs if their profits are being protected by the high price. Also the high price may discourage firms from producing alternative goods which they could produce more efficiently or which are in higher demand, but which nevertheless have a lower (free-market) price.

TC4
p 20

Pause for thought

Draw a supply and demand diagram with the price of labour (the wage rate) on the vertical axis and the quantity of labour (the number of workers) on the horizontal axis. What will happen to employment if the government raises wages from the equilibrium to some minimum wage above the equilibrium?

One of the best-known examples of governments fixing high minimum prices is the Common Agricultural Policy (CAP) of the European Union. This is examined in Box 3.5.

Setting a maximum (low) price

If the government sets a **maximum price** below the equilibrium (a price ceiling), there will be a shortage: $Q_d - Q_s$ in Figure 3.9. Price will not be allowed to rise to eliminate this shortage. The government may set maximum prices to prevent them rising above a certain level. This will normally be done for reasons of fairness. In wartime, or times of famine, the government may set maximum prices for basic goods so

that poor people can afford to buy them.

The resulting shortages, however, create further problems. If the government merely sets prices and does not intervene further, the shortages are likely to lead to the following:

■ Allocation on a 'first come, first served' basis. This is likely to lead to queues developing, or firms adopting waiting lists. Queues were a common feature of life in the former communist Eastern European countries where governments kept prices below the level necessary to equate demand and supply.

■ Firms deciding which customers should be allowed to buy: e.g., giving preference to regular customers.

Neither of the above may be considered to be fair. Certain needy people may be forced to go without. Therefore, the government may adopt a system of **rationing** – a system commonly used in wartime as a way of coping with shortages. People could be issued with a set number of coupons for each item rationed.

A major problem with maximum prices is likely to be the emergence of **underground (or shadow) markets** (see Case Study 3.7 in MyEconLab), where customers, unable to buy enough in legal markets, may well be prepared to pay very high prices: prices above P_e in Figure 3.9.

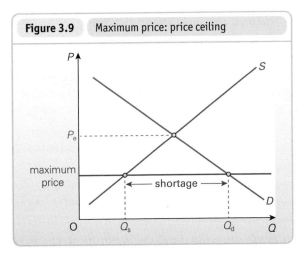

| **Figure 3.9** | Maximum price: price ceiling |

Definitions

Maximum price A price ceiling set by the government or some other agency. The price is not allowed to rise above this level (although it is allowed to fall below it).

Rationing Where the government restricts the amount of a good that people are allowed to buy.

Underground or shadow markets Where people ignore the government's price and/or quantity controls and sell illegally at whatever price equates illegal demand and supply.

BOX 3.5 AGRICULTURE AND MINIMUM PRICES

A problem of surpluses

Governments in many countries intervene in agricultural markets. The problems of fluctuating prices, dependency on foreign food imports, and the maintenance of farmers' and farm workers' incomes are but a few of the reasons for such intervention. The form that government intervention takes varies, from a series of subsidies or tax reliefs for farmers, to the more formal fixing of high minimum prices or direct payments.

Until recent years, the fixing of high minimum prices was the main policy used by the European Union in its Common Agricultural Policy (CAP). Here 'Intervention Boards' of the EU bought up any surpluses that resulted at a given 'intervention' price, usually set above the equilibrium.

The effects of this system are illustrated in the diagram, which shows the demand and supply of a particular agricultural product. Assume that the EU demand is D_{EU} and that EU supply is S_{EU}. Assume also that the world price is P_w. This will be the equilibrium price, since any shortage at P_w (i.e. $b - a$) will be imported at that price. Thus before intervention, EU demand is Q_{d1} and EU supply is Q_{s1} and imports are $Q_{d1} - Q_{s1}$.

Now assume that the EU sets an intervention price of P_i. At this high price, there will be a surplus of $d - e$ (i.e. $Q_{s2} - Q_{d2}$). Assume for the moment that none of this surplus is exported. It will all, therefore, be bought by the appropriate Intervention Board. The cost to the EU of buying this surplus is shown by the total shaded area ($edQ_{s2}Q_{d2}$: i.e. the surplus multiplied by the intervention price). Unless the food is thrown away or otherwise disposed of, there will obviously then be the additional costs of storing this food: costs that have been very high in some years as wine 'lakes' and grain and dairy 'mountains' have built up.

An alternative to storing the food is for the Board to sell the surpluses on the world market at the world price (P_w). In this case, the net cost to the Intervention Board would only be the pink area $edcf$: in other words, the amount purchased by the Board ($d - e$) multiplied by the difference in price paid by the Board and the price it receives on the world market ($P_i - P_w$).

Alternatively, export subsidies could be paid to farmers who sell on world markets to bring the amount they receive

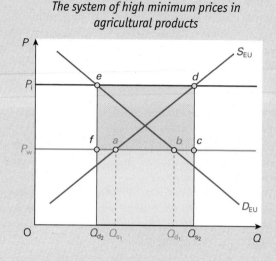

The system of high minimum prices in agricultural products

up to the intervention price: i.e. a subsidy of $P_i - P_w$. Here the Board would only need to purchase what had not been managed to be sold.

Over time the high prices will encourage farmers to produce more. Indeed they know the Intervention Boards will buy as much as they offer for sale. This results in a rightward shift in the supply curve and hence an even greater surplus.

Assessing the system of high minimum prices

The justifications for such a policy are that it stabilises domestic prices for farmers, reduces dependency on food imports by boosting domestic production and it boosts farmers' incomes. This also encourages them to invest in agriculture, which results in a growth in agricultural productivity.

Price support has, however, been criticised on a number of counts:

- Food surpluses were a costly waste of scarce resources.
- The system had harmful effects on the environment (see Case Study 3.9 in MyEconLab). Farmers boosted output by using

---

Another problem is that maximum prices reduce the quantity produced of an already scarce commodity. For example, artificially low prices in a famine are likely to reduce food supplies: if not immediately, then at the next harvest, because of less being sown. In many developing countries, governments control the price of basic foodstuffs in order to help the urban poor. The effect, however, is to reduce incomes for farmers, who are then encouraged to leave the land and flock into the ever-growing towns and cities.

To minimise these types of problem the government may attempt to reduce the shortage by encouraging supply: by drawing on stores, by direct government production, or by giving subsidies or tax relief to firms.

Alternatively, it may attempt to reduce demand: by the production of more alternative goods (e.g. home-grown vegetables in times of war) or by controlling people's incomes.

An example of a maximum price is considered in Case Study 3.8 in MyEconLab. The 'price' in this case is the rent paid by tenants for private rented accommodation.

> **Pause for thought**
>
> *Many governments intervene in the market for private rented accommodation including setting a maximum rent payable by tenants. Consider the arguments for and against rent controls.*

more chemical fertilisers and pesticides; and they gained land by removing hedgerows, trees and ponds. This caused pollution and affected wildlife and their habitats.

- The system increased inequalities within agriculture. Only larger farmers were able to boost output and gain more income. These tended to be located near each other, so only some EU regions gained.
- Prices for some agricultural commodities were kept higher than others, so producers of some commodities gained much more than others.
- Higher food prices penalise poor consumers, who spend a larger proportion of their income on food than do the rich.
- Subsidised EU exports have had a doubly damaging effect on agriculture in developing countries: (a) exporters of foodstuffs find it very difficult to compete with subsidised EU exports; (b) farmers in developing countries who are producing for their domestic market find that they cannot compete with cheap imports of food from the EU. Agriculture in the developing world thus declines. Farmers' incomes are too low to invest in the land. Many migrate to the overcrowded cities, with little or no paid employment.
- Trade disputes arose because export subsidies gave EU exports an unfair advantage and took export markets from other exporting countries.

Reforming the CAP

As a result of these problems, various reforms to the CAP have been implemented. Early reforms included a reduction in intervention prices and land being taken out of production ('set aside'). Price cuts boosted EU demand, while price cuts and set aside reduced EU supply. This considerably reduced the amount of subsidised EU exports.

There was also a move, begun in 1992, from price support to giving 'direct aid' to farmers, unrelated to current production. Direct aid removes the incentive for farmers to produce surpluses.

The policy of 'set aside' was abolished from 2008 following what has become known as the '2008 CAP Health Check'. This also saw a further boost to the shift from price support to direct aid. Under the Health Check reform, by the end of 2013 no more than 5 per cent of CAP expenditure involved export refunds and intervention purchases compared with over 90 per cent in 1992.

In order to try to help the environment directly and support the rural community more generally, 'Rural Development' policy makes grants and other incentives available for farmers to farm less intensively or to diversify into alternative rural industries (such as tourism and forestry).

Further reforms were agreed in 2013 for the 2014–20 period. Their key objectives are:

- *Enhanced competitiveness of EU agriculture.* The intent of the reform is to enhance market mechanisms, with the single largest change being the removal of quotas. From 2015 EU producers of sugar, wine and milk are able to meet increasing world demand by increasing their output. Conversely if demand for a product falls, farmers are no longer supported to produce up to a quota.
- *Sustainable EU agriculture.* This involves toughening up environmental requirements placed on farmers alongside a more strategic rural development policy. Thirty per cent of the Rural Development budget is reserved for voluntary measures that are beneficial for the environment; there are start-up payments for young farmers; and member states have the flexibility to adopt other redistributive schemes based on their own needs.
- *An effective and efficient CAP.* There are simplified regulations and a budget that is capped at 2013 levels, thus falling in real terms. This translates into a total CAP ceiling for 2014–20 of €408 billion.

These reforms are wide-ranging and many consider they are long overdue. The growth in both the number and diversity of member states had made the CAP unsustainable and increasingly inefficient. As the reforms are rolled out, commentators are looking ahead to assess just how well they will deliver for the EU and the world.

> *What is the effect on output of replacing high minimum prices with grants to farmers unrelated to current production?*

BOX 3.6 | **THE EFFECT OF IMPOSING TAXES ON GOODS** | EXPLORING ECONOMICS

Who ends up paying?

Another example of government intervention in markets is the imposition of taxes on goods. These indirect taxes, as they are called, include taxes such as value added tax (VAT) and excise duties on cigarettes, petrol and alcoholic drinks.

These taxes can be a fixed amount per unit sold – a 'specific tax'. An example is the tax on petrol, which is set at so much per litre. Alternatively, they can be a percentage of the price, or value added, at each stage of production – an '*ad valorem* tax'. An example is VAT.

When a tax is levied on a good or service, this has the effect of shifting the supply curve upwards by the amount of the tax (see diagram (a)). In the case of a specific tax, it will be a parallel shift, since the amount of the tax is the same at all prices.

But why does the supply curve shift upwards by the amount of the tax? In diagram (a), the supply curve (S) shows that to supply Q_1, producers need to receive a price of P_1. Now a tax is levied of an amount shown by the arrow. For producers to continue receiving P_1 and hence producing Q_1, the price charged to consumers has to be $P_1 + $ tax. Thus the new supply curve is shown by the red line S_T

The incidence of the tax

What will be the effect of the tax on the price and the quantity sold? This is illustrated in diagram (b). Before the tax is imposed, Q_1 units are sold at a price of P_1. The effect of the tax is to shift the supply curve to S_T Price rises to P_2 and quantity falls to Q_2.

Notice, however, that price does not rise by the full amount of the tax, because the demand curve is downward sloping. The amount of the tax is $P_2 - C$, whereas the price increase is only $P_2 - P_1$. Thus the burden or incidence of such taxes is distributed between consumers and producers.

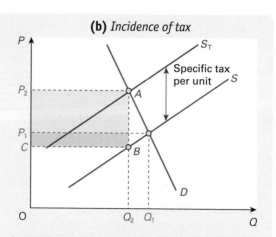

(b) *Incidence of tax*

Consumers pay to the extent that price rises. Producers pay to the extent that this rise in price is not sufficient to cover the tax.

We can also show in diagram (b) the revenue the government receives from the tax. The tax per unit is $P_2 - C$ and the quantity sold is Q_2 (shown by the distance CB). Thus the revenue raised is the total area of the shaded rectangle, P_2ABC.

The rise in price from P_1 to P_2 multiplied by the number of goods sold (Q_2) (the green area) is the amount of the tax passed on to consumers and thus represents the consumers' share of the tax. The remainder (the lilac area) is the producers' share. This is the amount by which the producers' net price is below the original price (i.e. $P_1 - C$) multiplied by Q_2.

Elasticity and the incidence of taxation

It is easy to see that the less elastic is demand:

■ the less quantity sold falls and hence the greater the revenue the government raises from the tax;
■ the more price rises and hence the greater the proportion of the tax paid by consumers.

Thus in most countries, cigarettes, petrol and alcohol are the major targets for indirect taxes. Demand for each of them is high and relatively inelastic, and so taxes on them raise a lot of revenue and do not curb demand significantly. Indeed, in the UK, fuel duty (a specific tax) and VAT (an *ad valorem* tax), together account for between 60 and 75 per cent of the cost of petrol, depending on the price of petrol.

> **?** *Demand tends to be more elastic in the long run than in the short run. Assume that a tax is imposed on a good that was previously untaxed. How will the incidence of this tax change as time passes?*

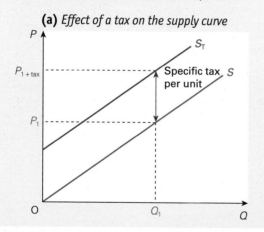

(a) *Effect of a tax on the supply curve*

Recap

1. The government may fix minimum or maximum prices. If a minimum price is set above the equilibrium price, a surplus will result. If a maximum price is set below the equilibrium price, a shortage will result.

2. Minimum prices are set as a means of protecting the incomes of suppliers or creating a surplus for storage in case of future reductions in supply. If the government is not deliberately trying to create a surplus, it must decide what to do with it.

3. Maximum prices are set as a means of keeping prices down for the consumer. The resulting shortage will cause queues, waiting lists or the restriction of sales by firms to favoured customers. Alternatively, the government could introduce a system of rationing. If it does, then underground markets are likely to arise. This is where goods are sold illegally above the maximum price.

QUESTIONS

1. Draw a diagram with two supply curves, one steeply sloping and one gently sloping. Ensure that the two curves cross. Draw a demand curve through the point where they cross and mark the equilibrium price and quantity. Now assume that the demand curve shifts to the right. Show how the shape of the supply curve will determine just what happens to price and quantity.

2. Which of the following will have positive signs and which will have negative ones? (a) price elasticity of demand; (b) income elasticity of demand (normal good); (c) income elasticity of demand (inferior good); (d) cross elasticity of demand (with respect to changes in price of a substitute good); (e) cross elasticity of demand (with respect to changes in price of a complementary good); (f) price elasticity of supply.

3. Demand for oil might be relatively elastic over the longer term, and yet it could still be observed that over time people consume more oil (or only very slightly less) despite rising oil prices. How can this apparent contradiction be explained?

4. Is the demand curve for a particular football club's season tickets the same as that facing any other football club? Explain.

5. Assume that a football club has the following demand curve for season tickets: $Q_d = 50\,000 - 50P$.
   a. What quantity of season tickets is demanded when season tickets are free ($P = 0$)?
   b. At what price do season tickets cease to be bought ($Q = 0$)?
   c. Using the information from (a) and (b) sketch the demand curve for the club.
   d. What amount of season tickets is demanded at £600 and £700? What revenue is generated from season ticket sales at each price?
   e. Using the average (mid-point) formula in Box 3.1 estimate the price elasticity between £600 and £700.
   f. What can we say about the price elasticity of demand between the points on the demand curve corresponding to season ticket prices of £600 and £700?
   g. Between what price range does raising season ticket prices increase revenues from season ticket sales?

6. How might a firm set about making the demand for its brand less elastic?

7. Assuming that a firm faces an inelastic demand and wants to increase its total revenue, in what direction should it change its price? Is there any limit to how far it should go in changing its price in this direction?

8. Why are both the price elasticity of demand and the price elasticity of supply likely to be greater in the long run?

9. Which are likely to have the highest cross elasticity of demand: two brands of coffee, or coffee and tea? Explain.

10. Redraw both diagrams in Figure 3.7, only this time assume that it was an initial shift in supply that caused price to change in the first place.

11. What are the advantages and disadvantages of speculation from the point of view of (a) the consumer; (b) firms?

12. Give some examples of decisions you have taken recently that were made under conditions of uncertainty. With hindsight do you think you made the right decisions?

13. Assume that the (weekly) market demand and supply of tomatoes are given by the figures shown below:

Price (£ per kilo)	4.00	3.50	3.00	2.50	2.00	1.50	1.00
Q_d (000 kilos)	30	35	40	45	50	55	60
Q_s (000 kilos)	80	68	62	55	50	45	38

   a. What are the equilibrium price and quantity?
   b. What will be the effect of the government fixing a minimum price of (i) £3.00 per kilo; (ii) £1.50 per kilo?
   c. Suppose that the government paid tomato producers a subsidy of £1.00 per kilo. (i) Give the new supply schedule. (ii) What will be the new equilibrium price? (iii) How much will this cost the government?
   d. Alternatively, suppose that the government guaranteed tomato producers a price of £2.50 per kilo. (i) How many tomatoes would it have to buy in order to ensure that all the tomatoes produced were sold? (ii) How much would this cost the government?
   e. Alternatively, suppose it bought all the tomatoes produced at £2.50. (i) At what single price would it have to sell them in order to dispose of the lot? (ii) What would be the net cost of this course of action?

14. Think of two things that are provided free. In each case, identify when and in what form a shortage might occur. In what ways are/could these shortages be dealt with? Are they the best solution to the shortages?

15. Think of some examples where the price of a good or service is kept below the equilibrium. In each case consider the advantages and disadvantages of the policy.

MyEconLab

This book can be supported by MyEconLab, which contains a range of additional resources, including an online homework and tutorial system designed to test and build your understanding.

You need both an access card and a course ID to access MyEconLab:

1. Is your lecturer using MyEconLab? Ask your lecturer for your course ID.

2. Has an access card been included with the book at a reduced cost? Check the inside back cover of the book.

3. If you have a course ID but no access card, go to: http://www.myeconlab.com/ to buy access to this interactive study programme.

ADDITIONAL CASE STUDIES IN THE *ESSENTIALS OF ECONOMICS* MyEconLab (www.pearsoned.co.uk/sloman)

3.1 **Shall we put up our price?** This uses the concept of price elasticity of demand to explain why prices are higher where firms face little or no competition.

3.2 **Any more fares?** Pricing on the buses: an illustration of the relationship between price and total revenue.

3.3 **Income elasticity of demand and the balance of payments.** This examines how a low income elasticity of demand for the exports of many developing countries can help to explain their chronic balance of payments problems.

3.4 **Elasticities of demand for various foodstuffs.** An examination of the evidence about price and income elasticities of demand for food in the UK.

3.5 **What we pay to watch sport.** Consideration of the demand function for season tickets to watch spectator sports like football.

3.6 **The role of the speculator.** This assesses whether the activities of speculators are beneficial or harmful to the rest of society.

3.7 **Underground markets.** How underground markets can develop when prices are fixed below the equilibrium.

3.8 **Rent control.** An analysis of the potential impact of rent controls on the private rental market.

3.9 **The CAP and the environment.** This case shows how the system of high intervention prices had damaging environmental effects. It also examines the more recent measures the EU has adopted to reverse the effects.

3.10 **The fallacy of composition.** An illustration of how something that applies to an individual may not apply to a larger group. The example is taken from agriculture.

3.11 **The Cobweb model.** An outline of the theory that explains price fluctuations in terms of time lags in supply.

3.12 **Dealing in futures markets.** How buying and selling in futures markets can reduce uncertainty.

WEB APPENDICES

3.1 **Point elasticity.** An alternative way of measuring elasticity.

3.2 **Risk and uncertainty.** An analysis of consumer decision making when knowledge is imperfect.

The supply decision

So far we have assumed that supply curves are generally upward sloping: that a higher price will encourage firms to supply more. But just how much will firms choose to supply at each price? It depends largely on the amount of profit they will make. If a firm can increase its profits by producing more, it will normally do so.

Profit is made by firms earning more from the sale of goods than they cost to produce. A firm's total profit is thus the difference between its total sales revenue (*TR*) and its total costs of production (*TC*). In order then to discover how a firm can maximise its profit or even get a sufficient level of profit, we must first consider what determines costs and revenue.

In Sections 4.1 and 4.2 we examine short-run and long-run costs respectively. Over the short run a firm will be limited in what inputs it can expand. For example, a manufacturing company might be able to use more raw materials, or possibly more labour, but it will not have time to open up another factory. Over the long run, however, a firm will have much more flexibility. It can, if it chooses, expand the whole scale of its operations.

In Section 4.3 we turn to the revenue side and see how a firm's revenue varies with output. Then in Section 4.4 we put revenue and cost together to see how profit is determined. We see how profit varies with output and how the point of maximum profit is found.

Finally, in Section 4.5 we consider why firms' behaviour may deviate from the traditional profit-maximising model. In some circumstances they may have an alternative aim; or perhaps there may be several potentially conflicting aims held by different stakeholders in the firm. There might, for example, by a conflict between the owners of the firm and those running it. Consequently, a firm's behaviour will depend on just what its aims are.

After studying this chapter, you should be able to answer the following questions:

- What is the relationship between inputs and outputs in both the short and long run?
- How do costs vary with output and just what do we mean by 'costs'?
- What are meant by 'economies of scale' and what are the reasons for such economies?
- How does a firm's sales revenue vary with output?
- How do we measure profits?
- At what output will a firm maximise its profits? How much profit will it make at this output?
- Why might firms choose not to maximise profits? What other objectives might firms follow?

4.1 PRODUCTION AND COSTS: SHORT RUN

How do a firm's costs vary with output over the short term?

The cost of producing any level of output will depend on the amount of inputs used and the price the firm must pay for them. Let us first focus on the quantity of inputs used.

> **KEY IDEA 14**
> *Output depends on the amount of resources and how they are used.* Different amounts and combinations of inputs will lead to different amounts of output. If output is to be produced efficiently, inputs should be combined in the optimum proportions.

Short-run and long-run changes in production

If a firm wants to increase production, it will take time to acquire a greater quantity of certain inputs. For example, a manufacturer can use more electricity by turning on switches, but it might take a long time to obtain and install more machines, and longer still to build a second or third factory.

If, then, the firm wants to increase output in a hurry, it will be able to increase the quantity of only certain inputs. It can use more raw materials, more fuel, more tools and possibly more labour (by hiring extra workers or offering overtime to its existing workforce). But it will have to make do with its existing buildings and most of its machinery.

The distinction we are making here is between **fixed factors** and **variable factors**. A *fixed* factor is an input that cannot be increased within a given time period (e.g. buildings). A *variable* factor is one that can.

The distinction between fixed and variable factors allows us to distinguish between the short run and the long run.

The short run. The **short run** is a time period during which at least one factor of production is fixed. In the short run, then, output can be increased only by using more variable factors. For example, if an airline wanted to carry more passengers in response to a rise in demand, it could possibly accommodate more passengers on existing flights if there were space. It could possibly increase the number of flights with its existing fleet, by hiring more crew and using more fuel. But in the short run it could not buy more aircraft: there would not be time for them to be built.

The long run. The **long run** is a time period long enough for all inputs to be varied. Given long enough, a firm can build a second factory and install new machines.

The actual length of the short run will differ from firm to firm. It is not a fixed period of time. Thus if it takes a farmer a year to obtain new land, buildings and equipment, the short run is any time period up to a year and the long run is any time period longer than a year. On the other hand, if

it takes an airline two years to obtain an extra aircraft, the short run is any period up to two years and the long run is any period longer than two years.

For the remainder of this section we will concentrate on *short-run* production and costs. We will look at the long run in Section 4.2.

Production in the short run: the law of diminishing returns

Production in the short run is subject to *diminishing returns*. You may well have heard of 'the law of diminishing returns': it is one of the most famous of all 'laws' of economics. To illustrate how this law underlies short-run production let us take the simplest possible case where there are just two factors: one fixed and one variable.

Take the case of a farm. Assume that the fixed factor is land and the variable factor is labour. Since the land is fixed in supply, output per period of time can be increased only by increasing the amount of workers employed. But imagine what would happen as more and more workers crowded on to a fixed area of land. The land cannot go on yielding more and more output indefinitely. After a point the additions to output from each extra worker will begin to diminish.

We can now state the **law of diminishing (marginal) returns**.

> **KEY IDEA 15**
> *The law of diminishing marginal returns.* When increasing amounts of a variable factor are used with a given amount of a fixed factor, there will come a point when each extra unit of the variable factor will produce less extra output than the previous unit.

> **Definitions**
>
> **Fixed factor** An input that cannot be increased in supply within a given time period.
>
> **Variable factor** An input that *can* be increased in supply within a given time period.
>
> **Short run** The period of time over which at least one factor is fixed.
>
> **Long run** The period of time long enough for *all* factors to be varied.
>
> **Law of diminishing (marginal) returns** When one or more factors are held fixed, there will come a point beyond which the extra output from additional units of the variable factor will diminish.

| BOX 4.1 | DIMINISHING RETURNS IN THE BREAD SHOP | CASE STUDIES & APPLICATIONS |

Is the baker using his loaf?

Just up the road from where John lives is a bread shop. Like many others, he buys his bread there on a Saturday morning. Not surprisingly, Saturday morning is the busiest time of the week for the shop and as a result it takes on extra assistants.

During the week only one assistant serves the customers, but on a Saturday morning there used to be five serving. But could they serve five times as many customers? No, they could not. There were diminishing returns to labour.

The trouble is that certain factors of production in the shop are fixed:

- The shop is a fixed size. It gets very crowded on a Saturday morning. Assistants sometimes have to wait while customers squeeze past each other to get to the counter, and with five serving, the assistants themselves used to get in each other's way.

- There is only one cash till. Assistants frequently had to wait while other assistants used it.
- There is only one pile of tissue paper for wrapping the bread. Again the assistants often had to wait.

The fifth and maybe even the fourth assistant ended up serving very few extra customers.

John is still going to the same bread shop and it still has only one till and one pile of tissue paper. But now only three assistants are employed on a Saturday! The shop, however, is just as busy.

? *How would you advise the baker as to whether he should (a) employ four assistants on a Saturday; (b) extend his shop, thereby allowing more customers to be served on a Saturday morning?*

Box 4.1 illustrates the law of diminishing returns in relation to a small retailer. Box 4.2 shows how the law can have potentially dire implications for us and the future inhabitants of our planet. This theme is also pursued in an article on the Sloman News Site, 'Tackling diminishing returns in food production'. Meanwhile Case Study 4.3 in MyEconLab looks at diminishing returns to the application of nitrogen fertiliser on farmland.

The relationship between inputs and output is explained in more detail in Web Appendix 4.1, which looks at the short-run 'production function'.

Measuring costs of production

We are now ready to look at short-run costs. First of all, we will need to define just what we mean by costs. The term is used differently by economists and accountants.

When measuring costs, economists always use the concept of **opportunity cost**. Remember from Chapter 1 how we defined opportunity cost. It is the cost of any activity measured in terms of the *sacrifice* made in doing it: in other words, the cost measured in terms of the opportunities forgone.

How do we apply this principle of opportunity cost to a firm? First we must discover what factors of production it is using. Then we must measure the sacrifice involved. To do this it is necessary to put factors into two categories.

Factors not owned by the firm: explicit costs

The opportunity cost of those factors not already owned by the firm is simply the price that the firm has to pay for them. Thus if the firm uses £100 worth of electricity, the opportunity cost is £100. The firm has sacrificed £100 that could have been spent on something else.

These costs are called **explicit costs** because they involve direct payment of money by firms.

Factors already owned by the firm: implicit costs

When the firm already owns factors (e.g. machinery), it does not as a rule have to pay out money to use them. Their opportunity costs are thus **implicit costs**. They are equal to what the factors could earn for the firm in some alternative use, either within the firm or hired out to some other firm.

Pause for thought

Assume that a farmer decides to grow wheat on land that could be used for growing barley. Barley sells for £100 per tonne. Wheat sells for £150 per tonne. Seed, fertiliser, labour and other costs of growing crops are £80 per tonne for both wheat and barley. What are the farmer's costs and profit per tonne of growing wheat?

Here are some examples of implicit costs:

- A firm owns some buildings. The opportunity cost of using them is the rent it could have received by letting them out to another firm.
- A firm draws £250 000 from the bank out of its savings in order to invest in new plant and equipment.

Definitions

Opportunity cost Cost measured in terms of the best alternative forgone.

Explicit costs The payments to outside suppliers of inputs.

Implicit costs Costs that do not involve a direct payment of money to a third party, but which nevertheless involve a sacrifice of some alternative.

BOX 4.2   MALTHUS AND THE DISMAL SCIENCE OF ECONOMICS

Population growth + diminishing returns = starvation

KI 15 p 76

KI 1 p 5

The law of diminishing returns has potentially cataclysmic implications for the future populations of the world.

If the population of the world grows rapidly, then food output may not keep pace with it. There will be diminishing returns to labour as more and more people crowd on to the limited amount of land available.

This is already a problem in some of the poorest countries of the world, especially in sub-Saharan Africa. The land is barely able to support current population levels. Only one or two bad harvests are needed to cause mass starvation – witness the appalling famines in recent years in Ethiopia and the Sudan.

The relationship between population and food output was analysed as long ago as 1798 by the Reverend Thomas Robert Malthus (1766–1834) in his *Essay on the Principle of Population*. This book was a bestseller and made Robert Malthus perhaps the best known of all social scientists of his day.

Malthus argued as follows:

I say that the power of population is indefinitely greater than the power in the earth to produce subsistence for man.

Population when unchecked, increases in a geometrical ratio. Subsistence increases only in an arithmetical ratio. A slight acquaintance with numbers will show the immensity of the first power in comparison with the second.[1]

What Malthus was saying is that world population tends to double about every 25 years or so if unchecked. It grows geometrically, like the series: 1, 2, 4, 8, 16, 32, 64, etc. But food output, because of diminishing returns, cannot keep pace with this. It is likely to grow at only an arithmetical rate, like the series: 1, 2, 3, 4, 5, 6, 7, etc. It is clear that population, if unchecked, will soon outstrip food supply.

So what is the check on population growth? According to Malthus, it is starvation. As population grows, so food output per head will fall until, with more and more people starving, the death rate will rise. Only then will population growth stabilise at the rate of growth of food output.

Have Malthus's gloomy predictions been borne out by events? Two factors have mitigated the forces that Malthus described:

■ The rate of population growth tends to slow down as countries become more developed. Although improved health prolongs life, this tends to be more than offset by a decline in the birth rate as people choose to have smaller families. This is illustrated in the table below. Population growth peaked in the 1960s, has slowed substantially since then and is projected to slow further in future decades.

■ Technological improvements in farming have greatly increased food output per hectare. These include better fertilisers and the development of genetically modified crops. (see Case Study 4.3 in MyEconLab for an example.)

The growth in food output has thus exceeded the rate of population growth in developed countries and in some developing countries too. Nevertheless, the Malthusian spectre is very real for some of the poorest developing countries, which are simply unable to feed their populations satisfactorily. It is these poorest countries of the world which have some of the highest rates of population growth – around 3 per cent per annum in many African countries.

A further cause for concern arises from the move in Asia towards a westernised diet, with meat and dairy products playing a larger part. This further increases pressure on the land, since cattle require considerably more grain to produce meat than would be needed to feed humans a vegetarian diet.

A third factor is cited by some commentators, who remain unconvinced of the strength of Malthus's gloomy prognostication for the world. They believe that he seriously underestimated humankind's capacity to innovate; perhaps human ingenuity is one resource that doesn't suffer from diminishing returns (see Section 9.6).

World population levels and growth: actual and projected

Year	World population (billions)	Average annual rate of increase (%)		
		World	More developed regions	Less developed regions
1950	2.5			
		1.8	1.2	2.1
1960	3.0			
		2.0	1.0	2.4
1970	3.7			
		1.9	0.7	2.2
1980	4.5			
		1.7	0.6	2.1
1990	5.3			
		1.4	0.3	1.7
2000	6.1			
		1.2	0.3	1.4
2010	6.9			
		1.1	0.3	1.3
2020	7.7			
		0.9	0.1	1.0
2030	8.4			
		0.7	0.1	0.8
2040	9.0			
		0.6	0.0	0.6
2050	9.6			

Source: from World Population Prospects: The 2012 Revision (United Nations, Department of Economic and Social Affairs), http://esa.un.org/unpd/wpp/, Reprinted with the permission of the United Nations

? *Why might it be possible for there to be a zero marginal productivity of labour on many family farms in poor countries and yet just enough food for all the members of the family to survive?*

---

[1] T.R. Malthus, *First Essay on Population* (Macmillan, 1926), pp. 13–14.

The opportunity cost of this investment is not just the £250 000 (an explicit cost), but also the interest it thereby forgoes (an implicit cost).

■ The owner of the firm could have earned £50 000 per annum by working for someone else. This £50 000, then, is the opportunity cost of the owner's time.

If there is no alternative use for a factor of production, as in the case of a machine designed to make a specific product, and if it has no scrap value, the opportunity cost of using it is *zero*. In such a case, if the output from the machine is worth more than the cost of all the *other* inputs involved, the firm might as well use the machine rather than let it stand idle.

What the firm paid for the machine – its **historic cost** – is irrelevant. Not using the machine will not bring that money back. It has been spent. These are sometimes referred to as 'sunk costs'.

Costs and output

A firm's costs of production depend on its output. The reason is simple. The more it produces, the greater the quantity of factors of production it must use. The more factors it uses, the greater its costs will be. More precisely, this relationship depends on two elements:

■ *The productivity of the factors.* The greater their productivity, the smaller will be the quantity of them that is needed to produce a given level of output, and hence the lower will be the cost of that output.
■ *The price of the factors.* The higher their price, the higher will be the costs of production.

In the short run, some factors used by the firm are fixed in supply. Their total costs, therefore, are fixed, in the sense that they do not vary with output. Rent on land is a **fixed cost**. It is the same whether the firm produces a lot or a little.

The total cost of variable factors, however, does vary with output. The cost of raw materials is a **variable cost**. The more that is produced, the more raw materials are used and therefore the higher is their total cost.

Total cost (*TC*) is thus total fixed cost (*TFC*) plus total variable cost (*TVC*)

Average and marginal cost

In addition to total costs (fixed and variable), there are two other categories of costs that are particularly important for our analysis of profits. These are average cost and marginal cost.

Average cost (*AC*) is cost per unit of production:

$$AC = TC/Q$$

Thus if it costs a firm £20 000 to produce 100 units of a product, the average cost would be £200 for each unit (£20 000/100).

Like total cost, average cost can be divided into the two components, fixed and variable. In other words, average

cost equals **average fixed cost** (*AFC = TFC/Q*) plus **average variable cost** (*AVC = TVC/Q*):

$$AC = AFC + AVC$$

Marginal cost (*MC*) is the *extra* cost of producing *one more unit*, that is the rise in total cost per one unit rise in output:

$$MC = \frac{\Delta TC}{\Delta Q}$$

where Δ means 'a rise in'.

For example, assume that a firm is currently producing 100 0000 boxes of matches a month. It now increases output by 1000 boxes (another batch): Δ*Q* = 1000. Assume that, as a result, total costs rise by £500: Δ*TC* = £500. What is the cost of producing one more box of matches? It is:

$$MC = \frac{\Delta TC}{\Delta Q} = \frac{£500}{1000} = 50p$$

(Note that all marginal costs are variable, since, by definition, there can be no extra fixed costs as output rises.) Table 4.1 shows costs for an imaginary firm, firm X, over a given period of time (e.g. a week). The table shows how average and marginal costs can be derived from total costs. It is assumed that total fixed costs are £12 000 (column 2) and that total variable costs are as shown in column 3.

The figures for *TVC* have been chosen to illustrate the law of diminishing returns. Initially, *before* diminishing returns set in, *TVC* rises less and less rapidly as more variable factors are added. For example, in the case of a factory with a fixed supply of machinery, initially as more workers are taken on the workers can do increasingly specialist tasks and make a fuller use of the capital equipment. Above a certain output (three units in Table 4.1), diminishing returns set in. Given that extra workers (the extra variable factors) are producing less and less extra output, the extra units of output they do produce will be costing more and more in

Definitions

Historic costs The original amount the firm paid for factors it now owns.

Fixed costs Total costs that do not vary with the amount of output produced.

Variable costs Total costs that do vary with the amount of output produced.

Total cost The sum of total fixed costs and total variable costs: *TC = TFC + TVC*.

Average (total) cost Total cost (fixed plus variable) per unit of output: *AC = TC/Q = AFC + AVC*

Average fixed cost Total fixed cost per unit of output: *AFC = TFC/Q*

Average variable cost Total variable cost per unit of output: *AVC = TVC/Q*

Marginal cost The cost of producing one more unit of output: *MC = ΔTC/ΔQ*

Table 4.1   Costs for firm X

Output (Q) (1)	TFC (£000) (2)	TVC (£000) (3)	TC (TFC+ TVC) (£000) (4)	AFC (TFC/Q) (£000) (5)	AVC (TVC/Q) (£000) (6)	AC (TC/Q) (£000) (7)	MC (ΔTC/ΔQ) (£000) (8)
0	12	0	12	–	–	–	
							10
1	12	10	22	12	10	22	
							6
2	12	16	28	6	8	14	
							5
3	12	21	33	4	7	11	
							7
4	12	28	40	3	7	10	
							12
5	12	40	52	2.4	8	10.4	
							20
6	12	60	72	2	10	12	
							31
7	12	91	103	1.7	13	14.7	

terms of wage costs. Thus *TVC* rises more and more rapidly. You can see this by examining column 3.

The figures in the remaining columns in Table 4.1 are derived from columns 1 to 3. Look at the figures in each of the columns and check how the figures are derived. Note the figures for marginal cost are plotted between the lines to illustrate that marginal cost represents the increase in costs as output increases from one unit to the next. We can use the figures in Table 4.1 to draw *MC*, *AFC*, *AVC* and *AC* curves.

KI 15
p76 *Marginal cost (MC).* The shape of the *MC* curve follows directly from the law of diminishing returns. Initially, in Figure 4.1, as more of the variable factor is used, extra units of output cost less than previous units. *MC* falls.

Beyond a certain level of output, diminishing returns set in. This is shown as point *x*. Thereafter *MC* rises. Additional units of output cost more and more to produce, since they require ever-increasing amounts of the variable factor.

Pause for thought

Before you read on, can you explain why the marginal cost curve will always cut the average cost curve at its lowest point?

Average fixed cost (AFC). This falls continuously as output rises, since total fixed costs are being spread over a greater and greater output.

Average (total) cost (AC). The shape of the *AC* curve depends on the shape of the *MC* curve. As long as new units of output cost less than the average, their production must pull the average cost down. That is, if *MC* is less than *AC*, *AC* must be falling. Likewise, if new units cost more than the average, their production must drive the average up. That is, if *MC* is greater than *AC*, *AC* must be rising. Therefore, the *MC* curve crosses the *AC* curve at its minimum point (point *z* in Figure 4.1). This relationship between averages and marginals is explored in Box 4.3.

Pause for thought

Why is the minimum point of the AVC curve at a lower level of output than the minimum point of the AC curve?

Average variable cost (AVC). Since $AVC = AC - AFC$, the *AVC* curve is simply the vertical difference between the *AC* and the *AFC* curves. Note that as *AFC* gets less, the gap between *AVC* and *AC* narrows. Since all marginal costs are variable (by definition, there are no marginal fixed costs), the same relationship holds between *MC* and *AVC* as it did between *MC* and *AC*. That is, if *MC* is less than *AVC*, *AVC* must be falling, and if *MC* is greater than *AVC*, *AVC* must be rising. Therefore, as with the *AC* curve, the *MC* curve crosses the *AVC* curve at its minimum point (point *y* in Figure 4.1).

Figure 4.1   Average and marginal costs

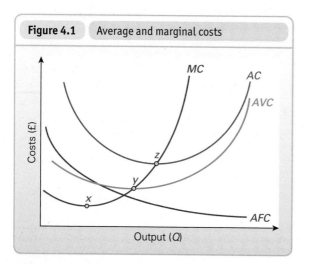

| BOX 4.3 | THE RELATIONSHIP BETWEEN AVERAGES AND MARGINALS | EXPLORING ECONOMICS |

In this chapter we have just examined the concepts of *average* and *marginal* cost. We shall be coming across several other average and marginal concepts later on. It is useful at this stage to examine the general relationship between averages and marginals. In all cases there are three simple rules that relate them.

To illustrate these rules, consider the following example.

Imagine over the first four matches of the football season Sloman FC have conceded a total of 8 goals, and so an average of 2 goals per match.

Now assume in their next match they concede a further 2 goals (the marginal goals conceded). This will not affect Sloman FC's average goals conceded per match. It will remain at 2. Their sixth match is against the much-feared Garratt FC who put 8 goals past the hapless keeper. This worsens the team's defensive record, with the average number of goals conceded per match rising; not to 8, of course, but to 3. This is found by dividing the total number of goals conceded (18) by the number of matches (6).

If then in the next match they manage to 'keep a clean sheet' with no goals conceded, this will pull the average goals conceded per match back down.

From this example we can derive the three universal rules about averages and marginals:

- If the marginal equals the average, the average will not change.
- If the marginal is above the average, the average will rise.
- If the marginal is below the average, the average will fall.

? An opening batsman for a university cricket club scores the following number of runs in five successive innings:

Innings:	1	2	3	4	5
Runs:	20	20	50	10	0

These can be seen as the marginal number of runs from each innings. Calculate the total and average number of runs after each innings. Show how the average and marginal scores illustrate the three rules above.

| BOX 4.4 | COSTS AND THE ECONOMIC VULNERABILITY OF FIRMS | CASE STUDIES & APPLICATIONS |

The behaviour of costs and firms' financial well-being

The economic environment in which firms operate is highly uncertain and yet, while some firms fail, others grow and succeed. What is it that makes some firms more vulnerable to the economic environment, while other firms are much more insulated? In this box, we look at one aspect of the answer to this question by focusing on both the shape and movements of a firm's average cost curves. How do these affect firms' economic vulnerability?

Type 1 economic vulnerability – average costs and changing levels of output

A typical firm will have a U-shaped average cost curve. It falls at first, reflecting rapidly falling average fixed costs, as they are spread over a greater output, plus a more efficient

deployment of variable factors of production. Then, as diminishing marginal returns become relatively more important than falling average fixed costs, average costs rise. An important determinant of a firm's vulnerability is how quickly average costs first fall and then rise as output changes.

Consider two firms, A and B. Each firm's average cost curve is shown in Figure (a). Assume, for simplicity, that each firm achieves minimum average cost at point x, namely at the same output Q_0 and at the same average cost, AC_0.

Now consider what would happen if, because of a deterioration in the macroeconomic environment, both firms were to experience a fall in demand and, as a result, cut output to Q_1.

With a U-shaped AC curve, both firms see per-unit costs rise, but firm A's unit costs rise significantly faster than firm B's, because firm A has a very steep AC curve.

(a) *Average cost for firms A and B: change in output*

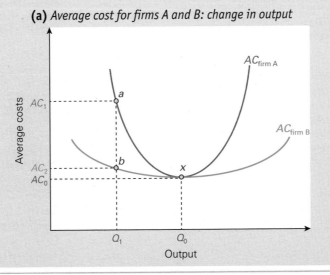

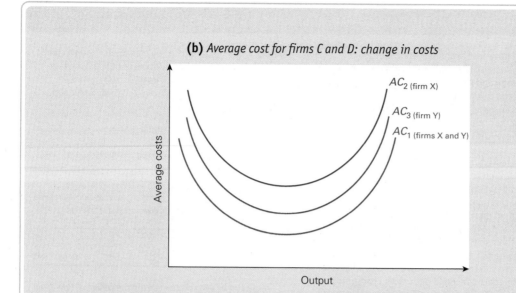

(b) *Average cost for firms C and D: change in costs*

The same fall in quantity pushes firm A's average costs up from AC_0 to AC_1 (point *a*) but only causes firm B's costs to increase to AC_2 (point *b*) as firm B's AC curve is very flat – sometimes called flute-shaped.

Returning to point *x*, consider now the effect of an improvement in the macroeconomic environment which leads both firms to increase output in response to higher demand. Again, firm A's costs rise more rapidly than firm B's.

Therefore, firm A is much more susceptible to any change in demand than firm B. Any small decrease (or increase) in output will have a significant effect on firm A's costs and hence on its profit margin and profits, making it a much more vulnerable firm.

So, what affects the steepness of the AC curve and hence makes one firm more vulnerable than another?

■ *The ratio of fixed factors to variable factors.* The higher the ratio, the more likely a firm is to face a steep AC curve. Total fixed costs do not change with output and hence, if output falls, it implies that its high fixed costs are being spread over fewer and fewer units of output and this causes average costs to rise rapidly.

■ *Flexibility in the use of inputs.* A firm that is relatively inflexible in its use of inputs may find that a cut in production results in its average cost rising rapidly. Similarly if it wishes to expand output beyond Q_0, it may find it difficult to do so without incurring considerable extra costs, for example by employing expensive agency staff or hiring expensive machinery.

Type 2 economic vulnerability – average costs and the purchasing of inputs

Most firms purchase inputs to the production process from other companies, but their reliance on other firms and, in some cases on materials where there is a volatile global market, can vary significantly. The second type of economic vulnerability concerns a firm's reliance on external or bought-in factors of production (inputs).

Some firms can be be heavily dependent on oil or other commodities and as such, if the price of these change, it can have a very big effect on the firm's costs of production, its profit margins and its profit. During periods of rising national and global output the demand for commodities increases and their prices rise (see Box 2.4). Firms that are heavily dependent on commodities can therefore experience a significant effect on its production costs with its AC curve shift vertically upwards by a considerable extent. In contrast, for a firm that does not use much oil or other commodities during production, or has alternative inputs, changes in the global price of oil or another input may cause only a very small shift in the AC curve.

In Figure (b), both firms X and Y have the same shaped AC curve, which we will assume is initially the same (i.e. AC_1). However, firm X is very dependent on oil, whereas firm Y is not.

Assume that oil prices now rise. This leads to a large upwards shift in firm X's AC curve from AC_1 to AC_2, but a smaller upwards shift in firm Y's AC curve from AC_1 to AC_3. There is a much larger cost penalty imposed on firm X than on firm Y, due to the reliance on oil as a factor of production.

In 2010, oil prices rose significantly (see Boxes 2.4 and 5.3), so firms which were big users of oil, either directly into the production process or for transporting their inputs and produce, saw their costs rise and their profits eroded. However, in late 2014 and early 2015, oil prices fell considerably and so those firms which were heavily dependent on oil saw their AC curves shift downwards significantly, thereby helping to increase their profits. Other firms which were less reliant on oil, however, did not benefit so much from low global prices for oil.

? *Is it possible for a firm to suffer from both types of economic vulnerability discussed in this box?*

Recap

1. Production in the short run is subject to diminishing returns. As greater quantities of the variable factor(s) are used, so each additional unit of the variable factor will add less to output than previous units: i.e. output will rise less and less rapidly.

2. When measuring costs of production, we should be careful to use the concept of opportunity cost. In the case of inputs not owned by the firm, the opportunity cost is simply the explicit cost of purchasing or hiring them. It is the price paid for them. In the case of inputs already owned by the firm, it is the implicit cost of what the factor could have earned for the firm in its best alternative use.

3. As some factors are fixed in supply in the short run, their total costs are fixed with respect to output. In the case of variable factors, their total cost increases as more output is produced and hence as more of them are used. Total cost can be divided into total fixed and total variable cost.

4. Marginal cost is the cost of producing one more unit of output. It will probably fall at first but will start to rise as soon as diminishing returns set in.

5. Average cost, like total cost, can be divided into fixed and variable costs. Average fixed cost will decline as more output is produced. The reason is that the total fixed cost is being spread over a greater and greater number of units of output. Average variable cost will tend to decline at first, but once the marginal cost has risen above it, it must then rise. The same applies to average cost.

4.2 PRODUCTION AND COSTS: LONG RUN

How do a firm's costs vary with output over the longer term?

In the long run, *all* factors of production are variable. There is time for the firm to build a new factory (maybe in a different part of the country), to install new machines, to use different techniques of production, and in general to combine its inputs in whatever proportion and in whatever quantities it chooses.

Looking to the long run, then, a firm will have to make a number of decisions: about the scale of its operations and the techniques of production it will use. These decisions will affect the costs of production. It is important, therefore, to get them right.

The scale of production

If a firm were to double all of its inputs – something it could do in the long run – would it double its output? Or would output more than double or less than double? We can distinguish three possible situations:

Constant returns to scale. This is where a given percentage increase in inputs will lead to the same percentage increase in output.

Increasing returns to scale. This is where a given percentage increase in inputs will lead to a larger percentage increase in output.

Decreasing returns to scale. This is where a given percentage increase in inputs will lead to a smaller percentage increase in output.

Notice the terminology here. The words 'to scale' mean that *all* inputs increase by the same proportion. Decreasing returns to *scale* are therefore quite different from diminishing *marginal* returns (where only the *variable* factor increases). The differences between marginal returns to a variable factor and returns to scale are illustrated in Table 4.2.

In the short run, input 1 is assumed to be fixed in supply (at 3 units). Output can be increased only by using more of the variable factor (input 2). In the long run, however, both input 1 and input 2 are variable.

In the short-run situation, diminishing returns can be seen from the fact that output increases at a decreasing rate (25 to 45 to 60 to 70 to 75) as input 2 is increased. In the long-run situation, the table illustrates increasing returns to scale. Output increases at an *increasing* rate (15 to 35 to 60 to 90 to 125) as both inputs are increased.

Table 4.2	Short-run and long-run increases in output					
Short run			**Long run**			
Input 1	**Input 2**	**Output**	**Input 1**	**Input 2**	**Output**	
3	1	25	1	1	15	
3	2	45	2	2	35	
3	3	60	3	3	60	
3	4	70	4	4	90	
3	5	75	5	5	125	

Economies of scale

KI 14
p 76

The concept of increasing returns to scale is closely linked to that of **economies of scale**. A firm experiences economies of scale if costs per unit of output fall as the scale of production increases. Clearly, if a firm is getting increasing returns to scale from its factors of production, then as it produces more it will be using smaller and smaller amounts of factors per unit of output. Other things being equal, this means that it will be producing at a lower average cost.

There are a number of reasons why firms are likely to experience economies of scale. Some are due to increasing returns to scale; some are not.

Specialisation and division of labour. In large-scale plants, workers can do more simple, repetitive jobs. With this **specialisation and division of labour** less training is needed; workers can become highly efficient in their particular job, especially with long production runs; there is less time lost by workers switching from one operation to another; and supervision is easier. Workers and managers can be employed who have specific skills in specific areas.

Indivisibilities. Some inputs are of a minimum size: they are indivisible. The most obvious example is machinery. Take the case of a combine harvester. A small-scale farmer could not make full use of one. They only become economical to use, therefore, on farms above a certain size. The problem of **indivisibilities** is made worse when different machines, each of which is part of the production process, are of a different size. For example, if there are two types of machine, one producing 6 units a day, the other packaging 4 units a day, a minimum of 12 units per day will have to be produced, involving two production machines and three packaging machines, if all machines are to be fully utilised.

The 'container principle'. Any capital equipment that contains things (e.g. blast furnaces, oil tankers, pipes, vats) tends to cost less per unit of output the larger its size. The reason has to do with the relationship between a container's volume and its surface area. A container's cost depends largely on the materials used to build it and hence roughly on its surface area. Its output depends largely on its volume. Large containers have a bigger volume relative to surface area than do small containers. For example, a container with a bottom, top and four sides, with each side measuring 1 metre, has a volume of 1 cubic metre and a surface area of 6 square metres (6 surfaces of 1 square metre each). If each side were doubled in length to 2 metres, the volume would be 8 cubic metres and the surface area 24 square metres (6 surfaces of 4 square metres each). Thus an eightfold increase in capacity has been gained at only a fourfold increase in the container's surface area, and hence an approximate fourfold increase in cost.

Greater efficiency of large machines. Large machines may be more efficient in the sense that more output can be gained for a given amount of inputs. For example, only one worker may be required to operate a machine, whether it be large or small. Also, a large machine may make more efficient use of raw materials.

By-products. With production on a large scale, there may be sufficient waste products to make some by-product.

Multi-stage production. A large factory may be able to take a product through several stages in its manufacture. This saves time and cost moving the semi-finished product from one firm or factory to another. For example, a large cardboard-manufacturing firm may be able to convert trees or waste paper into cardboard and then into cardboard boxes in a continuous sequence.

All the above are examples of **plant economies of scale**. They are due to an individual factory or workplace or machine being large. There are other economies of scale that are associated with the *firm* being large – perhaps with many factories.

Organisational economies. With a large firm, individual plants can specialise in particular functions. There can also be centralised administration of the firms. Often, after a merger between two firms, savings can be made by **rationalising** their activities in this way.

Spreading overheads. There are some expenditures that are only economic when the *firm* is large, such as research and development: only a large firm can afford to set up a research laboratory. This is another example of indivisibilities, only this time at the level of the firm rather than the plant. The greater the firm's output, the more these **overhead costs** are spread.

Financial economies. Large firms may be able to obtain finance at lower interest rates than small firms, as they are perceived as having lower default risks or have more power

---

Definitions

Economies of scale Where increasing the scale of production leads to a lower cost per unit of output.

Specialisation and division of labour Where production is broken down into a number of simpler, more specialised tasks, thus allowing workers to acquire a high degree of efficiency.

Indivisibilities The impossibility of dividing a factor into smaller units.

Plant economies of scale Economies of scale that arise because of the large size of the factory.

Rationalisation The reorganising of production (often after a merger) so as to cut out waste and duplication and generally to reduce costs.

Overheads Costs arising from the general running of an organisation, and only indirectly related to the level of output.

to negotiate a better deal. Additionally, they may be able to obtain certain inputs more cheaply by buying in bulk. (These are examples of economies of scale which are not the result of increasing returns to scale.)

Economies of scope. Often a firm is large because it produces a range of products. This can result in each individual product being produced more cheaply than if it was produced in a single-product firm.

The reason for these **economies of scope** is that various overhead costs and financial and organisational economies can be shared among the products. For example, a firm that produces a whole range of CD players, DVD players and recorders, amplifiers, games consoles, TVs and so on can benefit from shared marketing and distribution costs and the bulk purchase of electronic components.

Many companies will experience a variety of economies of scale and you can find examples in practice from a variety of sources. On the Sloman News Site, you will find blogs that discuss economies of scale, such as those experienced by companies using cloud computing (Operating in a cloud), the possibility of achieving economies of scale through takeovers (Take over?) and whether big supermarkets can use economies of scale to their advantage (Supermarket wars: a pricing race to the bottom). The economies of scale for large cloud providers is also discussed in numerous articles, including an article by Randy Bias[2] and another that considers the case of Microsoft.[3]

> **Pause for thought**
>
> *Which of the economies of scale we have considered are due to increasing returns to scale and which are due to other factors?*

Diseconomies of scale

When firms get beyond a certain size, costs per unit of output may start to increase. There are several reasons for such **diseconomies of scale**:

- Management problems of co-ordination may increase as the firm becomes larger and more complex, and as lines of communication get longer. There may be a lack of personal involvement by management.
- Workers may feel 'alienated' if their jobs are boring and repetitive, and if they feel an insignificantly small part of a large organisation. Poor motivation may lead to shoddy work.

- Industrial relations may deteriorate as a result of these factors and also as a result of the more complex interrelationships between different categories of worker.
- Production-line processes and the complex interdependencies of mass production can lead to great disruption if there are hold-ups in any one part of the firm.

Whether firms experience economies or diseconomies of scale depends on the conditions applying in each individual firm.

The size of the whole industry

As an *industry* grows in size, this can lead to **external economies of scale** for its member firms. This is where a firm, whatever its own individual size, benefits from the *whole industry* being large. For example, the firm may benefit from having access to specialist raw material or component suppliers, labour with specific skills, firms that specialise in marketing the finished product, and banks and other financial institutions with experience of the industry's requirements. What we are referring to here is the **industry's infrastructure**: the facilities, support services, skills and experience that can be shared by its members. This is one reason why we often see industrial clusters emerge.

The member firms of a particular industry might, however, experience **external diseconomies of scale**. For example, as an industry grows larger, this may create a growing shortage of specific raw materials or skilled labour. This will push up their prices, and hence the firms' costs.

The relationship between inputs and outputs in the long run is examined in Web Appendices 4.2 and 4.3. These look at ways of combining inputs so as to minimise costs for a given output or maximise output for a given cost.

[KI 14] *[p 76]*

Long-run average cost

We turn now to *long-run* cost curves. Since there are no fixed factors in the long run, there are no long-run fixed costs. For

> **Definitions**
>
> **Economies of scope** Where increasing the range of products produced by a firm reduces the cost of producing each one.
>
> **Diseconomies of scale** Where costs per unit of output increase as the scale of production increases.
>
> **External economies of scale** Where a firm's costs per unit of output decrease as the size of the whole *industry* grows.
>
> **Industry's infrastructure** The network of supply agents, communications, skills, training facilities, distribution channels, specialised financial services, etc., that supports a particular industry.
>
> **External diseconomies of scale** Where a firm's costs per unit of output increase as the size of the whole industry increases.

[2]Randy Bias, 'Understanding Cloud Datacenter Economies of Scale', *cloudscaling*, 4 October 2010 (http://www.cloudscaling.com/blog/cloud-computing/understanding-cloud-datacenter-economies-of-scale/).

[3]Charles Babcock, 'Microsoft: "Incredible Economies Of Scale" Await Cloud Users', *InformationWeek*, 5 November 2011 (http://www.informationweek.com/cloud/software-as-a-service/microsoft-incredible-economies-of-scale-await-cloud-users/d/d-id/1097690?).

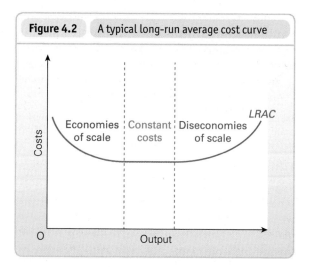

Figure 4.2 A typical long-run average cost curve

example, the firm may rent more land in order to expand its operations. Its rent bill therefore goes up as it expands its output. All costs, then, in the long run are variable costs.

Although it is possible to draw long-run total, marginal and average cost curves, we will concentrate on **long-run average cost (*LRAC*) curves**. These can take various shapes, but a typical one is shown in Figure 4.2.

It is often assumed that as a firm expands, it will initially experience economies of scale and thus face a downward-sloping *LRAC* curve. After a point, however, all such economies will have been achieved and thus the curve will flatten out. Then, possibly after a period of constant *LRAC*, the firm will get so large that it will start experiencing diseconomies of scale and thus a rising *LRAC*. At this stage, production and financial economies begin to be offset by the managerial problems of running a giant organisation.

The effect of this is to give a saucer-shaped curve, as in Figure 4.2.

Assumptions behind the long-run average cost curve
We make three key assumptions when constructing long-run average cost curves:

Factor prices are given. At each level of output it is assumed that a firm will be faced with a given set of factor prices. If factor prices *change*, therefore, both short- and long-run cost curves will shift. Thus an increase in nationally negotiated wage rates would shift the curves upwards.

However, factor prices might be different at *different* levels of output. For example, one of the economies of scale that many firms enjoy is the ability to obtain bulk discount on raw materials and other supplies. In such cases the curve does *not* shift. The different factor prices are merely experienced at different points along the curve, and are reflected in the shape of the curve. Factor prices are still given for any particular level of output.

The state of technology and factor quality are given. These are assumed to change only in the *very* long run (see page 87). If a firm gains economies of scale, it is because it is exploiting *existing* technologies and/or making better use of the existing availability of factors of production. As technology improves, the curves will shift downwards.

Firms choose the least-cost combination of factors for each output. The assumption here is that firms operate efficiently: that they choose the cheapest possible way of producing any level of output. If the firm did not operate efficiently, it would be producing at a point above the *LRAC* curve.

The relationship between long-run and short-run average cost curves

Take the case of a firm that has just one factory and faces a short-run average cost curve, illustrated by *SRAC*$_1$ in Figure 4.3.

In the long run, it can build more factories. If it thereby experiences economies of scale (due, say, to savings on administration), each successive factory will allow it to produce with a new lower *SRAC* curve. Thus with two factories it will face curve *SRAC*$_2$; with three factories curve *SRAC*$_3$; and so on. Each *SRAC* curve corresponds to a particular amount of the factor that is fixed in the short run: in this case, the factory. (Many more *SRAC* curves could be drawn

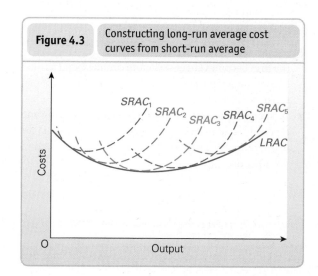

Figure 4.3 Constructing long-run average cost curves from short-run average

between the ones shown, since factories of different sizes could be built or existing ones could be expanded.)

From this succession of short-run average cost curves we can construct a long-run average cost curve. This is shown in Figure 4.3. This is known as the **envelope curve**, since it envelops the short-run curves.

Long-run cost curves in practice

Firms do experience economies of scale. Some experience continuously falling *LRAC* curves; others experience economies of scale up to a certain output and thereafter constant returns to scale.

Evidence is inconclusive on the question of diseconomies of scale. There is little evidence to suggest the existence of *technical* diseconomies, but the possibility of diseconomies due to managerial and industrial relations problems cannot be ruled out.

Some evidence on economies of scale in the UK is considered in Box 4.4.

Postscript: decision making in different time periods

We have distinguished between the short run and the long run. Let us introduce two more time periods to complete the picture. The complete list then reads as follows.

Very short run (immediate run). *All* factors are fixed. Output is fixed. The supply curve is vertical. On a day-to-day basis a firm may not be able to vary output at all. For example, a flower seller, once the day's flowers have been purchased from the wholesaler, cannot alter the amount of flowers available for sale on that day. In the very short run, all that may remain for a producer to do is to sell an already produced good.

KI 15
p 76 *Short run.* At least one factor is fixed in supply. More can be produced, but the firm will come up against the law of diminishing returns as it tries to do so.

Long run. All factors are variable. The firm may experience constant, increasing or decreasing returns to scale. But although all factors can be increased or decreased, they are of a fixed *quality*.

Very long run. All factors are variable, and their quality and hence productivity can change. Labour productivity can increase as a result of education, training, experience and social factors. The productivity of capital can increase as a result of new inventions (new discoveries) and innovation (putting inventions into practice).

Improvements in factor quality will reduce costs and thus shift the short- and long-run cost curves downwards.

Just how long the 'very long run' is will vary from firm to firm. It will depend on how long it takes to develop new techniques, new skills or new work practices.

It is important to realise that decisions *for* all four time periods can be made *at* the same time. Firms do not make short-run decisions *in* the short run and long-run decisions *in* the long run. They can make both short-run and long-run decisions today. For example, assume that a firm experiences an increase in consumer demand and anticipates that it will continue into the foreseeable future. It thus wants to increase output. Consequently, it makes the following four decisions *today*:

- *Very short run.* It accepts that for a few days it will not be able to increase output. It informs its customers that they will have to wait. It may temporarily raise prices to choke off some of the demand.
- *Short run.* It negotiates with labour to introduce overtime working as soon as possible, to tide it over the next few weeks. It orders extra raw materials from its suppliers. It launches a recruitment drive for new labour so as to avoid paying overtime longer than is necessary.
- *Long run.* It starts proceedings to build a new factory. The first step may be to discuss requirements with a firm of consultants.
- *Very long run.* It institutes a programme of research and development and/or training in an attempt to increase productivity.

> ### Pause for thought
>
> *Why are Christmas trees and fresh foods often sold cheaply on Christmas Eve? Why do shops find it most profitable to lower the price of these items to the point where the price elasticity of demand equals −1?*

Although we distinguish these four time periods, it is the middle two we are primarily concerned with. The reason for this is that there is very little the firm can do in the *very* short run. And in the *very* long run, although the firm will obviously want to increase the productivity of its inputs, it will not be in the position to make precise calculations of how to do it. It will not know precisely what inventions will be made, or just what will be the results of its own research and development.

> ### Definition
>
> **Envelope curve** A long-run average cost curve drawn as the tangency points of a series of short-run average cost curves.

BOX 4.5 MINIMUM EFFICIENT SCALE

The extent of economies of scale in practice

Two of the most important studies of economies of scale have been those made by C. F. Pratten[4] in the late 1980s and by a group advising the European Commission[5] in 1997. Both studies found strong evidence that many firms, especially in manufacturing, experienced substantial economies of scale.

In a few cases long-run average costs fell continuously as output increased. For most firms, however, they fell up to a certain level of output and then remained constant.

The extent of economies of scale can be measured by looking at a firm's *minimum efficient scale (MES)*. The *MES* is the size beyond which no significant additional economies of scale can be achieved: in other words, the point where the *LRAC* curve flattens off. In Pratten's studies he defined this level as the minimum scale above which any possible doubling in scale would reduce average costs by less than 5 per cent (i.e. virtually the bottom of the *LRAC* curve). In the diagram *MES* is shown at point *a*.

The *MES* can be expressed in terms either of an individual factory or of the whole firm. Where it refers to the minimum efficient scale of an individual factory, the *MES* is known as the *minimum efficient plant size (MEPS)*.

The *MES* can then be expressed as a percentage of the total size of the market or of total domestic production. Table (a), based on the Pratten study, shows *MES* for plants and firms in various industries. The first column shows *MES* as a percentage of total UK production. The second column shows *MES* as a percentage of total EU production. Table (b), based on the 1997 study, shows *MES* for various plants as a percentage of total EU production.

Expressing *MES* as a percentage of total output gives an indication of how competitive the industry could be. In some industries (such as footwear and carpets), economies

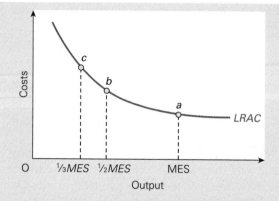

[4]Pratten, C.F. 'A survey of the economies of scale', in *Research on the 'Costs of Non-Europe'*, Vol. 2 (Office for Official Publications of the European Communities, Luxembourg, 1988).

[5]European Commission/Economists Advisory Group Ltd, 'Economies of Scale', *The Single Market Review, Sub-series V, Vol. 4.* (Office for Official Publications of the European Communities, Luxembourg, 1997).

of scale were exhausted (i.e. *MES* was reached) with plants or firms that were still small relative to total UK production and even smaller relative to total EU production. In such industries there would be room for many firms and thus scope for considerable competition.

In other industries, however, even if a single plant or firm were large enough to produce the whole output of the industry in the UK, it would still not be large enough to experience the full potential economies of scale: the *MES* is greater than 100 per cent. Examples from Table (a) include factories producing cellulose fibres, and car manufacturers. In such industries there is no possibility of competition. In fact, as long as the *MES* exceeds 50 per cent there will not be room for more than one firm large enough to gain full economies of scale. In this case the industry is said to be a *natural monopoly*. As we shall see in the next few chapters, when competition is lacking, consumers may suffer by firms charging prices considerably above costs.

A second way of measuring the extent of economies of scale is to see how much costs would increase if production were reduced to a certain fraction of *MES*. The normal fractions used are $\frac{1}{2}$ or $\frac{1}{3}$ *MES*. This is illustrated in the diagram.

Recap

1. In the long run, a firm is able to vary the quantity it uses of all factors of production. There are no fixed factors and hence no long-run fixed costs.

2. If it increases all factors by the same proportion, it may experience constant, increasing or decreasing returns to scale.

3. Economies of scale occur when costs per unit of output fall as the scale of production increases. This can be the result of a number of factors, some of which are directly due to increasing (physical) returns to scale. These include the benefits of specialisation and division of labour, the use of larger and more efficient machines, and the ability to have a more integrated system of production. Other economies of scale arise from the financial and administrative benefits of large-scale organisations.

4. When constructing long-run cost curves it is assumed that factor prices are given, that the state of technology is given and that firms will choose the least-cost method of production for each given output.

5. The *LRAC* curve can be downward sloping, upward sloping or horizontal, depending in turn on whether there are economies of scale, diseconomies of scale or neither. Typically *LRAC* curves are drawn as saucer-shaped (or as l-shaped). As output expands, initially there are economies of scale. When these are exhausted the curve will become flat. When the firm becomes very large it may begin to experience diseconomies of scale. If this happens, the *LRAC* curve will begin to slope upwards again.

6. An envelope curve can be drawn which shows the relationship between short-run and long-run average cost curves. The *LRAC* curve envelops the short-run *AC* curves: it is 'tangential' to them (i.e. just touches them).

7. Four distinct time periods can be distinguished. In addition to the short- and long-run periods, we can also distinguish the very short- and very long-run periods. The very short run is when all factors are fixed. The very long run is where not only the quantity of factors but also their quality is variable (as a result of changing technology etc.).

Table (a)

Product	MES as % of production		% additional cost at $\frac{1}{2}$ MES
	UK	EU	
Individual plants			
Cellulose fibres	125	16	3
Rolled aluminium semi-manufactures	114	15	15
Refrigerators	85	11	4
Steel	72	10	6
Electric motors	60	6	15
TV sets	40	9	9
Cigarettes	24	6	1.4
Ball-bearings	20	2	6
Beer	12	3	7
Nylon	4	1	12
Bricks	1	0.2	25
Tufted carpets	0.3	0.04	10
Shoes	0.3	0.03	1
Firms			
Cars	200	20	9
Lorries	104	21	7.5
Mainframe computers	>100	[n.a.]	5
Aircraft	100	[n.a.]	5
Tractors	98	19	6

Source: see footnote 4

Point *b* corresponds to $\frac{1}{2}$ MES; point *c* to $\frac{1}{3}$ MES. The greater the percentage by which LRAC at point *b* or *c* is higher than at point *a*, the greater will be the economies of scale to be gained by producing at MES rather than at $\frac{1}{2}$ MES or $\frac{1}{3}$ MES. For example, in Table (a) greater economies of scale can be

Table (b)

Plants	MES as % of total EU production
Aerospace	12.19
Tractors and agricultural machinery	6.57
Electric lighting	3.76
Steel tubes	2.42
Shipbuilding	1.63
Rubber	1.06
Radio and TV	0.69
Footwear	0.08
Carpets	0.03

Source: see footnote 5

gained by moving from $\frac{1}{2}$ MES to MES in the production of electric motors than of cigarettes.

The main purpose of the studies was to determine whether the single EU market is big enough to allow both economies of scale and competition. The tables suggest that in all cases, other things being equal, the EU market is indeed large enough for this to occur. The second study also found that 47 of the 53 manufacturing sectors analysed had scope for further exploitation of economies of scale.

In the 2007–13 research framework the European Commission agreed to fund a number of research projects to conduct further investigations of MES across different industries and to consider the impact of the expansion of the EU.

1. Why might a firm operating with one plant achieve MEPS and yet not be large enough to achieve MES? (Clue: are all economies of scale achieved at plant level?)

2. Why might a firm producing bricks have an MES that is only 0.2 per cent of total EU production and yet face little effective competition from other EU countries?

4.3 REVENUE

How does a firm's revenue vary with its level of sales?

Remember that we defined a firm's total profit as its total revenue minus its total costs of production. In the last two sections we looked at costs. We now turn to revenue.

As with costs, we distinguish between three revenue concepts: total revenue (*TR*), average revenue (*AR*) and marginal revenue (*MR*).

Total, average and marginal revenue

Total revenue (TR)

Total revenue is the firm's total earnings per period of time from the sale of a particular amount of output (*Q*).

For example, if a firm sells 1000 units (*Q*) per month at a price of £5 each (*P*), then its monthly total revenue will be £5000: in other words, £5 × 1000 (*P* × *Q*). Thus:

$$TR = P \times Q$$

Definition

Total revenue A firm's total earnings from a specified level of sales within a specified period: $TR = P \times Q$

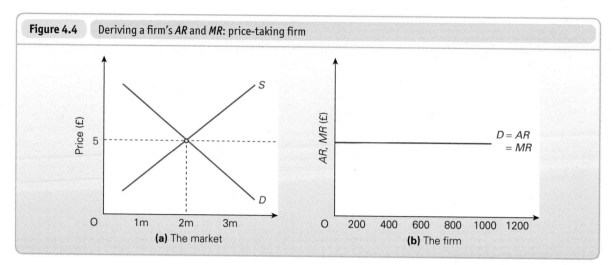

Figure 4.4 Deriving a firm's *AR* and *MR*: price-taking firm

(a) The market

(b) The firm

Average and marginal revenue curves when price is not affected by the firm's output

Average revenue

If a firm is very small relative to the whole market, it is likely to be a **price taker.** That is, it has to accept the price given by the intersection of demand and supply in the whole market. But, being so small, it can sell as much as it is capable of producing at that price. This is illustrated in Figure 4.4.

Average revenue (AR)

Average revenue is the amount that the firm earns per unit sold. Thus:

$$AR = TR/Q$$

So if the firm earns £5000 (*TR*) from selling 1000 units (*Q*), it will earn £5 per unit. But this is simply the price! Thus:

$$AR = P$$

(The only exception to this is when the firm is selling its products at different prices to different consumers. In this case *AR* is simply the (weighted) average price.)

Marginal revenue (MR)

Marginal revenue is the extra total revenue gained by selling one more unit (per time period). So if a firm sells an extra 20 units this month compared with what it expected to sell, and in the process earns an extra £100, then it is getting an extra £5 for each extra unit sold: *MR* = £5. Thus:

$$MR = \Delta TR/\Delta Q$$

We now need to see how each of these three revenue concepts (*TR*, *AR* and *MR*) varies with output. We can show this relationship graphically in the same way as we did with costs.

The relationship will depend on the market conditions under which a firm operates. A firm that is too small to be able to affect market price will have different-looking revenue curves from a firm that is able to choose the price it charges. Let us examine each of these two situations in turn.

Diagram (a) shows market demand and supply. Equilibrium price is £5. Diagram (b) looks at the demand for an individual firm that is tiny relative to the whole market. (Look at the difference in the scale of the horizontal axes in the two diagrams.)

Being so small, any change in its output will be too insignificant to affect the market price. It thus faces a horizontal demand 'curve' at this price. It can sell 200 units, 600 units, 1200 units or whatever without affecting this £5 price.

Average revenue is thus constant at £5. The firm's average revenue curve must therefore lie along exactly the same line as its demand curve.

Marginal revenue

In the case of a horizontal demand curve, the marginal revenue curve will be the same as the average revenue curve, since selling one more unit at a constant price (*AR*) merely adds that amount to total revenue. If an extra unit is sold at a constant price of £5, an extra £5 is earned.

Average and marginal revenue curves when price varies with output

Rather than accepting (or taking) the market price, firms would generally prefer to be a **price maker**. This will be

Definitions

Average revenue Total revenue per unit of output. When all output is sold at the same price, average revenue will be the same as price: $AR = TR/Q = P$

Marginal revenue The extra revenue gained by selling one more unit per period of time: $MR = \Delta TR/\Delta Q$

Price taker A firm that is too small to be able to influence the market price.

Price maker A firm that can choose the price it charges; it faces a downward-sloping demand curve. If, however, it alters its price, this will affect the quantity sold: a fall in price will lead to more being sold; a higher price will lead to less.

the case when a firm faces a downward-sloping demand curve. Generally, the larger its share of the market, the less elastic will be its demand curve, as there are probably fewer substitutes.

As a price maker, the firm can choose to lower its price and thereby sell more. Alternatively, it could raise its price, and earn more per unit sold, if it was willing to accept a fall in sales. Firms will tend to benefit from being price makers, as is discussed in an article from Harvard Business School.[6]

The curves (AR and MR) will look quite different when price does vary with the firm's output.

Average revenue

Remember that average revenue equals price. If, therefore, the price has to be reduced to sell more output, average revenue will fall as output increases.

Table 4.3 gives an example of a firm facing a downward-sloping demand curve. The demand curve (which shows how much is sold at each price) is given by the first two columns.

Note that, as in the case of a price-taking firm, the demand curve and the AR curve lie along exactly the same line (see Figure 4.5). The reason for this is simple: $AR = P$, and thus the curve relating price to quantity (the demand curve) must be the same as that relating average revenue to quantity (the AR curve).

Marginal revenue

When a firm faces a downward-sloping demand curve, marginal revenue will be less than average revenue, and may even be negative. But why?

If a firm is to sell more per time period, it must lower its price (assuming it does not advertise). This will mean lowering the price not just for the extra units it hopes to sell, but also for those units it would have sold had it not lowered the price.

Thus the marginal revenue is the price at which it sells the last unit, *minus* the loss in revenue it has incurred by reducing the price on those units it could otherwise have sold at the higher price. This can be illustrated with Table 4.3.

Assume that price is currently £7. Two units are thus sold. The firm now wishes to sell an extra unit. It lowers the price to £6. It thus gains £6 from the sale of the third unit, but loses £2 by having to reduce the price by £1 on the two units it could otherwise have sold at £7. Its net gain is therefore £6 − £2 = £4. This is the marginal revenue: it is the extra revenue gained by the firm from selling one more unit. Try using this method to check out the remaining figures for MR in Table 4.3. (Note that in the table the figures for MR are entered in the spaces between the figures for the other three columns.)

There is a simple relationship between marginal revenue and *price elasticity of demand*. Remember from Chapter 3 (pages 54–5) that if demand is price elastic, a *decrease* in price will lead to a proportionately larger increase in the quantity demanded and hence to an *increase* in revenue. Marginal revenue will thus be positive. If, however, demand is inelastic, a decrease in price will lead to a proportionately smaller increase in sales. In this case the price reduction will more than offset the increase in sales and as a result revenue will fall. Marginal revenue will be negative.

If, then, marginal revenue is a positive figure (i.e. if sales per time period are 4 units or less in Figure 4.5), the demand curve will be elastic at that quantity, since a rise in quantity sold (as a result of a reduction in price) would lead to a rise in total revenue. If, on the other hand, marginal revenue is negative (i.e. at a level of sales of 5 or more units in Figure 4.5), the demand curve will be inelastic at that quantity, since a rise in quantity sold would lead to a *fall* in total revenue.

Thus the demand (AR) curve of Figure 4.5 is elastic to the left of point r and inelastic to the right.

Table 4.3	Revenues for a firm facing a downward-sloping demand curve		
Q (units)	P = AR (£)	TR (£)	MR (£)
1	8	8	
			6
2	7	14	
			4
3	6	18	
			2
4	5	20	
			0
5	4	20	
			−2
6	3	18	
			−4
7	2	14	

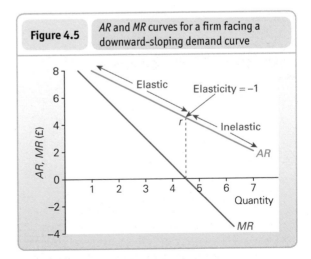

Figure 4.5 AR and MR curves for a firm facing a downward-sloping demand curve

[6]Benson P. Shapiro, 'Commodity Busters: be a Price Maker not a Price Taker', *Working Knowledge* (Harvard University, 10 February 2003).

Shifts in revenue curves

We saw in Chapter 2 that a change in *price* will cause a movement along a demand curve. It is similar with revenue curves, except that here the causal connection is in the other direction. Here we ask what happens to revenue when there is a change in the firm's *output*. Again the effect is shown by a movement along the curves.

A change in any *other* determinant of demand, such as tastes, income or the price of other goods, will shift the demand curve. As this change affects the price at which each level of output can be sold, there will be a shift in all three revenue curves. An increase in revenue is shown by a vertical shift upwards; a decrease by a shift downwards.

Recap

1. Total revenue (*TR*) is the total amount a firm earns from its sales in a given time period. It is simply price times quantity: $TR = P \times Q$.

2. Average revenue (*AR*) is total revenue per unit: $AR = TR/Q$. In other words, $AR = P$.

3. Marginal revenue is the extra revenue earned from the sale of one more unit per time period: $MR = \Delta TR/\Delta Q$.

4. The *AR* curve will be the same as the demand curve for the firm's product. In the case of a price taker, the demand curve and hence the *AR* curve will be a horizontal straight line and will also be the same as the *MR* curve.

5. A firm that faces a downward-sloping demand curve must obviously also face the same downward-sloping *AR* curve. The *MR* curve will also slope downwards, but will be below the *AR* curve and steeper than it.

6. When demand is price elastic, marginal revenue will be positive. When demand is price inelastic, marginal revenue will be negative.

7. A change in output is represented by a movement along the revenue curves. A change in any other determinant of revenue will shift the curves up or down.

4.4 PROFIT MAXIMISATION

How much output should a firm produce if it wants to maximise its profit?

We are now in a position to put costs and revenue together to find the output at which profit is maximised, and also to find out how much that profit will be. We take the case of a firm facing a downward-sloping demand curve, whose revenue, costs and profit are shown in Table 4.4.

Finding the maximum profit that the firm can make is a two-stage process. The first stage is to find the profit-maximising output. To do this we use the *MC* and *MR* curves. The second stage is to find out just how much profit is at this output. To do this we use the *AR* and *AC* curves.

Stage 1: Using marginal curves to arrive at the profit-maximising output

There is a very simple **profit-maximising rule**: if profits are to be maximised, *MR must equal MC*. From Table 4.4 it can be seen that $MR = MC$ at an output of 3. This is shown as point *e* in Figure 4.6.

But why are profits maximised when $MR = MC$? The simplest way of answering this is to see what the position would be if *MR* did not equal *MC*.

Referring to Figure 4.6, at a level of output below 3, *MR* exceeds *MC*. This means that by producing more units there will be a bigger addition to revenue (*MR*) than to cost (*MC*). Total profit will *increase*. As long as MR exceeds MC, profit can be increased by increasing production.

At a level of output above 3, *MC* exceeds *MR*. All levels of output above 3 thus add more to cost than to revenue and hence *reduce* profit. As long as MC exceeds MR, profit can be increased by cutting back on production.

Profits are thus maximised where $MC = MR$: at an output of 3. This can be confirmed by reference to the *TΠ* column in Table 4.4.

| Table 4.4 | | Revenue, cost and profit | | | | | | |

Q (units)	P=AR (£)	TR (£)	MR (£)	TC (£)	AC (£)	MC (£)	TΠ (£)	AΠ (£)
0	9	0		6	–		−6	–
			8			4		
1	8	8		10	10		−2	−2
			6			2		
2	7	14		12	6		2	1
			4			2		
3	6	18		14	4.67		4	1.33
			2			4		
4	5	20		18	4.5		2	0.5
			0			7		
5	4	20		25	5		−5	−1
			−2			11		
6	3	18		36	6		−18	−3
			−4			20		
7	2	14		56	8		−42	−6

Definition

Profit-maximising rule Profit is maximised where marginal revenue equals marginal cost.

TC 2
p 11

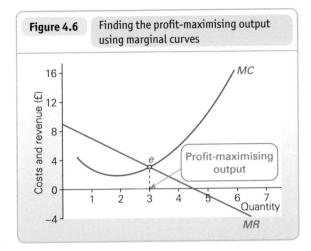

Figure 4.6 Finding the profit-maximising output using marginal curves

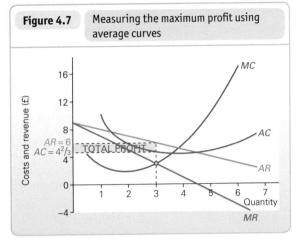

Figure 4.7 Measuring the maximum profit using average curves

Students worry sometimes about the argument that profits are maximised when $MR = MC$. Surely, they say, if the last unit is making no profit, how can profit be at a *maximum*? The answer is very simple. If you cannot add anything more to a total, the total must be at the maximum. Take the simple analogy of going up a hill. When you cannot go any higher, you must be at the top.

Stage 2: Using average curves to measure the size of the profit

Once the profit-maximising output has been discovered, we then use the average curves to measure the *amount* of profit at the maximum. Both marginal and average curves corresponding to the data in Table 4.4 are plotted in Figure 4.7.

First, average profit ($A\Pi$) is found. This is simply $AR - AC$. At the profit-maximising output of 3, this gives a figure for $A\Pi$ of $£6 - £4\frac{2}{3} = £1\frac{1}{3}$. Then total profit is obtained by multiplying average profit by output:

$$T\Pi = A\Pi \times Q$$

This is shown as the shaded area. It equals $£1\frac{1}{3} \times 3 = £4$. This can again be confirmed by reference to the $T\Pi$ column in Table 4.4.

Pause for thought

What will be the effect on a firm's profit-maximising output of a rise in fixed costs?

Some qualifications

Long-run profit maximisation

Assuming that the AR and MR curves are the same in the long run as in the short run, long-run profits will be maximised at the output where MR equals the *long-run MC*. The reasoning is the same as with the short-run case.

The meaning of 'profit'

One element of cost is the opportunity cost to the owners of the firm incurred by being in business. This is the minimum return that the owners must make on their capital in order to prevent them from eventually deciding to close down and perhaps move into some alternative business. It is a *cost* since, just as with wages, rent, etc., it has to be covered if the firm is to continue producing. This opportunity cost to the owners is sometimes known as **normal profit**, and is *included in the cost curves*.

What determines this normal rate of profit? It has two components. First, someone setting up in business invests capital in it. There is thus an opportunity cost. This is the interest that could have been earned by lending it in some riskless form (e.g. by putting it in a savings account in a bank). Nobody would set up a business unless they expected to earn at least this rate of profit. Running a business is far from riskless, however, and hence a second element is a return to compensate for risk. Thus:

Normal profit (%) = Rate of interest on a riskless loan
+ A risk premium

The risk premium varies according to the line of business. In those businesses with fairly predictable patterns, such as food retailing, it is relatively low. Where outcomes are very uncertain, as in mineral exploration or the manufacture of fashion garments, it is relatively high.

Thus if owners of a business earn normal profit, they will (just) be content to remain in that industry. If they earn more than normal profit, they will also (obviously) prefer to stay in this business. If they earn less than normal profit, then after a time they will consider leaving and using their capital for some other purpose.

Given that normal profits are included in costs, any profit that is shown diagrammatically (e.g. the shaded area

---

Definition

Normal profit The opportunity cost of being in business. It consists of the interest that could be earned on a riskless asset, plus a return for risk taking. It is counted as a cost of production.

BOX 4.6 | **THE LOGIC OF LOGISTICS**

Driving up profits

One key to a company's success is the logistics of its operations. 'Logistics' refers to the management of the inflow of resources to a company and the outflow of finished goods from it; in other words it refers to 'supply-chain management'. This includes the purchasing of raw materials, transporting them, production sequencing, stock control, delivery to wholesalers or retailers, and so on.

Logistics depends on the provision of high-quality and timely information. As IT systems have become increasingly sophisticated, they have enabled modern developments in logistics to transform the operation of many industries.

Driving down costs

With the widespread use of containerisation and development of giant distribution companies, such as UPS and DHL, transporting materials and goods around the world has become much faster and much cheaper. Instead of having to make parts in-house, companies can now use the logistics industry to obtain them at lower cost elsewhere, often from the other side of the world.

With improved systems for ordering materials, and deliveries becoming more and more reliable, firms no longer need keep large stocks of parts; they simply buy them as they need them. The same opportunity to save costs lies with the finished product: a company can keep lower levels of stocks when its own delivery mechanisms are more efficient.

The globalisation of logistics, with increasing use of the Internet, has resulted in a hugely complex logistics industry. Firms that were once solely concerned with delivery are now employed to manage companies' supply chains and achieve substantial cost savings for them.

Driving up revenues

Efficient logistics has not just resulted in lower costs. The flexibility it has given firms has allowed many to increase their sales.

Carrying lower levels of stocks and switching from supplier to supplier, with the process often being managed by a logistics company, can allow companies to change the products they offer more rapidly. They can be more responsive to consumer demand and thereby increase their sales.

A well-known example of a company benefiting from this approach is Primark. This low-cost fashion retailer focuses much more on buying, logistics and supply-chain management, than on branding or advertising.

1. *What dangers are there in keeping stocks to a minimum and relying on complex supply chains?*
2. *Which industries do you think would benefit most from reduced transport times for their finished products? Think of an industry, other than low-cost fashion, which would benefit from the ability to switch rapidly the products offered.*

---

in Figure 4.7) must therefore be over and above normal profit. It is known by several alternative names: **supernormal profit**, pure profit, economic profit, abnormal profit, producer's surplus (or sometimes simply profit). They all mean the same thing: the excess of total profit over normal profit.

Loss minimising

Sometimes there is no output at which the firm can make a profit. Such a situation is illustrated in Figure 4.8: the *AC* curve is above the *AR* curve at all levels of output.

In this case, the output where $MR = MC$ will be the loss-minimising output. The amount of loss at the point where $MR = MC$ is shown by the shaded area in Figure 4.8.

Whether or not to produce at all

The short run. Fixed costs have to be paid even if the firm is producing nothing at all. Rent has to be paid, business rates have to be paid, and so forth. Providing, therefore, that the firm is more than covering its *variable* costs, it can go some way to paying off these fixed costs and therefore will continue to produce.

It will shut down if it cannot cover its variable costs: that is, if the *AVC* curve is above, or the *AR* curve is below,

that illustrated in Figure 4.9. This situation is known as the **short-run shut-down point**.

The long run. All costs are variable in the long run. If, therefore, the firm cannot cover its long-run average costs (which include normal profit), it will close down. The **long-run shut-down point** will be where the *AR* curve is tangential to (i.e. just touches) the *LRAC* curve.

Definitions

Supernormal profit (also known as pure profit, economic profit, abnormal profit, producer's surplus or simply profit). The excess of total profit above normal profit.

Short-run shut-down point Where the *AR* curve is tangential to the *AVC* curve. The firm can only just cover its variable costs. Any fall in revenue below this level will cause a profit-maximising firm to shut down immediately.

Long-run shut-down point Where the *AR* curve is tangential to the *LRAC* curve. The firm can just make normal profits. Any fall in revenue below this level will cause a profit-maximising firm to shut down once all costs have become variable.

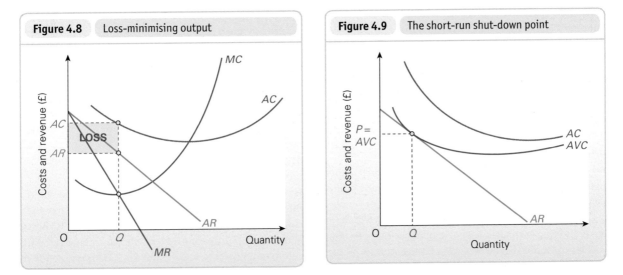

Figure 4.8 Loss-minimising output

Figure 4.9 The short-run shut-down point

Recap

1. Total profit equals total revenue minus total cost.

2. Graphically, profits are maximised at the output where marginal revenue equals marginal cost. Having found this output, the level of maximum profit can be found by finding the average profit ($AR - AC$) and then multiplying it by the level of output.

3. Normal profit is the minimum profit that must be made to persuade a firm to stay in business in the long run. It is counted as part of the firm's costs. Supernormal profit is any profit over and above normal profit.

4. For a firm that cannot make a profit at any level of output, the point where $MR = MC$ represents the loss-minimising output.

5. In the short run, a firm will close down if it cannot cover its variable costs. In the long run, it will close down if it cannot make normal profits.

4.5   PROBLEMS WITH TRADITIONAL THEORY

Are firms rational?

In Section 2.5 we considered why consumers might behave 'irrationally' and so make choices which do not maximise their own welfare. Can the same be true of firms? Why might firms deviate from 'rationality' and make choices which do not maximise profit? In other words, why might they deviate from the profit-maximising rule identified in Section 4.4? Two broad reasons are: the complexity and uncertainty of the environment in which firms operate and alternative objectives to that of profit maximisation. We now consider these in more detail.

Explaining actual producer behaviour

Lack of information

The main difficulty in trying to maximise profits is a *lack of information*. Firms operate in very complex environments, dealing with large amounts of imperfect information and uncertainty about both the present and the future.

One consequence is that firms are unlikely to know precisely the nature of their demand and *MR* curves. While firms will know how much they are selling at the moment, this only gives them one point on their demand curve and no point at all on their *MR* curve. In order to make even an informed guess of marginal revenue, they must have some idea of how responsive demand will be to a change in price. But how are they to estimate this price elasticity? Whilst market research may help, it is frequently unreliable.

But there is also the problem that firms operate in a changing environment where cost and revenue curves shift. If a firm chooses a price and output that maximises profits this year, it may as a result jeopardise profits in the future. Therefore, firms often face the problem of deciding the time period over which they should be seeking to maximise profits.

For example, a firm may be considering whether to invest in new expensive equipment which results in costs rising in the short run and thus short-run profits fall. However, if the quality of the product increases, demand is likely to increase over the longer run. Furthermore, its variable costs are likely to decrease if the new equipment is more

KI 11
p 59

efficient. Consequently, long-run profit is likely to increase, but probably by a highly uncertain amount.

Therefore, managers may resort to using rules of thumb or other shortcuts when making decisions. One approach is **average cost or mark-up pricing**. Here producers work out the price by simply adding a certain percentage (mark-up) for profit on top of average costs (average fixed costs plus average variable costs).

Alternative aims

An even more fundamental attack on the traditional theory of the firm is that firms do not even *aim* to maximise profits (even if they could).

The traditional theory of the firm assumes that it is the *owners* of the firm who make price and output decisions. It is reasonable to assume that owners *will* want to maximise profits. However, in **public limited companies** (see Case Study 4.1 in MyEconLab) the shareholders are the owners and presumably will want the firm to maximise profits so as to increase their dividends and the value of their shares. Shareholders elect directors. Directors in turn employ professional managers who are often given considerable discretion in making decisions. There is therefore a *separation between the ownership and control* of a firm. But, what are the objectives of managers? Will *they* want to maximise profits, or will they have some other aim, for example higher salaries, greater power or prestige, better working conditions, greater sales, etc.?

Managers will still have to ensure that *sufficient* profits are made to keep shareholders happy, but that may be very different from *maximising* profits. Alternative theories of the firm to those of profit maximisation, therefore, tend to assume that large firms are **profit satisficers**. That is, managers strive hard for a minimum target level of profit, but are less interested in profits above this level.

Perhaps the most well-known alternative theory of the firm is that of **sales revenue maximisation**. It may be that the success of managers, and in particular sales managers, is judged according to the level of the firm's sales. Sales figures are an obvious barometer of the firm's health. Managers' salaries, power and prestige may depend directly on sales revenue. The firm's sales representatives may be paid commission on their sales. Thus sales revenue maximisation may be a more dominant aim in the firm than profit maximisation, particularly if it has a dominant sales department.

In the case of a sales revenue maximiser, rather than obeying the '$MR = MC$ rule' of profit maximisation, the firm will continue to expand output until producing more units ceases to increase revenue. In other words, it will produce output until the marginal revenue from the last unit is zero: i.e. $MR = 0$ (assuming that at least normal profits are made at this output). An important consequence of this is that a sales revenue maximiser will produce a *greater* level of output than a profit maximiser. This is because it will continue to increase output so long as this increases total revenue even when additional units increase costs by more than they increase revenue. You can see this by inspecting

Figure 4.6 (on page 93). Profit is maximised at an output of 3; sales revenue is maximised at an output between 4 and 5.

> ### Pause for thought
>
> *Draw a diagram with MC and MR curves. Mark the output (a) at which profits are maximised; (b) at which sales revenue is maximised.*

Asymmetric information and the principal–agent problem

Firms employ people with specialist knowledge and skills to carry out specific tasks. They can be seen as 'agents' of their employer. This can give rise to what in economics is known as the **principal–agent problem** whereby it becomes difficult for employers to ensure that the 'agents' are acting in their best interests. Can the owners of a firm ever be sure that the appointed managers, as well as other staff too, are pursuing practices consistent with the maximisation of profit?

In large firms there can often be a complex chain of principal–agent relationships. But these relationships have an inherent danger for the principal: there is **asymmetric information** between the two sides. The agent knows more about the situation than the principal – of course, this is part of the reason why the principal employs the agent in the first place. The danger is that the agent may well not act in the principal's best interests, and may be able to get away with it because of the principal's imperfect knowledge.

Because of asymmetric information firms frequently have mechanisms for monitoring the performance of workers, such as annual performance reviews. Further, there may be *incentives* for agents to behave in the principals' interests. For example, managers' salaries could be closely linked to the firm's profitability or bonuses paid dependent on the outcomes of the performance reviews.

> ### Definitions
>
> **Average cost or mark-up pricing** Where firms set the price by adding a profit mark-up to average cost.
>
> **Public limited company** A company owned by its shareholders. Shareholders' liability is limited to the value of their shares. Shares may be bought and sold publicly – on the stock market.
>
> **Profit satisficing** Where decision makers in a firm aim for a target level of profit rather than the absolute maximum level.
>
> **Sales revenue maximisation** An alternative theory which assumes that managers aim to maximise the firm's short-run total revenue.
>
> **Principal–agent problem** Where people (principals), as a result of lack of knowledge, cannot ensure that their best interests are served by their agents.
>
> **Asymmetric information** Where one party in an economic relationship (e.g. an agent) has more information than another (e.g. the principal).

TC 4
p 20

KEY IDEA 16

Principal–agent problem Where people (principals), as a result of a lack of knowledge, cannot ensure that their best interests are served by their agents. Agents may take advantage of this asymmetry of information to the disadvantage of the principals.

Attitudes to risk

KI 13
p 66

Trying to maximise any objective can be risky. For example, if a firm tries to maximise its market share by aggressive advertising or price cutting, it might invoke a strong response from its rivals. The resulting war may drive it out of business. Concern with survival, therefore, may make firms cautious.

Economists have long identified over-optimism as a trait seen in many people. Consequently, some firms are likely to be adventurous and prepared to take risks. Adventurous firms are most likely to be those dominated by a powerful and ambitious individual – an individual who is risk loving and therefore prepared to take gambles.

The more dispersed the decision-making power is in a firm, however, and the more worried managers are about their own survival, the more cautious are their policies likely to be. They may, for example, prefer to stick with what have been popular products, and to expand steadily. If a firm is too cautious, however, it may not survive. It may find that it loses markets to more aggressive competitors.

> **Pause for thought**
>
> *Why might it present problems for a firm if managers are over-confident? Can you think of any reasons why managers might be more inclined to optimism than most other people?*

Recap

1. Traditional theory assumes profit-maximising behaviour by firms. Two major criticisms of this are: (a) firms may not have the information to maximise profits; (b) they may not even want to maximise profits.

2. The complexity of the environment in which firms operate may mean that firms adopt simple 'rules of thumb' such as applying a mark-up over costs when determining prices.

3. In many companies there is likely to be a separation between ownership and control. It is the managers who make the decisions, and managers may look to maximise their own utility rather than that of the owners (e.g. shareholders). The problem of managers not pursuing the same goals as the owners is an example of the principal–agent problem.

QUESTIONS

1. Up to roughly how long is the short run in the following cases?
   a. A mobile disco.
   b. Electricity power generation.
   c. A small grocery retailing business.
   d. 'Superstore Hypermarkets plc'.

   In each case specify your assumptions.

2. Given that there is a fixed supply of land in the world, what implications can you draw from the law of diminishing returns about the effects of an increase in world population on food output per head?

3. The following are some costs incurred by a shoe manufacturer. Decide whether each one is a fixed cost or a variable cost or has some element of both.
   a. The cost of leather.
   b. The fee paid to an advertising agency.
   c. Wear and tear on machinery.
   d. Business rates on the factory.
   e. Electricity for heating and lighting.
   f. Electricity for running the machines.
   g. Basic minimum wages agreed with the union.
   h. Overtime pay.
   i. Depreciation of machines as a result purely of their age (irrespective of their condition).

4. What economies of scale is a large department store likely to experience?

5. Why are many firms likely to experience economies of scale up to a certain size and then diseconomies of scale after some point beyond that?

6. Name some industries where external economies of scale are gained. What are the specific external economies in each case?

7. Examine Figure 4.2 (on page 86). What would (i) the firm's long-run total cost curve, and (ii) its long-run marginal cost curve, look like?

8. Under what circumstances is a firm likely to experience a flat-bottomed *LRAC* curve?

9. Draw a downward-sloping demand curve. Now choose scales for both axes. Read off various points on the demand curve and use them to construct a table showing price and quantity. Use this table to work out the figures for a marginal revenue column. Now use these figures to draw an *MR* curve.

10. Copy Figure 4.5 (which is based on Table 4.3). Now assume that incomes have risen and that, as a result, two more units per time period can be sold at each price. Construct a new table and plot the resulting new *AR* and *MR* curves on your diagram. Are the new curves parallel to the old ones? Explain.

11. Using the data in Table 4.3, construct a *total revenue* curve and mark the parts of the curve where the price elasticity of demand is (a) elastic; (b) unit elastic; (c) inelastic.

12. From the information given in the following table, construct a table like Table 4.4.

Q	0	1	2	3	4	5	6	7
P	12	11	10	9	8	7	6	5
TC	2	6	9	12	16	21	28	38

13. Use your table to draw a diagram like Figure 4.7. Use this diagram to show the profit-maximising output and the level of maximum profit. Confirm your findings by reference to the table you have constructed.

14. Normal profits are regarded as a cost (and are included in the cost curves). Explain why.

15. What determines the size of normal profit? Will it vary with the general state of the economy?

16. A firm will continue producing in the short run even if it is making a loss, providing it can cover its variable costs. Explain why. Just how long will it be willing to continue making such a loss?

17. The price of pocket calculators and digital watches fell significantly in the years after they were first introduced, and at the same time demand for them increased substantially. Use cost and revenue diagrams to illustrate these events. Explain the reasoning behind the diagram(s) you have drawn.

18. The table below shows the average cost and average revenue (price) for a firm at each level of output.

Output	1	2	3	4	5	6	7	8	9	10
AC (£)	7.00	5.00	4.00	3.30	3.00	3.10	3.50	4.20	5.00	6.00
AR (£)	10.00	9.50	9.00	8.50	8.00	7.50	7.00	6.50	6.00	5.50

a. Construct a table to show *TC*, *MC*, *TR* and *MR* at each level of output (put the figures for *MC* and *MR* mid-way between the output figures).

b. Using *MC* and *MR* figures, find the profit-maximising output.

c. Using *TC* and *TR* figures, check your answer to (b).

d. Plot the *AC*, *MC*, *AR* and *MR* figures on a graph.

e. Mark the profit-maximising output and the *AR* and *AC* at this output.

f. Shade in an area to represent the level of profits at this output.

19. In February 2000, Unilever, the giant consumer products company, announced that it was to cut 25 000 jobs, close 100 plants and rely more on the Internet to purchase its supplies. It would use part of the money saved to increase promotion of its leading brands, such as Dove skin-care products, Lipton tea, Omo detergents and Calvin Klein cosmetics. The hope was to boost sales and increase profits. What was the likely effect of meeting these targets on its total costs, total revenue, average costs and average revenue? Give reasons for your answer.

20. Would it be possible for firms to calculate their maximum-profit output if they did not use marginal cost and marginal revenue concepts?

21. What is meant by the principal–agent problem? Give two examples of this problem that you have come across in your own experience.

22. 'A firm will always prefer to make more profit rather than less.' Do you agree with this statement? Is it compatible with alternatives to the profit-maximising theory of the firm?

MyEconLab

This book can be supported by MyEconLab, which contains a range of additional resources, including an online homework and tutorial system designed to test and build your understanding.

You need both an access card and a course ID to access MyEconLab:

1. Is your lecturer using MyEconLab? Ask your lecturer for your course ID.

2. Has an access card been included with the book at a reduced cost? Check the inside back cover of the book.

3. If you have a course ID but no access card, go to: http://www.myeconlab.com/ to buy access to this interactive study programme.

ADDITIONAL CASE STUDIES IN *THE ESSENTIALS OF ECONOMICS* MyEconLab (www.pearsoned.co.uk/sloman)

4.1 **The legal and organisational structure of firms.** This case looks at the distinction between sole proprietorships, partnerships, private limited companies and public limited companies. It also distinguishes between U-form, M-form and H-form organisations.

4.2 **Division of labour in a pin factory.** This is the famous example of division of labour given by Adam Smith in his *Wealth of Nations* (1776).

4.3 **Diminishing returns to nitrogen fertiliser.** This case study provides a good illustration of diminishing returns in practice by showing the effects on grass yields of the application of increasing amounts of nitrogen fertiliser.

4.4 **The fallacy of using historic costs.** This looks at the example of the pricing of Christmas trees.

4.5 **Followers of fashion.** This case study examines the effects of costs on prices of fashion-sensitive goods.

4.6 **Cost curves in practice.** What do cost curves look like when fixed factors are divisible?

4.7 **Putting on a duplicate.** This examines the effects on marginal costs of additional passengers on a coach journey.

WEB APPENDICES

4.1 **The short-run production function.** An analysis of how output varies with increases in the quantity of the variable factor used. The appendix looks at the concepts of total, average and marginal product.

4.2 **The optimum combination of factors.** This appendix examines how factors can be combined so as to minimise costs for any given output. It uses the concept of marginal product and develops the 'equi-marginal principle' developed in Web Appendix 2.1.

4.3 **Isoquant analysis.** This develops a model to show the optimum combination of factors to minimise costs for any given output or maximise output for any given cost. The analysis is similar to indifference analysis, developed in Web Appendix 2.2.

Market structures

As we saw in Chapter 4, a firm's profits are maximised where its marginal cost equals its marginal revenue: $MC = MR$. But we will want to know more than this.

Assuming that a firm does want to maximise profits, what determines the *amount* of profit that it will make? Will its profits be large, or just enough for it to survive, or so low that it will be forced out of business? Will the price charged to the consumer be high or low? And, more generally, will the consumer benefit from the decisions a firm makes?

The answers to these questions depend on the amount of competition that a firm faces. A firm in a highly competitive environment will behave quite differently from a firm facing little or no competition. In particular, a firm facing competition from many other firms will be forced to keep its prices down and be as efficient as possible, simply to survive.

Even if a firm faces only one or two rivals, competition might be quite intense. Firms might put a lot of effort into producing more efficiently or into developing new or better products in order to gain a larger share of the market. They may, however, collude with each other to keep prices up.

When firms face little or no competition (like the local water company or a major pharmaceutical company), they may have considerable power over prices and we may end up paying a lot more.

In this chapter we look at different types of market and how well they serve the consumer.

After studying this chapter, you should be able to answer the following questions:

- What determines the degree of market power of a firm?
- Why does operating under conditions of perfect competition make being in business a constant battle for survival?
- How do firms get to become monopolies and remain so?
- At what price and output will a monopolist maximise profits and how much profit will it make?
- How well or badly do monopolies serve the consumer compared with competitive firms?
- How are firms likely to behave when there are just a few of them competing ('oligopolies')? Will they engage in all-out competition or will they collude with each other?
- What strategic games are oligopolists likely to play in their attempt to out do their rivals? What determines the output of these 'games'?
- Why may firms charge different consumers different prices for an identical product?

5.1 THE DEGREE OF COMPETITION

How much competition does a firm face?

It is traditional to divide industries into categories according to the degree of competition that exists between the firms within the industry. There are four such categories.

At one extreme is **perfect competition** where there are very many firms competing. Each firm is so small relative to the whole industry that it has no power to influence price. It is a price taker. At the other extreme is **monopoly**, where there is just one firm in the industry, and hence no competition from *within* the industry. In the middle comes **monopolistic competition**, which involves quite a lot of firms competing and where there is freedom for new firms to enter the industry, and **oligopoly**, where there are only a few firms and where entry of new firms is restricted.

Definitions

Perfect competition A market structure where there are many firms; where there is freedom of entry into the industry; where all firms produce an identical product; and where all firms are price takers.

Monopoly A market structure where there is only one firm in the industry.

Monopolistic competition A market structure where, like perfect competition, there are many firms and freedom of entry into the industry, but where each firm produces a differentiated product and thus has some control over its price.

Oligopoly A market structure where there are few enough firms to enable barriers to be erected against the entry of new firms.

To distinguish more precisely between these four categories, the following must be considered:

- How freely firms can enter the industry. Is entry free or restricted? If it is restricted, just how great are the barriers to the entry of new firms?
- The nature of the product. Do all firms produce an identical product, or do firms produce their own particular brand or model or variety?
- The degree of control the firm has over price. Is the firm a price taker or can it choose its price, and if so, how will changing its price affect its profits? What we are talking about here is the nature of the demand curve it faces. How elastic is it? If the firm puts up its price, will it lose (a) all its sales (a horizontal demand curve), or (b) a large proportion of its sales (a relatively elastic demand curve), or (c) just a small proportion of its sales (a relatively inelastic demand curve)?

> **KEY IDEA 17**
>
> *Market power benefits the powerful at the expense of others.* When firms have market power over prices, they can use this to raise prices and profits above the perfectly competitive level. Other things being equal, the firm will gain at the expense of the consumer. Similarly, if consumers or workers have market power they can use this to their own benefit.

Table 5.1 shows the differences between the four categories.

| Table 5.1 | Features of the four market structures |

Type of market	Number of firms	Freedom of entry	Nature of product	Examples	Implication for demand curve for firm
Perfect competition	Very many	Unrestricted	Homogeneous (undifferentiated)	Cabbages, carrots (these approximate to perfect competition)	Horizontal. The firm is a price taker
Monopolistic competition	Many/several	Unrestricted	Differentiated	Builders, restaurants	Downward sloping, but relatively elastic. The firm has some control over price
Oligopoly	Few	Restricted	1. Undifferentiated or 2. Differentiated	1. Petrol 2. Cars, electrical appliances	Downward sloping, relatively inelastic but depends on reactions of rivals to a price change
Monopoly	One	Restricted or completely blocked	Unique	Many prescription drugs, local water company	Downward sloping, more inelastic than oligopoly. The firm has considerable control over price

The market structure under which a firm operates will determine its behaviour. Firms under perfect competition behave quite differently from firms that are monopolists, which behave differently again from firms under oligopoly or monopolistic competition.

This behaviour (or 'conduct') in turn affects the firm's performance: its prices, profits, efficiency, etc. In many cases it also affects other firms' performance: *their* prices, profits, efficiency, etc. The collective conduct of all the firms in the industry affects the whole industry's performance.

Economists thus see a causal chain running from market structure to the performance of that industry:

Structure → Conduct → Performance

This does not mean, however, that all firms operating in a particular market structure will behave in exactly the same way. It is for this reason that government policy towards firms – known as 'competition policy' – prefers to focus on the *conduct* of individual firms, rather than simply on the market structure within which they operate.

The conduct of firms can actually affect the development of the market structure. For example, the interaction between firms may influence the development of new products or new production methods, and may encourage or discourage the entrance of new firms into the industry.

It is also important to note that some firms with different divisions and products may operate in more than one market structure. As an example, consider the case of Microsoft. Its Internet Explorer competes with more successful rivals, such as Chrome and Firefox, and, as a result, has little market power in the browser market. Its Office products, by contrast, have a much bigger market share and dominate the word processor, presentation and spreadsheet markets.

In looking at how market structure influences firms' behaviour we begin our analysis with the two extreme market structures: perfect competition and monopoly (Sections 5.2 and 5.3). Then we turn to look at the two intermediate cases of monopolistic competition and oligopoly (Sections 5.4 and 5.5).

These two intermediate cases are sometimes referred to collectively as **imperfect competition**. The vast majority of firms in the real world operate under imperfect competition. It is still worth studying the two extreme cases, however, because they provide a framework within which to understand the real world. Some industries tend more to the competitive extreme, and thus their performance corresponds to some extent to perfect competition. Other industries tend more to the other extreme, for example when there is one dominant firm and a few much smaller firms. In such cases their performance corresponds more to monopoly.

> ### Pause for thought
>
> *Give one more example in each of the four market categories in Table 5.1.*

> ### Recap
>
> 1. There are four alternative market structures under which firms operate. In ascending order of firms' market power, they are: perfect competition, monopolistic competition, oligopoly and monopoly.
> 2. The market structure under which a firm operates affects its conduct, which in turn affects its performance.

5.2 PERFECT COMPETITION

What happens when there are very many firms all competing against each other? Is this good for us as consumers?

The theory of perfect competition illustrates an extreme form of capitalism. In it, firms are entirely subject to market forces. They have no power whatsoever to affect the price of the product. The price they face is determined by the interaction of demand and supply in the whole *market*.

Assumptions

The model of perfect competition is built on four assumptions:

■ Firms are *price takers*. There are so many firms in the industry that each one produces an insignificantly small proportion of total industry supply, and therefore has *no power whatsoever* to affect the price of the product. It faces a horizontal demand 'curve' at the market price: the price determined by the interaction of demand and supply in the whole market.

■ There is complete *freedom of entry* into the industry for new firms. Existing firms are unable to stop new firms setting up in business. Setting up a business takes time,

> ### Definition
>
> **Imperfect competition** The collective name for monopolistic competition and oligopoly.

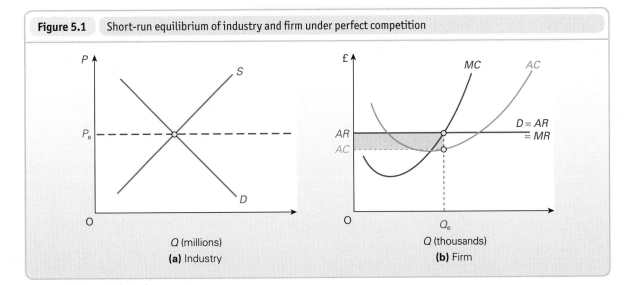

Figure 5.1 Short-run equilibrium of industry and firm under perfect competition

(a) Industry

(b) Firm

however. Freedom of entry, therefore, applies in the long run.

- All firms produce an *identical product*. (The product is 'homogeneous'.) There is therefore no branding or advertising.
- Producers and consumers have *perfect knowledge* of the market. That is, producers are fully aware of prices, costs and market opportunities. Consumers are fully aware of price, quality and availability of the product.

These assumptions are very strict. Few, if any, industries in the real world meet these conditions. Certain agricultural markets are perhaps closest to perfect competition. The market for certain fresh vegetables, such as potatoes, is an example.

Nevertheless, despite the lack of real-world cases, the model of perfect competition plays a very important role in economic analysis and policy. Its major relevance is as an 'ideal type' against which to compare real-world markets. Indeed, many argue that achieving perfect competition would bring a number of important advantages, such as keeping prices down to marginal cost and preventing firms from making supernormal profit over the long run. The model can thus be used as a benchmark against which to judge the shortcomings of particular industries. However, we shall also see that it has disadvantages, when compared with other market structures.

Pause for thought

It is sometimes claimed that the market for various stocks and shares is perfectly competitive, or nearly so. Take the case of the market for shares in a large company, such as BP. Go through each of the four assumptions above and see if they apply in this case. (Don't be misled by the first assumption. The 'firm' in this case is not BP itself, but rather the owners of the shares.)

The short-run equilibrium of the firm

In the **short run** we assume that the number of firms in the industry cannot be increased; there is simply not time for new firms to enter the market.

Figure 5.1 shows a short-run equilibrium for both industry and a firm under perfect competition. Both parts of the diagram have the same scale for the vertical axis. The horizontal axes have totally different scales, however. For example, if the horizontal axis for the firm were measured in, say, thousands of units, the horizontal axis for the whole industry might be measured in millions or tens of millions of units, depending on the number of firms in the industry.

Let us examine the determination of price, output and profit in turn.

Price

The price is determined in the industry by the intersection of demand and supply. Being a price taker, the firm faces a horizontal demand (or average revenue) 'curve' at this price. It can sell all it can produce at the market price (P_e), but nothing at a price above P_e.

Output

The firm will maximise profit where marginal cost equals marginal revenue ($MR = MC$), at an output of Q_e. Note that, since the price is not affected by the firm's output, marginal revenue will equal price (see page 90 and

Definition

Short run under perfect competition The period during which there is too little time for new firms to enter the industry.

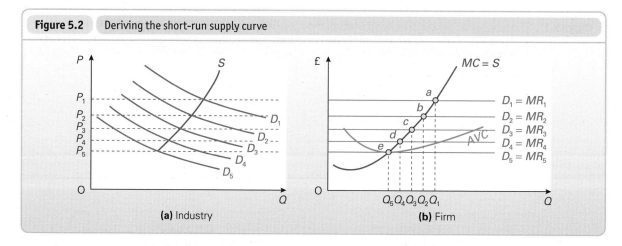

Figure 5.2 Deriving the short-run supply curve

(a) Industry

(b) Firm

Figure 4.4). Thus the firm's *MR* 'curve' and *AR* 'curve' (= demand 'curve') are the same horizontal straight line.

Profit

TC 2
p 11
If the average cost (*AC*) curve (which includes normal profit) dips below the average revenue (*AR*) 'curve', the firm will earn supernormal profit. Supernormal profit per unit at Q_e is the vertical difference between *AR* and *AC* at Q_e. Total supernormal profit is the shaded rectangle in Figure 5.1 (i.e. profit per unit times quantity sold).

The short-run supply curve

The *firm's* short-run supply curve will be its (short-run) marginal cost curve. But why? A supply curve shows how much will be supplied at each price: it relates quantity to price. The marginal cost curve relates quantity to marginal cost. But, under perfect competition, given that $P = MR$, and $MR = MC$, P must equal MC. Thus the supply curve and the *MC* curve will follow the same line.

For example, in Figure 5.2(b), if price were P_1, profits would be maximised at Q_1 where $P_1 = MC$. Thus point *a* is one point on the supply curve. At a price of P_2, Q_2 would be produced. Thus point *b* is another point on the supply curve, and so on.

So, under perfect competition, the firm's supply curve
KI 15
p 76
depends entirely on production costs. This demonstrates why the firm's supply curve is upward sloping. Since marginal costs rise as output rises (due to diminishing marginal returns), a higher price will be necessary to induce the firm to increase its output.

Note that the firm will not produce at a price below *AVC* (see page 94 above). Thus the supply curve is only that portion of the *MC* curve above point *e*.

What will be the short-run supply curve of the whole *industry*? This is simply the sum of the short-run supply curves (and hence *MC* curves) of all the firms in the industry. Graphically this will be a *horizontal* sum, since it is *quantities* that are being added.

Pause for thought

Will the industry supply be zero below a price of P_5 in Figure 5.2?

The long-run equilibrium of the firm

In the **long run**, if typical firms are making supernormal
TC 4
p 20
profits, new firms will be attracted into the industry. Likewise, if existing firms can make supernormal profits by increasing the scale of their operations, they will do so, since all factors of production are variable in the long run.

The effect of the entry of new firms and/or the expan-
KI 6
p 20
sion of existing firms is to increase industry supply. This is illustrated in Figure 5.3. At a price of P_1 supernormal profits are earned. The industry supply curve will thus shift to the right as new firms enter. This in turn leads to a fall in price.

Supply will go on increasing, and price falling, until firms are making only normal profits. This will be when price has fallen to the point where the demand 'curve' for
TC 6
p 37
the firm just touches the bottom of its long-run average cost curve. Q_L is thus the long-run equilibrium output of the firm, with P_L the long-run equilibrium price.

Since the *LRAC* curve is tangential to (i.e. just touching) all possible short-run *AC* curves (see Section 4.2), the full long-run equilibrium will be as shown in Figure 5.4 where:

$$LRAC = AC = MC = MR = AR$$

Definition

The long run under perfect competition The period of time that is long enough for new firms to enter the industry.

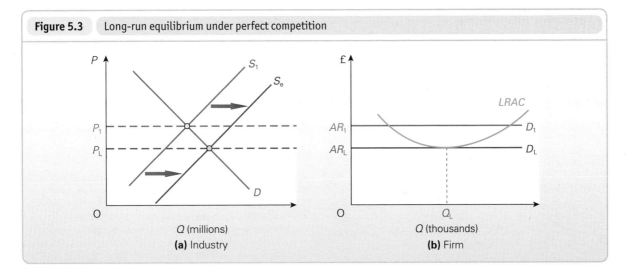

Figure 5.3 Long-run equilibrium under perfect competition

(a) Industry

(b) Firm

The incompatibility of perfect competition and substantial economies of scale

Why is perfect competition so rare in the real world – if it even exists at all? One important reason for this has to do with economies of scale.

In many industries, firms may have to be quite large if they are to experience the full potential economies of scale. But perfect competition requires there to be *many* firms. Firms must therefore be small under perfect competition: too small in most cases for economies of scale.

Once a firm expands sufficiently to achieve economies of scale, it will usually gain market power. It will be able to undercut the prices of smaller firms, which will thus be driven out of business. Perfect competition is destroyed.

Perfect competition could exist in any industry, therefore, only if there were no (or virtually no) economies of scale.

Is perfect competition good for consumers?

Generally it is argued that perfect competition is a 'good thing', and that the more perfect an industry becomes, the better. We explore the arguments in Section 5.3 (pages 110–11) after we have looked at monopoly, but at this stage the main points in favour of perfect competition can be identified:

- Price equals marginal cost. Why is this desirable? To answer this, consider what would happen if they were not equal. If price were greater than marginal cost, this would mean that consumers were putting a higher value (*P*) on the production of extra units than they cost to produce (*MC*). Therefore more ought to be produced. If price were less than marginal cost, consumers would be putting a lower value on extra units than they cost to produce. Therefore less ought to be produced. When they are equal, therefore, production levels are just right. But, as we shall see later, it is only under perfect competition

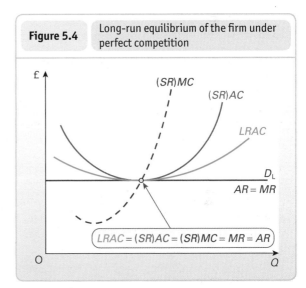

Figure 5.4 Long-run equilibrium of the firm under perfect competition

$$LRAC = (SR)AC = (SR)MC = MR = AR$$

that $MC = P$. This idea of producing just the right amount of the product is referred to as **allocative efficiency**.

- The combination of (long-run) production being at minimum average cost and the firm making only normal profit keeps prices at a minimum.

- Perfect competition is a case of 'survival of the fittest'. Inefficient firms will be driven out of business, since they will not be able to make even normal profits. This encourages firms to be as efficient as possible and, where possible, to invest in new improved technology. This

KI 17
p 101

BOX 5.1   E-COMMERCE

A return of power to the people?

The relentless drive towards big business in recent decades has seen many markets become more concentrated and increasingly dominated by large producers. And yet forces are at work that are undermining this dominance and bringing more competition to markets. One of these forces is *e-commerce*.

In this case study, we will consider the impact of e-commerce on market structures and power.

What do we mean by e-commerce?

E-commerce is a shorthand term for buying and selling products through electronic means, in most cases through the Internet. It involves a number of processes including marketing, purchase transactions and payments. This is a fast-moving sector; only a decade ago, buying something online might have involved sending an email order via your computer. Now we are genuinely surprised if even small firms don't have straightforward online processes, including a variety of payment mechanisms.

The growth in online shopping has been spectacular and shows no sign of slowing down. The chart shows the rise in online retail sales as a proportion of all retail sales in the UK between 2007 and 2015. Note that the proportion of Internet sales rises each year in the run-up to Christmas as many people buy gifts online.

Moving markets back towards perfect competition?

Let us reconsider three of the assumptions of perfect competition and the impact of e-commerce on them: a large number of firms; freedom of entry; and perfect knowledge.

A large number of firms. With the global reach of the Internet, the number of firms in any market has increased. Firms must now compete with others across the world, as consumers have access to the global marketplace. Firms must keep an eye on the prices and products of competitors worldwide and be aware of the continual emergence of new smaller businesses.

Freedom of entry. The Internet has had a key role to play here, reducing the costs of business start-ups. The traditional idea of rented office space, large start-up and fixed costs is no longer the only way to run a business. Small online

companies have been created from home, with little more than a computer, and many companies are transferring their purchases to the Internet, finding that prices can be significantly cheaper.

Marketing costs for small Internet-based companies can be relatively low, especially with powerful search engines and many of these new online companies are more specialist, relying on interest 'outsourcing' (buying parts, equipment and other supplies through the Internet) rather than making everything themselves. They are also more likely to use delivery firms rather than having their own transport fleet.

Not only do all the above factors make markets more price competitive, but they also bring other benefits. Costs are driven down, as firms economise on stock holding, rely more on outsourcing and develop more efficient relationships with suppliers. 'Procurement hubs', online exchanges and trading communities are now well established in many industries. All of these factors have made it relatively cheap for new firms to set up and begin trading over the Internet. Many of these firms are involved in 'B2C' (business-to-consumers) e-commerce, where they are selling directly to us as consumers. However, many have begun to sell to other firms, known as 'B2B' (business-to-business).

One particularly interesting example is eBay and the way in which it has caused a blurring between firms and consumers. Setting up a small business from home is now incredibly easy and, via eBay, consumers can become businesses with just one click. With around 130 million active users worldwide and hundreds of thousands of users running a business via eBay in the UK, buying and selling 'junk' has become a viable source of income. Estimates suggest that at any one time, there are over 800 million 'listings' on eBay.

eBay itself is an example of a business that expanded with the growth of the Internet. Founded in 1995, eBay grew rapidly, reaching half a million users and revenues of $4.7 billion in the USA within three years. In 2014, eBay's revenue was $17.9 billion, up from $8.7 billion five years earlier. In more recent years it has experienced some difficulties from increased competition, as there are many

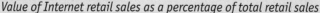

Value of Internet retail sales as a percentage of total retail sales

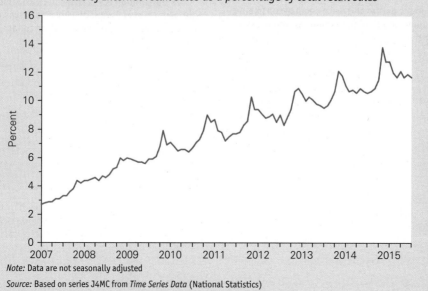

Note: Data are not seasonally adjusted

Source: Based on series J4MC from *Time Series Data* (National Statistics)

other sites offering similar services. However, eBay's global reach and volume of customers, courtesy of the Internet, have enabled rapid growth to continue. Although it is just one company, the fact that it has millions of users, acting as businesses, means that it has provided a highly competitive environment.

The increase in competition from the rise of e-commerce, in whatever form, has led to firms' demand curves becoming more price elastic. This is especially the case for goods which are cheap to transport or for services, such as travel agents, insurance and banking. While some large firms, such as Amazon, do provide competition for the more traditional firms, the greater freedom of entry for new firms that has been created by the Internet is providing an ever-increasing degree of competition, as more and more small businesses are set up every day. This has also created a more innovative environment, with a rapidly growing range of products.

Perfect knowledge. The Internet has also added to consumer knowledge. There are some obvious ways: e.g. facts, and figures through sites such as Wikipedia, where to eat, what to read, etc. However, it has also improved consumer knowledge through greater transparency. Online shopping agents such as Kelkoo and Google and online comparison sites, such as GoCompare and MoneySupermarket, can quickly locate a list of alternative suppliers and their prices. There is greater information on product availability, quality and consumer feedback. Virtual shopping malls, full of e-retailers, place the high street retailer under intense competitive pressure.

We have seen evidence of this online competition, with the down fall of some well-known high street retailers, such as HMV, Comet, Peacocks and Borders. Although the weak trading conditions following the economic downturn after 2007 were partly to blame, it has also been the sheer volume of competition these companies face from the Internet. HMV faces steep competition from companies like Amazon, as DVDs, Blu-ray and CDs can be sold much more cheaply online. LoveFilm and Netflix also provide a new way of watching films.

Google shopping allows consumers to compare prices on larger consumer durables such as fridges, cookers and washing machines, and with the large supermarkets offering such items online and price comparisons being so easy, consumers are finding bargains on the Internet. These competitive pressures from online retailing certainly added to the woes of Comet and other companies.

It is not just the traditional consumer that has benefited from greater knowledge. Many firms are also consumers, purchasing inputs from other firms. It is now commonplace for firms to use the Internet to search for cheaper sources of supply. This is even more relevant now that many firms operate in a worldwide marketplace and can source their supplies from across the globe.

What are the limits to e-commerce?

In 20 years, will we be doing all our shopping on the Internet? Will the only shopping centres be virtual ones? Although e-commerce is revolutionising some markets, it is unlikely that things will go anything like that far.

The benefits of 'shop shopping' are that you get to see the good, touch it and use it. You can have instant possession of it: you don't have to wait. Many people like wandering around the shops, meeting friends, seeing what takes their fancy, trying on clothes, browsing through DVDs, and so on. 'Retail therapy' for many is a leisure activity. Many consumers are willing to pay a 'premium' for these advantages.

Online shopping is limited by current technology and infrastructure. The quality of Internet access has improved significantly as broadband has become widely available, but online purchases can still be hampered by busy sites or slow connections.

And what if deliveries are late or fail completely? The busiest time for Internet shopping is in the run-up to Christmas. In 2011 Yodel, the UK's second largest household delivery company (after the Royal Mail), failed to deliver around 15 000 parcels per day as Christmas approached.[1] Similar problems occurred in 2014, when, 10 days before Christmas, Yodel announced that it was no longer collecting parcels for delivery due to a backlog (see articles in the *Guardian*[2] and the Mail Online[3]). Their delivery infrastructure simply could not cope with the increase in demand from online shopping and, clearly, over three years, it had not found a solution.

Additionally, online shopping requires access to a credit or debit card, which might not be available to everyone, particularly younger consumers and those on low incomes.

Also costs might not be as low as expected. How efficient is it to have many small deliveries of goods? How significant are the lost cost savings from economies of scale that larger producers or retailers are likely to generate?

There has also been concern that e-commerce can itself result in substantial monopoly power. As the leading 'marketplace' platform, bringing together buyers and sellers, eBay has the advantages of a well-known brand and market dominance. The consequence is that it can extract surplus from the traders who use its services. In 2008 eBay sellers called for a boycott of the site, following changes in the fees being charged and the removal of their ability to leave feedback on buyers. However, the profits eBay makes has attracted other firms into this area. Amazon Marketplace, ASOS and Not on the High Street are giving independent traders the opportunity to sell through well-known companies and providing competition to eBay.

Nevertheless, e-commerce has made many markets, both retail and B2B, more competitive. This is especially so for services and for goods whose quality is easy to identify online. Many firms are being forced to face up to having their prices determined by the market.

1. *Why may the Internet work better for replacement buys than for new purchases?*
2. *Give three examples of products that are particularly suitable for selling over the Internet and three that are not. Explain your answer.*
3. *As eBay has grown in size it has acquired substantial monopoly power. What are the barriers to entry for other companies wishing to act as a marketplace for B2C and B2B business?*

[1] 'Surge in online orders hits deliveries', *Financial Times*, 23 December 2011.

[2] 'Yodel warns of parcel backlog as Christmas deliveries face delay', *Guardian*, 12 December 2014.

[3] Ben Wilkinson, 'Delivery firm Yodel's boss forced into apology after delays mean thousands of customers may not receive parcels in time for Christmas', Mail Online, 24 December 2014.

idea of production at minimum cost and of costs being driven down is known as **productive efficiency.**

In general, it can be argued that perfectly competitive markets result in economic efficiency.

> **KEY IDEA 18**
>
> *Economic efficiency* is achieved when each good is produced at the minimum cost and where consumers get maximum benefit from their income.

Recap

1. The assumptions of perfect competition are: a very large number of firms, complete freedom of entry, a homogeneous product and perfect knowledge of the good and its market by both producers and consumers.

2. In the short run, there is not time for new firms to enter the market, and thus supernormal profits can persist. In the long run, however, any supernormal profits will be competed away by the entry of new firms.

3. The short-run equilibrium for the firm is where the price, as determined by demand and supply in the market, is equal to marginal cost. At this output the firm will be maximising profit.

4. The long-run equilibrium is where the market price is just equal to firms' long-run average cost.

5. There can be no substantial economies of scale to be gained in a perfectly competitive industry. If there were, the industry would cease to be perfectly competitive as the large, low-cost firms drove the small, high-cost ones out of business.

5.3   MONOPOLY

What happens when there is only one firm in the market? Do we as consumers suffer?

What is a monopoly?

This may seem a strange question because the answer appears obvious. A monopoly exists when there is only one firm in the industry.

But whether an industry can be classed as a monopoly is not always clear. It depends on how narrowly the industry is defined. For example, a textile company may have a monopoly on certain types of fabric, but it does not have a monopoly on fabrics in general. The consumer can buy fabrics other than those supplied by the company. A rail company may have a monopoly over rail services between two cities, but it does not have a monopoly over public transport between these two cities. People can travel by coach or air. They could also use private transport. Consider the blog on the Sloman News Site, which asks *Is Amazon a monopolist?*[4]

To some extent, the boundaries of an industry are arbitrary. What is more important for a firm is the amount of monopoly *power* it has, and that depends on the closeness of substitutes produced by rival industries. The Post Office, before 2006, had a monopoly over the delivery of letters, but it faced competition in communications from telephone, faxes and email. Now, with the ending of the monopoly over the delivery of letters, the Post Office criticises the 'unfair' competition it faces from other firms,

such as whistl, which delivers mail, packets and parcels, but *only* in more profitable urban areas. An article from *Post and Parcel*[5] considers this competition to the Royal Mail.

Barriers to entry

For a firm to maintain its monopoly position, there must be barriers to the entry of new firms. As we shall see, barriers also exist under oligopoly, but in the case of monopoly they must be high enough to block the entry of new firms. Barriers can take various forms.

Economies of scale. If the monopolist's costs go on falling significantly up to the output that satisfies the whole market, the industry may not be able to support more than one producer. This case is known as **natural monopoly.** It is particularly likely if the market is small. For example, two bus companies might find it unprofitable to serve the same

---

Definitions

Productive efficiency A situation where firms are producing the maximum output for a given amount of inputs, or producing a given output at the least cost.

Natural monopoly A situation where long-run average costs would be lower if an industry were under monopoly than if it were shared between two or more competitors.

KI 17
p 101

[4]http://pearsonblog.campaignserver.co.uk/?p=14509

[5]http://postandparcel.info/62638/news/companies/royal-mails-challenger-tnt-post-uk-to-rebrand-as-whistl/

routes, each running with perhaps only half-full buses, whereas one company with a monopoly of the routes could make a profit. The blog post *Fair Fares?*[6] on the Sloman News Site considers the bus industry. Electricity transmission via a national grid is another example of a natural monopoly.

Even if a market could support more than one firm, a new entrant is unlikely to be able to start up on a very large scale. Thus the monopolist that is already experiencing economies of scale can charge a price below the cost of the new entrant and drive it out of business. If, however, the new entrant is a firm already established in another industry, it may be able to survive this competition.

Network economies. When a product or service is used by everyone in the market, there are benefits to all users from having access to other users. One example of **network economies** comes from the use of Microsoft's products (see Case Study 5.4 in MyEconLab). Firms benefit from lower training costs because individuals who have learnt to use Microsoft products elsewhere can be readily absorbed into the firm. Individuals benefit too because they do not have to learn to use new software when they move to another organisation and the learning costs are fairly low as a new version of the software is introduced.

Other contemporary examples include eBay, which, by providing such large network economies, makes it very difficult for other online auction houses to compete, while Adobe provides application software and web services for creating, reading and managing PDF files. These portable document files, to give them their full name, can be used to present documents regardless of software, hardware and operating systems.

Economies of scope. A firm that produces a *range* of products is also likely to experience a lower average cost of production. For example, a large pharmaceutical company producing a range of drugs and toiletries can use shared research, marketing, storage and transport facilities across its range of products. These lower costs make it difficult for a new single-product entrant to the market, since the large firm will be able to undercut its price and drive it out of the market.

Product differentiation and brand loyalty. If a firm produces a clearly differentiated product, where the consumer associates the product with the brand, it will be very difficult for a new firm to break into that market.

In 1908 James Spengler invented, and patented, the electric vacuum cleaner. Later that year he sold the patent to his cousin's husband, William Hoover, who set about putting mass production in place. Decades after their legal monopoly (see below) ran out, people still associate vacuum-cleaning with Hoover and many of us would say that we are going to 'Hoover the carpet', despite using a Dyson, or other machine.

Other examples of strong brand image include Guinness, Kellogg's Cornflakes, Coca-Cola, Nescafé and Sellotape (or Scotch Tape in the USA). In many cases, strong brand presence would not be enough to *block* entry, but it might well reinforce other barriers.

Lower costs for an established firm. An established monopoly is likely to have developed specialised production and marketing skills. It is more likely to be aware of the most efficient techniques and the most reliable and/or cheapest suppliers. It is likely to have access to cheaper finance. It is thus likely to be operating on a lower average total cost curve. New firms would therefore find it hard to compete and would be likely to lose any price war.

Ownership of, or control over, key inputs or outlets. If a firm governs the supply of vital inputs (say, by owning the sole supplier of some component part), it can deny access to these inputs to potential rivals. On a world scale, the de Beers company has a monopoly in fine diamonds because all diamond producers market their diamonds through de Beers. In the UK, the 'Big Six' energy suppliers are involved in both production/generation and retailing to consumers. As we shall see in Box 5.4 (on page 125), this makes it difficult for smaller suppliers to enter the market, as they have had to buy wholesale from one of the Big Six.

Legal protection. The firm's monopoly position may be protected by patents on essential processes, by copyright, by various forms of licensing (allowing, say, only one firm to operate in a particular area) and by tariffs (i.e. customs duties) and other trade restrictions to keep out foreign competitors. Examples of monopolies protected by patents include most new medicines developed by pharmaceutical companies (e.g. anti-AIDS drugs), Microsoft's Windows operating systems, and agrochemical companies, such as Monsanto, with various genetically modified plant varieties and pesticides.

While patents do help monopolists to maintain their market power, they are also essential in encouraging new product innovation, as R&D is very expensive. Patents allow firms that engage in R&D to reap the rewards of that investment. This is thought by many economists to be important in driving the long-term growth of the economy (see Section 9.6).

> **Definition**
>
> **Network economies** The benefits to consumers of having a network of other people using the same product or service.

Mergers and takeovers. The monopolist can put in a takeover bid for any new entrant. The sheer threat of takeovers may discourage new entrants.

Retained profits and aggressive tactics. An established monopolist is likely to have some retained profits behind it. If a new firm enters the market, the established firm could start a price war, mount a massive advertising campaign, offer attractive after-sales service and introduce new brands to compete with the new entrant. Using its retained profits, it can probably sustain losses until the new entrant leaves the market, returning its monopoly status.

Equilibrium price and output

Since there is, by definition, only one firm in the industry, the firm's demand curve is also the industry demand curve.

Compared with other market structures, demand under monopoly tends to be less elastic at each price. The monopolist can raise its price and consumers have no alternative firm to turn to within the industry. They either pay the higher price, or go without the good altogether.

Unlike the firm under perfect competition, the monopoly firm is thus a 'price maker'. It can choose what price to charge. Nevertheless, it is still constrained by its demand curve. A rise in price will reduce the quantity demanded.

As with firms in other market structures, a monopolist will maximise profit where $MR = MC$. In Figure 5.5 profit is maximised at Q_m. The supernormal profit obtained is shown by the shaded area.

These profits will tend to be larger, the less elastic is the demand curve (and hence the steeper is the MR curve), and thus the bigger is the gap between MR and price (AR). The actual elasticity will depend on whether reasonably close substitutes are available in *other* industries. The demand for a rail service will be much less elastic (and the potential for profit greater) if there is no bus service to the same destination.

Since there are barriers to the entry of new firms, a monopolist's supernormal profits will not be competed away in the long run. The only difference, therefore, between short-run and long-run equilibrium is that in the long run the firm will produce where $MR = long\text{-}run\ MC$.

Monopoly versus perfect competition: which best serves the public interest?

Because it faces a different type of market environment, the monopolist will produce a quite different output and at a quite different price from a perfectly competitive industry. Let us compare the two.

Short-run price and output. Figure 5.6 compares the profit-maximising position for an industry under monopoly with that under perfect competition. Note that we are comparing the monopoly with the whole *industry* under perfect competition. That way we can assume, for sake of comparison, that they both face the same demand curve. We also assume for the moment that they both face the same cost curves.

The monopolist will produce Q_1 at a price of P_1. This is where $MC = MR$. If the same industry were under perfect competition, however, it would produce at Q_2 and P_2 – a higher output and a lower price. But why? The reason is that for each of the firms in the industry – and it is at this level that the decisions are made – marginal revenue is the same as price. Remember that the *firm* under perfect competition faces a perfectly elastic demand (AR) curve, which also equals MR (see Figure 5.1). Thus producing where $MC = MR$ also means producing where $MC = P$. When *all* firms under perfect competition do this, price and quantity in the *industry* will be given by P_2 and Q_2 in Figure 5.6.

In the short run, therefore, it would seem (other things being equal) that perfect competition better serves the consumer's interest than does monopoly.

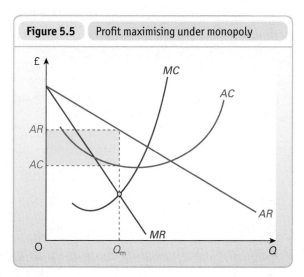

| **Figure 5.5** | Profit maximising under monopoly |

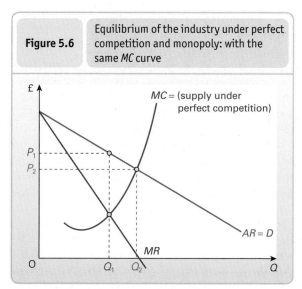

| **Figure 5.6** | Equilibrium of the industry under perfect competition and monopoly: with the same *MC* curve |

Long-run price and output. Under perfect competition, free-dom of entry eliminates supernormal profit and forces firms to produce at the bottom of their *LRAC* curve. The effect, therefore, is to keep long-run prices down. Under monopoly, however, barriers to entry allow profits to remain supernormal in the long run. The monopolist is not forced to operate at the bottom of the *AC* curve. Thus, other things being equal, long-run prices will tend to be higher, and hence output lower, under monopoly.

Pause for thought

If the shares in a monopoly (such as a water company) were very widely distributed among the population, would the shareholders necessarily want the firm to use its monopoly power to make larger profits?

Thus, again, it would *seem* that perfect competition bet-ter serves the consumer's interests. But this assumes that the cost curves are the *same* under both perfect competition and monopoly. Let us, therefore, turn to costs.

Costs under monopoly. The sheer survival of a firm in the long run under perfect competition requires that it uses the most efficient known technique, and develops new techniques wherever possible. The monopolist, however, sheltered by barriers to entry, can still make large profits even if it is not using the most efficient technique. It has less incentive, therefore, to be efficient. For this reason, costs may be *higher* under monopoly (another criticism of monopoly).

On the other hand, the monopoly may be able to achieve substantial economies of scale due to larger plant, centralised administration and the avoidance of unneces-sary duplication (e.g. a monopoly water company would eliminate the need for several sets of rival water mains under each street). If this results in an *MC* curve substan-tially below that of the same industry under perfect compe-tition, the monopoly may even produce a *higher* output at a *lower* price.

Another reason why a monopolist may operate with lower costs is that it can use part of its supernormal profits for research and development and investment. It may not have the same *incentive* to become as efficient as the per-fectly competitive firm which is fighting for survival, but it may have a much greater *ability* to become efficient than has the small firm with limited funds.

Although a monopoly faces no competition in the goods market, it may face an alternative form of compe-tition in financial markets. A monopoly, with potentially low costs, which is currently run inefficiently, is likely to be subject to a takeover bid from another company. This **competition for corporate control** may thus force the monopoly to be efficient in order to prevent being taken over.

Innovation and new products. The promise of supernormal prof-its, protected perhaps by patents, may encourage the develop-ment of new (monopoly) industries producing new products. It is this chance of making monopoly profits that encourages many people to take the risks of going into business.

Potential competition or potential monopoly? The theory of contestable markets

Potential competition

The theory of contestable markets argues that what is cru-cial in determining price and output is not whether an industry is *actually* a monopoly or competitive, but whether there is the real *threat* of competition.

If a monopoly is protected by high barriers to entry – say, it owns all the raw materials – then it will be able to make supernormal profits with no fear of competition.

If, however, another firm *could* take over from it with lit-tle difficulty, it will behave much more like a competitive firm. The threat of competition has a similar effect to actual competition.

As an example, consider a catering company that is given permission by a factory to run its canteen. The cater-ing company has a monopoly over the supply of food to the workers in that factory. If, however, it starts charging high prices or providing a poor service, the factory could offer the running of the canteen to an alternative catering com-pany. This threat may force the original catering company to charge 'reasonable' prices and offer a good service.

Perfectly contestable markets

A market is **perfectly contestable** when the costs of entry and exit by potential rivals are zero, and when such entry can be made very rapidly. In such cases, the moment the possibility of earning supernormal profits occurs, new firms will enter, thus driving profits down to a normal level. The sheer threat of this happening, so the theory goes, will ensure that the firm already in the market will (a) keep its prices down, so that it just makes normal profits, and (b) produce as efficiently as possible, taking advantage of any economies of scale and any new technology. If the existing firm did not do this, entry would take place, and potential competition would become actual competition.

Contestable markets and natural monopolies

So why in such cases are the markets not *actually* perfectly competitive? Why do they remain monopolies?

Definitions

Competition for corporate control The competition for the control of companies through takeovers.

Perfectly contestable market A market where there is free and costless entry and exit.

BOX 5.2   **BREAKING SKY'S MONOPOLY ON LIVE PREMIER LEAGUE FOOTBALL**

The sky is the limit for the English Premier League

The early days of Sky

The structure of English football was changed with the formation of the FA Premier League (EPL) for the 1992–3 football season. One justification for this was the promise of higher payments by TV companies. Live league football had been shown on free-to-air television throughout the 1980s and the clubs were very aware that this was potentially a very lucrative source of revenue.

The first contract to acquire the live and exclusive FA Premier League football broadcasting rights for the United Kingdom and Republic of Ireland was worth £191 million over five seasons. A consequence of Sky being awarded the contract was that live top-flight English league football was no longer available on terrestrial and free-to-air television. Those who wanted to watch live football matches on television had to sign up with Sky, buying both a basic package and the additional Sky sports channels; Sky thus had a monopoly.

Attempts to reduce monopoly power

Both the Premier League and Sky's coverage proved to be hugely successful with viewers and advertisers and this was reflected in the price paid for subsequent packages. The one starting in 1997 cost Sky £670 million for four seasons, while in 2003 BSkyB, as the company was now formally known, paid over £1 billion for exclusive rights for three seasons.

However, over this period the European Commission was expressing increasing concern about the extent of Sky's monopoly. The Commission started legal proceedings in 2002, filing a statement of objections, but was thwarted when the League agreed a new contract with Sky before ironing out an EC-approved deal.

At this time Sky did agree to sub-license up to eight 'top quality Premier League matches' each season to another broadcaster in order to win European approval. The Commission trumpeted this pledge as meaning 'that for the first time in the history of the Premier League free-to-air television will have a realistic opportunity to show live Premier League matches'. These hopes were dashed, however, when no rival broadcaster met the asking price set by Sky.

Auctioning the TV rights to the EPL

In 2005 the European Commission announced that Sky's monopoly would be broken. From 2007, the next set of rights, for a three-season period, would be sold in six 'balanced' packages of 23 games per season, with no broadcaster allowed more than five packages. The Commission claimed the deal would give fans 'greater choice and better value'.

However, concern was expressed about the impact on incomes of the Premiership clubs. While some commentators expected a more competitive process to result in roughly the same total income as was paid by Sky in 2003 (just over £1 billion), others suggested that Sky had originally paid a premium for the guarantee that it would be the sole broadcaster and that the introduction of competitive bidding would result in a fall in the revenues paid to clubs.

In May 2006 the bidding process for the rights for 2007–10 was completed. Sky won four of the six available packages and showed 92 live Premiership matches per season, while Setanta, an Irish-based satellite broadcaster, won the remaining two packages and showed 46 games per season. Between them, they paid £1.7 billion.

The same process was undertaken in 2009 for the 2010–11 to 2013–14 seasons. This time the rights fetched just short of £1.8 billion.

But, this was just the start of the riches for the EPL. Auctions took place in 2012 (2013–14 to 2016–17) and in 2015 (2017–18 to 2020–21). By now Setanta had folded, with BT entering this market in 2012.

Despite the opening up of 'competition', the total amount paid under the 'non-monopoly' schemes rocketed. Extraordinary sums of money were now being brought into the 'beautiful game'. In 2012, the agreed payment from BT and Sky combined was over £3 billion for three seasons, while in 2015 it had risen to £5.1 billion. Therefore, both auctions saw the payments for the rights rise by around 70 per cent.

The most likely reason has to do with economies of scale and the size of the market. To operate on a minimum efficient scale, the firm may have to be so large relative to the market that there is only room for one such firm in the industry. If a new firm does come into the market, then one or other of the two firms will not survive the competition. The market is simply not big enough for both of them.

If, however, there are no entry or exit costs, new firms will be perfectly willing to enter even though there is only room for one firm, provided they believe that they are more efficient than the existing firm. The existing firm, knowing this, will be forced to produce as efficiently as possible and with only normal profit.

The importance of costless exit

Setting up in a new business usually involves large expenditures on plant and machinery. Once this money has been committed, it becomes fixed costs. If these fixed costs are no higher than those of the existing firm, then the new firm could win the battle. But, of course, there is always the risk that it might lose.

But does losing the battle really matter? Can the firm not simply move to another market?

It does matter if there are substantial costs of exit. This will be the case if the capital equipment cannot be transferred to other uses – for example, a new blast furnace constructed by a new rival steel company. In this case, these fixed costs are known as **sunk costs**. The losing firm is left

Definition
Sunk costs Costs that cannot be recouped (e.g. by transferring assets to other uses).

The 2015 auction process

The 2015 auction saw Sky and BT pay £5.136 billion to broadcast 168 live Premier League matches. So how did the auction process work?

The broadcast rights for these matches were split into seven different packages, labelled A through to G, and placed in seven different auctions. Interested companies were invited to make an offer for any of the packages. However, these were 'sealed-bid' auctions; when broadcasters made their bid, they knew neither whether other firms had also made a bid or the size of any other bids. Another constraint was that no one firm was allowed to win more than five of the auctions. When the auction finishes the EPL only releases information about the winning offers.

Some of the packages are worth more than others to the broadcasters. The first five packages (A–E) each contain the rights for 28 games per season, while the other two packages (F and G) contain the rights for 14 matches. In some of the packages all of the games kick off at the same time and on the same day. For example, all 28 games in package 'A' kick off at 12.30 p.m. on a Saturday. Others contain more of a mixture. Some of the games in package E take place on a Monday evening, while others take place on a Friday evening. Given the potential advertising revenue and number of viewers, the most valuable package is D, which has 28 games that kick off at 4.00 p.m. on a Sunday.

Another factor that influences the value of a package is the number of 'first picks'. In any given week, more than one broadcaster might want to screen the same match. To overcome this problem, each package is allocated a number of first, second, third, fourth and fifth 'picks'. For example, package D came with 18 first and 10 fourth round picks. There is also a maximum and a minimum limit on the number of times games including a specific team can be broadcast.

Outcome of the 2015 auction

Sky won the auctions for packages A, C, D, E and G for a price of £4.17 billion. It would pay £1.392 billion to broadcast 126 live games per season, an average payment of £11.047 million per game. In the previous deal it paid £760 million for the rights to broadcast 116 live games per season, which is an average payment of £6.552 million per game. The new deal represented a cost increase of 68.6 per cent per game. However, the number of first picks Sky has secured in the new deal increases from 20 to 26.

BT won the auctions for packages B and F for a price of £960 million. It would pay £320 million for the rights to broadcast 42 live games per season – an average payment of £7.619 million per game. In the previous deal it paid £246 million per year for the rights to broadcast 38 live games per season, which is an average payment of £6.474 million per game. The new deal represents an increase in costs of 17.7 per cent per game for BT.

Sky stated that it will cover the increase in the price it has paid for the rights with efficiency savings. However, many observers believe that it will ultimately result in significant increases in the subscription rates for Sky Sports. The impact of the deal on Sky's profit may well depend on the willingness of its customers to pay higher prices.

As for BT, the 2015 auction marked a continuation of its strategy to win over customers from Sky by bundling its TV offering with highly profitable broadband and phone services. It conducted a fairly aggressive pricing strategy, undercutting Sky and offering live football 'free' to those taking phone and broadband packages. This helps explain the increasing prices broadcasters are willing to pay to screen live EPL matches.

1. *What other examples of monopoly power exist in football? Could this power be reduced?*
2. *Assess the impact of the pay broadcasters' emergence over the past 20 years on (a) football fans, (b) other viewers.*
3. *What are the challenges that would face another telecommunications company wishing to enter the market?*

---

with capital equipment it cannot use. The firm may therefore be put off entering in the first place. The market is not perfectly contestable, and the established firm can make supernormal profit.

If, however, the capital equipment can be transferred, the exit costs will be zero (or at least very low), and new firms will be more willing to take the risks of entry. For example, a rival coach company may open up a service on a route previously operated by only one company, and where there is still only room for one operator. If the new firm loses the resulting battle, it can still use the coaches it has purchased. It simply uses them for a different route. The cost of the coaches is not a sunk cost.

Costless exit, therefore, encourages firms to enter an industry, knowing that, if unsuccessful, they can always transfer their capital elsewhere.

The lower the exit costs, the more contestable the market. This implies that firms already established in other similar markets may provide more effective competition against monopolists, since they can simply transfer capital from one market to another. For example, studies of airlines in the USA show that entry to a particular route may be much easier for an established airline, which can simply transfer aircraft from one route to another.

Contestability and the consumer's interests

The more contestable the market, the more will a monopoly be forced to act like a firm under perfect competition. If, therefore, a monopoly operates in a perfectly contestable market, it might bring the 'best of both worlds' for the consumer. Not only will it be able to

KI 18
p 108

achieve low costs through economies of scale, but also the potential competition will keep profits and hence prices down.

Pause for thought

Think of two examples of highly contestable monopolies (or oligopolies). How well is the consumer's interest served?

Recap

1. A monopoly is where there is only one firm in an industry. In practice, it is difficult to determine where a monopoly exists because it depends on how narrowly an industry is defined.

2. Barriers to the entry of new firms will normally be necessary to protect a monopoly from competition. Such barriers include economies of scale (making the firm a natural monopoly or at least giving it a cost advantage over new (small) competitors), control over supplies of inputs or over outlets, patents or copyright, and tactics to eliminate competition (such as takeovers or aggressive advertising).

3. Profits for the monopolist will be maximised (as for other firms) where $MC = MR$.

4. If demand and cost curves are the same in a monopoly and a perfectly competitive industry, the monopoly will produce a lower output and at a higher price than the perfectly competitive industry.

5. On the other hand, any economies of scale will, in part, be passed on to consumers in lower prices, and the monopolist's high profits may be used for research and development and investment, which in turn may lead to better products at possibly lower prices.

6. Potential competition may be as important as actual competition in determining a firm's price and output strategy.

7. The threat of this competition is greater, the lower are the entry and exit costs to and from the industry. If the entry and exit costs are zero, the market is said to be perfectly contestable. Under such circumstances an existing monopolist will be forced to keep its profits down to the normal level if it is to resist entry of new firms. Exit costs will be lower, the lower are the sunk costs of the firm.

5.4 MONOPOLISTIC COMPETITION

What happens if there are quite a lot of firms competing, but each firm tries to attract us to its particular product or service?

Very few markets in practice can be classified as perfectly competitive or as a pure monopoly. The vast majority of firms do compete with other firms, often quite aggressively, and yet they are not price takers: they do have some degree of market power. Most markets, therefore, lie between the two extremes of monopoly and perfect competition, in the realm of 'imperfect competition'. As we saw in Section 5.1, there are two types of imperfect competition: namely, monopolistic competition and oligopoly.

Monopolistic competition is nearer to the competitive end of the spectrum. It can best be understood as a situation where there are a lot of firms competing but where each firm does nevertheless have some degree of market power (hence the term 'monopolistic' competition): each firm has some discretion as to what price to charge for its products.

Assumptions

- There are *quite a large number of firms*. As a result each firm has only a small share of the market, and therefore its actions are unlikely to affect its rivals to any great extent. What this means is that each firm in making its decisions does not have to worry how its rivals will react.

It assumes that what its rivals choose to do will *not* be influenced by what it does.

This is known as the assumption of **independence**. (As we shall see later, this is not the case under oligopoly. There we assume that firms believe that their decisions *do* affect their rivals, and that their rivals' decisions will affect them. Under oligopoly we assume that firms are *inter*dependent.)

- There is *freedom of entry* of new firms into the industry. If any firm wants to set up in business in this market, it is free to do so.

In these two respects, therefore, monopolistic competition is like perfect competition.

- Unlike perfect competition, however, each firm produces a product or provides a service in some way different from its rivals. As a result it can raise its price

Definition

Independence (of firms in a market) Where the decisions of one firm in a market will not have any significant effect on the demand curves of its rivals.

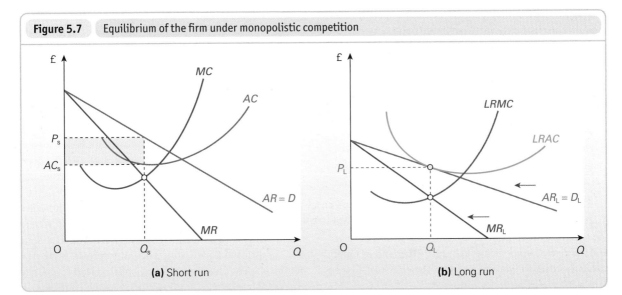

Figure 5.7 Equilibrium of the firm under monopolistic competition

(a) Short run

(b) Long run

without losing all its customers. Thus its demand curve is downward sloping, albeit relatively elastic given the large number of competitors to which customers can turn. This is known as the assumption of **product differentiation**.

Petrol stations, restaurants, hairdressers and builders are all examples of monopolistic competition.

A typical feature of monopolistic competition is that, although there are many firms in the industry, there is only one firm in a particular location. This applies particularly in retailing. There may be several newsagents in a town, but only one in a particular street. In a sense, therefore, it has a local monopoly. People may be prepared to pay higher prices there to avoid having to go elsewhere.

> **Pause for thought**
>
> *An example of monopolistic competition is provided by fast-food restaurants. What other businesses are in competition with fast-food restaurants and what determines the closeness of this competition?*

Equilibrium of the firm

Short run

As with other market structures, profits are maximised at the output where $MC = MR$. The diagram is the same as for the monopolist, except that the AR and MR curves are more elastic. This is illustrated in Figure 5.7(a). As with perfect competition, it is possible for the monopolistically competitive firm to make supernormal profit in the short run. This is shown as the shaded area.

Just how much profit the firm will make in the short run depends on the strength of demand: the position and elasticity of the demand curve. The further to the right the demand curve is relative to the average cost curve, and the less elastic the demand curve is, the greater will be the firm's short-run profit. Thus a firm whose product is considerably differentiated from its rivals may be able to earn considerable short-run profits.

> **Pause for thought**
>
> *Which of these two items is a petrol station more likely to sell at a discount: (a) oil; (b) sweets? Why?*

Long run

If typical firms are earning supernormal profit, new firms will enter the industry in the long run. As new firms enter, they will take some of the customers away from the established firms. The demand for the established firms' product will therefore fall. Their demand (AR) curve will shift to the left, and will continue doing so as long as supernormal profits remain and thus new firms continue entering.

Long-run equilibrium will be reached when only normal profits remain: when there is no further incentive for new firms to enter. This is illustrated in Figure 5.7(b). The firm's demand curve settles at D_L, where it just touches the firm's *LRAC* curve. Output will be Q_L: where $AR_L = LRAC$. (At any other output, *LRAC* is greater than AR and thus less than normal profit would be made.)

KI 6
p 20

TC 2
p 11

TC 8
p 59

> **Definition**
>
> **Product differentiation** Where one firm's product is sufficiently different from its rivals' to allow it to raise the price of the product without customers all switching to the rivals' products. A situation where a firm faces a downward-sloping demand curve.

There is a crucial difference between monopolistic competition and perfect competition in the transition from the short run to the long-run, even though the long-run equilibrium of normal profits for the firm is the same in both market structures:

- Under perfect competition, when new firms enter (or leave) the market, it is the industry supply curve that shifts, which changes the market price and leaves just normal profits.
- Under monopolistic competition, however, the entry of new firms is reflected by shifting an established firm's demand curve inwards and this eliminates the supernormal profits.

As all firms under monopolistic competition are producing a slightly differentiated product, each firm is different and hence we cannot create an industry demand or supply curve. Instead, we have to focus on the effect on a given firm when new firms enter the market.

Non-price competition

One of the biggest problems with the simple model in Figure 5.7 is that it concentrates on price and output decisions. In practice, the profit-maximising firm under monopolistic competition will also need to decide the exact variety of product to produce and how much to spend on advertising it. This will lead the firm to take part in **non-price competition.**

Non-price competition involves two major elements: product development and advertising.

The major aims of *product development* are to produce a product that will sell well (i.e. one in high or potentially high demand) and one that is different from rivals' products (i.e. has a relatively inelastic demand owing to lack of close substitutes). For shops or other firms providing a service, 'product development' takes the form of attempting to provide a service which is better than, or at least different from, that of rivals: personal service, late opening, certain lines stocked, and so on.

The major aim of *advertising* is to sell the product. This can be achieved not only by informing people of the product's existence and availability, but also by trying to persuade them to purchase it. Like product development, successful advertising will both increase demand and make the firm's demand curve less elastic, since it stresses the specific characteristics of this firm's product over its rivals' (see Box 3.2).

Product development and advertising not only increase a firm's demand and hence revenue, but also involve increased costs. So how much should a firm advertise, say to maximise profits?

For any given price and product, the optimal amount of advertising is where the revenue from *additional* advertising (MR_A) is equal to its cost (MC_A). As long as $MR_A > MC_A$, additional advertising will add to profit. But extra amounts spent on advertising are likely to lead to smaller and smaller increases in sales. Thus MR_A falls, until $MR_A = MC_A$. At that point no further profit can be made. It is at a maximum.

> **Pause for thought**
>
> *Why will additional advertising lead to smaller and smaller increases in sales?*

Several problems arise with this analysis. These include:

- The effect of product development and advertising on demand will be difficult for a firm to forecast.
- Product development can affect a firm's future costs. For example, it may impact on production costs or 'aftercare' costs, such as servicing and repair.
- Product development and advertising are likely to have different effects at different prices. Profit maximisation, therefore, will involve the more complex choice of the optimum combination of price, type of product, and level and variety of advertising.

Monopolistic competition and the public interest

Comparison with perfect competition
It is often argued that monopolistic competition leads to a less efficient allocation of resources than perfect competition.

Figure 5.8 compares the long-run equilibrium positions for two firms. One firm is under perfect competition and

> **Definition**
>
> **Non-price competition** Competition in terms of product promotion (advertising, packaging, etc.) or product development.

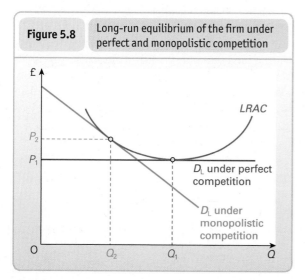

| **Figure 5.8** | Long-run equilibrium of the firm under perfect and monopolistic competition |

thus faces a horizontal demand curve. It will produce an output of Q_1 at a price of P_1. The other is under monopolistic competition and thus faces a downward-sloping demand curve. It will produce the lower output of Q_2 at the higher price of P_2. A crucial assumption here is that a firm would have the *same* long-run average cost (*LRAC*) curve in both cases. Given this assumption, monopolistic competition has the following disadvantages:

- Less will be sold and at a higher price.
- Firms will not be producing at the least-cost point.

By producing more, firms would move to a lower point on their *LRAC* curve. Thus firms under monopolistic competition are said to have **excess capacity**. In Figure 5.8 this excess capacity is shown as $Q_1 - Q_2$. In other words, monopolistic competition is typified by quite a large number of firms (e.g. petrol stations), all operating at less than optimum output, and thus being forced to charge a price above that which they could charge if they had a bigger turnover.

So how does this affect the consumer? Although the firm under monopolistic competition may charge a higher price than under perfect competition, the difference may be very small. Although the firm's demand curve is downward sloping, it is still likely to be highly elastic due to the large number of substitutes. Furthermore, the consumer may benefit from monopolistic competition by having a greater variety of products to choose from. Each firm may satisfy some particular requirement of particular consumers.

Comparison with monopoly

The arguments are very similar here to those when comparing perfect competition and monopoly.

On the one hand, freedom of entry for new firms and hence the lack of long-run supernormal profits under monopolistic competition are likely to help keep prices down for the consumer and encourage cost saving. On the other hand, monopolies are likely to achieve greater economies of scale and have more funds for investment and research and development.

Recap

1. Monopolistic competition occurs where there is free entry to the industry and quite a large number of firms operating independently of each other, but where each firm has some market power as a result of producing differentiated products or services.

2. In the short run, firms can make supernormal profits. In the long run, however, freedom of entry will drive profits down to the normal level. The long-run equilibrium of the firm is where the (downward-sloping) demand curve just touches the long-run average cost curve.

3. The long-run equilibrium is one of excess capacity. Given that the demand curve is downward sloping, the point where it just touches the *LRAC* curve will not be at the bottom of the *LRAC* curve. Increased production would thus be possible at *lower* average cost.

4. Firms under monopolistic competition may engage in non-price competition, in the forms of product development and advertising, in order to maintain an advantage over their rivals.

5. Monopolistically competitive firms, because of excess capacity, may have higher costs, and thus higher prices, than perfectly competitive firms, but consumers may gain from a greater diversity of products.

6. Monopolistically competitive firms may have fewer economies of scale than monopolies and conduct less research and development, but the competition may keep prices lower than under monopoly. Whether there will be more or less choice for the consumer is debatable.

5.5 OLIGOPOLY

What happens if there are just a few firms that dominate the market? Will they compete or get together?

Oligopoly occurs when just a few firms between them share a large proportion of the industry. Some of the best-known companies are oligopolists, including Ford, Coca-Cola, BP and Nintendo. On the Sloman News Site, you will find many blogs written about different oligopolies and it is both useful and interesting to compare the outcomes. Some examples of powerful oligopolies include toothbrush manufacturers, supermarkets and energy.

There are, however, significant differences in the structure of industries under oligopoly and similarly significant differences in the behaviour of firms. The firms may produce a virtually identical product (e.g. metals, chemicals, sugar, petrol). Most oligopolists, however, produce differentiated products (e.g. cars, toiletries, soft drinks, electrical appliances). Much of the competition between such oligopolists is in terms of the marketing of their particular brand.

Definition

Excess capacity (under monopolistic competition) In the long run firms under monopolistic competition will produce at an output below their minimum-cost point.

The two key features of oligopoly

Despite the differences between oligopolies, there are two crucial features that distinguish oligopoly from other market structures.

Barriers to entry

Unlike firms under monopolistic competition, there are various barriers to the entry of new firms. These are similar to those under monopoly (see pages 108–10). The size of the barriers, however, will vary from industry to industry. In some cases entry is relatively easy, whereas in others it is virtually impossible, perhaps due to patent protection or prohibitive research and development costs.

Interdependence of the firms

Because there are only a few firms under oligopoly, each firm has to take account of the others. This means that they are mutually dependent: they are **interdependent**. Each firm is affected by its rivals' actions. If a firm changes the price or specification of its product, for example, or the amount of its advertising, the sales of its rivals will be affected. The rivals may then respond by changing their price, specification or advertising.

No firm can therefore afford to ignore the actions and reactions of other firms in the industry. It is this feature that differentiates oligopolies from the other market structures. It is illustrated in the blog post *Pizza price wars*.

> **KEY IDEA 19**
> *People often think and behave strategically.* How you think others will respond to your actions is likely to influence your own behaviour. Firms, for example, when considering a price or product change will often take into account the likely reactions of their rivals.

It is impossible, therefore, to predict the effect on a firm's sales of, say, a change in the price of its product without first making some assumption about the reactions of other firms. Different assumptions will yield different predictions. For this reason there is no single generally accepted theory of oligopoly. Firms may react differently and unpredictably.

Competition and collusion

Oligopolists are pulled in two different directions:

- The interdependence of firms may make them wish to *collude* with each other. If they can club together and act as if they were a monopoly, they could jointly maximise industry profits.
- On the other hand, they will be tempted to *compete* with their rivals to gain a bigger share of industry profits for themselves.

These two policies are incompatible. The more fiercely firms compete to gain a bigger share of industry profits, the smaller these industry profits will become! For example, price competition drives down the average industry price, while competition through advertising raises industry costs. Either way, industry profits fall.

Sometimes firms will collude; sometimes they will not. The following sections examine first **collusive oligopoly** (both open and tacit), and then **non-collusive oligopoly**.

Collusive oligopoly

When firms under oligopoly engage in collusion, they may agree on prices, market share, advertising expenditure, etc. Such collusion reduces the uncertainty they face. It reduces the fear of engaging in competitive price cutting or retaliatory advertising, both of which could reduce total industry profits and probably each individual firm's profit.

KI 17 p 101

A cartel

A formal collusive agreement is called a **cartel**. The cartel will maximise profits if it acts like a monopoly, with members behaving as if they were a single firm. This is illustrated in Figure 5.9.

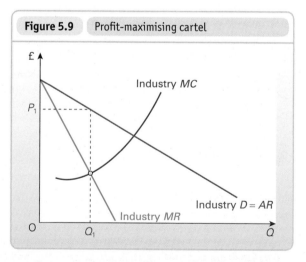

| **Figure 5.9** | Profit-maximising cartel |

TC 2
p 11 The total market demand curve is shown with the corresponding market *MR* curve. The cartel's *MC* curve is the *horizontal* sum of the *MC* curves of its members (since we are adding the *output* of each of the cartel members at each level of marginal cost). Profits are maximised at Q_1 where $MC = MR$. The cartel must therefore set a price of P_1 (at which Q_1 will be demanded).

Having agreed on the cartel price, the members may then compete against each other using *non-price competition*, to gain as big a share of resulting sales (Q_1) as they can.

Alternatively, the cartel members may somehow agree to divide the market between them. Each member would be given a **quota**. The sum of all the quotas must add up to Q_1. If the quotas exceeded Q_1, either there would be output unsold if price remained fixed at P_1, or the price would fall.

But if quotas are to be set by the cartel, how will it decide the level of each individual member's quota? The most likely method is for the cartel to divide the market between the members according to their current market share. That is the solution most likely to be accepted as 'fair'.

Pause for thought

If this 'fair' solution were adopted, what effect would it have on the industry MC curve in Figure 5.9?

In many countries, including the UK, cartels are illegal. They are seen by the government as a means of driving up prices and profits, and thereby as being against the public interest. Where open collusion is illegal, firms may simply break the law, or get round it. For example, in February 2007, the European Commission imposed a record fine of €992 million on four lift and escalator manufacturers for operating a price-fixing cartel (see Case Study 5.18 in MyEconLab).

Alternatively, firms may stay within the law, but still *tacitly* collude by watching each other's prices and keeping theirs
KI 19 similar. Firms may tacitly 'agree' to avoid price wars or
p 118 aggressive advertising campaigns.

Tacit collusion

One form of **tacit collusion** is where firms keep to the price that is set by an established leader. The leader may be the largest firm: the firm that dominates the industry. This is known as **dominant firm price leadership**. Alternatively, the price leader may simply be the one that has proved to be the most reliable to follow: the one that is the best barometer of market conditions. This is known as **barometric firm price leadership**.

Dominant firm price leadership. This is a 'sequential game', where one firm (the leader) moves first and then the followers, having observed the leader's choice of price, move second. We will discuss sequential games in more detail in Section 5.6.

But, how does the leader set the price? This depends on the assumptions it makes about its rivals' reactions to its price changes. If it assumes that rivals will simply follow it by making exactly the same percentage price changes up or down, then a simple model can be constructed. This is illustrated in Figure 5.10. The leader assumes that it will maintain a constant market share (say, 50 per cent).

The leader will maximise profits where its marginal revenue is equal to its marginal cost. It knows its current position on its demand curve (say, point *a*). It then estimates how responsive its demand will be to industry-wide price changes and thus constructs its demand and *MR* curves on that basis. It then chooses to produce Q_L at a price of P_L: at point *l* on its demand curve (where $MC = MR$). Other firms then follow that price. Total market demand will be Q_T, with followers supplying that portion of the market not supplied by the leader: namely, $Q_T - Q_L$.

There is one problem with this model. That is, the assumption that the followers will want to maintain a constant market share. It is possible that if the leader raises its price, the followers may want to supply more at this new price. On the other hand, the followers may decide merely to maintain their market share for fear of invoking

Figure 5.10	A price leader aiming to maximise profits for a given market share

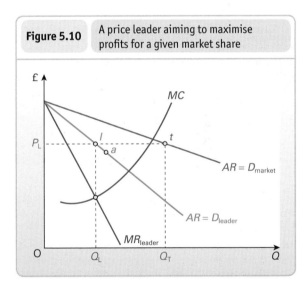

BOX 5.3   OPEC – THE RISE AND FALL AND RISE AGAIN OF A CARTEL

The history of the world's most famous cartel

OPEC is probably the best known of all cartels. It was set up in 1960 by the five major oil-exporting countries: Saudi Arabia, Iran, Iraq, Kuwait and Venezuela. Today it has 12 members. OPEC's stated objectives are:

- The co-ordination and unification of the petroleum policies of member countries.
- The stabilisation of oil markets to secure an efficient, economic and regular supply of petroleum to consumers, a steady income to producers and a fair return on capital for those investing in the petroleum industry.

The years leading up to 1960 had seen the oil-producing countries increasingly in conflict with the international oil companies, which extracted oil under 'concessionary agreement'. Under this scheme, oil companies were given the right to extract oil in return for royalties. This meant that the oil-producing countries had little say over output and price levels.

The early years

Despite the formation of OPEC in 1960, it was not until 1973 that control of oil production was effectively transferred from the oil companies to the oil countries, with OPEC making the decisions on how much oil to produce and thereby determining its oil revenue. By this time OPEC consisted of 13 members.

OPEC's pricing policy over the 1970s consisted of setting a market price for Saudi Arabian crude (the market leader), and leaving other OPEC members to set their prices in line with this: a form of dominant 'firm' price leadership.

As long as demand remained buoyant, and was price inelastic, this policy allowed large price increases with consequent large revenue increases. In 1973–4, after the Arab–Israeli War, OPEC raised the price of oil from around $3 per barrel to over $12. The price was kept at roughly this level until 1979. And yet the sales of oil did not fall significantly.

 Illustrate what was happening here on a demand and supply diagram. Remember that demand was highly inelastic and was increasing over time.

After 1979, however, following a further increase in the price of oil from around $15 to $40 per barrel, demand did fall. This was largely due to the recession of the early 1980s (although this recession was in turn largely caused by governments' responses to the oil price increases).

The use of quotas

Faced by declining demand, OPEC after 1982 agreed to limit output and allocate production quotas in an attempt to keep the price up. A production ceiling of 16 million barrels per day was agreed in 1984.

The cartel was beginning to break down, however, due to the following:

- The world recession and the resulting fall in the demand for oil.
- Growing output from non-OPEC members.
- 'Cheating' by some OPEC members who exceeded their quota limits.

Oil prices

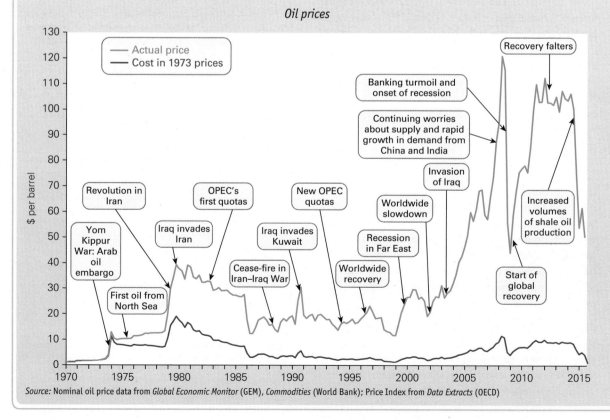

Source: Nominal oil price data from *Global Economic Monitor* (GEM), *Commodities* (World Bank); Price Index from *Data Extracts* (OECD)

With a glut of oil, OPEC could no longer maintain the price. The 'spot' price of oil (the day-to-day trading price of oil on the open market) was falling, as the graph shows.

The trend of lower oil prices was reversed in the late 1980s. With the world economy booming, the demand for oil rose and along with it the price. Then in 1990 Iraq invaded Kuwait and the Gulf War ensued. With the cutting-off of supplies from Kuwait and Iraq, the supply of oil fell and there was a sharp rise in its price.

But with the ending of the war and the recession of the early 1990s, the price rapidly fell again and only recovered slowly as the world economy started expanding once more.

On the demand side, the development of energy-saving technology plus increases in fuel taxes led to a relatively slow growth in consumption. On the supply side, the growing proportion of output supplied by non-OPEC members, plus the adoption in 1994 of a relatively high OPEC production ceiling of 24½ million barrels per day, meant that supply more than kept pace with demand.

The situation for OPEC deteriorated further in the late 1990s, following the recession in the Far East. Oil demand fell by some 2 million barrels per day. By early 1999, the price had fallen to around $10 per barrel – a mere $1.40 in 1973 prices! In response, OPEC members agreed to cut production by 4.3 million barrels per day. The objective was to push the price back up to around $18–20 per barrel.

But with the Asian economy recovering and the world generally experiencing more rapid economic growth, the price rose rapidly and soon overshot the $20 mark. By early 2000 it had reached $30: a tripling in price in just 12 months. With the world economy then slowing down, however, the price rapidly fell back, reaching $18 in November 2001.

However, in late 2001 the relationship between OPEC and non-OPEC oil producers changed. The 10 members of the OPEC cartel decided to cut production by 1.5 million barrels a day. This followed an agreement with five of the major oil producers outside of the cartel to reduce their output too, the aim being to push oil prices upwards and then stabilise them at around $25 per barrel.

The alliance between OPEC and non-OPEC oil producers is the first such instance of its kind in the oil industry. As a result, it seemed that OPEC might now once again be able to control the market for oil.

The price surge of 2003–8...

But how successfully could this alliance cope with crisis? With worries over an impending war with Iraq and a strike in Venezuela, the oil price rose again in late 2002, passing the $30 mark in early 2003. OPEC claimed that it could maintain supply and keep prices from surging even with an Iraq war, but with prices rising rapidly above $30, many doubted that it could.

In 2004 the situation worsened with supply concerns related to the situation in Iraq, Saudi Arabia, Russia and Nigeria, and the oil price rose to over $50 in October 2004. OPEC tried to relax the quotas, but found it difficult to adjust supply sufficiently quickly to make any real difference to the price.

From 2006, oil prices increased more sharply than they ever had before and, for the first time in years, the real price of oil exceeded that seen in the 1970s. The major cause of the increases was very substantial increases in demand, particularly from India and China, coupled with continuing concerns about supply. The implications of the sharp price increases were substantial: inflationary pressures built up across the world, while the income of OPEC nations doubled in the first half of 2008.

By July 2008 the price had reached $147. Some analysts were predicting a price of over $200 per barrel by the end of the year.

... and then the fall

But then, with the growing banking turmoil and fears of a recession, the price began to fall, and rapidly so, reaching $34 by the end of the year – less than a quarter of the price just five months previously. It then hovered around the $40 mark in the first quarter of 2009. While this was good news for the consumer, it was potentially damaging for investment in oil exploration and development and also for investment in alternative energy supplies.

OPEC responded to the falling price by announcing cuts in production, totalling some 14 per cent between August 2008 and January 2009. But with OPEC producing less than a third of global oil output, this represented less than 5 per cent of global production. Nevertheless, as global demand recovered, so oil prices rose again from 2009 peaking in March 2012 at $118.

The fragility of economic growth, especially in Europe where many governments were 'tightening their belts' in the face of growing concerns over levels of borrowing, began to put a brake on demand. The price of oil was to average close to $104 over 2013.

However, as we saw in Box 2.4, prices were to fall steeply from summer 2014. This was largely a result of the increased output in non-OPEC countries of non-conventional deposits, such as in shale formations. Consequently, OPEC's market share has waned.

OPEC responded to the increased supply, not by cutting output, but by announcing that it would retain output at current levels even if oil prices dropped as low as $40. What it was relying on was the fact that production from shale oil wells, although often involving low marginal costs, lasts only two or three years. Investment in new shale oil wells, by contrast, is often relatively expensive. By OPEC maintaining production, it was hoping to use its remaining market power to reduce supply of competitors over the medium to long term (see the blog post *A crude indicator of the economy (Part 2)* on the Sloman Economics News Site).

The recent history of OPEC illustrates the difficulty of using supply quotas to achieve a particular price. With demand being price inelastic but income elastic (responsive to changes in world income, such as rising demand from China), and with considerable speculative movements in demand, the equilibrium price for a given supply quota can fluctuate wildly.

What conditions facilitate the formation of a cartel? Which of these conditions were to be found in the oil market in (a) the early 1970s; (b) the mid-1980s; (c) the mid-2000s?

retaliation from the leader, in the form of price cuts or an aggressive advertising campaign.

Barometric firm price leadership. A similar exercise can be conducted by a barometric firm. Although the firm is not dominating the industry, its price will be followed by the others. It merely tries to estimate its demand and *MR* curves – assuming, again, a constant market share – and then produces where $MR = MC$ and sets price accordingly.

In practice, which firm is taken as the barometer may frequently change. Whether we are talking about oil companies, car producers or banks, any firm may take the initiative in raising prices. If the other firms are merely waiting for someone to take the lead – say, because costs have risen – they will all quickly follow suit. For example, if one of the bigger building societies or banks raises its mortgage rates by 1 per cent, this is likely to stimulate the others to follow suit.

Other forms of tacit collusion. An alternative to having an established leader is for there to be an established set of simple 'rules of thumb' that everyone follows.

One such example is **average cost pricing**. Here producers, instead of equating *MC* and *MR*, simply add a certain percentage for profit on top of average costs. Thus, if average costs rise by 10 per cent, prices will automatically be raised by 10 per cent. This is a particularly useful rule of thumb in times of inflation, when all firms will be experiencing similar cost increases.

Pause for thought

If a firm has a typically shaped average cost curve and sets prices 10 per cent above average cost, what will its supply curve look like?

Another rule of thumb is to have certain **price benchmarks**. Thus clothes may sell for £19.99, £24.99 or £49.99 (but not £20.01 or £25.01, etc.). If costs rise, then firms simply raise their price to the next benchmark, knowing that other firms will do the same.

Rules of thumb can also be applied to advertising (e.g. you do not criticise other firms' products, only praise your own); or to the design of the product (e.g. lighting manufacturers tacitly agreeing not to bring out an everlasting light bulb).

Factors favouring collusion

Collusion between firms, whether formal or tacit, is more likely when firms can clearly identify with each other or some leader and when they trust each other not to break agreements. It is easier for firms to collude if the following conditions apply:

- There are only very few firms, all well known to each other.
- They are open with each other about costs and production methods.

- They have similar production methods and average costs, and are thus likely to want to change prices at the same time and by the same percentage.
- They produce similar products and can thus more easily reach agreements on price.
- There is a dominant firm.
- There are significant barriers to entry and thus there is little fear of disruption by new firms.
- The market is stable. If industry demand or production costs fluctuate wildly, it will be difficult to make agreements, partly due to difficulties in predicting and partly because agreements may frequently have to be amended. There is a particular problem in a declining market where firms may be tempted to undercut each other's price in order to maintain their sales.
- There are no government measures to curb collusion.

Non-collusive oligopoly: the breakdown of collusion

In some oligopolies, there may be only a few (if any) factors favouring collusion. In such cases, the likelihood of price competition is greater.

Even if there is collusion, there will always be the temptation for individual oligopolists to 'cheat', by cutting prices or by selling more than their allotted quota. The danger, of course, is that this would invite retaliation from the other members of the cartel, with a resulting price war. Price would then fall and the cartel could well break up in disarray.

When considering whether to break a collusive agreement, even if only a tacit one, a firm will ask: (1) 'How much can we get away with without inviting retaliation?' and (2) 'If a price war does result, will we be the winners? Will we succeed in driving some or all of our rivals out of business and yet survive ourselves, and thereby gain greater market power?'

The position of rival firms, therefore, is rather like that of generals of opposing armies or the players in a game. It is a question of choosing the appropriate *strategy*: the strategy that will best succeed in outwitting your opponents. The strategy a firm adopts will, of course, be concerned not just with price but also with advertising and product development.

Definitions

Average cost pricing Where a firm sets its price by adding a certain percentage for (average) profit on top of average cost.

Price benchmark A price that is typically used. Firms, when raising a price, will usually raise it from one benchmark to another.

Non-collusive oligopoly: assumptions about rivals' behaviour

Even though oligopolists might not collude, they will still need to take account of rivals' likely behaviour when deciding their own strategy. In doing so they will probably look at rivals' past behaviour and make assumptions based on it. There are three well-known models, each based on a different set of assumptions.

Assumption that rivals produce a given quantity: the Cournot model

One assumption is that rivals will produce a particular *quantity*. This is most likely when the market is stable and the rivals have been producing a relatively constant quantity for some time. The task, then, for the individual oligopolist is to decide its own price and quantity given the presumed output of its competitors.

The earliest model based on this assumption was developed by the French economist Augustin Cournot in 1838. The **Cournot model** (which is developed in Web Appendix 5.2) takes the simple case of just two firms (a **duopoly**) producing an identical product: e.g., two electricity generating companies supplying the whole country.

This is illustrated in Figure 5.11 which shows the profit-maximising price and output for Firm A. The total market demand curve is shown as D_M. Assume that Firm A believes that its rival, Firm B, will produce Q_{B1} units. Thus Firm A perceives its own demand curve (D_{A1}) to be Q_{B1} units less than total market demand. In other words, the horizontal gap between D_M and D_{A1} is Q_{B1} units. Given its perceived demand curve of D_{A1}, its marginal revenue curve will be MR_{A1} and the profit-maximising output will be Q_{A1}, where $MR_{A1} = MC_A$. The profit-maximising price will be P_{A1}.

If Firm A believed that Firm B would produce *more* than Q_{B1}, its perceived demand and *MR* curves would be further to the left and the profit-maximising quantity and price would both be lower.

At the same time as Firm A makes an assumption about Firm B's output, Firm B will also be making an assumption about how much it thinks Firm A will produce. This is therefore a 'simultaneous game', as both firms are making their decisions at the same time, as we will discuss in Section 5.6.

Profits in the Cournot model. Industry profits will be *less* than under a monopoly or a cartel. The reason is that price will be lower than the monopoly price. This can be seen from Figure 5.11. If this were a monopoly, then to find the profit-maximising output, we would need to construct an *MR* curve corresponding to the market demand curve (D_M). This would intersect with the *MC* curve at a higher output than Q_{A1} and a *higher* price (given by D_M).

Nevertheless, profits in the Cournot model will be higher than under perfect competition, since price is still above marginal cost.

Assumption that rivals set a particular price: the Bertrand model

An alternative assumption is that rival firms set a particular price and stick to it. This scenario is more realistic when firms do not want to upset customers by frequent price changes or want to produce catalogues which specify prices. The task, then, for a given oligopolist is to choose its own price and quantity in the light of the prices set by rivals.

The most famous model based on this assumption was developed by another French economist, Joseph Bertrand, in 1883. Bertrand again took the simple case of a duopoly, but its conclusions apply equally to oligopolies with three or more firms.

The outcome is one of price cutting until all supernormal profits are competed away. The reason is simple. If Firm A assumes that its rival, Firm B, will hold price constant, then Firm A should undercut this price by a small amount and as a result gain a large share of the market. At this point, Firm B will be forced to respond by cutting its price. What we end up with is a price war until price is forced down to the level of average cost, with only normal profits remaining.

As with the Cournot model above, this is also a simultaneous move game, except here the variable of interest is price. The supermarket industry is a good example of a market where price wars are a constant feature: see, for example, the blog on the Sloman News Site titled *Supermarket price wars and the effect on suppliers*.

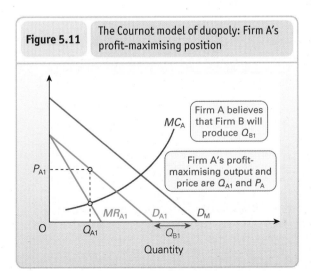

Figure 5.11	The Cournot model of duopoly: Firm A's profit-maximising position

Firm A believes that Firm B will produce Q_{B1}

Firm A's profit-maximising output and price are Q_{A1} and P_A

MC_A

P_{A1}

MR_{A1} D_{A1} D_M

O Q_{A1} Q_{B1}

Quantity

Nash equilibrium. The equilibrium outcome in either the Cournot or Bertrand models is not in the *joint* interests of the firms. In each case, total profits are less than under a monopoly or cartel. But, in the absence of collusion, the outcome is the result of each firm doing the best it can, given its assumptions about what its rivals are doing. The resulting equilibrium is known as a **Nash equilibrium** after John Nash, a US mathematician (and subject of the film *A Beautiful Mind*) who introduced the concept in 1951. We will return to this concept in Section 5.6.

In practice, when competition is intense, as in the Bertrand model, the firms may seek to collude long before profits have been reduced to a normal level. Alternatively firms may put in a **takeover bid** for their rival(s).

The kinked demand-curve assumption

In 1939 a theory of non-collusive oligopoly was developed simultaneously on both sides of the Atlantic: in the USA by Paul Sweezy and in the UK by R. L. Hall and C. J. Hitch. This **kinked demand theory** has since become perhaps the most famous of all theories of oligopoly. The model seeks to explain how it is that, even when there is no collusion at all between oligopolists, prices can nevertheless remain stable.

The theory is based on two asymmetrical assumptions:

■ If an oligopolist cuts its price, its rivals will feel forced to follow suit and cut theirs, to prevent losing customers to the first firm.

■ If an oligopolist raises its price, however, its rivals will *not* follow suit since, by keeping their prices the same, they will thereby gain customers from the first firm.

On these assumptions, each oligopolist will face a demand curve that is *kinked* at the current price and output (see Figure 5.12). A rise in price will lead to a large fall in sales as customers switch to the now relatively lower-priced rivals. The firm will thus be reluctant to raise its price. Demand is relatively elastic above the kink. On the other hand, a fall in price will bring only a modest increase in sales, since rivals lower their prices too and therefore customers do not switch. The firm will thus also be reluctant to lower its price. Demand is relatively inelastic below the kink. Thus oligopolists will be reluctant to change prices at all.

This price stability can be shown formally by drawing in the firm's marginal revenue curve, as in Figure 5.13.

To see how this is done, imagine dividing the diagram into two parts either side of Q_1. At quantities less than Q_1 (the left-hand part of the diagram), the *MR* curve will correspond to the shallow part of the *AR* curve. At quantities greater than Q_1 (the right-hand part), the *MR* curve will correspond to the steep part of the *AR* curve. To see how this part of the *MR* curve is constructed, imagine extending the steep part of the *AR* curve back to the vertical axis. This and the corresponding *MR* curve are shown by the dotted lines in Figure 5.13.

As you can see, there will be a gap between points *a* and *b*. In other words, there is a vertical section of the *MR* curve

between these two points. Profits are maximised where $MC = MR$. Thus, if the *MC* curve lies anywhere between MC_1 and MC_2 (i.e. between points *a* and *b*), the profit-maximising price and output will be P_1 and Q_1. Thus prices will remain stable *even with a considerable change in costs*.

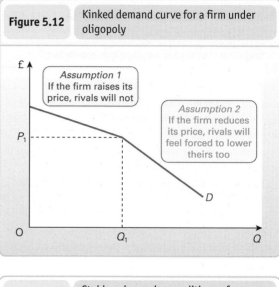

| **Figure 5.12** | Kinked demand curve for a firm under oligopoly |

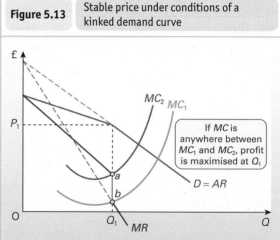

| **Figure 5.13** | Stable price under conditions of a kinked demand curve |

Definitions

Nash equilibrium The position resulting from everyone making their optimal decision based on their assumptions about their rivals' decisions. Without collusion, there is no incentive for any firm to move from this position.

Takeover bid Where one firm attempts to purchase another by offering to buy the shares of that company from its shareholders.

Kinked demand theory The theory that oligopolists face a demand curve that is kinked at the current price, demand being significantly more elastic above the current price than below. The effect of this is to create a situation of price stability.

| BOX 5.4 | THE POWER OF OLIGOPOLY | CASE STUDIES & APPLICATIONS |

Energising competition in the UK energy sector

A well-known oligopoly is the energy sector. It is dominated by six big firms (the 'Big Six'), which sell to over 90 per cent of UK households. You can find many articles about the energy sector on the Sloman News Site, considering the barriers to entry (*Making UK energy supply more competitive*), referral to the CMA (*CMA referral for energy sector*) and the savings that are possible from switching suppliers (*Do people have the energy to switch?*).

Barriers to entry

As with most oligopolies, a key problem in the energy sector is the existence of barriers to entry. In this industry the big six energy suppliers are involved in both generation of power and the local distribution of it. This illustrates the concept of **vertical integration**. They also offer 'dual-fuel' deals, where customers can receive a discount from buying electricity and gas from the same supplier. This illustrates the concept of **horizontal integration**.

The vertical integration, in particular, has made it difficult for smaller suppliers to enter the market, as they have had to buy wholesale from one of the Big Six. Thus a key focus of the industry regulator, Ofgem, has been how to reduce the barriers to entry to make the market more competitive. Through an increased number of suppliers, competition should increase and this should keep prices down, thereby benefiting households.

In June 2014, following months of political pressure, Ofgem referred[7] the industry to the Competition and Markets Authority (CMA)[8] to see if there was a possible breach of a dominant market position. Ofgem asked the CMA to investigate accusations of profiteering by the Big Six and discuss mechanisms to reduce structural barriers to entry that undermine competition, including the potential breaking up of these dominant firms. The Chief Executive of Ofgem, Dermot Nolan, said:

> A CMA investigation should ensure there are no barriers to stop effective competition bearing down on prices and delivering the benefits of these changes to consumers.[9]

Consumer inertia

As well as the traditional barriers to entry discussed above, new competitors face another obstacle, which also acts to reduce competition between existing firms. In some sense it is a form of brand loyalty, where customers are reluctant to switch to an alternative supplier, making it difficult for new entrants to attract customers.

However, in the case of energy firms, a big criticism levelled at the Big Six was that it was 'impossible' to switch. By 2011, there were more than 300 different tariffs available to domestic consumers and, although choice is often seen as a benefit of competition, there appears to have been too much choice, leading to very confused consumers. This then created inertia, whereby households simply stayed with their existing supplier, even if they were not the cheapest. The suppliers were thus accused of exploiting these 'loyalty' customers. An updated Issues Statement, by the CMA, said:

Comparing all available domestic tariffs – including those offered by the independent suppliers – we calculate that, over the period Quarter 1 2012 to Quarter 2 2014, over 95% of the dual fuel customers of the Six Large Energy Firms could have saved by switching tariff and/or supplier and that the average saving available to these customers was between £158 and £234 a year (depending on the supplier).[10]

By making it difficult for customers to switch between tariffs and between companies, competition is limited and this can make it very difficult for new firms to enter the market and gain a sufficient number of customers to make a profitable business.

Decisions of the regulators

In 2013, Ofgem introduced a full set of pricing rules in the retail sector. Energy companies had to publish simple 'per-unit' prices, allowing customers to compare tariffs at a glance. The aim of this was to encourage consumers to switch to the cheapest tariff and hence create a more competitive market, where companies are forced to offer the best deals to retain their customers.

Furthermore, from March 2014, the Big Six and the largest independent generators have had to trade fairly with independent suppliers or face penalties. In particular, they have to publish prices up to two years in advance to ensure more effective competition.

In both the wholesale and retail sector, Ofgem, and more recently the CMA, have taken continuous steps to break down the barriers to entry in the industry in an attempt to make the market genuinely competitive.

However, critics suggest that the current reforms have still not gone far enough, with the combined market share of the Big Six remaining well above 90 per cent in both sectors.

> *The Big Six have been required to open up their finances to greater scrutiny and publish prices up to two years in advance. How will this help to boost competition?*

Definitions

Vertical integration A business growth strategy that involves expanding within an existing market, but at a different stage of production. Vertical integration can be 'forward', such as moving into distribution or retail, or 'backward', such as expanding into extracting raw materials or producing components.

Horizontal integration A business growth strategy that involves expanding within an existing market at the same stage of production by moving into allied products. An example would be an electricity supplier moving into gas supply or a car manufacturer moving into the production of coaches or heavy goods vehicles.

[7] https://www.ofgem.gov.uk/press-releases/ofgem-refers-energy-market-full-competition-investigation
[8] https://www.gov.uk/cma-cases/energy-market-investigation
[9] 'Ofgem refers the energy market for a full competition investigation', *Press Release*, Ofgem, 26 June 2014.

[10] *Energy Market Investigation: Updated Issues Statement*, Competition and Markets Authority, 18 February 2015.

Oligopoly and the consumer

If oligopolists act collusively and jointly maximise industry profits, they will in effect be acting together as a monopoly. In such cases, prices may be very high. This is clearly not in the best interests of consumers.

Furthermore, in two respects, oligopoly may be more disadvantageous than monopoly:

- Depending on the size of the individual oligopolists, there may be less scope for economies of scale to mitigate the effects of market power.
- Oligopolists are likely to engage in much more extensive advertising than a monopolist. This will raise costs. Consumers could thus end up paying higher prices, though it may lead to product development and better information about the product's characteristics.

These problems will be less severe, however, if oligopolists do not collude, if there is some degree of price competition and if barriers to entry are weak. For example, in the Bertrand model, prices end up being set at the perfectly competitive level.

Also the power of oligopolists in certain markets may to some extent be offset if they sell their product to other powerful firms. Thus oligopolistic producers of baked beans or soap powder sell a large proportion of their output to giant supermarket chains, which can use their market power to keep down the price at which they purchase these products. This phenomenon is known as **countervailing power**.

In some respects, oligopoly has *advantages* to society over other market structures:

- Oligopolists, like monopolists, can use part of their supernormal profit for research and development. Unlike monopolists, however, oligopolists will have a considerable *incentive* to do so. If the product design is improved, this may allow the firm to capture a larger share of the market, and it may be some time before rivals can respond with a similarly improved product. If, in addition, costs are reduced by technological improvement, the resulting higher profits will improve the firm's capacity to withstand a price war.
- Non-price competition through product differentiation may result in greater choice for the consumer. Take the case of tablets or mobile phones. Non-price competition has led to a huge range of different products of many different specifications, each meeting the specific requirements of different consumers.

> ### Pause for thought
>
> *Assume that two brewers announce that they are about to merge. What information would you need to help you decide whether the merger would be in the consumer's interests?*

It is difficult to draw any general conclusions, since oligopolies differ so much in their performance.

> ### Definition
>
> **Countervailing power** Where the power of a monopolistic/oligopolistic seller is offset by powerful buyers which can prevent the price from being pushed up.

Recap

1. An oligopoly is where there are just a few firms in the industry with barriers to the entry of new firms. Firms recognise their mutual dependence.

2. Oligopolists want to maximise their joint profits. This tends to make them collude to keep prices high. On the other hand, they want the biggest share of industry profits for themselves. This tends to make them compete.

3. They are more likely to collude if there are few of them; if they are open with each other; if they have similar products and cost structures; if there is a dominant firm; if there are significant entry barriers; if the market is stable; and if there is no government legislation to prevent collusion.

4. Collusion can be open or tacit.

5. A formal collusive agreement is called a 'cartel'. A cartel aims to act as a monopoly. It can set price and leave the members to compete for market share, or it can assign quotas. There is always a temptation for cartel members to 'cheat' by undercutting the cartel price if they think they can get away with it and not trigger a price war.

6. Tacit collusion can take the form of price leadership. This is where firms follow the price set by either a dominant firm in the industry or one seen as a reliable 'barometer' of market conditions. Alternatively, tacit collusion can simply involve following various rules of thumb such as average cost pricing and benchmark pricing.

7. Even when firms do not collude they will still have to take into account their rivals' behaviour.

8. In the Cournot model firms assume that their rivals' output is given and then choose the profit-maximising price and output in the light of this assumption. The resulting price and profit are lower than under monopoly, but still higher than under perfect competition.

9. In the Bertrand model firms assume that their rivals' price is given. This will result in prices being competed down until only normal profits remain.

10. In the kinked demand-curve model, firms are likely to keep their prices stable unless there is a large shift in costs or demand.

11. Whether consumers benefit from oligopoly depends on the particular oligopoly and how competitive it is; whether there is any countervailing power; whether the firms engage in extensive advertising and of what type; whether product differentiation results in a wide range of choice for the consumer; and how much of the profits are ploughed back into research and development.

5.6 GAME THEORY

Thinking strategically about rivals

Economists use **game theory** to model the strategic interactions between 'players', such as firms, where those choices affect the interests of others. As we have seen, the behaviour of a firm under non-collusive oligopoly depends on how it thinks its rivals will react to its decisions. By using game theory we can try to understand the decisions that these firms make in relation to variables like price, advertising and product development.

While we focus here on the strategic interaction between firms, game theory can be applied to a huge range of areas. In the BBC News article, 'What exactly is "game theory"?',[11] we can see the application of game theory by the Greek Finance Minister, Yanis Varoufakis, in 2015, in his approach to negotiations over Greek debt.

Pause for thought

Can you think of other examples within economics where game theory could help to analyse the choices made by individuals, groups or organisations?

Single-move games

The simplest type of 'game' is a single-move or single-period game. This involves just one 'move' by each firm involved. Take the case of two or more firms bidding for a contract. When the bids have all been made, the contract will be awarded to the lowest bidder; the 'game' is over.

Simple dominant strategy games

Consider the case where there are just two firms with identical costs, products and demand. They are both considering which of two alternative prices to charge. Table 5.2 shows typical profits they could each make.

Let's assume that at present both firms (X and Y) are charging a price of £2 and that they are each making a profit of £10 million, giving a total industry profit of £20 million. This is shown in the top left-hand cell (A).

Now assume they are both (independently) considering reducing their price to £1.80. In making this decision they will need to take into account what their rival might do, and how this will affect them. Let's consider X's position. In our simple example there are just two things that its rival, firm Y, might do. Either Y could cut its price to £1.80, or it could leave its price at £2. What should X do?

To answer this question we need to take each of firm Y's two possible actions and look at firm X's best response to each. If we assume that firm Y chooses a price of £2, firm X could decide to keep its price at £2 giving it £10m in profit. This is shown by cell A. Alternatively, firm X could cut its price to £1.80 and earn £12m in profit, in cell B. Firm X's best response is therefore to cut price to £1.80, preferring a profit of £12m to one of £10m.

What about if we now assume that firm Y charges £1.80 – how should firm X best respond? If firm X charged £2, we would end up in cell C and firm X would earn only £5m in profit. On the other hand, firm X could also cut its price to £1.80, moving us to cell D, and it would earn £8m profit. By comparing these two profit outcomes, we can see that firm X's best response to firm Y lowering its price to £1.80 is to cut its own price to £1.80 as well, preferring a profit of £8m to a profit of £5m.

Note that firm Y will argue along similar lines, cutting price to £1.80 as well, no matter what it assumes that firm X will do.

This game is known as a **dominant strategy game** since, no matter what the other firm decides, each firm will make the same decision to cut price. As we saw in the Cournot and Bertrand models above, the equilibrium outcome where there is no collusion between the firms (cell D in this game) is known as a *Nash equilibrium*.

However, it is important to note that the profits earned by each firm in the Nash equilibrium (cell D) are lower than they would have been had the firms colluded and charged the higher price (cell A). Each firm would have

Table 5.2 Profits for firms X and Y at different prices

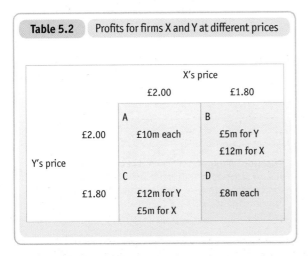

		X's price	
		£2.00	£1.80
Y's price	£2.00	**A** £10m each	**B** £5m for Y £12m for X
	£1.80	**C** £12m for Y £5m for X	**D** £8m each

Definitions

Game theory (or the theory of games) The study of alternative strategies that oligopolists may choose to adopt, depending on their assumptions about their rivals' behaviour.

Dominant strategy game Where the *same* policy is suggested by different strategies.

[11]Chris Stokel-Walker, 'What exactly is "game theory"?', *BBC News Magazine*, 18 February 2015.

earned £10 million (cell A). But if they did collude, both would be tempted to cheat and cut prices. This is known as the **prisoners' dilemma**. An example is given in Box 5.5. You can also watch the scene on YouTube[12] from the film *A Beautiful Mind,* where John Nash (played by Russell Crowe) begins to formulate the famous 'Nash equilibrium' concept.

More complex games

More complex 'games' can be devised with more than two firms, many alternative prices, differentiated products and various forms of non-price competition (e.g. advertising). We may also see 'games', where the best response for each firm depends on the assumptions made, meaning there is no dominant strategy. Consider the pay-off matrix in Table 5.3.

If firm X assumes that firm Y will charge £20, then firm X will either earn £6m in profit if it charges £25 or £5m in profit if it charges £19. Firm X's best response would be to charge £25 (cell A). However, if it assumes that firm Y will charge £15, then firm X's best response will now be to charge £19, preferring £4m in profit (cell D) to £3m in profit (cell C). We no longer have a dominant strategy. Firm X's best response depends on its assumption about Y's price.

> **Pause for thought**
>
> *What is firm Y's best response to each of firm X's possible choices in the game shown in Table 5.3? Does it have a dominant strategy in this game?*

In many situations, firms will have a number of different options open to them and a number of possible reactions by rivals. Such games can become highly complex.

The better the firm's information about (a) its rivals' costs and demand, (b) the likely reactions of rivals to its actions and (c) the effects of these reactions on its own profit, the better the firm's 'move in the game' is likely to be. It is similar to a card game: the more you know about your opponents' cards and how your opponents are likely to react to your moves, and the better you can calculate the effects of their moves on you, the better your moves in the game are likely to be.

Multi-move games

In many situations firms will *react* to what their rivals do; their rivals, in turn, will react to what they do. In other words, the game moves back and forth from one 'player' to the other like a game of chess or cards. Firms will still have to think strategically (as you do in chess), considering the likely responses of their rivals to their own actions. These multiple-move games are known as *repeated games* or *extensive-form games*.

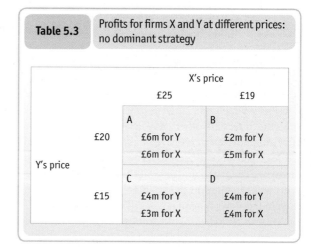

Table 5.3	Profits for firms X and Y at different prices: no dominant strategy	

		X's price	
		£25	£19
Y's price	£20	**A** £6m for Y £6m for X	**B** £2m for Y £5m for X
	£15	**C** £4m for Y £3m for X	**D** £4m for Y £4m for X

One of the simplest repeated games is the *tit-for-tat*. This is where a firm will cut prices, or make some other aggressive move, *only* if the rival does so first. To illustrate this repeated game let us look again at the example we considered in Table 5.2, but this time we will extend it beyond one time period.

Assume that firm X is adopting the tit-for-tat strategy. If firm Y cuts its price from £2.00 to £1.80, then firm X will respond in round 2 by also cutting its price. The two firms will end up in cell D – worse off than if neither had cut their price. If, however, firm Y had left its price at £2.00 then firm X would respond by leaving its price unchanged too. Both firms would remain in cell A with a higher profit than cell D.

As long as firm Y knows that firm X will respond in this way, it has an incentive not to cut its price. Thus it is in X's interests to make sure that Y clearly 'understands' how X will react to any price cut. In other words, X will make a threat.

The importance of threats and promises

In many situations, an oligopolist will make a threat or promise that it will act in a certain way. As long as the threat or promise is **credible** (i.e. its competitors believe it), the firm can gain and it will influence its rivals' behaviour.

Take the simple situation where a large oil company, such as Esso, states that it will match the price charged by any competitor within a given radius. Assume that competitors believe this 'price promise' but also that Esso will not

TC4 p20

> **Definitions**
>
> **Prisoners' dilemma** Where two or more firms (or people), by attempting independently to choose the best strategy for whatever the other(s) are likely to do, end up in a worse position than if they had co-operated in the first place.
>
> **Credible threat (or promise)** One that is believable to rivals because it is in the threatener's interests to carry it out.

BOX 5.5 **THE PRISONERS' DILEMMA**

Game theory is relevant not just to economics. A famous non-economic example is the prisoners' dilemma.

Nigel and Amanda have been arrested for a joint crime of serious fraud. Each is interviewed separately and given the following alternatives:

- First, if they say nothing, the court has enough evidence to sentence both to a year's imprisonment.
- Second, if either Nigel or Amanda alone confesses, he or she is likely to get only a three-month sentence but the partner could get up to 10 years.
- Third, if both confess, they are likely to get three years each.

These outcomes are illustrated in the diagram. What should Nigel and Amanda do?

Let us consider Nigel's dilemma. Should he confess in order to get the short sentence (the maximax strategy)? This is better than the year he would get for not confessing. There is, however, an even better reason for confessing. Suppose Nigel doesn't confess but, unknown to him, Amanda does confess. Then Nigel ends up with the long sentence (cell B). Nigel's best strategy is always to confess.

Amanda is in the same dilemma and so the result is simple. When both prisoners act in their own self-interest by confessing, they both end up with relatively long prison terms (cell D). Only when they collude will they end up with relatively short ones, the best combined solution (cell A). However, for each of these prisoners, the more certain they are that their compatriot will maintain their innocence, the greater the incentive for them to confess and reduce their sentence!

Of course the police know this and will do their best to prevent any collusion. They will keep Nigel and Amanda in separate cells and try to persuade each of them that the other is bound to confess.

Thus the choice of strategy depends on:

- Nigel's and Amanda's risk attitudes: i.e. are they 'risk lovers' or 'risk averse'?
- Nigel's and Amanda's estimates of how likely the other is to own up.

1. *Why is this a dominant strategy 'game'?*
2. *How would Nigel's choice of strategy be affected if he had instead been involved in a joint crime with Rikki, Kate, Amrita and Dave, and they had all been caught?*

The prisoners' dilemma is a good illustration of *the fallacy of composition*: what applies at the level of the individual does not apply to the group as a whole. It might be in the individual's interests to confess. It is clearly not in the interests of both, however, for both to confess.

| KEY IDEA 20 | *The fallacy of composition.* What applies in one case will not necessarily apply when repeated in all cases. |

Let's now look at two real-world examples of the prisoners' dilemma.

Standing up to see the action!

Dean is following his beloved Leicester City at yet another match. Leicester break forward at rapid pace. With the prospect of a goal he stands to get a better view. Others follow his lead: after all, if they stayed sitting, they would not see at all.

In this Nash equilibrium, most people are worse off, since, except for tall people, their view is likely to be worse and they lose the comfort of sitting down. If only Dean and others like him could just sit down!

Too much advertising

Why do firms spend so much on advertising? If they are aggressive, they do so to get ahead of their rivals (the maximax approach). If they are cautious, they do so in case their rivals increase their advertising (the maximin approach).

Although in both cases it may be in the individual firm's best interests to increase advertising, the resulting Nash equilibrium is likely to be one of excessive advertising: the total spent on advertising (by all firms) is not recouped in additional sales.

3. *Give one or two other examples (economic or non-economic) of the prisoners' dilemma.*

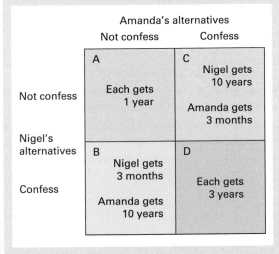

Alternatives for Nigel and Amanda

| | Amanda's alternatives | |
	Not confess	Confess
Nigel's alternatives — Not confess	A — Each gets 1 year	C — Nigel gets 10 years / Amanda gets 3 months
Nigel's alternatives — Confess	B — Nigel gets 3 months / Amanda gets 10 years	D — Each gets 3 years

Figure 5.14	A decision tree

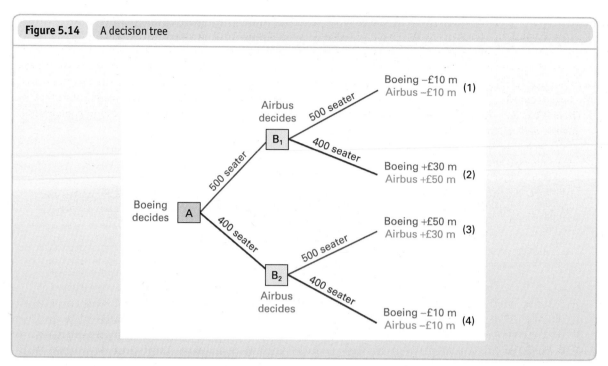

try to *undercut* their price. In the simple situation where there is only one other filling station in the area, what price should it charge? Clearly it should charge the price that would maximise its profits, assuming that Esso will charge the *same* price. In the absence of other filling stations in the area, this is likely to be a relatively high price.

Pause for thought

Assume that there are two major oil companies operating filling stations in an area. The first promises to match the other's prices. The other promises to sell at 1p per litre cheaper than the first. Describe the likely sequence of events in this 'game' and the likely eventual outcome. Could the promise of the second company be seen as credible?

Now assume that there are several filling stations in the area. What should the company do now? Its best bet is probably to charge the same price as Esso and hope that no other company charges a lower price and forces Esso to cut its price. Assuming that Esso's threat is credible, other companies are likely to reason in a similar way.

The importance of timing

Most decisions by oligopolists are made by one firm at a time rather than simultaneously by all firms. Sometimes a firm will take the initiative. At other times it will respond to decisions taken by other firms. Here we are considering a 'sequential game' where the 'order of play' is important.

Take the case of a new generation of large passenger aircraft that can fly further without refuelling. Assume that there is a market for a 500-seater version of this type of aircraft and a 400-seater version, but that the market for each size of aircraft is not big enough for the two manufacturers, Boeing and Airbus, to share it profitably. Let us also assume that the 400-seater market would give an annual profit of £50 million to a single manufacturer and that the 500 seater would give an annual profit of £30 million, but that if both manufacturers produced the same version, they would each make an annual loss of £10 million.

Assume that Boeing announces that it is building the 400-seater aircraft. What should Airbus do? The choice is illustrated in Figure 5.14. This diagram is called a **decision tree** and shows the sequence of events. The small square at the left of the diagram is Boeing's decision point (point A). If it had decided to build the 500-seater aircraft, we would move up the top branch. Airbus would now have to make a decision (point B_1). If it too built the 500-seater aircraft, we would move to outcome 1: a loss of £10m for both manufacturers. Clearly, with Boeing building a 500-seater aircraft, Airbus would choose the 400-seater aircraft: we would move to outcome 2, with Boeing making a profit of £30m and Airbus a profit £50m. Airbus would be very pleased!

Boeing's best strategy at point A, however, would be to build the 400-seater aircraft. We would then move

---

Definition

Decision tree (or game tree) A diagram showing the sequence of possible decisions by competitor firms and the outcome of each combination of decisions.

KI 19
p 118

to Airbus's decision point B_2. In this case, it is in Airbus's interests to build the 500-seater aircraft. Its profit would be only £30m (outcome 3), but this is better than the £10m loss if it too built the 400-seater aircraft (outcome 4). With Boeing deciding first, the Nash equilibrium will thus be outcome 3.

There is clearly a **first-mover advantage** here. Once Boeing has decided to build the more profitable version, Airbus is forced to build the less profitable one. Naturally, Airbus would like to build the more profitable one and be the first mover. Which company succeeds in going first depends on how advanced they are in their research and development and in their production capacity.

More complex decision trees. The aircraft example is the simplest version of a decision tree, with just two companies and each one making only one key decision. In many business situations, much more complex trees could be constructed. The 'game' would be more like chess, with many moves and several options on each move. If there were more than two companies, the decision tree would be more complex still.

> **Pause for thought**
>
> *Give an example of decisions that two firms could make in sequence, each one affecting the other's next decision.*

Recap

1. Game theory is a way of modelling behaviour in strategic situations where the outcome for an individual or firm depends on the choices made by others. It enables us to examine various strategies that firms can adopt when the outcome of each is not certain.

2. The simplest type of 'game' is a single-move or single-period game. Many single-period games have predictable outcomes, no matter what assumptions each firm makes about its rivals' behaviour. Such games are known dominant strategy games.

3. Non-collusive oligopolists will have to work out a price strategy. By making the best decisions based on assumptions about their rivals' behaviour we can arrive at a Nash equilibrium. However, a 'Nash' equilibrium may not always be the best strategy for the firms collectively. It is possible that both could do better by co-operating or colluding.

4. In multiple-move games, play is passed from one 'player' to the other sequentially. Firms will respond not only to what firms do, but also to what they say they will do. To this end, a firm's threats or promises must be credible if they are to influence rivals' decisions.

5. A firm may gain a strategic advantage over its rivals by being the first one to take action (e.g. launch a new product). A decision tree can be constructed to show the possible sequence of moves in a multiple-move game.

5.7 PRICE DISCRIMINATION

In what situations will firms be able to charge different prices to different consumers? How will we as consumers benefit or lose from the process?

Up until this point in the chapter it has been assumed that a firm sells each unit of its output for the same price. This is sometimes referred to as *uniform pricing*. However, if a firm implements a uniform pricing policy then it is missing out on potential profit. Given that some customers gain a higher utility from the product and thus have a greater willingness to pay, they would have still purchased the good if the price was higher.

The firm might be tempted to increase prices to try to capture some of this consumer surplus and convert it into profit. However, it faces a trade-off. A higher price will increase the profit *per transaction*, but it will also cause some of its customers to stop buying the product. These would be the people gaining a lower utility and hence putting a lower valuation on the product.

This trade-off could be avoided, however, if the firm could charge a higher price to those customers with a high valuation for the product (i.e. gaining a high utility) and a lower price to those consumers with a lower valuation for

the product. Firms can do this by implementing a strategy of **price discrimination**.

If the cost to a firm of supplying different customers does not vary then price discrimination can be defined in the following way: it is the practice of selling the same or similar products to different customers for different prices.

If the costs of supplying the good to different customers *do* vary, then the previous definition is incomplete. Hence, we identify price discrimination as the situation where the

> **Definition**
>
> **First-mover advantage** When a firm gains from being the first to take action.
>
> **Price discrimination** Where a firm sells the same or similar product at different prices and the difference in price cannot be fully accounted for by any differences in the costs of supply.

mark-up of price (*P*) over the marginal cost (*MC*) of supplying the product varies between different sales.

Third-degree price discrimination

The most common type of price discrimination, which economists refer to as **third-degree price discrimination**, is where a firm charges a different price to different groups of consumers. In doing so, the firm looks to identify some consumer characteristic, trait or attribute that could be used as a basis to split them into different groups. For example, consumers could be divided by age (e.g. adults and children) or by location (e.g. rich areas and poor areas). In other words, groups of consumers are categorised in some way and then charged a price accordingly.

To be successful the characteristic must have three important properties:

■ It must be relatively easy for the firm to observe.
■ It must provide some indication of the consumer's willingness to pay: i.e. consumers allocated to one group should generally be less price sensitive at any given price than those allocated to another group – in other words, price elasticity of demand must differ between the groups.
■ It must allow consumers to be split into separate markets so that consumers are unable simply to switch from the higher- to the lower-priced market. For example, people should not able to purchase the product in the lower-priced market and re-sell it in the higher-priced one.

Table 5.4 provides some examples of the types of characteristics that can be used as the basis for third-degree price discrimination.

Second-degree price discrimination

Another form of price discrimination, known as **second-degree price discrimination**, involves customers being offered a range of different prices for the same or similar product by the firm. This frequently involves companies offering discounts when larger quantities are purchased. Examples include the use by supermarkets of promotions such as 'buy two, get an additional one free' or electricity companies charging a high price for the first so many kilowatts and then a lower rate for additional kilowatts.

Another example concerns the timing of a purchase. For example, airlines may charge a lower price for people booking earlier, but as the aircraft fills up the seat prices rise (see Case Study 5.25 in MyEconLab). This is not third-degree price discrimination as the airline is not dividing customers into, say, business and leisure travellers, but rather letting people's price elasticity of demand reveal itself. Thus people wanting to travel at the last minute, who may indeed be business travellers, but could be people responding to a family emergency, are likely to have a lower price elasticity of demand and thus will be willing to pay a higher price than people who booked early.

First-degree price discrimination

First-degree price discrimination is the rarest form of price discrimination. It occurs when sellers charge each consumer the maximum price they are willing to pay. Stallholders in a bazaar may attempt to do this by initially asking a very high price. Then, as haggling takes place and the price is bid down, a price is settled on that represents the most the consumer is willing to pay.

> **Pause for thought**
>
> *Demonstrate on a market demand curve how successful first-degree price discrimination would eliminate consumer surplus.*

> ### Definitions
>
> **Third-degree price discrimination** Where a firm divides consumers into different groups based on some characteristic that is relatively easy to observe and acceptable to the consumer. The firm then charges a different price to consumers in different groups, but the same price to all the consumers within a group.
>
> **Second-degree price discrimination** Where a firm charges customers different prices for the same (or similar) product depending on the amount or time purchased.
>
> **First-degree price discrimination** Where a firm charges each consumer for each unit the maximum price they are willing to pay for that unit.

TC8 p 59

Table 5.4	Examples of third-degree price discrimination
Characteristic	**Example**
Age	16–25 or senior rail card; half price children's tickets in the cinema.
Gender	'Ladies' night' in a bar or club where men pay the full price for drinks while women can get the same drinks at a discounted price.
Location	Pharmaceutical companies often charge different prices for the same medicine/drug in different countries. Consumers in the USA are often charged more than those from other countries.
Occupation	Apple, Microsoft and Orange provide price discounts to employees of educational institutions.
Business or individual	Publishers of academic journals charge much lower subscription rates to individuals than university libraries.
Past buying behaviour	Firms often charge new customers a lower price than existing customers for the same product or service as an 'introductory offer'.

Advantages to the firm

As we have seen, there are various ways in which firms can engage in discriminatory pricing. Case Study 5.23 in MyEconLab discusses alternative types of price discrimination in more detail. The key point here is that price discrimination allows the firm to earn a higher *revenue* from any given level of sales. To demonstrate this consider Figure 5.15 which represents a firm's demand curve.

If the firm is to sell 200 units without price discrimination, it must charge a price of P_1. The total revenue it earns is shown by the blue area. If, however, it can practise second- or third-degree price discrimination by selling 150 of those 200 units at the higher price of P_2, it will gain the red striped area in addition to the blue area.

You can also see what would happen if the firm could practise first-degree price discrimination: i.e. charge each consumer the maximum price they are prepared to pay for each unit of the product. In this case, its revenue would be the whole area under the demand curve.

Another advantage the firm gains by price discrimination is that it may be able to use it to drive competitors out of business. If a firm has a monopoly in one market (e.g. the home market), it may be able to charge a high price due to its relatively inelastic demand, and thus make high profits. If it is under oligopoly in another market (e.g. the export market), it may use the high profits in the first market to subsidise a very low price in the oligopolistic market, thus forcing its competitors out of business.

Large bus companies in the UK have been accused of doing this (see Case Study 5.17 in MyEconLab). They use the profits made from the high fares on routes where they face no competition to subsidise fares on routes where they do face competition, often from a small rival attempting to break into the market. The aim is to drive the small company out of business. Sometimes on these routes, the large company charges fares that are below cost (thereby making a temporary loss on these routes). This practice is known as **predatory pricing**.

Price discrimination and the consumer

No clear-cut decision can be made over the desirability of price discrimination from the point of view of the consumer. Some people will benefit from it; others will lose. Those paying the higher price will probably feel that price discrimination is unfair to them. On the other hand, those charged the lower price may thereby be able to obtain a good or service they could otherwise not afford: e.g. concessionary bus or train fares for senior citizens.

Competition. As explained above, a firm may use price discrimination to drive competitors out of business. On the other hand, it might use its profits from its high-priced market to break into another market and withstand a possible price war. Competition is thereby increased.

Profits. Price discrimination raises a firm's profits. This could be seen to be against the interests of the consumer, especially if the average price of the product is raised. On the other hand, the higher profits may be reinvested and lead to lower costs in the future.

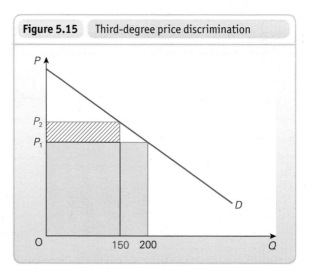

Figure 5.15 Third-degree price discrimination

| BOX 5.6 | PROFIT-MAXIMISING PRICES AND OUTPUT FOR A THIRD-DEGREE PRICE DISCRIMINATING FIRM | EXPLORING ECONOMICS |

Identifying different prices in different markets

Assuming that a firm wishes to maximise profits, what discriminatory prices should it charge and how much should it produce?

Assume that the firm sells an identical product in two separate markets H and L with demand and *MR* curves in each market as shown in panels (a) and (b) of the diagram – a case of third-degree price discrimination.

Equilibrium for a single-price firm. If the firm were unable to split its customers into these two different groups, then a market demand curve could be derived. This is illustrated in panel (c) and is obtained by horizontally aggregating the demand curves in panels (a) and (b).

The market demand curve is the same as the demand curve in market H from point *g* to *h*. This is because no consumers in market L are willing to pay a price above *d*. As the price falls below *d* both consumers in market H and L are willing to buy the good, so horizontal aggregation of both demand curves must take place from this point onwards. This creates a kink in the market demand curve at point *h*.

This kink also creates a discontinuity in the *MR* curve between points *j* and *k*. To simplify the explanation, it is also assumed that the firm's marginal cost is constant and that it has no fixed costs. Thus $AC = MC$.

To maximise profit, it would produce where the market marginal revenue equals marginal cost: i.e. $MR_M = MC$. This occurs at point *l* in panel (c). It would therefore produce an output of Q^* and sell all of this output at the same price of P^*.

Equilibrium under third-degree price discrimination. What happens if the firm could now charge a different price to the customers in market H from those in market L? At the single price of P^* the price elasticity of demand in market H is lower than it is in market L. (Note that demand is nevertheless elastic in both markets at this price as *MR* is positive.) Therefore the firm could increase its profits by charging a price above P^* in market H and below P^* in market L. This is illustrated in panels (a) and (b).

In market H the profit-maximising firm should produce where $MR_H = MC$. Therefore it should sell an output of Q_H for a price of P_H. In market L it should produce where $MR_L = MC$ at point *f*. Therefore it should sell an output of Q_L for a price of P_L. Note that P_L is below P^*, while P_H is above P^*.

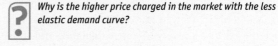 *Why is the higher price charged in the market with the less elastic demand curve?*

Profit-maximising output under third-degree price discrimination

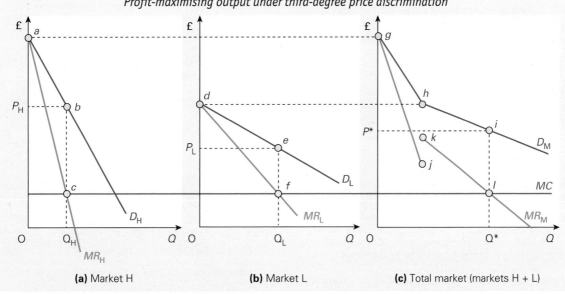

(a) Market H   **(b)** Market L   **(c)** Total market (markets H + L)

Recap

1. First-degree price discrimination is where is consumer is charged the maximum he or she is prepared to pay. Second-degree price discrimination is where the same consumer is charged different prices according to the amount, timing or other features of the purchase. Third-degree price discrimination is where consumers are divided into groups and the groups with the lower price elasticity of demand are charged the higher prices.

2. Price discrimination allows the firm to earn a higher revenue from a given level of sales.

3. Some people will gain from price discrimination; others will lose. It is likely to be particularly harmful when it is used as a means of driving competitors from the market (predatory pricing).

QUESTIONS

1. A perfectly competitive firm faces a price of £14 per unit. It has the short-run cost schedule shown in the table below.

Output	0	1	2	3	4	5	6	7	8
TC (£)	10	18	24	30	38	50	66	91	120

   a. Copy the table and put in additional rows for average cost and marginal cost at each level of output. (Enter the figures for marginal cost in the space between each column.)

   b. Plot *AC, MC* and *MR* on a diagram.

   c. Mark the profit-maximising output.

   d. How much (supernormal) profit is made at this output?

   e. What would happen to the price in the long run if this firm were typical of others in the industry? Why would we need to know information about long-run average cost in order to give a precise answer to this question?

2. If the industry under perfect competition faces a downward-sloping demand curve, why does an individual firm face a horizontal demand curve?

3. On a diagram similar to Figure 5.3, show the long-run equilibrium for both firm and industry under perfect competition. Now assume that the demand for the product falls. Show the short-run and long-run effects.

4. If supernormal profits are competed away under perfect competition, why will firms have an incentive to become more efficient?

5. Is it a valid criticism of perfect competition to argue that it is incompatible with economies of scale?

6. As an illustration of the difficulty in identifying monopolies, try to decide which of the following are monopolies: British Telecom; your local evening newspaper; a water company; the village post office; the Royal Mail; Interflora; the London Underground; ice creams in the cinema; Guinness; food sold in a train buffet car; Tipp-Ex; the board game 'Monopoly'.

7. Try this brain teaser. A monopoly would be expected to face an inelastic demand. After all, there are no direct substitutes. And yet, if it produces where *MR = MC, MR* must be positive, and demand must therefore be elastic. Therefore the monopolist must face an elastic demand! Can you solve this conundrum?

8. For what reasons would you expect a monopoly to charge (a) a higher price, and (b) a lower price, than if the industry were operating under perfect competition?

9. In which of the following industries are exit costs likely to be low: (a) steel production; (b) market gardening; (c) nuclear power generation; (d) specialist financial advisory services; (e) production of fashion dolls; (f) production of a new drug; (g) contract catering; (h) mobile discos; (i) car ferry operators? Are these exit costs dependent on how narrowly the industry is defined?

10. Think of three examples of monopolies (local or national) and consider how contestable their markets are.

11. Think of 10 different products or services and estimate roughly how many firms there are in the market. You will need to decide whether 'the market' is a local one, a national one or an international one. In what ways do the firms compete in each of the cases you have identified?

12. Assume that a monopolistically competitive industry is in long-run equilibrium. On a diagram like Figure 5.7, show the effect of a fall in demand on a firm's price and profit in (a) the short run and (b) the long run.

13. Imagine there are two types of potential customer for jam sold by a small food shop. The one is the person who has just run out and wants some now. The other is the person who looks in the cupboard, sees that the pot of jam is less than half full and thinks, 'I will soon need some more'. How will the price elasticity of demand differ between these two customers?

14. Why may a food shop charge higher prices than supermarkets for 'essential items' and yet very similar prices for delicatessen items?

15. Firms under monopolistic competition generally have spare capacity. Does this imply that if, say, half of the petrol stations were closed down, the consumer would benefit? Explain.

16. Will competition between oligopolists always reduce total industry profits?

17. In which of the following industries is collusion likely to occur: bricks, beer, margarine, cement, crisps, washing powder, carpets?

18. Devise a box diagram like that in Table 5.2 (page 127), only this time assume that there are three firms each considering the two strategies of keeping price the same or reducing it by a set amount. Is the game still a 'dominant strategy game'?

19. What do you understand by a 'repeated game'? Give examples of how the outcomes from a repeated game may differ from those in single-move games.

20. Which of the following are examples of effective countervailing power?

    a. Power stations buying coal from a large mining company.

    b. A large office hiring a photocopier from Xerox.

    c. Marks & Spencer buying clothes from a garment manufacturer.

    d. A small village store (but the only one for miles around) buying food from a wholesaler.

21. Is it the size of the purchasing firm that is important in determining its power to keep down the prices charged by its suppliers?

22. If a cinema could sell all its seats to adults in the evenings at the end of the week, but only a few on Mondays and Tuesdays, what price discrimination policy would you recommend to the cinema in order for it to maximise its weekly revenue?

23. Think of two examples of price discrimination. In what ways do the consumers gain or lose? What information would you need to be certain in your answer?

MyEconLab

This book can be supported by MyEconLab, which contains a range of additional resources, including an online homework and tutorial system designed to test and build your understanding.

You need both an access card and a course ID to access MyEconLab:

1. Is your lecturer using MyEconLab? Ask your lecturer for your course ID.

2. Has an access card been included with the book at a reduced cost? Check the inside back cover of the book.

3. If you have a course ID but no access card, go to: http://www.myeconlab.com/ to buy access to this interactive study programme.

ADDITIONAL CASE STUDIES IN THE *ESSENTIALS OF ECONOMICS* MyEconLab (www.pearsoned.co.uk/sloman)

5.1 **Is perfect best?** An examination of the meaning of the word 'perfect' in perfect competition.

5.2 **B2B electronic marketplaces.** This case study examines the growth of firms trading with each other over the Internet (business-to-business or 'B2B') and considers the effects on competition.

5.3 **Concentration ratios.** One way of measuring the degree of market power in an industry.

5.4 **Windows cleaning.** The examination of Microsoft's market dominance by the US Justice Department.

5.5 **Airline deregulation in the USA and Europe.** Whether the deregulation of various routes has led to more competition and lower prices.

5.6 **Competition in the pipeline?** Monopoly in the supply of gas.

5.7 **X-inefficiency.** A type of inefficiency suffered by many large firms, resulting in a wasteful use of resources.

5.8 **Edward Chamberlin (1899–1967).** The birth of the monopolistic competition model.

5.9 **The motor vehicle repair and servicing industry.** A case study of monopolistic competition.

5.10 **Curry wars.** Monopolistic competition in the take-away food market.

5.11 **Bakeries: oligopoly or monopolistic competition?** A case study on the bread industry, showing that small-scale local bakeries can exist alongside giant national bakeries.

5.12 **Oligopoly in the brewing industry.** A case study showing how the UK brewing industry is becoming more concentrated.

5.13 **Supermarket wars?** Is there genuine competition or tacit collusion in the UK supermarket sector?

5.14 **The global vitamin cartel.** A case study showing oligopolistic collusion in the production and sale of vitamins.

5.15 **Cut throat competition.** An examination of the barriers of entry to the UK razor market

5.16 **Cartels set in concrete, steel and cardboard.** This examines some of the best-known Europe-wide cartels of recent years.

5.17 **Competition on the buses?** An examination of the impact of the deregulation of UK bus services in the mid-1980s.

5.18 **A lift to profits?** The EC imposes a record fine on four companies operating a lift and escalator cartel.

5.19 **Merger activity.** This examines mergers in Europe: their causes and consequences.

5.20 **A product's life cycle.** How market conditions vary at different stages in a product's life.

5.21 **Peak load pricing.** An example of price discrimination.

5.22 **How do UK companies set prices?** A summary of the findings of a Bank of England survey on how firms set prices in practice.

5.23 **First, second and third.** An examination of how economists classify different types of price discrimination.

5.24 **Easy pricing.** How low-cost airlines, such as easyJet and Ryanair, use price discrimination to increase their revenue.

WEB APPENDICES

5.1 **Measuring monopoly power.** An examination of how the degree of monopoly power possessed by a firm can be measured.

5.2 **The Cournot model.** An extension of the analysis given in the text.

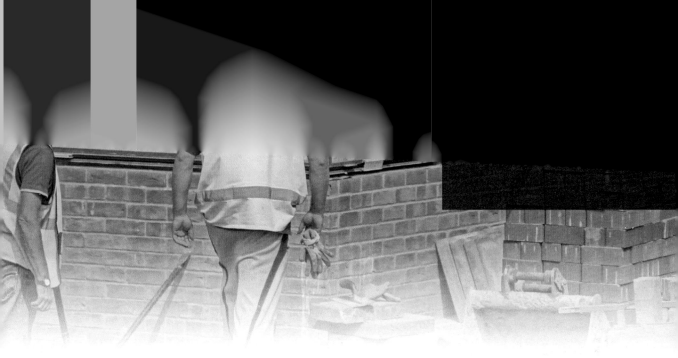

Wages and the distribution of income

Following the financial and economic crisis of the late 2000s there has been heightened interest in the seemingly very large sums that some workers appear to earn and, not least, some of those working in the banking sector. Some see the large divergences in earnings, particularly during difficult economic times, as symbolic of a crisis in capitalism. However, are such claims justified? In this chapter, we consider just why it is that some bankers, pop stars and footballers earn such large incomes. Why, on the other hand, do cleaners, hospital porters and workers in clothing factories earn very low incomes?

The explanation for differences in wages lies in the working of labour markets. In the first part of the chapter we will consider how labour markets operate. In particular, we will focus on the determination of wage rates in different types of market: ones where employers are wage takers, ones where they can choose the wage rate, and ones where wage rates are determined by a process of collective bargaining.

In Section 6.3 we ask the more general question of why some people are rich and others poor, and consider the degree of inequality in our society: a society that includes the super-rich, with their luxury yachts and their villas abroad, and people living in slum conditions, with not enough to feed and clothe themselves or their children properly; a society where people begging in the streets are an all too familiar sight.

The chapter closes with a consideration of what can be done to reduce inequality. Is the solution to tax the rich very heavily so that the money can be redistributed to the poor? Or might this discourage people from working so hard? Would it be better, then, to focus on benefits and increase the support for the poor?

After studying this chapter, you should be able to answer the following questions:

- How are wage rates determined in a perfect labour market?
- What are the determinants of the demand and supply of labour and their respective elasticities?
- What forms of market power exist in the labour market and what determines the power of employers and labour?
- What effects do powerful employers and trade unions have on wages and employment?
- How can we measure the extent of inequality in income and wealth and how has inequality changed over time?
- What are the causes of inequality?
- What can the government do to reduce inequality?

6.1 WAGE DETERMINATION IN A PERFECT MARKET

Why are some people paid higher wage rates than others?

Perfect labour markets

When looking at the market for labour, it is useful to make a similar distinction to that made in goods markets: the distinction between perfect and imperfect markets. That way we can gain a clearer understanding of the effects of power, or lack of it, in the labour market. Although in practice few labour markets are totally perfect, many do at least approximate to it.

The key assumption of a perfect labour market is that everyone is a **wage taker**. In other words, neither employers nor employees have any economic power to affect wage rates. This situation is not uncommon. Small employers are likely to have to pay the 'going wage rate' to their employees, especially where the employee is of a clear category, such as an electrician, a bar worker, a data analyst or a porter. As far as employees are concerned, being a wage taker means competing with other identical workers and not being a member of a union and therefore not being able to use collective bargaining to push up the wage rate.

Wage rates and employment under perfect competition are determined by the interaction of the market demand and supply of labour. This is illustrated in Figure 6.1. The curves show the total number of hours workers would supply and the number of hours of labour firms would demand for each wage rate in a particular labour market. The equilibrium market wage rate is W_e, where demand equals supply. Equilibrium employment in terms of the total number of hours people are employed in the market is Q_e.

Generally it would be expected that the supply and demand curves slope the same way as in goods markets.

The higher the wage rate paid for a certain type of job, the more workers will want to do that job and, generally, the more hours each will be willing to work. This gives an upward-sloping supply curve of labour. On the other hand, the higher the wage rate that employers have to pay, the less labour they will want to employ. They may simply produce less output, or they may substitute other factors of production, like machinery, for labour. Thus the demand curve for labour slopes downwards.

We now turn to look at the supply and demand for labour in more detail.

The supply of labour

As we have seen, the supply of labour in each market will typically be upward sloping. The *position* of the market supply curve of labour will depend on the number of people willing and able to do the job at each given wage rate. This depends on three things:

- The number of qualified people.
- The non-wage benefits or costs of the job, such as the pleasantness or otherwise of the working environment, job satisfaction or dissatisfaction, status, power, the degree of job security, holidays, perks and other fringe benefits.
- The wages and non-wage benefits in alternative jobs.

A change in the wage rate will cause a movement along the supply curve. A change in any of these other three determinants will shift the whole curve.

> #### Pause for thought
>
> *Which way will the supply curve shift if the wage rates in alternative jobs rise?*

The elasticity of supply of labour

How *responsive* will the supply of labour be to a change in the wage rate? If the market wage rate goes up, will a lot more labour become available or only a little? This responsiveness (elasticity) depends on (a) the difficulties and costs of changing jobs and (b) the time period.

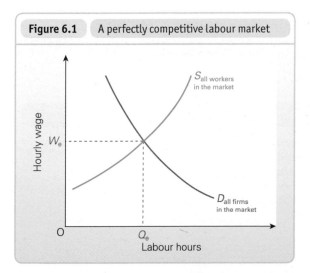

Figure 6.1 A perfectly competitive labour market

$S_{\text{all workers in the market}}$

W_e

$D_{\text{all firms in the market}}$

Hourly wage

O Q_e

Labour hours

> #### Definition
>
> **Wage taker** An employer (or employee) who is unable to influence the wage rate.

Another way of looking at the elasticity of supply of labour is in terms of the **mobility of labour**: the willingness and ability of labour to move to another job, whether in a different location (geographical mobility) or in a different industry (occupational mobility). The mobility of labour (and hence the elasticity of supply of labour) will be higher when there are alternative jobs in the same location, when alternative jobs require similar skills and when people have good information about these jobs.

It is also much higher in the long run, when people have the time to acquire new skills and when the education system has had time to adapt to the changing demands of industry.

The demand for labour: the marginal productivity theory

The market demand curve for labour will typically be downward sloping. To see why, let us examine how many workers an individual firm will want to employ.

In the previous two chapters, when we were looking at the production of goods, we assumed that firms aim to maximise profits. The theory of labour demand is based on the same assumption. This theory is generally known as the **marginal productivity theory**.

The profit-maximising approach

How many workers should a firm employ in order to maximise profits? The firm will answer this question by weighing up the costs of employing extra labour against the benefits. It will use exactly the same principles as in deciding how much output to produce.

In the goods market, the firm will maximise profits where the marginal cost of producing an extra unit of a *good* equals the marginal revenue from selling it: $MC = MR$.

In the labour market, the firm will maximise profits where the marginal cost of employing an extra *worker* equals the marginal revenue that the worker's output earns for the firm: MC of labour = MR of labour. The reasoning is simple. If an extra worker adds more to a firm's revenue than to its costs, the firm's profits will increase. It will be worth employing that worker.

But as more workers are employed, diminishing returns to labour will set in (see page 76). Each extra worker will produce less than the previous one, and thus earn less revenue for the firm. Eventually the marginal revenue from extra workers will fall to the level of their marginal cost. At that point, the firm will stop employing extra workers. There are no additional profits to be gained. Profits are at a maximum.

Measuring the marginal cost and revenue of labour

Marginal cost of labour (MC_L). This is the extra cost of employing one more worker. Under perfect competition the firm is too small to affect the market wage. It faces a horizontal supply curve. In other words, it can employ as many workers as it chooses at the market wage rate. Thus the additional cost of employing one more person will simply be the wage rate: $MC_L = W$.

Marginal revenue of labour (MRP_L). The marginal revenue that the firm gains from employing one more worker is called the **marginal revenue product of labour** (MRP_L). The MRP_L is found by multiplying two elements – the *marginal physical product* of labour (MPP_L) and the marginal revenue gained by selling one more unit of output (MR):

$$MRP_L = MPP_L \times MR$$

The MPP_L is the extra output produced by the last worker. Thus if the last worker produces 100 tonnes of output per week (MPP_L), and if the firm earns an extra £2 for each additional tonne sold (MR), then the worker's MRP is £200. This extra worker is adding £200 to the firm's revenue.

The profit-maximising level of employment for a firm

The MRP_L curve is illustrated in Figure 6.2. As more workers are employed, there will come a point when diminishing returns set in (point x). Thereafter the MRP_L curve slopes

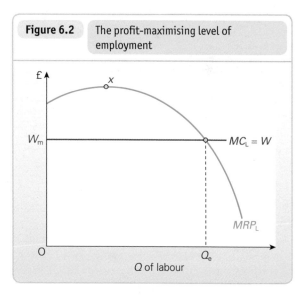

Figure 6.2 The profit-maximising level of employment

Definitions

Mobility of labour The willingness and ability of labour to move to another job.

Marginal productivity theory The theory that the demand for a factor depends on its marginal revenue product.

Marginal revenue product (of a factor) The extra revenue a firm earns from employing one more unit of a variable factor: $MRP_{factor} = MPP_{factor} \times MR_{good}$

Patterns in employment

The UK labour market has undergone great change in recent years. Advances in technology, changes in the pattern of output, a need to be competitive in international markets and various social changes have all contributed to changes in work practices and in the structure and composition of the workforce.

Major changes include the following.

Structural change. The UK has experienced a long-term decline in agricultural employment. From around 22 per cent of jobs in the 1840s, agriculture's share of total jobs had fallen to less than 9 per cent by 1900, 5 per cent by 1950 and by the mid-2010s to around 1.3 per cent. The manufacturing sector too has seen a decline in its share of jobs, but its decline began from the 1960s when the sector generated around 35 per cent of jobs. By 1990 this had halved to 17 per cent and by the mid- 2010s to under 8 per cent.

By contrast, jobs in the service industries have grown steadily since the Second World War when just under half of jobs were in the service sector. By 1990 this had risen to 70 per cent and to around 83 per cent in the mid-2010s.

A rise in female participation rates. In the 10-year period from 2005, women constituted 46 per cent of the paid labour force compared with 36 per cent at the beginning of the 1970s. The rise in participation rates is strongly associated with the growth in the service sector and the creation of part-time positions (see below). This helps to explain why men still supply a significant majority of the total number of hours worked in the economy. In the first half of the 2010s, males typically supplied over 61 per cent of hours worked, albeit lower than the average of 71 per cent seen across the 1970s.

A rise in part-time employment. In the early 1970s approximately one in six workers in the UK was part-time. This figure had risen to one-fifth of workers by the mid-1980s and, as the chart shows, the share of part-time employment in total employment figure has averaged close to 27 per cent in the first half of the 2010s.

Part-time jobs are overwhelmingly held by females. In the early 2010s around 80 per cent of part-time jobs were held by females; however, this share has fallen, having been close to 90 per cent in the early 1990s. The growth in part-time work reflects the growth in the service sector, where many jobs are part-time.

Growth in workers with second jobs. The UK has also seen considerable growth in the number of workers with more than one job. Some 1.2 million employees (3.9 per cent of those employed) had second jobs in 2014, of which 58 per cent were female. This compares with 702 000 (2.9 per cent of those employed) in 1984, of which 46 per cent were female.

Growth in self-employed workers. In 2014, 4.6 million employees were classified as self- employed, an historic high. This meant that 15 per cent of employees were now self-employed as compared with 11 per cent in 1984. The share was in line with the EU average. Self-employed workers tend to be older than the overall workforce. In 2014 around 43 per cent of self-employed employees were aged 50 or over as compared with 27 per cent of all employees. Around one-quarter of those self-employed were in 'skilled trades', such as construction, carpentry and joinery.

---

downwards. The figure also shows the MC_L 'curve' at the current market wage W_m.

Profits are maximised at an employment level of Q_e, where MC_L (i.e. the wage rate, W) = MRP_L. Why? At levels of employment less than Q_e, MRP_L exceeds MC_L. The firm will increase profits by employing more labour. At levels of employment greater than Q_e, MC_L exceeds MRP_L. In this case the firm will increase profits by reducing employment.

Derivation of the firm's demand curve for labour

No matter what the wage rate, the quantity of labour demanded will be found from the intersection of W and MRP_L (see Figure 6.3). At a wage rate of W_1, Q_1 labour is demanded (point *a*); at W_2, Q_2 is demanded (point *b*); at W_3, Q_3 is demanded (point *c*).

Thus the MRP_L curve shows the quantity of labour employed at each wage rate. But this is just what the demand curve for labour shows. Thus the MRP_L curve is the demand curve for labour.

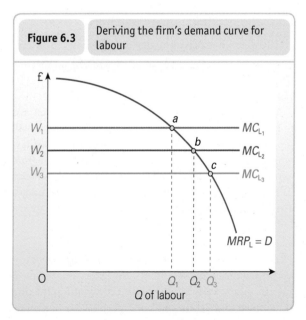

| Figure 6.3 | Deriving the firm's demand curve for labour |

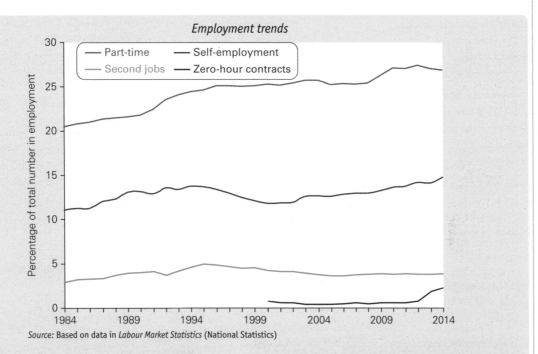

Employment trends

Source: Based on data in *Labour Market Statistics* (National Statistics)

A rise in the proportion of workers employed on fixed-term contracts, or on a temporary or casual basis. Many firms nowadays prefer to employ only their core workers/managers on a permanent ('continuing') basis. They feel that it gives them more flexibility in responding to changing market conditions to have the remainder of their workers employed on a short-term basis, and, perhaps, to make use of agency staff or to contract out work (see Case Study 6.2 in MyEconLab).

Consequently, this has seen a growth in no guaranteed hour contracts (NGHCs), more commonly referred to as zero-hour contracts. At the end of 2014 it was estimated

that 697 000 employees were employed on such contracts, which constitutes some 2.3 per cent of all employees (see chart). This figure rose sharply after 2011, when only 190 000 employees or 0.6 per cent of employees had been on zero-hour contracts.

1. *Write a short briefing note identifying some of the key long-term changes in UK employment patterns.*
2. *What potential issues might policy makers face as employment patterns change over time?*

There are three determinants of the demand for labour by a firm:

- The wage rate. This determines the position *on* the demand curve: i.e. the quantity demanded.
- The productivity of labour (MPP_L). This determines the position *of* the demand curve.
- The demand for the good being produced. The higher the demand for the good, the higher will be its price, and hence the higher will be MR, and thus MRP_L. This too determines the position of the demand curve. It shows how the demand for labour (and other factors) is a **derived demand**: i.e. one derived from the demand for the good. For example, the higher the demand for houses, and hence the higher their price, the higher will be the demand for bricklayers.

Pause for thought

If the productivity of a group of workers rises by 10 per cent, will the wage rate they are paid also rise by 10 per cent? Explain why or why not.

A change in the wage rate is represented by a movement along the demand curve for labour. A change in the productivity of labour or in the demand for the good *shifts* the curve.

Definition

Derived demand The demand for a factor of production depends on the demand for the good that uses it.

Market demand and its elasticity

For the same reason that the firm's demand for labour is downward sloping, so the whole market demand for labour will be downward sloping. At higher wage rates, firms in total will employ less labour.

The *elasticity* of this market demand for labour (with respect to changes in the wage rate) depends on various factors. Elasticity will be greater:

The greater the price elasticity of demand for the good. A rise in the wage rate, being a cost of production, will drive up the price of the good. If the market demand for the good is elastic, this rise in price will lead to a lot less being sold and hence a lot fewer people being employed.

The easier it is to substitute labour for other factors and vice versa. If labour can be readily replaced by other inputs (e.g. machinery), then a rise in the wage rate will lead to a large reduction in labour as workers are replaced by these other inputs.

The greater the wage cost as a proportion of total costs. If wages are a large proportion of total costs and the wage rate rises, total costs will rise significantly; therefore production will fall significantly, and so too will the demand for labour.

The longer the time period. Given sufficient time, firms can respond to a rise in wage rates by reorganising their production processes. For example, they could introduce robot production lines.

Wages and profits under perfect competition

The wage rate (*W*) is determined by the interaction of demand and supply in the labour market. This will be equal to the value of the output that the last person produces (MRP_L).

Profits to the individual firm arise from the fact that the MRP_L curve slopes downward (diminishing returns), with the last worker adding less to the revenue of firms than previous workers already employed.

If *all* workers in the firm receive a wage equal to the *MRP* of the last worker, everyone but the last worker will receive a wage *less* than their *MRP*. This excess of MRP_L over *W* of previous workers provides a surplus to the firm over its wages bill (see Figure 6.4). Part of this will be required for paying non-wage costs; part will be profits for the firm.

Perfect competition between firms will ensure that profits are kept down to *normal* profits. If the surplus over wages is such that *supernormal* profits are made, new firms will enter the industry. The price of the good (and hence MRP_L) will fall, and the wage rate will be bid up, until only normal profits remain.

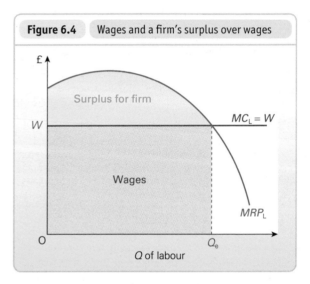

Figure 6.4 Wages and a firm's surplus over wages

6.2 WAGE DETERMINATION IN IMPERFECT MARKETS

How are wage rates affected by big business and by unions?

Firms with power

In the real world, many firms have the power to influence wage rates: they are not wage takers. This is one of the major types of labour market 'imperfection'.

When a firm is the only employer of a particular type of labour, this situation is called a **monopsony**. Royal Mail used to be a monopsony employer of postal workers.[1] Another example is when a factory is the only employer of certain types of labour in that district. It therefore has local monopsony power. When there are just a few employers, this is called **oligopsony**.

KI 17
p 101 Monopsonists (and oligopsonists too) are 'wage setters' not 'wage takers'. Thus a large employer in a small town may have considerable power to resist wage increases or even to force wage rates down. The National Health Service has considerable power in setting wages for health workers in the UK.

Such firms face an upward-sloping supply curve of labour. This is illustrated in Figure 6.5. If the firm wants to take on more labour, it will have to pay a higher wage rate to attract workers away from other industries. But conversely, by employing less labour it can get away with paying a lower wage rate. The supply curve shows the wage rate that must be paid to attract a given quantity of labour. The wage rate it pays is the *average cost* to the firm of employing labour (AC_L): i.e. the cost per worker. The supply curve is also therefore the AC_L curve.

The *marginal* cost of employing one more worker (MC_L) will be above the wage (AC_L): see Figure 6.5. The reason is that the wage rate has to be raised to attract extra workers.

Thus MC_L will be the new higher wage paid to the new employee *plus* the small rise in the total wages bill for existing employees: after all, they will be paid the higher wage too.

The profit-maximising employment of labour would be at Q_1, where $MC_L = MRP_L$. The wage (found from the AC_L curve) would thus be W_1.

If this had been a perfectly competitive labour market, employment would have been at the higher level Q_2, with the wage rate at the higher level W_2, where $W = MRP_L$. What in effect the monopsonist is doing, therefore, is forcing the wage rate down by restricting the number of workers employed.

The role of trade unions

How can unions influence the determination of wages, and what might be the consequences of their actions?

The extent to which unions will succeed in pushing *KI 17* up wage rates depends on their power and willingness to *p 101* take action. It also depends on the power of firms to resist and on their ability to pay higher wages. In particular, the scope for unions to gain a better deal for their members depends on the sort of market in which the employers are producing.

Unions facing competitive employers

If the employers are producing under perfect or monopolistic competition, wage rates can only rise at the expense of employment. Firms are earning just normal profit. Thus if unions force up the wage rate, the marginal firms will go bankrupt and leave the industry. Fewer workers will be employed. The fall in output will lead to higher prices. This will enable the remaining firms to pay a higher wage rate.

Figure 6.6 illustrates these effects. If unions succeed in raising the wage rate from W_1 to W_2, employment will fall from Q_1 to Q_2. There will be a surplus of people ($Q_3 - Q_2$) wishing to work in this industry for whom no jobs are available.

The union faces a second effect. Not only will jobs be lost as a result of the higher wage rate, but also there is a possibility that those in danger of losing their job will leave the union and undercut the union wage (unless employers have an agreement with the union not to employ non-unionised labour).

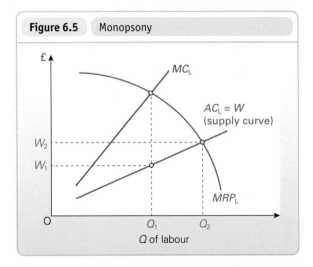

Figure 6.5 Monopsony

£

MC_L

$AC_L \equiv W$ (supply curve)

W_2

W_1

MRP_L

O Q_1 Q_2

Q of labour

Definitions

Monopsony A market with a single buyer or employer.

Oligopsony A market with just a few buyers or employers.

---

[1] Until 2005, Royal Mail had a statutory monopoly in the delivery of letters.

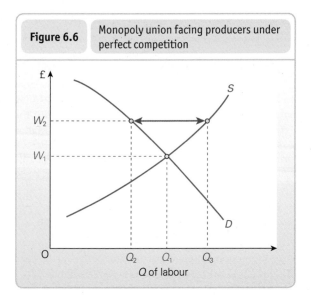

Figure 6.6 Monopoly union facing producers under perfect competition

In a competitive goods market, wage rates can only be increased without a reduction in the level of employment if, as part of the bargain, the productivity of labour is increased. This is called a **productivity deal**. The *MRP* curve, and hence the *D* curve in Figure 6.6, shifts to the right.

Pause for thought

At what wage rate in Figure 6.6 would employment be maximised: (a) W_1; (b) a wage rate above W_1; (c) a wage rate below W_1? Explain.

Bilateral monopoly

It is common to find the strongest unions where there is a monopsonistic labour market. In these circumstances we can think of the union monopoly as a counterweight to the power of a monopsony employer.

What will the wage rate be under these circumstances? What will the level of employment be? Unfortunately, economic theory cannot give a precise answer. There is no 'equilibrium' level as such (see Box 6.2). Ultimately the wage rate and level of employment will depend on the relative bargaining strengths and skills of unions and management.

Strange as it may seem, unions may be in a better position to make substantial gains for their members when they are facing a powerful employer. There is often considerable scope for them to increase wage rates *without* this leading to a reduction in employment, or even for them to increase both the wage rate *and* employment. The reason is that if firms have power in the *goods* market too, and are making supernormal profit, then there is scope for a powerful union to redistribute some of these profits to wages.

The actual wage rate under bilateral monopoly is usually determined through a process of negotiation or 'collective bargaining'. The outcome of this bargaining will depend on a wide range of factors, which vary substantially from one industry or firm to another.

Collective bargaining

Sometimes, when unions and management negotiate, *both* sides can gain from the resulting agreement. For example, the introduction of new technology may allow higher wages, improved working conditions and higher profits. Usually, however, one side's gain is the other's loss. Higher wages mean lower profits.

The outcome of the negotiations will depend on the relative bargaining strengths of both sides. In bargaining there are various threats or promises that either side can make. For these to be effective, of course, the other side must believe that they will be carried out – that the threats are credible.

Union *threats* might include strike action, **picketing, working to rule** or refusing to co-operate with management, for example in the introduction of new technology. Alternatively, in return for higher wages or better working conditions, unions might *offer* no-strike agreements, increased productivity, or long-term deals over pay.

In turn, employers might *threaten* employees with redundancies or reduced benefits. Alternatively, they might *offer*, in return for lower wage increases, better rewards such as productivity bonuses, profit-sharing schemes, more holiday or greater job security.

Industrial action imposes costs on both unions and firms. Union members lose pay; firms lose revenue. It is usually in both sides' interests, therefore, to settle by negotiation. Nevertheless, to gain the maximum advantage, each side must persuade the other that it will carry out its threats if pushed.

The approach described so far has essentially been one of confrontation. The alternative is for both sides to concentrate on increasing the total net income of the firm by co-operating on ways to increase efficiency or the quality of the product. This approach is more likely when unions and management have built up an atmosphere of trust over time.

Definitions

Productivity deal Where, in return for a wage increase, a union agrees to changes in working practices that will increase output per worker.

Picketing Where people on strike gather at the entrance to the firm and attempt to dissuade workers or delivery vehicles from entering.

Working to rule Where union members are instructed to stick to the letter of their job description and to refuse to take on any extra duties.

BOX 6.2 WAGES UNDER BILATERAL MONOPOLY

All to play for?

There is no single equilibrium wage rate under bilateral monopoly. This box shows why.

Assume first that there is no union. The diagram shows that a monopsonist employer will maximise profits by employing Q_1 workers at a wage rate of W_1 (Q_1 is where $MRP_L = MC_L$).

What happens when a union is introduced into this situation? Wages will now be set by negotiation between the union and management. Once the wage rate has been agreed, the employer can no longer drive the wage rate down by employing fewer workers. If it tried to pay less than the agreed wage, it could well be faced by a strike, and thus have a zero supply of labour!

Similarly, if the employer decided to take on *more* workers, it would not have to *increase* the wage rate as long as the negotiated wage were above the free-market wage: as long as the wage rate were above that given by the supply curve S_1.

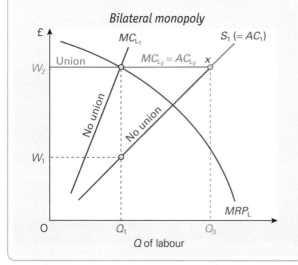

Bilateral monopoly

The effect of this is to give a new supply curve that is horizontal up to the point where it meets the original supply curve. For example, let us assume that the union succeeds in negotiating a wage rate of W_2. The supply curve will be horizontal at this level to the left of point x. To the right of this point it will follow the original supply curve S_1, since to acquire more than Q_3 workers it would have to raise the wage rate above W_2.

If the supply curve is horizontal to the left of point x at a level of W_2, so too will be the MC_L curve. The reason is simply that the extra cost to the employer of taking on an extra worker (up to Q_3) is merely the negotiated wage rate: no rise has to be given to existing employees. If MC_L is equal to the wage, the profit-maximising employment ($MC_L = MRP_L$) will now be where $W = MRP_L$. At a negotiated wage rate of W_2, the firm will therefore choose to employ Q_1 workers.

What this means, therefore, is that the union can push the wage rate up from W_1 to W_2 and the firm will still *want* to employ Q_1. In other words, a wage rise can be obtained *without* a reduction in employment.

The union could go further still. By threatening industrial action, it may be able to push the wage rate above W_2 and still insist that Q_1 workers are employed (i.e. no redundancies). The firm may be prepared to see profits drop right down to normal level rather than face a strike and risk losses. The absolute upper limit to the wage rate will be that at which the firm is forced to close down.

KI 13
p 66

?

1. If the negotiated wage rate were somewhere between W_1 and W_2, how would the resulting level of employment compare with that at W_1?
2. What in practice will determine just how much the agreed wage rate is above W_1?

Union membership. Trade union membership in the UK stands at about 6.5 million (25.6 per cent of employees) in the mid-2010s. This number is around half of that seen in the late 1970s. The fall in membership can be explained by a number of factors: the shift to a service-based economy; continued privatisation and the introduction of private-sector management practices, such as local pay bargaining; and contracted-out services into many of the remaining parts of the public sector. More women working and more part-time and casual work, with many people having no guaranteed hours, so-called 'zero-hour contracts' (see Box 6.1), are also contributory factors, as are the attitudes of many firms to union recognition.

Union membership remains highest in areas of the public sector with high levels of monopsony power, such as education, but there is no doubt that, even here, their power has declined.

Case Study 6.6 in MyEconLab charts the rise and decline of the labour movement in the UK.

The efficiency wage hypothesis

We have seen that a union may be able to force an employer to pay a wage above the market-clearing rate. But it may well be in employers' interests to do so, even in non-unionised sectors.

One explanation for this phenomenon is the **efficiency wage hypothesis**. This states that the productivity of workers rises as the wage rate rises. As a result, employers are frequently prepared to offer wage rates above the

KI 18
p 108

Definition

Efficiency wage hypothesis The hypothesis that the productivity of workers is affected by the wage rate that they receive.

market-clearing level, attempting to balance increased wage costs against gains in productivity. But why may higher wage rates lead to higher productivity? There are three main explanations.

Less 'shirking'. In many jobs it is difficult to monitor the effort that individuals put into their work. Workers may thus get away with shirking or careless behaviour. The business could attempt to reduce shirking by imposing a series of sanctions, the most serious of which would be dismissal. The greater the wage rate currently received, the greater will be the cost to the individual of dismissal, and the less likely it is, therefore, that workers will shirk. The business will benefit not only from the additional output, but also from a reduction in the costs of having to monitor workers' performance.

As a consequence, the **efficiency wage rate** for the business will be the 'true' profit-maximising wage rate for the firm. In this interpretation, the efficiency wage rate is the actual equilibrium wage rate determining the equilibrium level of employment.

Reduced labour turnover. If workers receive on-the-job training or retraining, then to lose a worker once the training has been completed is a significant cost to the business. Labour turnover, and hence its associated costs, can be reduced by paying a wage above the market-clearing rate. By paying such a wage rate, the business is seeking a degree of loyalty from its employees.

Improved morale. A simple reason for offering higher wage rates is to motivate the workforce – to create the feeling that the firm is a 'good' employer that cares about its employees. As a consequence, workers might be more industrious and more willing to accept the introduction of new technology (with the reorganisation that it involves).

The paying of efficiency wages will depend upon the type of work involved. Workers who occupy skilled positions, especially where the business has invested time in their training (thus making them costly to replace), are likely to receive relatively high efficiency wages. By contrast, workers in unskilled positions, where shirking can be easily monitored, where little training takes place and where workers can be easily replaced, are unlikely to command an 'efficiency wage premium'. In such situations, rather than keeping wage rates high, the business will probably try to pay as little as possible.

TC 4
p 20

Definition

Efficiency wage rate The profit-maximising wage rate for the firm after taking into account the effects of wage rates on worker motivation, turnover and recruitment.

Recap

1. Where a firm has monopoly power in employing labour, it is known as a 'monopsonist'. Such a firm will employ workers to the point where $MRP_L = MC_L$. Since the wage is below MC_L, the monopsonist, other things being equal, will employ fewer workers at a lower wage than would be employed in a perfectly competitive labour market.

2. If a union has monopoly power, its power to raise wages will be limited if the employer operates under perfect or monopolistic competition in the goods market. A rise in wage rates will force the employer to cut back on employment, unless there is a corresponding rise in productivity.

3. In a situation of bilateral monopoly (where a monopoly union faces a monopsony employer) the union may have considerable scope to raise wage rates above the monopsony level. There is no unique equilibrium wage. The wage rate will depend on the outcome of a process of collective bargaining between union and management.

4. Collective bargaining is the process by which employers and unions negotiate wage levels and the terms and conditions of employment. Both sides can use threats and promises to determine the outcome of the negotiating process. The success of such threats and promises depends upon factors such as the power of the union or the employer; attitudes and the determination to win; scope for compromise; negotiating skills; information; and the role of government.

5. The efficiency wage hypothesis states that a firm might pay a wage premium to: reduce shirking; reduce labour turnover; improve the quality of labour recruited; and stimulate worker morale. The level of efficiency wage rates will largely be determined by the types of job workers do, and the level and scarcity of the skills they possess.

6.3 INEQUALITY

How do we assess the extent of inequality?

Types of inequality

There a number of different ways of looking at the distribution of income and wealth and so assessing the extent of inequality.

The distribution of income

There are three broad ways of examining the distribution of income.

The size distribution of income. First we can look at how evenly incomes are distributed among the population. This is known as the **size distribution of income**. It can be expressed between *households*, or between *individual earners*, or between *all individuals*. It can be expressed either *before* or *after* the deduction of taxes and the receipt of benefits. For example, we might want to know the proportion of pre-tax national income going to the richest 10 per cent of households.

The functional distribution of income. We could also look at the distribution between different *factors of production*, known as the **functional distribution of income**. At the *broader* level, we could look at the distribution between the general factor categories: labour, land and capital. At a *narrower* level, we could look at distribution within the factor categories. Why are some jobs well paid while others are badly paid? Why are rents higher in some areas than in others?

Distribution by groups of people. Finally we could look at the **distribution of income by class of recipient**. This can be by *class of person*: women, men, single people, married people, people within a particular age group or ethnic group, and so on. Alternatively, it can be by *geographical area*. Typically, this is expressed in terms of differences in incomes between officially defined regions within a country.

When the distribution of income is analysed different measures of income can be used. These reflect the different stages of redistribution and, hence, the impact of government intervention. Households' **original income** is made up of employment income, income from financial products and income from occupational pensions. When we add to original income any cash benefits paid by government, such as state pensions, we have **gross income**. Next, after deducting direct taxes, such as income tax and national insurance contributions, we have **disposable income**. If we now deduct indirect taxes, like value added tax (VAT) and other expenditure taxes, we have **post-tax income**. Finally, we can attempt to add on the estimated value of *benefits in kind*, such as health and education, and, in doing so, obtain **final income**.

Table 6.1 shows the size distribution in the UK for original and post-tax income. The population is divided into five equal-sized groups or 'quintiles'.

Table 6.1	Distribution of UK income by quintile group of households									
	1980		**1990**		**2000/1**		**2010/11**		**2013/14**	
Household income group	Original income	Post-tax income	Original income	Post-tax income	Original income	Post-tax income	Original income	Post-tax income	Original income	Post-tax income
Lowest 20%	2	9	2	6	2	6	3	7	3	7
Next 20%	10	13	7	10	7	11	7	12	8	12
Middle 20%	18	17	17	16	15	16	14	16	15	16
Next 20%	26	23	26	23	25	23	24	22	24	23
Highest 20%	44	38	51	45	50	45	51	44	50	42
All	100	100	100	100	100	100	100	100	100	100

Source: The effects of taxes and benefits on household income, 2014/15 – Reference Tables, Table 26 (National Statistics, 2015)

Figure 6.7   Lorenz curve

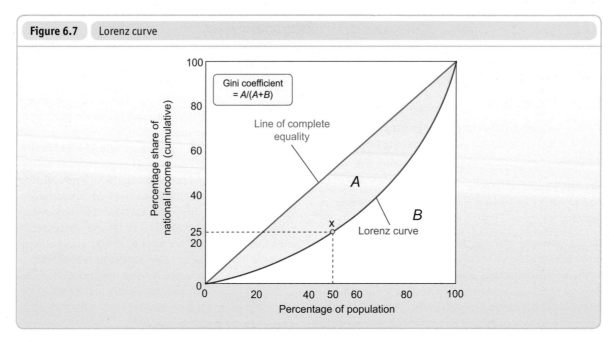

The following points can be drawn from these statistics:

■ In 2013/14, the richest 20 per cent of households earned 50 per cent of original income, and even after the deduction of taxes their share of post-tax income was still 42 per cent.

■ The poorest 20 per cent, by contrast, earned a mere 3 per cent of original income, and even after the receipt of benefits their share of post-tax income was only 7 per cent.

Inequality grew dramatically in the 1980s and 1990s in the UK and many other countries. Between 1980 and 2000/1, the share of post-tax income of the poorest 40 per cent of households fell from 22 per cent to 17 per cent; while the share of the top 20 per cent grew from 38 per cent to 45 per cent. After 2000, income inequality declined slightly. In the 2000s, this was largely the result of minimum wages and more generous benefits in the form of tax credits. In the period following the financial crisis of 2007–8, this was largely the result of many people on top incomes receiving somewhat less.

The distribution of wealth

KI 21
P 148

Income is a *flow*. It measures the receipt of money per period of time (e.g. £25 000 per year). Wealth, by contrast, is a *stock*. It measures the value of a person's assets at a particular point in time.

The distribution of wealth can be measured as a size distribution (how evenly it is distributed among the population); as a functional distribution (the proportion of wealth held in various forms, such as dwellings, land, company shares, bank deposits, etc.); or according to the holders of wealth, classified by age, sex, geographical area, etc.

KEY IDEA 21
Stocks and flows. A stock is a quantity of something at a given point in time. A flow is an increase or decrease in something over a specified period of time. This is an important distinction and a common cause of confusion.

Measuring the size distribution of income

Two of the most widely used methods for measuring inequality are the *Lorenz curve* and the *Gini coefficient*. We introduce them here in the context of the inequality of income but they can also be used to measure the inequality of wealth.

Lorenz curve

Figure 6.7 shows a hypothetical **Lorenz curve**. The horizontal axis measures percentages of the population from the poorest to the richest. Thus the 50 per cent point represents the poorest 50 per cent of the population. The vertical axis measures the percentage of national income they receive.

The curve starts at the origin: zero people earn zero incomes. If income were distributed totally equally, the Lorenz curve would be a straight 45° line. The 'poorest' 20 per cent of the population would earn 20 per cent of national income; the 'poorest' 50 per cent would earn

Definition

Lorenz curve A curve showing the proportion of national income (or wealth) earned by any given percentage of the population (measured from the poorest upwards).

Figure 6.8 Gini coefficients for selected OECD countries, based on disposable income: 2011 or 2012

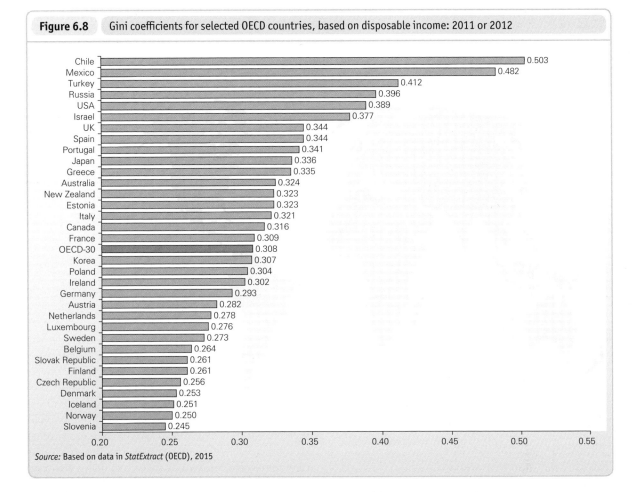

Source: Based on data in *StatExtract* (OECD), 2015

50 per cent, and so on. The curve ends up at the top right-hand corner, with 100 per cent of the population earning 100 per cent of national income.

In practice, the Lorenz curve will 'hang below' the 45° line. Point *x*, for example, shows a country where the poorest 50 per cent of households receive only 25 per cent of national income. The further the curve drops below the 45° line, the greater will be the level of inequality.

The Lorenz curve is quite useful for showing the change in income distribution over time. From 1949 to 1979 the curve for the UK moved inwards towards the 45° line, suggesting a lessening of inequality. Then from 1979 to 1990 it moved downwards away from the 45° line, suggesting a deepening of inequality. Since 1990 it has remained approximately the same.

The problem with simply comparing Lorenz curves by eye is that it is imprecise. This problem is overcome by using Gini coefficients.

Gini coefficient

The **Gini coefficient** is a precise way of measuring the position of the Lorenz curve. It is the ratio of the area between the Lorenz curve and the 45° line to the whole area below the 45° line. In Figure 6.7 this is the ratio of the shaded area *A* to the whole area (*A* + *B*), sometimes expressed as a percentage.

If income is totally equally distributed so that the Lorenz curve follows the 45° line, area *A* disappears and the Gini coefficient is zero. As inequality increases, so does area *A*. The Gini coefficient rises. In the extreme case of total inequality, where one person earns the whole of national income, area *B* would disappear and the Gini coefficient would be 1. Thus the Gini coefficient will be between 0 and 1. The higher it is, the greater is the inequality.

In 1977 the *post-tax* Gini coefficient in the UK was 0.294. With the growth in inequality during the 1980s, the coefficient steadily increased and stood at 0.406 in 1990. The it gradually fell until the mid-1990s and then rose again to reach 0.406 again by 2001/2. It then gradually fell during the 2000s to stand at 0.368 at the end of the decade. In the first part of the 2010s it average 0.37.

Figure 6.8 shows the Gini coefficients for a selection of countries in 2011 or 2012. These are based on *disposable income*. As you can see, several northern European countries

> **Definition**
>
> **Gini coefficient** The area between the Lorenz curve and the 45° line divided by the total area under the 45° line.

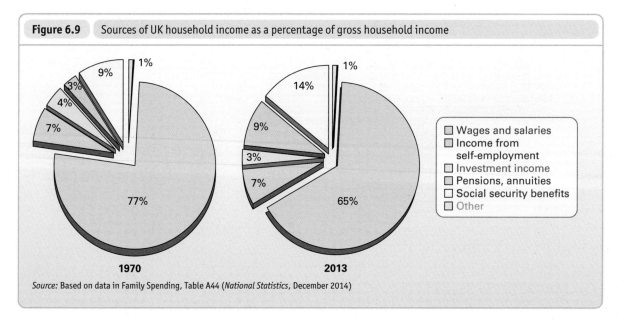

Figure 6.9   Sources of UK household income as a percentage of gross household income

1970

2013

Wages and salaries
Income from
  self-employment
Investment income
Pensions, annuities
Social security benefits
Other

Source: Based on data in Family Spending, Table A44 (*National Statistics*, December 2014)

were among those countries with the lowest Gini coefficients and hence were the most equal. The most unequal in the sample was Chile. The average across the OECD[2] countries was 0.308, more equal than the USA (0.389) and slightly more than the UK (0.344).

The functional distribution of income

Distribution of income by source

Figure 6.9 shows the sources of gross household incomes in 1970 and 2013. Wages and salaries constitute by far the largest element. However, their share fell from 77 per cent to 65 per cent of national income over this period. Conversely, the share coming from social security benefits and pensions rose from 12 per cent to 23 per cent, reflecting the growing proportion of the population past retirement age.

In contrast to wages and salaries, investment income (dividends, interest and rent) accounts for a relatively small percentage of household income – a mere 3 per cent in 2013. This partly reflects the historically very low rates of interest paid on savings accounts.

Despite the growth of small businesses and the increased numbers of people being 'employed' on a freelance basis, the proportion of incomes coming from self-employment has remained at around 7 per cent.

The overall shares illustrated in Figure 6.9 hide the fact that the sources of gross income differ quite markedly between different income groups. These differences are shown in Table 6.2.

Column (1) shows that higher-income groups get a larger proportion of their income from wages and salaries

than do lower-income groups. As would be expected, the poor tend to get a larger proportion of their incomes from social security benefits than do people further up the income scale (see column (5)).

It is interesting to note that the second poorest 20 per cent of households have a larger proportion of their income from pensions and annuities than any other group. Pensioners are clustered in this group because they tend to be fairly poor (pensions being less than wages), but not as poor as unemployed people or as families on low incomes.

We can see from the table that the proportion of income coming from profits, rent and interest (column (3)) varies little between the income groups. The exception is for the richest income group and even here its significance tends to be concentrated among the very richest. The conclusion from this, plus the fact that investment incomes account for only 3 per cent of household incomes in total, is that incomes from capital and land are of only relatively minor significance in explaining income inequality.

Distribution of wages and salaries by occupation

The major cause of differences in incomes between individuals in employment is the differences in wages and salaries between different occupations. Differences in full-time wages and salaries are illustrated in Figure 6.10. This shows the average gross weekly earnings of full-time adult workers in the nine highest- and five lowest-paid occupations in the UK in 2014. As you can see, there are considerable differences in pay between different occupations.

Differences in weekly earnings are mainly the result of differences in hourly rates of pay (see Box 6.3), but are also partly explained by differences in the number of hours worked (including the amount of overtime).

[2]The Organization for Economic Cooperation and Development. A group of 34 industrialised countries; 30 of them provide data on income distribution.

Table 6.2	Sources of UK household income as a percentage of total household gross weekly income by quintile groups: 2013						

Gross household weekly incomes (quintiles)	Wages and salaries	Income from self-employment	Income from investments	Pensions and annuities	Social security benefits	Other	Total
	(1)	(2)	(3)	(4)	(5)	(6)	(7)
Lowest 20%	10	4	2	9	74	1	100
Next 20%	32	5	2	17	42	2	100
Middle 20%	53	6	2	16	21	2	100
Next 20%	71	7	2	9	9	2	100
Highest 20%	78	8	5	5	2	1	100
All households	65	7	3	9	14	1	100

Source: *Family Spending*, Tables A39 and A44 (National Statistics, 2014)

Figure 6.10	Highest- and lowest-paid occupations – mean full-time gross weekly earnings (excluding overtime) (£): 2014

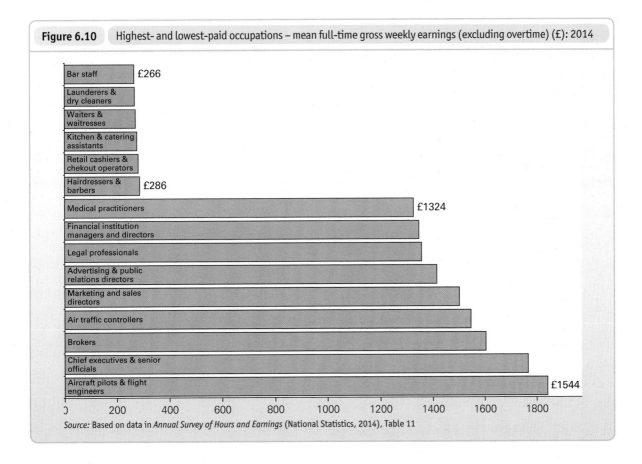

Source: Based on data in *Annual Survey of Hours and Earnings* (National Statistics, 2014), Table 11

Pause for thought

If fringe benefits (such as long holidays, company cars, free clothing/uniforms, travel allowances and health insurance) were included, do you think the level of inequality would increase or decrease? Explain why.

Since the late 1970s, wage differentials have widened. Part of the explanation lies in a shift in the demand for labour. Many firms have adopted new techniques that require a more highly educated workforce. Wage rates in some of these skilled occupations have increased substantially.

BOX 6.3 **EQUAL PAY FOR EQUAL WORK?**

Wage inequalities between men and women

Women earn less than men. How much less depends on how earnings are measured, but on the most widely used definition, mean gross earnings per hour of full-time workers, women in the UK in 2014 earned some 14 per cent less than men. This is based on figures in the Annual Survey of Hours and Earnings (ASHE). As the chart shows, the gender wage gap has narrowed in recent years. And this trend has been continuing for much longer. Women typically earned 37 per cent less in 1970, 26 per cent less by 1980, 23 per cent less by 1990 and 20 per cent less by 2000.

A similar picture of gender inequality in pay can be seen throughout the EU. In 2013, women's gross average hourly pay was 16.4 per cent less than men's. The figure varies from one country to another. For example, in Germany women earned 21.6 per cent less, in France 15.2 per cent less and in Italy 7.3 less.

The inequality between male and female earnings can in part be explained by the fact that men and women are occupationally segregated. Seeing that women predominate in poorly paid occupations, the difference in earnings is somewhat to be expected. But if you consider Table (b), you can see that quite substantial earnings differentials persist within particular occupations.

?

1. *If we were to look at weekly rather than hourly pay and included the effects of overtime, what do you think would happen to the pay differentials in the figure below?*
2. *In the table opposite which of the occupations have a largely female workforce?*

So why has this inequality persisted? There are a number of possible reasons:

- The marginal productivity of labour in typically female occupations may be lower than in typically male occupations. This may in part be due to simple questions of physical strength. Very often, however, it is due to the fact that women tend to work in more labour-intensive occupations. If there is less capital equipment per female worker than there is per male worker, then it would be expected that the marginal product of a woman would be less than that of a man. Evidence from the EU as a whole suggests that occupational segregation is a significant factor in explaining pay differences.
- Many women take career breaks to have children. For this reason, employers are sometimes more willing to invest money in training men (thereby increasing their marginal productivity), and more willing to promote men.
- Women tend to be less geographically mobile than men. If social norms are such that the man's job is seen as somehow more 'important' than the woman's, then a couple will often move if necessary for the man to get promotion. The woman, however, will have to settle for whatever job she can get in the same locality as her partner. Additionally this may reduce a woman's bargaining power when negotiating for wage increases in her current job, if her employer knows that her outside options are more limited than a man's would be.

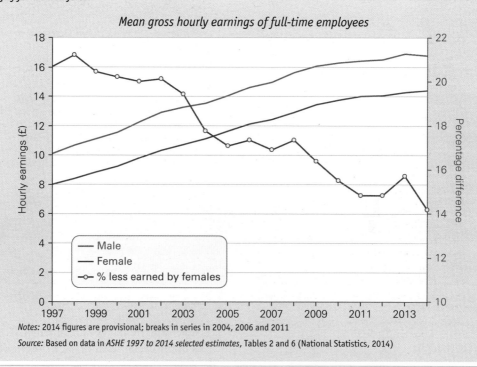

Mean gross hourly earnings of full-time employees

Notes: 2014 figures are provisional; breaks in series in 2004, 2006 and 2011

Source: Based on data in ASHE 1997 to 2014 selected estimates, Tables 2 and 6 (National Statistics, 2014)

Average hourly pay, excluding overtime, for selected occupations, full-time UK employees on adult rates, 2014

Occupation	Men	Women	Women's pay as a % of men's
	£ per hour		
Chief executives and senior officials	51.27	36.88	71.9
Medical practitioners	36.50	28.91	79.2
Solicitors	41.27	33.74	81.8
Laboratory technicians	13.14	10.96	83.4
Senior police officers	29.83	25.12	84.2
Librarians	17.13	14.44	84.3
Accountants	22.57	19.16	84.9
Communication operators	15.11	13.95	92.3
Management consultants & business analysts	23.69	21.96	92.7
Sales and retail assistants	8.74	8.12	92.9
Secondary school teachers	2.83	21.24	93.0
Assemblers and routine operatives	8.86	8.34	94.1
Hairdressers, barbers	7.91	7.55	95.4
Nurses	17.36	16.62	95.7
Bar staff	7.04	6.75	95.9
Social workers	17.45	16.76	96.0
Chefs	8.79	8.63	98.2
All occupations	**16.77**	**14.39**	**85.8**
Average gross weekly pay (incl. overtime)	673.00	539.20	80.1
Average weekly hours worked (incl. overtime)	40.20	37.50	
Average weekly overtime	1.40	0.60	

Source: Annual Survey of Hours and Earnings (National Statistics, 2014)

- A smaller proportion of women workers are members of unions than men. Even when they are members of unions, these are often in jobs where unions are weak (e.g. clothing industry workers and shop assistants).
- Around three-quarters of part-time workers in the UK today are female. While this proportion has fallen from around 90 per cent in the early 1980s, it remains significant. Part-time workers often have less bargaining power, less influence and less chance of obtaining promotion.
- Custom and practice. Despite equal pay legislation, many jobs done wholly or mainly by women continue to be low paid, irrespective of productivity.

- Prejudice. In many jobs women are discriminated against when it comes to promotion, especially to senior positions. A report published in 2015 for the UK government[3] confirmed that women remain seriously underrepresented in boardrooms. Of the FTSE 100 companies, only 23.5 per cent of board members were women (but nearly double the figure of 12.5 per cent in 2011). This phenomenon is known as the 'glass ceiling' and it is very difficult to legislate against. Businesses can simply claim that the 'better' person was promoted or that women do not put themselves forward. The report suggests various measures to increase the number of female board members, including discussions with chairmen on the issue, Women on Boards conferences, pressure from investors and requiring companies to report on their diversity policies.

Which of the above reasons could be counted as economically 'irrational' (i.e. paying different wage rates to women and men for other than purely economic reasons)? Certainly the last two would classify. Paying different wage rates on these grounds would not be in the profit interests of the employer.

Some of the others, however, are more difficult to classify. The causes of the inequality in wage rates may be traced back beyond the workplace: perhaps to the educational system or to a culture that discourages women from being so aggressive in seeking promotion.

It is interesting to consider the role that maternity pay and leave may play in the continuation of unequal incomes between women and men. In July 2008 Nicola Brewer, Chief Executive of the Equality and Human Right Commission, gave a speech in which she called for a rethinking of family policy. In particular she suggested that over-generous treatment of mothers, compared with fathers, was a contributory factor in continuing inequality. Ms Brewer argued that the UK's approach perpetuated the view that childcare was a women's issue rather than a parental one.

Her views, and those of others, have influenced recent developments in 'family-friendly' policies and from 2014 both parents have the right to share up to a year of parental leave. However, until this is widely accepted as the 'norm' and is used equally by men and women, employers may retain the view that women are less valuable and productive employees.

?
3. If employers were forced to give genuinely equal pay for equal work, how would this affect the employment of women and men? What would determine the magnitude of these effects?
4. How could family policy ensure that parents are able to work, while reducing pay differentials?
5. What measures could a government introduce to increase the number of women getting higher-paid jobs?

---

[3]'Women on Boards', *Davies Review Annual Report 2015* (GOV.UK, March 2015.)

Table 6.3	Sources of British household wealth as a percentage of total household wealth by income quintile groups: 2010–12			
Gross household annual incomes (quintiles)	Net property wealth	Physical wealth	Net financial wealth	Private pension wealth
	(1)	(2)	(3)	(4)
Lowest 20%	51	18	10	20
Next 20%	45	15	10	30
Middle 20%	39	13	11	37
Next 20%	36	12	12	41
Highest 20%	33	9	17	41

Note: Physical wealth in the Wealth and Assets Survey relates to vehicles and to the contents and valuables held within properties

Source: Wealth and Assets Survey (National Statistics, 2014)

At the same time there has been a decline in the number of unskilled jobs in industry, and, along with it, a decline in the power of unions to represent such people. Where low-skilled jobs remain, there is intense pressure on employers to reduce wage costs if they are competing with companies based in developing countries, where wage rates are much lower.

As prospects for the unskilled decline in industry, so people with few qualifications increasingly compete for low-paid service-sector jobs (e.g. in supermarkets, fast-food outlets and call centres). The growth in people seeking part-time work has also kept wage rates down in this sector.

The distribution of wealth

The Wealth and Assets Survey finds that the median level of gross income in the UK for the 2010–12 period was £32 100, while the median level of household wealth was £218 400. Therefore, median wealth was found to be seven times larger than median annual gross income.

Table 6.3 shows the composition of household wealth in Great Britain for 2010–12 for different income groups. For the two poorest income groups, net property wealth, namely property wealth after deducting any outstanding debts secured on property, is by far the largest component of wealth (see column (1)). However, for the two richest income groups private pension wealth is the largest component (see column (4)).

The proportion of wealth contributed by physical wealth (i.e. vehicles and contents and valuables within property) tends to decrease with income (see column (2)). Finally, net financial wealth, namely financial assets (savings, etc.) less financial liabilities (debts), accounts for a similar proportion of wealth in the first four quintiles, but makes a more

significant contribution to household wealth for those in the richest quintile (see column (3)).

Figure 6.11 shows how the inequality of wealth is far greater than inequality of income in Britain. It plots the Lorenz curves for both the distribution of gross income and household wealth in Great Britain for the 2010–12 period. The wealthiest 25 per cent of households owned 75 per cent of total household wealth in Great Britain while the richest 25 per cent of households by income received 55 per cent of total gross annual income.

Causes of wealth inequality

The four major causes of inequality in the distribution of wealth are as follows:

- *Inheritance*. This allows inequality to be perpetuated from one generation to another.
- *Income inequality*. People with higher incomes can save more.
- *Different propensities to save*. People who save a larger proportion of their income will build up a bigger stock of wealth.
- *Entrepreneurial and investment talent/luck*. Some people are successful in investing their wealth and making it grow rapidly.

Even though wealth is still highly concentrated, there was a significant reduction in inequality of wealth up to the early 1990s. From 1971 to 1991 the Gini coefficient of wealth fell a full 16 percentage points from 0.80 to 0.64. A major reason for this was the increased taxation of inherited wealth. Since 1991, however, this reduction in inequality has been reversed somewhat. This can be explained by lower levels of inheritance tax and substantial rises in property prices and share values.

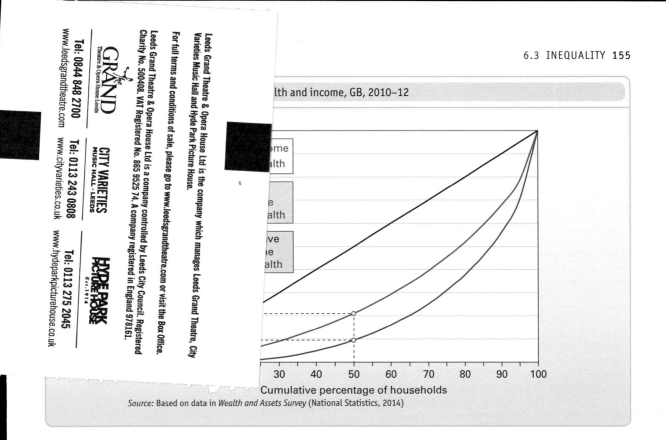

...lth and income, GB, 2010–12

Cumulative percentage of households

Source: Based on data in *Wealth and Assets Survey* (National Statistics, 2014)

Causes of inequality

We turn now to identify the major causes of inequality. The problem has many dimensions and there are many factors that determine the pattern and depth of inequality. It is thus wrong to try to look for a single cause, or even the major one. The following are possible determinants of inequality:

- Inequality of wealth. People with wealth are able to obtain an income other than from their own labour (e.g. from rent or dividends on shares).
- Differences in ability. People differ in intelligence, strength, etc. Some of these differences are innate and some are acquired through the process of 'socialisation' – education, home environment, etc.
- Differences in attitude. Some people are adventurous, willing to take risks, willing to move for better jobs, keen to push themselves forward. Others are much more cautious.
- Differences in qualifications. These are reflections of a number of things: ability, attitudes towards study, access to good education, income of parents, etc.
- Differences in hours worked. Some people do a full-time job plus overtime, or a second job; others work only part-time.
- Differences in job utility/disutility. Other things being equal, unpleasant or dangerous jobs will need to pay higher wages.

- Differences in power. Monopoly power in the supply of factors or goods, and monopsony power in the demand for factors, are unequally distributed in the economy.
- Differences in the demand for goods. Workers employed in expanding industries will tend to have a higher marginal revenue product because their output has a higher market value.
- Differences in household composition. The greater the number of dependants relative to income earners, the poorer the average household member will be (other things being equal). Similarly, the greater the number of retired people relative to economically active individuals, the poorer the household will tend to be.
- Discrimination by race, sex, age, social background, etc.
- Degree of government support. The greater the support for the poor, the less will be the level of inequality in the economy.
- Unemployment. When unemployment levels are high, this is one of the major causes of poverty.

KI 13
p 66

TC 5
p 23

Pause for thought

Which of these causes of inequality are reflected in differences in the marginal revenue product of labour?

BOX 6.4 MINIMUM WAGE LEGISLATION

A way of helping the poor?

The Labour government introduced a statutory UK minimum wage in April 1999. The rate was £3.60 per hour for those aged 22 and over, and £3.00 for those between 18 and 21 (the 'development rate'). In 2004 an additional rate was introduced for 16- and 17-year-olds and in 2010 for apprentices aged 16–18 and those aged 19 in the first year of their apprenticeship. The rates have been increased every year and from October 2015 were £6.70, £5.30, £3.87 and £3.30. However, as the chart shows, after adjusting for inflation, the real value of the minimum wage fell after 2008/9.

As of January 2015, 22 of the 28 EU member countries had a national minimum wage. These rates varied considerably. But, three broad groupings can be identified: one where minimum wages were lower than €500 a month (Bulgaria, Romania, Lithuania, the Czech Republic, Hungary, Latvia, Slovakia, Estonia, Croatia and Poland), an intermediate set where minimum wages range from €500 to less than €1000 a month (Portugal, Greece, Malta, Spain and Slovenia) and a final set where the national minimum wage was €1000 or above per month (UK, France, Ireland, Germany, the Netherlands, Belgium and Luxembourg).

The call for a minimum wage in the UK grew during the 1990s as the number of low-paid workers increased. There were many people working as cleaners, security guards and shop assistants who were receiving pittance rates of pay, sometimes less than £2 per hour. Several factors explain the growth in the size of the low-pay sector.

Lower demand for unskilled labour. Increased rates of unemployment since the early 1980s had shifted the balance of power from workers to employers. Employers were able to force many wage rates downwards, especially those of unskilled and semi-skilled workers.

Growth in part-time employment. Changes in the structure of the UK economy, particularly the growth in the service sector and the growing proportion of women seeking work, had led to an increase in part-time employment and zero-hour contracts, with many part-time workers not receiving the same rights and hourly pay as their full-time equivalents until 2000.

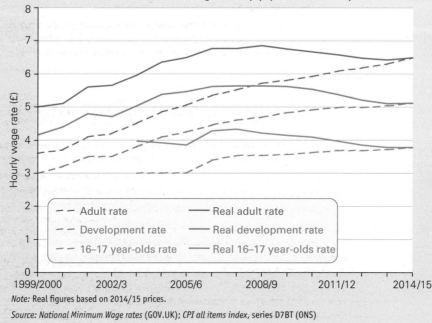

National minimum wage rates (£) (actual and real)

Note: Real figures based on 2014/15 prices.

Source: *National Minimum Wage rates* (GOV.UK); *CPI all items index*, series D7BT (ONS)

Changes in labour laws. The abolition of 'wages councils' in 1993, which had set legally enforceable minimum hourly rates in various low-paid industries, and the introduction of various new laws to reduce the power of labour had left low-paid workers with little protection.

Assessing the arguments

The principal argument against imposing a national minimum wage concerns its impact on employment. If you raise wage rates above the equilibrium level, there will be surplus labour: i.e. unemployment (see Figure 6.6 on page 144). However, the impact of a national minimum wage on employment is not so simple.

In the case of a firm operating in *competitive* labour and goods markets, the demand for low-skilled workers is relatively wage sensitive. Any rise in wage rates, and hence prices, by this firm alone would lead to a large fall in sales and hence in employment. But given that *all* firms face the minimum wage, individual employers are more able to pass on higher wages in higher prices, knowing that their competitors are doing the same.

When employers have a degree of monopsony power, however, it is not even certain that they would want to reduce employment. Remember what we argued in Box 6.2 (on page 145) when we were examining the effects of unions driving up wages. The argument is the same with a minimum wage. The minimum wage can be as high as W_2 and the firm will still want to employ as many workers as at W_1. The point is that the firm can no longer drive down the wage rate by employing fewer workers, so the incentive to cut its workforce has been removed.

In the long run, the effect on unemployment will depend on the extent to which the higher wages are compensated by higher labour productivity.

Evidence from the USA and other countries suggests that modest increases in the minimum wage have had a neutral effect upon employment. Similarly in the UK, there is little evidence to suggest that from 1999 employers responded by employing fewer workers. In fact, until 2008, unemployment rates fell, due to the fact that in the years following the introduction of the minimum wage there was a buoyant economy and increasing labour market flexibility.

Whether there would continue to be little effect if the minimum wage were to rise substantially is another matter. The issue, then, seems to be how *high* can the minimum wage be set before unemployment begins to rise?

Impact of the minimum wage in the UK

According to research from the Resolution Foundation published in October 2014, around 1.2 million workers now benefit from the national minimum wage (NMW), compared to just over 600 000 when introduced in 1999, while another 1.3 million earn within 50p of the legal hourly rate. These figures include high numbers of female workers, part-time workers and people from ethnic minorities.

One concern for economists, when assessing the national minimum wage, is that living costs, and particularly housing costs, vary substantially across the economy. There have been suggestions that *local* minimum wages rates should be set, to ensure a more efficient outcome.

However, there has been a more vociferous campaign for a 'living wage' – one which would lift those working full-time out of poverty. The Living Wage Foundation has estimated that for 2015 the UK average hourly wage would need to have been £7.85, while in London, where the cost of living is highest, this would have required an hourly rate of £9.15.

In his 2015 Summer Budget, George Osborne announced that a statutory 'national living wage (NLW)' would be introduced in April 2016 for workers aged 25 and above. At £7.20, this would be 50p more than the NMW of £6.70. Whether this should be seen as a 'living wage' or merely a top-up on the minimum wage is debatable. Nevertheless, the Conservative government plans for the NLW to be 60 per cent of median hourly earnings by 2020.

Of course a weakness of using a minimum wage as a means of relieving poverty is that it only affects the employed; yet one of the main causes of poverty is unemployment. This, in part, explains the focus on getting adults into work as the major plank of poverty-relief policy in the UK. It is apparent that a minimum wage rate cannot be the sole answer to poverty and must be considered in conjunction with benefits.

?

1. *If an increase in wage rates for low-paid workers leads to their being more motivated, how would this affect the marginal revenue product and the demand for such workers? What implications does your answer have for the effect on employment in such cases? (See pages 145–6 on the efficiency wage hypothesis.)*
2. *If a rise in the minimum wage encourages employers to substitute machines for workers, will this necessarily lead to higher long-term unemployment in (a) that industry and (b) the economy in general?*

BOX 6.5 **INEQUALITY AND ECONOMIC GROWTH** *CASE STUDIES & APPLICATIONS*

Macroeconomic implications of income inequality

What is the relationship between the degree of inequality in a country and the rate of economic growth? The traditional answer is that there is a trade-off between the two. Increasing the rewards to those who are more productive or who invest encourages a growth in productivity and capital investment, which, in turn, leads to faster economic growth. Redistribution from the rich to the poor, by contrast, is argued to reduce incentives by reducing the rewards from harder work, education, training and investment. Risk taking, it is claimed, is discouraged.

Recent evidence from the OECD and the IMF, however, suggests that when income inequality rises, economic growth *falls*. Inequality has grown massively in many countries, with average incomes at the top of the distribution seeing particular gains, while many at the bottom have experienced actual declines in real incomes or, at best, little or no growth. This growth in inequality can be seen in a rise in countries' Gini coefficients. The OECD average Gini coefficient rose from 0.29 in the mid-1980s to 0.32 in 2011–12. This, claims the OECD, has led to a loss in economic growth of around 0.35 percentage points per year.

But why should a rise in inequality lead to lower economic growth? According to the OECD, the main reason is that inequality reduces the development of skills of the lower-income groups and reduces social mobility. By hindering the accumulation of human capital – the knowledge, skills, competencies and other attributes embodied in people which help to produce goods, services or ideas – income inequality undermines education opportunities for disadvantaged individuals, lowering social mobility and hampering skills development. (Human capital is discussed further in Box 9.5.)

The lower educational attainment applies to both the length and quality of education: people from poorer backgrounds on average leave school or college earlier and with lower qualifications.

But if greater inequality generally results in lower economic growth, will a redistribution from rich to poor necessarily result in faster economic growth? According to the OECD:

Anti-poverty programmes will not be enough. Not only cash transfers but also increasing access to public services, such as high-quality education, training and healthcare, constitute long-term social investment to create greater equality of opportunities in the long run.

Thus redistribution policies need to be well designed and implemented and focus on raising incomes of the poor through increased opportunities to increase their productivity. Simple transfers from rich to poor via the tax and benefits system may, in fact, undermine economic growth. According to the IMF:

That equality seems to drive higher and more sustainable growth does not in itself support efforts to redistribute. In particular, inequality may impede growth at least in part because it calls forth efforts to redistribute that themselves undercut growth. In such a situation, even if inequality is bad for growth, taxes and transfers may be precisely the wrong remedy.

? *Identify policy measures that would both reduce inequality and increase income growth.*

Recap

1. Inequality can be examined by looking at the size distribution of income, the functional distribution of income, the distribution of income by recipient and the distribution of wealth.

2. The distribution of income and wealth can be illustrated by means of a Lorenz curve. The greater the inequality, the more bowed the curve will be towards the bottom right-hand corner.

3. The distribution can also be measured by a Gini coefficient. This will give a figure between 0 (total equality) and 1 (total inequality).

4. Wages and salaries constitute by far the largest source of income, and thus inequality can be explained mainly in terms of differences in wages and salaries. Nevertheless state benefits are an important moderating influence on inequality and constitute the largest source of income for the poorest 20 per cent of households. Investment earnings are only a minor determinant of income except for some of the very richest households.

5. Inequality in wages and salaries largely reflects differences in the productivity of workers, consumer demand, power and discrimination. Other determinants of income inequality include differences in household composition, inequality of wealth, unemployment and the level of government benefits.

6. The distribution of wealth is less equal than the distribution of income.

How can income be redistributed from rich to poor? What will be the effects of doing so?

In this section we will look at policies to redistribute incomes more equally, and in particular we will focus on the use of government social security benefits and taxation. In doing so, we will be focusing on the economic and social goal of 'equity' and so the distributive role for government identified in Chapter 1 (see page 21).

> **KEY IDEA 22** *Equity* is where income or wealth is distributed in a way that is considered to be fair or just. Note that an equitable distribution is not the same as a totally equal distribution and that different people have different views on what is equitable.

Taxation

If taxes are to be used as a means of achieving greater equality, the rich must be taxed proportionately more than the poor. The degree of redistribution will depend on the degree of 'progressiveness' of the tax. In this context, taxes may be classified as follows:

- **Progressive tax.** As people's income (Y) rises, the percentage of their income paid in the tax (T) rises. In other words, the average rate of tax (T/Y) rises. Income taxes are progressive (but much less progressive in the UK than they used to be).
- **Regressive tax.** As people's income rises, the percentage of their income paid in the tax falls: T/Y falls.
- **Proportional tax.** As people's income rises, the percentage of their income paid in the tax stays the same: T/Y is constant.

Therefore, progressiveness is defined in term of what happens to the *average* rate of tax as income rises. The more progressive a tax, the more it will redistribute incomes away from the rich. Regressive taxes will have the opposite effect, since they tax the rich proportionately less than the poor.

Details of tax rates in the UK are given in Case Study 6.14 on the book's website. This case study also examines how progressive or regressive the various types of tax are.

Problems with using taxes to redistribute incomes

How successfully can taxes redistribute income and at what economic cost?

Taxation takes away income. It can thus reduce the incomes of the rich. But no taxes, however progressive, can *increase* the incomes of the poor. This will require subsidies (i.e. benefits).

But what about tax cuts? Can bigger tax cuts not be given to the poor? This is possible only if the poor are already paying taxes in the first place. Take the two cases of income tax and taxes on goods and services:

- Income tax. If the government cuts income tax, then anyone currently paying it will benefit. A cut in tax *rates* will give proportionately more to the rich, since they have a larger proportion of taxable income relative to total income. An increase in personal *allowances*, on the other hand, will give the same *absolute* amount to everyone above the new tax threshold. This will therefore represent a smaller proportionate gain to the rich. In either case, however, there will be no gain at all to those people below the tax threshold. They paid no income tax in the first place and therefore gain nothing at all from income tax cuts.

  Increasing personal allowances was a major priority of the Liberal Democrats in the UK Coalition government of 2010–15. Over the five years, annual personal allowances were increased from £6475 to £10 600.

- Taxes on goods and services. Since taxes such as VAT and excise duties on alcoholic drinks, tobacco, petrol and gambling are generally regressive, any cut in their rate will benefit the poor proportionately more than the rich. A more dramatic effect would be obtained by cutting the rate most on those goods consumed relatively more by the poor (e.g. on domestic fuel).

The government may not wish to cut the overall level of taxation, given its expenditure commitments. In this case, it can switch the burden of taxes from regressive to progressive taxes, if it wishes to benefit the very poor.

Taxation and incentives

Tax changes affect incomes and/or prices. This, in turn, will change the incentives to consume and produce. Higher income taxes, for example, could discourage people from working. Higher taxes on certain products could discourage their consumption and hence production.

The whole question of taxation, choices and incentives can be highly charged politically. For instance, many countries, including the UK, have attempted since the 1980s to reduce both the basic and higher rates of income tax. While this has implications for the distribution of income, the

> **Definitions**
>
> **Progressive tax** A tax whose average rate with respect to income rises as income rises.
>
> **Regressive tax** A tax whose average rate with respect to income falls as income rises.
>
> **Proportional tax** A tax whose average rate with respect to income stays the same as income rises.

primary economic objective behind the tax changes has been to increase the incentive to work. According to the economic right, although high and progressive income taxes can lead to a more equal distribution of income they are likely to result in a smaller national output. Alternatively, by cutting taxes there will be a bigger national output but less equally divided. If many on the political left are correct, however, by raising income taxes we can have both a more equal society and a *bigger* national output: there is no trade-off.

The key to analysing these arguments is to distinguish between the *income effect* and the *substitution effect* of raising taxes. Raising income tax does two things:

■ It reduces disposable incomes. People therefore are encouraged to work *more* in an attempt to maintain their consumption of goods and services. This is called the **income effect**. 'I have to work more to make up for the higher taxes', a person might say.

■ It reduces the opportunity cost of leisure. Since higher income taxes reduce take-home pay, an extra hour taken in leisure now involves a smaller sacrifice in consumption. Thus people may substitute leisure for consumption, and work less. This is called the **substitution effect**. 'What is the point of doing overtime', another person might say, 'if so much of the overtime pay is going in taxes?'

The relative size of the income and substitution effects is likely to differ for different types of people. For example, the *income* effect is likely to dominate for those people with a substantial proportion of long-term commitments, such as those with families, with mortgages and other debts. They may feel forced to work *more* to maintain their disposable income. Clearly for such people, higher taxes are *not* a disincentive to work. The income effect is also likely to be relatively large for people on higher incomes, for whom an increase in tax rates represents a substantial cut in income.

The *substitution* effect is likely to dominate for those with few commitments: those whose families have left home, the single, and second-income earners in families where that second income is not relied on for 'essential' consumption. A rise in tax rates for these people is likely to encourage them to work less.

Although high-income earners may work more when there is a tax *rise*, they may still be discouraged by a steeply progressive tax *structure*. If they have to pay very high marginal rates of tax, it may simply not be worth their while seeking promotion or working harder (see Case Study 6.16 in MyEconLab).

One final point should be stressed. For many people there is no choice in the amount they work. The job they do dictates the number of hours worked, irrespective of changes in taxation.

Pause for thought

How will tax cuts affect the willingness of women with employed partners to return to paid work after having brought up a family? (Clue: think about the size of the income and substitution effects.)

Benefits

Benefits can be either benefits in kind or cash benefits.

Benefits in kind

Individuals receive other forms of benefit from the state, not as direct monetary payments, but in the form of the provision of free or subsidised goods or services. These are known as **benefits in kind**. The two largest items in most countries are health care and education. They are very differently distributed, however. This difference can largely be explained on age grounds. Old people use a large proportion of health services, but virtually no education services.

Benefits in kind tend to be consumed roughly equally by the different income groups. Nevertheless they do have some equalising effect, since they represent a much larger proportion of poor people's income than rich people's. They have a far smaller redistributive effect, however, than cash benefits.

Cash benefits

Means-tested benefits. **Means-tested benefits** are available only to those whose income (and savings in some instances) fall below a certain level. To obtain such benefits, therefore, people must apply for them and declare their personal circumstances to the authorities.

The benefits could be given as grants or merely as loans. They could be provided as general income support or for the meeting of specific needs, such as rents, fuel bills and household items.

Definitions

Income effect of a tax rise Tax increases reduce people's incomes and thus encourage people to work more.

Substitution effect of a tax rise Tax increases reduce the opportunity cost of leisure and thus encourage people to work less.

Benefits in kind Goods or services which the state provides directly to the recipient at no charge or at a subsidised price. Alternatively, the state can subsidise the private sector to provide them.

Means-tested benefits Benefits whose amount depends on the recipient's income or assets.

Figure 6.12 Social benefits as a percentage of GDP

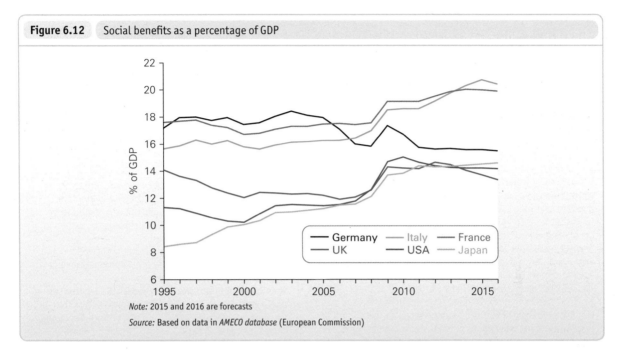

Note: 2015 and 2016 are forecasts

Source: Based on data in *AMECO database* (European Commission)

Universal benefits. **Universal benefits** are those that everyone is entitled to, irrespective of their income, if they fall into a certain category or fulfil certain conditions. Examples include state pensions, and unemployment, sickness and invalidity benefits.

Figure 6.12 shows the expenditure on social cash benefits in selected countries since 1995. These include unemployment, sickness, invalidity, maternity, family, survivors' and housing benefits and state pensions. As you can see, benefits as a percentage of GDP (national income) vary from one country to another. For instance, the percentage shares in Japan, the USA and the UK are significantly below those in France and Italy.

Differences between countries reflect a multitude of factors: some economic, but others not. Amongst the reasons are: differences in the coverage and levels of particular benefits, rates of unemployment, incomes, rates of economic growth and demographic factors such as the age structure of the population. But cultural and historic traditions can matter too, such as views concerning the role of governments – a theme we shall pick up again in Chapter 7.

The system of benefits in the UK and their redistributive effects are examined in Case Study 6.17 in MyEconLab.

Benefits and the redistribution of income

It might seem that means-tested benefits are a much more efficient system of redistributing income from the rich to the poor: the money is directed to those most in need. With universal benefits, by contrast, many people may receive them who have little need for them. Do families with very high incomes need child benefit? Would it not be better for the government to redirect the money to those who are genuinely in need? For example, in the UK, from January 2013, families where at least one parent earned more than £50 000

would have their child benefit reduced; and this would be reduced to zero when one parent earned over £60 000.

There are, however, serious problems in attempting to redistribute incomes by the use of means-tested benefits:

■ Not everyone entitled to means-tested benefits applies for them, whether from ignorance of what is available, from the complexities of claiming or from reluctance to reveal personal circumstances. Thus some of the poorest families may receive no support.

■ The levels of income above which people become ineligible for benefits may be set too low. Even if they were raised, there will always be some people just above these levels who will still find difficulties.

■ Means tests based purely on *income* (or even universal benefits based on broad categories) ignore the very special needs of many poor people. A person earning £120 a week living in a small, well-appointed flat with a low rent will have less need of assistance than another person who also earns £120 per week but lives in a cold, draughty and damp house with large bills to meet. If means tests are to be really fair, then *all* of a person's circumstances need to be taken into account.

The tax/benefit system and the problem of disincentives: the 'poverty trap'

When means-tested benefits are combined with a progressive income tax system, there can be a serious problem of disincentives. As poor people earn more money, so not only

Definition

Universal benefits Benefits paid to everyone in a certain category irrespective of their income or assets.

| BOX 6.6 | UK TAX CREDITS | CASE STUDIES & APPLICATIONS |

An escape from the poverty trap?

Tax credits were introduced in the UK in 1999 in the form of Working Families Tax Credit, which was replaced in 2003 by the Working Tax Credit (WTC) and Child Tax Credit (CTC). These credits are given either as tax relief or as a cash benefit.

Working Tax Credit was designed for working people on low incomes. To be eligible for the basic amount (up to £1960 in 2015/16), people without children aged 25 or over had to work at least 30 hours per week. People with children, the over 50s returning to work, the over 60s and the disabled had to work at least 16 hours per week. Couples and lone parents could receive an additional amount (up to £2010 in 2015/16). There was a further addition for anyone with children who worked at least 30 hours per week, or for couples who jointly worked at least 30 hours per week. This was designed as an incentive for people to move from part-time to full-time work. In 2015/16 recipients of WTC could also get help with their childcare worth up to £122.50 extra per week for one child, or £210 extra for two or more children, depending on how much they earned. WTC tapers off for incomes over a threshold amount (£6420 in 2015/16).

Child Tax Credit provided support to families with children, whether or not anyone in the family works. It is paid in addition to WTC and child benefit. There was a basic rate (£545 in 2015/16) and an amount for each child (up to £2780 in 2015/16). Again, relief tapers off for incomes over a threshold amount (£16 105 in 2015/16).

Apart from targeting support at poorer families, these tax credits were designed to improve incentives to work, by reducing the poverty trap (see page 161). In other words, the aim was to reduce the financial penalties for parents working by tapering off more slowly the rate at which benefits are lost. With a lost-benefit rate of 41 per cent, the combined marginal tax plus lost-benefit rate (the 'marginal deduction rate') is typically around 73 per cent, depending on a person's marginal rate of tax and national insurance and other means-tested benefits received.

Although the introduction of these tax credits did reduce the typical marginal deduction rate for poor families, it remained very high. For many poor parents, therefore, the incentive to work was still relatively low. What is more, a lower taper rate brings *more* families into the tax credit system. While this is good, in terms of providing support for them, the result is more of a disincentive for parents in such families to work extra hours, or to take a better job, since the marginal deduction rate is now higher. In other words, although they are better off, they will take home less for each extra hour worked.

WTC and CTC illustrate the general problem of providing support to poor people which is affordable for taxpayers without creating disincentives to work. The more gently the support tapers off (and hence the less the disincentive to earn extra money), the more costly it is to finance and hence the higher the tax rates that are needed elsewhere. The problems with using negative income taxes are explored in Case Study 6.17 in MyEconLab.

A major criticism of the way in which tax credits were employed was the complexity of the system. This complexity had two consequences: first, it reduced take up and, secondly, it made the system administratively costly and prone to errors.

A universal approach

In 2011 Iain Duncan Smith, the Secretary of State for Work and Pensions, announced plans fundamentally to reform the benefit system with the introduction of a new Universal Credit. His intention was radically to 'simplify the system to make work pay and combat worklessness and poverty'.[4] The new credit has been described as an integrated working-age credit providing a basic allowance with additional elements for children, disability, housing and caring.

The Universal Credit was launched in 2013 with a series of local pilots. It was to differ from the previous system in that it supports people both in and out of work, replacing Working Tax Credit, Child Tax Credit, Housing Benefit, Income Support, income-based Jobseeker's Allowance and income-related Employment and Support Allowance.

It was hoped that the design of the Universal Credit would address the concerns tax credits raise:

- Smoother taper rates, lessening the impact of the poverty trap and ensuring work pays.
- Removing the distortions that over-reward individuals working a certain number of hours, notably 16 or 30 hours with WTCs.
- Bringing together of in-work and out-of-work benefits, reducing the risks and transactions costs for those moving into work.
- Lower administrative costs, with benefits being overseen by a single body, the Department for Work and Pensions, rather than the multiple agencies involved previously.

However, the higher levels of support promised in the White Paper were accompanied by a warning to those out of work. The government would be applying a stronger level of conditionality: those who can work would be expected to do so.

Following the local pilots, there was considerable slippage in the timescale for its national implementation. There were also concerns that in moving people to the new system there would be delays in payments. The hope was that the roll-out of the Universal Credit would be largely complete by the end of 2017.

Economists sometimes refer to an 'unemployment trap'. People are discouraged from taking work in the first place. Explain how such a 'trap' arises. Will the Universal Credit create an unemployment trap? What are the best ways of eliminating, or at least reducing, the unemployment trap?

---

[4]*Universal Credit: welfare that works,* http://www.dwp.gov.uk/policy/welfare-reform/legislation-and-key-documents/universal-credit/ (DWP)

do they start paying income taxes and national insurance, but also they begin losing means-tested benefits. Theoretically, it is possible to have a marginal tax plus lost-benefit rate in excess of 100 per cent. In other words, for every extra £1 earned, taxes and lost benefits add up to more than £1. High marginal tax plus lost-benefit rates obviously act as a serious disincentive. What is the point of getting a job or trying to earn more money, if you end up earning little more or actually losing money?

This situation is known as the **poverty trap**. People are trapped on low incomes with no realistic means of bettering their position.

The problem of the poverty trap would be overcome by switching to a system of universal benefits unrelated to income. For example, *everyone* could receive a flat payment from the state fixed at a sufficiently high level to cover their basic needs. There would still be *some* disincentive, but this would be confined to an income effect: people would not have the same need to work if the state provided a basic income. But there would no longer be the disincentive to work caused by a resulting *loss* of benefits (a substitution effect).

The big drawback with universal benefits, however, is their cost. If they were given to everyone and were large enough to help the poor, their cost would be enormous. Thus although the benefits themselves would not create much disincentive effect, the necessary taxation to fund them almost certainly would.

There is no ideal solution to this conundrum. On the one hand, the more narrowly benefits are targeted on the poor, the greater the problem of the poverty trap. On the other hand, the more widely they are spread, the greater the cost of providing any given level of support to individuals.

A compromise proposal is that of a **negative income tax**. This is examined in Case Study 6.17 in MyEconLab. Box 6.6 examines the use of tax credits – a form of negative income tax – in the UK.

> ### Pause for thought
>
> *Does the targeting of benefits to those in greatest need necessarily increase the poverty trap?*

> ### Definitions
>
> **Poverty trap** Where poor people are discouraged from working or getting a better job because any extra income they earn will be largely taken away in taxes and lost benefits.
>
> **Negative income tax** A combined system of taxes and benefits. Below a certain level of income people pay a negative tax: in other words they receive benefits. As people earn more, they gradually lose their benefits until beyond a certain level they begin paying taxes – the tax becomes positive.

Recap

1. Taxes can be categorised as progressive, regressive or proportional. Progressive taxes have the effect of reducing inequality. The more steeply progressive they are, the bigger the reduction in inequality.

2. Taxes on their own cannot increase the incomes of the poor. Cutting taxes, however, *can* help the poor if the cuts are carefully targeted.

3. Using taxes to redistribute incomes can cause disincentives. Raising taxes has two effects on the amount people wish to work. On the one hand, people will be encouraged to work more in order to maintain their incomes. This is the income effect. On the other hand, they will be encouraged to substitute leisure for income (i.e. to work less), since an hour's leisure now costs less in forgone income. This is the substitution effect. The relative size of the income and substitution effects will depend on the nature of the tax change. The substitution effect is more likely to outweigh the income effect for those with few commitments, for people just above the tax threshold of the newly raised tax and in cases where the highest rates of tax are increased.

4. Benefits can be cash benefits or benefits in kind. They can be universal or means tested. Universal benefits include child benefit, state pensions, unemployment benefits, and sickness and invalidity benefits. Benefits in kind include health care, education and free school meals.

5. Means-tested benefits can be specifically targeted to those in need and are thus more 'cost-effective'. However, there can be serious problems with such benefits, including: limited take-up, time-consuming procedures for claimants, some relatively needy people falling just outside the qualifying limit and inadequate account taken of *all* relevant circumstances affecting a person's needs.

6. The poverty trap occurs when the combination of increased taxes and reduced benefits removes the incentive for poor people to earn more. The more steeply progressive this combined system is at low incomes, the bigger the disincentive effect.

QUESTIONS

1. If a firm faces a shortage of workers with very specific skills, it may decide to undertake the necessary training itself. If, on the other hand, it faces a shortage of unskilled workers, it may well offer a small wage increase in order to obtain the extra labour. In the first case it is responding to an increase in demand for labour by attempting to shift the supply curve. In the second case it is merely allowing a movement along the supply curve. Use a demand and supply diagram to illustrate each case. Given that elasticity of supply is different in each case, do you think that these are the best policies for the firm to follow?

2. For what types of reason does the marginal revenue product differ between workers in different jobs?

3. Why, do you think, are some of the lowest-paid jobs the most unpleasant?

4. The wage rate a firm has to pay and the output it can produce vary with the number of workers as shown in the table below (all figures are hourly). Assume that output sells at £2 per unit.

Number of workers	1	2	3	4	5	6	7	8
Wage rate (AC_L) (£)	3	4	5	6	7	8	9	10
Total output (TPP_L)	10	22	32	40	46	50	52	52

   a. Copy the table and add additional rows for TC_L, MC_L, TRP_L and MRP_L. Put the figures for MC_L and MRP_L in the spaces between the columns.
   b. How many workers will the firm employ in order to maximise profits?
   c. What will be its hourly wage bill at this level of employment?
   d. How much hourly revenue will it earn at this level of employment?
   e. Assuming that the firm faces other (fixed) costs of £30 per hour, how much hourly profit will it make?
   f. Assume that the workers now form a union and that the firm agrees to pay the negotiated wage rate to all employees. What is the maximum to which the hourly wage rate could rise without causing the firm to try to reduce employment below that in (b) above? (See the diagram in Box 6.2.)
   g. What would be the firm's hourly profit now?

5. The figures shown in the table at the top of the next column are for a monopsonist employer. Fill in the missing figures for columns (3) and (4). How many workers should the firm employ if it wishes to maximise profits?

Number of workers (1)	Wage rate (£) (2)	Total cost of labour (£) (3)	Marginal cost of labour (£) (4)	Marginal revenue product (£) (5)
1	100	100		
			110	230
2	105	210		
			120	240
3	110	330		
				240
4	115			
				230
5	120			
				210
6	125			
				190
7	130			
				170
8	135			
				150
9	140			
				130
10	145			

6. To what extent can trade unions be seen to be (a) an advantage, (b) a disadvantage to (i) workers in unions, (ii) employers bargaining with unions, (iii) non-union members in firms where there is collective bargaining, (iv) workers in non-unionised jobs?

7. Identify four groups of workers, two with very high wages and two with very low wages. Explain why they get the wages they do.

8. Do any of the following contradict marginal productivity theory: (a) wage scales related to length of service (incremental scales); (b) nationally negotiated wage rates; (c) discrimination; (d) firms taking the lead from other firms in determining this year's pay increase?

9. For what reasons is the average gross weekly pay of women only around four-fifths of that of men in the UK (see Box 6.3)?

10. Does the existence of overtime tend to increase or decrease inequality?

11. Distinguish between proportional, progressive and regressive taxation. Could a progressive tax have a constant marginal rate?

12. If a person earning £20 000 per year pays £2000 in a given tax and a person earning £40 000 per year pays £3200, is the tax progressive or regressive? Explain.

13. A proportional tax will leave the distribution of income unaffected. Why should this be so, given that a rich person will pay a larger absolute amount than a poor person?

14. Under what circumstances would a rise in income tax act as (a) a disincentive and (b) an incentive to effort?

15. Who is likely to work harder as a result of a cut in income tax rates – a person on a high income or a person on a low income? Why? Would your answer be different if personal allowances were zero?

16. What tax changes (whether up or down) will both have a positive incentive effect and redistribute incomes more equally?

17. What is meant by 'the poverty trap'? Would a system of universal benefits be the best solution to the problem of the poverty trap?

18. How would you go about deciding whether person A or person B gets more personal benefit from each of the following: (a) an electric fire; (b) a clothing allowance of £x; (c) draught-proofing materials; (c) child benefit? Do your answers help you in deciding how best to allocate benefits?

MyEconLab

This book can be supported by MyEconLab, which contains a range of additional resources, including an online homework and tutorial system designed to test and build your understanding.

You need both an access card and a course ID to access MyEconLab:

1. Is your lecturer using MyEconLab? Ask your lecturer for your course ID.

2. Has an access card been included with the book at a reduced cost? Check the inside back cover of the book.

3. If you have a course ID but no access card, go to: http://www.myeconlab.com/ to buy access to this interactive study programme.

ADDITIONAL CASE STUDIES IN THE *ESSENTIALS OF ECONOMICS* MyEconLab (www.pearsoned.co.uk/sloman)

6.1 **Labour as a factor of production.** An examination of some of the ethical consequences of treating labour as an 'input' into production.

6.2 **Flexible labour markets.** This looks at the changes in the ways that firms organise their workforces.

6.3 **Telecommuters.** This case study looks at the growth in the number of people working from home.

6.4 **Life at the mill.** Monopsony in Victorian times as reported by Friedrich Engels.

6.5 **Poverty in the past.** Extreme poverty in Victorian England.

6.6 **The rise and decline of the labour movement.** A brief history of trade unions in the UK.

6.7 **How useful is marginal productivity theory?** How accurately does the theory describe employment decisions by firms?

6.8 **Profit-sharing.** An examination of the case for and against profit-sharing as a means of rewarding workers.

6.9 **Immigration, the Single European Market and the UK labour market.** This case study looks at efforts to quantify the impact of immigration on the UK labour market following the expansion of the EU in 2004.

6.10 **How can we define poverty?** This examines different definitions of poverty and, in particular, distinguishes between absolute and relative measures of poverty.

6.11 **How to reverse the UK's increased inequality.** Recommendations of the Rowntree Foundation.

6.12 **Adam Smith's maxims of taxation.** This looks at the principles of a good tax system as identified by Adam Smith.

6.13 **Taxation in the UK.** This case study looks at the various types of tax in the UK. It gives the current tax rates and considers how progressive the system is.

6.14 **The poll tax.** This case charts the introduction of the infamous poll tax (or 'community charge') in the UK and its subsequent demise.

6.15 **The Laffer curve.** This curve suggests that raising tax rates beyond a certain level will reduce tax revenue. But will cutting tax rates increase revenue?

6.16 **The UK benefit system, more than 60 years on.** This considers the evolution of the UK benefit system and its impact on the distribution of income.

6.17 **Negative income tax and redistribution.** This case looks at the possible effects of introducing negative income taxes (tax credits).

6.18 **The squeezed middle.** What have been the effects on people on 'middle incomes' by successive governments to support poor families?

WEB APPENDICES

6.1 **Deriving the individual's supply curve of labour.** This uses indifference analysis (see Web Appendix 2.2) to explain the shape of an individual worker's supply curve of labour and explains why at high wage rates the curve may become backward bending.

6.2 **Economic rent and transfer earnings.** This appendix examines a way of classifying the earnings of a factor of production and shows how these earnings depend on the price elasticity of supply of the factor.

Chapter 7

Market failures and government policy

To what extent should we rely on markets to allocate resources? In recent years, governments throughout the world have tended to put more reliance on markets as the means of allocating resources. Policies of privatisation, deregulation, cutting government expenditure and taxes have been widely adopted by governments of all political persuasions.

Despite this increased reliance on markets, markets often fail. At a general level, while we observe the tendency for a country's national income to increase over time, it is inherently unstable and its distribution unequal. But, more than this, we witness and contribute to activities that adversely affect the lives of others, no more so than our impact on the environment. At the same time, many aspects of our lives seem to be dominated by the interests of big business and the quality of many of the goods we buy is very poor.

While both the extent and nature of government involvement in economies vary from one country to another, all governments are still expected to play a major role. This involvement ranges from supporting and regulating businesses, to the passing of laws to protect the individual, to providing or enabling access to key services such as education, health care and law and order, to social protection in the form of pensions and social security, to the provision of infrastructure, such as a country's rail track or road network.

In this chapter we identify the various ways in which the market fails to look after society's interests (Sections 7.1–7.4). Then we look at how the government can set about putting right these failings (Sections 7.5–7.7). Then we look at some of the shortcomings of governments, and ask: should we have more or less intervention? In the final section we turn to problems of the environment as a case study in market failure and government intervention.

After studying this chapter, you should be able to answer the following questions:

- What is the meaning of a 'socially efficient' allocation of resources and to what extent will a perfectly competitive market achieve social efficiency?
- For what reasons do real-world markets fail to achieve social efficiency?
- How can governments put right the failings of the market?
- How successful are they likely to be?
- How can economists explain environmental degradation?
- What policies can be pursued to achieve environmental sustainability?

7.1 SOCIAL EFFICIENCY

Is this something that the free market will achieve?

In order to decide the optimum amount of government intervention, it is first necessary to identify the various social goals that intervention is designed to meet. Two of the major objectives of government intervention identified by economists are **equity** and **social efficiency**.

Equity

KI 22
p 148 Most people would argue that the free market fails to lead to a *fair* distribution of resources, if it results in some people living in great affluence while others live in dire poverty. In
KI 21
p 159 Chapter 6 we considered how economists look to measure the degree of inequality in the distribution of income and wealth. Clearly what constitutes 'fairness' is a highly contentious issue: those on the political right generally have a quite different view from those on the political left. Nevertheless, most people would argue that the government does have some duty to redistribute incomes from the rich to the poor through the tax and benefit system, and perhaps to provide various forms of legal protection for the poor (such as a minimum wage rate).

In other words, government has a *redistributive* role to play (see page 21). Having looked at the causes of inequality and policies of redistribution in Chapter 6. we focus here on the second issue: that of social efficiency.

Social efficiency

KI 18
p 108 If the marginal benefits to society – or 'marginal social benefits' (*MSB*) – of producing (or consuming) any given good or service exceed the marginal costs to society – or 'marginal social costs' (*MSC*) – then it is said to be socially efficient to produce (or consume) more. For example, if people's gains from having additional motorways exceed *all* the additional costs to society (both financial and non-financial), then it is socially efficient to construct more motorways.

If, however, the marginal social costs of producing (or consuming) any good or service exceed the marginal social benefits, then it is socially efficient to produce (or consume) less.

It follows that if the marginal social benefits of any activity are equal to the marginal social costs, then the current level is the optimum. To summarise: to achieve social efficiency in the production of any good or service, the following should occur:

TC2
p 11 $MSB > MSC \rightarrow$ produce more
$MSC > MSB \rightarrow$ produce less
$MSB = MSC \rightarrow$ keep production at its current level

Similar rules apply to consumption. For example, if the marginal social benefits of consuming more of any good or service exceed the marginal social cost, then society would benefit from more of the good being consumed.

Social efficiency is an example of 'allocative efficiency': in other words, the best allocation of resources between alternative uses.

> **KEY IDEA 23**
> **TC 10**
> *Allocative efficiency in any activity is achieved where any reallocation would lead to a decline in net benefit.* It is achieved where marginal benefit equals marginal cost. Private efficiency is achieved where marginal private benefit equals marginal private cost (*MB = MC*). Social efficiency is achieved where marginal social benefit equals marginal social cost (*MSB = MSC*).

The concept of allocative efficiency is another of our threshold concepts (no. 10). It is a threshold concept, because to understand it is to understand how to make the most of scarce resources: and scarcity is the core problem of economics for all of us.

In the real world, however, the market rarely leads to social efficiency: the marginal social benefits of most goods and services do not equal the marginal social costs. Part of the problem is that many of our actions have spillover effects on other people (these are known as 'externalities'), part is a lack of competition, part is a lack of knowledge by both producers and consumers, and part is the fact that markets may take a long time to adjust to any disequilibrium, given the often considerable short-run immobility of factors of production.

> **KEY IDEA 24**
> *Markets generally fail to achieve social efficiency.* There are various types of market failure. Market failures provide one of the major justifications for government intervention in the economy.

In this chapter we examine these various 'failings' of the free market and what the government can do to rectify the situation. We also examine why the government itself may fail to achieve social efficiency.

General equilibrium

Markets are in a constant state of flux. Demand changes as consumer tastes change and as income changes; supply changes as technology, the availability of natural resources and costs change. These changes in demand and supply cause markets to adjust to a new equilibrium.

> **Definitions**
>
> **Social efficiency** Production and consumption at the point where *MSB = MSC*.
>
> **Equity** A fair distribution of resources.

At any one time, it is useful to look at the overall equilibrium towards which markets are heading: the **general equilibrium** of all markets.

> **KEY IDEA 25**
>
> *General equilibrium.* The situation where all individual markets in the economy are in equilibrium: in other words, where demand equals supply in all markets. If demand or supply changes in any market, there are likely to be ripple effects into other markets (i.e. for substitute or complementary goods, in both demand and supply), until a new general equilibrium is reached. This is Threshold Concept 11.
>
> **TC 11**

The concept of general equilibrium is a threshold concept because it gives us an insight into how market forces apply to a whole economy, and not just to its individual parts. It is about seeing how the whole jigsaw fits together and how changes ripple throughout the economy.

We can then ask whether this general equilibrium is socially efficient, or whether a reallocation of resources in the economy would lead to greater social efficiency.

An economy where all markets are perfectly competitive and where there are no externalities *will* be socially efficient when there is a state of general equilibrium. Why will this be so? Take the case of goods markets. In any given goods markets, the consumer will achieve private efficiency where marginal utility (i.e. marginal benefit) equals price (see Section 2.1, on page 32); and the producer where marginal cost equals price (see Section 5.2, page 103). Given that all producers and consumers face the same market price, in equilibrium marginal utility will equal marginal cost.

But will this be socially efficient? In the absence of externalities, benefits from consumption are confined to the consumers themselves. In other words, as members of society, their benefit is the whole social benefit. Thus $P = MU = MSB$. Likewise, the costs of production are confined to the producers: there are no costs imposed on *other* members of society. Thus $P = MC = MSC$.

To summarise:

$$MU = MSB = P = MC = MSC$$

and hence:

$$MSB = MSC$$

Thus equilibrium in any market under perfect competition with no externalities is socially efficient. When this applies to all markets, then general equilibrium is socially efficient.

Web Appendix 7.1 looks at social efficiency in more detail.

7.2   MARKET FAILURES: EXTERNALITIES AND PUBLIC GOODS

What will happen if certain markets are 'missing'?

Externalities

The market will not lead to social efficiency if the actions of producers or consumers affect people *other than themselves*. As we saw above, these effects on other people are known as **externalities**: they are the side-effects, or 'third-party' effects, of production or consumption. Externalities can be either desirable or undesirable. Whenever other people are affected beneficially, there are said to be **external benefits**. Whenever other people are affected adversely, there are said to be **external costs**.

So far in this book it has been assumed that there are no externalities. As far as consumption is concerned, we have assumed that the only people who benefit are the customers who purchase the good and derive pleasure from it.

Likewise we have assumed that all the opportunity costs to society in the production of a good are incurred by the firm producing it. These include the payments for the time/effort of the workers in the form of wages, the cost of raw materials and the opportunity cost of using capital goods. Society misses out on the best alternative things that these factor inputs could have produced.

> **KEY IDEA 26**
>
> *Externalities are spillover costs or benefits.* Where these exist, even an otherwise perfect market will fail to achieve social efficiency.

In the presence of externalities the full benefit to society (the **social benefit**) from the consumption of any good is

Definition

General equilibrium Where all the millions of markets throughout the economy are in a simultaneous state of equilibrium.

Externalities Costs or benefits of production or consumption experienced by society but not by the producers or consumers themselves. Sometimes referred to as 'spillover' or 'third-party' costs or benefits.

External benefits Benefits from production (or consumption) experienced by people *other* than the producer (or consumer).

External costs Costs of production (or consumption) borne by people *other* than the producer (or consumer).

Social benefit Private benefit plus externalities in consumption.

the private benefit enjoyed by consumers *plus* any externalities of consumption (positive or negative). Likewise the full cost to society (the **social cost**) of the production of any good or service is the private cost faced by firms *plus* any externalities of production (positive or negative).

There are four major types of externality.

External costs of production (MSC > MC) with no external costs/benefits of consumption (MSB = MPB)

When a chemical firm dumps waste into a river or pollutes the air, the community bears costs additional to those borne by the firm. There are marginal external costs (MEC_p) of chemical production. This is illustrated in Figure 7.1. In this example we assume that they begin with the first unit of production and increase at a constant rate.

The marginal *social* costs (*MSC*) of chemical production will equal the marginal private costs (*MPC*) plus the marginal external costs from production (MEC_p). This means that the *MSC* curve is above the *MPC* curve. The vertical distance between them is equal to the MEC_p. It is also assumed that there are no externalities in consumption, which means that the marginal social benefit (*MSB*) curve is the same as the marginal private benefit (*MPB*) curve.

Firms will maximise profit where marginal *private* cost (*MPC*) equals marginal revenue (*MR*). But under perfect competition, firms are price takers and thus can sell as much as they chose at the market price. Thus, for them, $P = AR = MR$ (see Section 5.2 on pages 103–4). This makes the *industry MPC* curve also the market supply curve, since at any price firms will choose to supply the output where price equals marginal cost. Thus in Figure 7.1, $S = MPC$.

The market demand curve will be the sum of individuals' demand curves, which are equal to their marginal utility curves (see Section 2.1 on page 32). In the context of consumption, marginal utility is the same thing as marginal private benefit. As we are assuming there are no externalities on the consumption side, $D = MPB = MSB$.

Competitive market forces, with producers and consumers only responding to private costs and benefits, will result

in a market equilibrium at point *a* in Figure 7.1: i.e. where demand equals supply. The market equilibrium price is P_{pc}, while the market equilibrium quantity is Q_{pc}.

At P_{pc}, *MPB* is equal to *MSB*. The market price reflects both the private and social benefits from the last unit consumed. However, the presence of external costs in production means that $MSC > MPC$.

The socially optimal output would be Q^*, where $P = MSB = MSC$. This is illustrated at point *c* and clearly shows how external costs of production in a perfectly competitive market result in overproduction: i.e. $Q_{pc} > Q^*$. From society's point of view, too much waste is being dumped in rivers. Society therefore suffers a welfare loss.

We can show this welfare loss diagrammatically. If we compare the sum of the marginal social costs of units produced between Q_{pc} and Q^* with the marginal social benefits of these units we can see that this welfare loss is the area *abc*. This is the **deadweight welfare loss** of the overproduction.

The problem of external pollution costs arises in a free-market economy because no one has legal ownership of the air or rivers and no one, therefore, can prevent or charge for their use as a dump for waste. Such a 'market' is *missing*. Control must, therefore, be left to the government or local authorities.

Other examples of external costs of production include extensive farming that destroys hedgerows and wildlife, and global warming caused by CO_2 emissions from power stations.

External benefits of production (MSC < MC) with no external costs/benefits of consumption (MSB = MPB)

If a forestry company plants new woodlands, there is a benefit not only to the company itself, but also to the world through a reduction of CO_2 in the atmosphere (forests are a carbon sink). In this case there are marginal external benefits (MEB_p) of production. These are shown in Figure 7.2. We assume that they begin with the first tree planted but that the marginal benefit declines with each additional tree. In other words, the MEB_p is a downward-sloping line.

> **Pause for thought**
>
> *Why are marginal external benefits typically likely to decline as output increases? Why in some cases might marginal external benefits be constant at all levels of output or even increase as more is produced?*

Given these positive externalities, the marginal *social* cost (*MSC*) of providing timber is less than the marginal private cost: $MSC = MPC - MEB_p$. This means that the *MSC* curve

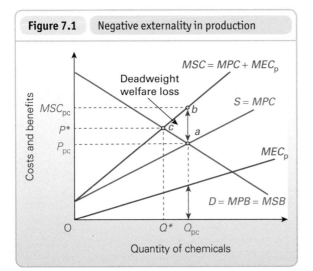

Figure 7.1 Negative externality in production

> **Definitions**
>
> **Social cost** Private cost plus externalities in production.
>
> **Deadweight loss** The loss in welfare arising from a socially inefficient allocation of resources.

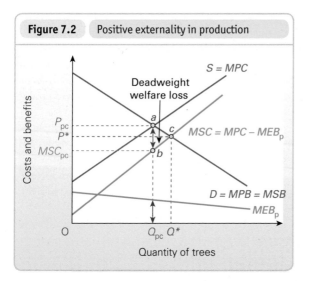

Figure 7.2 Positive externality in production

Quantity of trees

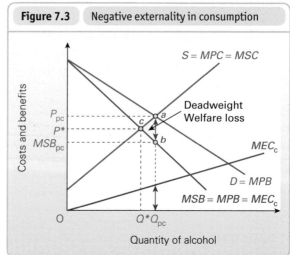

Figure 7.3 Negative externality in consumption

Quantity of alcohol

is *below* the MPC curve. The vertical distance between the curves is equal to the MEB_p. Once again, it is assumed that there are no externalities in consumption so that $MSB = MPB$.

Competitive market forces will result in an equilibrium output of Q_{pc}, where market demand (= MPB) equals market supply (= MPC) (point *a*). The socially efficient level of output, however, is Q': i.e. where $MSB = MSC$ (point *c*). The external benefits of production thus result in a level of output *below* the socially efficient level. From society's point of view not enough trees are being planted. The deadweight welfare loss caused by this underproduction is illustrated by the area *abc*. Output is not being produced between Q_{pc} and Q' even though $MSB > MSC$.

Another example of external benefits in production is that of research and development. If other firms have access to the results of the research, then clearly the benefits extend beyond the firm that finances it. Since the firm only receives the private benefits, it will conduct a less than optimal amount of research.

External costs of consumption (MSB < MB) with no external costs/benefits of production (MSC = MPC)

Drinking alcohol can sometimes lead to marginal external costs of consumption. For example, there are the extra nightly policing costs to deal with the increased chance of social disorder. Public health costs may also be greater as a direct consequence of people's drinking behaviour: e.g. through an increase in hospitalisations. It may also lead to a number of alcohol-related road accidents. These marginal external costs of consumption (MEC_c) result in the marginal social benefit of alcohol consumption being lower than the marginal private benefit: i.e. $MSB = MPB - MEC$.

This is illustrated in Figure 7.3, where the MSB curve is below the MPB curve. In this example it is assumed that there are no externalities in production so that $MSC = MPC$.

Competitive market forces will result in an equilibrium output of Q_{pc} (point *a*) whereas the socially efficient level of output is Q': i.e. where $MSB = MSC$ (point *c*). The external costs of consumption result in level of output *above* the

socially efficient level: i.e. $Q_{pc} > Q'$. From society's point of view, too much alcohol is being produced and consumed. The deadweight welfare loss caused by this overconsumption is illustrated by the area *abc*.

Other possible examples of negative externalities of consumption include taking a journey by car, noisy radios in public places, the smoke from cigarettes and litter.

External benefits of consumption (MSB > MB) with no external costs/benefits of production (MSC = MPC)

How do people travel to a city centre to go shopping on a Saturday? How do people travel to a football match? If they use the train, then other people benefit, as there is less congestion and exhaust fumes and fewer accidents on the roads. These marginal external benefits of consumption (MEB_c) result in the marginal social benefit of rail travel being *greater* than the marginal private benefit (i.e. $MSB = MPB + MEB_c$).

This is illustrated in Figure 7.4, where the MSB curve is above the MPB curve. The vertical distance between the curves is equal to the MEB_c. Once again it is assumed that there are no externalities in production so that $MSC = MPC$.

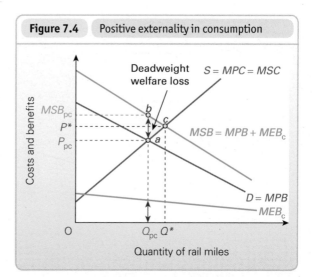

Figure 7.4 Positive externality in consumption

Quantity of rail miles

| BOX 7.1 | THE TRAGEDY OF THE COMMONS | EXPLORING ECONOMICS |

The depletion of common resources

Common resources are not owned but are available free of charge to anyone. Examples include the air we breathe and the oceans for fishing. Like public goods, they are non-excludable. For example, in the absence of intervention, fishing boats can take as many fish as they are able from the open seas. There is no 'owner' of the fish to stop them. As long as there are plentiful stocks of fish, there is no problem.

But as more people fish the seas, so fish stocks are likely to run down. This is where common resources differ from public goods. There *is* rivalry. One person's use of a common resource diminishes the amount available for others. This result is an overuse of common resources. This is why many fish stocks are severely depleted, why rainforests are disappearing (cut down for timber or firewood), why many roads are congested and why the atmosphere is so polluted (being used as a common 'dump' for emissions). In each case, a resource that is freely available is overused. This has become known as the **tragedy of the commons**.

How can we analyse the overuse of common resources? The simplest way is in terms of externalities. When I use a common resource, I am reducing the amount available for others. I am imposing a cost on other people: an external cost. If I am motivated by self-interest, I will not take these external costs into account and so an overuse of the resource occurs.

Another way of analysing it is to examine the effect of one person's use of a resource on other people's output externalities. Take the case of fishing grounds. In the diagram the horizontal axis measures the use of this common resource, say in terms of the number of fishing boats per day. The average cost of operating a boat (e.g. the wages of the crew and the fuel) is taken to be constant and is thus equal to the marginal cost. For the sake of simplicity, the price of fish is also assumed to be constant.

As the number of boats increases and fish stocks decline, so each extra boat entering will add less and less to the total catch. The revenue added by each extra boat is the marginal revenue product (*MRP*). In this case the additional collective revenue from each extra boat declines. Eventually, at point B_2, no more fish can be caught: $MRP = 0$. The catch is at the maximum. The average revenue product (*ARP*) is the revenue earned per boat: i.e. the total value of the catch divided by the number of boats.

The average and marginal revenue product curves have to be interpreted with care. Say one additional boat enters the fishing ground. The *MRP* curve shows the extra revenue accruing to the boat operators collectively. It does *not* show the revenue actually earned by the additional boat. The extra boat gets an average catch (which has been reduced somewhat because of the additional boat) and hence gains the average revenue product of all the boats.

What will be the equilibrium? Note first that the optimal number of boats for the boat operators collectively is B_1, where the marginal cost of an extra boat equals its marginal revenue product. In other words, this maximises the collective profit. At point B_1, however, there will be an incentive for extra boats to enter the fishery because the average revenue product (i.e., the return that an additional boat gets) is greater than the cost of operating the boat.

More boats will enter as long as the value earned by each boat (*ARP*) is greater than the cost of operating it: as long as the *ARP* curve is above the $AC = MC$ line. Equilibrium is reached with B_3 boats: considerably above the collective profit-maximising number. Note also that the way the diagram is drawn, marginal revenue product is negative. The last boat has *decreased* the total value of the catch.

In many parts of the world, fish stocks have become so severely depleted that governments, individually or collectively, have had to act. Measures have included quotas on catches or the number of boats, minimum net mesh sizes (to allow young fish to escape), or banning fishing altogether in certain areas or for certain species.

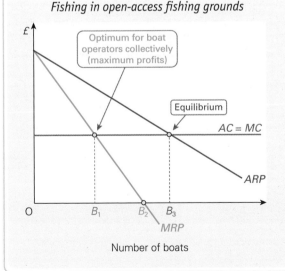

Fishing in open-access fishing grounds

 To what extent can the following be regarded as common resources: (a) rainforests; (b) children's playgrounds in public parks; (c) silence in a library; (d) the internet?

KI 26 p 168

KI 2 p 7

External benefits of consumption result in a level of output below the socially efficient level: i.e. $Q_{pc} < Q^*$. From society's point of view not enough journeys are being made by train. The deadweight welfare caused by this under consumption is illustrated by the area *abc*.

Other examples of external benefits of consumption include the beneficial effects for other people from someone using a deodorant, parents getting their children vaccinated and people planting flowers in their front garden.

To summarise: whenever there are external benefits, there will be too little produced or consumed. Whenever there are external costs, there will be too much produced or consumed. The market will not equate *MSB* and *MSC*.

The above arguments have been developed in the context of perfect competition, with prices given to the producer or consumer by the market. Externalities also occur in all other types of market.

Public goods

There is a category of goods where the positive externalities are so great that the free market, whether perfect or imperfect, may not produce at all. They are called **public goods**. Examples include lighthouses for private pleasure craft,[1] pavements, flood-control dams, public drainage, public services such as the police and even government itself.

Public goods have two important characteristics: *non-rivalry* and *non-excludability*.

- If I consume a bar of chocolate, it cannot then be consumed by someone else. If, however, I enjoy the benefits of street lighting, it does not prevent you or anyone else doing the same. There is thus what we call **non-rivalry** in the consumption of such goods. These goods tend to have large external benefits relative to private benefits. This makes them socially desirable, but privately unprofitable. No single individual would pay to have a pavement built along his or her street. The private benefit would be too small relative to the cost. And yet the social

benefit to all the other people using the pavement may far outweigh the cost.

- If I spend money erecting a flood-control dam to protect my house, my neighbours will also be protected by the dam. I cannot prevent them enjoying the benefits of my expenditure. This feature of **non-excludability** means that they would get the benefits free, and would therefore have no incentive to pay themselves. This is known as the **free-rider problem**.

Pause for thought

Which of the following have the property of non-rivalry: (a) a can of drink; (b) public transport; (c) a commercial radio broadcast; (d) the sight of flowers in a public park?

> **KEY IDEA 27**
>
> *The free-rider problem.* People are often unwilling to pay for things if they can make use of things other people have bought. This problem can lead to people not purchasing things that would be to the benefit of themselves and other members of society.

When goods have these two features, the free market will simply not provide them. Thus these public goods can only be provided by the government or by the government subsidising private firms to do so. However, it is important to note that not all goods and services produced by the public sector come into the category of 'public goods and services': thus education and health are publicly provided, but they *can* be, and indeed are, privately provided as well.

Definitions

Public good A good or service that has the features of non-rivalry and non-excludability and as a result would not be provided by the free market.

Non-rivalry Where the consumption of a good or service by one person will not prevent others from enjoying it.

Non-excludability Where it is not possible to provide a good or service to one person without it thereby being available to others to enjoy.

Free-rider problem Where it is not possible to exclude other people from consuming a good that someone has bought.

---

[1] As far as commercial ships are concerned, it is practical to levy a charge. Merchant ships and larger commercial pleasure craft calling at UK and Irish ports are charged 'light dues', which are used to finance lighthouse services.

Recap

1. Social efficiency will be achieved where $MSC = MSB$ for each good and service. In practice, however, markets fail to achieve social efficiency. One reason for this is the existence of externalities.

2. Externalities are spillover costs or benefits. Whenever there are external costs, the market will (other things being equal) lead to a level of production and consumption *above* the socially efficient level. Whenever there are external benefits, the market will (other things being equal) lead to a level of production and consumption *below* the socially efficient level.

3. Public goods will not be provided by a free market. The problem is that they have large external benefits relative to private benefits and without government intervention it would not be possible to prevent people having a 'free ride' and thereby escaping contributing to their cost of production.

7.3 MARKET FAILURES: MONOPOLY POWER

What problems arise from big business?

KI 24
p 167

Whenever markets are imperfect, whether as pure monopoly or monopsony, or whether as some form of imperfect competition, the market will fail to equate MSB and MSC, even if there are no externalities. Take the case of monopoly. A monopoly will produce less than the socially efficient output. This is illustrated in Figure 7.5. A monopoly faces a downward-sloping demand curve, and therefore marginal revenue is below average revenue ($= P = MSB$). Profits are maximised at an output of Q_1, where marginal revenue equals marginal cost (see Figure 5.5 on page 110). If there are no externalities, the socially efficient output will be at the higher level of Q_2, where $MSB = MSC$.

Deadweight loss under monopoly

Consumer and producer surplus

One way of analysing the welfare loss that occurs under monopoly is to use the concepts of *consumer* and *producer surplus*.

We first came across consumer surplus in Chapter 2 (see Box 2.1 on page 33). It is the excess of consumers' total benefit (or 'utility') from consuming a good over their total expenditure on it.

Producer surplus is similar to supernormal profit (see Section 4.4). The two concepts are illustrated in Figure 7.6. The diagram shows an industry that is initially under perfect competition and then becomes a monopoly (but faces the same revenue and cost curves).

Let us start by examining consumer and producer surplus under *perfect competition*.

Consumer surplus. Under perfect competition the industry will produce an output of Q_{pc} at a price of P_{pc}, where $MC = P$ ($= AR$): i.e. at point *a* (see pages 110–11).

Consumers' total benefit is given by the area under the demand curve (the sum of all the areas 1–7). The reason for this is that each point on the demand curve shows how much the last consumer is prepared to pay (i.e. the benefit to the marginal consumer). The area under the demand curve thus shows the total of all these marginal benefits from zero consumption to the current level: i.e. it gives total benefit.

Consumers' total expenditure is $P_{pc} \times Q_{pc}$ (areas 4 + 5 + 6 + 7).

Consumer surplus is the difference between total benefit and total expenditure: in other words, the area between the price and the demand curve (areas 1 + 2 + 3).

Producer surplus. **Producer surplus** is the difference between total revenue and total variable cost.

Total variable cost is the area under the MC curve (areas 6 + 7). The reason for this is that each point on the marginal cost curve shows what the last unit costs to produce. The area under the MC curve thus gives all the marginal costs starting from an output of zero to the current output: i.e. it gives total variable costs.

Total revenue is $P_{pc} \times Q_{pc}$ (areas 4 + 5 + 6 + 7).

Definitions

Consumer surplus The excess of what a person would have been prepared to pay for a good (i.e. the utility) over what that person actually pays.

Producer surplus The excess of total revenue over total variable cost.

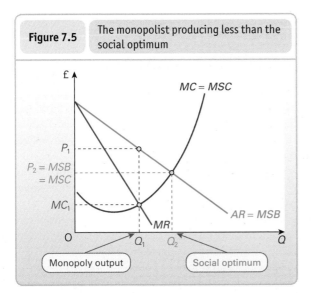

Figure 7.5 The monopolist producing less than the social optimum

Monopoly output — Q_1

Social optimum — Q_2

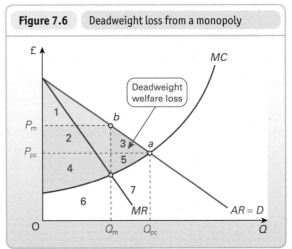

Figure 7.6 Deadweight loss from a monopoly

Producer surplus is thus the area between the price and the *MC* curve (areas 4 + 5).[2]

Total (private) surplus. Total consumer plus producer surplus is therefore the area between the demand and *MC* curves. This is shown by the total shaded area (areas 1 + 2 + 3 + 4 + 5).

The effect of monopoly on total surplus

KI 17
p 101

What happens when the industry is under *monopoly*? The firm will produce where $MC = MR$, at an output of Q_m and a price of P_m (at point *b* on the demand curve). Total revenue is $P_m \times Q_m$ (areas 2 + 4 + 6). Total cost is the area under the *MC* curve (area 6). Thus producer surplus is areas 2 + 4. This is clearly a *larger* surplus than under perfect competition (since area 2 is larger than area 5): monopoly profits are larger than profits under perfect competition.

Consumer surplus, however, will be much smaller. With consumption at Q_m, total benefit to consumers is given by areas 1 + 2 + 4 + 6, whereas consumer expenditure is given by areas 2 + 4 + 6. Consumer surplus, then, is simply area 1. (Note that area 2 has been transformed from consumer surplus to producer surplus.)

KI 24
p 167

Total surplus under monopoly is therefore areas 1 + 2 + 4: a smaller surplus than under perfect competition.

'Monopolisation' of the industry has resulted in a loss of total surplus of areas 3 + 5. The producer's gain is less than consumers' loss. This net loss of total surplus is the deadweight welfare loss of monopoly.

Conclusions

As was shown in Section 5.3, there are possible social *advantages* from powerful firms – advantages such as economies of scale and more research and development. These advantages may outweigh deadweight loss from monopoly power. It can be argued that an ideal situation would be where firms are large enough to gain economies of scale and yet were somehow persuaded or compelled to produce where $P = MC$ (assuming no externalities).

> **Pause for thought**
>
> *Assume that a monopoly existed in an industry where there were negative externalities. Could the socially efficient output be Q_m in Figure 7.6? If so, would this make monopoly socially efficient?*

Recap

1. Monopoly power will (other things being equal) lead to a level of output below the socially efficient level.

2. This will result in deadweight welfare loss, which is the loss in total producer and consumer surplus.

3. Consumer surplus is the excess of what consumers are prepared to pay (which is how we measure the benefit to consumers) over what they actually pay. Producer surplus is the excess of total revenue over total cost (i.e. total profit).

4. The effect of monopoly will be to give a higher producer surplus than under perfect competition, but a much lower consumer surplus. Thus total surplus is lower.

5. There are potential gains from monopoly, such as economies of scale and higher investment. Such gains have to be offset against the deadweight loss.

7.4 OTHER MARKET FAILURES

In what other ways may a market fail to make the best use of scarce resources?

Ignorance and uncertainty

Perfect competition assumes that consumers, firms and factor suppliers have perfect knowledge of costs and benefits. In the real world there is often a great deal of ignorance and uncertainty. Thus people are unable to equate marginal benefit with marginal cost.

Consumers purchase many goods only once or a few times in a lifetime. Cars, washing machines, televisions and other consumer durables fall into this category. Consumers may not be aware of the quality of such goods until they have purchased them, by which time it is too late. Advertising may contribute to people's ignorance by misleading them as to the benefits of a good.

Firms are often ignorant of market opportunities, prices, costs, the productivity of labour (especially white-collar workers), the activity of rivals, etc.

Many economic decisions are based on expected future conditions. Since the future can never be known for certain, many decisions may turn out to be wrong.

In some cases it may be possible to obtain the information through the market. There may be an agency that

---

[2]As the sum of marginal costs gives total variable costs, it does not include *fixed* costs. Total profit, therefore, is less than total producer surplus. Total profit is total producers' surplus minus total fixed costs.

will sell you the information, or a newspaper, magazine or website that contains the information. In such cases you will have to decide whether the cost to you of obtaining the information is worth the benefit it will provide you. A problem here is that you may not have sufficient information to judge how reliable the information is that you are obtaining!

Protecting people's interests

Dependants

People do not always make their own economic decisions. They are often dependent on decisions made by others. Parents make decisions on behalf of their children; partners on each other's behalf; younger adults on behalf of old people; managers on behalf of shareholders, etc.

A free market will respond to these decisions, however good or bad they may be, whether they be in the interest of the dependant or not. Thus the government may feel it necessary to protect dependants.

Poor economic decision making by individuals on their own behalf

The government may feel that people need protecting from poor economic decisions that they make on their *own* behalf. It may feel that in a free market people will consume too many harmful things. Thus if the government wants to discourage smoking and drinking, it can put taxes on tobacco and alcohol. In other words, it can use taxes to try to affect the choices that people make. In more extreme cases, it could make various activities illegal: activities such as driving over the limit, certain types of gambling, and the sale and consumption of drugs.

On the other hand, the government may feel that people consume too little of things that are good for them: things such as education, health care and sports facilities. Such goods are known as **merit goods**. The government could either provide them free or subsidise their production.

The principal–agent problem

> **Pause for thought**
>
> *How do merit goods differ from public goods?*

KI 16
p 97 The problem of dependants is an example of the principal–agent problem that we introduced in Chapter 4 (see page 96). One of the features of a complex modern economy is that people (principals) have to employ others (agents) to carry out their wishes. If you want to go on holiday, it may be easier to go to a travel agent to sort out the arrangements than to do it all yourself. Likewise, if you want to buy a house, it is more convenient to go to an estate agent. The point is that these agents have specialist knowledge and can save you, the principal, a great deal of time and effort. This

is merely an example of the benefits of specialisation and the division of labour.

It is the same with firms. As we saw in Chapter 4, they employ people with specialist knowledge and skills to carry out specific tasks. Companies frequently employ consultants to give them advice, or engage the services of specialist firms such as an advertising agency. It is the same with the employees of the company. They can be seen as 'agents' of their employer. In the case of workers, they can be seen as the agents of management. Junior managers are the agents of senior management. Senior managers are the agents of the directors, who are themselves agents of the shareholders. Some argue that the complexity of principal–agent relationships in large firms results in a 'divorce' between the owners of the firm (the shareholders), who are the principals, and the controllers of the firm (the managers), who are the shareholders' agents.

These relationships have an inherent danger for the principal: there is **asymmetric information** between the two sides. The agent knows more about the situation than the principal – in fact, this is part of the reason why the principal employs the agent in the first place. The danger is that the agent may well not act in the principal's best interests, and may be able to get away with it because of the principal's imperfect knowledge. The estate agent trying to sell you a house may not tell you about the noisy neighbours or that the vendor is prepared to accept a much lower price. A second-hand car dealer may 'neglect' to tell you about the rust on the underside of the car or that it has a history of unreliability.

So how can principals tackle the problem? There are two elements in the solution:

■ They must have some way of *monitoring* the performance of their agents (see page 96). For example, a business might employ efficiency experts to examine the operation of its management.
■ There must also be *incentives* for agents to behave in the principals' interests. This might involve making payments to agents conditional on meeting specific objectives.

TC 4
p 20

In a competitive market, managers' and shareholders' interests are more likely to coincide. Managers have to ensure that the company remains efficient or it may not survive the competition and they might lose their jobs. In monopolies and oligopolies, however, where supernormal profits

> **Definitions**
>
> **Merit goods** Goods which the government feels that people should consume but tend to underconsume and which therefore ought to be subsidised or provided free.
>
> **Asymmetric information** Where one party in an economic relationship (e.g. an agent) has more information than another (e.g. the principal).

BOX 7.2 | **SHOULD HEALTH-CARE PROVISION BE LEFT TO THE MARKET?**

A case of multiple market failures

In the UK, the National Health Service provides free hospital treatment, a free general practitioner service and free prescriptions for certain categories of people (such as pensioners and children). Their marginal cost to the patient is thus zero. Of course, these services use resources and they thus have to be paid for out of taxes.

But why are these services not sold directly to the patient, thereby saving the taxpayer money? There are, in fact, a number of reasons why the market would fail to provide the optimum amount of health care.

The issue of equity

KI 22
p 159

This is a problem connected with the distribution of income. Because income is unequally distributed, some people will be able to afford better treatment than others, and the poorest people may not be able to afford treatment at all. On grounds of equity, therefore, it is argued that health care should be provided free – at least for those on low incomes.

The concept of equity that is usually applied to health care is that individuals should be able to access treatment according to their medical need rather than according to their ability to pay.

[?] 1. *Does this argument also apply to food and other basic goods?*

Difficulty for people in predicting their future medical needs

KI 13
p 66

If you were suddenly taken ill and required a major operation, it could be very expensive indeed for you if you had to pay. On the other hand, you may go through life requiring very little if any medical treatment. In other words, there is great uncertainty about your future medical needs. As a result it would be very difficult to plan your finances and budget for possible future medical expenses if you had to pay for treatment.

Medical insurance provides a solution to this problem, but there remains a problem of equity. Would the chronically sick or very old be able to obtain cover and, if so, would they be able to afford the premiums? This issue of 'gaps' in an insurance-based system means that some form of intervention on grounds of equity may be needed, even if most provision is private.

Externalities

Health care generates a number of benefits *external* to the patient. If you are cured of an infectious disease, for example, it is not just you who benefits but also others, since you will not infect them. In addition, if you have a job you will be able to get back to work, thus reducing the disruption there. These external benefits of health care could be quite large.

KI 26
p 168

If the sick had to pay the cost of their treatment, they may decide not to be treated – especially if they are poor. They will consider the costs and benefits they might experience, but may not take into account the effect that their illness has on other people. The market, by equating *private* benefits and costs, would produce too little health care.

Patient ignorance

Markets only function well to allocate resources efficiently if the consumer has the information to make informed decisions.

---

can often be relatively easily earned, the interests of shareholders and managers are likely to diverge. Here it will be in shareholders' interests to institute incentive mechanisms that ensure that their agents, the managers, are motivated to strive for profitability.

Immobility of factors and time lags in response

Even under conditions of perfect competition, factors may be very slow to respond to changes in demand or supply. Labour, for example, may be highly immobile both occupationally and geographically. This can lead to large price changes and hence to large supernormal profits and high wages for those in the sectors of rising demand or falling costs. The long run may be a very long time coming!

In the meantime, there will be further changes in the conditions of demand and supply. Thus the economy is in a constant state of disequilibrium and the long run never comes. As firms and consumers respond to market signals and move towards equilibrium, so the equilibrium position moves and the social optimum is never achieved.

Whenever monopoly/monopsony power exists, the problem is made worse as firms or unions put up barriers to the entry of new firms or factors of production.

> **KEY IDEA 28** *The problem of time lags.* Many economic actions can take a long time to take effect. This can cause problems of instability and an inability of the economy to achieve social efficiency.

Macroeconomic goals

As we shall see later in the book, the key macroeconomic objectives relate in one way or another to the total level of spending or the total level of output in an economy. These objectives include strong and stable rates of economic growth, full employment, stable prices and a balance of international payments. Unfortunately the free market is unlikely to achieve these objectives simultaneously.

In the late 2000s and early 2010s an increasingly important macroeconomic goal for many governments was to

For many products that we buy, we have a pretty good idea how much we will like them. In the case of health care, however, 'consumers' (i.e. patients) may have very poor knowledge. If you have a pain in your chest, it may be simple muscular strain, or it may be a symptom of heart disease. You rely on the doctor (the *supplier* of the treatment) to give you the information: to diagnose your condition. Two problems could arise here with a market system of allocating health care.

KI 16
p 97

The first is that unscrupulous doctors might advise more expensive treatment than is necessary; they might even have an agreement with certain drugs companies that they will try to persuade you to buy an expensive branded product rather than an identical cheaper version. The problem will also exist in an insurance-based system, where the doctor may be even more inclined to over-supply if the patient has sufficient cover. This illustrates the principal–agent problem and the problem of asymmetric information (see page 96).

The second is that patients suffering from the early stages of a serious disease might not consult their doctor until the symptoms become acute, by which time it might be too late to treat the disease, or very expensive to do so. With a health service that is free at the point of use, however, a person is likely to receive an earlier diagnosis of serious conditions.

Oligopoly

KI 17
p 101

If doctors and hospitals operated in the free market as profit maximisers, it is unlikely that competition would drive down their prices. Instead they might collude to fix standard prices for treatment, so as to protect their incomes. Even if doctors did compete openly, it is unlikely that consumers would have enough information to enable them to 'shop around' for the best value.

We have to be careful though: to argue that the market system will fail to provide an optimal allocation of health-care resources does not in itself prove that *free provision* will result in optimal provision. For example, with no charge for GP appointments it is likely that some patients will consult their doctors over trivial complaints. The result will be excessive consumption, with consumption beyond the socially efficient point.

In the USA there is much more reliance on *private medical insurance* with only very poor people getting free treatment. Alternatively, the government may simply *subsidise* health care, so as to make it cheaper rather than free. This is the case with prescriptions and dental treatment in the UK, where many people have to pay part of the cost of treatment. Also the government can *regulate* the behaviour of the providers of health care, to prevent exploitation of the patient. Thus only people with certain qualifications are allowed to operate as doctors, nurses, pharmacists, etc.

?

2. *If health care is provided free, the demand is likely to be high. How is high demand likely to be dealt with? Is this a good way of dealing with the issue?*

3. *Go through each of the market failures identified in this box. In each case, consider what alternative policies are open to a government to tackle them. What are the advantages and disadvantages of these alternatives?*

---

ensure the stability of the financial system. This is an example of where a market failure in a particular sector is highly significant in other sectors too. In this case, intense competition among financial institutions and weaknesses in systems of regulation led to unsustainable lending practices and to the collapse or near-collapse of financial institutions around the world (see Chapter 10 for more on the financial system).

Parts C and D of this book examine the various macroeconomic problems and the methods of government intervention in more detail.

How far can economists go in advising governments?

Certain goals, such as growth in national income, changes in the distribution of income and greater efficiency, are relatively easy to quantify. Others, such as enlightenment or the sense of community well-being, are virtually impossible to quantify. For this reason, economics tends to concentrate on the means of achieving a relatively narrow range of goals. The danger is that by economists concentrating on a limited number of goals, they may well influence the policy makers – the government, local authorities, various pressure groups, etc. – into doing the same, and thus into neglecting other, perhaps important social goals.

Different objectives are likely to conflict. For example, economic growth may conflict with greater equality. In the case of such 'trade-offs', all the economist can do is to demonstrate the effects of a given policy, and leave the policy makers to decide whether the benefits in terms of one goal outweigh the costs in terms of another goal.

TC 1
p 7

KEY IDEA 29

Societies face trade-offs between economic objectives. For example, the goal of faster growth may conflict with that of greater equality; the goal of lower unemployment may conflict with that of lower inflation (at least in the short run). This is an example of opportunity cost: the cost of achieving more of one objective may be achieving less of another. The existence of trade-offs means that policy makers must make choices.

> **Recap**
>
> 1. Ignorance and uncertainty may prevent people from consuming or producing the levels they would otherwise choose. Information may sometimes be provided (at a price) by the market, but it may be imperfect and in some cases not available at all.
>
> 2. Markets may respond sluggishly to changes in demand and supply. The time lags in adjustment can lead to a permanent state of disequilibrium and to problems of instability.
>
> 3. In a free market there may be inadequate provision for dependants and an inadequate output of merit goods. Also, because of asymmetric information, agents may not always act in the best interests of their principals.
>
> 4. Although economists cannot make ultimate pronouncements on the rights and wrongs of the market – that involves making moral judgements (and economists here are no different from any other person) – they can point out the consequences of the market and of various government policies, and also the trade-offs that exist between different objectives.

7.5 GOVERNMENT INTERVENTION: TAXES AND SUBSIDIES

Will taxing the bad and subsidising the good solve the problem of externalities?

Faced with all the problems of the free market, what is a government to do?

There are several policy instruments that the government can use. At one extreme it can totally replace the market by providing goods and services itself. At the other extreme it can merely seek to persuade producers, consumers or workers to act differently. Between the two extremes the government has a number of instruments it can use to change the way markets operate. These include taxes, subsidies, laws and regulatory bodies. In this and the next two sections we examine these different forms of government intervention.

The use of taxes and subsidies

A policy instrument particularly favoured by many economists is that of taxes and subsidies. They can be used for two main purposes: (a) to promote greater social efficiency by altering the composition of production and consumption, and (b) to redistribute incomes. We examined their use for the second purpose in the last chapter. Here we examine their use to achieve greater social efficiency.

When there are imperfections in the market, social efficiency will not be achieved. Marginal social benefit (*MSB*) will not equal marginal social cost (*MSC*). A different level of output would be more desirable. Taxes and subsidies can be used to correct these imperfections. Essentially the approach is to tax those goods or activities where the market produces too much, and subsidise those where the market produces too little.

Taxes and subsidies to correct externalities

The rule here is simple: the government should impose a tax equal to the marginal external cost (or grant a subsidy equal to the marginal external benefit). This is known as a Pigouvian tax (or Pigouvian subsidy) named after the economist Arthur Pigou.

Previously we examined the impact of external costs of pollution created by the chemical industry as a whole. We will now focus on one firm in that industry, which otherwise is perfectly competitive. Our firm is thus a price taker. Assume that this particular chemical company emits smoke from a chimney and thus pollutes the atmosphere. This creates external costs for the people who breathe in the smoke. The marginal social cost of producing the chemicals thus exceeds the marginal private cost to the firm: $MSC > MC$.

This is illustrated in Figure 7.7. In this example it is assumed the marginal external pollution cost begins with the first unit of production but remains constant. Hence the MEC_p is drawn as a horizontal line. The vertical distance between the MC and MSC curves is equal to the MEC_p. The marginal pollution cost (the externality) is shown by the vertical distance between the MC and MSC curves. The firm produces Q_1 where $P = MC$ (its profit-maximising output), but in doing so takes no account of the external pollution costs it imposes on society.

If the government now imposes a tax on production equal to the marginal pollution cost, it will effectively 'internalise' the externality. The firm will have to pay an amount in tax equal to the external cost it creates. It will therefore now maximise profits at Q_2, where $P = MC + tax$. But this is the socially optimum output where $MSB = MSC$.

Taxes and subsidies to correct for monopoly

If the problem of monopoly that the government wishes to tackle is that of *excessive profits*, it can impose a lump-sum tax on the monopolist – that is, a tax of a fixed absolute amount irrespective of how much the monopolist produces, or the price it charges. Since a lump-sum

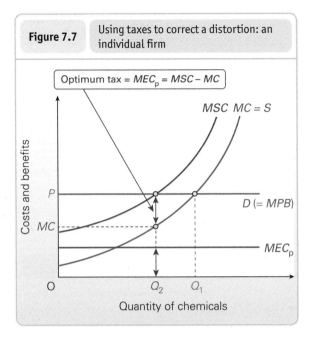

Figure 7.7 Using taxes to correct a distortion: an individual firm

Optimum tax = $MEC_p = MSC - MC$

Disadvantages of taxes and subsidies

Unfeasible to use different tax and subsidy rates. Each firm produces different levels and types of externalities and operates under different degrees of imperfect competition. It would be administratively very difficult and expensive, if not impossible, to charge every offending firm its own particular tax rate (or grant every relevant firm its own particular rate of subsidy). Even in the case of pollution where it is possible to measure a firm's emissions, there would still have to be a different tax rate for each pollutant and even for each environment, depending on its ability to absorb the pollutant and the number of people affected.

Using combinations of lump-sum taxes and per-unit subsidies to correct monopoly distortions to price, output and profit would also probably be impractical. Given that cost and revenue curves differ substantially from one firm to another, separate tax and subsidy rates would be needed for each firm. An army of tax inspectors would be necessary to administer the system!

Lack of knowledge. Even if a government did decide to charge a tax equal to each offending firm's marginal external costs, it would still have the problem of measuring those costs and apportioning blame. The damage to lakes and forests from acid rain has been a major concern since the beginning of the 1980s. But just how serious is that damage? What is its current monetary cost? How long-lasting is the damage?

tax is an additional *fixed* cost to the firm, and hence will not affect the firm's marginal cost, it will not reduce the amount that the monopolist produces (which *would* be the case with a per-unit tax). Two examples of such taxes are the 'windfall tax' imposed in 1997 by the UK Labour government on the profits of various privatised utilities, and in 2005 on the profits of oil companies operating in the North Sea following large increases in world oil prices.

If the government is concerned that the monopolist produces less than the socially efficient output, it could give the monopolist a *per-unit subsidy* (which would encourage the monopolist to produce more). But would this not *increase* the monopolist's profit? The answer to this is to impose a harsh lump-sum tax in addition to the subsidy. The tax would not undo the subsidy's benefit of encouraging the monopolist to produce more, but it could be used to reduce the monopolist's profits below the original (i.e. pre-subsidy) level.

Advantages of taxes and subsidies

Many economists favour the tax/subsidy solution to market imperfections (especially the problem of externalities) because it still allows the market to operate. It forces firms to take on board the full social costs and benefits of their actions. It is also adjustable according to the magnitude of the problem.

Moreover, if firms are taxed for polluting, they are encouraged to find cleaner ways of producing. The tax acts as an incentive over the longer run to reduce pollution. Likewise, by subsidising *good* practices, firms are given the incentive to adopt more good practices.

> **Pause for thought**
>
> *Why is it easier to use taxes and subsidies to tackle the problem of car exhaust pollution than to tackle the problem of peak-time traffic congestion in cities?*

Just what and who are to blame? These are questions that cannot be answered precisely. It is thus impossible to fix the 'correct' pollution tax on, say, a particular coal-fired power station.

Despite these problems, it is nevertheless possible to charge firms by the amount of a particular emission. For example, firms could be charged for chimney smoke by so many parts per million of a given pollutant. Although it is difficult to 'fine-tune' such a system so that the charge reflects the precise number of people affected by the pollutant and by how much, it does go some way to internalising the externality. As Box 7.3 (on page 190) shows, many countries in recent years have introduced 'green' taxes, seeing them as an effective means of protecting the environment.

TC 4
p 20

> ### Recap
>
> 1. Taxes and subsidies are one means of correcting market distortions.
>
> 2. Externalities can be corrected by imposing tax rates equal to the size of marginal external costs, and granting rates of subsidy equal to marginal external benefits.
>
> 3. Taxes and subsidies can also be used to affect monopoly price, output and profit. Subsidies can be used to persuade a monopolist to increase output (and reduce price) to the competitive level. Lump-sum taxes can then be used to reduce monopoly profits without affecting the new price or output.
>
> 4. Taxes and subsidies have the advantages of 'internalising' externalities and of providing incentives to reduce external costs. On the other hand, they may be impractical to use when different rates are required for each case, or when it is impossible to know the full effects of the activities that the taxes or subsidies are being used to correct.

7.6 GOVERNMENT INTERVENTION: LAWS AND REGULATION

Should the government try to stop 'bad behaviour' by big business?

Laws prohibiting or regulating undesirable structures or behaviour

Laws are frequently used to correct market imperfections. Laws can be of three main types: those that prohibit or regulate behaviour that imposes external costs, those that prevent firms providing false or misleading information, and those that prevent or regulate monopolies and oligopolies.

Advantages of legal restrictions

- They are usually simple and clear to understand and are often relatively easy to administer. For example, various polluting activities could be banned or restricted.
- When the danger is very great, or when the extent of the danger is not as yet known, it might be much safer to ban various practices altogether (e.g. the use of various toxic chemicals) rather than to rely on taxes.
- When a decision needs to be taken quickly, it might be possible to invoke emergency action. For example, in a city like Athens it has been found to be simpler to ban or restrict the use of private cars during a chemical smog emergency than to tax their use.
- Because consumers suffer from imperfect information, consumer protection laws can make it illegal for firms to sell shoddy or unsafe goods, or to make false or misleading claims about their products.

KI 16
p 97

Disadvantages of legal restrictions

The main problem is that legal restrictions tend to be a rather blunt weapon. If, for example, a firm were required to reduce the effluent of a toxic chemical to 20 tonnes per week, there would be no incentive for the firm to reduce it further. With a tax on the effluent, however, the more the firm reduced the effluent, the less tax it would pay. Thus with a system of taxes there is a *continuing* incentive to cut pollution, to improve safety, or whatever.

Regulatory bodies

Rather than using the blunt weapon of general legislation to ban or restrict various activities, a more 'subtle' approach can be adopted. This involves the use of various regulatory bodies. Having identified possible cases where action might be required (e.g. potential cases of pollution or misleading information), the regulatory body would probably conduct an investigation and then prepare a report containing its findings and recommendations. It might also have the power to enforce its decisions or this might be up to some higher authority.

EU competition policy

In most industrial countries, governments have in place a 'competition policy' which attempts to control the worst abuses of market power. Relevant EU legislation is contained in Articles 101 and 102 of the 2009 Treaty of the Functioning of the European Union. Additional regulations covering mergers came into force in 1990 and were amended in 2004. Further minor amendments have been put in place since then, which have focused on specific market regulation.

Restrictive practices. Article 101 is concerned with oligopolistic collusion. It is designed to prevent collusive *behaviour* rather than oligopolistic *structures* (i.e. the simple existence of co-operation between firms).

Practices considered anti-competitive include firms colluding to do any of the following:

- Fix prices (i.e. above competitive levels).
- Limit production, markets, technical development or investment.
- Share out markets or sources of supply.
- Charge discriminatory prices or operate discriminatory trading conditions, such as to benefit the colluding parties and disadvantage others.

■ Make other firms who sign contracts with any of the colluding firms accept unfavourable obligations which, by their nature, have no connection with the subject of such contracts.

If companies are found guilty of undertaking any of these anti-competitive practices that are in contravention of Article 101, they are subject to financial penalties.

Abuse of market power. Article 102 relates to the abuse of market power and has also been extended to cover mergers. As with Article 101, it is the *behaviour* of firms that is the target of the legislation. The following are cited as examples of abuses of market power. As you can see, they are very similar to those in Article 101.

■ Charging unfairly high prices to consumers, or paying unfairly low prices to suppliers.
■ Limiting production, markets or technical developments to the detriment of consumers.
■ Using price discrimination or other discriminatory practices to the detriment of certain parties.
■ Making other firms that sign contracts with it to accept unfavourable obligations which, by their nature, have no connection with the subject of such contracts.

Under Article 102, such practices can be banned and firms can be fined where they are found to have abused a dominant position.

The two Articles predominately apply to firms trading between EU members and so do not cover monopolies or oligopolies operating solely within a member country.

Merger policy. Under current regulations (2004), mergers that would significantly reduce competition in the EU are prohibited. This normally, therefore, applies to large mergers. For example, a merger could be blocked if there were concerns that the new firm would have significant market power that might lead to higher prices for consumers.

The merger must also have an 'EU dimension'. This is defined as where no more than two-thirds of each firm's EU-wide business is conducted in a single member state. If a firm does conduct more than two-thirds of its business in one country then investigation of the merger would be the responsibility of that member state's competition authority.

UK competition policy

There have been substantial changes to UK competition policy since the first legislation was introduced in 1948. The current approach is based on the 1998 Competition Act and the 2002 Enterprise Act, together with Part 3 of the 2013 Enterprise and Regulatory Reform Act.

The Competition Act brought UK policy in line with EU policy, detailed above. The Act has two key sets (or 'chapters') of prohibitions. Chapter I prohibits various restrictive practices, and mirrors EU Article 101. Chapter II prohibits various abuses of monopoly power, and mirrors EU Article 102. The Enterprise Act strengthened the Competition Act and introduced new measures for the control of mergers.

The 2013 Act resulted in the setting up of a new regulatory body, the Competition and Markets Authority (CMA), which took over the work of its predecessors, the Office for Fair Trading and the Competition Commission.

Restrictive practices. The 1998 Competition Act brought UK restrictive practices policy more into line with EU policy. For example, the way fines were calculated and implemented for anti-competitive behaviour was changed so that it was more comparable to the method used by the European Commission: i.e. the penalties imposed could be up to 10 per cent of the firm's annual turnover.

The types of practices that constitute 'cartel agreements' were also made more consistent with EU policy: e.g. price fixing, limiting supply, sharing out markets, limiting supply or bid-rigging.

It is a *criminal* offence to engage in cartel agreements (i.e. horizontal, rather than vertical, collusive agreements between firms), irrespective of whether there are appreciable effects on competition. Convicted offenders can receive a prison sentence of up to five years and/or an unlimited fine. Prosecutions can be brought by the Serious Fraud Office or the CMA. The CMA also has substantial powers to enter premises, seize documents and require people to answer questions or provide information.

Abuse of market power. Under the Chapter II prohibition of the 1998 Competition Act, it is illegal for a dominant firm to exercise its market power in such a way as to reduce competition. Any suspected case is investigated by the CMA, which uses a two-stage process in deciding whether an abuse has taken place.

The first stage is to establish whether a firm has a position of dominance, where 'dominance' normally involves the firm having at least a 40 per cent share of the market. If the firm *is* deemed to be dominant, the second stage involves the CMA having to decide whether the firm's practices constitute an abuse of its position. It specifies the same four types of market abuse as does Article 102 (see above).

The simple *existence* of any of these practices may not constitute an abuse. The CMA has to decide whether their *effect* is to restrict competition. This may require a detailed investigation to establish whether competition is restricted or distorted. If this is found to be the case, the CMA decides what actions must be taken to remedy the situation.

Merger policy. A merger or takeover is investigated by the CMA if the target company has a UK turnover that exceeds £70 million, or if the merger results in the new company having a market share of 25 per cent or more.

UK policy is similar to EU policy. The CMA conducts a preliminary or Phase 1 investigation to see whether competition is likely to be threatened. There is a statutory deadline of 40 working days to complete Phase 1, by which point the CMA has to decide whether there is a significant chance that the merger would result in a substantial lessening of competition (SLC). If the CMA concludes that this might be the case, it begins Phase 2 of the process – a much more in- depth assessment. If no SLC issues are raised, the merger is allowed to go ahead.

There is a 24-week statutory time limit for Phase 2 decisions to be made, by which point the CMA has to decide whether (a) to allow the merger to go ahead unconditionally, (b) to allow it go ahead subject to the firms meeting certain legally binding conditions, (c) to prohibit the merger. In the 10 years between 2004–5 and 2013–14 only nine mergers were prohibited out of the 110 Phase 2 investigations that took place.

UK regulation of privatised utilities

In the UK there are also regulatory bodies for each of the major privatised utilities. These regulators are as follows: the Office for Gas and Electricity Markets (Ofgem), the Office of Communications (Ofcom), the Office of Rail and Road (ORR) and the Office of Water Services (Ofwat).

As well as supervising the competitive behaviour of the privatised utility, they set terms under which the industries have to operate. For example, the ORR sets the terms under which rail companies have access to track and stations. The terms set by the regulator can be reviewed by negotiation between the regulator and the industry. If agreement cannot be reached, the CMA acts as an appeal court and its decision is binding.

The regulator for each industry also sets limits to the prices that certain parts of the industry can charge. These parts are those where there is little or no competition, for example the charges made to electricity and gas retailers by National Grid, the owner of the electricity grid and major gas pipelines.

The price-setting formulae have largely been of the 'RPI minus X' variety (although other factors, including competition and excessive profits, are also taken into account). What this means is that the industries can raise their prices by the rate of increase in the retail price index (i.e. by the rate of inflation) *minus* a certain percentage (X) to take account of expected increases in efficiency. Thus if the rate of inflation were 3 per cent, and if the regulator considered that the industry (or firm) could be expected to reduce its costs by 2 per cent ($X = 2\%$), then price rises would be capped at 1 per cent. The $RPI - X$ system is thus an example of **price-cap regulation**. The idea of this system of regulation is that it forces the industry to pass cost savings on to the consumer. (The $RPI - X$ system is considered further in Case Study 7.4 in MyEconLab.)

Pause for thought

What other forms of intervention are likely to be necessary to back up the work of regulatory bodies?

Definition

Price-cap regulation Where the regulator puts a ceiling on the amount by which a firm can raise its price.

Recap

1. Laws can be used to regulate activities that impose external costs, to regulate monopolies and oligopolies, and to provide consumer protection. Legal controls are often simpler and easier to operate than taxes, and are safer when the danger is potentially great. Nevertheless, legal controls tend to be rather a blunt weapon, although discretion can sometimes be allowed in the administration of the law.

2. Regulatory bodies can be set up to monitor and control activities that might be against the public interest (e.g. anti-competitive behaviour of oligopolists).

3. Competition policy in most countries recognises that monopolies, mergers and restrictive practices can bring both costs and benefits to the consumer. Generally, though, restrictive practices tend to be more damaging to consumers' interests than simple monopoly power or mergers.

4. The focus of both EU and UK legislation is on anti-competitive practices rather than on the simple existence of agreements between firms or market dominance. Practices that are found after investigation to be detrimental to competition are prohibited and heavy fines can be imposed, even for a first offence.

5. Regulation in the UK of privatised utilities has involved setting up regulatory offices for the separate industries. These generally operate informally, using negotiation and bargaining to persuade the industries to behave in the public interest. They also set the terms under which the firms can operate (e.g. access rights to the respective grid).

6. As far as prices are concerned, in many cases privatised utilities are not controlled, as the industries are sufficiently competitive. Where the regulator deems that competition is insufficient, the industries are normally required to abide by an 'RPI minus X' formula. This forces them to pass potential cost reductions on to the consumer.

7.7 OTHER FORMS OF GOVERNMENT INTERVENTION

What other means does the government have to correct market failures?

Changes in property rights

One cause of market failure is the limited nature of property rights. If someone dumps a load of rubble in your garden, you can insist that it is removed. If, however, someone dumps a load of rubble in their *own* garden, but which is next door to yours, what can you do? You can still see it from your window. It is still an eyesore. But you have no property rights over the next-door garden.

Property rights define who owns property, to what uses it can be put, the rights other people have over it and how it may be transferred. By *extending* these rights, individuals may be able to prevent other people imposing costs on them, or charge them for doing so.

The socially efficient level of charge would be one that was equal to the marginal external cost (and would have the same effect as the government charging a tax on the firm of that amount: see Figure 7.7). The **Coase theorem**[3] states that in an otherwise perfectly competitive market, the socially efficient charge *will* be levied. But why?

Let us take the case of river pollution by a chemical works that imposes a cost on people fishing in the river. If property rights to the river were now given to the fishing community they could impose a charge on the chemical works per unit of output. If they charged *less* than the marginal external cost, they would suffer more from the last unit (in terms of lost fish) than they were being compensated. If they charged *more*, and thereby caused the firm to cut back its output below the socially efficient level, they would be sacrificing receiving charges that would be greater than the marginal suffering. It will be in the sufferers' best interests, therefore, to charge an amount *equal* to the marginal externality.

> **Pause for thought**
>
> *If the sufferers had no property rights, show how it would still be in their interests to 'bribe' the firm to produce the socially efficient level of output.*

In most instances, however, this type of solution is totally impractical. It is impractical when *many* people are *slightly* inconvenienced, especially if there are many culprits imposing the costs. For example, if I were disturbed by noisy lorries outside my home, it would not be practical to negotiate with every haulage company involved. What if I wanted to ban the lorries from the street but my next-door

neighbour wanted to charge them 10p per journey? Who gets their way?

The extension of private property rights becomes more practical where the parties involved are few in number, are easily identifiable and where the costs are clearly defined. Thus a noise abatement Act could be passed which allowed me to prevent my neighbours playing noisy radios, having noisy parties or otherwise disturbing the peace in my home. The onus would be on me to report them. Or I could agree not to report them if they paid me adequate compensation.

But even in cases where only a few people are involved, there may still be the problem of litigation. Justice may not be free, and there may be concerns that companies or rich individuals can afford 'better' justice than individuals on more modest incomes. The rich can employ top lawyers. Even if I have a right to sue a large company for dumping toxic waste near me, I may not have the legal muscle to win.

Finally there is a broader question of *equity*. The extension of private property rights may favour the rich (who tend to have more property) at the expense of the poor. Ramblers may get great pleasure from strolling across a great country estate, along public rights of way. This may annoy the owner. If the owner's property rights are now extended to exclude the ramblers, is this a social gain?

Of course, equity considerations can also be dealt with by altering property rights, but in a different way. *Public* property like parks, open spaces, libraries and historic buildings could be extended. Also the property of the rich could be redistributed to the poor. Here it is less a question of the rights that ownership confers, and more a question of altering the ownership itself.

> **Pause for thought**
>
> *Would it be a good idea to extend countries' territorial waters in order to bring key open-seas fishing grounds within countries' territory? Could this help to solve the problem of over-fishing?*

Provision of information

When ignorance or asymmetric information is a reason for market failure, the direct provision of information by the

> **Definition**
>
> **The Coase theorem** By sufferers from externalities doing deals with perpetrators (by levying charges or offering payments), the externality will be 'internalised' and the socially efficient level of output will be achieved.

---

[3]Named after Ronald Coase, who developed the theory. See his 'The problem of social cost', *Journal of Law and Economics* (1960).

government or one of its agencies may help to correct that failure. An example is the information on jobs provided by job centres to those looking for work. They thus help the labour market to work better and increase the elasticity of supply of labour.

Another example is the provision of consumer information – for example, on the effects of smoking, or of eating certain foodstuffs. Another is the provision of government statistics on prices, costs, employment, sales trends, etc. This enables firms to plan with greater certainty.

The direct provision of goods and services

In the case of public goods and services, such as streets, pavements, seaside illumination and national defence, the market may completely fail to provide. In this case the government must take over the role of provision. Central government, local government or some other public agency could provide these goods and services directly. Alternatively, they could pay private firms to do so. The public would pay through central and local taxation.

But just what quantity of the public good should be provided? How can the level of public demand or public 'need' be identified? Should any charge at all be made to consumers for each unit consumed?

With a pure public good, once it is provided the marginal cost of supplying one more consumer is zero. Take the case of a lighthouse. Once it is constructed and in operation, there is no extra cost of providing the service to additional passing ships. Even if it were *possible* to charge ships each time they make use of it, it would not be socially desirable. Assuming no external costs, MSC is zero. Thus $MSB = MSC$ at a price of zero. Zero is thus the socially efficient price.

But what about the construction of a new public good, like a new road or a new lighthouse? How can a rational decision be made by the government as to whether it should go ahead? This time the marginal cost is not zero: extra roads and lighthouses cost money to build. The solution is to identify all the costs and benefits to society from the project (private and external) and to weigh them up. This is known as **cost–benefit analysis** (see Web Appendix 7.2 for details of how cost–benefit analysis is conducted). If the social benefits of the project exceed the social costs, then it would be socially efficient to go ahead with it. Many proposed public projects are subjected to cost–benefit analysis in order to assess their desirability.

The government could also provide goods and services directly which are *not* public goods. Examples include health and education. We can identify various reasons why such things are provided free, or at well below cost, which link to one or more of the broad reasons for intervention identified in Section 1.5 (see pages 21–3). These factors include:

Social justice. Society may feel that these things should not be provided according to ability to pay. Rather they should be provided as of right: an equal right based on need.

Large positive externalities. People other than the consumer may benefit substantially. If a person decides to get treatment for an infectious disease, other people benefit by not being infected. A free health service thus helps to combat the spread of disease.

Dependants. If education were not free, and if the quality of education depended on the amount spent, and if parents could choose how much or little to buy, then the quality of children's education would depend not just on their parents' income, but also on how much they cared. A government may choose to provide such things free in order to protect children from 'bad' parents. A similar argument is used for providing free prescriptions and dental treatment for all children.

Ignorance. Consumers may not realise how much they will benefit. If they had to pay, they may choose (unwisely) to go without. Providing health care free may persuade people to consult their doctors before a complaint becomes serious.

Macroeconomic benefits. Public provision of services such as health and education can positively affect the economy's human capital (see Boxes 6.5 and 9.5) and so the potential effectiveness of the workforce and, in turn, the economy's productive potential.

Nationalisation and privatisation

Another possible solution to market failure, advocated by some on the political left, is nationalisation. If industries are not being run in the public interest by the private sector, then bring them into public ownership. Problems of monopoly power, externalities, inequality, etc., can be dealt with directly if these industries are run with the public interest, rather than private gain, at heart.

In the late 1940s and early 1950s the Labour government of the time nationalised many of the key transport, communications and power industries, such as the railways, freight transport, airlines, coal, gas, electricity and steel.

However, by the mid-1970s the performance of the nationalised industries was being increasingly questioned. A change of policy was introduced in the early 1980s, when successive Conservative governments engaged in an extensive programme of 'privatisation', returning virtually all of the nationalised industries back to the private sector. These included telecommunications, gas, water, steel, electricity and the railways.

By 1997, the year the Conservatives left office, with the exception of the rail industry in Northern Ireland and

> ### Definition
>
> **Cost–benefit analysis** The identification, measurement and weighing up of the costs and benefits of a project in order to decide whether or not it should go ahead.

the water industry in Northern Ireland and Scotland, the only nationalised industry remaining in the UK was the Post Office (including post offices and mail). The Post Office and Royal Mail were split in 2012 and Royal Mail was privatised in October 2013. Post Office Ltd remains state owned but, under the 2011 Postal Services Act, there is the option for it to become a mutual organisation in the future.

Other countries have followed similar programmes of privatisation in what has become a worldwide phenomenon. Privatisation has been seen as a means of revitalising ailing industries and as a golden opportunity to raise revenues to ease budgetary problems.

In 2008, however, many governments returned to the use of nationalisation, in order to 'rescue' banks which were at risk of going bankrupt. This was facilitated by the EU giving permission for member states to support financial institutions, subject to conditions under EU state-aid rules.

Arguments for and against privatisation

The principal argument in favour of privatisation is that it exposes industries to *market forces*, from which will flow the benefits of greater efficiency, faster growth and greater responsiveness to the wishes of the consumer.

If privatisation involves splitting an industry into competing companies, this greater competition in the goods market may force the companies to drive down costs and reduce prices in order to stay in business.

Privatised companies do not have direct access to government finance. To finance investment they must now go to the market: they must issue shares or borrow from banks or other financial institutions. In doing so, they will be competing for funds with other companies, and thus must be seen as capable of using these funds profitably.

Market discipline will also be enforced by shareholders. Shareholders want a good return on their shares and will thus put pressure on the privatised company to perform well. The competition for corporate control (see page 111) thus provides incentives for firms to be efficient.

However, some industries have the characteristic of being a natural monopoly (see pages 108–9). In such cases, the market forces argument for privatisation largely breaks down if a public monopoly is simply replaced by a private monopoly. | KI 17 | p 101 |

Critics also point to the fact that various industries may create substantial external benefits and yet may be privately unprofitable. A railway or an underground line, for example, may considerably ease congestion on the roads, thus benefiting road as well as rail users. Other industries may cause substantial external costs. A coal-fired power station, for example, may pollute the atmosphere and cause acid rain. Will such externalities be ignored under privatisation? | KI 26 | p 168 |

In assessing these arguments, a lot depends on the toughness of government legislation and the attitudes and powers of regulatory agencies (see Section 7.6) after privatisation.

Recap

1. An extension of property rights may allow individuals to prevent others imposing costs on them, or to charge them for so doing. This is not practical, however, when many people are affected to a small degree, or where several people are affected but differ in their attitudes towards what they want done about the 'problem'.

2. The government may provide information in cases where the private sector fails to provide an adequate level.

3. The government may also provide goods and services directly. These could be in the category of public goods or other goods where the government feels that provision by the market is inadequate.

4. Another potential approach to market failure is to bring some industries under public control. However, many countries have over recent decades embarked on programmes of privatisation. An important argument in favour of privatisation has been the potential of greater competition, not only in the goods market but in the market for finance and for corporate control. However, critics point to problems arising from industries characterised by natural monopoly or significant externalities.

7.8 MORE OR LESS INTERVENTION?

Can the government always put things right?

Government intervention in the market can itself lead to problems. The advocates of privatisation, for example, argue that, as well as benefiting from the discipline of market forces, privatised industries are free of government interference and are able make more rational economic decisions and plan with greater certainty.

However, the general case for less government intervention is not that the market is the *perfect* means of achieving

given social goals, but rather that the problems created by intervention are greater than the problems overcome by that intervention.

Drawbacks of government intervention

Lack of market incentives. Though the market may be imperfect, it does tend to encourage efficiency by allowing the | TC 4 | p 20 |

efficient to receive greater rewards. Government intervention, whether this is nationalisation, welfare payments, the use of subsidies, guaranteed prices or wages, etc., removes market forces or cushions their effect. Therefore, it may remove certain useful incentives. Subsidies, for example, may allow inefficient firms to survive, while welfare payments may be argued to discourage effort.

Shifts in government policy. The economic efficiency of industry may suffer if government intervention changes too frequently. It makes it difficult for firms to plan if they cannot predict tax rates, subsidies, price and wage controls, etc.

Shortages and surpluses. If the government intervenes by fixing prices at levels other than the equilibrium, this will create either shortages or surpluses (see Section 3.7).

If the price is fixed *below* the equilibrium, there will be a shortage. For example, if the rent of social housing is fixed below the equilibrium in order to provide affordable housing for low-income households, demand will exceed supply. In the case of such shortages the government will have to adopt a system of waiting lists, or rationing, or giving certain people preferential treatment. Alternatively it will have to allow allocation to be on a first-come, first-served basis or allow queues to develop. Black markets are likely to occur.

If the price is fixed *above* the equilibrium price, there will be a surplus. Such surpluses are obviously wasteful. (The problem of food surpluses in the EU was examined in Box 3.5.)

Poor information. The government may not know the full costs and benefits of its policies. It may genuinely wish to pursue the interests of consumers or any other group and yet may be unaware of people's wishes or misinterpret their behaviour.

Bureaucracy and inefficiency. Government intervention involves administrative costs. The more wide-reaching and detailed the intervention, the greater the number of people and material resources that will be involved. These resources may be used wastefully.

Lack of freedom for the individual. Government intervention involves a loss of freedom for individuals to make economic choices. The argument is not just that the pursuit of individual gain is seen to lead to the social good, but that it is desirable in itself that individuals should be as free as possible to pursue their own interests with the minimum of government interference: that minimum being largely confined to the maintenance of laws consistent with the protection of life, liberty and property.

Advantages of the free market

Although markets in the real world are not perfect, even imperfect markets can be argued to have positive advantages over government provision or even government regulation. These might include the following.

Automatic adjustments. Government intervention requires administration. A free-market economy, on the other hand, leads to automatic, albeit imperfect, adjustment to demand and supply changes.

Dynamic advantages of capitalism. The chances of making high monopoly/oligopoly profits will encourage businesspeople to invest in new products and new processes and techniques. It thereby encourages innovation which has macroeconomic benefits too. While prices may be high initially, consumers will gain from the extra choice of products. Furthermore, if profits are high, new firms will sooner or later break into the market and competition will ensue.

> ### Pause for thought
>
> *Are there any features of free-market capitalism that would discourage innovation?*

A high degree of competition even under monopoly/oligopoly. Even though an industry at first sight may seem to be highly monopolistic, competitive forces may still work as a result of the following:

- A fear that excessively high profits might encourage firms to attempt to break into the industry (assuming that the market is contestable).
- Competition from closely related industries (e.g. coach services for rail services, or electricity for gas).
- The threat of foreign competition.
- Countervailing powers (see page 126). Large powerful producers often sell to large powerful buyers. For example, the power of detergent manufacturers to drive up the price of washing powder is countered by the power of supermarket chains to drive down the price at which they purchase it. Thus power is to some extent neutralised.
- The competition for corporate control (see page 111).

Should there be more or less intervention in the market?

No firm conclusions can be drawn in the debate between those who favour more and those who favour less government intervention, for the following reasons:

- The debate involves many moral, social and political issues which cannot be settled by economic analysis. For example, it could be argued that freedom to set up in business and freedom from government regulation are desirable for their own sake. As a fundamental ethical point of view this can be disputed, but not disproved.
- In principle, the issue of whether a government ought to intervene in any situation could be settled by weighing

up the costs and benefits of that intervention. However, such costs and benefits, even if they could be identified, are extremely difficult if not impossible to measure, especially when the costs are borne by different people from those who receive the benefits and when externalities are involved.

- Often the effect of more or less intervention simply cannot be predicted: there are too many uncertainties.

Nevertheless, economists can make a considerable contribution to analysing problems of the market and the effects of government intervention.

Recap

1. Government intervention in the market may lead to shortages or surpluses; it may be based on poor information; it may be costly in terms of administration; it may stifle incentives; it may be disruptive if government policies change too frequently; it may remove certain liberties.

2. By contrast, a free market leads to automatic adjustments to changes in economic conditions; the prospect of monopoly/oligopoly profits may stimulate risk taking and hence research and development and innovation; there may still be a high degree of actual or potential competition under monopoly and oligopoly.

3. It is impossible to draw firm conclusions about the 'optimum' level of government intervention. This is partly due to the moral/political nature of the question, partly due to the difficulties of measuring costs and benefits of intervention/non-intervention, and partly due to the difficulties of predicting the effects of government policies, especially over the longer term.

7.9 THE ENVIRONMENT: A CASE STUDY IN MARKET FAILURE

How can economists contribute to the environmental debate?

The environmental problem

Scarcely a day goes by without some environmental issue or other featuring in the news: another warning about global warming; a company fined for illegally dumping waste; a drought or flood blamed on pollution/global warming; smog in some major cities. Also attempts by policy makers to improve the environment are often controversial and hit the headlines: e.g., the impact of government climate change policies on the size of people's energy bills.

Why does the environment appear to be so misused and policies that attempt to improve the situation so controversial? To answer these questions we have to understand the nature of the economic relationship between humans and the natural world.

The environment as a resource
We all benefit from the environment in three ways:

- as an amenity to be enjoyed
- as a source of primary products (food, raw materials and other resources)
- as a place where we can dump waste.

KI 2
p 7 Unfortunately these three different uses are often in conflict with each other. For example, we extract and burn fossil fuels such as coal, oil and gas, for power generation and industrial uses. However, the extraction of these fuels may have a negative impact on the amenity value of the environment. One only has to think of some of the concerns raised by people about the impact of drilling for shale gas

on the appearance of their local communities. The burning of fossil fuels also creates greenhouse gases that are emitted into the atmosphere and cause climate change. Some of the CO_2 gets absorbed into the oceans, which increases their level of acidity and kills marine life.

Policies that try to reduce our current use of the environment as a source of primary products and/or reduce the volume of emissions we generate come at cost. These higher costs are often passed on to consumers in the form of higher prices – an outcome they often dislike and complain about.

The subject of environmental degradation lies clearly within the realm of economics, since it is a direct consequence of production and consumption decisions. So how can economic analysis help us to understand the nature of the problem and design effective policies that will result in the optimal use of the environment? What will be the impact of these policies on households and firms?

Market failures

An unregulated market system may fail to provide an adequate protection for the environment for a number of reasons.

Externalities. We saw in Section 7.2 how pollution could *KI 26* be classified as a 'negative externality' of production or *p 168* consumption.

In the case of production, there are marginal external costs (*MEC*), which means that the marginal social costs (*MSC*) are greater than the marginal private costs (*MC*) to the polluter.

The failure of the market system to equate *MSC* and marginal social benefit (*MSB*) is due to either consumers or firms lacking the appropriate property rights. Because no one owns the environment, there is no one to enforce property rights over it. If a company pollutes the air that I breathe, I cannot stop it because the air does not belong to me.

KI 27 *The environment as a common resource.* The air, the seas
p 172 and many other parts of the environment are not privately owned. They are a global 'commons'. As such, it is extremely difficult to exclude non-payers from consuming the benefits they provide. Because of this property of 'non-excludability' (see page 172), the environment can often be consumed at a zero price. If the price of any good or service to the user is zero, there is no incentive to economise on its use.

Many parts of the environment, however, are *scarce*: there is *rivalry* in their use. As people increase their use of the environment, it may prevent other or rival consumers from enjoying it. We saw in Box 7.1 how over-fishing in the open oceans can lead to the depletion of fish stocks.

Ignorance. There have been many cases of people causing environmental damage without realising it, especially when the effects build up over a long time. Take the case of aerosols. It was not until the 1980s that scientists connected their use to ozone depletion. Even when the problems are known to scientists, consumers may not appreciate the full environmental costs of their actions. So even if people would like to be more 'environmentally friendly' in their activities, they might not have the knowledge to be so.

KI 28 *Intergenerational problems.* The environmentally harmful
p 176 effects of many activities are long term, whereas the benefits are immediate. Thus consumers and firms are frequently prepared to continue with various practices and leave future generations to worry about their environmental consequences. The problem, then, is a reflection of the importance that people attach to the present relative to the future.

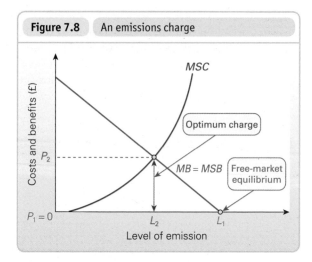

| Figure 7.8 | An emissions charge |

Pause for thought

Look through the categories of possible market failings in Sections 7.1 to 7.4. Are there any others, in addition to the four we have just identified, that will result in a socially inefficient use of the environment?

Policy alternatives

Charging for use of the environment (as a resource or a dump)

TC 5 One way of 'pricing the environment' is for the govern-
p 23 ment to impose **environmental charges** on consumers or firms. Thus *emissions charges* could be levied on firms discharging waste. Another example is the use of *user charges* to

households for sewage disposal or rubbish collection. The socially efficient level of environmental use would be where the marginal social benefits and costs of that use were equal. This is illustrated in Figure 7.8, which shows the emission of toxic waste into a river by a chemical plant.

It is assumed that all the benefits from emitting the waste into the river accrue to the firm (i.e. there is no external benefit). Marginal private and marginal social benefits are thus the same (*MB = MSB*). The curve slopes downwards because, with a downward-sloping demand curve for the *good*, higher output will have a lower marginal benefit, and so too will the waste associated with it.

But what about the marginal costs? Without charges, **KI 26**
the marginal private cost of using the river for emitting the **p 168** waste is zero. The pollution of the river, however, imposes an external cost on those living by the river or using it for fishing or water supply. The marginal external cost rises as the river becomes less and less able to cope with increased levels of emission. As there is no private cost, the marginal social cost is the same as the marginal external cost.

Without a charge, the firm will emit L_1, since this is **TC 10**
where its private marginal cost (= 0) equals its private mar- **p 167** ginal benefit. The socially efficient level of emission is L_2 and the socially efficient level of emission charge, therefore, is P_2.

Environmental ('green') taxes and subsidies

Rather than charging for environmental use, a tax could be imposed on the output (or consumption) of a good, wherever external environmental costs are generated. These are known as **green taxes**. In this case, the good already has

Definition

Environmental charges Charges for using natural resources (e.g. water or national parks), or for using the environment as a dump for waste (e.g. factory emissions or sewage).

a price: the tax has the effect of increasing the price. To achieve a socially efficient output, the rate of tax should be equal to the marginal external cost (see Figure 7.7 on page 179). The alternative is to subsidise activities that reduce pollution (such as the installation of loft insulation). Here the rate of subsidy should be equal to the marginal external benefit.

Although green taxes and subsidies are theoretically a means of achieving social efficiency, they do have serious limitations (see Box 7.3).

Laws and regulations

The traditional way of tackling pollution has been to set maximum permitted levels of emission or resource use, or minimum acceptable levels of environmental quality, and then to fine firms contravening these limits. Clearly, there have to be inspectors to monitor the amount of pollution, and the fines have to be large enough to deter firms from exceeding the limit.

Virtually all countries have environmental regulations of one sort or another. For example, the EU has over 200 items of legislation covering areas such as air and water pollution, noise, the marketing and use of dangerous chemicals, waste management, the environmental impacts of new projects (such as power stations, roads and quarries), recycling, depletion of the ozone layer and global warming.

Given the uncertainty over the environmental impacts of pollutants, especially in the longer term, it is often better to play safe and set tough emissions standards or standards for environmental impact ('ambient' standards). These could always be relaxed at a later stage if the effects turn out not to be so damaging, but it might be too late to reverse damage if the effects turn out to be more serious. Taxes may be a more sophisticated means of reaching a socially efficient output, but regulations are usually more straightforward to devise, easier to understand by firms and easier to implement.

Education

People's attitudes are very important in determining the environmental consequences of their actions. Fortunately for the environment, people are not always out simply to maximise their own self-interest. If they were, then why would people often buy more expensive 'green' products, such as environmentally friendly detergents? The answer is that many people like to do their own little bit, however small, towards protecting the environment.

This is where education can come in. If children, and adults for that matter, were made more aware of environmental issues and the consequences of their actions, then people's consumption habits could change and more pressure would be put on firms to improve their 'green credentials'.

Tradable permits

A policy measure that has grown in popularity in recent years is that of **tradable permits**. This is a combination of regulations and market-based systems. A maximum permitted level of emission is set for a given pollutant for a given factory, and the firm is given a permit to emit up to this amount. If it emits less than this amount, it is given a credit for the difference, which it can then use in another of its factories, or sell to other firms. These other firms are then allowed to emit that amount *over* their permitted level. Thus the overall level of emissions is given by regulations, whereas their distribution is determined by the market.

Take the example of firms A and B, which are currently producing 12 units of a pollutant each. Now assume that a standard is set permitting them to produce only 10 units each. If firm A managed to reduce the pollutant to 8 units, it would be given a credit for 2 units. It could then sell this to firm B, enabling B to continue emitting 12 units. The effect would still be a total reduction of 4 units between the two firms. However, the trade in pollution permits allows pollution reduction to be concentrated where it can be achieved at lowest cost. In our example, if it cost firm B more to reduce its pollution than firm A, the permits could be sold from A to B at a price that was profitable to both (i.e. at a price above the cost of emission reduction to A, but below the cost of emission reduction to B). Given the resulting reduced cost of pollution control, it might be politically easier to impose tougher standards (i.e. impose lower permitted levels of emission).

The principle of tradable permits can be used as the basis of international agreements on pollution reduction. Each country could be required to achieve a certain percentage reduction in a pollutant (e.g. carbon dioxide, CO_2, or sulphur dioxide, SO_2), but any country exceeding its reduction could sell its right to these emissions to other (presumably richer) countries.

A similar principle can be adopted for using natural resources. Thus fish quotas could be assigned to fishing boats or fleets or countries. Any parts of these quotas not used could then be sold.

In the EU, a carbon Emissions Trading Scheme (ETS) has been in place since January 2005 as part of the EU's approach to meeting its targets under the Kyoto Treaty (see Case Study 7.8 in MyEconLab). This scheme is examined in Box 7.4.

Assessing the system of tradable permits. The main advantage of tradable permits is that they combine the simplicity of regulations with the benefits of achieving pollution reduction in

---

Definitions

Green tax A tax on output designed to charge for the adverse effects of production on the environment. The socially efficient level of a green tax is equal to the marginal environmental cost of production.

Tradable permits Each firm is given a permit to produce a given level of pollution. If less than the permitted amount is produced, the firm is given a credit. This can then be sold to another firm, allowing it to exceed its original limit.

BOX 7.3 GREEN TAXES

Their growing popularity in the industrialised world

Increasingly countries are introducing 'green' taxes in order to discourage pollution as goods are produced, consumed or disposed of. The table shows the range of green taxes used around the world and the chart shows green tax revenues as a percentage of GDP in a sample of 20 OECD countries alongside the weighted OECD average.

As can be seen, green taxes are typically higher than average in Scandinavian countries, reflecting the strength of their environmental concerns. They are lowest in the USA. By far the largest green tax revenues come from fuel taxes. Fuel taxes are relatively high in the UK and so, therefore, are green tax revenues.

There are various problems, however, with using taxes in the fight against pollution.

Identifying the socially efficient tax rate. It will be difficult to identify the appropriate amount of tax for each firm, given that each one is likely to produce different amounts of pollutants for any given level of output. Even if two firms produce identical amounts of pollutants, the environmental damage might be quite different, because the ability of the environment to cope with it will differ between the two locations. Also, the number of people suffering will differ (a factor that is very important when considering the *human* impact of pollution). What is more, the harmful effects are likely to build up over time, and predicting these effects is fraught with difficulty.

Problems of demand inelasticity. The less elastic the demand for the product, the less effective will a tax be in cutting production and hence in cutting pollution. Thus taxes on petrol would have to be very high indeed to make significant reductions in the consumption of petrol and hence significant reductions in the exhaust gases that contribute towards global warming and acid rain.

Redistributive effects. Many green taxes are regressive. The poor spend a higher proportion of their income on domestic fuel than the rich. A 'carbon tax' on such fuel therefore has

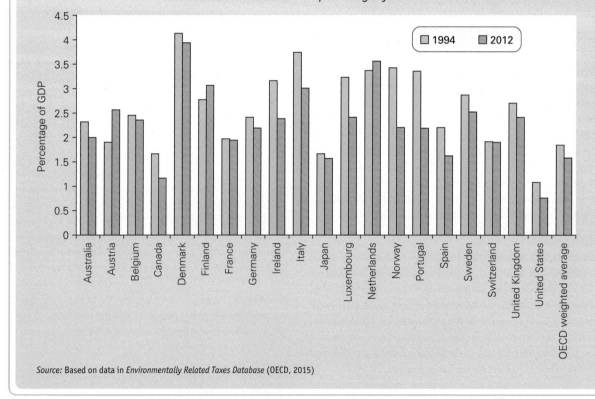

Green tax revenues as a percentage of GDP

Source: Based on data in *Environmentally Related Taxes Database* (OECD, 2015)

TC 4
p 20 the most efficient way. There is also the advantage that firms have a financial incentive to cut pollution. This might then make it easier for governments to impose tougher standards (i.e. impose lower permitted levels of emission).

There are, however, various problems with tradable permits. One is the possibility that trade will lead to pollution being concentrated in certain geographical areas. Another is that it may reduce the pressure on dirtier factories (or countries) to cut their emissions. Additionally, the system will lead to significant cuts in pollution only if the permitted levels are low. Once the system is in place, the government might then feel that the pressure is off to *reduce* the permitted levels. In early 2011, a further problem came to light, when the EU ETS suspended trading

Types of environmental taxes and charges

Motor fuels	Other goods	Air transport
Leaded/unleaded	Batteries	Noise charges
Diesel (quality differential)	Plastic carrier bags	Aviation fuels
Carbon/energy taxation	Glass containers	**Water**
Sulphur tax	Drink cans	Water charges
Other energy products	Tyres	Sewage charges
Carbon/energy tax	CFCs/halons	Water effluent charges
Sulphur tax or charge	Disposable razors/cameras	Manure charges
NO_2 charge	Lubricant oil charge	**Direct tax provisions**
Methane charge	Oil pollutant charge	Tax relief on green investment
Agricultural inputs	Solvents	Taxation on free company cars
Fertilisers	**Waste disposal**	Employer-paid commuting expenses taxable
Pesticides	Municipal waste charges	Employer-paid parking expenses taxable
Manure	Waste-disposal charges	Commuter use of public transport tax deductible
Vehicle-related taxation	Hazardous waste charges	
Sales tax depends on car size	Landfill tax or charges	
Road tax depends on car size	Duties on waste water	

the effect of redistributing incomes away from the poor. The poor also spend a larger proportion of their income on food than do the rich. Taxes on agriculture, designed to reduce the intensive use of fertilisers and pesticides, also tend to hit the poor proportionately more than the rich.

Not all green taxes, however, are regressive. The rich spend a higher proportion of their income on motoring than the poor. Thus petrol and other motoring taxes could have a progressive effect.

Problems with international trade. If a country imposes pollution taxes on its industries, its products will become less competitive in world trade. To compensate for this, it may be necessary to give the industries tax rebates for exports. Also taxes would have to be imposed on imports of competitors' products from countries where there is no equivalent green tax.

Evidence on the adverse effect of environmental taxes on a country's exports is inconclusive, however. Over the long term, in countries with high environmental taxes (or other tough environmental measures), firms will be stimulated to invest in low-pollution processes and products. This will later give such countries a competitive advantage if *other* countries then impose tougher environmental standards.

Effects on employment. Reduced output in the industries affected by green taxes will lead to a reduction in employment. If, however, the effect was to encourage investment in new cleaner technology, employment might not fall. Furthermore, employment opportunities could be generated elsewhere, if the extra revenues from the green taxes were spent on alternative products (e.g. buses and trains rather than cars).

Despite these problems, such taxes can still move output closer to the socially efficient level. What is more, they do have the major advantage of providing a continuing incentive to firms to find cleaner methods of production and thereby save more on their tax bills.

> **?** *Is it a good idea to use the revenues from green taxes to subsidise green alternatives (e.g. using petrol taxes for subsidising rail transport)? Consider the implications for wider tax policy in your answer.*

in permits following identification of a substantial fraud worth €7.5 million.

> **Pause for thought**
>
> *To what extent does the introduction of tradable permits lead to a lower level of total pollution (as opposed to its redistribution)?*

How much can we rely on governments?

If governments are to be relied upon to set the optimum green taxes or regulations, several conditions must be met.

First, they must have the will to protect the environment. But governments are accountable to their electorates and must often appease various pressure groups, such as representatives of big business. In the USA, for example, there has been great resistance to cuts in greenhouse gases

BOX 7.4   TRADING OUR WAY OUT OF CLIMATE CHANGE

The EU carbon trading system

The EU introduced a carbon Emissions Trading Scheme (EU ETS) in January 2005 as its principal policy to meet environmental targets set by the international treaty, the Kyoto Protocol (which entered into force in February 2005). Article 17 of this treaty supported the use of emissions trading and a similar scheme had already reduced emissions of both sulphur dioxide and nitrous oxide in the USA. The EU ETS created a market in carbon permits or allowances. Its ultimate objective is to give companies greater financial incentives to reduce their emissions of CO_2.

Phases I and II

The first phase of the scheme ran from January 2005 until December 2007. Around 12 000 industrial plants across 27 countries were allocated approximately 2.2 billion CO_2 permits, called Emission Unit Allowances (EUAs). Each EUA issued to a firm gives it the right to emit one tonne of carbon dioxide into the atmosphere. The factories covered by the scheme were collectively responsible for around 40 per cent of the EU's CO_2 emissions each year.

Companies that do not have enough EUAs to match their annual emissions can purchase additional EUAs to cover the difference, while those that reduce their emissions are able to sell any surplus EUAs for a profit. Companies are able to trade directly with each other or via brokers operating throughout Europe.

At the end of December 2007 all existing allowances became invalid and the second Trading Period began, to last until the end of 2012. Although this was run under the same general principles as Trading Period 1, it also allowed companies to use 'Joint Implementation' and 'Clean Development Mechanism' credits earned under the Kyoto Protocol's project-based mechanisms (see Case Study 7.8 in MyEconLab). In other words, companies could offset emissions in the EU against emission reductions they achieve in countries outside the EU.

Phase III

Phase III of the EU ETS came into operation on 1 January 2013. It built on the experience gained from operating Phases I and II of the system and included two significant changes.

Move to an EU-wide cap. The cap on total emissions in both Phases I and II of the system were set in a decentralised manner. Each member state had to develop a National Allocation Plan (NAP). The NAP set out the total cap on emissions for that country, the total quantity of EUAs that would be issued and how they would be assigned to each industrial plant or factory. Each NAP had to be approved by the European Commission before it could be implemented. The numerous NAPs have been replaced in Phase III of the EU ETS by a single EU-wide cap on the volume of emissions and on the

total number of EUAs to be issued. The size of this EU-wide cap is to be reduced by 1.74 per cent per year so that emissions in 2020 are 21 per cent lower than 2005.

Move to auctioning permits. In Phase I and II of the EU ETS the majority of EUAs were freely allocated to the plants and factories covered by the scheme. The number of EUAs each factory would receive was based on their current emissions. The European Commission allowed member states to auction up to a maximum of 5 per cent of the EUAs in Phase I and 10 per cent in Phase II. However, this option was seldom chosen.

In Phase III a big increase is planned in the proportion of EUAs that are auctioned. Since 2013 most of the firms in the power sector have already had to purchase all of their allowances by auction. The average in other sectors is planned to increase from 20 per cent in 2013 to 70 per cent by 2020. Only firms in manufacturing and the power industry in certain member states will continue to be allocated the majority of their allowances at no charge.

It has also been recommended by the EU that half of the revenue generated from the auctions should be used to fund measures to reduce greenhouse gas emissions.

In December 2009, the EU also agreed to a '20–20–20' package to tackle climate change. This would involve cutting greenhouse gases by 20 per cent by 2020 compared with 1990 levels, raising the use of renewable energy sources to 20 per cent of total energy usage and cutting energy consumption by 20 per cent.

Much of the emissions reductions would be achieved by tighter caps under the ETS, with binding national targets for non-ETS sectors, such as agriculture, transport, buildings and services. However, over half of the reductions could be achieved by international carbon trading, where permits could be bought from abroad: e.g. under the Clean Development Mechanism.

Assessing the ETS

The introduction of the world's largest market-based policy to address climate change was welcomed by many economists and policy makers. However, others have raised concerns about both the operation of the scheme and its likely impact on overall emissions.

The size of the cap. What matters crucially for the impact of the scheme is the total number of permits issued by the authorities: i.e. the size of the overall cap. If the supply of the permits exceeds demand in the secondary market then the price will be relatively low and firms will lack the necessary incentives to invest in new energy-efficient technology.

Some people have argued that the number of EUAs issued in the past has been far too generous. One reason for this

from the automobile, power and various other industries, many of which have powerful representation in Congress. One of the problems is that many of the environmental effects of our actions today will be on future generations, but governments represent today's generation, and

today's generation may not be prepared to make the necessary sacrifices. This brings us back to the importance of education.

Secondly, it must be possible to identify just what the optimum is. This requires a knowledge of just what the

may have been the de-centralised manner in which the EUAs were allocated through the NAPs. This gave some countries a strong incentive to game the system by setting an aggregate cap in its NAP that was greater than the volume of emissions actually being produced. By doing this, costs could be kept down for firms operating in that country, which would help to maintain its national economic competitiveness.

Another reason why the number of EUAs may have been too great is because of successful lobbying of governments by firms. In particular they may have exaggerated claims about the potential negative impact of issuing fewer EUAs on their costs and future competitiveness.

This over-allocation of EUAs clearly seems to have been a problem in Phase I of the scheme. Emission levels across the EU actually rose by 1.9 per cent while the price of EUAs fell from a peak of €30 to just €0.02.

The scrutiny of NAPs by the EU became more rigorous in Phase II of the scheme and the cap on emissions was tightened by 7 per cent. However, there were still big variations between countries, and it appears that the Commission still had limited capacity to check the accuracy of each NAP. Phase III of the system seems to have addressed some of these issues with the removal of the NAPs and the introduction of a single EU-wide cap.

Move from free allocation of permits to auctions. Another major issue with Phases I and II of the scheme was that the majority of EUAs were freely allocated to plants and factories. It was argued by many policy makers that this was important because firms needed time to adjust gradually to a system where they would have to start paying for the pollution they generated. Some people were particularly concerned that selling the permits for a positive price would have large adverse effects on some firms' costs. This might make it increasingly difficult for them to compete with companies outside the EU. However, after the system was introduced, there were accusations that firms in the power sector had simply used the free allocation of permits to make 'windfall profits'.

The increasing use of auctioning in Phase III of the scheme has been adopted to address this issue. It is also assumed that, after eight years of experience with permits, firms will be better able to adapt to having to buy EUAs.

Other concerns included:

- The annual rate of decline in the number of EUAs issued being determined at the beginning of the trading period. Although this provides certainty for firms, it also reduced the ability of the scheme to respond to changing conditions.

  This was clearly illustrated during the global economic downturn. The reduction in industrial output resulted in much lower emissions and this put

downward pressure on the price of EUAs. With EUAs trading at such a low price there was very little incentive for firms to reduce their pollution levels. This led to some debate about whether the cap should be tightened within Phase II to take account of this, though this did not in fact happen.

- Some countries appearing to have set tough targets in their NAPs, while others appearing to have 'gamed' the system. This raised issues about the equity of the scheme.
- A perceived lack of willingness to prosecute those infringing the rules.
- Credits earned through Credit Development Mechanisms and Joint Implementation coming from new investments that would have taken place anyway. These 'bogus' credits then enabled companies to maintain their emission levels.

Transport emissions. From 2012 the EU ETS scheme was also extended to aircraft emissions. Originally the scheme was supposed to cover emissions from all flights either arriving or departing from airports in the EU. Following a huge outcry from the aviation industry, the scheme was temporarily amended so that it would only include flights whose arrival and departure were both at EU airports. This was known as 'Stop the Clock' and an initial cap was set at 86 million tonnes of CO_2.

Plans to bring shipping emissions within the scheme have been delayed. Shipping is a large and growing source of emissions. As a first step towards cutting these, the European Commission has proposed that owners of large ships using EU ports should report their verified emissions from 2018.

Similarly, road transport, responsible for around 20 per cent of all emissions, remains outside the scheme.

Overall, it is still difficult to assess the impact of the ETS, even though we are now well inside Phase III of the scheme. Disaggregating the effect of emission allowances from the effects of other economic factors and policy changes is enormously complicated. However, there is general agreement that the systems and processes set in place do have the potential to be effective. The question remains, however, whether there is the political will to tighten the cap in order to reduce emissions further.

Consider a situation where all firms are of identical size and each is allocated credits that allows it to produce 10 per cent less than its current emissions. How would this compare with a situation where permits are allocated to 90 per cent of firms only? Consider both efficiency and equity in your answer.

environmental effects are of various activities, such as the emission of CO_2 into the atmosphere, and that is something on which scientists disagree.

Finally, there is the problem that many environmental issues are global and not just local or national. Many

require concerted action by governments around the world. The history of international agreements on environmental issues, however, is plagued with difficulties between countries, which seem concerned mainly with their own national interests.

BOX 7.5　THE PROBLEM OF URBAN TRAFFIC CONGESTION

Does Singapore have the answer?

Singapore has some 280 vehicles per kilometre of road (this compares with 271 in Hong Kong, 222 in Japan, 77 in the UK, 75 in Germany and 37 in the USA). The average car in Singapore is driven some 18 000 kilometres per year, but with low car ownership (see below), this translates into a relatively low figure for kilometres travelled by car per person. What is more, cars flow relatively freely: the average car speed during peak hours is estimated to be as high as 29 km/h on main roads and 64 km/h on expressways. So are there lessons that we can learn from Singapore in tackling traffic congestion?

The problem of traffic congestion

Traffic congestion is a classic example of the problem of externalities.

When people use their cars, not only do they incur private costs (petrol, wear and tear on the vehicle, tolls, the time taken to travel, etc.), but also they impose costs on other people. These external costs include the following:

■ *Congestion costs: time.* When a person uses a car on a congested road, it will add to the congestion. This will therefore slow down the traffic even more and increase the journey time of other car users.
■ *Congestion costs: monetary.* Congestion increases fuel consumption, and the stopping and starting increases the costs of wear and tear. When a motorist adds to congestion, therefore, there will be additional monetary costs imposed on other motorists.
■ *Environmental costs.* When motorists use a road they reduce the quality of the environment for others. Cars emit fumes and create noise. This is bad enough for pedestrians and other car users, but can be particularly distressing for people living along the road. Driving can cause accidents – a problem that increases as drivers become more impatient because of delays.

Exhaust gases cause long-term environmental damage and are one of the main causes of the greenhouse effect and of the increased acidity of lakes and rivers and the poisoning of forests. They can also cause long-term health problems (e.g. for asthma sufferers).

The socially efficient level of road usage

These externalities mean that road usage will be above the social optimum. This is illustrated in the diagram. Costs and benefits are shown on the vertical axis and are measured in money terms. Thus any non-monetary costs or benefits (such as time costs) must be given a monetary value. The horizontal axis measures road usage in terms of cars per minute passing a specified point on the road.

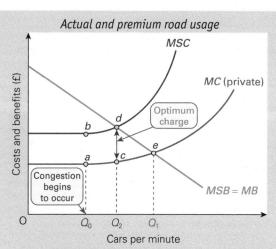

Actual and premium road usage

For simplicity it is assumed that there are no external benefits from car use and that therefore marginal private and marginal social benefits are the same. The MSB curve is shown as downward sloping. The reason for this is that different road users put a different value on any given journey. If the marginal (private) cost of making the journey were high, only those for whom the journey had a high marginal benefit would travel along the road. If the marginal cost of making the journey fell, more people would make the journey: people choosing to make the journey as long as the marginal cost of the journey was less than the marginal benefit. Thus the greater the number of cars, the lower the marginal benefit.

The marginal (private) cost curve (*MC*) is likely to be constant up to the level of traffic flow at which congestion begins to occur. This is shown as point *a* in the diagram. Beyond this point, marginal cost is likely to rise as time costs increase (i.e. journey times lengthen) and as fuel consumption rises.

The marginal social cost curve (*MSC*) is drawn above the marginal private cost curve. The vertical difference between the two represents the external costs. Up to point *b*, external costs are simply the environmental costs. Beyond point *b*, there are also external congestion costs, since additional road users slow down the journey of other road users. These external costs get progressively greater as traffic grinds to a halt.

The actual level of traffic flow will be at Q_1, where marginal private costs and benefits are equal (point *e*). The socially efficient level of traffic flow, however, will be at the lower level of Q_2 where marginal social costs and benefits are equal (point *d*). In other words, there will be an excessive level of road usage.

So what can governments do to 'internalise' these externalities?

The Singapore solution

In contrast to its neighbours, many of which are suffering more acute urban traffic congestion problems, Singapore has an integrated transport policy. This includes the following:

- Restricting the number of new car licences, and allowing their price to rise to the corresponding equilibrium. This makes car licences in Singapore among the most expensive in the world.
- A 154-kilometre-long mass rail transit (MRT) system with subsidised fares. Trains are comfortable, clean and frequent. Stations are air-conditioned.
- A programme of building new estates near MRT stations.
- Cheap, frequent buses, serving all parts of the island.

But it is in respect to road usage that the Singaporean authorities have been most innovative.

Area licences. The first innovation came in 1975 when the Area Licensing Scheme (ALS) was introduced. The city centre was made a restricted zone. Motorists who wished to enter this zone had to buy a ticket (an 'area licence') at any one of 33 entry points. Police were stationed at these entry points to check that cars had paid and displayed. This scheme was extended to the major expressways in 1995 with the introduction of the Road Pricing Scheme (RPS).

The Vehicle Quota System. Then in 1990 a quota system for new cars was established. The government decides the total number of cars that the country should have, and issues just enough licences each month to maintain that total. These licences (or 'Certificates of Entitlement') are for 10 years and are offered at auction. Their market price varies from around £10 000 to £40 000.

Partly as a result of the quota system, there are only 114 private cars per 1000 population. This is only a fraction of the figure for European countries.

A problem with the licences is that they are a once-and-for-all payment, which does not vary with the amount that people use their car. In other words, their marginal cost (for additional miles driven) is zero. Many people feel that, having paid such a high price for their licence, they ought to use their car as much as possible in order to get value for money!

Electronic road pricing. With traffic congestion steadily worsening, it was recognised that something more had to be done. Either the Area Licensing Scheme had to be widened, or some other form of charging had to be adopted. The decision was taken to introduce electronic road pricing (ERP). This alternative would not only save on police labour costs, but enable charge rates to be varied according to levels of congestion, times of the day, and locality.

What, then, would be the optimum charge? If the objective is to reduce traffic from Q_1 to Q_2 in the diagram, then a charge of $d - c$ should be levied.

Since 1998 all vehicles in Singapore have been fitted with an in-vehicle unit (IU). Every journey made requires the driver to insert a smart card containing pre-paid units into the IU. On specified roads, overhead gantries read the IU and deduct the appropriate charge from the card. If a car does not have sufficient funds on its smart card, the car's details are relayed to a control centre and a fine is imposed. The system has the benefit of operating on three-lane highways and does not require traffic to slow down.

The ERP system operates on roads subject to congestion and charges can vary every 5, 20 or 30 minutes according to predicted traffic flows. Rates are published in advance for a three-month period. A review of traffic conditions takes place every quarter and the results can lead to rates being adjusted in future periods. The system is thus very flexible to allow traffic to be kept at the desired level.

Satellite tracking. The authorities in Singapore are now testing the use of a Global Navigation Satellite System. This would remove the need for the overhead gantries. It would also make it possible to alter the size of the charge with the length of the congested road the driver has travelled along.

The ERP system was expensive to set up, however. Cheaper schemes have been adopted elsewhere, such as Norway and parts of the USA. These operate by funnelling traffic into a single lane in order to register the car, but they have the disadvantage of slowing the traffic down.

One message is clear from the Singapore solution. Road pricing alone is not enough. Unless there are fast, comfortable and affordable public transport alternatives, the demand for cars will be highly price inelastic. People have to get to work!

1. *Referring to a town or city with which you are familiar, consider what would be the most appropriate mix of policies to deal with its traffic congestion problems.*
2. *Explain how, by varying the charge debited from the smart card according to the time of day or level of congestion, a socially optimal level of road use can be achieved.*

Recap

1. The effects of population pressures and market failures have led to growing environmental degradation.

2. The market fails to achieve a socially efficient use of the environment because large parts of the environment are a common resource, because production or consumption often generates environmental externalities, because of ignorance of the environmental effects of our actions, and because of a lack of concern for future generations.

3. One approach to protecting the environment is to impose charges for using the environment or taxes per unit of output. The problem with these methods is in identifying the appropriate charges or tax rates, since these will vary according to the environmental impact.

4. Another approach is to use laws and regulations, such as making certain practices illegal or putting limits on discharges. This is a less sophisticated alternative to taxes or charges, but it is safer when the environmental costs of certain actions are unknown.

5. Education can help to change attitudes towards the environment and the behaviour of consumers and firms.

6. Tradable permits are a mix of regulations and market-based systems. Firms are given permits to emit a certain level of pollution and these can then be traded. A firm that can reduce its pollution relatively cheaply below its permitted level can sell this credit to another firm that finds it more costly to do so. The system is an efficient and administratively cheap way of limiting pollution to a designated level. It can, however, lead to pollution being concentrated in certain areas and can reduce the pressure on firms to find cleaner methods of production.

7. Although governments can make a major contribution to reducing pollution, government action is unlikely to lead to the optimum outcome (however defined). Governments may be more concerned with short-run political considerations and will not have perfect information.

QUESTIONS

1. The table below gives the costs and benefits of an imaginary firm operating under perfect competition whose activities create a certain amount of pollution. (It is assumed that the costs of this pollution to society can be accurately measured.)

Output (units)	Price per unit (MSB) (£)	Marginal (private) costs to the firm (MC) (£)	Marginal external (pollution) costs (MEC) (£)	Marginal social costs (MSC = MC + MEC) (£)
1	100	30	20	50
2	100	30	22	52
3	100	35	25	60
4	100	45	30	75
5	100	60	40	100
6	100	78	55	133
7	100	100	77	177
8	100	130	110	240

a. What is the profit-maximising level of output for this firm?

b. What is the socially efficient level of output?

c. Why might the marginal pollution costs increase in the way illustrated in this example?

2. In Figure 7.1 (page 169) the *MSC* curve is drawn as being steeper than the *MPC* curve. Under what circumstances would they be parallel?

3. Give additional examples of each of the four types of externality to those given on pages 169–72.

4. Give some examples of public goods (other than those given on page 172). Does the provider of these goods or services (the government or local authority) charge for their use? If so, is the method of charging based on the amount of the good people use? Is it a good method of charging? Could you suggest a better method?

5. Distinguish between publicly provided goods, public goods and merit goods.

6. Name some goods or services provided by the government or local authorities that are not public goods.

7. Some roads could be regarded as a public good, but some could be provided by the market. Which types of road could be provided by the market? Why? Would it be a good idea?

8. Assume that you have decided to buy an LED television. How do you set about ensuring that you make the right choice between the available makes?

9. Assume that you wanted the information given in (a)–(h) below. In which cases could you (i) buy perfect information; (ii) buy imperfect information; (iii) obtain information without paying for it; (iv) not obtain information?
   a. Which washing machine is the more reliable?
   b. Which of two jobs that are vacant is the more satisfying?
   c. Which builder will repair my roof most cheaply?
   d. Which builder will make the best job of repairing my roof?
   e. Which builder is best value for money?
   f. How big a mortgage would it be wise for me to take out?
   g. What course of higher education should I follow?
   h. What brand of washing powder washes whiter?

   In which cases are there non-monetary costs to you of finding out the information? How can you know whether the information you acquire is accurate or not?

10. Make a list of pieces of information a firm might want to know and consider whether it could buy the information and how reliable that information might be.

11. Assume that a country had no state education at all. For what reasons might the private education system not provide the optimal allocation of resources to and within education?

12. Assume that a firm discharges waste into a river. As a result, the marginal social costs (*MSC*) are greater than the firm's marginal (private) costs (*MC*). The table below shows how *MC*, *MSC*, *AR* and *MR* vary with output. Assume that the marginal private benefit (*MB*) is given by the price (*AR*). Assume also that there are no externalities on the consumption side, and that therefore *MSB* = *MB*.

Output	1	2	3	4	5	6	7	8
MC	23	21	23	25	27	30	35	42
MSC	35	34	38	42	46	52	60	72
TR	60	102	138	168	195	219	238	252
AR	60	51	46	42	39	36.5	34	31.5
MR	60	42	36	30	27	24	19	14

a. How much will the firm produce if it seeks to maximise profits?

b. What is the socially efficient level of output (assuming no externalities on the demand side)?

c. How much is the marginal external cost at this level of output?

d. What size of tax would be necessary for the firm to reduce its output to the socially efficient level?

e. Why is the tax less than the marginal externality?

f. Why might it be equitable to impose a lump-sum tax on this firm?

g. Why will a lump-sum tax not affect the firm's output (assuming that in the long run the firm can still make at least normal profit)?

13. On a diagram similar to Figure 7.7 (on page 179), demonstrate how a subsidy can correct for an external benefit.

14. Why might it be better to ban certain activities that cause environmental damage rather than to tax them?

15. To what extent could property rights (either public or private) be successfully extended and invoked to curb the problem of industrial pollution (a) of the atmosphere, (b) of rivers, (c) by the dumping of toxic waste, (d) by the erection of ugly buildings and (e) by the creation of high levels of noise?

16. What protection do private property rights in the real world give to sufferers of noise (a) from neighbours, (b) from traffic, (c) from radios at the seaside?

17. How suitable are legal restrictions in the following cases?

a. Ensuring adequate vehicle safety (e.g. that tyres have sufficient tread or that the vehicle is roadworthy).

b. Reducing traffic congestion.

c. Preventing the abuse of monopoly power.

d. Ensuring that mergers are in the public interest.

e. Ensuring that firms charge a price equal to marginal cost.

18. How would you evaluate the following?

a. The external effects of building a reservoir in an area of outstanding natural beauty.

b. The external effects of acid rain pollution from a power station.

19. Many economists have argued that a form of 'congestion tax' ought to be imposed on motorists who use their cars on busy roads, to take account of the external costs they impose on other road users and pedestrians. Compare the relative advantages and disadvantages of the following measures:

a. Increasing the rate of duty on petrol.

b. Increasing the annual road fund licence.

c. Using a system such as that in Singapore (see Box 7.5), where charges are deducted from a pre-paid smart card inserted into a device in the car. Charges vary according to the time of day and/or the level of congestion.

d. Installing cameras that record number plates of cars in a designated zone, and then fining their owners if a daily fixed fee for driving in the zone has not been paid (this system is used in London).

e. Setting up toll booths to charge motorists for using certain stretches of road.

f. The use of bus and cycle lanes at peak times.

g. Subsidising public transport.

20. Give examples of how the government intervenes to protect the interests of dependants from bad economic decisions taken on their behalf.

21. What are the possible arguments in favour of fixing prices (a) below and (b) above the equilibrium? Are there any means of achieving the same social goals without fixing prices?

22. Make out a case for (a) increasing and (b) decreasing the role of the government in the allocation of resources.

MyEconLab

This book can be supported by MyEconLab, which contains a range of additional resources, including an online homework and tutorial system designed to test and build your understanding.

You need both an access card and a course ID to access MyEconLab:

1. Is your lecturer using MyEconLab? Ask your lecturer for your course ID.

2. Has an access card been included with the book at a reduced cost? Check the inside back cover of the book.

3. If you have a course ID but no access card, go to: http://www.myeconlab.com/ to buy access to this interactive study programme.

ADDITIONAL CASE STUDIES IN THE ESSENTIALS OF ECONOMICS MYECONLAB (www.pearsoned.co.uk/sloman)

7.1 Corporate social responsibility. An examination of social responsibility as a goal of firms and its effect on business performance.

7.2 The police as a public service. The extent to which policing can be classified as a public good.

7.3 Deadweight loss from taxes on goods and services. This shows the welfare loss from the imposition of a tax, which must be weighed against the redistributive and other gains from the tax.

7.4 Regulating privatised industries. This looks at the system of regulation applied to the major privatised industries in the UK.

7.5 Libertarianism. The views of the 'neo-Austrian' right that market capitalism has dynamic advantages in creating incentives to innovate and take risks.

7.6 Public choice theory. This examines how economists have attempted to extend their analysis of markets to the field of political decision making.

7.7 Perverse subsidies. An examination of the use of subsidies around the world that are harmful to the environment.

7.8 Selling the environment. The market-led solution to the Kyoto Protocol.

7.9 Are we all green now? Changing attitudes to the environment.

7.10 A deeper shade of green. Different approaches to environmental sustainability.

7.11 Restricting car access to Athens. A case study that examines how the Greeks have attempted to reduce local atmospheric pollution from road traffic.

7.12 The right track for reform? How successful has rail privatisation been in the UK?

7.13 Can the market provide adequate protection for the environment? This explains why markets generally fail to take into account environmental externalities.

7.14 Environmental auditing. Are businesses becoming greener? A growing number of firms are subjecting themselves to an 'environmental audit' to judge just how 'green' they are.

WEB APPENDICES

7.1 Private and social efficiency. This appendix uses general equilibrium analysis to show how a perfect market economy in the absence of externalities will lead to a socially optimal allocation of resources.

7.2 Cost–benefit analysis. A technique to help decide whether or not a project should go ahead.

WEBSITES RELEVANT TO PART B

Numbers and sections refer to websites listed in the Web Appendix and hotlinked from this book's website at www.pearsoned.co.uk/sloman.

- For news articles relevant to Part B, follow the *News* link from MyEconLab or Google the Sloman Economics News site.
- For economic data, see sites in section B and particularly sites B1, 3, 5, 14, 21, 27, 29, 31–33, 38, 39. For data on the housing market, see sites B7–11.
- For student resources relevant to Part B, see sites C1–7, 9, 10, 14, 19, 25; D3.
- For general news on markets, market failure and government intervention, see sites in section A, and particularly A1–5, 7–9, 18, 19, 22, 23, 24, 31, 35, 36. See also links to newspapers worldwide in A38, 39, 42–44; and see A41 for links to economics news articles from newspapers worldwide.
- For sites favouring the free market, see C17; E34. See also C18 for the development of ideas on the market and government intervention.
- For information on agriculture and the Common Agricultural Policy, see sites E14 and G9.
- For sites that look at companies, their scale of operation and market share, see B32, D2; E4, 10; G7, 8.
- For information on poverty and inequality, see sites B18; E9, 13, 40.
- For information on taxes, benefits and the redistribution of income, see E9, 25, 30, 36; G5, 13.
- UK and EU departments relevant to competition policy can be found at sites E10; G7, 8.
- UK regulatory bodies can be found at sites E4, 11, 15, 16, 19, 21, 22.
- For information on taxes and subsidies, see E18, 25, 30, 36; G13. For use of green taxes, see E2, 14, 30; G11; H5.
- For information on health and the economics of health care, see E8; H8, 9. See also links in I8 and 17.
- For the economics of the environment, see links in I11. For policy on the environment and transport, see E2, 7, 11, 14, 29; G10, 11, 19. See also H11.

Macroeconomics

Aggregate demand and the national economy

We turn now to *macroeconomics*. This will be the subject for this third part of the book and most of the final part.

In particular, we will be examining five key topics. The first is national output. What determines the size of national output? What causes it to grow? Why do growth rates fluctuate? Why do economies sometimes surge ahead and at other times languish in recession?

The second is employment and unemployment. What causes unemployment? If people who are unemployed want jobs, and if consumers want more goods and services, then why does our economy fail to provide a job for everyone who wants one?

The third is the issue of inflation. Why is it that the general level of prices always seems to rise, and only rarely fall? Why is inflation a problem? But why, if prices do fall, might that be a bad thing too? Why do countries' central banks, such as the Bank of England, set targets for the rate of inflation? And why is that target positive (e.g. 2 per cent) rather than zero?

The fourth issue is the financial system. We look at the role that financial institutions play in modern economies. In doing so, we analyse the financial crisis of the late 2000s, the initial responses of policy makers to limit the adverse impact on economies and the subsequent responses to try to prevent a similar crisis reoccurring.

The final topic, which is the subject of the final part of the book, concerns a country's economic relationships with other countries. We look at international trade and investment and at the flows of foreign currencies around the world.

In this chapter, after a preliminary look at the range of macroeconomic issues, we then focus on the first of these issues: national output. In doing this we identify the key purchasers of goods and services in the economy and the ways in which these purchasers are connected. We analyse the potential determinants of their spending and so the factors that can influence the aggregate level of expenditure in the economy.

After studying this chapter, you should be able to answer the following questions:

- What are the key macroeconomic issues faced by all countries?
- Who are the key groups of purchasers whose demands determine the total level of spending on a country's goods and services?
- What are the various flows of incomes around the economy? What causes these flows to expand or contract?
- How do we measure national output?
- What factors influence the level of spending by firms, households and government?
- What determines the level of national output at any one time?
- What is the effect on national income of an increase in spending?

8.1 INTRODUCTION TO MACROECONOMICS

What issues does macroeconomics tackle?

The first half of the book was concerned with microeconomics. We saw how it focuses on individual parts of the economy and with the demand and supply of particular goods and services and resources.

The issues addressed by macroeconomists, by contrast, relate in one way or another to the *total* level of spending in the economy (aggregate demand) or the *total* level of output (aggregate supply). Many of these issues are ones on which elections are won or lost. Is the economy growing and, if so, how rapidly? How can we avoid, or get out of, recessions? What causes unemployment and how can the rate be got down? Why is inflation a problem and what can be done to keep it a modest levels? What will happen to interest rates and if they were to change what would be their economic impact? How big a problem is government debt? Are banks lending too much or too little?

If there were agreement about the answers to these questions, macroeconomics would be simpler – but less interesting! As it is, macroeconomics is often characterised by lively debate. Economists can take different views on the importance of macroeconomic issues, their causes and the appropriate policy responses. They can also disagree about how to analyse macroeconomic phenomena and, therefore, the actual approach to take in modelling macroeconomic relationships.

We shall be looking at these different views throughout this third part of the book. This is not to suggest that economists always disagree and we will also identify some general points of agreement, at least among the majority of economists.

Problems of prediction. Another factor in addressing these questions is the difficulty of forecasting what will happen. It is relatively easy to explain things once they have happened. Predicting what is going to happen is another matter. Few economists – or anyone else – foresaw the global banking crisis, credit crunch and subsequent economic downturn of the late 2000s. Even those who thought banks had too little capacity to absorb losses and were making too many risky loans, could not predict exactly when a crisis would occur.

The role of expectations. A crucial element in macroeconomic activity is people's expectations. If people are optimistic about the future, consumers may be more inclined to spend and firms more inclined to invest. If they are pessimistic, spending may fall. But what drives these expectations? Again, this is a topic of lively debate.

Politics. Then there is the political context. Governments may be unwilling to take unpopular measures, especially when an election looms. So, should they give responsibility for decisions to other bodies? In many countries, interest rates are not set by the government but by the central bank. In the UK, for example, it is the Bank of England that sets interest rates at the monthly meetings of the Monetary Policy Committee.

So just what are the macroeconomic issues that we will be studying in the following chapters? We can group them under the following headings: economic growth, unemployment, inflation and the economic relationships with the rest of the world, the financial well-being of individuals, businesses and other organisations, governments and nations, and the relationship between the financial system and the economy. We will be studying other issues too, such as consumer behaviour, finance and taxation, but these still link to these major macroeconomic issues and, more generally, to how economies function.

Key macroeconomic issues

Economic growth

To measure how quickly an economy is growing we need a means of measuring the value of a nation's output. The measure we use is **gross domestic product (GDP)**. However, to compare changes in output from one year to the next we must eliminate those changes in GDP which simply result from changes in prices. When we have done so, we can then analyse **rates of economic growth**. Governments hope to achieve a high rate of economic growth over the long term: in other words, growth that is sustained over the years and is not just a temporary phenomenon. They also try to achieve *stable* growth, avoiding both recessions and excessive short-term growth that cannot be sustained. In practice, however, this can often prove difficult to achieve, as recent history has shown.

Figure 8.1 shows how growth rates have fluctuated over the years for four economies.[1] As you can see, in all four cases there has been considerable volatility in their growth rates. Therefore, while we observe most economies around the world growing over the long term, growth is highly variable in the short term with periods, like the late 2000s,

KI 1
p 5

> **Definitions**
>
> **Gross domestic product (GDP)** The value of output produced within a country, typically over a 12-month period.
>
> **Rate of economic growth** The percentage increase in output between two moments of time, typically over a 12-month period.

---

[1]Note that EU-15 stands for the 15 member countries of the EU prior to 1 May 2004: Austria, Belgium, Denmark, Germany, Greece, Finland, France, Ireland, Italy, Luxembourg, Netherlands, Portugal, Spain, Sweden and the UK.

Figure 8.1 Growth rates in selected industrial economies, 1965–2016

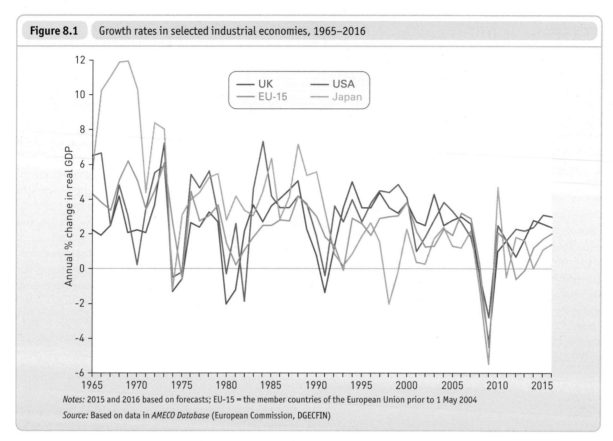

Notes: 2015 and 2016 based on forecasts; EU-15 = the member countries of the European Union prior to 1 May 2004

Source: Based on data in *AMECO Database* (European Commission, DGECFIN)

when economies experience negative rates of growth and so contract. The fact that growth fluctuates in this way is fundamental to our understanding of economies. The inherent instability of economies is our next threshold concept.

> **KEY IDEA 30**
> **TC 12**
> *Economies suffer from inherent instability.* As a result, economic growth and other macroeconomic indicators tend to fluctuate. This is Threshold Concept 12. It is a threshold concept because it is vital to recognise the fundamental instability in market economies. Analysing the ups and downs of the 'business cycle' occupies many macroeconomists.

Unemployment

Reducing unemployment is another major macroeconomic aim of governments, not only for the sake of the unemployed themselves, but also because it represents a waste of human resources and because unemployment benefits are a drain on government revenues.

Unemployment in the 1980s and early 1990s was significantly higher than in the previous three decades. Then, in the late 1990s and early 2000s, it fell in some countries, such as the UK and USA. However, with the global economic crisis of that late 2000s many countries experienced rising rates of unemployment. This was exacerbated in the early 2010s by attempts, particularly across Europe, to reduce levels of government borrowing which depressed rates of economic growth. These patterns are illustrated in Figure 8.2, which shows unemployment rates (as a percentage of the labour force) for the same four economies.

In the UK, in recent years, there has been a move towards more flexible contracts, with many people's wages not keeping up with inflation and many working fewer hours than they would like. This has helped to reduce the rate of unemployment, but has created a problem of **underemployment**.

Inflation

By inflation we mean a general rise in prices throughout the economy. Government policy here is to keep inflation both low and stable. One of the most important reasons for this is that it will aid the process of economic decision making. For example, businesses will be able to set prices and wage rates, and make investment decisions with far more confidence.

We have become used to low **inflation rates** and in some countries, like Japan, periods of deflation, with a general fall in prices. Even though inflation rates rose in many countries in 2008 and then again in 2010–11, figures remained much lower than in the past; in 1975, UK inflation reached over 23 per cent. Figure 8.3 illustrates annual rates of consumer price inflation (annual percentage change in consumer prices) in the same four economies.

> **Definitions**
>
> **Underemployment** When people work fewer hours than they would like at their current wage rate.
>
> **Inflation rate (annual)** The percentage increase in prices over a 12-month period.

Figure 8.2 Standardised unemployment rates in selected industrial economies, 1965–2016

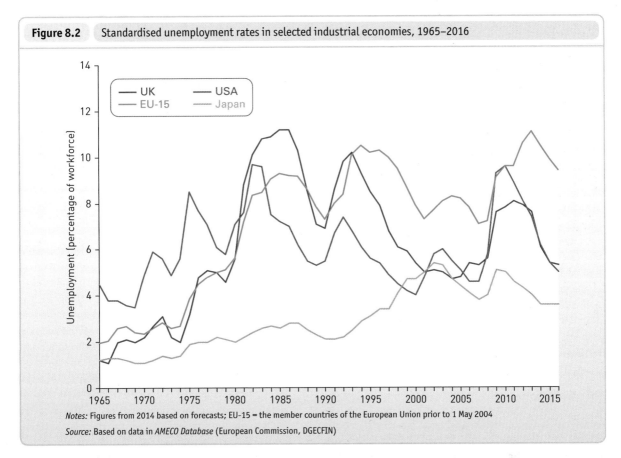

Notes: Figures from 2014 based on forecasts; EU-15 = the member countries of the European Union prior to 1 May 2004

Source: Based on data in *AMECO Database* (European Commission, DGECFIN)

Figure 8.3 Inflation rates in selected industrial economies, 1965–2016

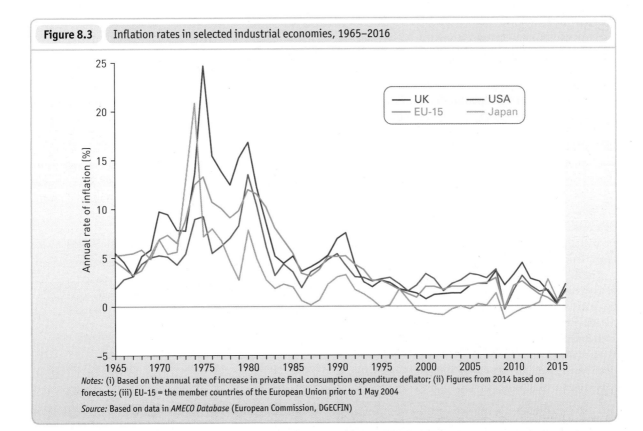

Notes: (i) Based on the annual rate of increase in private final consumption expenditure deflator; (ii) Figures from 2014 based on forecasts; (iii) EU-15 = the member countries of the European Union prior to 1 May 2004

Source: Based on data in *AMECO Database* (European Commission, DGECFIN)

In most developed countries, governments have a particular target for the rate of inflation. In the UK the target for the growth of consumer prices is 2 per cent. The Bank of England then adjusts interest rates to try to keep inflation on target (we see how this works in Chapter 12).

The balance of payments

A country's **balance of payments account** records all transactions between the residents of that country and the rest of the world. These transactions enter as either debit items or credit items. The debit items include all payments *to* other countries: these include the country's purchases of imports, the spending on investment it makes abroad and the interest and dividends paid to people abroad who have invested in the country. The credit items include all receipts *from* other countries: from the sales of exports, from inward investment expenditure and from interest and dividends earned from abroad.

The sale of exports and any other receipts from abroad earn foreign currency. The purchase of imports or any other payments abroad use up foreign currency. If we start to spend more foreign currency than we earn, one of two things must happen. Both are likely to be a problem.

The balance of payments will go into deficit. In other words, there will be a shortfall of foreign currencies. The government will therefore have to borrow money from abroad, or draw on its foreign currency reserves to make up the shortfall. This is a problem because, if it goes on too long, overseas debts will mount, along with the interest that must be paid; and/or reserves will begin to run low.

The exchange rate will fall. The **exchange rate** is the rate at which one currency exchanges for another. For example, the exchange rate of the pound into the dollar might be £1 = $1.50.

If the government does nothing to correct the balance of payments deficit, then the exchange rate must fall, for example to $1.45 or $1.40, or lower. (We will show just why this is so in Chapter 14.) A falling exchange rate is a problem because it pushes up the price of imports and may fuel inflation. Also, if the exchange rate fluctuates, this can cause great uncertainty for traders and can damage international trade and economic growth.

Sector accounts

KI 21
p 148
There are two main types of accounts used to show the financial position of individuals, businesses and other organisations, governments and nations.

The first type, known as a *balance sheet*, shows the *stock* of assets and liabilities. An *asset* is something owned by or owed to you. Thus money in your bank account is an asset. A *liability* is a debt: i.e. something you owe to someone else, such as outstanding balances on your credit card(s). At any given moment in time, we will be holding a certain amount of assets and liabilities. The same applies to organisations, governments and countries.

The second type, known as an *income and expenditure account* or *profit and loss* account, shows *flows* of incomes and expenditure. These are measured as so much *per period of time*. Thus a person's weekly wages would be an income flow; and spending, whether by cash, debit or credit card, would be an expenditure flow. Tax receipts would be an income flow for governments; and money spent on imports would be an expenditure flow for a country.

There are three key accounts which are compiled for the main sectors of the economy: the household, corporate and government sectors and the economy as whole.

- First, there is the *income account* which records the various flows of income alongside the amounts either spent or saved. Economic growth refers to the annual real growth in a country's income flows (i.e. after taking inflation into account).
- Secondly, there is the *financial account*. The financial *balance sheet* gives a complete record of the stocks of financial assets (arising from saving) and financial liabilities (arising from borrowing) of a sector, and include things such as currency, bank deposits, loans, bonds and shares. *Changes* in such balances over time (flows of new saving and borrowing) have been key in explaining the credit crunch and subsequent deep recession of the late 2000s/early 2010s.
- Thirdly, there is the *capital account* which records the stock of non-financial (physical) wealth, arising from acquiring or disposing of physical assets, such as property and machinery. *Changes* over time (inflows and outflows) in the capital balance sheets of the different sectors give important insights into relationships between the sectors of the economy and to possible growing tensions.

The *national balance sheet* is a measure of the wealth of a country. It can be presented so as to show the contribution of each sector and/or the composition of wealth. The balance of a sector's or country's stock of both financial and non-financial wealth is referred to as its *net worth*.

Figure 8.4 presents the national balance sheet for the UK since 1997. It shows the actual value (£) of the stock of net worth and its value relative to the value of output from domestic production over a 12-month period: i.e. annual gross domestic product (see the appendix to this chapter for an analysis of the measurement of GDP). In 2014, the net worth of the UK was £8.1 trillion, equivalent to 4.4 times the

---

Definitions

Balance of payments account A record of the country's transactions with the rest of the world. It shows the country's payments to or deposits in other countries (debits) and its receipts or deposits from other countries (credits). It also shows the balance between these debits and credits under various headings.

Exchange rate The rate at which one national currency exchanges for another. The rate is expressed as the amount of one currency that is necessary to purchase *one unit* of another currency (e.g. €1.25 = £1).

Figure 8.4   UK net worth

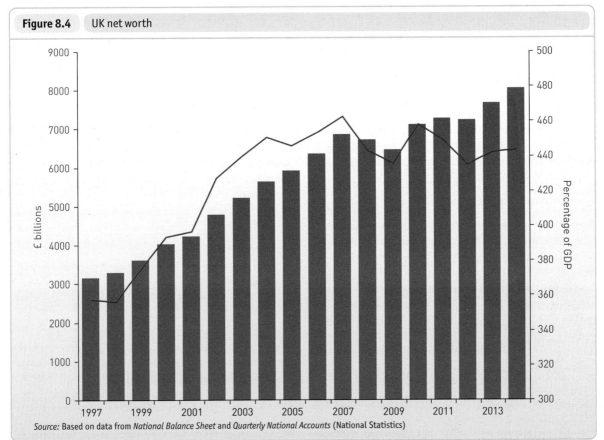

Source: Based on data from *National Balance Sheet* and *Quarterly National Accounts* (National Statistics)

country's annual GDP and equivalent to £125 000 per person. The stock of net worth fell for two consecutive years – 2008 and 2009 – at the height of the financial crisis and the economic slowdown.

These various accounts are part of an interconnected story detailing the financial well-being of a country's households, corporations and government. To illustrate how, consider what would happen if, over a period of time, you were to spend more than the income you receive – a deficit on your income account. To finance your excess spending you could perhaps draw on any financial wealth that you have accumulated through saving. Alternatively, you might fund some of your spending through a loan from a financial institution, such as a bank. Either way, your financial balance sheet will deteriorate. Or you may dispose of some physical assets, such as property, causing the capital balance sheet to deteriorate. But however your excess spending is financed, your net worth declines.

> **KEY IDEA 30** *Balance sheets affect peoples' behaviour.* The size and structure of governments', institutions' and individuals' liabilities (and assets too) affect economic well-being and can have significant effects on behaviour and economic activity.

The importance of balance sheet effects in influencing behaviour and, hence, economic activity has been recognised increasingly by both economists and policy makers, especially since the financial crisis of 2007–9. Yet there

remains considerable work to be done in understanding their effects and so in devising the most appropriate policies. KI 31 p 205

> **Pause for thought**
>
> *Is the balance of payments account an income and expenditure account or a balance sheet?*

Financial stability

A core aim of the government and the **central bank** is to ensure the stability of the financial system. After all, financial markets and institutions are an integral part of economies. Their well-being is crucial to the well-being of an economy.

Furthermore, because of the global interconnectedness of financial institutions and markets, problems can spread globally like a contagion. The financial crisis of the late 2000s showed how financially distressed financial institutions can

> **Definition**
>
> **Central bank** A country's central bank is banker to the government and the banks as a whole (see Section 10.2). In most countries the central bank operates monetary policy by setting interest rates and influencing the supply of money. The central bank in the UK is the Bank of England; in the eurozone it is the European Central Bank (ECB) and in the USA it is the Federal Reserve Bank (the 'Fed').

cause serious economic upheaval on a global scale. Therefore models of the macroeconomy need to incorporate financial markets and institutions and to capture the *interaction* between the financial system and the macroeconomy.

As we shall see in Chapter 10, a major part of the global response to the financial crisis has been to try to ensure that financial institutions are more financially resilient. In particular, financial institutions should have more loss-absorbing capacity and therefore be better able to withstand 'shocks' and deteriorating macroeconomic conditions.

Government macroeconomic policy

From the above issues we can identify a series of macroeconomic policy objectives that governments might typically pursue:

- High and stable economic growth.
- Low unemployment.
- Low inflation.
- The avoidance of balance of payments deficits and excessive exchange rate fluctuations.
- The avoidance of excessively financially-distressed sectors of the economy, including government.
- A stable financial system.

Unfortunately, these policy objectives may conflict. For example, a policy designed to accelerate the rate of economic growth may result in a higher rate of inflation, a balance of payments deficit and excessive lending. Governments are thus often faced with awkward policy choices, further demonstrating how societies face trade-offs between economic objectives (see Section 7.4).

KI 29
p 177

Recap

1. Macroeconomics, like microeconomics, looks at issues such as output, employment and prices; but it looks at them in the context of the whole economy.

2. Among the macroeconomic goals that are generally of most concern to governments are economic growth, reducing unemployment, keeping inflation low and stable, avoiding balance of payments and exchange rate problems, avoiding excessively financially-distressed economic agents (i.e. households, businesses and governments) and ensuring a stable financial system.

8.2 THE CIRCULAR FLOW OF INCOME MODEL

How is spending related to income and who are the key groups of purchasers in the economy?

One way in which the objectives are linked is through their relationship with **aggregate demand (AD)**. This is the total spending on goods and services made within the country by four groups of people: consumers on goods and services (C), firms on investment (I), the government on goods, services and investment (such as education, health and new roads) (G) and people abroad on this country's exports (X). From these four we have to subtract any imports (M) since aggregate demand refers only to spending on *domestic* firms. Thus:[2]

$$AD = C + I + G + X - M$$

TC 3
p 12

To show how the objectives are related to aggregate demand, we can use a simple model of the economy. This is the *circular flow of income* model and is shown in Figure 8.5. It is an extension of the model we looked at back in Chapter 1 (see Figure 1.5 on page 15).

If we look at the left-hand side of the diagram we can identify two major groups: *firms* and *households*. Each group has two roles. Firms are producers of goods and services; they are also the employers of labour and other factors of production. Households (which include all individuals) are the consumers of goods and services; they are also the

suppliers of labour and various other factors of production. In the diagram there is an inner flow and various outer flows of incomes between these two groups.

Before we look at the various parts of the diagram, a word of warning. Do not confuse *money* and *income*. Money is a stock concept. At any given time, there is a certain quantity of money in the economy (e.g. £12 trillion). But that does not tell us the level of national *income*. Income is a flow concept, measured as so much *per period of time*.

The relationship between money and income depends on how rapidly the money *circulates*: its 'velocity of circulation'. (We will examine this concept in detail later on.) If there is £1 trillion of money in the economy and each £1 on average is paid out as income twice each year, then annual national income will be £2 trillion.

Definition

Aggregate demand (AD) Total spending on goods and services made in the economy. It consists of four elements, consumer spending (C), investment (I), government spending (G) and the expenditure on exports (X), less any expenditure on foreign goods and services (M):
$AD = C + I + G + X - M.$

---

[2]An alternative way of specifying this is to focus on just the component of each that goes to domestic firms. We use a subscript 'd' to refer to this component (i.e. with the imported component subtracted). Thus $AD = C_d + I_d + G_d + X$.

Figure 8.5 The circular flow of income

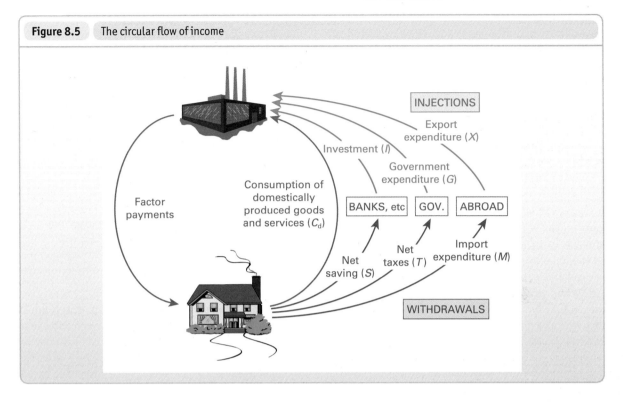

The inner flow, withdrawals and injections

The inner flow

Firms pay money to households in the form of wages and salaries, dividends on shares, interest and rent. These payments are in return for the services of the factors of production – labour, capital and land – that are supplied by households. Thus on the left-hand side of the diagram, money flows directly from firms to households as 'factor payments'.

Households, in turn, pay money to domestic firms when they **consume domestically produced goods and services** (C_d). This is shown on the right-hand side of the inner flow. There is thus a circular flow of payments from firms to households to firms, and so on.

If households spend *all* their incomes on buying domestic goods and services, and if firms pay out *all* this income they receive as factor payments to domestic households, and if the velocity of circulation does not change, the flow will continue at the same level indefinitely. The money just goes round and round at the same speed and incomes remain unchanged.

withdrawn. At the same time, incomes are injected into the flow from outside.

To help understand this we need to recognise that there other groups of purchasers (i.e. demanders). So far we have identified households and firms as two key groups in the economy. If we introduce government into our model we have a third group. While this increases the complexity of our model, it makes it more realistic and increases the ways in which the total spending on goods and services in the economy can be affected.

A fourth group in our economic model is overseas purchasers. This group comprises the foreign equivalents of our three domestic groupings. For instance, it includes French households and Japanese car manufacturers.

The final group in the model is financial institutions, such as banks and building societies, and they play a key role. These institutions provide the link between those who wish to borrow and those who wish to save. In other words, they are 'intermediaries', which allow some in the economy to save while others borrow. For instance, they can provide firms with the access to the credit they need to fund investment projects, such as the purchase of new machinery.

Pause for thought

Would this argument still hold if prices rose?

In the real world, of course, it is not as simple as this. Not all income gets passed on round the inner flow; some is

Definition

The consumption of domestically produced goods and services (C_d) The direct flow of payments from households to firms for goods and services produced within the country.

Let's now incorporate our additional purchasers and the financial system into our model. We begin by focusing on the withdrawals from and injections into the inner flow.

Withdrawals (W)

Only part of the incomes received by households will be spent on the goods and services of domestic firms. The remainder will be withdrawn from the inner flow. Likewise only part of the incomes generated by firms will be paid to UK households. The remainder of this will also be withdrawn. There are three forms of **withdrawals** (or 'leakages' as they are sometimes called).

Net saving (S). Saving is income that households choose not to spend but to put aside for the future. Savings are normally deposited in financial institutions such as banks and building societies. This is shown in the bottom centre of the diagram. Money flows from households to 'banks, etc'. What we are seeking to measure here, however, is the net flow from households to the banking sector. We therefore have to subtract from saving any borrowing or drawing on past savings by households to arrive at the *net* saving flow. Of course, if household borrowing exceeded saving, the net flow would be in the other direction: it would be negative.

Net taxes (T). When people pay taxes (to either central or local government), this represents a withdrawal of money from the inner flow in much the same way as saving: only in this case, people have no choice! Some taxes, such as income tax and employees' national insurance contributions, are paid out of household incomes. Others, such as VAT and excise duties, are paid out of consumer expenditure. Others, such as corporation tax, are paid out of firms' incomes before being received by households as dividends on shares. (For simplicity, however, taxes are shown in Figure 8.5 as leaving the circular flow at just one point. It does not affect the argument.)

When, however, people receive *benefits* from the government, such as unemployment benefits, child benefit and pensions, the money flows the other way. Benefits are thus equivalent to a 'negative tax'. These benefits are known as **transfer payments**. They transfer money from one group of people (taxpayers) to others (the recipients).

In the model, 'net taxes' (T) represent the *net* flow to the government from households and firms. It consists of total taxes minus benefits.

Import expenditure (M). Not all household consumption (C) is of totally home-produced goods (C_d). Households spend some of their incomes on imported goods and services, or on goods and services using imported components. Although the money that consumers spend on such goods initially flows to domestic retailers, it will eventually find its way abroad, either when the retailers or wholesalers themselves import them, or when domestic manufacturers purchase imported inputs to make their products.

This expenditure on imports constitutes the third withdrawal from the inner flow. This money flows abroad.

As we shall see, households are not the only group to purchase imported goods and services or goods and services using imported components: firms and government do too. These expenditures also contribute towards the sum of import expenditures (M) and affect the level of aggregate demand.

Total withdrawals are simply the sum of net saving, net taxes and the expenditure on imports:

$$W = S + T + M$$

Injections (J)

Only part of the demand for firms' output arises from consumers' expenditure. The remainder comes from other sources outside the inner flow. These additional components of aggregate demand are known as **injections** (J). There are three types of injection.

Investment on domestically produced goods (I_d). This is firms' spending on domestically produced goods and services after obtaining the money from various financial institutions – either past savings or loans, or through a new issue of shares. They may invest in plant and equipment or may simply spend the money on building up stocks of inputs, semi-finished or finished goods. Not all of the investment expenditure (I) undertaken by domestic firms is on totally home-produced goods. Investment expenditure on goods and services produced overseas contributes towards import expenditure (M).

Government expenditure on domestically produced goods and services (G_d). When the government (both central and local) spends money on goods and services produced by domestic firms, this counts as an injection. (Note that government expenditure in this model does *not* include state benefits. These transfer payments, as we saw above, are the equivalent of negative taxes and have the effect of reducing the T component of withdrawals.) As well as providing goods and services by purchasing from firms, governments can actually own and run operations themselves. In these cases, the wages of public-sector staff will also be a component of the government's expenditure and are a flow of factor payments to households.

Definitions

Withdrawals (W) (or leakages) Incomes of households or firms that are not passed on round the inner flow. Withdrawals equal net saving (S) plus net taxes (T) plus import expenditure (M): $W = S + T + M$.

Transfer payments Moneys transferred from one person or group to another (e.g. from the government to individuals) without production taking place.

Injections (J) Expenditure on the production of domestic firms coming from outside the inner flow of the circular flow of income. Injections equal investment (I_d) plus government expenditure (G_d) plus expenditure on exports (X).

As with investment, not all government purchases (G) are on totally home-produced goods and services. Expenditures on items made overseas contribute towards import expenditure (M).

Export expenditure (X). Money flows into the circular flow from abroad when households, firms and governments abroad buy our exports of goods and services.

Total injections are simply the sum of investment and government expenditure (both only on domestic products) and exports:

$$J = I_d + G_d + X$$

Aggregate demand, as we have seen, is the total spending on domestic firms. In other words it is the spending by the household sector on domestically produced goods and services (C_d), plus the three injections:

$$AD = C_d + J$$

The relationship between withdrawals and injections

There are indirect links between saving and investment via financial institutions, between taxation and government expenditure via the government (central and local), and between imports and exports via foreign countries. These links, however, do not guarantee that $S = I_d$ or $G_d = T$ or $M = X$.

Take investment and saving. The point here is that the decisions to save and invest are made by different people, and thus they plan to save and invest different amounts. Likewise the demand for imports may not equal the demand for exports. As far as the government is concerned, it may choose not to spend all its tax revenues: to run a 'budget surplus; or it may choose to spend more than it receives in taxes: to run a 'budget deficit' – by borrowing to make up the difference.

Thus planned injections (J) may not equal planned withdrawals (W).

The circular flow of income and the key macroeconomic objectives

If planned injections are not equal to planned withdrawals, what will be the consequences? If injections exceed withdrawals, the level of expenditure will rise: there will be a rise in aggregate demand. This extra spending will increase firms' sales and thus encourage them to produce more. Total output in the economy will rise. Thus firms will pay out more in wages, salaries, profits, rent and interest. In other words, national income will rise.

The rise in aggregate demand will tend to have the following effects upon the major macroeconomic objectives:

- There will be economic growth. The greater the initial excess of injections over withdrawals, the bigger will be the rise in national income.

- Unemployment will fall as firms take on more workers to meet the extra demand for output.
- The rate of inflation will tend to rise. The greater the rise in aggregate demand relative to the capacity of firms to produce, the more will firms find it difficult to meet the extra demand, and the more likely they will be to raise prices.
- The exports and imports part of the balance of payments will tend to deteriorate. The higher demand sucks more imports into the country, and higher domestic inflation makes exports less competitive and imports relatively cheaper compared with home-produced goods. Thus imports will tend to rise and exports will tend to fall.
- The increase in aggregate demand and its impact on income, consumption and saving will be recorded on the sector income accounts. These effects will impact on the financial and capital balance sheets of the various sectors and of the economy as a whole. An increase in national income allows economic agents to accumulate financial and non-financial assets and/or to reduce holdings of financial liabilities. Exactly how the balance sheets are affected depends on the actual behaviour of economic agents.

Pause for thought

What will be the effect on each of the objectives if planned injections are less than planned withdrawals?

Disequilibrium and a chain reaction

When injections do not equal withdrawals, a state of *disequilibrium* will exist: aggregate demand will rise or fall. Disequilibrium results in a chain reaction so as to bring the economy back to a state of equilibrium where injections are equal to withdrawals.

To illustrate this chain reaction, let us consider the situation again where injections exceed withdrawals. Perhaps there has been a rise in business confidence so that investment has risen. Or perhaps there has been a tax cut so that withdrawals have fallen. As we have seen, the excess of injections over withdrawals will lead to a rise in national income. But as national income rises, so households will not only spend more on domestic goods (C_d), but also save more (S), pay more taxes (T) and buy more imports (M). In other words, withdrawals will rise. This will continue until they have risen to equal injections. At that point, national income will stop rising, and so will withdrawals. Equilibrium has been reached.

In Sections 8.4 and 8.5 we return to the circular flow model to address in more detail how changes in aggregate demand could affect the level of national income. In other words, we will consider the chain reaction resulting from disequilibrium and its impact on an economy's size. But, now we consider in more detail the significance in money terms of our purchasers of goods and services that we identified in the model.

Recap

1. The circular flow of income model depicts the flows of money round the economy. The inner flow shows the direct flows between firms and households. Money flows from firms to households in the form of factor payments, and back again as consumer expenditure on domestically produced goods and services.

2. Not all incomes get passed on directly round the inner flow. Some is withdrawn in the form of net saving; some is paid in net taxes; and some goes abroad as expenditure on imports.

3. Likewise not all expenditure on domestic firms is by domestic consumers. Some is injected from outside the inner flow in the form of investment expenditure, government expenditure and expenditure on the country's exports.

4. The circular flow will be in equilibrium when planned injections equal planned withdrawals. But, planned injections and withdrawals are unlikely to be equal. This will result in a chain reaction that returns the economy to a position of equilibrium.

8.3 THE COMPONENTS OF AGGREGATE DEMAND

What are the main groups that spend money in the economy?

We have seen how the demand for the goods and services produced within a country originates from four broad groups of purchasers: households, firms, government and their foreign equivalents across the world:

$$AD = C + I + G + X - M$$

The circular flow model demonstrates the interdependence of these groups as well as the significance of the financial system. Changes in the behaviour of these purchasers and of financial institutions can have significant effects on the economy. One general point of agreement among most economists is that in the *short run* changes in aggregate demand can have a major impact on output and employment. In the long run, it is generally thought that changes

in aggregate demand will have much less impact on output and employment and much more effect on prices.

In this section we consider some of the possible influences on the expenditures by the purchasers of goods and services in order to develop an understanding of what drives *changes* in the level of aggregate demand. We then use our findings to develop a demand-driven model of the economy in Sections 8.4 and 8.5.

The magnitude of the components of aggregate demand

Before we look in detail at each of the components of aggregate demand, it is worth noting that their magnitude varies from country to country. Table 8.1 presents the average

---

Table 8.1	Composition of aggregate demand, % (average 1990–2012)					
	Household final consumption	Gross capital formation (public and private)	General government final consumption	Exports	Imports	External balance (X − M)
Australia	55.8	24.9	17.8	19.3	18.4	0.9
Brazil	61.7	18.6	20.5	11.4	12.5	−1.1
China	42.4	40.5	14.4	26.7	23.3	3.4
France	56.9	18.8	24.6	23.5	23.6	−0.1
Germany	58.5	19.2	19.0	34.1	31.1	3.0
India	61.5	30.2	11.6	14.2	17.6	−3.4
Ireland	48.7	22.8	18.0	72.3	60.6	11.6
Japan	57.9	24.4	17.3	12.0	11.3	0.7
Russia	47.5	25.4	18.4	28.8	18.4	10.4
Singapore	40.1	26.5	9.9	189.7	167.9	21.8
Sweden	49.6	17.9	29.5	41.5	37.6	3.9
UK	62.9	16.1	21.8	24.7	25.5	−0.8
USA	66.0	20.7	16.4	10.0	12.9	−2.8

Note: Based on constant-price data

Source: From *National Accounts Estimates of Main Aggregates* (United Nations Statistics Division), © (2015) United Nations. Reprinted with the permission of the United Nations, http://unstats.un.org

percentage composition of aggregate demand for a selection of countries over the period 1990 to 2012.

The first three columns show the volume of purchases made by each country's residents, whether on domestically produced goods or imports.

Of these three components we can see that for each country the largest is the expenditure share on final goods by households (which include non-profit institutions, such as clubs and societies). These figures help to explain why economic activity is sensitive to changes in household spending and why it is important to consider what factors may affect household spending.

To arrive at the figure for aggregate demand, we have to add the consumption on each country's products by people abroad (exports), but also subtract that part of the expenditure in the first three columns going on goods and services from abroad (imports).

Pause for thought

1. *What are the implications for economic growth rates of the figures for gross capital formation?*
2. *Why are the figures for exports and imports so high for Singapore and relatively high for Ireland and so low for the USA and Japan?*

Household consumption

As Table 8.1 shows, the largest component of aggregate demand is household consumption. Therefore, in trying to understand the determination of a nation's output and its changes from period to period, a good starting point is to consider what might affect the volume of purchases by households.

Disposable income. Perhaps the first determinant you think of as capable of explaining consumption is **disposable income**. Disposable income is the income that the household sector has available for spending or saving after deductions, such as income tax and payments to social insurance schemes (national insurance in the UK), and any additions, such as social benefits.

Evidence suggests that, over the long run, when people's disposable income rises, they will spend most of it. So if your disposable income rises from £20 000 at the age of 25 to £30 000 at the age of 35, you will spend most of this extra £10 000. In other words, an individual's long-run **marginal propensity to consume** is likely to be close to 1.

However, short-run changes in disposable income, such as those from one quarter of a year to the next, are relatively more variable than those in spending. This suggests that our short-run marginal propensity to consume will be smaller than it is over the longer term. One explanation is that households do not like their spending to vary too drastically in the short term. For example, many people's income varies with the time of year. Examples include those

working in the holiday industry or painting and decorating. However, such people are likely to spread their spending relatively evenly over the year.

Case Study 8.1 in MyEconLab looks at the evidence on how consumption varies with disposable income in both the short and long run.

Expected future incomes. Many people take into account both current and expected future incomes when planning their current and future consumption. You might have a relatively low income when you graduate, but can expect (you hope!) to earn much more in the future.

You are thus willing to take on more debts now in order to support your consumption, not only as a student but shortly afterwards as well, anticipating that you will be able to pay back these loans later. It is similar with people taking out a mortgage to buy a house. They might struggle to pay the interest at first, but hope that this will become easier over time.

In fact, the financial system (such as banks and building societies) plays an important part in facilitating this **smoothing of consumption** by households. You can borrow when your income is low and pay back the loans later on when your income is higher. Therefore, the financial system can provide households with greater flexibility over when to spend their expected future incomes.

The financial system and the attitude of lenders. The financial sector provides households with both longer-term loans and also short-term credit. But, financial institutions can affect the growth in consumption if their ability and willingness to provide credit changes. The global financial crises of the second half of the 2000s saw credit criteria tighten dramatically. A tightening of credit practices, such as reducing overdraft facilities or reducing income multiples (the size of loans made available relative to household incomes), weakens consumption growth. In contrast, a relaxation of lending practices, as seen in many countries during the 1980s, can strengthen consumption growth.

Changes in interest rates can affect household spending. For example, if interest rates rise, loans become more expensive for households to 'service'. **Debt-servicing costs** are the costs incurred in repaying the loans and the interest

---

Definitions

Disposable income Income after tax and other deductions and after the receipt of benefits.

Marginal propensity to consume (*mpc*) The proportion of a rise in income (ΔY) that goes on consumption (ΔC): i.e. $\Delta C/\Delta Y$

Consumption smoothing The act by households of smoothing their levels of consumption over time despite facing volatile incomes.

Debt-servicing costs The costs incurred when repaying debt, including debt interest payments.

payments on the loan. Where the rate of interest rate on debt is variable any changes in interest rates affect the cost of servicing the debt.

Pause for thought

In recent years there has been an increase in the use of individual voluntary arrangements (IVAs) whereby households who have got into financial trouble try to arrange a repayment schedule with their creditors. These arrangements often involve some of the debt being written off. What is the effect likely to be on borrowing? Is there a moral hazard here (see page 67)?

KI 21
p 148
Household wealth and the household sector's balance sheet. By borrowing and saving, households accumulate a stock of financial liabilities (debts), financial assets (savings) and physical assets (mainly property). The household sector's financial balance sheet details the sector's holding of financial assets and liabilities while its capital balance sheet details its physical assets. The balance of financial assets over liabilities is the household sector's net financial wealth. The household sector's net worth is the sum of its net financial wealth and its physical wealth.

KI 31
p 205
Changes to the household balance sheet will affect the sector's financial health – sometimes referred to as its level of financial distress. Such changes can have a significant impact on short-term prospects for household spending. For instance, a declining net worth to income ratio is an indicator of greater financial distress. This could be induced by falling house prices or falling share prices. In response to this, we might see the sector engage in precautionary saving, whereby households attempt to build up a buffer stock of wealth. This buffer stock acts as a form of security blanket. Alternatively, households may look to repay some of their outstanding debt.

Therefore, the impact of a worsening balance sheet may be to weaken spending, while improvements on the balance sheet may strengthen the growth of consumption. (The household balance sheet is discussed in Box 8.1.)

Consumer sentiment. If people are uncertain about their future income prospects, or fear unemployment, they are likely to be cautious in their spending. Surveys of consumer confidence are closely followed by policy makers (see Box 8.2) as an indicator of the level of future spending.

Expectations of future prices. If people expect prices to rise, they tend to buy durable goods such as furniture and cars before this happens. Conversely, if people expect prices to fall, they may wait. This has been a problem in Japan for many years, where periods of falling prices (deflation) led many consumers to hold back on spending, thereby weakening aggregate demand and hence economic growth.

The distribution of income. Poorer households will typically spend more than richer ones out of any additional income they receive. They have a higher marginal propensity to consume than the rich, with very little left over to save. A redistribution of national income from the poor to the rich will therefore tend to reduce the total level of consumption in the economy.

Tastes and attitudes. If people have a 'buy now, pay later' mentality, or a craving for consumer goods, they are likely to have a higher level of consumption than if their tastes are more frugal. The more 'consumerist' and materialistic a nation becomes, facilitated by its financial system, the higher will its consumption be for any given level of income.

The age of durables. If people's car, carpets, clothes, etc., are getting old, they will tend to have a high level of 'replacement' consumption, particularly after a recession when they had cut back on their consumption of durables. Conversely, as the economy reaches the peak of the boom, people are likely to spend less on durables as they have probably already bought the items they want.

Investment

There are five major determinants of investment.

Increased consumer demand. Investment is to provide extra capacity. This will only be necessary, therefore, if consumer demand increases. The bigger the increase in consumer demand, the more investment will be needed.

You might think that, since consumer demand depends on the level of national income, investment must too. But we are not saying that investment depends on the *level* of consumer demand; rather it depends on *how much it has risen*. If income and consumer demand are high but *constant*, there will be no point in firms expanding their capacity: no point in investing (other than to replace worn-out or out-of-date equipment).

The relationship between investment and *increased* consumer demand is examined by the 'accelerator theory'. (We will look at this theory in Section 9.4.)

Expectations. Since investment is made in order to produce output for the future, investment must depend on firms' expectations about future market conditions. But, future markets cannot be predicted with accuracy: they depend on consumer tastes, the actions of rivals and the whole state of the economy. Investment is thus *risky*.

TC 9
p 62

Investment depends crucially on business confidence in the future (see Box 8.2). In the short run, therefore, we could expect periods of economic uncertainty, such as in the recessions of the early 1990s and late 2000s, to reduce capital expenditure by firms.

BOX 8.1 | **THE HOUSEHOLD SECTOR BALANCE SHEETS** | CASE STUDIES & APPLICATIONS

Net worth

A country's national balance sheet details its net worth (i.e. wealth). This aggregates the net worth of the household sector, the corporate sector and the public sector. We consider here the net worth of the household sector and the extent to which this may influence consumption (C).[1] The sector's net worth is the sum of its *net financial wealth* and *non-financial assets*.

- The household sector's net financial wealth is the balance of financial assets over financial liabilities. Financial assets include moneys in savings accounts, shares and pension funds. Financial liabilities include debts secured against property, largely residential mortgages, and unsecured debts, such as overdrafts and unpaid balances on credit cards.
- Physical wealth is predominantly the sector's residential housing wealth and is, therefore, affected by changes in house prices.

The table summarises the net worth of the UK household sector. By the end of 2014 the sector had a stock of net worth estimated at over £9.44 trillion compared with £3.55 trillion at the end of 1997 – an increase of 166 per cent. This, of course, is a nominal increase, not a real increase, as part of it merely reflects the rise in asset prices.

To put the absolute size of net worth and its components into context we can express them relative to annual disposable income or GDP. This shows that the household sector's net worth in 2014 was equivalent to 8.1 times the flow of household disposable income in that year, or 5.2 times GDP. In 1997 it was 6.0 times and 4.0 times respectively. Despite the upward trend, in 2001 and 2008 net worth fell relative to both GDP and disposable income while in 2013 it fell relative to GDP.

Chart (a) plots the components of the household sector's net worth (the figures are percentages of disposable income). The ratio of the sector's net worth to disposable income peaked in 2007 at 769 per cent, compared with 603 per cent in 1997.

The chart shows the importance of non-financial wealth in the rise of net worth over this period. Non-financial wealth rose from 257 per cent of disposable income (£1.51 trillion) in 1997 to 469 per cent of disposable income (£4.39 trillion) in 2007. In 2014, although

non-financial wealth was a higher nominal figure (£5.24 trillion), as a proportion of disposable income it had fallen to 452 per cent. By contrast, the ratio of net *financial* wealth to disposable income peaked in 1999 at 395 per cent, and had fallen to 264 per cent by 2008 but had risen back to 362 per cent by 2014.

The 8.7% decline in net worth in 2008 was accompanied by a 9.1 per cent decline in net financial wealth and an 8.4 per cent fall in non-financial assets. The former was driven by a 34 per cent fall in the worth of holdings of shares and other equity as stock markets plummeted in the wake of the financial crisis, while the latter reflected a 9.5 per cent fall in the value of dwellings.

The household sector's net worth then rose each year from 2009 to 2014, sufficiently so to raise the ratio of net worth to disposable income above its 2007 peak.

Net financial wealth was 49.4 per cent higher in 2014 than in 2007, while the value of non-financial assets was 19.5 per cent higher. The rise in the value of net financial wealth was largely attributable to the rise in the value of securities other than shares held by households, which rose by 71 per cent.

Balance sheets and consumption

The state of the household sector's balance sheets affects the level of consumer spending (C) – something that was dramatically demonstrated in the credit crunch of 2008/9 and the subsequent recession and slow recovery. Here we examine the various types of effect.

Financial wealth

The household sector has experienced significant growth in the size of its financial balance sheet. This is captured by Chart (b), which shows the components of net financial wealth: financial assets and liabilities. The ratio of financial liabilities to disposable income rose from 105 per cent in 1997 to 168 per cent in 2007; people were taking on more and more debt relative to their incomes, fuelled by the ease of accessing credit – both consumer credit (loans and credit-card debt) and mortgages. Then, in the aftermath of the credit crunch, the ratio began to fall. By 2014, it stood at 145 per cent.

Summary of household sector balance sheets, 31 December 1997 and 2014

	1997			2014		
	£ billions	% of disposable income	% of GDP	£ billions	% of disposable income	% of GDP
Financial assets	2658.2	451.4	300.9	5883.1	506.9	323.9
Financial liabilities	617.6	104.9	69.9	1681.2	144.9	92.6
Net financial wealth	**2040.6**	**346.5**	**231.0**	**4201.9**	**362.1**	**231.3**
Non-financial assets	1511.8	256.7	171.1	5241.4	451.7	288.6
Net worth	**3552.3**	**603.2**	**402.1**	**9443.3**	**813.7**	**519.9**

Source: Based on data from National Balance Sheet, 2015 Estimates and Quarterly National Accounts (ONS)

[1] The household sector in the official statistics also includes 'non-profit institutions serving households (NPISH)' such as charities, clubs and societies, trade unions, political parties and universities.

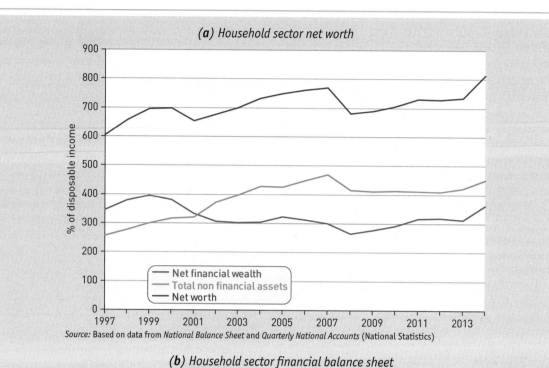

(a) Household sector net worth

Source: Based on data from *National Balance Sheet* and *Quarterly National Accounts* (National Statistics)

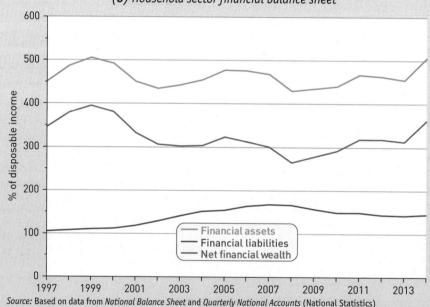

(b) Household sector financial balance sheet

Source: Based on data from *National Balance Sheet* and *Quarterly National Accounts* (National Statistics)

The longer-term increase in the sector's debt-to-income ratio up to 2007 meant that interest payments involved increasingly significant demands on household budgets and hence on the discretionary income households had for spending. This made the sector's spending more sensitive to changes in interest rates. This became a worry as recovery gathered pace from 2014. A rise in interest rates could place a substantial burden on households, thereby curbing consumer expenditure and causing the recovery to stall.

Higher debt-to-income levels can fuel people's concerns about the potential risks arising from debt. If the prospects for income growth are revised down or become more uncertain, people may decide to cut their spending in order to pay off some of their debts.

Non-financial assets
The accumulation of household debt has gone hand-in-hand with the growth of non-financial assets, mainly housing. This is not a coincidence, since an important reason for the growth in household debt has been the sector's acquisition

KI 13
p 66

KI 21
p 148

of property. *Secured debt* is debt where property acts as collateral. It accounts for nearly 90 per cent of household debt. Between 1998 and 2014 it grew on average by around 7 per cent per year. Over the same period, the stock of dwellings increased in value by around 8 per cent per year.

House prices display two characteristics: they are notoriously volatile in the short term but rise relative to general prices over the long term. House price volatility makes the net worth of the household sector volatile too. This impact of house price volatility on net worth had grown over the years as house prices had risen and hence the stocks of both housing assets and secured debt had risen. In 2013, 52 per cent of the household sector's net worth came from the value of dwellings. It had been as high as 57 per cent in 2007.

The precautionary effect. The volatility in net worth from volatile house prices (and potentially the prices of other assets, such as shares) can induce volatility in consumption. If asset prices are falling, households may respond by cutting their spending and increasing saving. This is a *precautionary effect*. Conversely, higher asset prices enable households to reduce saving and spend more.

The collateral effect. The trend for house prices to rise introduces another means by which the balance sheets affect spending: *a collateral effect*. As house prices rise, people's housing equity will tend to rise too. Housing equity is the difference between the value of the property and the value of any outstanding loan secured against it. House price movements affect the collateral that households have to secure *additional* lending.

When house prices are rising, households may look to borrowing additional sums from mortgage lenders for purposes other than transactions involving property or spending on major home improvements. This is known as *housing equity withdrawal* (HEW). These funds can then be used to fund consumption, purchasing other assets (e.g. shares) or repaying other debts.

When house prices fall, households have less collateral to secure additional lending to fund spending. In these circumstances people may wish to restore, at least partially, their housing equity by increasing mortgage repayments (negative HEW), thereby further reducing consumption.

The period from 2002 to 2007 was one of high levels of HEW, averaging close to £7.0 billion per quarter or 3.1 per cent of disposable income. From 2008 to 2014, however, HEW averaged *minus* £11.2 billion per quarter. This meant that households were *increasing* housing equity by the equivalent of 3.9 per cent of income per quarter – money that could have been spent on consumption. Case Study 8.7 in MyEconLab details the patterns in HEW and consumer spending.

> **?** *Draw up a list of the various factors that could affect the household balance sheet and then consider how these could impact on consumer spending.*

The cost and efficiency of capital equipment. If the cost of capital equipment goes down or machines become more efficient, the return on investment will increase. Firms will invest more. Technological progress is an important determinant here.

The rate of interest. The higher the rate of interest, the more expensive it will be for firms to finance investment, and hence the less profitable will the investment be. Economists keenly debate just how responsive total investment in the economy is to changes in interest rates.

The availability of finance. Investment requires financing. Retained earnings provide one possible source. Alternatively, firms could seek finance from banks, or perhaps issue debt instruments, such as bonds, or issue new shares. Therefore, difficulties in raising finance, such as seen in the late 2000s and into the early 2010s, can limit investment.

Government expenditure

As we saw in Figure 8.1, some government purchases can be categorised as capital expenditure. These are expenditures incurred in providing goods and services that will deliver longer-term consumption benefits, such as the education 'services' from school buildings.

The remaining expenditures involve the purchase of goods and services that are used or consumed in the short run. These other final consumption expenditures can involve day-to-day operational costs, such as paying teachers or purchasing items of stationery. Remember that government expenditures on benefits, grants and subsidies do not directly involve the purchase of a good or services, though they can affect aggregate demand through their impact on incomes. Therefore, these expenditures are treated as 'negative taxation'.

Government spending on goods and services is largely independent of the level of national income in the short term. The reason is as follows. In the months preceding the Budget each year, spending departments make submissions about their needs in the coming year. These are discussed with the Treasury and a sum is allocated to each department. That then (save for any unforeseen events) fixes government expenditure on goods and services for the following financial year. This will be a simplifying assumption we make when we construct our demand-driven model of the economy in Section 8.4.

However, the level of government expenditure can be affected by *changes* in national income, just as can private investment. In response to a recession, governments may to look to support the economy by increasing its purchases of goods and services to support aggregate demand.

BOX 8.2 SENTIMENT AND SPENDING

Does sentiment help to forecast spending?

Each month, consumers and firms across the EU are asked a series of questions, the answers to which are used to compile indicators of consumer and business confidence. For instance, consumers are asked about how they expect their financial position to change. They are offered various options such as 'get a lot better, 'get a lot worse' and balances are then calculated on the basis of positive and negative replies.[1]

Chart (a) plots economic sentiment in the EU across consumers and different sectors of business since 1985. The chart nicely captures the volatility of economic sentiment. This volatility is more marked amongst businesses than consumers and, in particular, in the construction sector.

Now compare the volatility of economic sentiment in Chart (a) with the annual rates of growth in household consumption and gross capital formation in Chart (b). You can see that volatility in economic sentiment is reflected in patterns of both consumer and investment expenditure. However, capital formation is significantly more volatile than household spending.

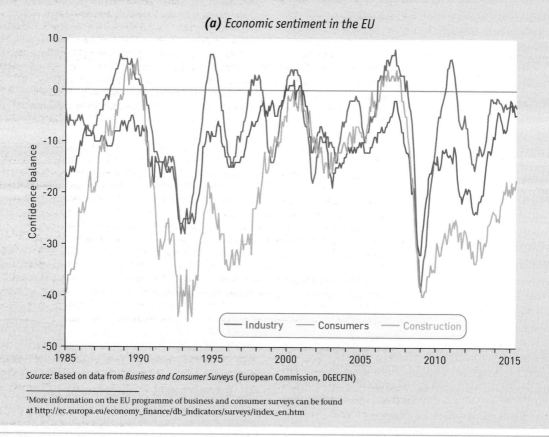

(a) Economic sentiment in the EU

Source: Based on data from *Business and Consumer Surveys* (European Commission, DGECFIN)

[1]More information on the EU programme of business and consumer surveys can be found at http://ec.europa.eu/economy_finance/db_indicators/surveys/index_en.htm

For instance, governments may use their discretion to bring forward capital projects to boost aggregate demand and provide employment. This type of boost to aggregate demand was witnessed in many countries, including the UK and USA, in response to the economic downturn of 2008/9.

Over the longer term, government expenditure *will* depend on national income. The higher the level of national income, the higher is the amount of tax revenue that the government receives, and hence the more it can afford to spend. The governments of richer nations clearly spend much more than those of developing countries.

Imports and exports

Imports

The sum of final expenditures by a country's households, firms and government is known as its **gross domestic final expenditure**. However, when estimating the country's

Definition

Gross domestic final expenditure Total expenditure by a country's residents on final goods and services. It thus includes expenditure on imports and excludes expenditure on exports.

What is less clear is the extent to which changes in sentiment *lead* to changes in spending. In fact, a likely scenario is that spending and sentiment interact. High rates of spending growth may result in high confidence through economic growth, which in turn leads to more spending. The reverse is the case when economic growth is subdued: low spending growth leads to a lack of confidence, which results in low spending growth and so low rates of economic growth.

What makes measures of confidence particularly useful is that they are published monthly. By contrast, measures of GDP and spending are published annually or quarterly and with a considerable time delay. Therefore, measures of confidence are extremely timely for policy makers and provide them with very useful information about the likely path of spending and output growth.

1. *What factors are likely to influence the economic sentiment of (i) consumers and (ii) businesses?*
2. *Could the trends in the economic sentiment indicators for consumers and businesses diverge?*

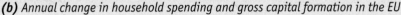

(b) *Annual change in household spending and gross capital formation in the EU*

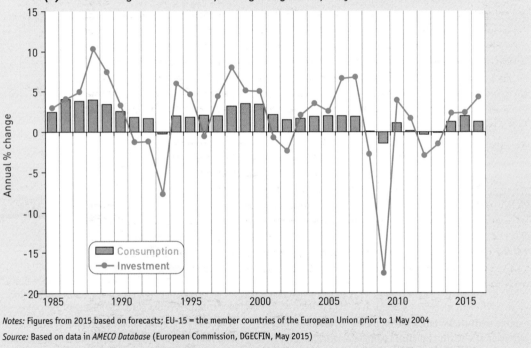

Notes: Figures from 2015 based on forecasts; EU-15 = the member countries of the European Union prior to 1 May 2004

Source: Based on data in *AMECO Database* (European Commission, DGECFIN, May 2015)

GDP we must subtract imports as they are not part of this nation's production.

But what determines the level of import expenditure?

National income. In part, the factors that affect consumption, investment and government expenditure will affect import expenditure too. This is because some proportion of the demands by households, firms and government is satisfied by consuming foreign goods. Therefore, one influence on imports will be national income. We would expect more to be spent on imports as domestic incomes rise.

Exchange rates. Another factor affecting the consumption of foreign goods will be the rates of exchange between the domestic and foreign currencies. These are typically expressed as the number of foreign currency units per unit of domestic currency, for example the number of euros per US dollar.

If the number of foreign currency units which can be exchanged for one unit of domestic currency increases, then an **appreciation** of the domestic currency has occurred. This will lead to a decrease in the domestic-currency price of imported foreign goods and services

> **Definition**
>
> **Appreciation** A rise in the exchange rate of the domestic currency with foreign currencies.

relative to domestically produced goods and services (since one unit of domestic currency buys more foreign currency). Therefore, we would expect an appreciation to increase the sale of imports. Conversely a **depreciation** will lead to a fall in imports.

Exports

Exports are sold to people abroad, and thus depend largely on *their* incomes, not on incomes at home. Nevertheless, there are two indirect links between a country's national income and its exports:

- Via other countries' circular flows of income. If domestic incomes rise, more will be spent on imports. But this will cause a rise in other countries' incomes and lead them to buy more imports, part of which will be this country's exports.

- Via the exchange rate. A rise in domestic incomes will lead to a rise in imports. Other things being equal, this will lead to a depreciation in the exchange rate (we examine the reasons for this in Chapter 14). This will make it cheaper for people in other countries to buy this country's exports. Export sales will rise.

Recap

1. Household spending (consumption) depends primarily on current and expected future disposable incomes and on the cost and availability of finance.

2. The financial system enables households to shift incomes across their lifetimes by borrowing or saving, but means that they accumulate stocks of assets and liabilities. Changes in the value of these assets and liabilities as well as in the costs of servicing debt can affect their spending.

3. Private investment expenditure involves a highly heterogeneous set of purchases, but is likely to be affected by changes in interest rates, changes in consumer demand and in business confidence.

4. Government expenditure decisions are affected by economic and social considerations, but the political context is important too.

5. Import expenditure, like the total expenditure of households, firms and government, is affected by the level of national income. The exchange rate is also an important determinant.

6. Export expenditure is likely to depend on income levels overseas and on the rate of exchange.

8.4 SIMPLE KEYNESIAN MODEL OF NATIONAL INCOME DETERMINATION

How do changes in aggregate demand affect national income?

Having looked at the determinants of aggregate demand, we are now ready to see what happens if aggregate demand changes. You will recall from Section 8.2 that there is general agreement that changes in aggregate demand can have significant effects in the short run on economic activity and, hence, on output and employment.

To see what these effects might look like, we shall apply in this and the next section what has become known as the 'simple Keynesian model'. Throughout we assume that prices are constant and hence there is an absence of inflation.

The analysis is based on the theory developed by John Maynard Keynes back in the 1930s, a theory that has had a profound influence on economics (see Case Studies 8.3 and 8.4 in MyEconLab). Keynes argued that, without government intervention to steer the economy, countries could lurch from unsustainable growth to deep and prolonged recessions.

The central argument is that the level of production in the economy depends on the level of aggregate demand. If people buy more, firms will produce more in response to this, providing they have spare capacity. If people buy less, firms will cut down their production and lay off workers. But just *how much*

will national income rise or fall as aggregate demand changes?

The Keynesian analysis of output and employment can be explained most simply by returning to the circular flow of income diagram. Figure 8.6 shows a simplified version of the circular flow model that we looked at in Section 8.2.

We saw in Section 8.2 that aggregate demand will be constant when the total levels of injections (J) equals the total level of withdrawals (W). But, if injections do not equal withdrawals, a state of disequilibrium exists. What will bring them back into equilibrium is a change in national income and employment.

Start with a state of equilibrium, where injections equal withdrawals. Now assume that there is a rise in injections. For example, firms increase their investment in response to a relaxation of banks' lending criteria. As a result aggregate demand ($C_d + J$) will be higher. Firms will respond

---

Definition

Depreciation A fall in the exchange rate of the domestic currency with foreign currencies.

Figure 8.6 The circular flow of income

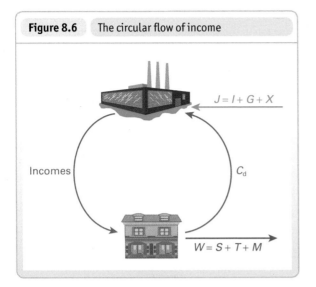

$J = I + G + X$

Incomes

C_d

$W = S + T + M$

to this increased demand by using more labour and other resources, and thus paying out more incomes (Y) to households. Household consumption will rise and so firms will sell more.

Firms will respond by producing more, and thus using more labour and other resources. Household incomes will rise again. Consumption and hence production will rise again, and so on. There will thus be a multiplied rise in incomes and employment. This is known as the **multiplier effect** and is an example of the 'principle of cumulative causation'.

KEY IDEA **31** | *The principle of cumulative causation.* An initial event can cause an ultimate effect that is much larger. This phenomenon of things building on themselves occurs throughout market economies. It is a fundamental principle in economics and is the thirteenth of our fifteen threshold concepts.

TC **13**

The process, however, does not go on forever. Each time household incomes rise, households save more, pay more taxes and buy more imports. In other words, withdrawals rise. When withdrawals have risen to match the increase in injections, equilibrium will be restored and national income and employment will stop rising. The process can be summarised as follows:

$J > W \rightarrow Y\uparrow \rightarrow W\uparrow$ until $J = W$

Similarly, an initial fall in injections (or rise in withdrawals) will lead to a multiplied fall in national income and employment:

$W > J \rightarrow Y\downarrow \rightarrow W\downarrow$ until $J = W$

Thus equilibrium in the circular flow of income can be at *any* level of output and employment.

Showing equilibrium with a Keynesian diagram

We now want to present our simple Keynesian model a little more formally. In Section 8.3 we considered some

of the key determinants of aggregate demand (AD). We saw that a number of factors are likely to affect AD and its components. However, when modelling we tend to simplify matters and so abstract from some of the complex realities of the real world. That is what we are going to do here to gain additional insights into the relationship between aggregate demand and national income.

The equilibrium level of national income can be shown on a 'Keynesian' diagram. This plots various elements of the circular flow of income (such as consumption, withdrawals, injections and aggregate demand) against national income (i.e. real GDP). There are two approaches to finding equilibrium: the withdrawals and injections approach; and the income and expenditure approach. Let us examine each in turn.

The withdrawals and injections approach

In Figure 8.7, national income (real GDP) (Y) is plotted on the horizontal axis; withdrawals (W) and injections (J) are plotted on the vertical axis.

In constructing Figure 8.7 we assume a *positive* relationship between national income and each of the withdrawals (saving, taxes and imports). This simplification of the behaviour of withdrawals allows us to draw an upward-sloping withdrawals line.

Pause for thought

Why might withdrawals be negative at very low levels of national income?

Figure 8.7 | Equilibrium national income: withdrawals equal injections

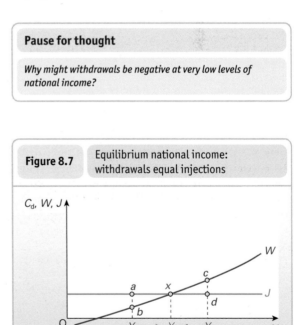

C_d, W, J

Definition

Multiplier effect An initial increase in aggregate demand of £xm leads to an eventual rise in national income that is greater than £xm.

Now we turn to the injections line. As we saw in Section 8.3, the impact of the current level of national income on the amount that businesses plan to invest, that the government plans to spend and that overseas residents plan to import from the UK (i.e. UK exports) may be slight and certainly debatable. Thus injections, for the simplicity of our model, are assumed to be independent of national income. The injections line, therefore, is drawn as a horizontal straight line. (This does not mean that injections are constant over time: merely that they are constant with respect to national income. If injections rise, the whole line will shift upwards.)

Withdrawals equal injections at point x in the diagram. Equilibrium national income is thus Y_e.

If national income were below this level, say at Y_1, injections would exceed withdrawals (by an amount $a - b$). This additional net expenditure injected into the economy would encourage firms to produce more. This in turn would cause national income to rise. But as people's incomes rose, so they would save more, pay more taxes and buy more imports. In other words, withdrawals would rise. There would be a movement up along the W curve. This process would continue until $W = J$ at point x.

If, on the other hand, national income were initially at Y_2, withdrawals would exceed injections (by an amount $c - d$). This deficiency of demand would cause production and hence national income to fall. As it did so, there would be a movement down along the W curve until again point x was reached.

The income and expenditure approach

In Figure 8.8 the 45° line out from the origin plots $C_d + W$ against Y. It is a 45° line because, by definition, $Y = C_d + W$. To understand this, consider what can happen to national income: either it must be spent on domestically produced goods (C_d) or it must be withdrawn from the circular flow – there is nothing else that can happen to it. Thus if Y were £1000 billion, then $C_d + W$ must also be £1000 billion. If you draw a line such that whatever value is plotted on the horizontal axis (Y) is also plotted on the vertical axis

($C_d + W$), the line will be at 45° (assuming that the axes are drawn to the same scale).

The green line plots aggregate demand. In this diagram it is known as the *aggregate expenditure line* (E). It consists of $C_d + J$: in other words, the total spending on the product of domestic firms (see Figure 8.6).

To show how this line is constructed, consider the brown line. This shows C_d. It is flatter than the 45° line. The reason is that for any given rise in national income, only *part* will be spent on domestic product, while the remainder will be withdrawn: i.e. C_d rises less quickly than Y. The proportion of the rise in national income which is spent on domestic goods and services is called the **marginal propensity to consume domestically produced goods (mpc_d)**. Therefore, if three-quarters of the rise in national income is spent on home-produced items, the mpc_d is ¾.

The E line consists of $C_d + J$. But we have assumed that J is constant with respect to Y. Thus the E line is simply the C_d line shifted upwards by the amount of J.

If aggregate expenditure exceeded national income, at say Y_1, there would be excess demand in the economy (of $e - f$). In other words, people would be buying more than was currently being produced. Firms would thus find their stocks dwindling and would therefore increase their level of production. In doing so, they would employ more factors of production. National income would thus rise. As it did so, C_d and hence E would rise. There would be a movement up along the E line. But because not all the extra income would be consumed (i.e. some would be withdrawn), expenditure would rise less quickly than income: the E line is flatter than the Y line. As income rises towards Y_e, the gap between Y and E gets smaller. Once point z is reached, $Y = E$. There is then no further tendency for income to rise.

If national income exceeded aggregate expenditure, at say Y_2, there would be insufficient demand for the goods and services currently being produced ($g - h$). Firms would find their stocks of unsold goods building up. They would thus respond by producing less and employing fewer factors of production. National income would thus fall and go on falling until Y_e was reached.

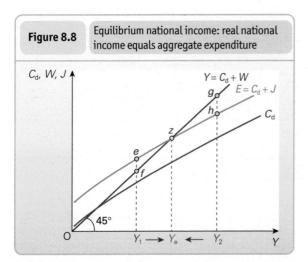

| **Figure 8.8** | Equilibrium national income: real national income equals aggregate expenditure |

Pause for thought

1. *Why does $a - b$ in Figure 8.7 equal $e - f$ in Figure 8.8?*
2. *Why does $c - d$ in Figure 8.7 equal $g - h$ in Figure 8.8?*

Note that if Y and E, and W and J, were plotted on the same diagram, point z (in Figure 8.8) would be vertically above point x (in Figure 8.7).

Definition

The marginal propensity to consume domestically produced goods (mpc_d) The proportion of a rise in national income that is spent on goods and services produced within the country.

Recap

1. In the simple Keynesian model, equilibrium national income is where withdrawals equal injections, and where national income equals the total expenditure on domestic products: where $W = J$ and where $Y = E$.

2. The relationships between national income and the various components of the circular flow of income can be shown on a diagram, where national income is plotted on the horizontal axis and the various components of the circular flow are plotted on the vertical axis.

3. Equilibrium national income can be shown on this diagram, either at the point where the W and J lines cross or where the E line crosses the 45° line (Y).

8.5 | THE MULTIPLIER

What will be the effect on output of a rise in spending?

In a demand-driven model of the economy, when injections rise (or withdrawals fall) national income will rise. But by how much? The answer is that there will be a *multiplied* rise in income: i.e. national income will rise by more than the rise in injections (or fall in withdrawals). The size of the **multiplier** is given by the letter k, where:

$$k = \Delta Y / \Delta J$$

Thus if injections rose by £10 million (ΔJ) and, as a result, national income rose by £30 million (ΔY), the multiplier would be 3.

But what determines the size of the rise in income (ΔY)? In other words, what determines the size of the multiplier? This can be shown graphically using either the withdrawals and injections approach or the income and expenditure approach from the previous section. (You may omit one, if you choose.)

The withdrawals and injections approach

Assume that injections rise from J_1 to J_2 in Figure 8.9. Equilibrium will move from point a to point b. Income will thus rise from Y_{e1} to Y_{e2}. But this rise in income (ΔY) is bigger than the rise in injections (ΔJ) that caused it.

This is the multiplier effect. It is given by $(c - a)/(b - c)$ (i.e. $\Delta Y / \Delta J$).

It can be seen that the size of the multiplier depends on the *slope of the W curve*. The flatter the curve, the bigger will be the multiplier: i.e. the bigger will be the rise in national income from any given rise in injections. The slope of the W curve is given by $\Delta W / \Delta Y$. This is the proportion of a rise in national income that is withdrawn, and is known as the **marginal propensity to withdraw** (*mpw*).

The point here is that the less is withdrawn each time money circulates, the more will be re-circulated and hence the bigger will be the rise in national income. The size of the multiplier thus varies inversely with the size of the *mpw*. The bigger the *mpw*, the smaller the multiplier; the smaller the *mpw*, the bigger the multiplier. In fact the **multiplier formula** is simply the inverse of the *mpw*:

$$k = 1/mpw$$

Thus if the *mpw* were ¼, the multiplier would be 4. So if J increased by £10 million, Y would increase by £40 million.

To understand why, consider what must happen to withdrawals. Injections have risen by £10 million, thus withdrawals must rise by £10 million to restore equilibrium ($J = W$). But with an *mpw* of ¼, this £10 million rise in withdrawals must be one-quarter of the rise in national

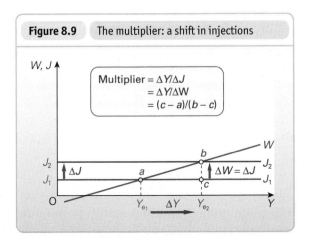

Figure 8.9 The multiplier: a shift in injections

Multiplier = $\Delta Y / \Delta J$
= $\Delta Y / \Delta W$
= $(c - a)/(b - c)$

Definitions

Multiplier The number of times by which a rise in national income (ΔY) exceeds the rise in injections (ΔJ) that caused it:

$$k = \Delta Y / \Delta J$$

Marginal propensity to withdraw The proportion of an increase in national income that is withdrawn from the circular flow of income:

$$mpw = \Delta W / \Delta Y$$

Multiplier formula The formula for the multiplier is:

$$k = 1/mpw \text{ or } 1/(1 - mpc_d)$$

income that has resulted from the extra injections. Thus Y must rise by £40 million.

An alternative formula uses the concept of the marginal propensity to consume domestically produced goods (mpc_d) that we introduced earlier. This, as we saw, is the proportion of a rise in national income that is spent on domestically produced goods, and thus is not withdrawn. Thus if a quarter of a rise in national income is withdrawn, the remaining three-quarters will re-circulate as C_d. Thus:

$$mpw + mpc_d = 1$$

and

$$mpw = 1 - mpc_d$$

Thus the alternative formula for the multiplier is:

$$k = 1/(1 - mpc_d)$$

But why is the multiplier given by the formula $1/mpw$? This can be illustrated by referring to Figure 8.9. The mpw is the slope of the W line. In the diagram this is given by the amount $(b - c)/(c - a)$. The multiplier is defined as $\Delta Y/\Delta J$. In the diagram this is the amount $(c - a)/(b - c)$. But this is merely the inverse of the mpw. Thus the multiplier equals $1/mpw$.[5]

The income and expenditure approach

Assume in Figure 8.10 that injections rise by £20 billion. The expenditure line thus shifts upwards by £20 billion to E_2. The same effect would be achieved by withdrawals falling by £20 billion, and hence consumption of domestically produced goods rising by £20 billion. Equilibrium national

income rises by £60 billion, from £100 billion to £160 billion (where the E_2 line crosses the Y line).

What is the size of the multiplier? It is $\Delta Y/\Delta J$: in other words, £60bn/£20bn = 3. This can be derived from the multiplier formula:

$$k = \frac{1}{1 - mpc_d}$$

The mpc_d is given by $\Delta C_d/\Delta Y$ = £40bn/£60bn = 2/3 (i.e. the slope of the C_d line). Thus:

$$k = \frac{1}{1 - {}^2/_3} = \frac{1}{{}^1/_3} = 3$$

The multiplier: a numerical illustration

The multiplier effect does not work instantaneously. When there is an increase in injections, whether investment, government expenditure or exports, it takes time before this brings about the full multiplied rise in national income.

Consider the following example. Let us assume for simplicity that the mpw is ½. This will give an mpc_d of ½ also. Let us also assume that investment (an injection) rises by £160 million and stays at the new higher level. Table 8.2 shows what will happen.

As firms purchase more machines and construct more factories, the incomes of those who produce machines and those who work in the construction industry will increase by £160 million. When this extra income is received by households, whether as wages or profits, half will be withdrawn (mpw = ½) and half will be spent on the goods and services of domestic firms. This increase in consumption thus generates additional incomes for firms of £80 million over and above the initial £160 million (which is still being generated in each time period). When this additional £80 million of incomes is received by households (round 2), again half will be withdrawn and half will go on consumption of domestic product. This increases national income by a further £40 million (round 3). And so each time we go around the circular flow of income, national income increases, but by only half as much as the previous time (mpc_d = ½).

Pause for thought

Think of two reasons why a country might have a steep E line, and hence a high value for the multiplier.

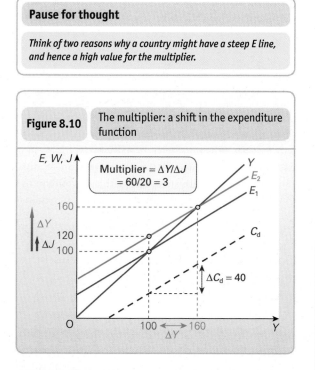

| Figure 8.10 | The multiplier: a shift in the expenditure function |

| Table 8.2 | The multiplier 'round' |

Round	ΔJ (£m)	ΔY (£m)	ΔC_d (£m)	ΔW (£m)
1	160	160	80	80
2	–	80	40	40
3	–	40	20	20
4	–	20	10	10
5	–	10	5	5
6	–	5	.	.
.	.	.	.	.
$1 \rightarrow \infty$	320	160	160	160

---

[5]In some elementary textbooks, the formula for the multiplier is given as $1/mps$ (where mps is the marginal propensity to save: the proportion of a rise in income saved). The reason for this is that it is assumed (for simplicity) that there is only one withdrawal, namely saving, and only one injection, namely investment. As soon as this assumption is dropped, $1/mps$ becomes the wrong formula.

If we add up the additional income generated in each round (assuming the process goes on indefinitely), the total will be £320 million: twice the rise in injections. The multiplier is 2.

The bigger the mpc_d (and hence the smaller the mpw), the more will expenditure rise each time national income rises, and hence the bigger will be the multiplier.

In the simple Keynesian model of the economy that we have applied in the final two sections of the chapter, national income is driven purely by changes in aggregate demand. Changes in aggregate demand result in multiplied changes in national income and employment. We have assumed that all prices are constant; in other words we have assumed a world without inflation. In the next chapter, we relax this assumption. This allows us to examine further the magnitude of changes to national income following changes in aggregate demand.

Recap

1. If injections rise (or withdrawals fall), there will be a multiplied rise in national income. The multiplier is defined as $\Delta Y/\Delta J$. Thus if a £10 million rise in injections led to a £50 million rise in national income, the multiplier would be 5.

2. The size of the multiplier depends on the marginal propensity to withdraw (mpw). The smaller the mpw, the less will be withdrawn each time incomes are generated round the circular flow, and thus the more will go round again as *additional* demand for domestic product.

3. The multiplier formula is $1/mpw$ or $1/(1 - mpc_d)$.

APPENDIX: MEASURING NATIONAL INCOME AND OUTPUT

Three routes: one destination

To assess how fast the economy has grown we must have a means of *measuring* the value of the nation's output. The measure we use is *gross domestic product* (GDP).

GDP can be calculated in three different ways, which should all result in the same figure. These three methods are illustrated in the simplified circular flow of income shown in Figure 8.A1.

The product method

The first method of measuring GDP is to add up the value of all the goods and services produced in the country, industry by industry. In other words, we focus on firms and add up all their production. Thus method number one is known as the *product method*.

In the national accounts these figures are grouped together into broad categories such as manufacturing, construction and distribution. The figures for the UK economy for 2013 are shown in the top part of Figure 8.A2.

When we add up the output of various firms we must be careful to avoid *double counting*. For example, if a manufacturer sells a television to a retailer for £200 and the retailer sells it to the consumer for £300, how much has this television contributed to GDP? The answer is *not* £500. We do not add the £200 received by the manufacturer to the £300 received by the retailer: that would be double counting. Instead we just count either the final value (£300) or the value added at each stage (£200 by the manufacturer + £100 by the retailer).

The sum of all the values added by all the various industries in the economy is known as **gross value added (GVA) at basic prices**.

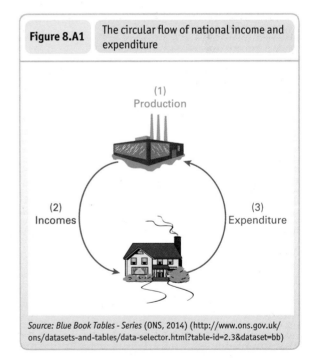

| Figure 8.A1 | The circular flow of national income and expenditure |

Source: Blue Book Tables - Series (ONS, 2014) (http://www.ons.gov.uk/ons/datasets-and-tables/data-selector.html?table-id=2.3&dataset=bb)

Definitions

Gross value added (GVA) at basic prices The sum of all the values added by all industries in the economy over a year. The figures exclude taxes on products (such as VAT) and include subsidies on products.

Figure 8.A2 UK GDP: 2013

UK GVA (product based measure): 2013	£m	% of GVA
Agriculture, forestry and fishing	9 937	0.7
Mining & quarrying; electricity & gas; water supply & sewerage	67 460	4.4
Manufacturing	147 697	9.7
Construction	92 363	6.1
Wholesale & retail trade; repair of motor vehicles	171 940	11.3
Hotels, restaurants & food services	43 044	2.8
Transportation; information & communication	159 424	10.5
Financial and insurance activities	122 587	8.0
Real estate	175 678	11.5
Public administration & defence	79 298	5.2
Education; human health & social work	206 336	13.5
Other services	249 540	16.4
GVA (gross value added at basic prices)	**1 525 304**	**100.0**

UK GVA by category of income: 2013		
Compensation of employees (wages and salaries)	877 883	57.6
Operating surplus (gross profit, rent and interest of firms government and other institutions)	523 351	34.3
Mixed incomes	98 848	6.5
Tax less subsidies on production (other than those on products) plus statistical discrepancy	25 222	1.7
GVA (gross value added at basic prices)	**1 525 304**	**100.0**

UK GDP: 2013	
GVA (gross value added at basic prices)	1 525 304
plus VAT and other taxes on products	194 735
less Subsidies on products	-6 737
GDP (at market prices)	**1 713 302**

How do we get from GVA to GDP? The answer has to do with taxes and subsidies on products. Taxes paid on goods and services (such as VAT and duties on petrol and alcohol) and any subsidies on products are *excluded* from gross value added (GVA), since they are not part of the value added in production. Nevertheless the way GDP is measured throughout the EU is at *market prices*: i.e. at the prices actually paid at each stage of production. Thus **GDP at market prices** (sometimes referred to simply as GDP) is GVA *plus* taxes on products *minus* subsidies on products. This is illustrated in the bottom part of Figure 8.A2.

The income method

The second approach is to focus on the incomes generated from the production of goods and services. A moment's reflection will show that this must be the same as the sum of all values added at each stage of production. Value added is simply the difference between a firm's revenue from sales and the costs of its purchases from other firms. This difference is made up of wages and salaries, rent, interest and profit. In other words, it consists of the incomes earned by those involved in the production process.

Since GVA is the sum of all values added, it must also be the sum of all incomes generated: the sum of all wages and salaries, rent, interest and profit.

The second part of Figure 8.A2 shows how these incomes are grouped together in the official statistics. As you can see, the total is the same as that in the top part of the figure, even though the components are quite different.

Note that we do not include transfer payments such as social security benefits and pensions. Since these are not payments for the production of goods and services, they are excluded from GVA. Conversely, part of people's gross income is paid in income taxes. Since it is this gross (pre-tax) income that arises from the production of goods and services, we count wages, profits, interest and rent *before* the deduction of income taxes.

As with the product approach, if we are working out GVA, we measure incomes before the payment of taxes on products or the receipt of subsidies on products, since it is these pre-tax and subsidy incomes that arise from the value added by production. When working out GDP, however,

Definitions

Gross domestic product (GDP) (at market prices)
The value of output produced within a country over a 12-month period in terms of the prices actually paid.
GDP = GVA + taxes on products − subsidies on products

we add in these taxes and subtract these subsidies to arrive at a *market price* valuation.

The expenditure method

The final approach to calculating GDP is to add up all expenditure on final output (which will be at market prices). This will include the following:

- Consumer expenditure (*C*). This includes all expenditure on goods and services by households and by non-profit institutions serving households (NPISH) (e.g. clubs and societies).
- Government expenditure (*G*). This includes central and local government expenditure on final goods and services. Note that it includes non-marketed services, such as health and education, but excludes transfer payments, such as pensions and social security payments.
- Investment expenditure (*I*). This includes investment in capital, such as buildings and machinery. It also includes the value of any increase (+) or decrease (−) in inventories (stocks), whether of raw materials, semi-finished goods or finished goods.
- Exports of goods and services (*X*).
- Imports of goods and services (*M*). These have to be *subtracted* from the total in order to leave just the expenditure on *domestic* product. In other words, we subtract the part of consumer expenditure, government expenditure and investment that goes on imports. We also subtract the imported component (e.g. raw materials) from exports.

$$\text{GDP (at market prices)} = C + I + G + X - M$$

Table 8.A1 shows the calculation of UK GDP by the expenditure approach.

From GDP to national income

Gross national income

Some of the incomes earned in the country will go abroad. These include wages, interest, profit and rent earned in this country by foreign residents and remitted abroad, and taxes on production paid to foreign governments and institutions (e.g. the EU). On the other hand, some of the incomes earned by domestic residents will come from abroad. Again, these can be in the form of wages, interest, profit or rent, or in the form of subsidies received from governments or institutions abroad. Gross *domestic* product, however, is concerned with those incomes generated *within* the country, irrespective of ownership. If, then, we are to take 'net income from abroad' into account (i.e. these inflows minus outflows), we need a new measure. This is **gross national income** (GNY).[6] It is defined as follows:

$$\text{GNY at market prices} = \text{GDP at market prices} + \text{Net income from abroad}$$

Thus GDP focuses on the value of domestic production, whereas GNY focuses on the value of incomes earned by domestic residents.

Net national income

The measures we have used so far ignore the fact that each year some of the country's capital equipment will wear out or become obsolete: in other words, they ignore **capital depreciation**. If we subtract an allowance for depreciation (or 'capital consumption') we get **net national income** (NNY):

$$\text{NNY at market prices} = \text{GNY at market prices} - \text{Depreciation}$$

Table 8.A2 shows GDP, GNY and NNY figures for the UK.

Table 8.A2	UK GDP, GNY and NNY at market prices: 2013
	£ million
Gross domestic product (GDP)	**1 713 302**
Plus net income from abroad	−13 132
Gross national income (GNY)	**1 700 170**
Less capital consumption (depreciation)	−227 981
Net national income (NNY)	**1 472 189**

Source: United Kingdom National Accounts (National Statistics)

Table 8.A1	UK GDP at market prices by category of expenditure, 2013	
	£ million	**% of GDP**
Consumption expenditure of households and NPISH (*C*)	1 110 807	64.8
Government final consumption (*G*)	346 774	20.2
Gross capital formation (*I*)	291 717	17.0
Exports of goods and services (*X*)	511 275	29.8
less Imports of goods and services (*M*)	−543 375	−31.7
Statistical discrepancy	−3 896	−0.2
GDP at market prices	**1 713 302**	**100.0**

Source: United Kingdom National Accounts (National Statistics)

Definitions

Gross national income (GNY) GDP plus net income from abroad.

Depreciation The decline in value of capital equipment due to age or wear and tear.

Net national income (NNY) GNY minus depreciation.

---

[6]In the official statistics, this is referred to as *GNI*. We use *Y* to stand for income, however, to avoid confusion with investment.

BOX 8.3   **THE DISTINCTION BETWEEN REAL AND NOMINAL VALUES**

Working out what is real

Which would you rather have: (a) a pay rise of 5 per cent when inflation is 2 per cent, or (b) a pay rise of 10 per cent when inflation is 9 per cent? Which debt would you rather have: (a) one where the interest rate is 10 per cent and inflation is 8 per cent, or (b) one where the interest rate is 5 per cent and the inflation rate is 1 per cent?

To answer these questions, you need to distinguish between real and nominal values. *Nominal values* are measured in current prices and take no account of inflation. Thus in the questions above, the nominal pay rises are (a) 5 per cent and (b) 10 per cent; the nominal interest rates are (a) 10 per cent and (b) 5 per cent. In each case it might seem that you are better off with alternative (b).

But if you opted for answers (b), you would be wrong. Once you take inflation into account, you would be better off in each case with alternative (a). What we need to do is to use *real values*. Real values take account of inflation. Thus in the first question, although the nominal pay rise in alternative (a) is 5 per cent, the real pay rise is only 3 per cent, since 2 of the 5 per cent is absorbed by higher prices. You are only 3 per cent better off in terms of what you can buy. In alternative (b), however, it is worse: the real pay rise is only 1 per cent, since 9 of the 10 per cent is absorbed by higher prices. Thus in real terms, alternative (a) is better.

In the second question, although in alternative (a) you are paying 10 per cent in nominal terms, your debt is being reduced in real terms by 8 per cent and thus you are paying a real rate of interest of only 2 per cent. In alternative (b), although the nominal rate of interest is only 5 per cent,

your debt is being eroded by inflation by only 1 per cent. The real rate of interest is thus 4 per cent. Again, in real terms, you are better off with alternative (a).

The distinction between real and nominal values is a threshold concept, as understanding the distinction is fundamental to assessing statistics about the economy. Often politicians will switch between real and nominal values depending on which are most favourable to them. Thus a government wishing to show how strong economic growth has been will tend to use nominal growth figures. On the other hand, the opposition will tend to refer to real growth figures, as these will be lower (assuming a positive inflation rate).

It's easy to make the mistake of using nominal figures when we should really be using real ones. This is known as **money illusion**: the belief that a rise in money terms represents a real rise.

?   *When comparing two countries' GDP growth rates, does it matter if we use nominal figures, provided we use them for both countries?*

Definition

Money illusion The belief that a rise in money terms represents a real rise. It is a situation where people think in nominal, rather than real, terms.

Households' disposable income

Finally, we come to a term called **households' disposable income**. It measures the income people have available for spending (or saving): i.e. after any deductions for income tax, national insurance, etc., have been made. It is the best measure to use if we want to see how changes in household income affect consumption.

How do we get from GNY at market prices to households' disposable income? We start with the incomes that firms receive[7] from production (plus income from abroad) and then deduct that part of their income that is *not* distributed to households. This means that we must deduct taxes that firms pay – taxes on goods and services (such as VAT), taxes on profits (such as corporation tax) and any other taxes – and add in any subsidies they receive. We must then subtract allowances for depreciation and any undistributed profits. This gives us the gross income that households receive from firms in the form of wages, salaries, rent, interest and distributed profits.

To get from gross income to what is available for households to spend, we must subtract the money that households pay in income taxes and national insurance contributions, but add all benefits to households such as pensions and child benefit.

Pause for thought

1. *Should we include the sale of used items in the GDP statistics? For example, if you sell your car to a garage for £2000 and it then sells it to someone else for £2500, has this added £2500 to GDP, or nothing at all, or merely the value that the garage adds to the car: i.e. £500?*
2. *What items are excluded from national income statistics which would be important to take account of if we were to get a true indication of a country's standard of living?*

Definitions

Households' disposable income The income available for households to spend: i.e. personal incomes after deducting taxes on incomes and adding benefits.

---

[7]We also include income from any public-sector production of goods or services (e.g. health and education) and production by non-profit institutions serving households.

Households' disposable income

= GNY at market prices – Taxes paid by firms

+ Subsidies received by firms – Depreciation

– Undistributed profits – Personal taxes + Benefits

Taking account of inflation

If we are to make a sensible comparison of one year's national income with another, we must take inflation into account. For example, if this year national income is 10 per cent higher than last year, but at the same time prices are also 10 per cent higher, then the average person will be no better off at all. There has been no *real* increase in income.

An important distinction here is between **nominal GDP** and **real GDP**.

	The distinction between nominal and real figures. Nominal figures are those using current prices, interest rates, etc. Real figures are figures corrected for inflation. This distinction is so important in assessing economic data that it is another of our threshold concepts.

Nominal GDP, sometimes called 'money GDP', measures GDP in the prices ruling at the time and thus takes no account of inflation. *Real* GDP, however, measures GDP in the prices that ruled in some particular year – the *base year*. Thus we could measure each year's GDP in, say, 2011 prices (known as 'GDP at constant 2011 prices'). This would enable us to see how much *real* GDP had changed from one year to another. In other words, it would eliminate increases in money GDP that were merely due to an increase in prices.

> ### Definitions
>
> **Nominal GDP** GDP measured in current prices. These figures take no account of inflation.
>
> **Real GDP** GDP measured in constant prices that ruled in a chosen base year, such as 2000 or 2006. These figures *do* take account of inflation. When inflation is positive, real GDP figures will grow more slowly than nominal GDP figures.

BOX 8.4	**TRYING TO MAKE SENSE OF ECONOMIC DATA**	CASE STUDIES & APPLICATIONS

The apparently puzzling case of Japanese GDP

When a country is experiencing inflation, nominal GDP will rise faster than real GDP. The reason is that part of the rise in nominal GDP can be explained simply by the rise in prices.

The chart shows nominal and real GDP in Japan and the UK. For both countries the base year is 2005 and thus in both nominal and real GDP are the same in that year.

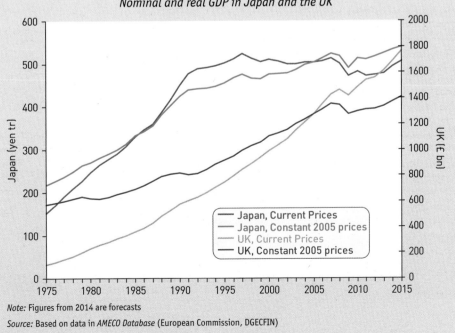

Nominal and real GDP in Japan and the UK

- Japan, Current Prices
- Japan, Constant 2005 prices
- UK, Current Prices
- UK, Constant 2005 prices

Note: Figures from 2014 are forecasts

Source: Based on data in *AMECO Database* (European Commission, DGECFIN)

The UK experienced inflation every year from 1975. Thus nominal GDP grew faster than real GDP. This can be seen from the graph, where before 2005, nominal GDP is *below* real GDP and after 2005, nominal GDP is *above* real GDP.

In Japan, however, things have been different with a period of prolonged deflation (negative inflation) since the mid-1990s. The average price of Japanese output typically fell by about 1 per cent each year between 1995 and 2015. One result of this was that the average price of Japanese produced goods and services in 1985 was the same as in 2005. Therefore, we observe nominal GDP *above* GDP at 2005 prices (real GDP) from the mid-1980s.

Similarly, after the 2005 base year we observe Japanese nominal GDP being *below* GDP at 2005 prices. In 2015, the average price of Japanese goods was 6 per cent lower than in 2005.

1. *If a country experiences a consistent rise in the average price level of domestically produced goods would we expect yearly real rates of economic growth to be higher or lower than nominal rates of growth? Explain your answer.*
2. *What effect would re-basing real GDP figures to a later year have on the figures if the country was experiencing (a) inflation; (b) deflation?*

QUESTIONS

1. The table below shows index numbers for real GDP (national output) for various countries (2007 = 100).

   Using the formula $G = (Y_t - Y_{t-1})/Y_{t-1} \times 100$ (where G is the rate of growth, Y is the index number of output, t is any given years and $t-1$ is the previous year):

   a. Work out the growth rate for each country for each year from 2008 to 2015.
   b. Plot the figures on a graph. Describe the pattern that emerges.

	2007	2008	2009	2010	2011	2012	2013	2014	2015
EU-15	100.0	100.3	95.8	97.8	99.4	98.8	98.7	99.9	101.7
UK	100.0	99.7	95.4	97.2	98.8	99.4	101.1	104.0	106.6
USA	100.0	99.7	96.9	99.4	101.0	103.3	105.6	108.2	111.5
Japan	100.0	99.0	93.5	97.8	97.4	99.1	100.7	100.7	101.8

   Source: AMECO Database (European Commission, DGECFIN)

2. For simplicity, taxes are shown as being withdrawn from the inner flow of the circular flow of income (see Figure 8.5 on page 207) at just one point. In practice, different taxes are withdrawn at different points. At what point of the flow would the following be paid: (a) income taxes people pay on the dividends they receive on shares; (b) VAT; (c) business rates; (d) employees' national insurance contributions?

3. In terms of the UK circular flow of income, are the following net injections, net withdrawals or neither? If there is uncertainty, explain your assumptions.
   a. Firms are forced to take a cut in profits in order to give a pay rise.
   b. Firms spend money on research.
   c. The government increases personal tax allowances.
   d. The general public invests more money in building societies.
   e. UK investors earn higher dividends on overseas investments.
   f. The government purchases US military aircraft.
   g. People draw on their savings to finance holidays abroad.
   h. People draw on their savings to finance holidays in the UK.
   i. The government runs a budget deficit (spends more than it receives in tax revenues) and finances it by borrowing from the general public.
   j. The government runs a budget deficit and finances it by printing more money.
   k. As consumer confidence rises, households decrease their precautionary saving.

4. How might we assess the financial well-being of households?

5. Identify the key purchasers of the goods and services produced within a country. Which of these groups of purchasers is the most significant in value terms?

6. Of what significance does the financial system have for household spending?

7. An economy is currently in equilibrium. The following figures refer to elements in its national income accounts.

	£bn
Consumption (total)	60
Investment	5
Government expenditure	8
Imports	10
Exports	7

a. What is the current equilibrium level of national income?

b. What is the level of injections?

c. What is the level of withdrawals?

d. Assuming that tax revenues are £7 billion, how much is the level of saving?

e. If national income now rises to £80 billion and, as a result, the consumption of domestically produced goods rises to £58 billion, what is the mpc_d?

f. What is the value of the multiplier?

g. Given an initial level of national income of £80 billion, now assume that spending on exports rises by £4 billion, spending on investment rises by £1 billion and government expenditure falls by £2 billion. By how much will national income change?

8. What is the relationship between the mpc_d and the mpw?

9. Assume that the multiplier has a value of 3. Now assume that the government decides to increase aggregate demand in an attempt to reduce unemployment. It raises government expenditure by £100 million with no increase in taxes. Firms, anticipating a rise in their sales, increase investment by £200 million, of which £50 million consists of purchases of foreign machinery. How much will national income rise? (Assume no other changes in injections.)

10. On a Keynesian diagram, draw three W lines of different slopes, all crossing the J line at the same point. Now draw a second J line above the first. Mark the original equilibrium and all the new ones corresponding to each of the W lines. Using this diagram, show how the size of the multiplier varies with the mpw.

11. Why does the slope of the E line in a Keynesian diagram equal the mpc_d? (Clue: draw an mpc_d line.)

12. On a Keynesian diagram, draw two E lines of different slopes, both crossing the Y line at the same point. Now draw another two E lines, parallel with the first two and crossing each other vertically above the point where the first two crossed. Using this diagram, show how the size of the multiplier varies with the mpc_d.

13. What factors could explain why some countries have a higher multiplier than others?

14. In 1974 the UK economy shrank by 2.5 per cent before shrinking by a further 1.5 per cent in 1975. However, the figures for GDP showed a rise of 12 per cent in 1974 and 24 per cent in 1975. What explains these apparently contradictory results?

MyEconLab

This book can be supported by MyEconLab, which contains a range of additional resources, including an online homework and tutorial system designed to test and build your understanding.

You need both an access card and a course ID to access MyEconLab:

1. Is your lecturer using MyEconLab? Ask your lecturer for your course ID.

2. Has an access card been included with the book at a reduced cost? Check the inside back cover of the book.

3. If you have a course ID but no access card, go to: http://www.myeconlab.com/ to buy access to this interactive study programme.

ADDITIONAL CASE STUDIES IN THE *ESSENTIALS OF ECONOMICS* MyEconLab (www.pearsoned.co.uk/sloman)

8.1 **How does consumption behave?** The case looks at evidence on the relationship between consumption and disposable income from the 1950s to the current day.

8.2 **The paradox of thrift.** How saving more can make the country worse off.

8.3 **John Maynard Keynes (1883–1946).** A profile of the great economist.

8.4 **The Keynesian revolution.** How Keynes' ideas revolutionised the approach to recession and mass unemployment and became economic orthodoxy in the 1950s and 60s.

8.5 **Keynes' views on the consumption function.** An analysis of how the assumptions made by Keynes affect the shape of the consumption function.

8.6 **The relationship between income and consumption.** Three alternative views of the consumption function.

8.7 **The explosion of UK household debt.** The growth of household debt in the UK since the mid-1990s and its potential impact on consumption.

8.8 **Trends in housing equity withdrawal (HEW).** An analysis of the patterns in HEW and consumer spending.

8.9 **Deriving the multiplier formula.** Using simple algebra to show how the multiplier formula is derived.

8.10 **The GDP deflator.** An examination of how GDP figures are corrected to take inflation into account.

8.11 **Simon Kuznets and the system of national income accounting.** This looks at the work of Simon Kuznets, who devised the system of national income accounting that is used around the world. It describes some of the patterns of economic growth that he identified.

8.12 **Comparing national income statistics.** The importance of taking the purchasing power of local currencies into account.

8.13 **Taking into account the redistributive effects of growth.** This case shows how figures for economic growth can be adjusted to allow for the fact that poor people's income growth would otherwise count for far less than rich people's.

8.14 **The use of ISEW.** An alternative measure to GDP for estimating economic welfare.

WEB APPENDIX

8.1 **Using GDP statistics.** How well do GDP statistics measure a country's standard of living?

Aggregate supply and growth

In this chapter we focus on the factors that influence the aggregate supply of goods and services to an economy. We begin by constructing the aggregate demand and supply (*AD/AS*) model. This has an advantage over the circular flow and Keynesian models introduced in Chapter 8: it allows us to consider the impact of demand and supply changes not only on the level of output (real GDP), but also on the general level of prices in the economy.

We then turn to look at the causes of economic growth. Why does real GDP grow over time and what determines its rate?

We start by looking at *short-run* growth: the growth in real GDP over a relatively short period of time, such as three months, a year or perhaps a few years. We will see that short-run growth rates fluctuate markedly from year to year. For instance, in some years the economy booms, with real growth rates well above the average. But, in other years, growth rates slow markedly and even become negative (i.e. a decline in output). These variations in growth tend to be cyclical: a phenomenon known as the *business cycle*. In this chapter we discuss the possible causes of the business cycle.

Then we consider the drivers of long-term economic growth: growth over many years. Long-term growth is important because it can raise the general standard of living. A key ingredient of long-term growth is technological progress. Therefore, we finish by considering what can be done to foster technological progress and whether or not this involves an active role for governments.

After studying this chapter, you should be able to answer the following questions:

- What can explain the slopes of the aggregate demand (*AD*) and aggregate supply (*AS*) curves? What variables cause the *AD* and *AS* curves to shift?
- What is the effect on the economy of an increase in spending? Will output increase; will prices increase; or will there be some combination of the two?
- What is meant by the 'business cycle' and how does the actual output produced in the economy relate to what could potentially be produced?
- What are the causes of short-term fluctuations in economic growth? What is the role of changes in aggregate demand and changes in aggregate supply in determining the course of the business cycle?
- What determines the rate of economic growth over the long term?
- How do changes in (a) investment and (b) technological progress affect the long-term growth rate?
- What factors influence the rate of technological progress?

9.1 THE *AD/AS* MODEL

Moving on from the circular flow model of the economy

In the last chapter, we assumed that a rise in aggregate demand would be reflected purely in terms of an increase in national output (real GDP). We assumed that prices would not change. In practice, a rise in aggregate demand is likely to lead to a rise not only in GDP, but also in prices throughout the economy.

The problem with both the circular flow model and the Keynesian multiplier model is that they take no account of just how firms make supply decisions: they assume that firms simply respond to demand. But supply decisions, as well as being influenced by current levels of demand, are also influenced by prices and costs. To be able to analyse the impact of changes in aggregate demand on national income *and* prices we make use of the aggregate demand–aggregate supply (*AD/AS*) model. This is illustrated in Figure 9.1.

As with demand and supply curves for individual goods, we plot quantity on the horizontal axis, except that now it is the *total quantity of national output*, (real) GDP; and we plot price on the vertical axis, except that now it is the *general* price level. Because the general price level relates to the prices of all domestically produced goods and services it is also known as the **GDP deflator**.

We now examine each curve in turn.

The aggregate demand curve

Remember what we said about aggregate demand in Chapter 8. It is the total level of spending on the country's products and consists of four elements: consumer spending on domestic products (C_d), private investment within the country (I_d), government expenditure on domestic goods and services (G_d) and expenditure on the country's exports (X). Thus:

$$AD = C_d + I_d + G_d + X$$

The aggregate demand curve shows how much national output (GDP) will be demanded at each level of prices. The level of prices in the economy is shown by a price index (see Web Appendix A).

But why will the *AD* curve slope downwards: why will people demand fewer products as prices rise? There are three main reasons:

- An **international substitution effect**. If prices rise, people will be encouraged to buy fewer of the country's products and more imports instead (which are now relatively cheaper); the country will also sell fewer exports (which are now less competitive). Thus imports (a withdrawal) will rise and exports (an injection) will fall. Aggregate demand, therefore, will be lower.

- An **inter-temporal substitution effect**. As prices rise, people will need more money to pay for their purchases. With a given supply of money in the economy, this will have the effect of driving up interest rates (we will explore this in Chapter 10). The effect of higher interest rates will be to discourage borrowing and encourage saving, with individuals postponing current consumption in favour of future consumption. The effect will be a reduction in spending and hence in aggregate demand.

- **Real balance effect.** If prices rise, the value of people's savings will be eroded. They may thus save more (and spend less) to compensate.

The above three effects are *substitution effects* of the rise in prices (see page 29). They involve a switch to *alternatives* – either imports or saving.

There may also be an *income effect*. This will occur when consumers' incomes do not rise as fast as prices, causing a fall in consumers' *real* incomes. Consumers cut down on consumption as they cannot afford to buy so much. Firms, on the other hand, with falling real wage costs, are likely to

TC 14 p 227

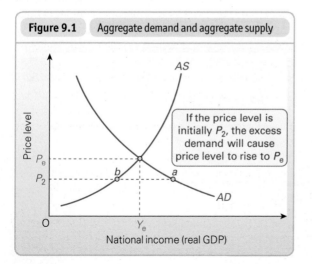

Figure 9.1   Aggregate demand and aggregate supply

If the price level is initially P_2, the excess demand will cause price level to rise to P_e

---

Definitions

GDP deflator The price index of all final domestically produced goods and services: i.e. all items that contribute towards GDP.

International substitution effect As prices rise, people at home and abroad buy less of this country's products and more of products from abroad.

Inter-temporal substitution effect Higher prices may lead to higher interest rates and thus less borrowing and more saving.

Real balance effect As the price level rises, the value of people's money assets falls. They therefore spend less in their attempt to protect the real value of their savings

find their profit per unit rising. However, they are unlikely to spend much more on investment, if at all, as consumer expenditure is falling. The net effect is a fall in aggregate demand.

If, however, consumers' money incomes rise at the *same* rate as prices, there will be no income effect (assuming no money illusion: see Box 8.3 on page 227): real incomes have not changed.

The aggregate supply curve

The aggregate supply curve shows the amount of goods and services that firms are willing to supply at any level of prices, other things remaining the same. The main variables that we hold constant when drawing the *short-run* aggregate supply curve are wage rates, the prices of other inputs, technology, and the labour force and the capital stock. Because these things obviously do change over time, we have to drop this assumption when drawing *long-run* aggregate supply curves. For now, we concentrate on the short-run *AS* curve.

Why do we assume that wage rates and other input prices are constant in the short run? Wage rates are frequently determined by a process of collective bargaining and, once agreed, will typically be set for a whole year, if not two. Even if they are not determined by collective bargaining, wage rates often change relatively infrequently. So too with the price of other inputs: except in perfect, or near perfect markets (such as the market for various raw materials), firms supplying capital equipment and other inputs tend to change their prices relatively infrequently. They do not immediately raise them when there is an increase in demand or lower them when demand falls. There is thus a 'stickiness' in both wage rates and the price of many inputs.

The short-run aggregate supply curve slopes upwards (as in Figure 9.1). In other words, the higher the level of prices, the more will be produced. The reason is simple: because we are holding wages and other input prices constant, as the prices of firms' products rise their profitability at each level of output will be higher than before. This will encourage them to produce more.

But what *limits* the increase in aggregate supply in response to an increase in prices? In other words, why is the aggregate supply curve not horizontal? There are two main reasons:

- *Diminishing returns*. With some factors of production fixed in supply, notably capital equipment, firms experience diminishing returns from their other factors, and hence have an upward-sloping marginal cost curve. In microeconomic analysis the upward-sloping cost curves of firms explain why the supply curves of individual goods and services slope upwards. Here in macroeconomics we are adding the supply curves of all goods and services and thus the aggregate supply curve also slopes upwards.

- *Growing shortages of certain variable factors*. As firms collectively produce more, even inputs that can be varied

may increasingly become in short supply. Skilled labour may be harder to find, for example.

Thus rising costs explain the upward-sloping aggregate supply curve. The more steeply costs rise as production increases, the less elastic will the aggregate supply curve be. It is likely that, as the level of GDP increases, and as full capacity is approached, so marginal costs will rise faster. The aggregate supply curve will thus tend to get steeper (as shown in Figure 9.1).

Equilibrium

The equilibrium price level will be where aggregate demand equals aggregate supply. To demonstrate this, consider what would happen if aggregate demand exceeded aggregate supply, for example at P_2 in Figure 9.1. The resulting shortages throughout the economy would drive up prices. This would cause a movement up *along* both the *AD* and *AS* curves until $AD = AS$, at a price level of P_e and a level of national income of Y_e.

Shifts in the AD or AS curves

If there is a change in the price level there will be a movement *along* the *AD* and *AS* curves. If any other determinant of *AD* or *AS* changes, the respective curve will shift. The analysis here is very similar to shifts and movements along demand and supply curves in individual markets (see pages 30–1 and 36).

The aggregate demand curve will shift if there is a change in any of its components: C_d, I_d, G_d or X. Thus if the government decides to spend more, or if customers spend more as a result of lower taxes, or if business confidence increases so that firms decide to invest more, the *AD* curve will shift to the right. A fall in any of these will cause the *AD* curve to shift to the left.

Similarly, the aggregate supply curve will shift if there is a change in any of the variables that are held constant when we plot the curve. Several of these variables, notably technology, the labour force and the stock of capital, change only slowly in the short run – normally shifting the curve gradually to the right. Wage rates (and other input prices) can change significantly in the short run, however, and are thus the major causes of shifts in the short-run supply curve.

What effect will an increase in the average wage rate have on the aggregate supply curve? Wages typically account for around 70 per cent of firms' costs. If, therefore, wages increase, costs increase and profitability falls, and this reduces the amount that firms wish to produce at any level of prices. Thus the aggregate supply curve shifts to the left. A similar effect will occur if other input prices increase. If, on the other hand, input prices fall, the aggregate supply curve shifts to the right.

An important input is oil. Changes in the price of oil can shift the aggregate supply curve. A dramatic example occurred in 1973–4 (see Box 5.3) when oil prices quadrupled over a very short period of time. This was an extreme example of what is known as a negative supply-side shock. A fall in oil prices, such as that which occurred in late 2014, would be an example of a positive supply-side shock.

> ### Pause for thought
>
> *Give some examples of events that could shift (a) the AD curve to the left; (b) the AS curve to the right.*

Effect of a shift in the aggregate demand curve

If there is an increase in aggregate demand, the *AD* curve will shift to the right. This will lead to a combination of higher prices and higher output, depending on the elasticity of the *AS* curve. The more elastic the *AS* curve, the more will output rise relative to prices. (We will consider the shape of the *AS* curve in more detail in Chapter 11.)

What we shall see is that the aggregate supply curve in the long run is generally much less elastic than the short-run curve and could be vertical.

KI 6
p 20

Recap

1. Equilibrium in the economy occurs where aggregate demand equals aggregate supply.

2. A diagram can be constructed to show aggregate demand and aggregate supply, with the price level on the vertical axis and national output (GDP) on the horizontal axis.

3. The *AD* curve is downward sloping, meaning that aggregate demand will be lower at a higher price level. The reason is that at higher prices there will be substitution effects: (a) there will be more imports and fewer exports; (b) interest rates will tend to be higher, resulting in reduced borrowing and increased saving; (c) people will be encouraged to save more to maintain the value of their savings. Also, if consumer incomes rise less quickly than prices, there will be an income effect too.

4. The *AS* curve is upward sloping because the higher prices resulting from higher demand will encourage firms to produce more (assuming that factor prices and technology are fixed).

5. A change in the price level will cause a movement along the *AD* and *AS* curves. A change in any other determinant of either *AD* or *AS* will cause a shift in the respective curve.

6. The amount that prices and output rise as a result of an increase in aggregate demand will depend on the shape of the *AS* curve.

7. A rise in aggregate demand, to the extent that it results in higher prices, will not have a full multiplier effect on real national income.

9.2 INTRODUCING ECONOMIC GROWTH

What is the historical pattern of economic growth and can we expect it to continue?

Despite the short-run volatility in the rate of growth associated with the business cycle, economies do experience increasing output over the long run. Short-run economic instability seems to go hand-in-hand with long-run growth.

These twin characteristics of growth are nicely captured in Figure 9.2, which plots for the UK both the *level* of real GDP (a measure of the economy's output) and annual percentage *changes* in real GDP. It shows that while the volume of output tends to grow over time, the rate of this growth is volatile, with occasional periods of negative growth (falling real GDP).

The distinction between actual and potential growth

Before examining the causes of economic growth, it is essential to distinguish between *actual* and *potential* economic growth. People frequently confuse the two.

Actual growth is the percentage increase in national output (real GDP) from one period to another. When statistics on growth rates are published, it is actual growth they are referring to. Figure 9.3 shows annual growth rates for four economies (it is the same as Figure 8.1).

Potential growth is the speed at which the economy *could* grow. It is the percentage annual increase in the economy's *capacity* to produce: the rate of growth in *potential output*.

> ### Definitions
>
> **Actual growth** The percentage annual increase in national output actually produced.
>
> **Potential growth** The percentage annual increase in the capacity of the economy to produce.

Figure 9.2 Output and economic growth in the UK since 1850

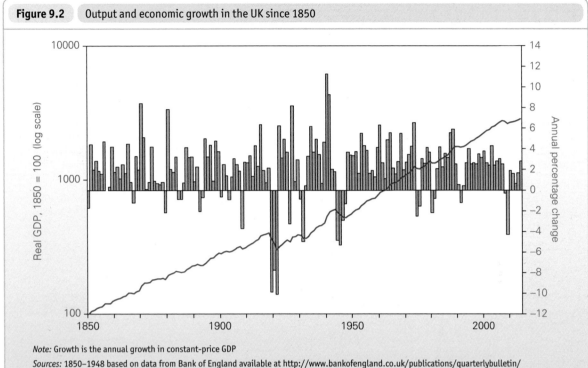

Note: Growth is the annual growth in constant-price GDP

Sources: 1850–1948 based on data from Bank of England available at http://www.bankofengland.co.uk/publications/quarterlybulletin/threecenturiesofdata.xls; from 1949 based on data from *Quarterly National Accounts* series IHYP and YBEZ (National Statistics)

Figure 9.3 Growth rates in selected industrialised economies, 1965–2016

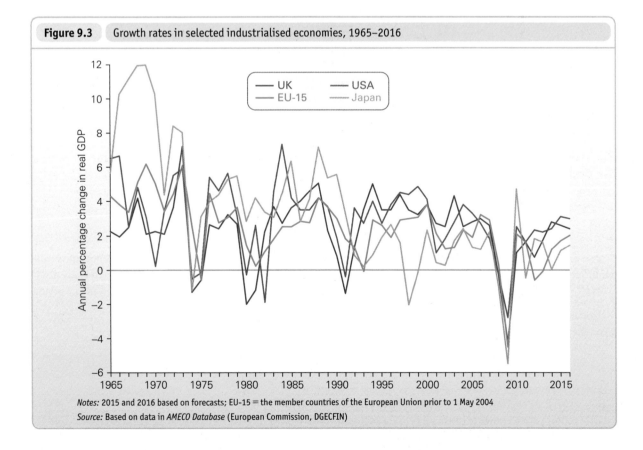

Notes: 2015 and 2016 based on forecasts; EU-15 = the member countries of the European Union prior to 1 May 2004

Source: Based on data in *AMECO Database* (European Commission, DGECFIN)

BOX 9.1 OUTPUT GAPS

An alternative measure of excess or deficient demand

If the economy grows, how fast and for how long can it grow before it runs into inflationary problems? On the other hand, what minimum rate must be achieved to avoid rising unemployment?

To answer these questions, economists have developed the concept of 'output gaps'.[1] As we have seen, the output gap is the difference between actual output and potential output: i.e. normal capacity output.

If actual output is below potential output (the gap is negative), there will be a higher than normal level of unemployment as firms are operating below their normal level of capacity utilisation. There will, however, be a downward pressure on inflation, resulting from a lower than normal level of demand for labour and other resources. If actual output is above potential output (the gap is positive), there will be excess demand and a rise in inflation.

[1] See Giorno et al., 'Potential output, output gaps and structural budget balances', *OECD Economic Studies*, no. 24, 1995.

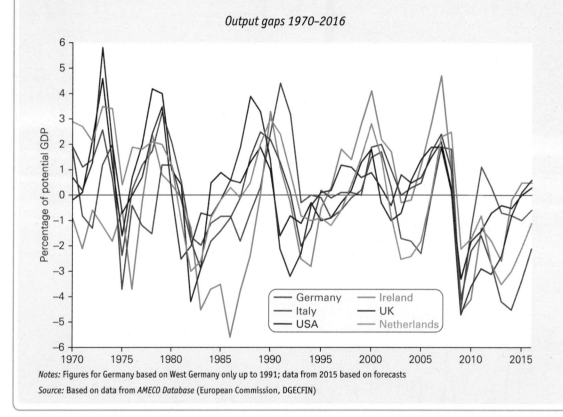

Output gaps 1970–2016

Percentage of potential GDP

— Germany — Ireland
— Italy — UK
— USA — Netherlands

Notes: Figures for Germany based on West Germany only up to 1991; data from 2015 based on forecasts

Source: Based on data from *AMECO Database* (European Commission, DGECFIN)

Two of the major factors contributing to potential economic growth are:

■ An increase in resources – natural resources, labour or capital.

■ An increase in the efficiency with which these resources are used, through advances in technology, improved labour skills or improved organisation.

Potential output (i.e. potential GDP) is the level of output when the economy is operating at 'normal capacity utilisation'. This allows for firms having a planned degree of spare capacity to meet unexpected demand or for hold-ups in supply. It also allows for some unemployment

as people move from job to job. Potential output is thus somewhat below full-capacity output, which is the absolute maximum that could be produced with firms working flat-out.

Definition

Potential output The economically sustainable level output that could be produced in the economy: i.e. one that involves a 'normal' level of capacity utilisation and does not result in rising inflation.

Generally, the gap will be negative in a recession and positive in a boom. In other words, output gaps follow the course of the business cycle.

But how do we measure output gaps? There are two principal statistical techniques.

De-trending techniques. This approach is a purely mechanical exercise which involves smoothing the actual GDP figures. In doing this, it attempts to fit a trend growth path along the lines of the dashed line in Figure 9.4. The main disadvantage of this approach is that it is not grounded in economic theory and therefore does not take into consideration those factors that economists consider to be important in determining output levels over time.

Production function approach. Many institutions, such as the European Union, use an approach which borrows ideas from economic theory. Specifically, it uses the idea of a production function which relates output to a set of inputs. Estimates of potential output are generated by using statistics on the size of a country's capital stock (see Box 9.3), the potential available labour input and, finally, the productivity or effectiveness of these inputs in producing output.

In addition to these statistical approaches use could be made of *business surveys*. In other words, we ask businesses directly. However, survey-based evidence can provide only a broad guide to rates of capacity utilisation and whether there is deficient or excess demand.

International evidence

The diagram shows output gaps for six countries from 1970 estimated using a production function approach. What is apparent from the chart is that all the countries have experienced significant output gaps, both positive and negative. This is consistent with a theme that we shall see throughout the second half of the book: economies are inherently volatile. In other words, countries experience business cycles.

The diagram does show that the characteristics of countries' business cycles can differ, particularly in terms of depth and duration. But, we also see evidence of an international business cycle (see pages 244–5) where national cycles appear to share characteristics. This is particularly stark in the late 2000s and early 2010s. Increasing global interconnectedness from financial and trading links meant that the financial crisis of the late 2000s spread like a contagion.

While output gaps vary from year to year, over the longer term the average output gap tends towards zero. As we can see from the table below, this means that for our selection of countries from 1970 the actual rate of economic growth is roughly the same as the potential rate.

**Average annual growth in actual and potential output,%
(1970–2015)**

	Average annual growth rates (%)	
	Actual output (real GDP)	Potential output
Germany	2.07	2.08
Ireland	4.19	4.20
Italy	1.87	1.94
Netherlands	2.28	2.35
UK	2.29	2.29
USA	2.81	2.85

Source: AMECO Database (European Commission, DGECFIN)

1. *Characterise the state of an economy during positive and negative output gaps.*
2. *Are all business cycles the same?*

The difference between actual and potential output is known as the **output gap**. Thus if actual output exceeds potential output, the output gap is positive: the economy is operating above normal capacity utilisation. If actual output is below potential output, the output gap is negative: the economy is operating below normal capacity utilisation. Box 9.1 looks at the output gap for five developed countries since 1970.

If the actual growth rate is less than the potential growth rate, there will be an increase in spare capacity and probably an increase in unemployment: the output gap will become more negative (or less positive). To close a negative output gap, the actual growth rate would temporarily have to exceed the potential growth rate. In the long run, however, the actual growth rate will be limited to the potential growth rate.

There are thus two major policy issues concerned with economic growth: the short-run issue of ensuring that actual growth is such as to keep actual output as close as possible to potential output; and the long-run issue of what determines the rate of potential economic growth.

Definition

Output gap The difference between actual and potential output. When actual output exceeds potential output, the gap is positive. When actual output is less than potential output, the gap is negative.

9.3 SHORT-TERM ECONOMIC GROWTH AND THE BUSINESS CYCLE

What is the pattern of economic growth from year to year?

Although growth in potential output varies to some extent over the years – depending on the rate of advance of technology, the level of investment and the discovery of new raw materials – it nevertheless tends to be much steadier than the growth in actual output.

As we have seen, actual growth tends to fluctuate. In some years there is a high rate of economic growth: the country experiences a boom. In other years, economic growth is low or even negative: the country experiences a slowdown or **recession**. This cycle of booms and recessions is known as the **business cycle** or **trade cycle**.

There are four 'phases' of the business cycle. They are illustrated in Figure 9.4.

1. *The upturn.* In this phase, a contracting or stagnant economy begins to recover, and growth in actual output resumes.
2. *The expansion.* During this phase, there is rapid economic growth: the economy is booming. A fuller use is made of resources, and the gap between actual and potential output narrows.
3. *The peaking out.* During this phase, growth slows down or even ceases.
4. *The slowdown, recession or slump.* During this phase, there is little or no growth or even a decline in output. Increasing slack develops in the economy.

A word of caution: do not confuse a high *level* of output with a high rate of *growth* in output. The level of output is highest in phase 3. The rate of growth in output is highest in phase 2 (i.e. where the curve is steepest).

Pause for thought

Figure 9.4 shows a decline in actual output in recession. Redraw the diagram, only this time show a mere slowing down of growth in phase 4.

Long-term output trend. A line can be drawn showing the trend of national output over time (i.e. ignoring the cyclical fluctuations around the trend). This is shown as the dashed line in Figure 9.4. If, over time, firms on average operate with a 'normal' degree of capacity utilisation, the trend output line will be the same as the potential output line. Also, if the average level of capacity that is unutilised stays constant from one cycle to another, the trend line will have the same slope as the full-capacity output line. In other words, the trend (or potential) rate of growth will be the same as the rate of growth of capacity.

If, however, the level of unutilised capacity changes from one cycle to another, then the trend line will have a different slope from the full-capacity output line. For example, if unemployment and unused industrial capacity *rise* from one peak to another, or from one trough to another, the trend line will move further away from the full-capacity output line (i.e. it will be less steep).

The business cycle in practice

The business cycle illustrated in Figure 9.4 is a 'stylised' cycle: it is smooth and regular. Drawing it this way allows us to make a clear distinction between each of the four phases. In practice, however, business cycles are highly irregular. They are irregular in two ways.

The length of the phases. Some booms are short lived, lasting only a few months or so. Others are much longer, lasting perhaps three or four years. Likewise some recessions are short while others are long.

The magnitude of the phases. Sometimes in phase 2, there is a very high rate of economic growth, perhaps 4 per cent per annum or more. On other occasions in phase 2, growth is much gentler. Sometimes in phase 4 there is a recession, with an actual decline in output, as occurred in 2008–9. On other occasions, phase 4 is merely a 'pause', with growth simply being low.

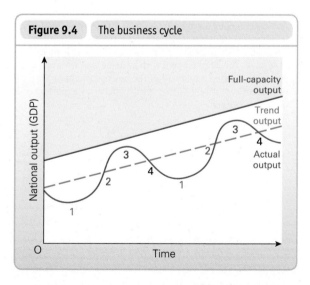

Figure 9.4 The business cycle

Definitions

Recession In official statistics, a recession is defined as when an economy experiences falling national output (negative growth) for two or more quarters.

Business cycle or trade cycle The periodic fluctuations of national output round its long-term trend.

The essence of the business cycle is the variability of economic growth. This is more readily apparent when, rather than looking at the levels of real GDP, we look at the rates of changes in real GDP. We can see this by revisiting Figure 9.2 (on page 235). While the plot of real GDP gives us a sense that growth is irregular, since if growth was constant we would have a straight line, it is by looking at the annual rates of change that we can see the true extent of this.

Recap

1. Actual growth must be distinguished from potential growth. The actual growth rate is the percentage annual increase in the output that is actually produced, whereas potential growth is the percentage annual increase in the normal capacity of the economy to produce (whether or not it is actually produced).

2. Actual growth will fluctuate with the course of the business cycle. The cycle can be broken down into four phases: the upturn, the expansion, the peaking out, and the slowdown or recession. In practice, the length and magnitude of these phases will vary: the cycle is thus irregular.

9.4 EXPLANATIONS OF THE BUSINESS CYCLE

Why isn't economic growth constant?

In this section we look at why growth in the short run tends to fluctuate. In other words, we examine the causes of the business cycle.

Fluctuations in aggregate demand

The focus of much of the analysis of business cycles is on why aggregate demand fluctuates. In other words, economists try to understand the factors that shift the *AD* curve in Figure 9.1 (on page 232). Keynesian economists, in particular, have taken this approach and then sought to devise appropriate stabilisation policies to iron out these fluctuations.

A more stable economy, they argue, will provide a better climate for investment and the growth of both individual businesses and the economy as a whole.

Consumption cycles

Spending by the household sector is the largest component of aggregate demand: consequently even relatively small changes in consumer behaviour can have a significant impact on the overall demand for firms' goods and services. As Figure 9.5 shows, annual rates of economic growth mirror those in household consumption. We saw in Section 8.3 (see pages 211–2) how household consumption is affected by a

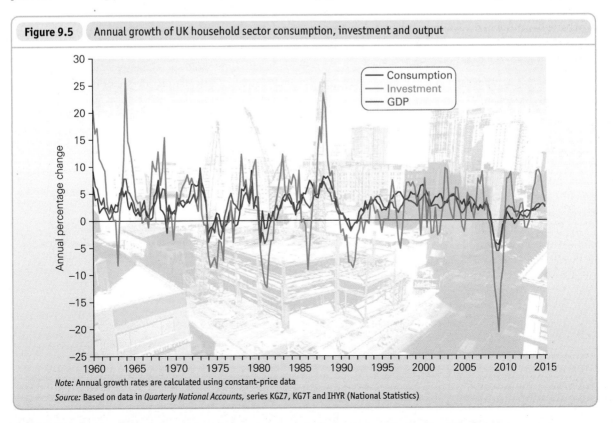

Figure 9.5 Annual growth of UK household sector consumption, investment and output

Note: Annual growth rates are calculated using constant-price data

Source: Based on data in *Quarterly National Accounts*, series KGZ7, KG7T and IHYR (National Statistics)

number of factors. Here we consider four that help to explain the contribution of consumption to the business cycle.

TC 9
p 62

Expectations of future incomes. If consumers believe that their incomes are likely to rise and that their jobs are secure, they are likely to spend more. Thus when the economy booms, consumer confidence is likely to rise, thereby further stimulating the economy. If, however, the economy is in recession and consumers are worried about their future income or that they may lose their job, they will probably cut back on spending. This is then likely to deepen the recession. In simple terms, the current spending plans of forward-looking households are dependent on expectations of future incomes.

Expectations of future prices. If people expect prices to rise, as is likely in a boom, they tend to buy durable goods such as furniture and cars before this happens. Again, this will give an additional boost to the economy. Conversely, if people expect prices to fall, as is likely in a recession, they may wait, thereby deepening the recession. This has been a problem in Japan for many years, where periods of falling prices (deflation) led many consumers to hold back on spending, thereby weakening aggregate demand and hence economic growth.

The age of durables. If people's car, carpets, clothes, etc., are getting old, they will tend to have a high level of 'replacement' consumption, particularly after a recession when they had cut back on their consumption of durables. This can help to stimulate a recovery from recession. Conversely, as the economy reaches the peak of the boom, people are likely to spend less on durables as they have probably already bought the items they want. This can then contribute to the ending of the boom. Thus spending on durable can help to explain the turning points: the upturn from recession and the downturn from a boom.

The availability or price of credit. In a boom, with bank deposits increasing and banks relatively confident about the future, banks may be willing to lend more or reduce the interest rate charged on credit relative to that paid on saving, thereby further stimulating consumer spending. In a recession, however, banks may fear people's ability to repay loans and may thus cut back on lending or raise the interest rate charged on credit relative to that paid on saving, thereby further dampening consumer demand.

In other words, banks take the path of output as a signal of the riskiness of lending: they perceive lending to be riskier in a recession than in a boom. This is significant because it can result in the overall flow of credit being dependent on the phase of the business cycle. If true, it creates an inherently destabilising mechanism *within* the economy.

The idea that the financial sector may amplify shocks to the macroeconomy when conditions in financial markets are affected by the state of the macroeconomy is known as the **financial accelerator**.

The **financial instability hypothesis** argues similarly that credit flows are likely to be pro-cyclical. The psychology of banks and investors is important here. After a period of sustained growth banks become more confident to lend while investors become more confident to borrow. However, the sustainability of lending becomes increasingly more fragile. The growth of debt on the balance sheets can only be sustained in the longer term by the growth in asset values (housing or financial assets) alongside buoyant income flows.

The financial instability hypothesis suggests that a point is reached, perhaps triggered by an economic shock, when confidence is replaced by pessimism. Credit criteria tighten, as they did in the late 2000s, and people look to improve their financial well-being by reducing their exposure to debt. This can trigger a **balance sheet recession**. The size of this effect could be very large since asset values will fall as large numbers of people look to sell assets. The financial instability hypothesis is considered further in Box 10.4 (on page 282).

KI 31
p 205

Both the financial accelerator and the financial instability hypothesis illustrate feedback loops between the financial sector and the macroeconomy.

Instability of investment

One of the factors contributing to the ups and downs of the business cycle is the instability of investment. Figure 9.5 shows that real investment spending (gross capital formation) is markedly more volatile than output (real GDP).

As with household spending, we would expect investment, and in particular private-sector investment, to be affected by expectations and financial market conditions. Therefore, changes in national income can lead to amplified changes in investment expenditure because of their impact on the financial sector.

Pause for thought

Other than looking at the current growth of economic output, how else can financial institutions assess the riskiness of their lending?

> **Definitions**
>
> **Financial accelerator** When a change in national income is amplified by changes in the financial sector, such as changes in interest rate differentials or the willingness of banks to lend.
>
> **Financial instability hypothesis** The idea that the financial system swings between robustness and fragility so generating cycles in credit and destabilising the macroeconomy.
>
> **Balance sheet recession** An economic slowdown or recession caused by private-sector agents looking to improve their financial well-being by increasing their saving and/or paying down debt.

Yet, the extent of the volatility in investment points to another type of accelerator effect. To understand this effect, remember that investment (except for replacement investment) provides businesses with *additional* capacity. This helps to explain why, in a recession, investment in new plant and equipment can all but disappear. After all, what is the point in investing in additional capacity if you cannot even sell what you are currently producing? When an economy begins to recover from a recession, however, and confidence returns, investment can rise very rapidly. In percentage terms, the rise in investment may be *several times that of the rise in income*. When the growth of the economy slows down, however, investment can fall dramatically.

The point is that investment depends not so much on the *level* of national income and consumer demand, as on their *rate of change*. Since this 'induced' investment is to provide *additional* capacity, it depends on how much demand has risen, not on its level. But growth rates change by much more than the level of output. For example, if economic growth is 1 per cent in 2015 and 2 per cent in 2016, then in 2016 output has gone up by 2 per cent, but growth has gone up by 100 per cent (i.e. it has doubled). Thus changes in investment tend to be much more dramatic than changes in national income. This is known as the **accelerator theory**. Box 9.2 gives an example of this accelerator effect.

Pause for thought

Under what circumstances would you expect a rise in national income to cause a large accelerator effect?

These fluctuations in investment, being injections into the circular flow of income, then have a multiplied effect on national income and will thus magnify the upswings and downswings of the business cycle.

Fluctuations in stocks

Firms hold stocks (or 'inventories') of finished goods. These stocks tend to fluctuate with the course of the business cycle, and these fluctuations in stocks themselves contribute to fluctuations in output.

Imagine an economy that is recovering from a recession. At first, firms may be cautious about increasing production: doing so may involve taking on more labour or making additional investment. Firms may not want to make these commitments if the recovery could soon peter out. They may, therefore, run down their stocks rather than increase output. Initially the recovery from recession will be slow.

If the recovery does continue, however, firms will start to gain more confidence and will increase their production. Also they will find that their stocks have got rather low and will

need building up. This gives a further boost to production, and for a time the growth in output will exceed the growth in demand. This extra growth in output will then, via the multiplier, lead to a further increase in demand.

Once stocks have been built up again, the growth in output will slow down to match the growth in demand. This slowing down in output will, via the accelerator and multiplier, contribute to the ending of the expansionary phase of the business cycle.

As the economy slows down, firms may for a time be prepared to carry on producing and build up stocks. The increase in stocks thus cushions the effect of falling demand on output and employment.

If the recession continues, firms will be unwilling to go on building up stocks. But as firms attempt to reduce their stocks back to the desired level, production will fall *below* the level of sales, despite the fact that sales themselves are lower. This could therefore lead to a dramatic fall in output and, via the multiplier, to an even bigger fall in sales.

Eventually, once stocks have been run down to the minimum, production will have to rise again to match the level of sales. This will contribute to a recovery and the whole cycle will start again.

Why do booms and recessions persist?

Why do booms and recessions last for several months or even years? There are two main reasons.

Time lags. It takes time for changes in injections and withdrawals to be fully reflected in changes in national income, output and employment. The multiplier process takes time. Moreover, consumers, firms and government may not all respond immediately to new situations. Their responses are spread out over a period of time.

'Bandwagon' effects. Once the economy starts expanding, growth expectations become buoyant. People think ahead and adjust their spending behaviour: they consume and invest more now. Likewise in a recession a mood of pessimism may set in. The effect is cumulative.

The multiplier and accelerator interact: they feed on each other. A rise in income causes a rise in investment (the accelerator). This, being an injection into the circular flow, causes a multiplied rise in income. This then causes a further accelerator effect, and a further multiplier effect, and so on. The increase in investment may be greater still if credit conditions ease. If so, the financial accelerator further amplifies the increase in national income.

Definition

Accelerator theory The *level* of investment depends on the *rate of change* of national income, and as a result tends to be subject to substantial fluctuations.

BOX 9.2 **THE ACCELERATOR: AN EXAMPLE** EXPLORING ECONOMICS

Demonstrating the instability of investment

The following example illustrates some important features of the accelerator. It looks at the investment decisions made by a firm in response to change in the demand for its product. The firm is taken as representative of firms throughout the economy. The example is based on various strict assumptions. These help to keep the analysis simple.

■ The firm's machines last exactly 10 years and then need replacing.
■ At the start of the example, the firm has 10 machines in place: one ten years old, one nine years old, one eight years old, one seven, one six, and so on. Thus one machine needs replacing each year.

■ Machines produce exactly 100 units of output per year. This figure cannot be varied.
■ The firm always adjusts its output and its stock of machinery to match consumer demand.

The example shows what happens to the firm's investment over a six-year period when there is first a substantial rise in consumer demand, then a levelling off and then a slight fall. It illustrates the following features of the accelerator (see the table below).

The accelerator effect

Year	0	1	2	3	4	5	6
Quantity demanded by consumers (sales)	1000	1000	2000	3000	3500	3500	3400
Number of machines required	10	10	20	30	35	35	34
Induced investment (I_i) (extra machines)		0	10	10	5	0	0
Replacement investment (I_r)		1	1	1	1	1	0
Total investment ($I_i + I_r$)		1	11	11	6	1	0

Investment will rise when the growth of national income (and hence consumer demand) is rising ($\Delta Y_{t+1} > \Delta Y_t$). Years 1 to 2 illustrate this. The rise in consumer demand is zero in year 1 and 1000 units in year 2. Investment rises from 1 to 11 machines. The growth in investment may be considerably greater than the growth in consumer demand, giving a large accelerator effect. Between years 1 and 2, consumer demand doubles but investment goes up by a massive *11* times!

Investment will be constant even when national income is growing, if the increase in income this year is the same as last year ($\Delta Y_{t+1} = \Delta Y_t$). Years 2 to 3 illustrate this. Consumer demand continues to rise by 1000 units, but investment is constant at 11 machines.

Investment will fall even if national income is still growing, if the rate of growth is slowing down ($\Delta Y_{t+1} < \Delta Y_t$). Years 3 to 4 illustrate this. Consumer demand rises now by 500 units (rather than the 1000 units last year). Investment falls from 11 to 6 machines.

If national income is constant, investment will be confined to replacement investment only. Years 4 to 5 illustrate this. Investment falls to the one machine requiring replacement.

If national income falls, even if only slightly, investment can be wiped out altogether. Years 5 to 6 illustrate this. Even though demand has fallen by only $^1/_{35}$, investment will fall to zero. Not even the machine that is wearing out will be replaced.

In practice, the accelerator will not be as dramatic and clear cut as this. The effect will be extremely difficult to predict for the following reasons:

■ Many firms may have spare capacity and/or carry stocks. This will enable them to meet extra demand without having to invest.
■ The willingness of firms to invest will depend on their confidence of *future* demand. Just because demand has currently risen, firms are not going to rush out and spend large amounts of money on machines that will last many years if it is quite likely that next year demand will fall back again.
■ Firms may make their investment plans a long time in advance and may be unable to change them quickly.
■ Even if firms decide to invest more, the producer goods industries may not have the capacity to meet a sudden surge in demand for machines.
■ Machines do not as a rule suddenly wear out. A firm could thus delay replacing machines and keep the old ones for a bit longer if it was uncertain about its future level of demand.

All these points tend to reduce the magnitude of the accelerator and to make it very difficult to predict. Nevertheless the effect still exists. Firms still take note of changes in consumer demand when deciding how much to invest. Evidence shows that fluctuations in investment are far more severe than fluctuations in national income.

? *If there is an initial change in injections or withdrawals, then theoretically this will set off a chain reaction between the multiplier and accelerator. Assuming that there is an initial rise in injections, trace through the multiplier and accelerator effects. Why is it unlikely that national income will go on rising more and more rapidly?*

Group behaviour. Individual consumers and businesses may take their lead from others and so mimic their behaviour. This helps to reinforce bandwagon effects.

For example, during the 2000s many financial institutions loosened their lending criteria. This helped to fuel unsustainable property booms in several countries, including the UK, Ireland and the USA. They engaged in a competitive race, offering evermore favourable terms for borrowers. Often the borrowers could only repay if their assets (e.g. property) appreciated in value, as they tend to do in a boom – but not in a recession. This mirrors the predictions of the financial instability hypothesis (see page 240).

This rush to lend meant that many banks over-extended themselves and operated with too little capital. This made them much more vulnerable to financial crises and much more likely to cut back lending dramatically in a downturn – as indeed they did from 2008.

Group behaviour can therefore help to amplify economic upturns and downturns. This illustrates how the interaction between economic agents affects macroeconomic aggregates, such as national income.

Why do booms and recessions come to an end? What determines the turning points?

If booms or recessions can last for some time, then why do they not go on for ever? Why do they come to an end?

Ceilings and floors. Actual output can go on growing more rapidly than potential output only as long as there is slack in the economy. As full employment is approached and as more and more firms reach full capacity, so a ceiling to output is reached.

At the other extreme, there is a basic minimum level of consumption that people tend to maintain. During a recession, people may not buy much in the way of luxury and durable goods, but they will still continue to buy food and other basic goods. There is thus a floor to consumption.

Echo effects. Durable consumer goods and capital equipment may last several years, but eventually they will need replacing. The replacement of goods and capital purchased in a previous boom may help to bring a recession to an end.

The accelerator. For investment to continue rising, consumer demand must rise at a faster and faster rate. If this does not happen, investment will fall back and the boom will break.

Sentiment and expectations. A change of sentiment and a sense that current rates of growth will not be sustained can lead people to adjust their spending behaviour, so contributing to the very slowdown that was expected. The impact of this will be amplified by bandwagon effects and group behaviour.

Random shocks. National or international political, social or natural events can affect the mood and attitudes of firms, governments and consumers, and thus affect aggregate demand.

Changes in government policy. In a boom, a government may become most worried by inflation and balance of trade deficits and thus pursue contractionary policies. In a recession, it may become most worried by unemployment and lack of growth and thus pursue expansionary policies. These government policies, if successful, will bring about a turning point in the cycle. This was the hope for the expansionary policies pursued by many governments during the global recession of the late 2000s.

Pause for thought

Why is it difficult to predict precisely when a recession will come to an end and the economy will start growing rapidly?

Keynesians argue that governments should attempt to reduce cyclical fluctuations by the use of active stabilisation policies. A more stable economy will provide a better climate for long-term investment, which will lead to faster growth in both potential and actual output. The policy traditionally favoured by Keynesians for stabilising the economy is *fiscal policy*. This is considered in Chapter 12.

Fluctuations in aggregate supply

While the mainstream view of business cycles stresses the importance of fluctuations in aggregate demand, it recognises that shifts in the aggregate supply curve in Figure 9.1 can also cause fluctuations in output. Sudden sharp changes to input prices, such as in the price of oil, could be one such cause.

But some economists, such as 'new classical economists', go further and argue that shifts in aggregate supply are the *primary* source of economic volatility. One particular theory is known as **real business cycle theory**. In a recession, according to the theory, aggregate supply curves will shift to the left (output falls), while in a boom aggregate supply curves shift to the right (output rises). But what makes aggregate supply shift in the first place, and why, after an initial shift, will the aggregate supply curve *go on* shifting, causing a recession or boom to continue?

Definition

Real business cycle theory The new classical theory which explains cyclical fluctuations in terms of shifts in aggregate supply, rather than aggregate demand.

The initial shifts in aggregate supply are caused by *impulses*. An impulse could come from a structural change: say, a shift in demand from older manufacturing industries to new service industries. Because of the immobility of labour, not all those laid off in the older industries will find work in the new industries. Structural unemployment (part of equilibrium unemployment) rises and output falls.

Alternatively, the impulse could be a change in technology. For example, a technological breakthrough in telecommunications could shift aggregate supply to the right. Or it could come from an oil price increase, shifting aggregate supply to the left.

The persistence of supply-side effects

Real business cycle theory stresses that the effects of impulses persist – aggregate supply *goes on* shifting. There are two main reasons. The first is that several changes may take months to complete. For example, a decline in demand for certain older industries, perhaps caused by growing competition from abroad, does not take place overnight. Likewise, a technological breakthrough does not affect all industries simultaneously.

The second reason is that these changes affect the profitability of investment. A positive shock (impulse) will raise investment levels, which will increase firms' capacity; hence the aggregate supply curve will shift to the right. Conversely, a negative shock (impulse) will reduce investment, causing the aggregate supply curve to shift to the left. Therefore, changes in the profitability of investment are said to amplify or 'propagate' the impact of the impulses through their effect on aggregate *supply*. This is in contrast to the multiplier effect where changes in investment affect output through their effect on aggregate demand (see pages 219 and 221–3).

Turning points

So far we have seen how the theory of real business cycles explains persistent rises or falls in aggregate supply. But how does it explain *turning points*? Why do recessions and booms come to an end? The most likely explanation is that, once a shock has worked its way through, aggregate supply will stop shifting. If there is then any shock in the other direction, aggregate supply will start moving back again. For example, after a period of recession, an eventual rise in business confidence will cause investment to rise and hence aggregate supply to shift back to the right. Since these 'reverse shocks' are likely to occur at irregular intervals, they can help to explain why real-world business cycles are themselves irregular.

Redefining the concept of the business cycle

While the ideas behind the real business cycle are controversial they do raise important questions about our understanding of the business cycle. The traditional view is of the business cycle as fluctuations in actual output around the economy's potential output. This view of the business cycle is the one illustrated in Figure 9.4. On the other hand, real

business cycle theory portrays the business cycle as upward and downward movements in the economy's potential output which then affect the economy's actual output.

Because the shocks in real business cycle models affect potential output and so affect the economy's growth path, these models merge the analysis of the short run and the long run. This has heralded a more general trend in macroeconomic modelling to analyse both the short-term impact of economic shocks and their potential long-term impact, regardless of whether the shocks emerge from the supply side or the demand side.

Therefore, while there continues to be keenly contested debates about the sources of economic volatility, the ways in which they are propagated and the role of policy makers, there is widespread recognition that shocks *can* have persistent or enduring effects on the economy.

An example of this has occurred in recent years. The deep recession following the financial crisis of 2008 led to a collapse in investment and this reduced aggregate supply as well as aggregate demand. When economic growth resumed in 2013 at pre-recession rates, real GDP was some 17 per cent lower than it would have been had the pre-recession growth rate of nearly 3 per cent continued from 2008 (see Figure 9.6). The financial crisis thus resulted in a reduction not just in actual GDP, but also in potential GDP as capacity was lost and investment in new capacity was reduced or abandoned.

Finance and trade

Economies evolve and so do our models and understanding of the determinants of the business cycle. Two important changes are (a) the increasing dependence of economies on the financial system (known as **financialisation**) and (b) the increasing interconnectedness between national economies.

Importance of the financial sector. The financial crisis of the late 2000s demonstrated how integral or systemically important some financial institutions have become in many modern-day economies. When analysing changes in national income, therefore, it is crucial to understand just how the financial system impacts on the economic choices made by individuals, firms and governments.

Global interdependence. We live in an interdependent world and the economic well-being of one country can have significant effects on another. This interdependence has grown for two main reasons.

> ### Definition
>
> **Financialisation** A term describing the significance of the financial system in our everyday lives and in influencing economic activity.

KI 28
p 176

Figure 9.6 Real GDP in the UK

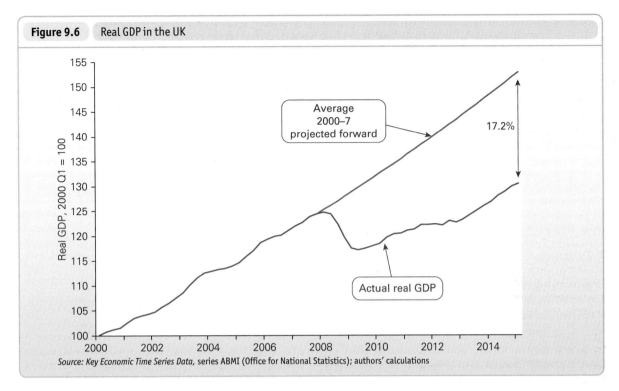

Source: Key Economic Time Series Data, series ABMI (Office for National Statistics); authors' calculations

First, there has also been a rapid growth in financial flows between countries, especially short-term financial flows. Financial systems are highly interconnected and some financial institutions are not just systemically important at a national level but at a global level too. **Global systemically important banks or G-SIBs** are banks which, through a series of measures, have been identified as significant players in the global financial system.

Secondly, many countries have seen their imports and exports grow more rapidly than the overall size of their economies (see Section 13.1 and Figure 13.1 on page 363).

One consequence of the growth in trade and financial interdependence is that the business cycles in different countries have become more synchronised, resulting in an **international business cycle**.

Recap

1. Keynesians explain cyclical fluctuations in the economy by examining the causes of fluctuations in the level of aggregate *demand*.

2. Financial institutions may use economic growth as an indicator of the riskiness of lending. This will affect the availability of credit or the price of credit. Weaker growth is likely to result in reduced flows of credit and a higher rate of interest on borrowing relative to that on saving. This creates a financial accelerator effect which amplifies the business cycle. The financial instability hypothesis argues that the financial system swings between fragility and robustness with changes in the confidence of banks and investors. Again, the result is credit cycles which generate macroeconomic instability.

3. A major part of the Keynesian explanation of the business cycle is the instability of investment. The accelerator theory helps to explain this instability. It relates the level of investment to *changes* in national income and consumer demand. An initial increase in consumer demand can result in a very large percentage increase in investment; but as soon as the rise in consumer demand begins to level off, investment will fall; and even a slight fall in consumer demand can reduce investment to virtually zero. Investment in stocks is also unstable and tends to amplify the business cycle.

4. Booms and recessions can persist because of time lags, 'bandwagon' and 'group' effects and the *interaction* of the multiplier, accelerator and credit cycles.

5. Turning points are explained by ceilings and floors to output, echo effects, the accelerator, expectations and sentiment, random shocks and swings in government policy.

6. Real business cycle theory focuses on aggregate supply shocks (impulses), which then persist for a period of time. Eventually their effect will peter out, and supply shocks in the other direction can lead to turning points in the cycle.

7. Explanations of national business cycles evolve as the way in which economic activity is conducted changes. Two important examples of this are financialisation and trade.

9.5 LONG-TERM ECONOMIC GROWTH

How does income per head today compare with that in the past?

Growth over the decades

While it is understandable that we are concerned with the ups and downs of the business cycle, when we step back and look at the longer span of history, these short-term fluctuations take on less significance. What we see is that economies tend to experience long-term economic growth, not long-term economic decline. This illustrated in Figure 9.7, which shows the path of real GDP in six developed countries since 1960.

Such growth cannot be explained by a closing of the gap between actual and potential output: by an expansion of aggregate demand leading to a fuller use of resources. Instead, the explanation lies on the supply side. Countries' economic *capacity* has increased.

Comparing the growth performance of different countries

An increase in economic capacity is reflected in a growth in the average output per worker and in the average output per head of the population (per capita). Table 9.1 shows the average annual growth in these two variables for several developed countries since the 1960s, alongside that for output (real GDP). The effect of even very small differences can have a significant effect when looked at over many years. Table 9.2 shows how many times greater output, output per person employed and output per capita in 2015 were compared with that in 1960.

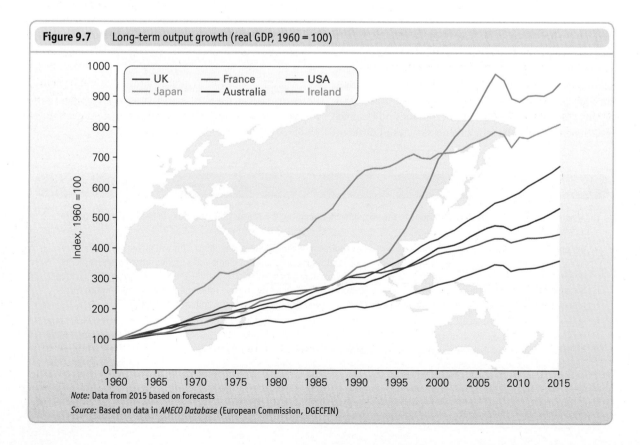

Figure 9.7   Long-term output growth (real GDP, 1960 = 100)

Legend: UK, France, USA, Japan, Australia, Ireland

Note: Data from 2015 based on forecasts

Source: Based on data in *AMECO Database* (European Commission, DGECFIN)

Table 9.1	Average annual growth rates (%) 1961–2015		
	Real GDP	Real GDP per worker	Real GDP per capita
Canada	3.3	1.3	2.0
France	2.8	2.3	2.1
Germany	2.4	1.9	2.1
Ireland	4.2	3.1	3.3
Italy	2.5	2.3	2.1
Japan	4.0	3.3	3.4
Netherlands	2.7	2.0	2.0
Spain	3.4	2.9	2.6
UK	2.4	1.9	2.0
USA	3.1	1.7	2.0

Note: German figures based on West Germany only up to 1991
Source: Based on data from *AMECO Database* (European Commission, DGECFIN)

Table 9.2	Output ratios, 2015 relative to 1960		
	Real GDP	Real GDP per worker	Real GDP per capita
Canada	5.8	2.0	2.9
France	4.5	3.5	3.2
Germany	4.1	2.5	2.7
Ireland	9.5	5.3	5.7
Italy	3.8	3.4	3.1
Japan	8.1	6.0	6.0
Netherlands	4.3	2.9	3.0
Spain	6.2	4.6	4.1
UK	3.6	2.8	2.9
USA	5.4	2.5	3.0

Note: German figures based on West Germany only up to 1991
Source: Based on data from *AMECO Database* (European Commission, DGECFIN)

Pause for thought

1. *Is it possible to have economic growth without an increase in output per worker? Explain.*
2. *Why may the rates of growth in average output per worker and in average output per head of the population differ?*

As you can see from these two tables, there has been a considerable difference in the rates of growth experienced by the different countries. Such differences have implications for the longer-term *living standards* of countries' populations. However, if economic growth is to give an indication of an increase in living standards, it has to be measured per head of the population (as shown in the final column in each table).

In general, GDP per capita in the richer developed countries has grown at a slower rate than in the less rich ones. The result has been a narrowing of the gap in living standards. For example, in 1950, GDP per head in the USA (in purchasing-power standard terms) was 2.5 times that in West Germany and 20 times that in Japan. By 2015, GDP per head in the USA was only 24 per cent higher than that in Germany and 47 per cent higher than that in Japan.

The next section explores the causes and effects of economic growth. But before we go on, a word of caution: long-term economic growth does not mean universal improvement. People are not necessarily happier; there are many stresses in modern living; the environment is in many respects more polluted; inequality has increased in most countries, especially over the past 20 years; for many people work is more demanding and the working day is longer than in the past; there is more crime and more insecurity. More is not always better.

Recap

1. The determinants of economic growth in the long run lie primarily on the supply side.
2. Most developed countries have experienced average annual rates of economic growth of more than 2 per cent over the past 50 years, but there have been considerable differences between countries.
3. The income gap between developed countries has tended to narrow as the less rich ones have grown faster than the richer ones.

9.6 EXPLANATIONS OF LONG-TERM GROWTH

Why is income per head today so much higher than a generation ago?

The causes of economic growth

The sources of growth in potential output can be grouped into two broad categories:

TC 15
p 248

- An increase in the *quantity* of factors. Here we would include an increase in the workforce or the average number of hours that people work, an increase in raw materials (e.g. discoveries of oil) and an increase in capital. Of these, for most countries it is an increase in the capital stock, brought about by investment, that is the most important source of growth.

- An increase in the *productivity* of factors. Here we would include an increase in the skills of workers, a more efficient organisation of inputs by management and more productive capital equipment. Most significant here is technological progress. Developments of computer technology, of new techniques in engineering, of lighter, stronger and cheaper materials, of digital technology in communications and of more efficient motors have all contributed to a massive increase in the productivity of capital. Machines today can produce much more output than machines in the past that cost the same to manufacture.

> **KEY IDEA**
> **34**
>
> **TC**
> **15**
>
> Long-term growth in a country's output depends on a growth in the quantity and/or productivity of its resources. Potential economic growth depends on a country's resources, technology and productivity. This is crucial to understanding what underlies the wealth of nations and why some countries have faster growth rates than others. It forms the 15th of our threshold concepts.

In this section, we will examine these two sources of growth, focusing first on capital accumulation (an increase in the *quantity* of capital) and then on technological progress (an increase in the *productivity* of factors).

Capital accumulation

An increase in capital per worker will generally increase output. In other words, the more equipment that is used by people at work, the more they are likely to produce. But to increase capital requires investment, and that investment requires resources – resources that could have been used for producing consumer goods. Thus more investment over the longer term requires more saving.

A simple model of economic growth

The rate of growth via capital accumulation depends on two things:

- The marginal capital/output ratio (k). This is the amount of extra capital (ΔK) divided by the extra annual output that it produces (ΔY). Thus $k = \Delta K / \Delta Y$. The lower the value of k, the higher is the productivity of capital (i.e. the less extra capital you need to produce extra output).

- The proportion of national income that is invested (i), which, assuming that all saving is invested, will equal the proportion of national income that is saved (s).

The formula for growth becomes:

$g = i/k$ (or $g = s/k$)

Thus if 20 per cent of national income went in new investment ($i = 20$ per cent), and if each £1 of new investment yielded 25p of extra income per year ($k = 4$), then the growth rate would be 5 per cent.

A simple example will demonstrate this. If national income is £100 billion, then £20 billion will be invested ($i = 20\%$). This will lead to extra annual output of £5 billion ($k = 4$). Thus national income grows to £105 billion: a growth of 5 per cent.

But what determines the rate of investment? There are a number of determinants. These include the confidence of businesspeople about the future demand for their products, the profitability of business, the tax regime, the rate of growth in the economy and the rate of interest.

The neoclassical growth model

Although the above model is a useful starting point for examining economic growth arising from increased capital, two qualifications need to be made.

- The first is that as capital per worker increases, so diminishing returns to capital are likely to set in. For example, if, in an office, you start equipping workers with PCs, at first output will increase very rapidly. But as more and more workers have their own PC rather than having to share, so the rate of increase in output slows down. When everyone has their own, output is likely to be at a maximum. Any additional PCs (of the same specification) will remain unused. Thus, for a given workforce, as the capital stock increases, so the marginal capital/output ratio (k) will rise and the growth rate will fall. **KI 15** **p 76**

- The second qualification is that, the larger the capital stock, the greater the proportion of investment that will **KI 21** **p 148**

| BOX 9.3 | GETTING INTENSIVE WITH PHYSICAL CAPITAL | EXPLORING ECONOMICS |

How quickly does it grow?

In this box we take a look at two issues relating to physical capital. First, we consider the components of physical capital that are recorded in a country's national accounts. Secondly, we compare the growth in physical capital with rates of economic growth for a sample of countries.

What is capital?

In a country's national accounts, physical capital consists of non-financial *fixed assets*. It does not include goods and services transformed or used up in the course of production; these are known as *intermediate goods and services*. Furthermore, it does not relate directly to the stock of human capital: the skills and attributes embodied in individuals that affect production (see Box 9.5).

A country's stock of fixed assets can be valued at its replacement cost, regardless of its age: this is its *gross* value. It can also be valued at its written-down value known as its *net* value. The net value takes into account the *consumption of capital* which occurs through wear and tear (depreciation) or when capital becomes naturally obsolescent.

The table shows that the estimated value of the *net* capital stock of the UK in 2013 was £3.98 trillion. This is considerably less than the 2013 estimate of human capital of £17.9 trillion (see Box 9.5). To put this into context, this is roughly 2.3 times the value of GDP.

The table shows that there are six broad categories of fixed assets. The largest of these by value is *dwellings*, which includes houses, bungalows and flats. Residential housing yields rental incomes for landlords and, more generally, provides all of us with important consumption services, most notably shelter.

The second largest component by value is *other buildings and structures*. This includes buildings, other than dwellings, and most civil engineering and construction work. It will include structures such as factories, schools and hospitals and the country's railway track.

The third largest component by value is *other machinery and equipment*. This is essentially plant and includes electricity and telephone lines, production equipment, tools, computers and other office equipment. Next by value is *intellectual property products*. This includes computer software, original works of literature or art and mineral

UK net capital stock

| | 2013 | | | Average real annual change,% | |
Type	£ billions	% of fixed assets	% of GDP	1997–2013	2008–13
Dwellings	1 670.8	42.0	97.5	1.3	0.4
Other buildings and structures	1 411.5	35.5	82.3	2.3	2.0
Other machinery and equipment	614.9	15.4	35.9	2.1	1.1
Intellectual property products	188.3	4.7	11.0	−0.7	−0.3
Transport equipment	89.5	2.2	5.2	0.2	0.1
Cultivated biological resources	6.4	0.2	0.4	3.8	5.0
All fixed assets	3 981.4	100.0	232.4	1.6	1.0

Sources: Based on data from *Capital Stocks, Consumption of Fixed Capital, 2014* and *Quarterly National Accounts,* series YBHA (National Statistics)

exploration. Then comes *transport equipment*, which includes vehicles such as lorries, fork-lift trucks and tractors. The smallest component by value is *cultivated biological resource*, which includes livestock and forests.

The final column of the table shows that on average from 1997 to 2013 the *volume* of the UK capital stock increased by 1.6 per cent per year. This was largely driven by growth in 'other machinery and equipment' and in 'other buildings and structures'. Since 2008 growth in the overall volume of the stock of fixed capital has fallen to only 1 per cent per year.

How does capital grow? An international comparison

In models of economic growth an important measure of the capital stock is the amount of capital per worker. This is also known as *capital intensity*. In the chart we plot the ratio of capital per worker in 2015 to that in 1960 (x-axis) against

ratio of real GDP per worker in 2015 to that in 1960 (y-axis) in a selection of developed countries.

For each country we observe an increase in capital intensity, although the rates of capital accumulation differ quite significantly. The data show that the UK ranks relatively lowly in terms of capital accumulation. In the UK the capital stock per worker is 2.4 times higher in 2015, compared with, for example, Japan where it is 5.6 times higher or France where it is 3.8 times higher.

We would expect that the higher the level of capital per worker, the greater will be the level of output (real GDP) per worker. This is largely borne out in the chart. However, while there is a statistical association between capital accumulation and economic growth, economic theory plays an important role in our understanding of this apparent relationship.

There is considerable debate about the determinants of capital accumulation and its significance for growth,

KI 31
p 205

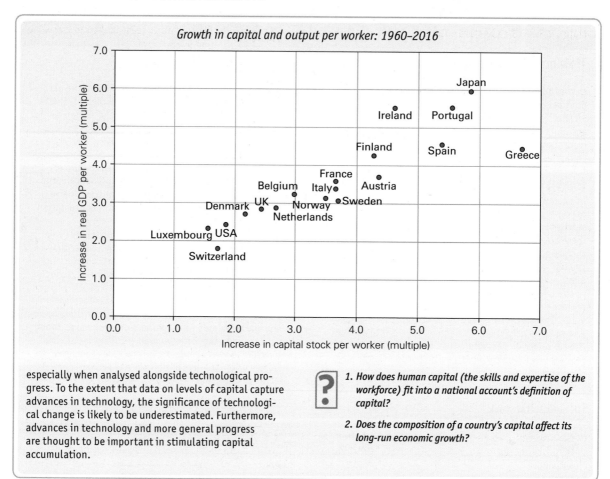

Growth in capital and output per worker: 1960–2016

especially when analysed alongside technological progress. To the extent that data on levels of capital capture advances in technology, the significance of technological change is likely to be underestimated. Furthermore, advances in technology and more general progress are thought to be important in stimulating capital accumulation.

?

1. *How does human capital (the skills and expertise of the workforce) fit into a national account's definition of capital?*

2. *Does the composition of a country's capital affect its long-run economic growth?*

be needed for replacement purposes, and the smaller the proportion that can be used for increasing the size of the capital stock.

Let us now incorporate these two qualifications into a model of growth. This is known as the **neoclassical** or **'Solow' growth model**, after the MIT economics professor and Nobel Prize winner, Robert Solow. This model is illustrated in Figure 9.8. The size of the capital stock (K) is measured on the horizontal axis; the level of national output (Y) is measured on the vertical axis. Assuming that the size of the workforce is constant, any increase in the capital stock means an increase in the average amount of capital per worker.

So how have we taken the two qualifications into account? First, consider the assumption of diminishing returns to capital. The Y curve shows that as the capital stock increases, so output increases. But, because of diminishing returns to capital the Y curve gets less and less steep. What will be the effect on investment? Increased output will mean increased saving and hence increased investment. This is shown by the investment curve (I). Note that

KI 15
p 76

the I curve has the same general shape as the Y curve because saving is assumed to be a given proportion of GDP. But, the higher the share of investment in GDP, the steeper will be this line.

Now consider our second qualification. There will be an increase in the amount of investment needed for replacement purposes as the capital stock increases. The depreciation (D) line shows the amount of depreciation of capital that takes place, and hence the amount of replacement investment required. The bigger the capital stock, the larger the amount of replacement investment required.

Definitions

Neoclassical analysis The analysis of market economics where it is assumed that individuals and firms are self-interested rational maximisers.

Solow growth model A model which explains economic growth in terms of the effects on the capital stock and output of a change in investment.

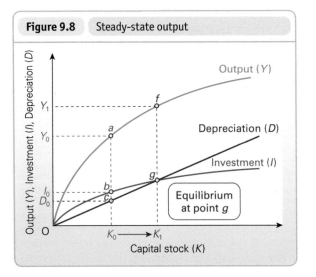

Figure 9.8 Steady-state output

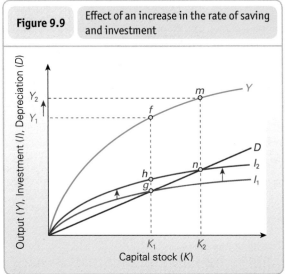

Figure 9.9 Effect of an increase in the rate of saving and investment

Assume initially that the size of the capital stock is K_0. This will generate an output of Y_0 (point a). This output, in turn, will generate saving and investment of I_0, but of this, D_0 will have to be used for replacement purposes. The difference $(b - c)$ will be available to increase the size of the capital stock. The capital stock will thus increase up to K_1 (point g). At this point, all investment will be required for replacement purposes. Output will therefore cease growing. Y_1 represents the **steady-state level of national income**.

Effect of an increase in the saving rate. If the saving rate increases, the investment curve will shift upwards. This is shown by a shift from I_1 to I_2 in Figure 9.9. Investment is now above that which is necessary to maintain the capital stock at K_1. The capital stock will grow, therefore, and so will national income. But this growth is only temporary. Once the capital stock has risen to K_2, all the new higher level of investment will be absorbed in replacing capital ($I = D$ at point n). National income stops rising. Y_2 represents the new steady-state national income.

Does this mean, therefore, that there is no long-term gain from an increase in the saving rate? There *is* a gain, to the extent that income per worker is now higher (remember that we are assuming a constant labour force), and this higher income will be received not just once, but every year from now on as long as the saving rate remains at the new higher level. There is no increase in the long-term *growth rate*, however. To achieve that, we would have to look to the other determinants of growth.

What should be clear from the above analysis is that, without technological progress or some other means of increasing output from a given quantity of inputs, long-term economic growth cannot be sustained.

Pause for thought

If there were a gradual increase in the saving rate over time, would this lead to sustained economic growth even without technological progress?

Human capital and education. The analysis of Figures 9.8 and 9.9 need not be confined to the stock of physical capital: machines, buildings, tools, etc. It can also apply to human capital. Human capital refers to the skills and expertise of workers that have been acquired through education and training. If part of saving is used for investment in education and training, then the productivity of workers will rise, and so will output.

In Figures 9.8 and 9.9, therefore, the horizontal axis measures both physical and human capital. An increase in either has the effect of increasing the steady-state level of national income. In Boxes 9.3 and 9.5 we consider both how physical capital and human capital respectively are treated in countries' national accounts and their rates of accumulation.

Technological progress

The effect of technological progress on output
Technological progress has the effect of increasing the output from a given amount of investment. This is shown in

Definition

Steady-state national income The long-run equilibrium level of national income. The level at which all investment is used to maintain the existing capital stock at its current level.

BOX 9.4   LABOUR PRODUCTIVITY

How effective is UK labour?

A country's potential output depends on the productivity of its factors of production, including labour.

There are two common ways of measuring labour productivity. The first is output per worker. This is the most straightforward measure to calculate. All that is required is a measure of total output and employment.

A second measure is output per hour worked. This has the advantage that it is not influenced by the *number* of hours worked. So for an economy like the UK, with a very high percentage of part-time workers on the one hand, and long average hours worked by full-time employees on the other, such a measure would be more accurate in gauging worker efficiency.

Both measures focus solely on the productivity of labour. If we want to account directly for the productivity of both labour *and* capital we need to consider the growth in *total* factor productivity (*TFP*). This measure analyses output relative to the amount of all factors used. Changes in total factor productivity over time provide a reasonable indicator of technical progress.

International comparisons of labour productivity

Charts (a) and (b) show comparative productivity levels of various countries and the G7 using GDP per hour worked. Chart (a) shows countries' productivity relative to the UK. As you can see, GDP per hour worked is lower in the UK than the other countries with the exception of Japan. For example, in 2014, compared with the UK, output per hour was 32 per cent higher in the USA and France and 33 per cent higher in Germany.

Compared with the rest of the G7 countries, UK output per hour was 20 per cent lower – the highest productivity gap since the series began in 1991. A major explanation of lower productivity in the UK is the fact that for decades it has invested a smaller proportion of its national income than most other industrialised nations. Nevertheless, until 2006 the gap had been narrowing with the rest of the G7. This was because UK productivity, although lower than in many other countries, was growing faster. This can be seen in Chart (b). Part of the reason for this was the inflow of investment from abroad.

Chart (c) compares labour productivity across both measures. Workers in the USA and the UK work longer hours than those in France and Germany. Thus whereas output *per hour worked* in the USA is on par with that in France and Germany, output *per person employed* in the USA is about 4 per cent higher than in France and 5 per cent higher than in Germany.

The evidence points to UK labour productivity being *lower* than that in the USA, France and Germany on both measures but higher than that in Japan. In understanding the growth in labour productivity it is generally agreed that we need to focus on three factors: physical capital (see Box 9.3), human capital (see Box 9.5), and innovation and technological progress. The significance of these for the UK productivity gap is considered further in Case Study 9.7 in MyEconLab.

1. *Identify some policies a government could pursue to stimulate labour productivity growth.*
2. *What could explain the differences in labour productivity between the five countries in Chart (c), and why do the differences vary according to which of the two measures is used?*

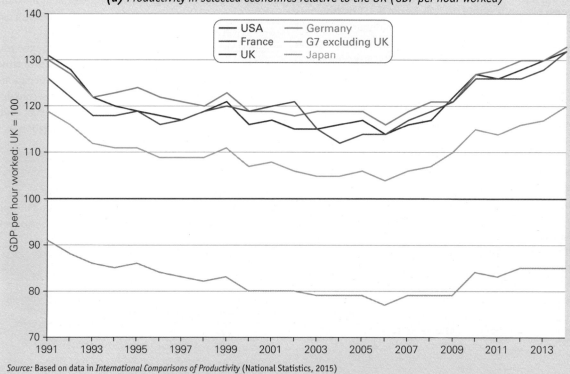

(a) Productivity in selected economies relative to the UK (GDP per hour worked)

Source: Based on data in *International Comparisons of Productivity* (National Statistics, 2015)

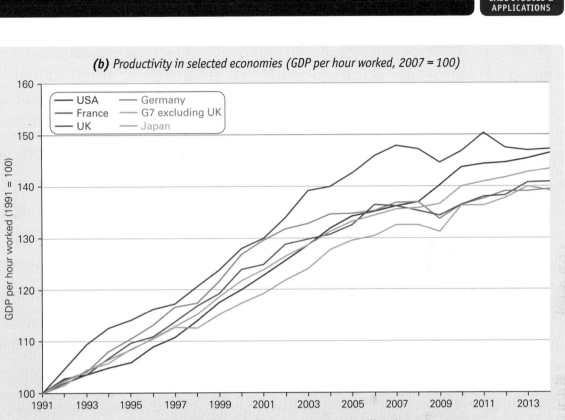

(b) *Productivity in selected economies (GDP per hour worked, 2007 = 100)*

Source: Based on data in *International Comparisons of Productivity* (National Statistics, 2015), rebased by authors

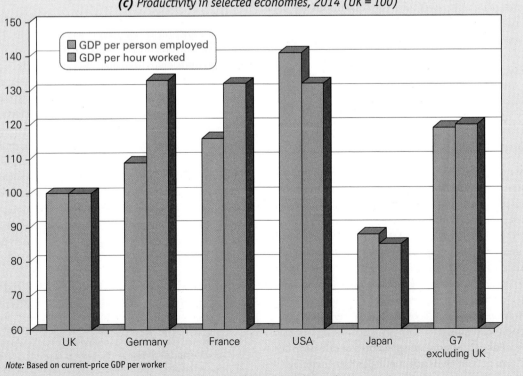

(c) *Productivity in selected economies, 2014 (UK = 100)*

Note: Based on current-price GDP per worker

Source: Based on data in *International Comparisons of Productivity* (National Statistics, 2015)

Figure 9.10   Effect of a technological advance

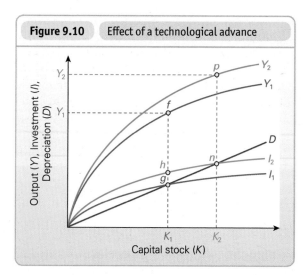

Figure 9.10. Initial investment and income curves are I_1 and Y_1; steady-state income is at a level of Y_1 (point f). A technological advance has the effect of shifting the Y line upwards, say to Y_2. The higher income curve leads to a higher investment curve (for a given rate of saving). This is shown by curve I_2. The new long-term equilibrium capital stock is thus K_2, and the new steady-state level of income is Y_2 (point p).

If there is a 'one-off' technological advance, the effect is the one we have just illustrated. National income rises to a higher level, but does not go on rising once the new steady-state level has been reached. But technological progress marches on over time. New inventions are made; new processes are discovered; old ones are improved. In terms of Figure 9.10, the Y curve *goes on* shifting upwards over time, as does the I curve too. The faster the rate of technological progress, the faster will the Y curve shift upwards and the higher will be the rate of economic growth.

Endogenous growth theory

TC 15
p 248
It should now be apparent that an increase in technological progress is essential if a country wants to achieve faster rates of growth in the long term. But is this purely in the lap of the scientists and engineers?

In the Solow growth model that we have been considering up to now, this is indeed the type of assumption made. In other words, technological progress is simply a 'given': it is exogenously determined. Thus whilst the neoclassical model identifies the importance of technological progress for enduring growth, it does not offer governments actual policy prescriptions.

So what can be done to speed up the rate of innovation? Can governments adopt policies that encourage scientific breakthroughs and technological developments? An **endogenous growth model** attempts to answer such

questions by incorporating technological advancement *within* the model.

Endogenous growth models stress the importance of research and development, education and training, and fostering innovation. As you can imagine, there is considerable interest and debate surrounding endogenous growth models, amongst not just academics, but policy makers too. Policy makers are clearly interested in pursuing policies that could make their country a world leader in innovation and technological advancement, especially if this helps to sustain higher long-run rates of economic growth, and so higher standards of living.

In such models, a major determinant of technological progress is the size and composition of the capital stock. As economies accumulate capital, they are likely to devote more resources to the development and maintenance of capital goods. In other words, they are likely to have a larger sector devoted to producing and developing capital goods. Therefore, the process of capital accumulation can raise the rate of technological progress and enable even further capital accumulation. A virtuous circle is created. Consequently, rather than looking at capital accumulation and technological progress as purely separate sources of long-term growth, the two are arguably interdependent.

Pause for thought

What is 'endogenous' about endogenous growth theory?

Investment in research and development can be encouraged through the use of patents and copyrights. These provide some protection to firms, enabling them to capture more of the benefits from their own ideas and thus providing them with an incentive to create and innovate. Furthermore, the striving for profit or the pursuit of competitive advantage over rivals, through either the design of innovative products and services or more cost-efficient production processes, are incentives that can drive this innovation and creativity.

But there are limits to the ability of firms to exclude other firms from prospering from their own ideas, such as the development of products, processes and people. The virtuous circle is thus reinforced by externalities: the spillover of ideas from one firm to another. New ideas cannot be put back into the metaphorical bottle once its lid is off.

Definition

Endogenous growth models Models where the rate of economic growth depends on the rate of technological progress and diffusion, both of which depend on size of the capital stock and the capital goods industries, and also on institutions, incentives and the role of government.

A model of endogenous technological progress

Endogenous growth models contain two key elements. The first is that technological progress is *dependent* on various economic factors such as the rate of investment in research and development. This could be included as an element in the investment (I) term, that is:

$$I = I_n + I_c$$

where I_n is investment in research and development of new technology (it could also include investment in training) and I_c is investment in capital that uses current technology. The greater the value of I_n/I_c, the faster will the Y curve (and I curve) shift upwards in Figure 9.8. Any policy, then, that increases the proportion of national income being devoted to R&D and training will increase the long-run rate of economic growth.

The second element is the responsiveness of national income to new technologies. This will depend in part on the extent to which innovations spill over to other firms, which duplicate or build on them, thereby adding to the increase in national income (ΔY). The greater the value of $\Delta Y/I_n$, the steeper will be the Y line in Figure 9.8 and the greater will be the rate of economic growth.

The values of I_n and $\Delta Y/I_n$ are thought to depend on structural and institutional factors within the economy and on the role of government. These include:

- Attitudes of businesses, such as their inclination to take risk.
- The willingness of financial institutions to lend to support investment opportunities.
- Tax incentives and government grants, for instance support for R&D.
- A research infrastructure (e.g. laboratories and the number and skills of researchers).
- The degree of competition within industries.
- The incentive to develop new products and services and/or to reduce costs.
- The magnitude of external spillovers from the generation of new products, processes and techniques.
- The stock of human capital.

> **Pause for thought**
>
> *List a series of factors that you think could influence the significance of spillovers from investment.*

As we have seen, endogenous growth models try to explain how the economy's production function shifts upwards over time. In some cases the production function may also become steeper – in other words, a given rise in the capital stock causes a larger rise in national income. The reason is that the benefits of the output from investment are not just captured by the firms doing the investing. Rather, some spill over to other firms. For example, firms may be able to duplicate or develop other firms' ideas. Consequently, these spillovers can positively impact on the overall marginal product of capital.

Policy implications

If there is a virtuous circle arising from firms investing and innovating, how are governments best placed to encourage it? Many economists argue that this requires supply-side policies – policies that impact directly on aggregate supply. Examples include policies to influence research and development, education and training, industrial organisation and work practices.

There is less agreement, however, as to whether these policies should focus on delivering market solutions or involve greater state intervention. We return to these themes in Section 12.4, which looks at a range of supply-side policies.

But encouraging investment does not just depend on effective supply-side policies. It also depends on the stability of the macroeconomic environment. It is not easy for businesses to plan ahead in times of great economic uncertainty. By contrast, the less the volatility in output (real GDP), the greater will be the confidence of business to innovate and invest. In Chapter 12, we also look at policies to stabilise aggregate demand: both fiscal and monetary policies.

As we saw earlier in the chapter, the idea that economic shocks can have persistent or enduring effects on the path of potential output has become a feature of many macroeconomic models. These shocks can originate from both the demand and supply sides. Either way, we need to understand the mechanisms by which such shocks are propagated and their significance for longer-term growth.

Some economists, however, argue that, given the inherent volatility of economies, governments should be more proactive. For instance, imperfections in the financial system which result in credit cycles can have a marked effect on flows of investment, including spending on research and development (see Section 9.4 for the financial accelerator and financial instability hypothesis). They argue that governments have a role to play in helping to stabilise aggregate demand so as to support and encourage firms to invest and increase potential output.

TC15 p 248

TC15 p 248

BOX 9.5　UK HUMAN CAPITAL

Estimating the capabilities of the labour force

The OECD (2001) defines human capital as the knowledge, skills, competencies and other attributes embodied in individuals or groups of individuals acquired during their life and used to produce goods, services or ideas in market circumstances.

In other words, human capital captures the capabilities embodied in people in the workforce that can affect both the nature and extent of production. While trends in human capital have implications for economic growth, there can be microeconomic effects too. For example, individuals with a lower stock of human capital may face a greater probability of unemployment or lower lifetime earnings. This has implications for inequality and social cohesiveness. But, how we do we go about measuring human capital?

Measuring human capital

In estimating an individual's human capital, a common approach is to estimate the present value of an individual's *remaining lifetime labour income*. This can be done for representative individuals in categories defined by gender, age and educational attainment. An assumption is then made about the working life of individuals. In compiling the UK estimates it is assumed that the remaining lifetime labour income of individuals aged 65 and over is zero. Then an approach known as *backwards recursion* is applied.

Backwards recursion involves first estimating the remaining lifetime labour income of someone aged 64 with a particular gender, age and educational level. The remaining lifetime income in this case is simply their current annual labour income for the year from their 64th birthday. For someone aged 63 it is their current annual labour income for the year from their 63rd birthday plus the present value[1] of the remaining lifetime income of someone aged 64 with the same gender, age and educational level. This continues back to someone aged 16. In calculating the remaining lifetime labour income of representative individuals, account is also taken of the probability that their level of education attainment may rise and, with it, their expected future earnings.

Further working assumptions are necessary to complete the calculations. Two of the most important are that: the rate of labour productivity growth is 2 per cent per annum and the discount rate is 3.5 per cent per annum, as recommended by HM Treasury's Green Book (2003) when undertaking appraisal and evaluation studies in central government.

Two measures of the stock of human capital are estimated. The first is for *employed* human capital. It is based on estimating the remaining lifetime labour income of those in employment. The second is *full* human capital. It includes the human capital of the unemployed. This assumes that the human capital of those currently unemployed should be valued at the remaining lifetime labour income of employed individuals with the same characteristics (gender, age and educational attainment). It ignores any so-called scarring effects from being unemployed, such as the depreciation of job-specific or transferable skills. Such effects are likely to increase the longer the duration of unemployment.

Estimates of human capital

The chart shows estimates of employed and full human capital in the UK since 2004. Both follow broadly similar patterns. Between 2004 and 2007, prior to the financial crisis, the stock of human capital increased steadily by a little over 2.5 per cent per annum. Employed human capital fell in each year from 2009 to 2013 and full human capital in each year from 2010 to 2013. The fall in full human capital has, however, been less pronounced because of the impact of rising unemployment on the employed human capital estimates.

In 2014, the UK's full human capital was £18.95 trillion while that for employed human capital was £18.22 trillion. This means that stock of human capital was between 10.2 and 10.6 times larger than annual GDP, depending on which measure of human capital is used. If we compare the figures for human capital with those for physical capital in Box 9.3, we can see that the estimated stock of human capital in the mid 2010s was about 4.5 times larger.

We can also analyse the *distribution* of human capital by a particular characteristic, such as educational attainment. In 2014 it is estimated that 36.1 per cent of UK employed human capital was embodied in the 27.0 per cent of the population who have a degree (or equivalent). In contrast, only 5.1 per cent of employed human capital was embodied in the 9.0 per cent of the working-age population with no formal qualifications.

Inequality and human capital

Research by the OECD and IMF[2] suggests that there is a correlation between inequality and human capital development and that this impacts on economic growth. Higher inequality reduces economic growth.

---

[1] 'Present value' in this case is the value in today's terms of income earned in the future. These incomes have to be reduced by the rate of interest that could have been earned if the income had been earned today instead of in the future. This process of reducing future incomes to present values is known as 'discounting'.

[2] 'See: *FOCUS on Inequality and Growth* (Directorate for Employment, Labour and Social Affairs, OECD, December 2014); and Jonathan D. Ostry, Andrew Berg, and Charalambos G. Tsangarides 'Redistribution, Inequality, and Growth', *IMF Staff Discussion Note* (IMF, February 2014).

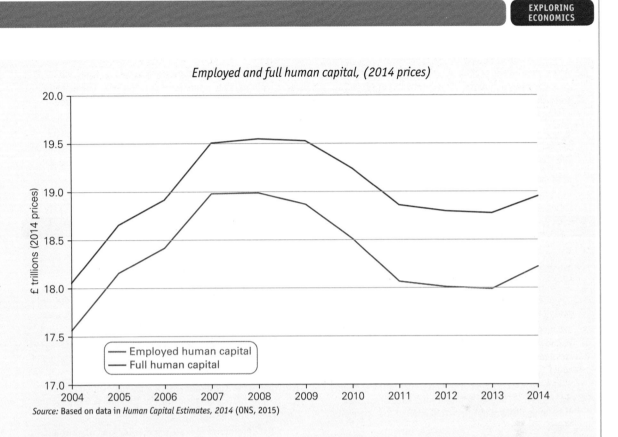

Employed and full human capital, (2014 prices)

Source: Based on data in *Human Capital Estimates, 2014* (ONS, 2015)

Traditionally it has been argued that there is a *trade-off* between inequality and economic growth: that higher inequality encourages economic growth. Increasing the rewards to those who are more productive or who invest, it is claimed, encourages a growth in productivity and capital investment, which, in turn, leads to faster economic growth. Redistribution from the rich to the poor, by contrast, is argued to reduce incentives by reducing the rewards from harder work, education, training and investment. Risk taking, it is claimed, is discouraged.

However, the OECD and IMF research suggests that when income inequality rises, economic growth falls. Inequality has grown massively in many countries, with average incomes at the top of the distribution seeing particular gains, while many at the bottom have experienced actual declines in real incomes or, at best, little or no growth. This growth in inequality, claims the OECD, has led to a loss in economic growth of around 0.35 percentage points per year over the past 25 years.

According to the OECD and IMF, inequality reduces the development of skills of the lower-income groups and reduces social mobility. The lower educational attainment applies both to the length and quality of education: people from poorer backgrounds tend to leave school or college earlier and with lower qualifications.

But if greater inequality generally results in lower economic growth, will a redistribution from rich to poor necessarily result in faster economic growth? Redistribution policies need to be well designed and implemented and focus on raising incomes of the poor through increased opportunities to increase their productivity. There needs to be increasing access to public services, such as high-quality education, training and health care. Simple transfers from rich to poor via the tax and benefits system may, in fact, undermine economic growth.

1. *In what ways might human capital and physical capital be complementary?*
2. *In what other ways could we consider the distribution of human capital?*

Recap

1. The determinants of economic growth in the long run lie primarily on the supply side. They can be put into two broad categories: an increase in the quantity of factors and an increase in the productivity of factors.

2. An increased saving rate will lead to higher investment and hence to an increase in the capital stock. This, in turn, will lead to a higher level of national income. A larger capital stock, however, will require a higher level of replacement investment. Once this has risen to absorb all the extra investment, national income will stop rising: growth will cease. An increased saving rate will therefore lead only to a rise in output, not to a long-term rise in the rate of growth.

3. A higher long-term rate of growth will normally require a faster rate of technological progress. Endogenous growth theories see capital accumulation and technological progress as interdependent sources of long-term growth. The rate of technological progress and its rate of diffusion depend on economic institutions and incentives. Supply-side policy could be used to alter these.

QUESTIONS

1. Why does the aggregate demand curve slope downwards? What factors would cause it to move to the left?

2. In what way will the nature of aggregate supply influence the effect of a change in aggregate demand on prices and real national income?

3. What shape do you think the aggregate supply curve would be at the current output if the economy was in a deep recession?

4. What shape of aggregate supply curve is assumed by the simple Keynesian demand-driven model of the economy introduced in Chapter 8? Under what circumstances is this shape likely to be a true reflection of the aggregate supply curve?

5. Referring to Figure 9.1, assume that the price level is currently above the equilibrium. Explain how the price level would return to its equilibrium level.

6. Why do cyclical swings seem much greater when we plot growth, rather than the level of output, on the vertical axis?

7. At what point of the business cycle is the country now? What do you predict will happen to growth over the next two years? On what basis do you make your prediction?

8. Why does investment in construction and producer goods industries tend to fluctuate more than investment in retailing and the service industries?

9. How can the interaction of the multiplier and accelerator explain cyclical fluctuations in national income? Why is it difficult to predict the size of the multiplier and accelerator?

10. Can governments induce cyclical fluctuations in national income? Can it ever be in the interests of governments to induce such volatility?

11. How regular are the cyclical patterns in real GDP during the course of a business cycle? In what ways could these patterns vary?

12. What do you understand by the concept of financialisation? Of what significance is this for our understanding of the determinants of the business cycle?

13. What are the determinants of long-run economic growth? Is long-run economic growth sustainable without technological progress?

14. What determines the rate of depreciation? What would happen if the rate of depreciation fell?

15. Explain the shapes of the I and Y curves in the Solow model of growth. What happens to these curves if the share of investment in national income rises?

16. What is the significance of the term 'endogenous' in endogenous growth theory? What, according to this theory, determines the long-run rate of economic growth?

17. What policy prescriptions do the neoclassical and endogenous growth theories offer policy makers looking to raise their country's long-run growth rate?

18. For what possible reasons may one country experience a persistently faster rate of economic growth than another?

19. What do the financial accelerator and the financial instability hypothesis imply about the determinants of longer-term rates of economic growth?

MyEconLab

This book can be supported by MyEconLab, which contains a range of additional resources, including an online homework and tutorial system designed to test and build your understanding.

You need both an access card and a course ID to access MyEconLab:

1. Is your lecturer using MyEconLab? Ask your lecturer for your course ID.

2. Has an access card been included with the book at a reduced cost? Check the inside back cover of the book.

3. If you have a course ID but no access card, go to: http://www.myeconlab.com/ to buy access to this interactive study programme.

ADDITIONAL CASE STUDIES IN THE *ESSENTIALS OF ECONOMICS* MyEconLab (www.pearsoned.co.uk/sloman)

9.1 **Introducing theories of economic growth.** An overview of classical and more modern theories of growth (a more detailed account of economic growth is given in Section 9.7).

9.2 **An international comparison of household wealth and indebtedness.** An examination of households' financial assets and liabilities relative to disposable income in seven developed countries (the G7).

9.3 **Business expectations and their effect on investment.** An examination of business surveys in Europe and the effects of business sentiment on investment.

9.4 **The multiplier/accelerator interaction.** A numerical example showing how the interaction of the multiplier and accelerator can cause cycles in economic activity.

9.5 **Has there been an accelerator effect since 1978?** An examination of the evidence for an accelerator effect in the UK.

9.6 **Modelling the financial accelerator.** This case looks at how we can incorporate the accelerator effect into the simple Keynesian model of the economy.

9.7 **The phases of the business cycle.** A demand-side analysis of the factors contributing to each of the four phases.

9.8 **Productivity performance and the UK economy.** A detailed examination of how the UK's productivity compares with that in other countries.

9.9 **The USA: is it a 'new economy'?** An examination of whether US productivity increases are likely to be sustained.

9.10 **Technology and economic change.** How to get the benefits from technological advance.

9.11 **UK industrial performance.** This examines why the UK has had a poorer investment record than many other industrial countries and why it has suffered a process of 'deindustrialisation'.

9.12 **The R&D Scoreboard.** An international comparison of spending by companies on research and development.

9.13 **The new economy.** Does globalisation bring economic success?

WEB APPENDIX

9.1 **Deriving a price index for the economy.** This explores how the process of chain linking is used to derive price indices for the components of aggregate demand and for the economy as a whole.

10

Banking, money and interest rates

In this chapter we are going to look at the important roles that money and the banking system play in the economy. Changes in the behaviour of financial institutions and in the amount of money can have a powerful effect on all the major macroeconomic indicators, such as inflation, unemployment, economic growth, exchange rates, the balance of payments and the financial well-being of different sectors of the economy, including financial institutions themselves. Furthermore, the financial crisis of the late 2000s has helped to demonstrate the systemic importance of financial institutions to the economy.

But why do changes in the money supply affect the economy? Well, the supply of money and the demand for money between them determine the *rate of interest*, and this has a crucial impact on aggregate demand and the performance of the economy generally. Furthermore, many aspects of economic activity are dependent on the availability of money.

The very first question addressed in this chapter is to define what is actually meant by money (not as easy as it may seem), and to examine its functions. Then in Sections 10.2 and 10.3 we look at the operation of the financial sector of the economy and its role in determining the supply of money. This sector has come in for considerable scrutiny in recent times, following the banking turmoil associated with the 'credit crunch' of 2007–9.

We then turn to look at the demand for money. Here we are not asking how much money people would like. The answer to that would probably be 'as much as possible'! What we are asking is: how much of people's assets do they want to hold in the form of money?

Then, in Section 10.5, we put supply and demand together to show how interest rates are determined, or how money supply must be manipulated to achieve a chosen rate of interest. We will see how changes in money supply and/or interest rates affect aggregate demand and the level of activity in the economy.

After studying this chapter, you should be able to answer the following questions:

- What are the functions of money?
- What determines the amount of money in the economy? What causes it to grow and what is the role of banks in this process?
- Why do central banks, such as the Bank of England and the European Central Bank, play a crucial role in the functioning of economies?
- What is the relationship between money and interest rates? What is the role of various financial institutions in this relationship?
- How will a change in the money supply affect the level of aggregate demand? How will this, in turn, affect the level of real GDP?

What is this thing called 'money'?

Before going any further we must define precisely what we mean by 'money' – not as easy a task as it sounds. Money is more than just notes and coin. In fact the main component of a country's money supply is not cash, but deposits in banks and other financial institutions. Only a very small proportion of these deposits are kept by the banks in their safes or tills in the form of cash. The bulk of the deposits appear merely as bookkeeping entries in the banks' accounts.

This may sound very worrying. Will a bank have enough cash to meet its customers' demands? The answer in the vast majority of cases is yes. Only a small fraction of a bank's total deposits will be withdrawn at any one time, and banks always seek to ensure that they have the ability to meet their customers' demands. The chances of banks running out of cash are very low indeed. The only circumstance where this could become possible is if people lost confidence in a bank and started to withdraw money in what is known as a 'run on the bank'. This happened with the Northern Rock Bank in September 2007. But in these circumstances the central bank or government would intervene to protect people's deposits by making more cash available to the bank or, in the last resort, by nationalising the bank (as happened with Northern Rock in February 2008).

What is more, the bulk of all but very small transactions are not conducted in cash at all. By the use of debit cards, credit cards and cheques, most money is simply transferred from the purchaser's to the seller's bank account without the need for first withdrawing it in cash.

What items should be included in the definition of money? To answer this we need to identify the *functions* of money.

The functions of money

The main purpose of money is for buying and selling goods, services and assets: i.e. as a medium of exchange. It also has two other important functions. Let us examine each in turn.

A medium of exchange

In a subsistence economy where individuals make their own clothes, grow their own food, provide their own entertainment, etc., people do not need money. If people want to exchange any goods, they will do so by barter. In other words, they will do swaps with other people.

The complexities of a modern developed economy, however, make barter totally impractical for most purposes (see Case Study 10.1 in MyEconLab). What is necessary is a **medium of exchange** that is generally acceptable as a means of payment for goods and services and as a means of payment for labour and other factor services. 'Money' is any such medium.

To be a suitable physical means of exchange, money must be light enough to carry around, must come in a number of denominations, large and small, and must not be easy to forge. Alternatively, money must be in a form that enables it to be transferred indirectly through some acceptable mechanism. For example, money in the form of bookkeeping entries in bank accounts can be transferred from one account to another by the use of mechanisms such as debit cards and direct debits.

A means of evaluation

Money allows the value of goods, services and assets to be compared. The value of goods is expressed in terms of prices, and prices are expressed in money terms. Money also allows dissimilar things, such as a person's wealth or a company's assets, to be added up. Similarly, a country's GDP is expressed in money terms. Money thus serves as a 'unit of account'.

A means of storing wealth

People need a means whereby the fruits of *today's* labour can be used to purchase goods and services in the *future*. People need to be able to store their wealth: they want a means of saving. Money is one such medium in which to hold wealth. It can be saved.

What should count as money?

What items, then, should be included in the definition of money? Unfortunately, there is no sharp borderline between money and non-money.

Cash (notes and coin) obviously counts as money. It readily meets all the functions of money. Goods (fridges, cars and cabbages) do not count as money. But what about various financial assets such as deposits in savings accounts and stocks and shares? Do they count as money? The answer is: it depends on how narrowly money is defined.

Countries thus use several different measures of money supply. All include cash, but they vary according to what additional items are included. To understand their significance and the ways in which money supply can be controlled, it is first necessary to look at the various types of account in which money can be held and at the various financial institutions involved.

Pause for thought

Why are debit cards not counted as money?

Definition

Medium of exchange Something that is acceptable in exchange for goods and services.

KI 31
p 205

KI 13
p 66

> **Recap**
>
> 1. Money's main function is as a medium of exchange. In addition, it is a means of evaluation and a means of storing wealth.
>
> 2. What counts as money depends on how narrowly it is defined. All definitions include cash, but they vary according to what other financial assets are included.

10.2 THE FINANCIAL SYSTEM

Where do banks and other financial institutions fit in?

In order to understand the role of the financial sector in determining the supply of money, it is important to distinguish different types of financial institution. Each type has a distinct part to play in determining the size of the money supply.

The key role of banks in the monetary system

By far the largest element of money supply is bank deposits. It is not surprising, then, that banks play an absolutely crucial role in the monetary system.

Banking can be divided into two main types: retail banking and wholesale banking. Most banks today conduct both types of business and are thus known as 'universal banks'.

Retail banking is the business conducted by the familiar high street banks, such as Barclays, HSBC, Lloyds, Royal Bank of Scotland, NatWest (part of the RBS group), Santander and TSB. They operate bank accounts for individuals and businesses, attracting deposits and granting loans at published rates of interest.

The other major type of banking is **wholesale banking**. This involves receiving large deposits from and making large loans to companies or other banks and financial institutions; these are known as wholesale deposits and loans. As far as companies are concerned, these may be for short periods of time to account for the non-matching of a firm's payments and receipts from its business. They may be for longer periods of time, for various investment purposes. Because wholesale deposits and loans often involve very large sums of money, banks compete against each other for them and negotiate individual terms with the firm to suit the firm's particular requirements.

In the past, there were many independent wholesale banks, known as investment banks. These included famous names such as Morgan Stanley, Rothschild, S G Hambros and Goldman Sachs. With the worldwide financial crisis of 2008, however, most of the independent investment banks merged with universal banks, which conduct both retail and wholesale activities.

The rise of large universal banks has caused concern, however. In the UK in 2010, the Coalition government set up the Independent Commission on Banking (ICB). It was charged with investigating the structure of the banking

system. It proposed *functional separation*: the ring-fencing of retail from wholesale banking. It was argued that, for the stability of the financial system, it was necessary to isolate the core activities of retail banks from the potential contagion from risky wholesale banking activities.

KI 13
p 66

The principal recommendations of the ICB were accepted and the Financial Services (Banking Reform) Act became law in December 2013. The Act defines core activities as facilities for accepting deposits, facilities for withdrawing money or making payments from deposit accounts and the provision of overdraft facilities. It gives regulators the power to exercise ring-fencing rules to ensure the effective provision of core activities. These include restricting the power of a ring-fenced body to enter into contracts and payments with other members of the banking group. The Act also gives the regulator restructuring powers so as to split banks up to safeguard their future.

Building societies. These are UK institutions that historically have specialised in granting loans (mortgages) for house purchase. But, like banks, they too are deposit-taking financial institutions and so compete for the deposits of the general public. In recent years, many building societies have converted to banks.

Banks and building societies are both examples of what are called **monetary financial institutions (MFIs)**. This term is used to describe all deposit-taking institutions which, as we will see later, also includes central banks (e.g. the Bank of England).

> **Definitions**
>
> **Retail banking** Branch, telephone, postal and Internet banking for individuals and businesses at published rates of interest and charges. Retail banking involves the operation of extensive branch networks.
>
> **Wholesale banking** Where banks deal in large-scale deposits and loans, mainly with companies and other banks and financial institutions. Interest rates and charges may be negotiable.
>
> **Monetary financial institutions (MFIs)** Deposit-taking financial institutions including banks, building societies and central banks.

| BOX 10.1 | FINANCIAL INTERMEDIATION | EXPLORING ECONOMICS |

What is it that banks do?

Banks and other financial institutions are known as *financial intermediaries*. They all have the common function of providing a link between those who wish to lend and those who wish to borrow. In other words, they act as the mechanism whereby the supply of funds is matched to the demand for funds. In this process, they provide five important services.

Expert advice

Financial intermediaries can advise their customers on financial matters: on the best way of investing their funds and on alternative ways of obtaining finance. This should help to encourage the flow of savings and the efficient use of them.

Expertise in channelling funds

Financial intermediaries have the specialist knowledge to be able to channel funds to those areas that yield the highest return. They also have the expertise to assess risks and to refuse loans for projects considered too risky or to charge a risk premium to others. This all encourages the flow of saving as it gives savers the confidence that their savings will be secure and earn a good rate of interest. Financial intermediaries also help to ensure that projects that are potentially profitable will be able to obtain finance. They help to increase allocative efficiency.

Maturity transformation

Many people and firms want to borrow money for long periods of time, and yet many depositors want to be able to withdraw their deposits on demand or at short notice. If people had to rely on borrowing directly from other people, there would be a problem here: the lenders would not be prepared to lend for a long enough period. If you had £100 000 of savings, would you be prepared to lend it to a friend to buy a flat if the friend was going to take 25 years to pay it back? Even if there was no risk whatsoever of your friend defaulting, most people would be totally unwilling to tie up their savings for so long.

This is where a bank or building society comes in. It borrows money from a vast number of small savers, who are able to withdraw their money on demand or at short notice. It then lends the money to house purchasers for a long period of time by granting mortgages (typically these are paid back over 20 to 30 years). This process whereby financial intermediaries lend for longer periods of time than they borrow is known as *maturity transformation*. They are able to do this because with a large number of depositors it is highly unlikely that they would all want to withdraw their deposits at the same time. On any one day, although some people will be withdrawing money, others will be making new deposits.

Risk transformation

You may be unwilling to lend money directly to another person in case they do not pay up. You are unwilling to take the risk. Financial intermediaries, however, by lending to large numbers of people, are willing to risk the odd case of default. They can absorb the loss because of the interest they earn on all the other loans. This spreading of risks is known as *risk transformation*. What is more, financial intermediaries may have the expertise to be able to assess just how risky a loan is.

Transmitting payments

In addition to channelling funds from depositors to borrowers, certain financial institutions have another important function. This is to provide a means of transmitting payments. Thus by the use of debit cards, credit cards, Internet and telephone banking, cheques, direct debits, etc., money can be transferred from one person or institution to another without having to rely on cash.

? *Which of the above are examples of economies of scale?*

Definitions

Financial intermediaries Financial institutions acting as a means of channelling funds from depositors to borrowers.

Maturity transformation The transformation of deposits into loans of a longer maturity.

Risk transformation The ability of financial institutions to spread risks by having a large number of clients.

Balance sheets

KI 31 p 205 Banks and building societies provide a range of **financial instruments**. These are financial claims, either by customers on the bank (e.g. deposits) or by the bank on its customers (e.g. loans). They are best understood by analysing the balance sheets of financial institutions, which itemise their liabilities and assets. A financial institution's liabilities are those financial instruments involving a financial claim on the financial institution itself. As we shall see, these are largely *deposits* by customers, such as current and savings accounts. Its assets are financial instruments involving a financial claim on a third party: these are *loans*, such as personal and business loans and mortgages.

The total liabilities and assets for UK MFIs are set out in the KI 31 p 205 balance sheet in Table 10.1. The aggregate size of the balance sheet in Spring 2015 was equivalent to around four times the UK's annual GDP. This is perhaps the simplest indicator of the significance of banks in modern economies, like the UK.

Both the *size* and *composition* of banks' balance sheets have become the focus of the international community's

Definition

Financial instruments Financial products resulting in a financial claim by one party over another.

| **Table 10.1** | Balance sheet of UK MFIs (end of April 2015) | | | | | | |

Sterling liabilities	£bn	%		Sterling assets	£bn	%
Sight deposits		42.9		Notes and coins	9.7	0.3
UK MFIs	126.4			Balances with UK central bank		9.4
UK public sector	15.3			Reserve balances	312.0	
UK private sector	1163.2			Cash ratio deposits	4.1	
Non-residents	144.0			Loans		11.0
Time deposits		31.2		UK MFIs	258.1	
UK MFIs	131.9			UK MFIs' CDs, etc.	4.5	
UK public sector	18.3			Non-residents	109.4	
UK private sector	708.7			Bills and acceptances	6.9	0.2
Non-residents	195.2			Reverse repos	261.1	7.7
Repos	250.9	7.4		Investments	438.8	13.0
CDs and other short-term papers	161.2	4.8		Advances	1901.2	56.3
Capital and other internal funds	414.0	12.3		Other assets	74.1	2.2
Other liabilities	45.7	1.4				
Total sterling liabilities	3374.8	100.0		**Total sterling assets**	3379.9	100.0
Foreign currency liabilities	3890.5			Total foreign currency assets	3885.4	
Total liabilities	7265.3			Total assets	7265.3	

Note: Data are not seasonally adjusted

Source: Based on data in *Bankstats* (*Monetary and Financial Statistics*), (Bank of England), June 2015

effort to ensure the stability of countries' financial systems. The growth of the aggregate balance sheet in the UK is considered in Box 10.2. But, it is to the composition of the balance sheet that we now turn.

Liabilities

Customers' deposits in banks and building societies are **liabilities** to these institutions. This means simply that the customers have the claim on these deposits and thus the institutions are liable to meet the claims.

There are four major types of deposit: sight deposits, time deposits, certificates of deposit and 'repos'.

Sight deposits. **Sight deposits** are any deposits that can be withdrawn on demand by the depositor without penalty. In the past, sight accounts did not pay interest. Today, however, there are many sight accounts that do. In fact, there is quite aggressive competition nowadays between banks to offer apparently very attractive interest rates on such accounts, although these are often on balances up to a relatively small amount.

The most familiar form of sight deposits are current accounts at banks. Depositors are issued with cheque books and/or debit cards (e.g. Visa debit or MasterCard's Maestro) that enable them to spend the money directly without first having to go to the bank and draw the money out in cash. In the case of debit cards, the person's account is electronically debited when the purchase is made and the card is 'swiped'

across the machine and the pin entered. This process is known as EFTPOS (electronic funds transfer at point of sale).

An important feature of current accounts is that banks often allow customers to be overdrawn. That is, they can draw on their account and make payments to other people in excess of the amount of money they have deposited.

Time deposits. **Time deposits** require notice of withdrawal. However, they normally pay a higher rate of interest than sight accounts. With some types of account, a depositor can withdraw a certain amount of money on demand, but there will be a penalty of so many days' lost interest. They are not cheque-book or debit-card accounts, although some allow customers to use cash cards. The most familiar form of time deposits are the deposit and savings accounts in banks and the various savings accounts in building societies. No overdraft facilities exist with time deposits.

A substantial proportion of time deposits are from the *banking sector*: i.e. other banks and other financial institutions. Interbank lending grew over the years up to 2008 as money markets were deregulated and as deposits increasingly moved from one currency to another to take advantage of different rates of interest between different countries. A large proportion of overseas deposits are from foreign banks.

Interbank lending virtually dried up in 2008–9, however. Banks became increasingly fearful that if they lent money to other banks, the other banks might default on payment. The reason was that many banks held assets based on mortgages granted to people unable to pay. As these assets fell in value, so banks became less and less able to raise enough money to pay back interbank loans.

Certificates of deposit. **Certificates of deposit (CDs)** are certificates issued by banks to customers (usually firms) for large deposits of a fixed term (e.g. £100 000 for 18 months). They can be sold by one customer to another, and thus provide a means whereby the holders can get money quickly if they need it without the *banks* that have issued the CD having to supply the money. (This makes them relatively 'liquid' to the depositor but 'illiquid' to the bank: we examine this below.) The use of CDs has grown rapidly in recent years. Their use by firms has meant that, at a wholesale level, sight accounts have become *less* popular.

Sale and repurchase agreements (repos). If banks have a temporary shortage of funds, they can sell some of their financial assets to other banks or to the central bank – the Bank of England in the UK and the European Central Bank in the eurozone (see below) – and later repurchase them on some agreed date, typically a fortnight later. These **sale and repurchase agreements (repos)** are in effect a form of loan – the bank borrowing for a period of time using some of its financial assets as the security for the loan. One of the major assets to use in this way are government bonds, normally called 'gilt-edged securities' or simply 'gilts' (see below). Sale and repurchase agreements involving gilts are known as *gilt repos*. Gilt repos play a vital role in the operation of monetary policy (see Section 12.2).

Capital and other funds. This consists largely of the share capital in banks. Since shareholders cannot take their money out of banks, it provides a source of funding to meet sudden increases in withdrawals from depositors and to cover bad debts. It is vital that banks have sufficient capital. As we shall see, an important part of the response to the financial crisis has been to require banks to hold relatively larger amounts of capital. At the end of 2008, the aggregate amount of sterling capital held by banks based in the UK was equivalent to 9.7 per cent of their sterling liabilities. By the end of 2014 this had risen to 13 per cent.

Assets

A bank's financial **assets** are its claims on others. There are three main categories of assets.

Cash and reserve balances in the central bank (Bank of England in the UK, ECB in the eurozone). Banks need to hold a certain amount of their assets as cash. This is largely used to meet the day-to-day demands of customers.

They also keep 'reserve balances' in the central bank. In the UK these earn interest at the Bank of England's repo rate (or 'Bank Rate' as it is called), if kept within an agreed target range. These are like the banks' own current accounts and are used for clearing purposes (i.e. for settling the day-to-day payments between banks). They can be withdrawn in cash on demand. With interbank lending being seen as too risky during the crisis of 2008, many banks resorted to depositing surplus cash in the Bank of England, even though the Bank Rate was lower than the interbank rate (known as 'LIBOR', which stands for the London Interbank Offered Rate).

In the UK, banks and building societies are also required to deposit a small fraction of their assets as 'cash ratio deposits' (CRDs) with the Bank of England. These cannot be drawn on demand and earn no interest. The Bank then invests these funds and the interest it earns helps to finance its operations to implement monetary policy and to ensure financial stability. As both this chapter and Chapter 12 detail, the financial crisis resulted in the Bank of England increasing the scale of its activities to ensure the stability of the financial system, including taking a greater supervisory role. Consequently, the size of CRDs was increased in 2013.

The increase in CRDs alongside an increase in reserve balances led to an increase in banks' cash and balances in the Bank of England. In 2015, they accounted for around 9 per cent of banks' sterling assets compared with just 4 per cent in 2010. Nonetheless, the vast majority of banks' assets remain in the form of various types of loan – to individuals and firms, to other financial institutions and to the government. These are 'assets' because they represent claims that the banks have on other people. Loans can be grouped into two types: short and long term.

Short-term loans. These are in the form of *market loans, bills of exchange* or *reverse repos*. The market for these various types of loan is known as the **money market**.

Definitions

Certificates of deposit (CDs) Certificates issued by banks for fixed-term interest-bearing deposits. They can be resold by the owner to another party.

Sale and repurchase agreements (repos) An agreement between two financial institutions whereby one in effect borrows from another by selling its assets, agreeing to buy them back (repurchase them) at a fixed price and on a fixed date.

Assets Possessions or claims held on others.

Money market The market for short-term loans and deposits.

BOX 10.2   **THE GROWTH OF BANKS' BALANCE SHEETS**

The rise of wholesale funding

Banks' traditional funding model relied heavily on deposits as the source of funds for loans. However, new ways for financial institutions to access funds to generate new loans evolved, especially in the years preceding the financial crisis of 2008. These reflected the deregulation of financial markets and the rapid pace of financial innovation.

Seeds of the crisis

Increasingly financial institutions made greater use of *wholesale funds*. These are funds obtained mainly from other

financial institutions. This coincided too with the emergence of a process known as *securitisation*. This involves the conversion of non-marketable banks' assets, such as residential mortgages, which have regular income streams (e.g. from payments of interest and capital), into assets that could be traded, known as 'tradable financial instruments'. These provide lenders who originate the loans with a source of funds for further loans. Therefore, securitisation became another means of obtaining funds from other financial institutions. Securitisation is discussed further in Box 10.3.

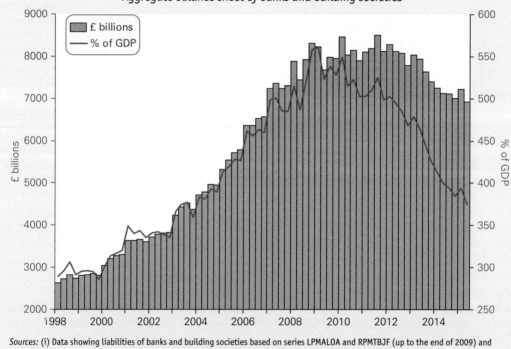

Aggregate balance sheet of banks and building societies

Sources: (i) Data showing liabilities of banks and building societies based on series LPMALOA and RPMTBJF (up to the end of 2009) and RPMB3UQ (from 2010) from *Statistical Interactive Database*, Bank of England (data published 2 June 2015, not seasonally adjusted). (ii) GDP data from series YBHA , Office for National Statistics (GDP figures are the sum of the latest four quarters)

- **Market loans** are made primarily to other banks or financial institutions. This interbank lending consists of (a) money lent 'at call' (i.e. reclaimable on demand or at 24 hours' notice); (b) money lent for periods up to one year, but typically a few weeks; (c) CDs (i.e. certificates of deposits made in other banks or building societies).
- **Bills of exchange** are loans either to companies (**commercial bills**) or to the government (**Treasury bills**). These are, in effect, an IOU, with the company issuing them (in the case of commercial bills), or the Bank of England on behalf of the government (in the case of Treasury bills), promising to pay the holder a specified sum on a particular date (the 'maturity date'), typically

Definitions

Market loans Short-term loans (e.g. money at call and short notice).

Bills of exchange Certificates promising to repay a stated amount on a certain date, typically three months from the issue of the bill. Bills pay no interest as such, but are sold at a discount and redeemed at face value, thereby earning a rate of discount for the purchaser.

Commercial bills Bills of exchange issued by firms.

Treasury bills Bills of exchange issued by the Bank of England on behalf of the government. They are a means whereby the government raises short-term finance.

KI 31
p 205

With an increasing use of money markets by financial institutions, vast sums of funds became available for lending. One consequence of this is illustrated in the chart: the expansion of the aggregate balance sheet. The balance sheet grew from £2½ trillion (3 times GDP) in 1998 to £8.5 trillion (5.6 times GDP) in 2010.

The growth in banks' balance sheets was accompanied by a change in their composition.

First, the profile of banks' assets became less liquid as they extended more long-term credit to households and firms. Assets generally became more risky too, as banks increasingly granted mortgages of 100 per cent or more of the value of houses – a problem for banks if house prices fell and they were forced to repossess.

Secondly, there was a general increase in the use of fixed-interest bonds as opposed to ordinary shares (equities) for raising capital. The ratio of bonds to equity capital is known as the *gearing (or leverage) ratio*. The increase in leverage meant that banks were operating with lower and lower levels of loss-absorbing capital, such as ordinary shares. If banks run at a loss, dividends on shares can be suspended; the payment of interest on fixed-interest bonds cannot. This meant that as the crisis unfolded, policy makers were facing a liquidity problem, not among one or two financial institutions, but across the financial system.

KI 20
p 129

The market failure we are describing is a form of *co-ordination failure* and is an example of the *'fallacy of composition'*. When one bank pursues increased earnings by borrowing from and lending to other financial institutions, this is not necessarily a problem. But, if many institutions build their balance sheets by borrowing from and lending to *each other*, then it becomes a problem for the whole financial system. The apparent increase in liquidity for individual banks, on which they base credit, is not an overall increase in liquidity for the financial system as a whole. The effect is to create a credit bubble.

KI 31
p 205

The dangers of the bubble for the financial system and beyond were magnified by the increasingly tangled web of interdependencies between financial institutions, both nationally and globally. There was a danger that this complexity was masking fundamental weaknesses of many financial institutions and too little overall liquidity.

The financial crisis

Things came to a head in 2007 and 2008. Once one or two financial institutions failed, such as Northern Rock in the UK in September 2007 and Lehman Brothers in the USA in September 2008, the worry was that failures would spread like a contagion. Banks could no longer rely on each other as their main source of liquidity.

The problems arising from the balance sheet expansion, increased leverage and a heightened level of maturity mismatch meant that central banks around the world, including the Bank of England, were faced with addressing a liquidity problem of huge proportions. They had to step in to supply central bank money to prevent a collapse of the banking system.

Subsequently, the international Basel Committee on Banking Supervision (see pages 269–72) agreed a set of measures, to be applied globally, designed to ensure the greater financial resilience of banks and banking systems. It is notable from the chart how the early 2010s saw a consolidation of the aggregate balance sheet of banks resident in the UK. By the end of the second quarter of 2015 the aggregate balance sheet stood at £6.9 trillion. This was equivalent to 3.7 times GDP, and comparable to levels seen back in 2004.

> **?** *Why do you think banks became reluctant to deposit moneys with other banks during the financial crisis of the late 2000s?*

Definition

Gearing or leverage (US term) The ratio of debt capital to equity capital: in other words, the ratio of borrowed capital (e.g. bonds) to shares.

---

three months later. Since bills do not pay interest, they are sold below their face value (at a 'discount') but redeemed on maturity at the face value. This enables the purchaser, in this case the bank, to earn a return. The market for new or existing bills is therefore as known as the **discount market**.

■ The price paid for bills will depend on demand and supply. For example, the more Treasury bills that are offered for sale (i.e. the higher the supply), the lower will be their equilibrium price, and hence the higher will be their rate of return (i.e. their rate of interest, or 'rate of discount').

■ **Reverse repos**. When a sale and repurchase agreement is made, the financial institution *purchasing* the assets (e.g. gilts) is, in effect, giving a short-term loan. The other party agrees to buy back the assets (i.e. pay back the loan) on a set date. The assets temporarily held by the bank making the loan are known as 'reverse repos'. Reverse repos are typically for one week, but can be for as little as overnight to as long as one year.

Definitions

Discount market An example of a money market in which new or existing bills are bought and sold.

Reverse repos Gilts or other assets that are purchased under a sale and repurchase agreement. They become an asset to the purchaser.

Longer-term loans. These consist primarily of loans to customers, both personal customers and businesses. These loans, also known as *advances*, are of four main types: fixed-term (repayable in instalments over a set number of years – typically, six months to five years), overdrafts (often for an unspecified term), outstanding balances on credit-card accounts and mortgages (typically for 25 years).

Investments. Banks also make investments. These are partly in government bonds (gilts), which are effectively loans to the government. The government sells bonds, which then pay a fixed sum each year as interest. Once issued, they can then be bought and sold on the stock exchange. Banks are normally only prepared to buy bonds that have less than five years to maturity (the date when the government redeems the bonds). Banks also invest in other financial institutions, including subsidiary financial institutions.

Taxing the banks

In January 2011, the UK introduced the bank levy: a tax on the liabilities of banks and building societies operating in the UK. The design of the levy built on proposals presented by the International Monetary Fund in June 2010. There were two key principles. First, the revenues raised should be able to meet the full fiscal costs of any future support for financial institutions. Secondly, it should provide banks with incentives to reduce risk-taking behaviour and so reduce the likelihood of future financial crises.

The UK bank levy has two rates: a full rate on taxable liabilities with a maturity of less than one year and a half rate on taxable liabilities with a maturity of more than one year. The intention is to discourage excessive short-term borrowing by the banks in their use of wholesale funding. The tax levy rates were intended to raise at least £2.5 billion each year. When introduced from January 2011 the full rate was set at 0.05 and the half rate at 0.025. However, rates were subsequently raised on several occasions. One reason behind this was that the shrinking balance sheets of MFIs (see Box 10.2) meant that revenues over the period 2011–12 to 2013–14 averaged only £2 billion each year. By April 2015 the full rate had risen to 0.21 per cent and the half rate to 0.105 per cent.

In designing the levy, policy makers excluded certain liabilities so as to discourage excessively risky lending and encourage banks to maintain sufficient funds to meet the demands of its depositors. For example, retail deposits insured by public schemes such as the UK's Financial Services Compensation Scheme are not subject to the levy. In trying to encourage small banks, the levy is not imposed on the first £20 billion of liabilities.

Unsurprisingly, the introduction of the levy drew some criticism from the banking sector, but this was to grow as levy rates were increased. In its Summer 2015 Budget, the new Conservative government announced significant changes to the way in which banks and building societies would be taxed. The changes looked to address the concerns from those that the existing arrangements were harming the ability of UK banks to support the macroeconomy and, in particular, to compete overseas.

The UK government announced a phased reduction in levy rates from January 2016, with the full rate due to fall to 0.1 per cent by January 2021. Additionally, for global banks with their headquarters in the UK, the bank levy would only be imposed on their UK balance sheet liabilities from January 2021 as opposed to their entire balance sheet.

Alongside the reduction in the levy rate a new tax on banks' profits (rather than liabilities) was introduced from January 2016. This was set at a rate of 8 per cent which is payable in addition to the tax on profits arising from UK corporation tax. The move means that more of the tax burden on banks is now aligned with their profitability. Nonetheless, this extra tax on banks' profits continues to recognise the particular risks that banks can pose for the macroeconomy.

Liquidity, profitability and capital adequacy

As we have seen, banks keep a range of liabilities and assets. The balance of items in this range is influenced by three important considerations: profitability, liquidity and capital adequacy.

Profitability

Profits are made by lending money out at a higher rate of interest than that paid to depositors. The average interest rate received by banks on their assets is greater than that paid by them on their liabilities.

Liquidity

The **liquidity** of an asset is the ease with which it can be converted into cash without loss. Cash itself, by definition, is perfectly liquid.

Some assets, such as money lent at call to other financial institutions, are highly liquid. Although not actually cash, these assets can be converted into cash virtually on demand with no financial penalty. Other short-term interbank lending is also very liquid. The only issue here is one of confidence that the money will actually be repaid. This was a worry in the financial crisis of 2008/9, when many banks stopped lending to each other on the interbank market for fear that the borrowing bank might become insolvent.

Other assets, such as gilts, can be converted into cash straight away by selling them on the stock exchange, but with the possibility of some financial loss, given that their market price fluctuates. Such assets, therefore, are not as liquid as money at call.

Other assets are much less liquid. Personal loans to the general public or mortgages can be redeemed by the bank

---

Definition

Liquidity The ease with which an asset can be converted into cash without loss.

only as each instalment is paid. This was why securitisation of mortgages became popular with banks as it effectively made their mortgage assets tradable and hence more liquid (see Boxes 10.2 and 10.3).

Banks must always be able to meet the demands of their customers for withdrawals of money. To do this, they must hold sufficient cash or other assets that can be readily turned into cash. In other words, banks must maintain sufficient liquidity.

The balance between profitability and liquidity

Profitability is the major aim of banks and most other financial institutions. However, the aims of profitability and liquidity tend to conflict. In general, the more liquid an asset, the less profitable it is, and vice versa. Personal and business loans to customers are profitable to banks, but highly illiquid. Cash is totally liquid, but earns no profit. Thus financial institutions like to hold a range of assets with varying degrees of liquidity and profitability.

For reasons of *profitability*, banks will want to 'borrow short' (at low rates of interest, such as on current accounts) and 'lend long' (at higher rates of interest, such as on personal loans). The difference in the average maturity of loans and deposits is known as the **maturity gap**. In general terms, the larger the maturity gap between loans and deposits, the greater the profitability. For reasons of *liquidity*, however, banks will want a relatively small gap: if there is a sudden withdrawal of deposits, banks will need to be able to call in enough loans.

The ratio of an institution's liquid assets to total assets (or liabilities) is known as its **liquidity ratio**. For example, if a bank had £100 million of assets, of which £10 million were liquid and £90 million were illiquid, the bank would have a 10 per cent liquidity ratio.

If a financial institution's liquidity ratio is too high, it will make too little profit. If the ratio is too low, there will be the risk that customers' demands may not be able to be met: this would cause a crisis of confidence and possible closure. Institutions thus have to make a judgement as to what liquidity ratio is best – one that is neither too high nor too low.

Balances in the central bank, short-term loans (i.e. those listed above) and government bonds with less than 12 months to maturity (and hence tradable now at near to their face value) would normally be regarded as liquid assets.

KI 13
p 66
Over the years, banks had reduced their liquidity ratios (i.e. the ratio of liquid assets to total assets). This was not a problem as long as banks could always finance lending to customers by borrowing on the interbank market. In 2008, however, banks became increasingly worried about bad debt. They thus felt the need to increase their liquidity ratios and hence cut back on lending and chose to keep a higher proportion of deposits in liquid form. In the UK, for example, banks substantially increased their level of reserves in the Bank of England.

Pause for thought

Why are government bonds that still have 11 months to run regarded as liquid, whereas overdrafts granted for a few weeks are not?

Capital adequacy

In addition to sufficient liquidity, banks must have sufficient capital (i.e. funds) to allow them to meet all demands from depositors and to cover losses if borrowers default on payment. Capital adequacy is a measure of a bank's capital relative to its assets, where the assets are weighted according to the degree of risk. The more risky the assets, the greater the amount of capital that will be required. **KI 13**
p 66

A measure of capital adequacy is given by the **capital adequacy ratio (CAR)**. This is given by the following formula:

$$CAR = \frac{\text{Common Equity Tier 1 capital } + \text{ Additional Tier 1 capital } + \text{ Tier 2 capital}}{\text{Risk-weighted assets}}$$

Common Equity Tier 1 (CET1) capital includes bank reserves (from retained profits) and ordinary share capital (equities), where dividends to shareholders vary with the amount of profit the bank makes. Such capital thus places no burden on banks in times of losses as no dividend need be paid. What is more, unlike depositors, shareholders cannot ask for their money back.

Additional Tier 1 (AT1) capital consists largely of preference shares. These pay a fixed dividend (like company bonds), but although preference shareholders have a prior claim over ordinary shareholders on company profits, dividends need not be paid in times of loss.

Tier 2 capital is subordinated debt with a maturity greater than five years. Subordinated debt holders only have a claim on a company after the claims of all other bond holders have been met.

Risk-weighted assets are the total value of assets, where each type of asset is multiplied by a risk factor. Under the internationally agreed Basel II accord, cash and government bonds have a risk factor of zero and are thus not included. Interbank lending between the major banks has a risk factor of 0.2 and is thus included at only 20 per cent of its value; residential mortgages have a risk factor of 0.35; personal loans, credit-card debt and overdrafts have a risk factor of 1;

Definitions

Maturity gap The difference in the average maturity of loans and deposits.

Liquidity ratio The proportion of a bank's total assets held in liquid form.

Capital adequacy ratio (CAR) The ratio of a bank's capital (reserves and shares) to its risk-weighted assets.

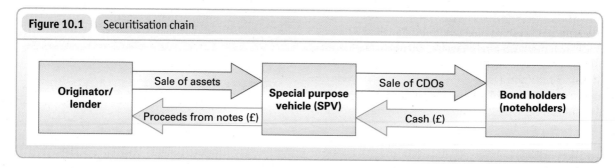

Figure 10.1 Securitisation chain

loans to companies carry a risk factor of 0.2, 0.5, 1 or 1.5, depending on the credit rating of the company. Thus the greater the average risk factor of a bank's assets, the greater will be the value of its risk-weighted assets, and the lower will be its CAR.

The greater the CAR, the greater the capital adequacy of a bank. Under Basel II, banks were required to have a CAR of at least 8 per cent (i.e. 0.08). They were also required to meet two supplementary CARs. First, banks needed to hold a ratio of Tier 1 capital to risk-weighted assets of at least 4 per cent and, secondly, a ratio of ordinary share capital to risk-weighted assets of at least 2 per cent. It was felt that these three ratios would provide banks with sufficient capital to meet the demands from depositors and to cover losses if borrowers defaulted. The financial crisis, however, meant a rethink (as we shall see below on pages 271–2).

Secondary marketing and securitisation

As we have seen, one way of reconciling the two conflicting aims of liquidity and profitability is for financial institutions to hold a mixture of liquid and illiquid assets. Another way is through the **secondary marketing** of assets. This is where holders of assets sell them to someone else before the maturity date. This allows banks to close the maturity gap for *liquidity* purposes, but maintain the gap for *profitability* purposes.

Certificates of deposit (CDs) are a good example of secondary marketing. CDs are issued for fixed-period deposits in a bank (e.g. one year) at an agreed interest rate. The bank does not have to repay the deposit until the year is up. CDs are thus illiquid liabilities for the bank, and they allow it to increase the proportion of illiquid assets without having a dangerously high maturity gap. But the holder of the CD in the meantime can sell it to someone else (through a broker). It is thus liquid to the holder. Because CDs are liquid to the holder, they can be issued at a relatively *low* rate of interest and thus allow the bank to increase its profitability.

Another example of secondary marketing is when a financial institution sells some of its assets to another financial institution. The advantage to the first institution is that it gains liquidity. The advantage to the second one is that it gains profitable assets. The most common method for the sale of assets has been through a process known as **securitisation**.

Securitisation occurs when a financial institution pools some of its assets, such as residential mortgages, and sells them to an intermediary known as a **special purpose vehicle (SPV)**. SPVs are legal entities created by the financial institution. In turn, the SPV funds its purchase of the assets by issuing bonds to investors (noteholders). These bonds are known as **collateralised debt obligations (CDOs)**. The sellers (e.g. banks) get cash now rather than having to wait and can use it to fund loans to customers. The buyers make a profit if the income yielded by the CDOs is as expected. Such bonds can be very risky, however, as the future cash flows may be *less* than anticipated.

The securitisation chain is illustrated in Figure 10.1. The financial institution looking to sell its assets is referred to as the 'originator' or the 'originator/lender'. Working from left to right, we see the originator/lender sells its assets to another financial institution, the SPV, which then bundles assets together into CDOs and sells them to investors (e.g. banks or pension funds) as bonds. Now, working from right to left, we see that by purchasing the bonds issued by the SPV, the investors provide the funds for the SPV's purchase of the lender's assets. The SPV is then able to use the proceeds from the bond sales (CDO proceeds) to provide the originator/lender with liquidity.

The effect of secondary marketing is to reduce the liquidity ratio that banks feel they need to keep. It has the effect of increasing their maturity gap.

Definitions

Secondary marketing Where assets are sold before maturity to another institution or individual.

Securitisation Where future cash flows (e.g. from interest rate or mortgage payments) are turned into marketable securities, such as bonds.

Special purpose vehicle (SPV) Legal entities created by financial institutions for conducting specific financial functions, such as bundling assets together into fixed-interest bonds and selling them.

Collateralised debt obligations (CDOs) These are a type of security consisting of a bundle of fixed-income assets, such as corporate bonds, mortgage debt and credit-card debt.

Dangers of secondary marketing. There are dangers to the banking system, however, from secondary marketing. To the extent that banks individually feel that they can operate with a lower liquidity ratio, so this will lead to a lower national liquidity ratio. This may lead to an excessive expansion of credit (illiquid assets) in times of economic boom.

Also, there is an increased danger of banking collapse. If one bank fails, this will have a knock-on effect on those banks which have purchased its assets. In the specific case of securitisation, the strength of the chain is potentially weakened if individual financial institutions move into riskier market segments, such as **sub-prime** residential mortgage markets. Should the income streams of the originator's assets dry up – for instance, if individuals default on their loans – then the impact is felt by the whole of the chain. In other words, institutions and investors are exposed to the risks of the originator's lending strategy.

The issue of securitisation and its impact on the liquidity of the financial system during the 2000s is considered in Box 10.3.

Strengthening international regulation of capital adequacy and liquidity

Capital adequacy

In the light of the financial crisis of 2008/9, international capital adequacy requirements were strengthened by the *Basel Committee on Banking Supervision* in 2010–11. The new 'Basel III' capital requirements, as they are called, will be phased in by 2019. They are summarised in Figure 10.2.

From 2013, banks continued to need a CAR of at least 8 per cent (i.e. 0.08). But, by 2015 were required to operate with a ratio of CET1 to risk-weighted assets of at least 4.5 per cent. The phased introduction of a *capital conservation buffer* from 2016 will raise the CET1 ratio to no less than 7 per cent by 2019. This will take the overall CAR to at least 10.5 per cent.

On top of this, national regulators will be required to assess the financial resilience across all financial institutions under its jurisdiction, particularly in light of economic conditions. This is **macro-prudential regulation**. If necessary, it will then apply a *counter-cyclical buffer* to all banks so increasing the CET1 ratio by up to a further 2.5 per cent. This will allow financial institutions to build up a capital buffer in boom times to allow it to be drawn on in times of recession or financial difficulty. It should also help to reduce the likelihood of financial institutions destabilising the economy by amplifying the business cycle.

Large global financial institutions, known as **global systemically important financial banks (G-SIBs)**, will be required to operate with a CET1 ratio of up to 2.5 per cent higher than other banks. The reason for this extra capital requirement is that the failure of such an institution could trigger a global financial crisis. This would potentially take the overall CAR for very large financial institutions in 2019 to 15.5 per cent (see Figure 10.2).

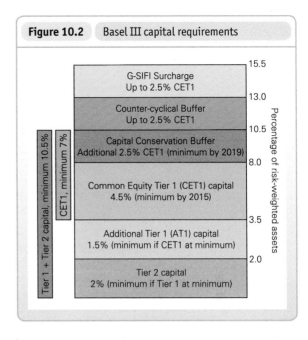

Figure 10.2 Basel III capital requirements

Liquidity

The financial crisis drew attention for the need of banks not only to hold adequate levels of capital but also to manage their liquidity better. The Basel III framework includes a *liquidity coverage ratio* (LCR). This requires that financial institutions have high-quality liquid assets (HQLAs) to cover the expected net cash flow over the next 30 days. Beginning in 2015, the minimum LCR ratio (HQLAs relative to the expected 30-day net cash flow) will rise from 60 per cent to 100 per cent by 2019.

Net stable funding ratio (NSFR)

As part of Basel III, it is intended to introduce a minimum *net stable funding ratio* (NSFR) by 2018. The NSFR is the ratio of stable liabilities to assets likely to require funding (i.e. assets where there is a likelihood of default or which could not be 'monetised' and thereby converted into money through their sale). The aim of having a minimum NSFR is to limit excessive risk from maturity transformation by taking a longer-term view of the funding profile of banks relative to their assets.

Definitions

Sub-prime debt Debt where there is a high risk of default by the borrower (e.g. mortgage holders who are on low incomes facing higher interest rates and falling house prices).

Macro-prudential regulation Regulation which focuses on the financial system as a whole and which monitors its impact on the wider economy.

Global systemically important banks (G-SIBs) Banks identified by a series of indicators as being significant players in the global financial system.

BOX 10.3 | THE RISE OF SECURITISATION

Spreading the risk or promoting a crisis?

The conflict between profitability and liquidity may have sown the seeds for the credit crunch that affected economies across the globe in the second half of the 2000s.

To understand this, consider the size of the 'advances' item in the banking sector's balance sheet – some 57 per cent of the value of sterling assets (see Table 10.1). The vast majority of these are to households. Advances secured against property have, in recent times, accounted for around 80 per cent by value of all household advances. *Residential mortgages* involve institutions lending long.

The number of UK residential mortgages has grown over time because of an increase in both the size of the housing stock and the proportion of households who are owner-occupiers. The number of households in the UK has increased from 19 million in 1971 to 27 million in 2014. Over the same period the owner-occupation rate has risen from 50 per cent to 64 per cent, though this is down from its peak of 70 per cent in 2002. The growth in the *value* of residential mortgages had been further fuelled by the long-term increase in house prices, including a period of strong and protracted growth between 1996 and 2008.

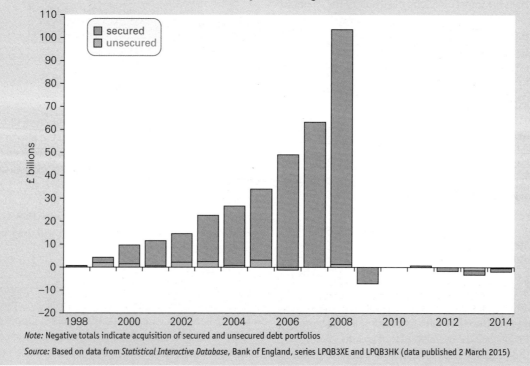

Net securitisations of MFI lending to individuals

Note: Negative totals indicate acquisition of secured and unsecured debt portfolios

Source: Based on data from *Statistical Interactive Database*, Bank of England, series LPQB3XE and LPQB3HK (data published 2 March 2015)

On the liabilities side, these will be weighted by their expected reliability – in other words, by the stability of these funds. This weighting will reflect the maturity of the liabilities and the likelihood of lenders withdrawing their funds. For example, Tier 1 and 2 capital will have a weighting of 100 per cent; term deposits with less than one year to maturity will have a weighting of 50 per cent; and unsecured wholesale funding will have a weighting of 0 per cent. The result of these weightings is a measure of stable funding.

On the assets side, these will be weighted by the likelihood that they will have to be funded over the course of one year. This means that they will be weighted by their liquidity, with more liquid assets requiring less funding.

Thus cash will have a zero weighting, while more risky assets will have weightings up to 100 per cent. The result is a measure of required funding.

Banks will need to hold a ratio of minimum stable liabilities to required funding (NSFR) of 100 per cent.

The central bank

The Bank of England is the UK's central bank. The European Central Bank (ECB) is the central bank for the countries using the euro. The Federal Reserve System (the Fed) is the USA's central bank. All countries with their own currency have a central bank and they fulfil two vital roles in the economy.

Securitisation of debt

One way in which individual institutions can achieve the necessary liquidity to expand the size of their mortgage lending (illiquid assets) is through *securitisation*. Securitisation grew especially rapidly in the UK and USA. In the UK this was particularly true amongst banks; building societies have historically made greater use of retail deposits to fund advances.

Figures from the Bank of England show that the value of lending to individuals which was securitised increased from just over £0.8 billion in 1998 to £103.7 billion in 2008 (see chart). As we can see from the chart, the majority of debt that has been securitised is secured debt: i.e. residential mortgages.

Securitisation is a form of financial engineering. It provides banks (originator/lenders) with liquidity and enables them to engage in further lending opportunities. It provides the special purpose vehicles with the opportunity to issue profitable securities.

The increase in securitisation up to 2008 highlights the strong demand amongst investors for these securities or 'collateralised debt obligations' (CDOs). The attraction of these fixed-income products for the noteholders was the potential for higher returns than on (what were) similarly rated products. However, investors have no recourse should people with mortgages fall into arrears or, worse still, default on their mortgages.

Risks and the sub-prime market

The securitisation of assets is not without risks for all those in the securitisation chain and consequently for the financial system as a whole.

The pooling of advances in itself *reduces* the cash-flow risk facing investors. However, there is a *moral hazard* problem here (see page 67). The pooling of the risks may encourage originator/lenders to lower their credit criteria by offering higher-income multiples (advances relative to annual household incomes) or higher loan-to-value ratios (advances relative to the price of housing).

Towards the end of 2006 the USA witnessed an increase in the number of defaults by households on residential mortgages. This was a particular problem in the sub-prime market – higher-risk households with poor credit ratings. Similarly, the number falling behind with their payments rose. This was on the back of rising interest rates.

These problems in the US sub-prime market were the catalyst for the liquidity problem that beset financial systems in 2007 and 2008. Where these assets were securitised, investors, largely other financial institutions, suffered from the contagion arising from arrears and defaults.

Securitisation also internationalised the contagion. Investors are global so that advances, such as a US family's residential mortgage, can cross national borders. This resulted in institutions writing off debts, a deterioration of their balance sheets, the collapse in the demand for securitised assets and the drying up of liquidity.

The chart shows the collapse of the market for securitised assets. The period from 2009 to 2014 was characterised by banks *buying back* CDOs from SPVs, including unsold ones.

? *Does securitisation necessarily involve a moral hazard problem?*

Definition

Moral hazard The temptation to take more risks when you know that someone else will cover the risks if you get into difficulties. In the case of banks taking risks, the 'someone else' may be another bank, the central bank or the government.

The first is to oversee the whole monetary system and ensure that banks and other financial institutions operate as stably and as efficiently as possible.

The second is to act as the government's agent, both as its banker and in carrying out monetary policy. The Bank of England traditionally worked in very close liaison with the Treasury, and there used to be regular meetings between the Governor of the Bank of England and the Chancellor of the Exchequer. Although the Bank may have disagreed with Treasury policy, it always carried it out. With the election of the Labour government in 1997, however, the Bank of England was given independence to decide the course of monetary policy. In particular, this meant that the Bank of England and not the government would now decide interest rates.

Another example of an independent central bank is the European Central Bank, which operates the monetary policy for the eurozone countries. Similarly, the Fed is independent of both the President and Congress, and its chairman is generally regarded as having great power in determining the country's economic policy. Although the degree of independence of central banks from government varies considerably around the world, there has been a general move in recent years to make central banks more independent.

If the UK were ever to adopt the euro, there would be a much reduced role for the Bank of England. At present, however, within its two broad roles, it has a number of different functions. Although we will consider the case of the Bank of England, the same principles apply to other central banks.

It issues notes

The Bank of England is the sole issuer of banknotes in England and Wales (in Scotland and Northern Ireland, retail banks issue banknotes). The amount of banknotes issued by the Bank of England depends largely on the demand for notes from the general public. If people draw more cash from their bank accounts, the banks will have to draw more cash from their balances in the Bank of England.

It acts as a bank

To the government. It keeps the two major government accounts: the 'Exchequer' and the 'National Loans Fund'. Taxation and government spending pass through the Exchequer. Government borrowing and lending pass through the National Loans Fund. The government tends to keep its deposits in the Bank of England to a minimum. If the deposits begin to build up (from taxation), the government will probably spend them on paying back government debt. If, on the other hand, it runs short of money, it will simply borrow more.

To banks. Banks' deposits in the Bank of England consist of reserve balances and cash ratio deposits (see Table 10.1). The reserve balances are used for clearing purposes between the banks, but are also a means by which banks can manage their liquidity risk. Therefore, the reserve balances provide banks with an important buffer stock of liquid assets.

To overseas central banks. Overseas central banks keep deposits of sterling (or euros in the case of the ECB) as part of their official reserves and/or for purposes of intervening in the foreign exchange market in order to influence the exchange rate of their currency. We will examine exchange rates in Chapter 12.

It operates the government's monetary policy

Monetary policy. The Bank of England's Monetary Policy Committee (MPC) sets the Bank Rate at its regular meetings. This nine-member committee consists of four experts appointed by the Chancellor of the Exchequer and four senior members of the Bank of England, plus the Governor in the chair.

By careful management of the liquidity of the financial system the Bank of England aims to keep market interest rates in line with Bank Rate. It is able to do this through operations in the money markets. These are known as **open-market operations (OMOs)**. If shortages of liquidity are driving up short-term interest rates above the desired level, the Bank of England purchases securities (gilts and/ or Treasury bills) on the open market: e.g. through reverse repos (a repo to the banks). This releases liquidity into the financial system and puts downward pressure on interest rates. Conversely, if excess liquidity is driving down interest rates, the Bank of England will sell more securities. When these are purchased, this will reduce banks' reserves and thereby put upward pressure on interest rates.

As the financial crisis unfolded it became increasingly difficult for the Bank to meet its monetary policy objectives while maintaining financial stability. New policies were thus adopted. October 2008 also saw the Bank of England stop short-term open-market operations. The key priority was now ensuring sufficient liquidity and so the focus switched to longer-term OMOs.

March 2009 saw the Bank begin a programme of **quantitative easing (QE)** (see Box 12.5). The aim was to increase the amount of money in the financial system and thereby stimulate bank lending and hence aggregate demand. QE involved the Bank creating electronic money and using it to purchase assets, mainly government bonds, predominantly from non-deposit-taking financial institutions, such as unit trusts, insurance companies and pension funds. These institutions would then deposit the money in banks, which could lend it to businesses and consumers for purposes of spending.

It provides liquidity, as necessary, to banks

Financial institutions engage in maturity transformation. While most customer deposits can be withdrawn instantly, financial institutions will have a variety of lending commitments, some of which span many years. Hence, the Bank of England acts as a 'liquidity backstop' for the banking system. It attempts to ensure that there is always an adequate supply of liquidity to meet the legitimate demands of depositors in banks.

Banks' reserve balances provide them with some liquidity insurance. However, the Bank of England needs other means by which to provide both individual banks and the banking system with sufficient liquidity. The financial crisis, for instance, saw incredible pressure on the aggregate liquidity of financial system. The result is that the UK has three principal insurance facilities.

Definitions

Open-market operations The sale (or purchase) of government securities in the open market which aim to reduce (or increase) the money supply and thereby affect interest rates.

Quantitative easing (QE) When the central bank increases the monetary base through an open market purchase of government bonds or other securities. It uses electronic money (reserve liabilities) created specifically for this purpose.

Index long-term repos (ILTRS). Each month the Bank of England provides MFIs with reserves for a six-month period secured against collateral and indexed against the Bank Rate. Financial institutions can borrow reserves against different levels of collateral. These levels reflect the quality and liquidity of the collateral. The reserves are distributed through an auction where financial institutions indicate, for their particular level of collateral, the number of basis points over the Bank Rate (the 'spread') they are prepared to pay. The resulting equilibrium interest rate, paid by all those borrowing, is that which balances the demand from MFIs with the supply of reserves made available. The Bank of England may subsequently provide a greater quantity of reserves if, from the bids, it observes a greater demand for it to provide liquidity insurance.

Discount window facility (DWF). This on-demand facility allows financial institutions to borrow government bonds (gilts) for 30 days against different classes of (less liquid) collateral. They pay a fee to do so. The size of the fee is determined by both the type and quantity of collateral being traded. The gilts can then be used in repo operations as a means of securing liquidity. Financial institutions can look to roll over the gilts obtained from the DWF beyond the normal 30 days if they are still short of liquidity.

Contingent term repo facility (CTRF). This is a facility which the Bank of England can activate in exceptional circumstances. As with the ILTRS, financial institutions can obtain liquidity secured against different levels of collateral through an auction. However, the terms, including the maturity of the funds, are intended to be more flexible.

It oversees the activities of banks and other financial institutions

The Bank of England requires all recognised banks to maintain adequate liquidity: this is called **prudential control**.

In May 1997, the Bank of England ceased to be responsible for the detailed supervision of banks' activities. This responsibility passed to the Financial Services Authority (FSA). But, the financial crisis of the late 2000s raised concerns about whether the FSA, the Bank of England and HM Treasury were sufficiently watchful of banks' liquidity and the risks of liquidity shortage. Some commentators argued that a much tighter form of prudential control should have been imposed.

The early 2010s saw the implementation of a new regulatory framework with an enhanced role for the Bank of England.

First, the Bank's *Financial Policy Committee (FPC)* was made responsible for *macro-prudential regulation*: i.e. regulation which takes a broader view of the financial system. It considers, for instance, the resilience of the financial system to possible shocks and its propensity to create macro-economic instability through excessive credit creation.

Secondly, the prudential regulation of individual firms was transferred from the FSA to the *Prudential Regulation Authority (PRA)*, a subsidiary of the Bank of England.

Meanwhile, the *Financial Conduct Authority (FCA)* took responsibility for consumer protection and the regulation of markets for financial services. The FCA is an independent body accountable to HM Treasury. The FSA was wound up.

It operates the government's exchange rate policy

The Bank of England manages the country's gold and foreign currency reserves on behalf of the Treasury. This is done through the **exchange equalisation account**. As we shall see in Chapter 14, by buying and selling foreign currencies on the foreign exchange market, the Bank of England can affect the exchange rate.

Pause for thought

1. Would it be possible for an economy to function without a central bank?
2. What effect would a substantial increase in the sale of government bonds and Treasury bills have on interest rates?

The role of the money markets

Money markets enable participants, such as banks, to lend to and borrow from each other. The financial instruments traded are short-term ones. As we have seen, central banks use money markets to exercise control over interest rates. But, they are very important too in widening the lending and borrowing opportunities for financial institutions.

We take the case of the London money market, which is normally divided into the 'discount' and 'repo' markets and the 'parallel' or 'complementary' market.

The discount and repo markets

The discount market. The **discount market** is the market for commercial or government bills. In the UK government bills are known as Treasury bills and operations are conducted by the Debt Management Office, usually on a weekly basis. Treasury bills involve short-term lending, say for one or three months, which, in conjunction with their low default risk, make them highly liquid assets. The term 'discount market' is used because the bills being traded are issued at a price below their face value: i.e. at a discount. On maturity the holder is paid the full face

---

Definitions

Prudential control The insistence by the Bank of England that banks maintain adequate liquidity.

Exchange equalisation account The gold and foreign exchange reserves account in the Bank of England.

Discount market The market for corporate bills and Treasury bills whose initial price is below the redemption value.

value and thus earns the difference between that and the discounted purchase price. The *rate* of discount on bills can be calculated by the size of the discount relative to the redemption value and is usually expressed as an annual percentage rate.

The discount market is also known as the 'traditional market' because it was the market in which many central banks traditionally used to supply central bank money to financial institutions. For instance, if the Bank of England wanted to increase liquidity in the banking system it could purchase from the banks Treasury bills which had yet to reach maturity. This process is known as **rediscounting**. The Bank of England would pay a price below the face value, thus effectively charging interest to the banks. The price could be set so that the 'rediscount rate' reflected the Bank Rate.

The repo market. The emergence of the repo market is a more recent development dating back in the UK to the 1990s. As we saw earlier, repos have become an important potential source of wholesale funding for financial institutions. But they are also an important means by which central banks can affect the liquidity of the financial system, not only to implement monetary policy but also to ensure financial stability.

By entering into a repo agreement the Bank of England can buy securities, such as gilts, from the banks (thereby supplying them with money) on the condition that the banks buy them back at a fixed price and on a fixed date. The repurchase price will be above the sale price. The difference is the equivalent of the interest that the banks are being charged for having what amounts to a loan from the Bank of England. The repurchase price (and hence the 'repo rate') is set by the Bank of England to reflect the Bank Rate chosen by the MPC.

The Bank of England first began using repo operations to manage the liquidity of the financial system in 1997 when it undertook daily operations, with the repurchases of securities usually occurring two weeks after the initial sale. This system was refined so that in 2006 operations became weekly and the repurchase period typically shortened to one week.

However, the financial crisis caused the Bank to modify its repo operations to manage liquidity for both purposes of monetary policy and increasingly to ensure financial stability. These changes included a widening of the securities eligible as collateral for loans and, as we saw above, a consequent suspension of short-term repo operations.

So central banks, like the Bank of England, are prepared to provide central bank money through the creation of reserves. Central banks are thus the ultimate guarantor of sufficient liquidity in the monetary system and, for this reason, are known as the **lender of last resort**.

As a means of supplying liquidity to troubled banks in various eurozone countries, the ECB in late 2011 and into 2012 issued a large amount of three-year repo loans

(just over €1 trillion). These long-term repo operations, or LTROs, were seen as vital for staving off a liquidity crisis and potential collapse of certain banks struggling with bad debts.

The parallel money markets

Like repo markets, complementary or parallel money markets have grown rapidly in recent years. In part, this reflects the opening up of markets to international dealing, the deregulation of banking and money market dealing, and the desire of banks to keep funds in a form that can be readily switched from one form of deposit to another, or from one currency to another.

Examples of parallel markets include the markets for certificates of deposit (CDs), foreign currencies markets (dealings in foreign currencies deposited short term in the country) and the interbank market. We focus here on the important interbank market (details on other parallel markets can be found in Case Study 10.10 in MyEconLab).

The interbank market. This involves wholesale loans from one bank to another from one day to up to several months. Banks with surplus liquidity lend to other banks, which then use this as the basis for loans to individuals and companies. The rate at which banks lend to each other is known as the IBOR (interbank offered rate). The IBOR has a major influence on the other rates that banks charge. In the eurozone, the IBOR is known as Euribor. In the UK, it is known as the LIBOR (where 'L' stands for 'London'). As interbank loans can be anything from overnight to 12 months, the IBOR will vary from one length of loan to another.

Interbank interest rates tend to be higher than those in the discount and repo markets and sensitive to the aggregate level of liquidity in the financial system.

As Figure 10.3 shows, during the financial crisis of 2008 interbank lending rates rose significantly above the Bank Rate. At the same time lending virtually ceased as banks became worried that the bank they were lending to might default.

> ### Pause for thought
>
> *Why should Bank of England determination of the rate of interest in the discount and repo markets also influence rates of interest in the parallel markets?*

> ### Definitions
>
> **Rediscounting bills of exchange** Buying bills before they reach maturity.
>
> **Lender of last resort** The role of the Bank of England as the guarantor of sufficient liquidity in the monetary system.

Figure 10.3 One–month LIBOR and Bank Rate

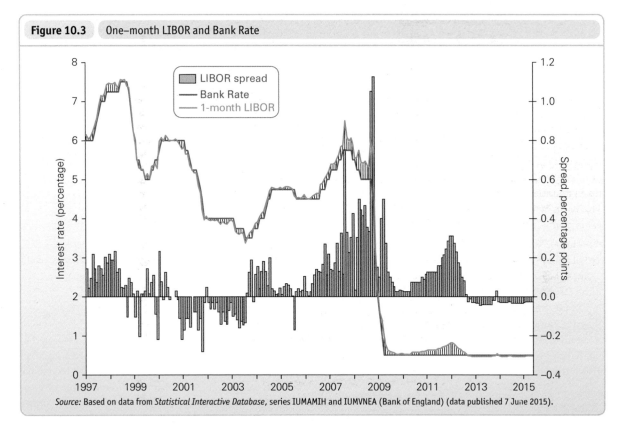

Source: Based on data from *Statistical Interactive Database*, series IUMAMIH and IUMVNEA (Bank of England) (data published 7 June 2015).

Recap

1. Central to the financial system are the retail and wholesale arms of banks. Between them they provide the following important functions: giving expert advice, channelling capital to areas of highest return, maturity transformation, risk transformation and the transmission of payments. Some of these banks had to be rescued by the government in 2008 – they were too important to the health of the economy to allow them to fail.

2. Banks' liabilities include both sight and time deposits. They also include certificates of deposit and repos. Their assets include: notes and coin, balances with the central bank, market loans, bills of exchange (Treasury bills and commercial bills), reverse repos, advances to customers (the biggest item – including overdrafts, personal loans, credit-card debt and mortgages) and investments (government bonds and interbank investments). In the years up to 2008 they had increasingly included securitised assets.

3. Banks aim to make profits, but they must also have a sufficient capital base and maintain sufficient liquidity. Liquid assets, however, tend to be relatively unprofitable and profitable assets tend to be relatively illiquid. Banks therefore need to keep a balance of profitability and liquidity in their range of assets.

4. The Bank of England is the UK's central bank. It issues notes; it acts as banker to the government, to banks and to various overseas central banks; it oversees the activities of banks and other financial institutions; it ensures sufficient liquidity for the financial sector; it operates the country's monetary and exchange rate policy.

5. The money market is the market in short-term deposits and loans. It consists of the discount and repo markets and the parallel money markets.

6. Through repos the Bank of England provides liquidity to the banks at the rate of interest chosen by the Monetary Policy Committee (Bank Rate). It is always prepared to lend in this way in order to ensure adequate liquidity in the economy. The financial crisis saw the Bank of England adapt its operations in the money market and introduce new mechanisms for providing liquidity insurance, including the Discount Window Facility and longer-term repos.

7. The parallel money markets consist of various markets in short-term finance between various financial institutions.

10.3 THE SUPPLY OF MONEY

How is it measured and what determines its size?

If money supply is to be monitored and possibly controlled, it is obviously necessary to measure it. But what should be included in the measure? Here we need to distinguish between the *monetary base* and *broad money*.

The **monetary base** (or 'high-powered money' or 'narrow money') consists of cash (notes and coin) in circulation outside the central bank.[1] In 1970, the stock of notes and coins in circulation in the UK was around £4 billion, equivalent to 7 per cent of annual GDP. By 2014 this had grown to around £70 billion, but equivalent to only about 4 per cent of annual GDP.

But the monetary base gives us a very poor indication of the effective money supply, since it excludes the most important source of liquidity for spending: namely, bank deposits – and most spending from these deposits is not by cash, but by debit card, direct debit, cheques, etc. The problem, however, is which deposits to include. We need to answer three questions:

- Should we include just sight deposits, or time deposits as well?
- Should we include just retail deposits, or wholesale deposits as well?
- Should we include just bank deposits, or building society (savings institution) deposits as well?

In the past there has been a whole range of measures, each including different combinations of these accounts. However, financial deregulation, the abolition of foreign exchange controls and the development of computer technology have led to huge changes in the financial sector throughout the world. This has led to a blurring of the distinctions between different types of account. It has also made it very easy to switch deposits from one type of account to another. For these reasons, the most usual measure that countries use for money supply is **broad money**, which in most cases includes both time and sight deposits, retail and wholesale deposits, and bank and building society (savings institution) deposits.

In the UK this measure of broad money is known as M4. In most other European countries and the USA, it is known as M3. There are, however, minor differences between countries in what is included.

In 1970, the stock of M4 in the UK was around £26 billion, equivalent to 50 per cent of annual GDP. By 2014 this had grown to £2.1 trillion, equivalent to about 120 per cent of annual GDP.

As we have seen, bank deposits of one form or another constitute by far the largest component of (broad) money supply. To understand how money supply expands and contracts, and how it can be controlled, it is thus necessary to understand what determines the size of bank deposits. Banks can themselves expand the amount of bank deposits, and hence the money supply, by a process known as 'credit creation'.

The creation of credit

To illustrate this process in its simplest form, assume that banks have just one type of liability – deposits – and two types of asset – balances with the central bank (to achieve liquidity) and advances to customers (to earn profit).

Banks want to achieve profitability while maintaining sufficient liquidity. Assume that they believe that sufficient liquidity will be achieved if 10 per cent of their assets are held as balances with the central bank. The remaining 90 per cent will then be in advances to customers. In other words, the banks operate a 10 per cent liquidity ratio.

Assume initially that the combined balance sheet of the banks is as shown in Table 10.2. Total deposits are £100 billion, of which £10 billion (10 per cent) are kept in balances with the central bank. The remaining £90 billion (90 per cent) are lent to customers.

Now assume that the government spends more money – £10 billion, say, on roads or education. It pays for this with cheques drawn on its account with the central bank. The

Table 10.2	Banks' original balance sheet		
Liabilities	**£bn**	**Assets**	**£bn**
Deposits	100	Balances with the central bank	10
		Advances	90
Total	100	Total	100

---

[1] Before 2006, there used to be a measure of narrow money called 'M0'. This included cash in circulation outside the Bank of England and banks' non-interest-bearing 'operational balances' in the Bank of England, with these balances accounting for a tiny proportion of the whole. Since 2006, the Bank of England has allowed banks to hold interest-bearing reserve accounts, which are much larger than the former operational balances. The Bank of England thus decided to discontinue M0 as a measure and focus on cash in circulation as its measure of the monetary base.

Definitions

Monetary base Notes and coin outside the central bank.

Broad money Cash in circulation plus retail and wholesale bank and building society deposits.

people receiving the cheques deposit them in their banks. Banks return these cheques to the central bank and their balances correspondingly increase by £10 billion. The combined banks' balance sheet now is shown in Table 10.3.

But this is not the end of the story. Banks now have surplus liquidity. With their balances in the central bank having increased to £20 billion, they now have a liquidity ratio of 20/110, or 18.2 per cent. If they are to return to a 10 per cent liquidity ratio, they need only retain £11 billion as balances at the central bank (£11 billion/£110 billion = 10 per cent). The remaining £9 billion they can lend to customers.

Assume now that customers spend this £9 billion in shops using their debit cards. Under the EFTPOS system the balances in the central bank of the customers' banks will duly be debited by £9 billion, but the balances in the central bank of the shopkeepers' banks will be credited by £9 billion: leaving *overall balances in the central bank unaltered*. There is still a surplus of £9 billion over what is required to maintain the 10 per cent liquidity ratio. The new deposits of £9 billion in the shopkeepers' banks, backed by balances in the central bank, can thus be used as the basis for *further* loans. Ten per cent (i.e. £0.9 billion) must be kept back in the central bank, but the remaining 90 per cent (i.e. £8.1 billion) can be lent out again.

When the money is spent and again transferred between banks, this £8.1 billion will still remain as surplus balances in the central bank and can therefore be used as the basis for yet more loans. Again, 10 per cent must be retained and the remaining 90 per cent can be lent out. This process goes on and on until eventually the position is as shown in Table 10.4.

Table 10.3	The initial effect of an additional deposit of £10 billion		
Liabilities	**£bn**	**Assets**	**£bn**
Deposits (old)	100	Balances with the central bank (old)	10
Deposits (new)	10	Balances with the central bank (new)	10
		Advances	90
Total	110	Total	110

Table 10.4	The full effect of an additional deposit of £10 billion		
Liabilities	**£bn**	**Assets**	**£bn**
Deposits (old)	100	Balances with the central bank (old)	10
Deposits (new: initial)	10	Balances with the central bank (new)	10
(new: subsequent)	90	Advances (old)	90
		Advances (new)	90
Total	200	Total	200

The initial increase in balances with the central bank of £10 billion has allowed banks to create new advances (and hence deposits) of £90 billion, making a total increase in money supply of £100 billion.

> **Pause for thought**
>
> *If banks choose to operate with a 5 per cent liquidity ratio and receive an extra £100 million of cash deposits: (a) What is the size of the bank deposits multiplier? (b) How much will total deposits have expanded after the multiplier has worked through? (c) How much will total credit have expanded?*

This effect is known as the **bank deposits multiplier**. In this simple example, with a liquidity ratio of $1/10$ (i.e. 10 per cent), the bank deposits multiplier is 10. An initial increase in deposits of £10 billion allowed total deposits to rise by £100 billion. In this simple world, therefore, the bank deposits multiplier is the inverse of the liquidity ratio (L):

$$\text{Bank deposits multiplier} = 1/L$$

The creation of credit: the real world

In practice, the creation of credit is not as simple as this. There are three major complications.

Banks' liquidity ratio may vary

Banks may choose a different liquidity ratio. At certain times, banks may decide that it is prudent to hold a bigger proportion of liquid assets. For example, if banks are worried about increased risks of default on loans, they may choose to hold a higher liquidity ratio to ensure that they have enough to meet customers' needs. This was the case in the late 2000s when many banks became less willing to lend to other banks for fear of the other banks' assets containing sub-prime debt. Banks, as a result, hoarded cash and became more cautious about granting loans.

On the other hand, there may be an upsurge in consumer demand for credit. Banks may be very keen to grant additional loans and thus make more profits, even though they have acquired no additional assets. They may simply go ahead and expand credit, and accept a lower liquidity ratio.

Customers may not want to take up the credit on offer. Banks may wish to make additional loans, but customers may not want to borrow. There may be insufficient demand. But will the banks not then lower their interest rates, thus encouraging

> **Definition**
>
> **Banks deposits multiplier** The number of times greater the expansion of bank deposits is than the additional liquidity in banks that causes it: $1/L$ (the inverse of the liquidity ratio).

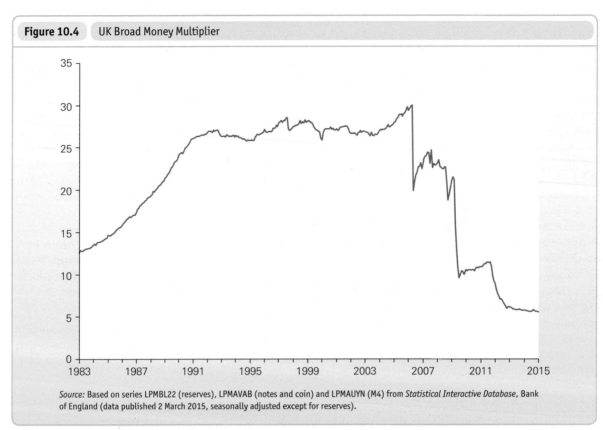

Figure 10.4 UK Broad Money Multiplier

Source: Based on series LPMBL22 (reserves), LPMAVAB (notes and coin) and LPMAUYN (M4) from *Statistical Interactive Database*, Bank of England (data published 2 March 2015, seasonally adjusted except for reserves).

people to borrow? Possibly; but if they lower the rate they charge to borrowers, they must also lower the rate they pay to depositors. But then depositors may switch to other institutions such as building societies.

> **Pause for thought**
>
> *How will an increased mobility of savings and other capital between institutions affect this argument?*

Banks may not operate a simple liquidity ratio

The fact that banks hold a number of fairly liquid assets, such as money at call, bills of exchange and certificates of deposit, makes it difficult to identify a simple liquidity ratio. If the banks use extra cash to buy such liquid assets, can they then use *these* assets as the basis for creating credit? It is largely up to banks' judgements on their overall liquidity position. In practice, therefore, the size of the bank deposits multiplier will vary and is thus difficult to predict in advance.

Some of the extra cash may be withdrawn by the public

If extra cash comes into the banking system, and as a result extra deposits are created, part of them may be held by households and non-bank firms (known in this context as the **non-bank private sector**) as cash outside the banks. In other words, some of the extra cash leaks out of the banking system. This will result in an overall multiplier effect that is smaller than the full bank deposits multiplier. This overall

multiplier is known as the **money multiplier**. It is defined as the change in total money supply expressed as a proportion of the change in the monetary base that caused it: $\Delta M_s/\Delta M_b$ (where M_s is total broad money supply and M_b is the monetary base).

TC 13
p 219

The broad money multiplier in the UK

In the UK, the principal money multiplier measure is the broad money multiplier. This is given by $\Delta M4/\Delta M_b$, where M_b in this case is defined as cash in circulation with the public and in banks' interest-bearing deposits (reserve accounts) at the Bank of England.

Another indicator of the broad money multiplier is simply the ratio of the *level of* (as opposed to change in) M4 relative to the *level of* cash in circulation with the public and banks' reserve accounts at the central bank. This 'levels' relationship is shown in Figure 10.4 and helps us to analyse the longer-term relationship between the stocks of broad money and the monetary base. From it we can see how

> **Definitions**
>
> **Non-bank private sector** Households and non-bank firms. In other words, everyone in the country other than banks and the government (central and local).
>
> **Money multiplier** The number of times greater the expansion of money supply (M_s) is than the expansion of the monetary base (M_b) that caused it: $\Delta M_s/\Delta M_b$.

broad money grew rapidly relative to the monetary base during the late 1980s and into the early 1990s. From the early 1990s to the mid-2000s, the level of M4 relative to the monetary base fluctuated in a narrow range.

From May 2006 the Bank of England began remunerating banks' reserve accounts at the official Bank Rate. This encouraged banks to increase their reserve accounts at the Bank of England and led to a sharp fall in the broad money multiplier. It then declined further during 2009. The significant decline in 2009 and again in 2011–12 coincided with the Bank of England's programme of asset purchases (quantitative easing) which led to a large increase in banks' reserves at the Bank of England. The point is that the increase in the monetary base did not lead to the same percentage increase in broad money, as banks were more cautious about lending and chose to keep higher reserves. The policy of quantitative easing is discussed more in Chapter 12.

In the next section we look at factors which help explain movements in the money multiplier and changes in the money supply.

Pause for thought

Which would you expect to fluctuate more, the money multiplier ($\Delta M_s/\Delta M_b$), or the simple ratio, M_s/M_b?

What causes money supply to rise?

Money supply can rise for a number of reasons. We examine each below.

Central bank action

The central bank may decide that the stock of money is too low and that this is keeping up interest rates and holding back spending in the economy. In such circumstances, it may choose to create additional money.

As we saw above (page 274), this was the case following the 2007/8 financial crisis when the Bank of England and the US Federal Reserve Bank embarked on programmes of *quantitative easing*. This involved the central bank creating electronic (narrow) money and using it to purchase assets, mainly government bonds. When the recipients of the money (mainly non-bank financial institutions) deposited it in banks, the banks could lend it to businesses and consumers for purposes of spending and, through the bank deposits multiplier, broad money supply would increase.

As we can see from Figure 10.5, however, this was not enough to prevent UK broad money supply falling for much of the period from 2010 to 2014.

Banks choose to hold a lower liquidity ratio

If banks collectively choose to hold a lower liquidity ratio, they will have surplus liquidity. The banks have tended to choose a lower liquidity ratio over time because of the increasing use of direct debits and debit-card and credit-card transactions.

Surplus liquidity can be used to expand advances, which will lead to a multiplied rise in broad money supply (e.g. M4).

An important trend up to the late 2000s was the growth in *interbank lending*. Table 10.1 (on page 264) showed that short-term loans to other banks (including overseas banks)

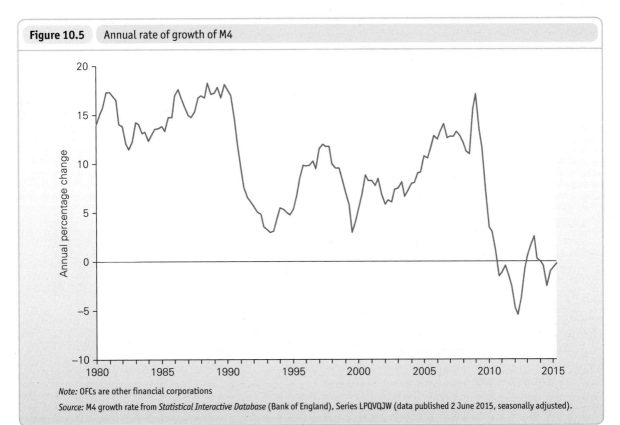

| Figure 10.5 | Annual rate of growth of M4 |

Note: OFCs are other financial corporations

Source: M4 growth rate from *Statistical Interactive Database* (Bank of England), Series LPQVQJW (data published 2 June 2015, seasonally adjusted).

BOX 10.4   CREDIT, MONEY AND MINSKY'S FINANCIAL INSTABILITY HYPOTHESIS

Are credit cycles inevitable?

Patterns in lending and the money supply

M4 is the UK's main broad aggregate measure of the money supply. It is defined as the UK non-bank private sector's holdings of notes and coins, sterling deposits and other short-term financial instruments issued by banks and building societies (up to five years).

As we can see from Figure 10.5 (see page 281) the growth of broad money is highly variable. Nonetheless, the weakness in the growth of M4 from the late 2000s was especially marked. An important reason for this was the collapse in the flows of credit from MFIs to the rest of the private sector. As we saw on earlier (pages 278–9), when banks grant credit, further deposits are created when the non-bank private sector looks to spend this credit. This can result in more credit being extended and more deposits being created.

Chart (a) shows annual *flows* of net lending to the non-bank private sector: the household sector, non-financial corporations and other financial corporations (OFCs). Net lending is *additional* credit and is calculated by subtracting repayments from the total amount of gross lending by banks and building societies.

The chart captures the marked growth in credit during the late 1980s, particularly to households which contributed to the stock of M4 (broad money) increasing at an average rate of 16 per cent year over the second half of the decade. A marked slowdown in the growth of credit followed the recession of the early 1990s. Private non-financial corporations reduced their holdings of bank debt during this period. Unsurprisingly M4 growth slowed too, with the annual growth

rate falling to only a little over 2 per cent during 1993.

From the mid-1990s up to the late 2000s we observe a period of prolonged and robust credit growth. Over the period 2006 to 2008 yearly net lending to the non-bank private sector averaged £292 billion. Again this helped to fuel the growth in M4. The average annual rate of growth in M4 over 2006 and 2007 was 13 per cent.

But, the story was to change dramatically from 2008 onwards as the 'credit crunch' began to bite. We began to see extraordinarily low levels of net lending to households – levels not seen since the late 1970s. Meanwhile non-financial corporations and OFCs began reducing their existing bank debts by more than they were acquiring new debts: i.e. net lending to these two sectors was negative.

While the repayment of debt by OFCs was aided by the Bank of England's programme of asset purchases (quantitative easing), the late 2000s marked a new phase in the credit cycle. But, how inevitable was this slump and the exuberance in lending that preceded it? How inevitable are credit cycles?

Minsky's credit cycles

Hyman Minsky (1919–1996) was an American economist, born of Belarusian parents. He is known for his work on understanding the relationship between the financial system and the macroeconomy. His 'financial instability hypothesis' proposes that financial cycles are an inherent part of the economic cycle and so are a key cause of the fluctuations in real GDP.

As we saw in Section 9.4 (pages 240–1), psychological influences are important in explaining the financial

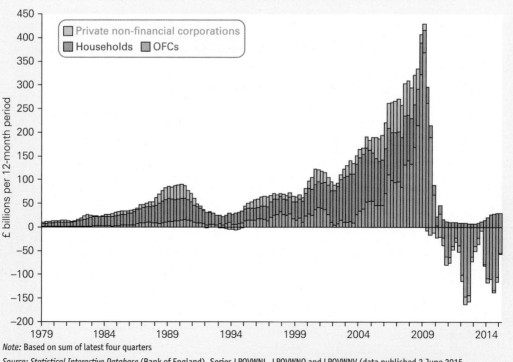

(a) *Annual flows of net lending to non-bank private sector*

Note: Based on sum of latest four quarters

Source: Statistical Interactive Database (Bank of England), Series LPQVWNL, LPQVWNQ and LPQVWNV (data published 2 June 2015, seasonally adjusted).

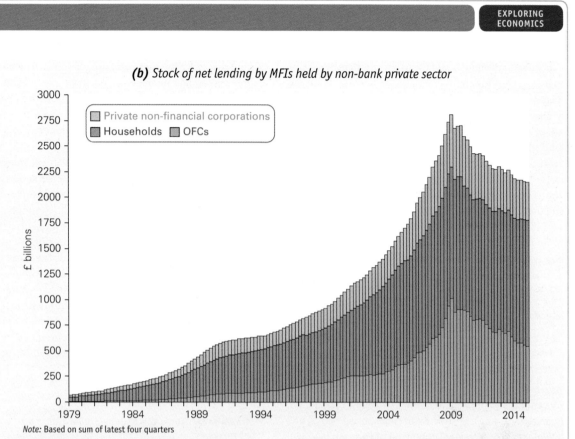

(b) *Stock of net lending by MFIs held by non-bank private sector*

Legend:
- Private non-financial corporations
- Households
- OFCs

Note: Based on sum of latest four quarters

Source: Statistical Interactive Database (Bank of England), Series LPQBC44, LPQBC56 and LPQBC57 (data published 2 June 2015, seasonally adjusted)

instability hypothesis. The extension of credit by MFIs can be seen to go through different phases. During these phases credit criteria and the ability of borrowers to afford their debts vary. Credit flows are therefore dependent on the state of the economy. Consequently, the accumulation of debt by the non-bank private sector is pro-cyclical: in other words, it helps to amplify the magnitude of the cycle.

Minsky argued that credit flows will tend to increase in a period of sustained growth. This causes banks and investors to develop a heightened euphoria and confidence in the economy and in the returns of assets. As a result, economic agents begin to take on bigger debts to acquire assets. These debts increasingly stretch their financial well-being. A point is reached, perhaps triggered by an economic shock or a tightening of economic policy, when the euphoria stops and confidence is replaced with pessimism. This is sometimes referred to as a 'Minsky moment'.

Some argue that a Minsky moment may have taken place in 2008/9. If we look at Chart (b) we can see that the private non-bank sector had become incredibly indebted to MFIs by this point. By the end of March 2009 its stock of MFI debt had peaked at £2.81 trillion, the equivalent to almost 290 per cent of annual GDP.

The consequence of a Minsky moment is that lenders reduce their lending while, more generally, economic agents look to increase their net worth (i.e. reduce debts or increase savings) to ensure their financial well-being. The data in the two charts appear consistent with this behaviour. These individual actions cause a decline in aggregate spending and in national income. In other

words, we observe a balance sheet economic slowdown or, as in the late 2000s, a balance sheet recession. Furthermore, the large-scale selling of assets to improve financial well-being causes the value of assets to fall. This paradoxical reduction of net worth is known as the 'paradox of debt'.

Minsky believed that credit cycles are an inherent feature of a free-market economy. Hence, the authorities will need to take action to moderate or thwart credit cycles so as to reduce economic instability. The significance given to macro-prudential regulation by policy makers in the response to the financial crisis can be seen as an example of a 'thwarting mechanism' to help mitigate the dangers posed to the economy by credit cycles.

While Minsky argued that the ingredients for economic volatility arising from financial instability are ever-present, some argue that other factors are needed for this instability to develop into a financial crisis. These factors may be part of a longer cycle of events. We could view the processes of financial deregulation and innovation that have characterised the past two to three decades as part of this longer cycle.

One interpretation of the financial crisis of the late 2000s is that it was the result of the interaction of the normal Minsky cycle (i.e. short-run variations in the accumulation of credit) with a longer cycle of events or a 'Minsky super-cycle'.

KI 31
p 205

? *What demand-side and supply-side factors influence the flows of net lending by financial institutions to the non-bank private sector?*

are now the largest element in banks' liquid assets. These assets may be used by a bank as the basis for expanding loans and thereby starting a chain of credit creation. But although these assets are liquid to an *individual bank*, they do not add to the liquidity of the banking system *as a whole*. By using them for credit creation, the banking system is operating with a lower *overall* liquidity ratio.

This was a major element in the banking crisis of 2008. By operating with a collectively low liquidity ratio, banks were vulnerable to people defaulting on debt, such as mortgages. The problem was compounded by the holding of sub-prime debt in the form of securitised assets. Realising the vulnerability of other banks, banks became increasingly unwilling to lend to each other. The resulting decline in interbank lending reduced the amount of credit created and so depressed the money supply (see Figure 10.5). In Box 10.4 we discuss in more detail the effect of credit cycles on the UK money supply.

> **Pause for thought**
>
> *What effects do debit cards and cash machines (ATMs) have on (a) banks' prudent liquidity ratios; (b) the size of the bank deposits multiplier?*

The non-bank private sector chooses to hold less cash

Households and firms may choose to hold less cash. Again, the reason may be a greater use of cards, direct debits, etc. This means that a greater proportion of the cash base will be held as deposits in banks rather than in people's wallets, purses or safes outside banks. The extra cash deposits allow banks to create more credit.

The above two reasons for an expansion of broad money supply (M4) are because more credit is being created for a given monetary base. As Figure 10.4 showed, the money multiplier rose substantially in the late 1980s and early 1990s and then gradually up to 2006.

The other two reasons for an expansion of money supply are reasons why the monetary base itself might expand.

An inflow of funds from abroad

When sterling is used to pay for UK exports and is deposited in UK banks by the exporters, credit can be created on the basis of it. This leads to a multiplied increase in the domestic money supply.

The money supply will also expand if depositors of sterling in banks overseas then switch these deposits to banks in the UK. This is a direct increase in the money supply. In an open economy like the UK, movements of sterling and other currencies into and out of the country can be very large. This can lead to large fluctuations in the money supply.

A public-sector deficit

A public-sector deficit is the difference between public-sector expenditure and public-sector receipts. To meet this deficit, the government has to borrow money by selling interest-bearing securities (Treasury bills and gilts). In general, the bigger the

public sector's deficit, the greater will be the growth in the money supply. Just how the money supply will be affected, however, depends on who buys the securities

Consider first the case where government securities are purchased by the non-bank private sector. The money supply will remain unchanged. When people or firms buy the bonds or bills, they will draw money from their banks. When the government spends the money, it will be redeposited in banks. There is no increase in money supply. It is just a case of existing money changing hands.

This is not the case when the securities are purchased by the banking sector, including the central bank. Consider the purchase of Treasury bills by commercial banks: there will be a multiplied expansion of the money supply. The reason is that, although banks' balances at the central bank will go down when the banks purchase the bills, they will go up again when the government spends the money. In addition, the banks will now have additional liquid assets (bills), which can be used as the basis for credit creation.

The government could attempt to minimise the boost to money supply by financing the deficit through the sale of gilts, since, even if these were partly purchased by the banks, they could not be used as the basis for credit creation.

> **Pause for thought**
>
> *Identify the various factors that could cause a fall in the money supply.*

The relationship between money supply and the rate of interest

Simple monetary theory often assumes that the supply of money is totally independent of interest rates. The money supply is **exogenous**. This is illustrated in Figure 10.6(a). The supply of money is assumed to be determined by the government or central bank ('the authorities'): what the authorities choose it to be, or what they allow it to be by their choice of the level and method of financing public-sector borrowing.

In practice, money supply is **endogenous**, with higher interest rates leading to increases in the supply of money. This is illustrated in Figure 10.6(b). The argument is that the supply of money is responding to the demand for money. If people start borrowing more money, the resulting shortage of money in the banks will drive up interest rates. But if banks

> **Definitions**
>
> **Exogenous money supply** Money supply that does not depend on the demand for money but is set by the authorities (i.e. the central bank or the government).
>
> **Endogenous money supply** Money supply that is determined (at least in part) by the demand for money.

Figure 10.6 The supply of money curve

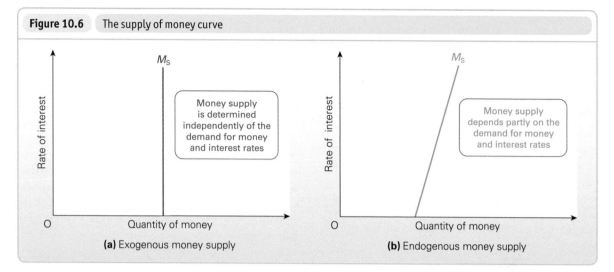

(a) Exogenous money supply

(b) Endogenous money supply

have surplus liquidity or are prepared to operate with a lower liquidity ratio, they will create extra credit in response to the increased demand and higher interest rates: money supply will expand. If banks find themselves short of liquidity, they can always borrow from the central bank through repos.

Some economists go further still. They argue that money supply is not only endogenous, but the 'curve' is effectively horizontal; money supply expands passively to match the demand for money. It is likely, however, that the shape will vary with the confidence of banks. In periods of optimism banks may be willing to expand credit to meet the demand from customers. In periods of pessimism, such as that following the financial crisis, banks may be unwilling to grant credit when customers seek it.

Recap

1. Money supply can be defined in a number of different ways, depending on what items are included. A useful distinction is between narrow money and broad money. Narrow money includes just cash and possibly banks' balances at the central bank. Broad money also includes deposits in banks and possibly various other short-term deposits in the money market. In the UK, M4 is the preferred measure of broad money. In the eurozone it is M3.

2. Bank deposits expand through a process of credit creation. If banks' liquid assets increase, they can be used as a base for increasing loans. When the loans are redeposited in banks, they form the base for yet more loans, and thus a process of multiple credit expansion takes place. The ratio of the increase of money to an expansion of the liquidity base is called the 'bank deposits multiplier'. It is the inverse of the liquidity ratio.

3. In practice, it is difficult to predict the precise amount by which money supply will expand if there is an increase in banks' liquidity. The reasons are that banks may choose to hold a different liquidity ratio; customers may not take up all the credit on offer; there may be no simple liquidity ratio, given the range of relatively liquid assets; and some of the extra cash may leak away into extra cash holdings by the general public.

4. (Broad) money supply will rise if (a) banks choose to hold a lower liquidity ratio and thus create more credit for an existing amount of liquidity; (b) the non-bank private sector chooses to hold less cash; (c) the government runs a deficit and some of it is financed by borrowing from the banking sector; (d) there is an inflow of funds from abroad.

5. Simple monetary theory assumes that the supply of money is independent of interest rates. In practice, a rise in demand for money, and hence a rise in interest rates, will often lead to an increase in money supply, though this may be affected by the confidence of banks.

10.4 THE DEMAND FOR MONEY

How much money do we want to hold at any one time?

The demand for money refers to the desire to *hold* money: to keep your wealth in the form of money, rather than spending it on goods and services or using it to purchase financial assets such as bonds or shares. It is usual to distinguish three reasons why people want to hold their assets in the form of money.

The transactions motive. Since money is a medium of exchange, it is required for conducting transactions. But since people only receive money at intervals (e.g. weekly or monthly) and not continuously, they require to hold balances of money in cash or in current accounts.

The precautionary motive. Unforeseen circumstances can arise, such as a car breakdown. Thus individuals often hold some additional money as a precaution. Firms too keep precautionary balances because of uncertainties about the timing of their receipts and payments. If a large customer is late in making payment, a firm may be unable to pay its suppliers unless it has spare liquidity.

The assets or speculative motive. Money is not just a medium of exchange, it is also a means of storing wealth (see page 261). Keeping some or all of your wealth as money in a bank account has the advantage of carrying no risk. It earns a relatively small, but safe rate of return. Some assets, such as company shares or bonds, may earn you more on average, but there is a chance that their price will fall. In other words, they are risky.

What determines the size of the demand for money?

What would cause the demand for money to rise? We now turn to examine the various determinants of the size of the demand for money (M_d). In particular, we will look at the role of the rate of interest. First, however, let us identify the other determinants of the demand for money.

Money national income. The more money people earn, the greater will be their expenditure and hence the greater the transactions demand for money. A rise in money ('nominal') incomes in a country can be caused either by a rise in real GDP (i.e. real output) or by a rise in prices, or by some combination of the two.

The frequency with which people are paid. The less frequently people are paid, the greater the level of money balances that will be required to tide them over until the next payment.

Financial innovations. The increased use of credit cards, debit cards and cash machines, plus the advent of interest-paying current accounts, have resulted in changes in the demand for money. The use of credit cards reduces both the transactions and precautionary demands. Paying once a month for goods requires less money on average than paying separately for each item purchased. Moreover, the possession of a credit card reduces or even eliminates the need to hold precautionary balances for many people. On the other hand, the increased availability of cash machines, the convenience of debit cards and the ability to earn interest on current accounts have all encouraged people to hold more money in bank accounts. The net effect has been an increase in the demand for money.

Speculation about future returns on assets. The assets motive for holding money depends on people's expectations. If they believe that share prices are about to fall on the stock market, they will sell shares and hold larger balances of money in the meantime. The assets demand, therefore, can be quite high when the price of securities is considered certain to fall. Some clever (or lucky) individuals anticipated the 2007–8 stock market decline. They sold shares and 'went liquid'.

Generally, the more risky such alternatives to money become, the more will people want to hold their assets as money balances in a bank or building society.

People also speculate about changes in the exchange rate. If businesses believe that the exchange rate is about to appreciate (rise), they will hold greater balances of domestic currency in the meantime, hoping to buy foreign currencies with them when the rate has risen (since they will then get more foreign currency for their money).

The rate of interest (or rate of return) on assets. In terms of the operation of money markets, this is the most important determinant. It is related to the opportunity cost of holding money. The opportunity cost is the interest forgone by not holding higher-interest-bearing assets, such as shares, bills or bonds. With most bank accounts today paying interest, this opportunity cost is less than in the past and thus the demand for money for assets purposes has increased.

But what is the relationship between money demand and the rate of interest? Generally, if rates of interest (or return) rise, they will rise more on shares, bills and bonds than on bank accounts. The demand for holding money in accounts will thus fall. The demand for money is thus inversely related to the rate of interest.

The demand for money curve

The demand for money curve with respect to interest rates is shown in Figure 10.7. It is downward sloping, showing that lower interest rates will encourage people to hold additional money balances.

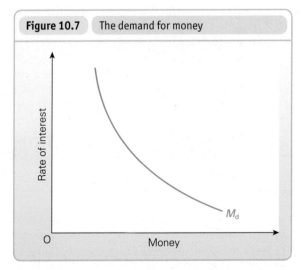

Figure 10.7   The demand for money

A change in interest rates is shown by a movement along the demand for money curve. A change in any other determinant of the demand for money (such as national income or expectations about exchange rate movements) will cause the whole curve to shift: a rightward shift representing an increase in demand; a leftward shift representing a decrease.

> **Pause for thought**
>
> *Which way is the demand for money curve likely to shift in each of the following cases? (a) Prices rise, but real incomes stay the same. (b) Interest rates abroad rise relative to domestic interest rates. (c) People anticipate that share prices are likely to fall in the near future.*

> **Recap**
>
> 1. The three motives for holding money are the transactions, precautionary and assets (or speculative) motives.
> 2. The demand for money will be higher, (a) the higher the level of money national income (i.e. the higher the level of real national income and the higher the price level), (b) the less frequently people are paid, (c) the greater the advantages of holding money in bank accounts, such as the existence of cash machines and the use of debit cards, (d) the more risky alternative assets become and the more likely they are to fall in value, and the more likely the exchange rate is to rise, and (e) the lower the opportunity cost of holding money in terms of interest forgone on alternative assets.
> 3. The demand for money curve with respect to interest rates is downward sloping.

10.5 EQUILIBRIUM

What effect do the demand and supply of money have on interest rates?

Equilibrium in the money market

Equilibrium in the money market occurs when the demand for money (M_d) is equal to the supply of money (M_s). This equilibrium is achieved through changes in the rate of interest.

In Figure 10.8, assume that the demand and supply of money are given by M_s and M_d. The equilibrium rate of interest is r_e and the equilibrium quantity of money is M_e. But why?

If the rate of interest were above r_e, people would have money balances surplus to their needs. They would use these to buy shares, bonds and other assets. This would drive up the price of these assets. But the price of assets is inversely related to interest rates. The higher the price of an asset (such as a government bond), the less any given interest payment will be as a percentage of its price (e.g. £10 as a percentage of £100 is 10 per cent, but as a percentage of £200 is only 5 per cent). Thus a higher price of assets will correspond to lower interest rates.

As the rate of interest fell, so there would be a contraction of the money supply (a movement down along the M_s curve) and an increase in the demand for money balances, especially speculative balances (a movement down along the M_d curve). The interest rate would go on falling until it reached r_e. Equilibrium would then be achieved.

Similarly, if the rate of interest were below r_e, people would have insufficient money balances. They would sell securities, thus lowering their prices and raising the rate of interest until it reached r_e.

A shift in either the M_s or the M_d curve will lead to a new equilibrium quantity of money and rate of interest at the new intersection of the curves. For example, a rise in the supply of money will cause the rate of interest to fall, whereas a rise in the demand for money will cause the rate of interest to rise.

In practice, there is no one single interest rate. Rather equilibrium in the money markets will be where demand and supply of the various financial instruments separately balance. Generally, however, different interest rates tend to move roughly together as the overall demand for money and other liquid assets (or their supply) changes. Table 10.5 gives some examples of interest rates on various financial instruments. It shows how the various rates of interest move together.

In many countries today interest rates have become a key tool of monetary policy. As we saw in Section 10.2, the Bank

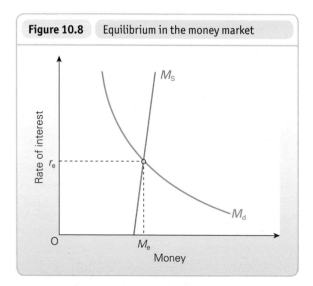

Figure 10.8 Equilibrium in the money market

Table 10.5	Selected rates of interest: January 1997 to January 2015 (monthly averages)						
Financial instrument	Period of loan	Rate of interest, per cent per annum					
		Average Jan 1997– Sept 2008	Average Oct 2008– Jan 2015	Jan 1997	Sept 2008	Jan 2009	Jan 2015
Call money	Overnight	5.15	0.58	5.90	4.89	1.34	0.45
Gilt repos	1 week	5.09	0.59	5.91	4.92	1.43	0.47
Interbank loans	1 month	5.25	0.74	6.14	5.57	1.71	0.48
Treasury bills	3 months	5.04	0.49	6.01	4.74	0.89	0.34
British government securities[1]	20 years	4.81	3.79	7.74	4.64	4.48	2.36
Bank and building society mortgages[2]	Variable (25 years typical)	6.87	4.28	7.18	6.95	4.73	4.56
Credit card	–	17.72	16.99	22.14	16.12	16.09	17.88
Official Bank Rate (policy rate)	–	5.18	0.63	5.94	5.00	1.50	0.50

[1] Zero coupon, nominal yields (series IUMALNZC)
[2] Standard variable rate for UK MFIs (series IUMTLMV)
Source: Statistical Interactive Database (Bank of England), 2 March 2015

of England conducts open-market operations to affect the general structure of interest rates. By doing so, it supplies an aggregate level of reserves such that, given the demand for money, it is able to keep interbank rates close to its chosen policy rate ('Bank Rate'). Then, this affects the general structure of the economy's interest rates. We can see how the significant reductions to the policy rate from late 2008 were typically mirrored by falls in other interest rates.

The link between the money and goods markets

A rise in money supply will cause a rise in aggregate demand. This, in turn, will then cause a multiplied rise in national income. The size of the rise in real national income (i.e. output) will depend on the degree of spare capacity in the economy. In this section we see how a rise in money supply causes a rise in aggregate demand. In Chapter 11 we see to what extent this rise in aggregate demand leads to a rise in national output, and to what extent it merely leads to a rise in prices.

There are two principal ways in which a rise in money supply causes a rise in aggregate demand. The first is via changes in interest rates – known as the **interest rate transmission mechanism**. The second is via changes in the exchange rate – known as the **exchange rate transmission mechanism.**

The interest rate transmission mechanism
The interest rate transmission mechanism is illustrated in the top part of Figure 10.9. It is a three-stage process:

■ A rise in money supply leads to a surplus of money at the current rate of interest. This results in a fall in the equilibrium rate of interest. This would be illustrated by a rightward shift in the M_s line in Figure 10.8, with the rate of interest falling to the point where this new M_s curve crossed the M_d curve.

■ This fall in the rate of interest then encourages firms to invest, since it is cheaper to borrow money to finance new buildings, machines, etc. A rise in investment would lead the injections (*J*) line in Figure 8.7 (see page 219) to move vertically upwards. It also encourages consumers to spend, since borrowing through credit cards and personal loans is now cheaper. At the same time, it discourages saving. This would lead to a downward shift in the withdrawals (*W*) line in Figure 8.7.

■ The net effect of these changes in injections and withdrawals is a rise in aggregate demand.

The overall effect of a change in money supply on national income will depend on the size of the effect in each of the three stages. The size of these effects is keenly debated by economists. The debates essentially focus on the shapes of the curves in Figures 10.8 and 8.7 and whether they are likely to shift.

Pause for thought

If everybody believes that the rate of interest will rise, what effect will an increase in the money supply have on the rate of interest? Why was this question relevant in the late 2000s?

Definitions

Interest rate transmission mechanism How a change in money supply affects aggregate demand via a change in interest rates.

Exchange rate transmission mechanism How a change in money supply affects aggregate demand via a change in exchange rates.

Figure 10.9 Monetary transmission mechanisms

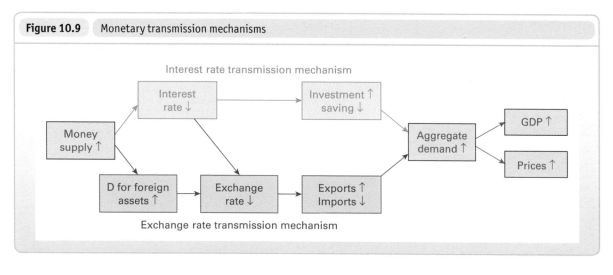

The exchange rate transmission mechanism

Exchange rates are determined by the demand and supply of currencies. (We will examine this in detail in Chapter 14.) If the supply of sterling on the foreign exchange market (e.g. from importers in the UK wishing to buy foreign currencies in order to buy foreign goods) exceeds the demand (e.g. from foreign companies wishing to obtain sterling to buy UK exports), the exchange rate will fall ('depreciate'). For example, the pound might depreciate from $1.65 to $1.50, or from €1.30 to €1.20. Conversely, if the demand for sterling exceeds the supply, the exchange rate will rise ('appreciate').

Changes in the money supply will not only affect interest rates, but also affect the demand and supply of the currency and thus have an effect on exchange rates. The change in the exchange rate will then affect aggregate demand. This 'exchange rate transmission mechanism' is illustrated in the bottom part of Figure 10.9.

Assume again that the money supply increases. This has the following effects:

■ Part of the excess money balances is used to purchase foreign assets. This therefore leads to an increase in the supply of domestic currency coming onto the foreign exchange markets.

■ As we have already seen, the excess supply of money in the domestic money market pushes down the rate of interest. This reduces the return on domestic assets below that on foreign assets. This, like the first effect,

leads to an increased demand for foreign assets and thus an increased supply of domestic currency on the foreign exchange market. It also reduces the demand for domestic assets by those outside the country, and thus reduces the demand for the domestic currency. This causes the exchange rate to fall (depreciate).

■ The fall in the exchange rate (e.g. from €1.25 to €1.20) means that people abroad have to pay less for a pound. This makes UK exports (an injection) cheaper and hence more are sold. People in the UK, by contrast, get less foreign currency for a pound. This makes imports (a withdrawal) more expensive and hence fewer are purchased.

■ Again, the net effect of these changes in injections and withdrawals is a rise in aggregate demand.

In both cases, the rise in aggregate demand then leads to a multiplied rise in national income (GDP). This, however, as we shall see in Section 11.2, may be wholly or partly offset by a rise in prices.

Pause for thought

What, do you think, determines the amount that real output rises as a result of a rise in the money supply? (We examine this in the next chapter.)

The relationship between the money and goods market is explored in more detail in Web Appendices 10.2 and 10.3, which look at the '*IS/LM*' and '*IS/MP*' models respectively.

Recap

1. Equilibrium in the money market is where the supply of money is equal to the demand. Equilibrium is achieved through changes in the interest rate.

2. The interest rate mechanism works as follows: a rise in money supply causes money supply to exceed money demand; interest rates fall; this causes investment to rise; this causes a multiplied rise in national income.

3. The exchange rate mechanism works as follows: a rise in money supply causes interest rates to fall; the rise in money supply plus the fall in interest rates cause an increased supply of domestic currency to come onto the foreign exchange market; this causes the exchange rate to depreciate; this will cause increased exports and reduced imports and hence a multiplied rise in national income.

QUESTIONS

1. Imagine that the banking system receives additional deposits of £100 million and that all the individual banks wish to retain their current liquidity ratio of 20 per cent.
   a. How much will banks choose to lend out initially?
   b. What will happen to banks' liabilities when the money that is lent out is spent and the recipients of it deposit it in their bank accounts?
   c. How much of these latest deposits will be lent out by the banks?
   d. By how much will total deposits (liabilities) eventually have risen, assuming that none of the additional liquidity is held outside the banking sector?
   e. How much of these are matched by (i) liquid assets; (ii) illiquid assets?
   f. What is the size of the bank deposits multiplier?
   g. If one-half of any additional liquidity is held outside the banking sector, by how much less will deposits have risen compared with (d) above?

2. What is meant by the terms *narrow money* and *broad money*? Does broad money fulfil all the functions of money?

3. Which, if any, of the following count as (broad) money? (a) A credit card. (b) A debit card. (c) A cheque book. (d) A bank deposit account pass book. (e) A building society pass book.

4. How does money aid the specialisation and division of labour?

5. What enables banks safely to engage in both maturity transformation and risk transformation?

6. Why do banks hold a range of assets of varying degrees of liquidity and profitability?

7. What is meant by the securitisation of assets? How might this be (a) beneficial and (b) harmful to banks and the economy?

8. What were the causes of the credit crunch and the banking crisis of the late 2000s?

9. Analyse the possible effects on banks' balance sheets of the following:
   a. The Basel III regulatory requirements.
   b. The UK bank levy.

10. What is measured by the CET1 ratio? What measures would a bank need to take in order to increase its CET1 ratio?

11. If banks choose to operate a 20 per cent liquidity ratio and receive extra cash deposits of £10 million, assuming that the general public do not wish to hold a larger total amount of cash balances outside the banks:
    a. How much credit will ultimately be created?
    b. By how much will total deposits have expanded?
    c. What is the size of the bank deposits multiplier?

12. If the government reduces the size of its public-sector net cash requirement, why might the money supply nevertheless increase more rapidly?

13. Why might the relationship between the demand for money and the rate of interest be an unstable one?

14. What effects will the following have on the equilibrium rate of interest? (You should consider which way the demand and/or supply curves of money shift.)
    a. Banks find that they have a higher liquidity ratio than they need.
    b. A rise in incomes.
    c. A growing belief that interest rates will rise from their current level.

MyEconLab

This book can be supported by MyEconLab, which contains a range of additional resources, including an online homework and tutorial system designed to test and build your understanding.

You need both an access card and a course ID to access MyEconLab:

1. Is your lecturer using MyEconLab? Ask your lecturer for your course ID.

2. Has an access card been included with the book at a reduced cost? Check the inside back cover of the book.

3. If you have a course ID but no access card, go to: http://www.myeconlab.com/ to buy access to this interactive study programme.

ADDITIONAL CASE STUDIES IN THE *ESSENTIALS OF ECONOMICS* MyEconLab (www.pearsoned.co.uk/sloman)

10.1 **Barter: its use in Russia in the 1990s.** When barter was used as an alternative to money.

10.2 **The attributes of money.** What makes something, such as metal, paper or electronic records, suitable as money?

10.3 **From coins to bank deposit money.** This case traces the evolution of modern money.

10.4 **Changes in the banking industry.** This considers the changing face of the banking industry and asks whether bigger is better.

10.5 **Are the days of cash numbered?** Does the increased use of credit and debit cards and direct debits mean that cash will become obsolete?

10.6 **Gresham's law.** Historic examples of 'bad' money driving out 'good' money as people hoard the 'good' money.

10.7 **German banking.** This case compares the tradition of German banks with that of UK retail banks. Although the banks have become more similar in recent years, German banks have a much closer relationship with industry.

10.8 **Bailing out the banks.** An overview of the concerted efforts made to rescue the banking system in the crisis of 2007/9.

10.9 **Changes in the operation of monetary policy in the UK.** A more detailed look at the evolution of Bank of England methods of controlling money and bank lending than that given on page 274.

10.10 **Parallel money markets.** A description of the variety of short-term financial instruments available in the parallel money markets.

10.11 **UK monetary aggregates.** This case shows how money supply is measured using both UK measures and euro-zone measures.

10.12 **Making money grow.** A light-hearted illustration of the process of credit creation.

10.13 **Consolidated MFI balance sheet.** A look at the consolidated balance sheet of UK monetary financial institutions (banks, building societies and the Bank of England).

WEB APPENDICES

10.1 **The money multiplier.** This appendix shows how the money multiplier is calculated.

10.2 *IS/LM* **analysis.** This appendix develops a model that brings together the goods and money markets in one diagram.

10.3 *IS/MP* **analysis.** This develops a more recent model of the goods and money markets based on the assumption that the central bank targets the rate of inflation.

Inflation and unemployment

In the previous chapters we have considered some of the influences on aggregate demand and aggregate supply as well as the importance of money and the financial system. In this chapter we draw on this analysis to consider two major macroeconomic issues: inflation and unemployment.

We have seen that the economy's price level is determined by aggregate demand and supply. In this chapter we will consider what determines the rate of *increase* in prices. In other words, what determines the rate of inflation? For instance, can it be affected by the growth in money supply?

We then turn to unemployment: its nature and causes. We see that it is determined by aggregate demand and supply, but this time for labour rather than for goods and services.

Having looked at inflation and unemployment separately, we then see how they are related. A crucial element in this relationship is people's expectations of inflation. This is the topic for Section 11.5.

In recent years, central banks around the world have set targets for the rate of inflation. This has had a profound effect on people's expectations and also on the relationships between inflation and unemployment. We look at these effects in Section 11.6.

After studying this chapter, you should be able to answer the following questions:

- What are the causes of inflation?
- Do changes in aggregate demand affect just prices or both prices and national output?
- How do changes in money supply impact on aggregate demand?
- What are the causes of unemployment?
- What is the relationship between unemployment and inflation, and is the relationship a stable one?
- How does a policy of targeting a rate of inflation affect the relationship between inflation and unemployment?

11.1 INFLATION

Price levels and inflation rates

Inflation refers to rising price levels; deflation refers to falling price levels. The annual rate of inflation measures the annual percentage *increase* in prices. If the rate of inflation is negative, then prices are falling and we are effectively measuring the rate of deflation.

Typically inflation relates to *consumer* prices. The government publishes a 'consumer prices index' (CPI) each month, and the annual rate of inflation is the percentage increase in that index over the previous 12 months.

A broader measure of inflation relates to the rate at which the prices of all domestically produced goods and services are changing. The price index used in this case is the *GDP deflator* (see page 232 and Case Study 8.9 in MyEconLab). Figure 11.1 shows the annual rates of change in the GDP deflator for the USA, Japan, the UK and the EU-15. As you can see, inflation was particularly severe in the mid-1970s, but rates have been relatively low in more recent years and indeed Japan has experienced falling prices.

You will also find rates of inflation reported for a variety of goods and services. For example, indices are published for commodity prices (see Box 2.4), for food prices, for house prices (see Box 2.2), for import prices, for prices after taking taxes into account, and so on. Their respective rates of inflation are simply their annual percentage increase. Likewise it is possible to give the rate of inflation of wage rates ('wage inflation').

Figure 11.2 shows three inflation rate measures for the UK from 2001. The three annual inflation rates have varied between –3 and 6 per cent over the period. Interestingly, from 2008 we see that the annual rate of CPI inflation – the Bank of England's target measure – consistently exceeded the annual growth of average weekly earnings. This meant that the purchasing power of average weekly earnings was being eroded by higher consumer prices.

Before we proceed, a word of caution: be careful not to confuse a rise or fall in the rate of *inflation* with a rise or fall in *prices*. An increase in the rate of inflation means a *faster* increase in prices. A fall in the rate of inflation means a *slower* increase in prices (but still an increase as long as the rate of inflation is positive).

Introduction to the causes of inflation

Demand-pull inflation

Demand-pull inflation is caused by continuing rises in aggregate demand. In Figure 11.3, the *AD* curve shifts to the

> #### Definition
>
> **Demand-pull inflation** Inflation caused by persistent rises in aggregate demand.

Figure 11.1	Inflation rates in selected industrial economies

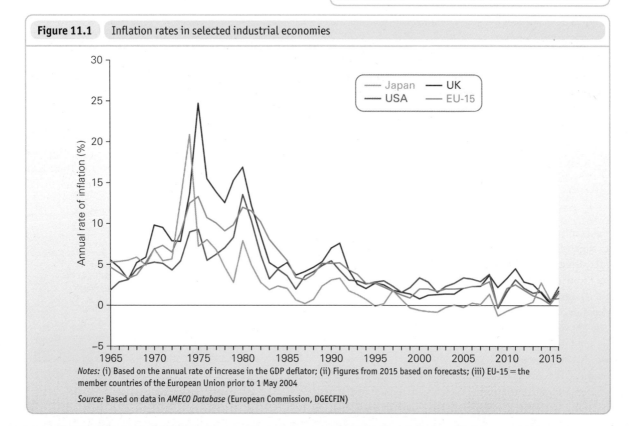

Notes: (i) Based on the annual rate of increase in the GDP deflator; (ii) Figures from 2015 based on forecasts; (iii) EU-15 = the member countries of the European Union prior to 1 May 2004

Source: Based on data in *AMECO Database* (European Commission, DGECFIN)

Figure 11.2 Selection of UK annual inflation rates

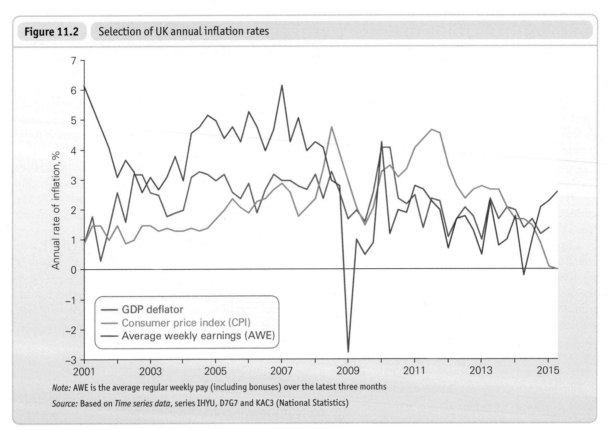

Note: AWE is the average regular weekly pay (including bonuses) over the latest three months

Source: Based on *Time series data*, series IHYU, D7G7 and KAC3 (National Statistics)

Figure 11.3 Demand-pull inflation

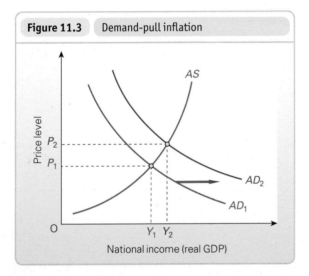

right (and continues doing so). Firms will respond to the rise in aggregate demand partly by raising prices and partly by increasing output (there is a move up along the *AS* curve). Just how much they raise prices depends on how much their costs rise as a result of increasing output. This in turn depends on how close actual output is to potential output. The less slack there is in the economy, the more will firms respond to a rise in demand by raising their prices. In other words, the steeper is the *AS* curve, the larger is the increase in prices. We consider this in more detail in Section 11.2.

Demand-pull inflation is typically associated with a booming economy. Many economists therefore argue that

it is the counterpart of demand-deficient unemployment. When the economy is in recession, demand-deficient unemployment will be high, but demand-pull inflation will be low. When, on the other hand, the economy is near the peak of the business cycle, demand-pull inflation will be high, but demand-deficient unemployment will be low.

Cost-push inflation

Cost-push inflation is associated with continuing rises in costs and hence continuing leftward (upward) shifts in the *AS* curve. Such shifts occur when costs of production rise *independently* of aggregate demand. If firms face a rise in costs, they will respond partly by raising prices and passing the costs on to the consumer, and partly by cutting back on production. This is illustrated in Figure 11.4. There is an upward shift in the aggregate supply curve: from AS_1 to AS_2.

Pause for thought

If there is a general rise in costs of production across the country, does this necessarily mean that there is pure cost-push inflation?

Definition

Cost-push inflation Inflation caused by persistent rises in costs of production (independently of demand).

BOX 11.1 | **INFLATION OR DEFLATION**

Where's the danger?

During the first half of the 2000s it appeared that inflation was no longer a serious worry in many developed economies. Instead, 'deflation' (i.e. falling prices) had become a source of concern. The Japanese economy had experienced deflation for a decade or so and central banks, including the US Federal Reserve and the European Central Bank, were sounding warnings that deflation was a real and present danger to us all.

One of the main causes of declining prices was the process of globalisation. Imports from low-cost countries, such as China and India, drove prices down. What is more, outsourcing call-centre, back-office and IT work to developing countries put downward pressure on wages. This downward effect on prices and wages in the USA and other developed economies was dubbed the 'China price' effect.

A return of inflation?

The global economy grew strongly after 2003. Between 2004 and 2007 global growth averaged 5.4 per cent each year. The UK and USA saw average annual economic growth rates of 3.1 and 2.9 per cent respectively. These, however, were dwarfed by China and India, which experienced growth rates of 12.1 per cent and 9.1 per cent respectively.

The rapid growth in aggregate demand in many OECD countries, such as the UK and USA, put upward pressure on prices and wages but, unlike previously, the 'China price' effect was beginning to *reinforce* this upward pressure.

By 2007–8, the growth in China, India and other rapidly developing countries was causing significant inflation in commodity prices: i.e. in the prices of raw materials and primary agricultural products. This emergence of rapid commodity price inflation can be seen in the chart.

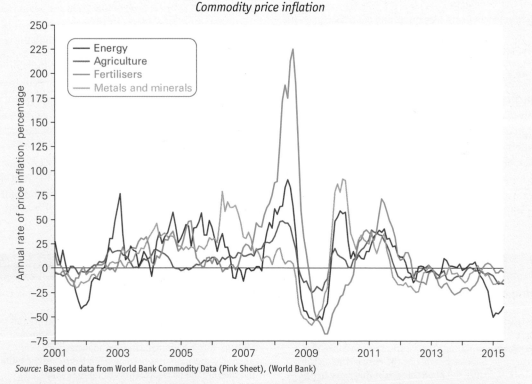

Commodity price inflation

Source: Based on data from World Bank Commodity Data (Pink Sheet), (World Bank)

Swinging between inflation and deflation

However, with the onset of recession in mid-2008, inflation started to fall. Once more there seemed to be a spectre of deflation. By 2009, many people were asking themselves why they should buy now when, by delaying, they might be able to get an item more cheaply later on. The effect of this would be a leftward shift in the *AD* curve, which forces prices down even further.

But the worry about deflation was short-lived. In 2010, the global economy expanded by 5.4 per cent and by a further 4.1 per cent in 2011. This was mirrored by the likes of China and India who saw their respective economies expand by 10.4 per cent and 10.3 per cent in 2010 and by 9.3 per cent and 6.6 per cent in 2011. In the UK, the annual rate of CPI inflation peaked at 5.2 per cent in the 12 months to September 2011, significantly above the Bank of England's central inflation target of 2 per cent.

The period 2012 to 2014 saw a slight easing of global growth, with the world economy expanding by around 3.3 per cent each year. This was reflected in a cooling of the rate of commodity price inflation. By 2014 commodity prices in general and oil prices in particular were falling. The fall in oil prices from around $100 per barrel to around $60 in the second half of the year reflected both worries for the prospects of economic growth, especially in the eurozone, and increased supply, especially from shale deposits in the USA. Falling commodity prices helped to moderate consumer price inflation rates. By February 2015, the annual rate of CPI inflation in the UK had fallen to 0 per cent and in the eurozone to –0.3 per cent.

1. *What long-term benefits might deflation generate for business and the economy in general?*
2. *Would an inflationary China price effect be an example of demand-pull or cost-push effect?*

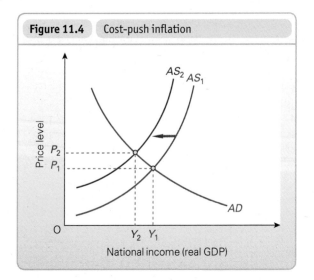

Figure 11.4 Cost-push inflation

This causes the price level to rise to P_2 and the level of output (real GDP) to *fall* to Y_2.

Just how much firms raise prices and cut back on production depends on the shape of the aggregate demand curve. The less elastic the *AD* curve, the less sales will fall as a result of any price rise, and hence the more will firms be able to pass on the rise in their costs to consumers as higher prices.

Note that the effect on output and employment is the opposite of demand-pull inflation. With demand-pull inflation, output and hence employment tend to rise because of the underlying rise in demand. With cost-push inflation, however, output and employment tend to fall.

It is important to distinguish between *single* shifts in the aggregate supply curve (known as 'supply shocks') and *continuing* shifts. If there is a single leftward shift in aggregate supply, there will be a single rise in the price level. For example, if the government raises the excise duty on oil, there will be a single rise in oil prices and hence in industry's fuel costs. This will cause *temporary* inflation while the price rise is passed on through the economy. Once this has occurred, prices will stabilise at the new level and the rate of inflation will fall back to zero again. If cost-push inflation is to continue over a number of years, therefore, the aggregate supply curve must *continually* shift to the left. If cost-push inflation is to *rise*, these shifts must get more rapid.

Rises in costs may originate from a number of different sources, such as trade unions pushing up wages, firms with monopoly power raising prices in order to increase their profits, or increases in international commodity prices. With the process of globalisation and increased international competition, cost-push pressures have tended to decrease in recent years. One major exception has been the oil shocks that have occurred from time to time. For example, the near tripling of oil prices from $51 per barrel in January 2007 to $147 per barrel in July 2008 and again from $41 per barrel in January 2009 to $126 per barrel in April 2011 put upward pressure on costs and prices around the world.

The interaction of demand-pull and cost-push inflation

Demand-pull and cost-push inflation can occur together, since wage and price rises can be caused both by increases in aggregate demand and by independent causes pushing up costs. Even when an inflationary process *starts* as either demand-pull or cost-push, it is often difficult to separate the two. An initial cost-push inflation may encourage the government to expand aggregate demand to offset rises in unemployment. Alternatively, an initial demand-pull inflation may strengthen the power of certain groups, who then

---

BOX 11.2 **COST-PUSH ILLUSION**

When rising costs are not cost-push inflation?

It is easy to get confused between demand-pull and cost-push inflation.

Frequently, inflationary pressures *seem* to come from the cost side. Shopkeepers blame their price rises on the rise in their costs – the wholesale prices they have to pay. The wholesalers blame their price rises on a rise in *their* costs – the prices they are charged by the various manufacturers. The manufacturers in turn blame rising raw material costs, rising wage rates, rising rents, and so on. Everyone blames their price rises on the rise in their costs.

But why have these costs risen?

It could well be due to a rise in aggregate *demand*! Wages may go up because of falling unemployment and a shortage of labour. Firms *have* to pay higher wages in order to recruit or maintain enough labour. Rents may rise because of the upsurge in demand. So too with raw materials: higher demand may pull up their prices too.

What we have then is a 'cost-push illusion'. Costs rise, it is true, but they rise because of an increase in demand.

So when does genuine cost-push inflation occur? This occurs when costs of production rise independently of demand. This will normally involve an increased use of monopoly power: unions becoming more powerful or militant and thus driving up wages; firms using their monopoly/oligopoly power to push up prices; commodity producers such as the OPEC countries forming cartels to push up their prices; the government using its power to raise indirect taxes (such as the increase in the UK in the standard rate of VAT from 17.5 to 20 per cent in January 2011).

In many cases, these cost-push or 'supply-side' shocks are one-off events and after an initial rise in prices, prices settle at the new higher level. There is thus only a temporary inflationary effect while these cost rises work through the economy.

If consumer demand rises and firms respond by raising prices, is this necessarily an example of demand-pull inflation? Could there be such a thing as demand-pull illusion? (Clue: why might consumer demand have risen?)

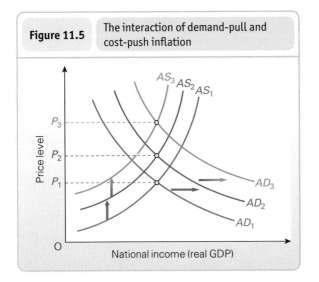

Figure 11.5 The interaction of demand-pull and cost-push inflation

Expectations and inflation

Workers and firms take account of the *expected* rate of inflation when making decisions.

Imagine that a union and an employer are negotiating a wage increase. Let us assume that both sides expect a rate of inflation of 2 per cent. The union will be happy to receive a wage rise somewhat above 2 per cent. That way, the members would be getting a *real* rise in incomes. The employers will be happy to pay a wage rise somewhat below 2 per cent. After all, they can put their price up by approximately 2 per cent, knowing that their rivals will do the same. The actual wage rise that the two sides agree on will thus be somewhere around 2 per cent.

Now let us assume that the expected rate of inflation is 10 per cent. Both sides will now negotiate around this benchmark, with the outcome being somewhere around 10 per cent.

Thus the higher the expected rate of inflation, the higher will be the level of pay settlements and price rises, and hence the higher will be the resulting actual rate of inflation.

In recent years the importance of expectations in explaining the actual rate of inflation has been increasingly recognised by economists. We examine this in Sections 11.4 and 11.5.

use this power to drive up costs. Either way, the result is likely to be continuing rightward shifts in the *AD* curve and upward shifts in the *AS* curve. Prices will carry on rising. This is illustrated in Figure 11.5.

Recap

1. Demand-pull inflation occurs as a result of continuing increases in aggregate demand.
2. Cost-push inflation occurs when there are continuing increases in the costs of production independent of rises in aggregate demand. Single 'supply shocks' will lead to one-off increases in prices but not to continuing inflation.
3. Expectations play a crucial role in determining the level of inflation. The higher people expect inflation to be, the higher it will be.

11.2 AGGREGATE DEMAND, INFLATION AND OUTPUT

How will changes in the level of spending affect inflation and output?

In the previous section we introduced the idea of demand-pull inflation: inflation caused by increases in aggregate demand. But what impact would we expect changes in aggregate demand to have on prices (P)? Will levels of national output (Y) change too?

The debate concerning the impact of changes in aggregate demand on prices and output can best be understood in terms of the nature of the aggregate supply (*AS*) curve. We will start with the short-run *AS* (*SRAS*) curve and then look at the long-run curve.

Assume that there is a rise in aggregate demand. The short-run effect on output and prices will depend on the shape of the *SRAS* curve. The new classical and monetarist position (at least in the long run) is that the result of the rise in demand will simply be a rise in prices. In contrast, the Keynesian position is that there will also (or even solely) be

a rise in national output. Let us examine the different analyses of the *SRAS* curve.

The short-run aggregate supply curve

Various approaches to analysing aggregate supply are illustrated in Figure 11.6.

The moderate position

The moderate or mainstream view is that the *SRAS* curve is upward sloping. As we saw in Section 9.1, this is because wages and many other input prices exhibit *some* 'stickiness' in the short term. A rise in demand will not simply be absorbed in higher input prices: in other words, output will rise too.

Nevertheless, as more variable factors are used, firms will experience diminishing returns. Marginal costs will rise.

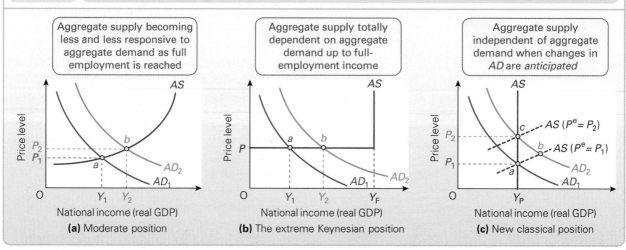

Figure 11.6   Different short-run aggregate supply curves

(a) Moderate position

(b) The extreme Keynesian position

(c) New classical position

The less the spare capacity in firms, the more rapidly marginal costs will rise for any given increase in output and hence the steeper will be the *SRAS* curve.

Therefore, the moderate view is that an increase in *AD* will have some effect on prices and some effect on output and employment (see Figures 11.6(a) and 11.9(a)). The extent of these effects will depend on the economy's current level of output relative to its potential level. The higher the actual output is relative to potential output, the steeper the *SRAS* becomes.

The extreme Keynesian position

The extreme Keynesian position (diagram (b)) is that up to a level of income that will generate full employment (Y_F) (similar to the concept of potential national income) the *SRAS* curve is *horizontal*. A rise in aggregate demand from AD_1 to AD_2 will raise output from Y_1 to Y_2, but there will be *no effect on prices* until full employment is reached.

In this extreme Keynesian model, aggregate supply up to the full-employment level is determined entirely by the level of aggregate demand. But there is no guarantee that aggregate demand will intersect aggregate supply at full employment. Therefore governments should manage aggregate demand by appropriate fiscal and monetary policies to ensure production at Y_F. We look at various macroeconomic policies in Chapter 12.

A recessionary gap. If the equilibrium level of national income (Y_e) is below the full-employment level (Y_F), there is what is known as a **recessionary or deflationary gap**. This situation is illustrated in Figure 11.7.

The **full-employment level of national income (Y_F)** (in other words, the potential level of output) is represented by the vertical line. The equilibrium level of national income is Y_e, where $W = J$ and $Y = E$. The recessionary gap is $a - b$: namely, the amount that the E line is below the 45° line at

the full-employment level of national income (Y_F). It is also $c - d$: the amount that injections fall short of withdrawals at the full-employment level of income.

If national income is to be raised from Y_e to Y_F, injections will have to be raised and/or withdrawals lowered so as to close the deflationary gap.

Note that the size of the recessionary gap is *less* than the amount by which Y_e falls short of Y_F. This illustrates the

Figure 11.7   The recessionary gap

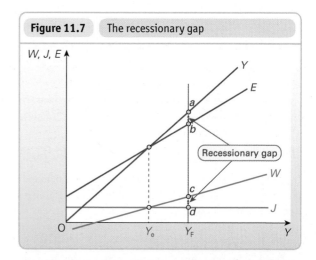

Definitions

Recessionary or deflationary gap The shortfall of aggregate expenditure below national income (and injections below withdrawals) at the full-employment level of national income.

Full-employment level of national income (real GDP) The level of national income (real GDP) at which there is no deficiency of demand.

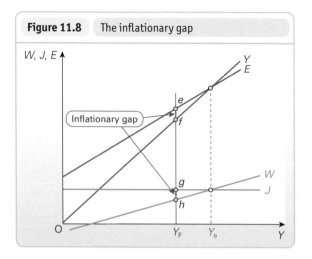

Figure 11.8 The inflationary gap

multiplier (see pages 221–3). If injections are raised by $a - b$ (i.e. $c - d$), national income will rise by $Y_F - Y_e$. The multiplier is thus given by:

$$\frac{Y_F - Y_e}{a - b}$$

An inflationary gap. If at the full-employment level of income, aggregate expenditure *exceeds* national income, there will be a problem of excess demand. Y_e will be above Y_F. The problem is that Y_F represents a real ceiling to output when the economy is working at normal capacity. In the short run, national income can only rise above this level by temporary measures, such as overtime working, which will put upward pressure on wages and prices. The result will therefore be demand-pull inflation.

This situation involves an **inflationary gap**. This is the amount by which aggregate expenditure exceeds national income, or injections exceed withdrawals, at the full-employment level of national income. This is illustrated by the gaps $e - f$ and $g - h$ in Figure 11.8.

To eliminate this inflation, the inflationary gap must be closed, either by raising withdrawals or by lowering injections.

Pause for thought

Assume that full-employment national income is £500 billion and that current national income is £450 billion. Assume also that the mpc_d is 4/5. (a) Is there an inflationary or deflationary gap? (b) What is the size of this gap?

The new classical position
In contrast, new classicists argue that the *SRAS* curve may be *vertical* at potential output (Y_p), as in Figure 11.6(c). This rests on two important assumptions. First, there is the assumption of **continuous market clearing**. This means that all markets continuously adjust to their equilibrium. Secondly, there is the assumption of **rational expectations**.

This means that people use all available information and predict inflation, or any other macroeconomic variable, as well as they can. The important point here is that forecasting errors are random so that, on average, people's expectations of inflation are correct.

The implication of continuous market clearing and rational expectations is that *anticipated* changes in aggregate demand will simply cause a change in prices, not a change in output and employment, even in the short run. Hence, an anticipated rise in aggregate demand will quickly work through both goods and factor markets into higher prices. There has been no increase in *real* aggregate demand. Output remains at its potential (normal capacity) level Y_p. Thus it is essential to keep (nominal) demand under control if *prices* are to be kept under control.

Unanticipated change in aggregate demand. An upward-sloping *SRAS* curve would be observable only if changes in aggregate demand were *unanticipated* and even then deviations in output from its potential level would be transitory. If, in Figure 11.6(c), aggregate demand were to rise unexpectedly, say from AD_1 to AD_2, people would not foresee the upward effect on general prices. Hence, workers and firms would have negotiated specific input prices, including wages, on the expectation that the general price level would be P_1. Therefore, the expected price level P^e is P_1 ($P^e = P_1$). As the general price level rises it is profitable for businesses to expand output levels. This is equivalent to the move from *a* to *b* in Figure 11.6(c).

Once people recognise these errors, however, output adjusts back to its potential level Y_p. The economy moves from point *b* to *c*. In the presence of rational expectations and continuous market clearing this adjustment is likely to happen relatively quickly. Hence to raise output and employment *supply-side* policies will be required. If successful, these will shift the vertical *AS* curve to the right.

Pause for thought

If there was an unexpected decrease in aggregate demand would new classicists expect output to fall below its potential level? Explain.

Definitions

Inflationary gap The excess of aggregate expenditure over income (and injections over withdrawals) at the full-employment level of national income.

Continuous market clearing The assumption that all markets in the economy continuously clear so that the economy is permanently in equilibrium.

Rational expectations Expectations based on the *current* situation. These expectations are based on the information people have to hand. While this information may be imperfect and therefore people will make errors, these errors will be random.

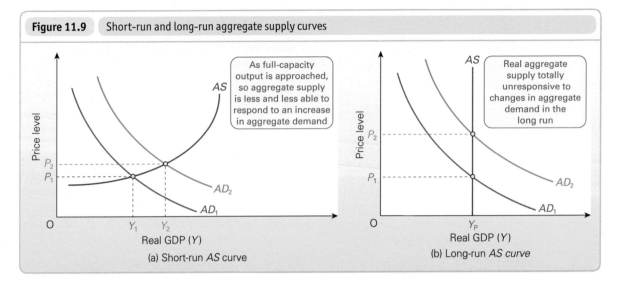

Figure 11.9 Short-run and long-run aggregate supply curves

As full-capacity output is approached, so aggregate supply is less and less able to respond to an increase in aggregate demand

(a) Short-run *AS* curve

Real aggregate supply totally unresponsive to changes in aggregate demand in the long run

(b) Long-run *AS curve*

The long-run aggregate supply curve

A vertical long-run AS curve

While new classical economists argue that the short-run *AS* curve is typically vertical, most economists argue that it is only the *long-run AS* curve that is vertical at the potential level of output (Y_p): see Figure 11.9(b). Any rise in nominal aggregate demand would lead simply to a rise in prices and no long-term increase in output at all.

The mainstream view is that long-term increases in output could occur only through rightward shifts in this vertical long-run *AS* curve, in other words through increases in potential output. To achieve this, governments should largely focus on supply-side policy, such as policies which help foster technological progress (see Chapter 9).

But why do these economists argue that the long-run *AS* curve is vertical? They justify this by focusing on the *interdependence of markets*. Assume initially that the economy is operating at the potential level of output (Y_p). Now assume that there is an increase in demand, such as from an

increase in government expenditure. The increase in aggregate demand will initially lead firms to raise both prices and output, for the reasons we gave above. In other words, the short-run aggregate supply curve is upward sloping. There is a movement from point *a* to point *b* in Figure 11.10. Output rises to Y_2.

However, as raw material and intermediate goods producers raise their prices, so this will raise the costs of production of firms using these inputs. A rise in the price of steel will raise the costs of producing cars and washing machines. At the same time, workers, seeing the prices of goods rising, will demand higher wages. Firms will be relatively willing to grant these wage demands, given that they are experiencing a buoyant demand from their customers. The effect of all this is to raise firms' *costs*, and hence their prices. As prices rise for any given level of output, so the short-run *AS* curve will shift upwards. This is shown by a move to $AS_{2(\text{short run})}$ in Figure 11.10. The economy moves from point *b* to point *c*. Thus output can only temporarily rise above the potential level (Y_p).

The long-run effect, therefore, of a rise in aggregate demand from AD_1 to AD_2 is a movement from point *a* to point *c*. The long-run aggregate supply curve passes through these two points. It is vertical at the potential level of output. A rise in aggregate demand will therefore have no long-run effect on output. The entire effect will be felt in terms of higher prices.

As we saw above, new classical economists go one step further. Because markets are very flexible, they argue, higher costs will be passed through into higher prices virtually instantly. What is more, people will typically anticipate this and hence take it into account *now*. These assumptions mean that the *short*-run aggregate supply curve will be vertical also (as in Figure 11.6(c)). Even if the change in aggregate demand and/or the impact on prices were a 'surprise', markets would still clear relatively quickly so that any impact on the economy's output would be transitory.

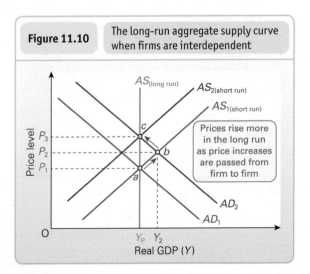

Figure 11.10 The long-run aggregate supply curve when firms are interdependent

Prices rise more in the long run as price increases are passed from firm to firm

An upward-sloping long-run AS curve

Some Keynesian economists, however, argue that the long-run *AS* curve is upward sloping, not vertical. Indeed, it may be even shallower than the short-run curve. For them, potential output is affected by changes in aggregate demand.

We saw in Chapter 9 that investment is crucial to long-run economic growth. The argument here is that with a rise in demand firms may be encouraged to invest in new plant and machinery. This increase in the stock of capital will increase the *capacity* of the economy to produce. In other words, the increase in aggregate demand will increase potential output. The result is that firms may well be able to increase output significantly in the long run with little or no increase in their prices. Their long-run *MC* curves are much flatter than their short-run *MC* curves.

Again assume initially that output is at the potential level. In Figure 11.11 this is shown as Y_{P1}. Aggregate demand then increases to AD_2. Equilibrium moves to point *b* with GDP at Y_2. The resulting increased investment shifts the short-run *AS* curve to the right. Equilibrium moves from point *b* to *d*. Point *d* is now at the new potential level of output, Y_{P2}. The long-run *AS* curve thus joins points *a* and *d*.

The way the diagram is drawn, the long-run *AS* curve is more elastic than the short-run curve. There is a relatively large increase in output and a relatively small increase in price. If the rise in costs had been more substantial, curve $AS_{2(short run)}$ could be above curve $AS_{1(short run)}$. In this case, although the long-run *AS* curve would still be upward sloping, it would be steeper than the short-run curves: point *d* would be above point *b*.

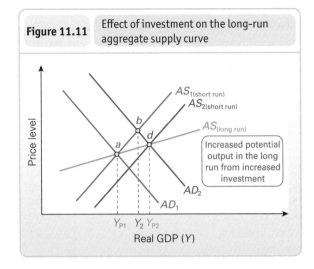

Figure 11.11 Effect of investment on the long-run aggregate supply curve

Pause for thought

If a shift in the aggregate demand curve from AD_1 to AD_2 in Figure 11.11 causes a movement from point a to point d in the long run, will a shift in the aggregate demand curve from AD_1 to AD cause a movement from point d back to point a in the long run?

The long-run *AS* curve will be steeper if the extra investment causes significant shortages of materials, machinery or labour. This is more likely when the economy is already operating near its full-capacity output. It will be flatter, and possibly even downward sloping, if the investment involves the introduction of new cost-reducing technology.

Recap

1. The impact of changes in aggregate demand on prices (and output) is affected by the nature of aggregate supply (*AS*) curve.

2. If nominal aggregate demand changes, then in the short run it is likely to affect real GDP (*Y*) according to the degree of slack in the economy. The short-run aggregate supply curve tends to be relatively elastic (except when the economy is operating close to or above potential output). This is because both wage rates and prices tend to be relatively sticky.

3. In the long run, according to many economists, the aggregate supply curve is vertical because price increases from any rise in aggregate demand tend to be passed on from one firm to another and feed into wage increases.

4. New classicists argue that that the *short-run* aggregate supply curve may be vertical too. This is because of the flexibility of markets and the ability of rational people to forecast the effect of expected changes in aggregate demand on prices.

5. Some argue, however, that the long-run aggregate supply curve may be upward sloping. If a sustained increase in demand leads to increased investment, this can have the effect of shifting the short-run aggregate supply curve to the right and making the long-run curve upward sloping, not vertical.

11.3 MONEY SUPPLY, AGGREGATE DEMAND AND INFLATION

How will changes in money supply affect spending, output and prices?

There is considerable debate around the impact of changes in the money supply on inflation. The debate focuses on not only how changes in aggregate demand affect inflation, as we have done up to this point, but also how changes in the money supply affect aggregate demand.

The 1970s saw the rise of monetarism. The most famous advocate of monetarism was Milton Friedman, who argued that inflation can be attributed entirely to increases in the money supply. The faster money supply expands, the higher will be the rate of inflation. New classical economists of today take a similar view. Excessive expansion of the money supply will lead simply to inflation. Keynesians, by contrast, see a much looser association between money and prices.

The debate can best be understood in terms of the **quantity theory of money**. The theory is simply that the level of prices in the economy depends on the quantity of money: the greater the supply of money, the higher will be the level of prices.

A development of the quantity theory is the *equation of exchange*. Focusing on this equation is the best way of understanding the debate over the relationship between money and prices.

The equation of exchange

The **equation of exchange** shows the relationship between the money value of spending and the money value of output (nominal GDP). This identity may be expressed as follows:

$$MV = PY$$

M is the supply of money in the economy (e.g. M4). *V* is its **velocity of circulation**. This is the number of times per year that money is spent on buying goods and services that have been produced in the economy that year (real GDP). *P* is the level of prices of domestically produced goods and services, expressed as an index, where the index is 1 in a chosen base year (e.g. 1990). Thus if prices today are double those in the base year, *P* is 2. *Y* is *real* national income (real GDP): in other words, the quantity of national output produced in that year measured in base-year prices.

PY is thus nominal GDP: i.e. GDP measured at current prices (see the Appendix to Chapter 8, page 227). For example, if GDP at base-year prices (*Y*) is £1 trillion and the price index is 2, then GDP at current prices (*PY*) is £2 trillion.

Pause for thought

If the money supply is cut by 10 per cent, what must happen to the velocity of circulation if there is no change in GDP at current prices?

MV is the total spending on the goods and services that make up GDP – in other words, (nominal) aggregate demand. For example, if money supply is £500 billion, and money, as it passes from one person to another, is spent on average four times a year on national output, then total spending (*MV*) is £2 trillion a year. But this too *must* equal GDP at current prices. The reason is that what is spent on output (by consumers, by firms on investment, by the government or by people abroad on exports) must equal the value of goods produced (*PY*).

The equation of exchange (or 'quantity equation') is true by definition. *MV* is *necessarily* equal to *PY* because of the way the terms are defined. Thus a rise in *MV must* be accompanied by a rise in *PY*. What a change in *M* does to *P*, however, is a matter of debate. The controversy centres on the impact of changes in the money supply on aggregate demand and then on the impact of changes in aggregate demand on output. We have seen that the latter depends crucially on the nature of the aggregate supply. We now focus on the relationship between money supply and aggregate demand, beginning with the short-run relationship.

Money and aggregate demand

The short run

Chapter 10 identified two ways in which changes in the money supply could affect aggregate demand: the interest rate and exchange rate transmission mechanisms. Taken together, the impact of an increase in the money supply can be summarised as follows:

1. A rise in money supply will lead to a fall in the rate of interest.
2. The fall in the rate of interest will lead to a rise in investment and other forms of borrowing. It will also lead to a fall in the exchange rate and hence a rise in exports and a fall in imports.
3. The rise in investment, and the rise in exports and fall in imports, will mean a rise in aggregate demand.

However, there is considerable debate over how these transmission mechanisms function.

How interest rate elastic is money demand? The demand for money as a means of storing wealth (the assets motive) can be large and highly responsive to changes in interest rates

---

Definitions

Quantity theory of money The price level (*P*) is directly related to the quantity of money in the economy (*M*).

Equation of exchange *MV = PY*. The total level of spending on GDP (*MV*) equals the total value of goods and services produced (*PY*) that go to make up GDP.

Velocity of circulation The number of times annually that money on average is spent on goods and services that made up GDP.

on alternative assets. Indeed, large sums of money move around the money market as firms and financial institutions respond to and anticipate changes in interest rates. Therefore, the demand for money curve in Figure 10.8 (see page 287) could be relatively flat. This is important because following an increase in money supply only a relatively small fall in interest rates on bonds and other assets may be necessary to persuade people to hold all the extra money in bank accounts. This greatly slows down the average speed at which money circulates. The fall in V may virtually offset the rise in M.

In other words, the more sensitive is the demand for money to changes in the rate of interest, the less impact changes in money supply have on aggregate demand.

How stable is the money demand function? Another criticism is that the demand for money is unstable and so the demand for money curve in Figure 10.8 is frequently moving. People hold speculative balances of money when they anticipate that the prices of other assets, such as shares, bonds and bills, will fall (and hence the rate of return or interest on these assets will rise).

There are many factors that could affect such expectations, such as changes in foreign interest rates, changes in exchange rates, statements of government intentions on economic policy, good or bad industrial news, or newly published figures on inflation or money supply. With an unstable demand for money, it is difficult to predict the effect of a change in money supply on interest rates and so on aggregate demand.

It has been largely for this reason that most central banks have preferred to control interest rates directly, rather than indirectly by controlling the money supply – although increasing the money supply through 'quantitative easing' was a major additional measure used to stimulate aggregate demand in the wake of the world recession. We examine the conduct of monetary policy in Chapter 12.

How interest rate elastic is spending? The problem here is that investment may be insensitive to changes in interest rates. Businesses are more likely to be influenced in their decision to invest by predictions of the future buoyancy of markets. Interest rates do have *some* effect on businesses' investment decisions, but the effect is unpredictable, depending on the confidence of investors.

Where interest rates are likely to have a stronger effect on spending is via mortgages. If interest rates go up, and mortgage rates follow suit, people will suddenly be faced with higher monthly repayments (debt servicing costs) and will therefore have to cut down their expenditure on goods and services.

How interest rate sensitive is the exchange rate? Also the amount that the exchange rate will depreciate is uncertain, since exchange rate movements, as we shall see in Chapter 14, depend crucially on expectations about trade

prospects and about future world interest rate movements. Thus the effects on imports and exports are also uncertain.

To summarise: the effects on total spending of a change in the money supply *might* be quite strong, but they could be weak. In other words, the effects are highly unpredictable.

$$M\uparrow \rightarrow V\downarrow(?) \rightarrow MV?$$

Keynesians use these arguments to criticise the use of monetary policy as a means of managing aggregate demand.

The long run

In the long run, there is a stronger link between money supply and aggregate demand. In fact, monetarists claim that in the long run V is determined *totally independently* of the money supply (M). Thus an increase in M will leave V unaffected and hence will directly increase expenditure (MV):

$$M\uparrow \rightarrow M\bar{V}\uparrow$$

where the bar over the V term means that it is **exogenously** determined: i.e. determined *independently* of M. But why do they claim this?

If money supply increases over the longer term, people will have more money than they require to hold. They will spend this surplus. Much of this spending will go on goods and services, thereby directly increasing aggregate demand.

The theoretical underpinning for this is given by the *theory of portfolio balance*. People have a number of ways of holding their wealth. They can hold it as money, or as financial assets such as bills, bonds and shares, or as physical assets such as houses, cars and televisions. In other words, people hold a whole portfolio of assets of varying degrees of liquidity – from cash to central heating.

If money supply expands, people will find themselves holding more money than they require: their portfolios are 'unnecessarily liquid'. Some of this money will be used to purchase financial assets and some, possibly after a period of time, to purchase *goods and services*. As more assets are purchased, this will drive up their price. This will effectively reduce their 'yield'. For bonds and other *financial* assets, this means a reduction in their rate of interest. For goods and services, it means an increase in their price relative to their usefulness or 'utility'.

The process will stop when a balance has been restored in people's portfolios. In the meantime, there will have been extra consumption and hence an increase in aggregate demand.

Definition

Exogenous variable A variable whose value is determined independently of the model of which it is part.

> **Recap**
>
> 1. The quantity equation $MV = PY$ can be used to analyse the possible relationships between money and prices.
>
> 2. In the short run, the velocity of circulation (V) may vary inversely, but unpredictably, with the money supply (M). The reason is that changes in money supply will have unpredictable and possibly rather weak effects on interest rates, and, similarly, changes in interest rates will have unpredictable and probably rather weak effects on aggregate demand. Thus spending (MV) will change by possibly only a small and rather unpredictable amount.
>
> 3. In the long run, there is a stronger link between money supply and aggregate demand.

11.4 UNEMPLOYMENT

If people want to consume more goods, why are so many people out of work?

Unemployment fluctuates with the business cycle. In recessions, such as those experienced by most countries in the early 1980s, early 1990s and the early and late 2000s, unemployment tends to rise. In boom years, such as the late 1980s, late 1990s and mid-2000s, it tends to fall. Figure 11.12 shows these cyclical movements in unemployment for selected countries.

As well as experiencing fluctuations in unemployment, most countries have experienced long-term changes in average unemployment rates. This is illustrated in Table 11.1, which shows average unemployment rates in a selection of industrialised countries. Average unemployment rates in the 1980s and 1990s were higher than in the 1970s, and average rates in the 1970s were, in turn, higher than in the 1960s. In certain countries, such as the UK and the USA, the late 1990s and early 2000s saw a long-term fall in unemployment.

However, the global financial crisis of the late 2000s and subsequent economic downturn saw a marked upward turn in unemployment rates. This was particularly so in countries where government finances were badly hit and where, as a result, governments looked to repair their balance sheets by restraining spending and/or raising taxes.

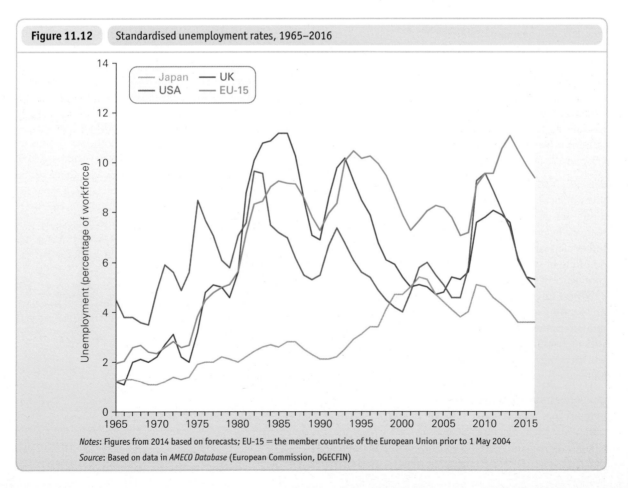

| Figure 11.12 | Standardised unemployment rates, 1965–2016 |

Notes: Figures from 2014 based on forecasts; EU-15 = the member countries of the European Union prior to 1 May 2004

Source: Based on data in *AMECO Database* (European Commission, DGECFIN)

Table 11.1	Average unemployment by decade (%)					
	1960s	**1970s**	**1980s**	**1990s**	**2000s**	**2010–16**
Australia	1.7	3.8	7.6	8.8	5.5	5.6
Canada	5.0	6.7	9.4	9.5	7.0	7.2
France	1.7	2.9	8.6	11.4	8.7	9.9
Germany	0.7	2.0	5.8	7.7	9.1	5.5
Greece	5.1	2.3	6.1	9.1	9.7	22.3
Ireland	5.3	7.5	14.2	12.0	5.4	12.2
Japan	1.3	1.7	2.5	3.1	4.7	4.2
Portugal	2.4	4.6	7.5	5.7	7.5	14.0
Spain	2.4	4.5	16.3	18.0	11.2	23.2
UK	1.6	3.5	9.5	8.0	5.4	6.9
USA	4.8	6.2	7.3	5.7	5.6	7.3
EU-15	2.2	3.5	8.4	9.5	7.9	10.2

Notes: (i) EU-15 = 15 members of the European Union prior to 1 May 2004; (ii) German figures relate to West Germany only up to 1991; (iii) Figures from 2015 are forecasts

Source: AMECO database (European Commission, DGECFIN, 2015)

In some countries, such as Ireland, Greece and Portugal, emergency loans had to be granted to help meet the rising costs of managing their rising stock of debt.

The meaning of 'unemployment'

Unemployment can be expressed either as a number (e.g. 2 million) or as a percentage (e.g. 5 per cent). But just who should be included in the statistics? Should it be everyone without a job? The answer is clearly no, since we would not want to include children and pensioners. We would probably also want to exclude those who were not looking for work, such as parents choosing to stay at home to look after children.

The most usual definition that economists use for the **number unemployed** is: 'those of working age who are without work, but who are available for work at current wage rates'. If the figure is to be expressed as a percentage, then it is a percentage of the total **labour force**. The labour force is defined as: 'those in employment (including the self-employed, those in the armed forces and those on government training schemes) plus those unemployed'. Thus

if 30 million people were employed and 2 million people were unemployed, the **unemployment rate** would be:

$$\frac{2}{30} \times 100 = 6.7\%$$

Official measures of unemployment

Claimant unemployment

Two common measures of unemployment are used in official statistics. The first is **claimant unemployment**. The claimant count is simply a measure of all those in receipt of unemployment-related benefits. In the UK claimants receive the Jobseeker's Allowance.

Claimant statistics have the advantage of being very easy to collect. However, they exclude all those of working age available for work at current wage rates, but who are *not* eligible for benefits. If the government changes the eligibility conditions so that fewer people are now eligible, this will reduce the number of claimants and hence the official number unemployed, even if there has been no change in the numbers with or without work.

Definitions

Number unemployed (economist's definition) Those of working age who are without work, but who are available for work at current wage rates.

Labour force The number employed plus the number unemployed.

Unemployment rate The number unemployed expressed as a percentage of the labour force.

Claimant unemployment Those in receipt of unemployment-related benefits.

BOX 11.3 **THE COSTS OF UNEMPLOYMENT**

CASE STUDIES & APPLICATIONS

Is it just the unemployed who suffer?

The most obvious cost of unemployment is to the *unemployed themselves*. There is the direct financial cost of the loss in their earnings, measured as the difference between their previous wage and their unemployment benefit. Then there are the personal costs of being unemployed. The longer people are unemployed, the more dispirited they may become. Their self-esteem is likely to fall, and they are more likely to succumb to stress-related illness.

Then there are the costs to the *family and friends* of the unemployed. Personal relations can become strained, and there may be an increase in domestic violence and the number of families splitting up.

Then there are the *broader costs to the economy*. Unemployment benefits are a cost borne by taxpayers. There may also have to be extra public spending on benefit offices, social services, health care and the police. What is more, unemployment represents a loss of output. In other words, actual output is below potential output. Apart from the lack of income to the unemployed themselves, this under utilisation of resources leads to lower incomes for other people too:

■ The government loses tax revenues, since the unemployed pay no income tax or national insurance, and, given that the unemployed spend less, they pay less VAT and excise duties.

■ Firms lose the profits that could have been made, had there been full employment.

■ Other workers lose any additional wages they could have earned from the higher national output.

What is more, the longer people remain unemployed, the more deskilled they tend to become. In other words, their stock of human capital declines. As we saw in Chapter 9, investment in human capital is considered by many as an important influence on an economy's potential output. Therefore, long-term unemployment reduces potential as well as actual income.

Finally there is some evidence that higher unemployment leads to increased crime and vandalism. This obviously imposes a cost on the sufferers.

The costs of unemployment are to some extent offset by benefits. If workers voluntarily quit their jobs to look for a better one, then they must reckon that the benefits of a better job more than compensate for their temporary loss of income. From the nation's point of view, a workforce that is prepared to quit jobs and spend a short time unemployed will be a more adaptable, more mobile workforce – one that is responsive to changing economic circumstances. Such a workforce will lead to greater allocative efficiency in the short run and more rapid economic growth over the longer run.

Long-term involuntary unemployment is quite another matter. The costs clearly outweigh any benefits, both for the individuals concerned and for the economy as a whole. A demotivated, deskilled pool of long-term unemployed is a serious economic and social problem.

? *How might an economist set about measuring the various costs of unemployment to family, friends and society at large?*

Standardised unemployment rates

Recognising the weaknesses of the claimant statistics, the UK government since 1998 has used the **standardised unemployment rate** as the main measure of unemployment. Sometimes known as ILO unemployment, this is the measure used by the International Labour Organization (ILO) and the Organization for Economic Cooperation and Development (OECD), two international organisations that publish unemployment statistics for many countries.

In this measure, the unemployed are defined as people of working age who are without work, available to start work within two weeks and *actively seeking employment* or waiting to take up an appointment. The figures are compiled from the results of national labour force surveys. In the UK the labour force survey is conducted quarterly.

But is the standardised unemployment rate likely to be higher or lower than the claimant unemployment rate? The standardised rate is likely to be higher to the extent that it includes people seeking work who are nevertheless not entitled to claim benefits, but lower to the extent that it excludes those who are claiming benefits and yet who are not actively seeking work. Clearly, the tougher the benefit regulations, the lower the claimant rate will be relative to the standardised rate. In the three months to September 2014, standardised unemployment in the UK (for those

aged 16 and over) was estimated at 1.96 million (6.0 per cent) while claimant count unemployment in September 2014 was measured at 0.95 million (2.8 per cent).

In many countries, female unemployment has traditionally been higher than male unemployment. Causes have included differences in education and training, discrimination by employers, more casual or seasonally related employment among women, and other social factors. In many countries, however, the position has changed in recent years. As you can see, in six of the ten economies in Table 11.2 male unemployment rates are higher than female rates. The main reason is the decline in many of the older industries, such as coal and steel, which employed mainly men. Across the whole EU, male and female unemployment rates are virtually the same.

Definition

Standardised unemployment rate The measure of the unemployment rate used by the ILO and OECD. The unemployed are defined as persons of working age who are without work, available for work and actively seeking employment.

Table 11.2	Standardised unemployment rates by age and gender, average April 2009 to March 2015					
	All ages			**Under 25**		
	Total	**Male**	**Female**	**Total**	**Male**	**Female**
France	9.7	9.7	9.8	23.9	24.1	23.6
Germany	5.9	6.2	5.6	8.7	9.4	7.8
Greece	20.5	17.7	24.2	46.0	40.3	52.6
Ireland	13.3	15.9	10.0	27.1	32.0	21.8
Italy	10.2	9.4	11.4	34.1	32.6	36.4
Netherlands	6.0	5.6	6.3	11.6	11.9	11.2
Poland	9.5	9.0	10.1	24.8	23.2	27.0
Portugal	13.8	13.7	13.9	32.8	31.6	34.1
Spain	22.7	22.3	23.2	48.5	49.7	47.1
Sweden	8.1	8.3	7.9	23.7	24.8	22.5
UK	7.4	8.0	6.8	19.8	22.1	17.2
USA	8.1	8.6	7.6	16.3	17.9	14.4
EU-15	10.1	10.1	10.2	21.6	22.6	20.6
EU-28	10.0	10.0	10.1	22.2	22.9	21.3

Source: Statistics Database, Eurostat (European Commission, 2015)

Table 11.2 also shows that unemployment rates in the under-25 age group are higher than the average, and substantially so in many countries. In the EU as a whole the unemployment rate of the under-25s in the six-year period from April 2009 to March 2015 was more than double the average rate; in Italy it was more than triple. There are various explanations for this, including the suitability (or unsuitability) of the qualifications of school leavers, the attitudes of employers to young people, and the greater willingness of young people to spend time unemployed looking for a better job or waiting to start a further or higher education course. The difference in rates is less in Germany, which has a well-established apprenticeship system.

Unemployment and the labour market

We now turn to the causes of unemployment. These causes fall into two broad categories: *equilibrium* unemployment and *disequilibrium* unemployment. To make clear the distinction between the two, it is necessary to look at how the labour market works.

Figure 11.13 shows the aggregate demand for labour and the aggregate supply of labour: that is, the total demand and supply of labour in the whole economy. The *real* average wage rate is plotted on the vertical axis. This is the average wage rate expressed in terms of its purchasing power: in other words, after taking prices into account.

The **aggregate supply of labour curve** (AS_L) shows the number of workers *willing to accept jobs* at each real wage rate. This curve is relatively inelastic, since the size of the workforce at any one time cannot change significantly. Nevertheless it is not totally inelastic because (a) a higher wage rate will encourage some people to enter the labour market (e.g. parents raising children), and (b) the unemployed will be more willing to accept job offers rather than continuing to search for a better paid job.

Figure 11.13	Disequilibrium unemployment

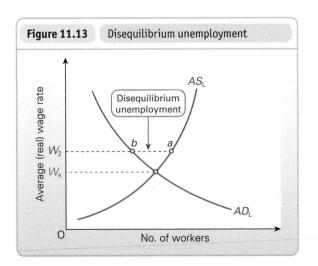

Definition

Aggregate supply of labour curve A curve showing the total number of people willing and able to work at different average real wage rates.

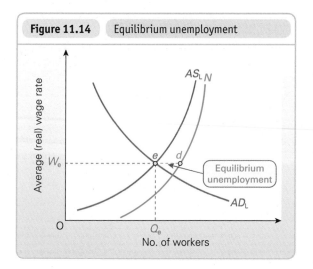

Figure 11.14   Equilibrium unemployment

The **aggregate demand for labour curve** (AD_L) slopes downwards. The higher the real wage rate, the more will firms attempt to economise on labour and to substitute other factors of production for labour.

The labour market is in equilibrium at a wage of W_e, where the demand for labour equals the supply. If the wage rate were above W_e, the labour market would be in a state of disequilibrium. At a wage rate of W_2, there is an excess supply of labour of $a - b$. This is called **disequilibrium unemployment**.

For disequilibrium unemployment to occur, two conditions must hold:

- The aggregate supply of labour must exceed the aggregate demand.
- There must be a 'stickiness' in wages. In other words, the wage rate must not immediately fall to We.

Even when the labour market *is* in equilibrium, however, not everyone looking for work will be employed. Some people will hold out, hoping to find a better job. The curve *N* in Figure 11.14 shows the total number in the labour force. The horizontal difference between it and the aggregate supply of labour curve (AS_L) represents the excess of people looking for work over those actually willing to accept jobs. Q_e represents the equilibrium level of employment and the distance $d - e$ represents the **equilibrium level of unemployment**. This is sometimes known as the *natural level of unemployment*.

TC 6
p 37

Types of disequilibrium unemployment

There are three possible causes of disequilibrium unemployment.

Real-wage unemployment

Real-wage unemployment is where trade unions use their monopoly power to drive wages above the market-clearing level. In Figure 11.13, the wage rate is driven up above W_e. Excessive real wage rates were blamed by the Thatcher and Major governments for the high unemployment of the 1980s and 1990s. The possibility of higher real-wage unemployment was also one of the reasons for their rejection of a national minimum wage.

Even though unions have the power to drive up wages in some industries, their power to do so has waned in recent years. Labour markets have become more flexible (see Case Study 6.2 in MyEconLab). What is more, the process of globalisation has meant that many firms face intense competition from rivals in China, India and many other countries. This makes it impossible for them to concede large pay increases. In many cases, they can simply use labour in other countries if domestic labour is too expensive. For example, many firms employ call-centre workers in India, where wages are much lower.

As far as the national minimum wage is concerned, evidence from the UK suggests that the rate has not been high enough to have significant adverse effects on employment (see Box 6.4 on page 156). However, with the introduction by the Conservative government of a higher minimum wage for people aged 25 and over, which it has dubbed the 'living wage', worries have been expressed by many businesses in low-wage sectors, such as retail and hospitality, that they may be forced to cut employment.

Demand-deficient or cyclical unemployment

Demand-deficient or cyclical unemployment is associated with recessions. As the economy moves into recession, consumer demand falls. Firms find that they are unable to sell their current level of output. For a time they may be prepared to build up stocks of unsold goods, but sooner or later

TC 12
p 202

Definitions

Aggregate demand for labour curve A curve showing the total demand for labour in the economy at different average real wage rates.

Disequilibrium unemployment Unemployment resulting from real wages in the economy being above the equilibrium level.

Equilibrium ('natural') unemployment The difference between those who would like employment at the current wage rate and those willing and able to take a job.

Real-wage unemployment Disequilibrium unemployment caused by real wages being driven up above the market-clearing level.

Demand-deficient or cyclical unemployment Disequilibrium unemployment caused by a fall in aggregate demand with no corresponding fall in the real wage rate.

they will start to cut back on production and cut back on the amount of labour they employ. In Figure 11.13 the AD_L curve shifts to the left. The deeper the recession becomes and the longer it lasts, the higher will demand-deficient unemployment become.

But if there is surplus labour, why do real wages not fall so as to eliminate the surplus? There are two main reasons, both of which help to explain why real wage rates did not fall during the recessions of the early 1980s and early 1990s.

Efficiency wages. The argument here is that wage rates fulfil two functions. The first is the traditional one of balancing the demand and supply of labour. The second is that of motivating workers. If real wage rates are reduced when there is a surplus of labour, then those workers already in employment may become dispirited and work less hard. If, on the other hand, firms keep wage rates up, then by maintaining a well-motivated workforce, by cutting down on labour turnover and by finding it easier to attract well-qualified labour, firms may find their costs are reduced: a higher real wage is thus more profitable for them. The maximum-profit real wage rate (the **efficiency wage rate**) is likely to be above the market-clearing real wage rate (see pages 145–6). Demand-deficient unemployment is likely to persist – more people would like to work at the efficiency wage than there are jobs available.

Insider power. If those still in employment (the insiders) are members of unions, while those out of work (the outsiders) are not, or if the insiders have special skills or knowledge that give them bargaining power with employers, while the outsiders have no influence, then there is no mechanism whereby the surplus labour – the outsiders – can drive down the real wage rate and eliminate the demand-deficient unemployment.

Even if real wages *did* fall, it may not solve the problem of demand-deficient unemployment. In fact, it might even make the problem worse. The reason is that this general cut in real wages throughout the economy would reduce workers' real incomes and hence reduce their *consumption of goods*. As the aggregate demand for goods fell, there would be a further reduction in demand for labour: the aggregate demand for labour curve would shift further to the left. The fall in real wages would be 'chasing' a leftward-shifting AD_L curve. As the real wage fell towards equilibrium, so the equilibrium real wage itself would be falling and equilibrium would not be reached. There would still be demand-deficient unemployment.

Pause for thought

If this analysis is correct, namely that a reduction in real wages will reduce the aggregate demand for goods, what assumption must we make about the relative proportions of wages and profits that are spent (given that a reduction in real wage rates will lead to a corresponding increase in rates of profit)?

Later, as the economy recovers and begins to grow again, so demand-deficient unemployment will start to fall again. Because demand-deficient unemployment fluctuates with the business cycle, it is sometimes referred to as 'cyclical unemployment'. Figure 11.12 (on page 304) showed such fluctuations in unemployment in various industrial countries.

Growth in the labour supply

If labour supply rises with no corresponding increase in the demand for labour, the equilibrium real wage rate will fall. If the real wage rate is 'sticky' downwards, unemployment will occur. This tends not to be such a serious cause of unemployment as demand deficiency, since the supply of labour changes relatively slowly. Nevertheless there is a problem of providing jobs for school and university leavers each year with the sudden influx of new workers onto the labour market.

Equilibrium unemployment (or natural unemployment)

If you look at Table 11.1 on page 305, you can see how unemployment in many countries was higher in the 1980s and 1990s than in the previous two decades. Part of the reason for this was the growth in equilibrium unemployment. In the 2000s, unemployment fell in many countries – at least until the financial crisis of 2007/8. Again, part of the reason for this was a change in equilibrium unemployment, but this time a fall.

Although there may be overall *macro*economic equilibrium, with the *aggregate* demand for labour equal to the *aggregate* supply, and thus no disequilibrium unemployment, at a *micro*economic level supply and demand may not match. In other words, there may be vacancies in some parts of the economy, but an excess of labour (unemployment) in others. This is equilibrium unemployment. There are various types of equilibrium unemployment.

Frictional (search) unemployment

Frictional (search) unemployment occurs when people leave their jobs, either voluntarily or because they are sacked or made redundant, and are then unemployed for a period of time while they are looking for a new job. They may not get the first job they apply for, despite a vacancy existing. The employer may continue searching, hoping to

Definitions

Efficiency wage rate The profit-maximising wage rate for the firm after taking into account the effects of wage rates on worker motivation, turnover and recruitment.

Frictional (search) unemployment Unemployment that occurs as a result of imperfect information in the labour market. It often takes time for workers to find jobs (even though there are vacancies) and in the meantime they are unemployed.

BOX 11.4 THE DURATION OF UNEMPLOYMENT

Taking a dip in the unemployment pool

A few of the unemployed may never have had a job and maybe never will. For most, however, unemployment lasts only a certain period. For some it may be just a few days while they are between jobs. For others it may be a few months. For others – the long-term unemployed – it could be several years. As Box 11.3 explains, long-term unemployment negatively affects a country's potential output, particularly by reducing a country's stock of human capital. Therefore, the length of time people spend unemployed is an important labour market issue.

Long-term unemployment is normally defined as those who have been unemployed for over 12 months. Chart (a) shows the composition of standardised unemployment in the UK by duration since the early 1990s. It shows how long-term unemployment fell from the mid-1990s until the economic downturn in the late 2000s. As a result, the percentage of unemployed people classified as long-term unemployed,

which had hit 45 per cent during 1994, fell to just below 20 per cent during 2004, before rising to 37 per cent in early 2014.

But what determines the average duration of unemployment? There are three important factors here.

The number unemployed (the size of the stock of unemployment)

Unemployment is a 'stock' concept: it measures a quantity of people unemployed at a particular point in time. The higher the stock of unemployment, the longer will tend to be the duration of unemployment. There will be more people competing for vacant jobs.

KI 21
p 148

The rate of inflow and outflow from the stock of unemployment

The people making up the unemployment total are constantly changing. Each week some people are made redundant or quit

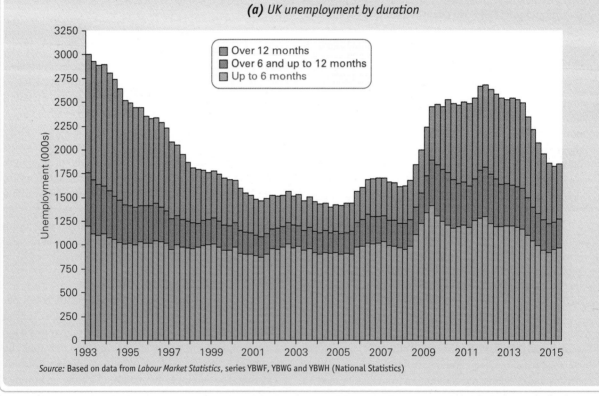

(a) UK unemployment by duration

Legend:
- Over 12 months
- Over 6 and up to 12 months
- Up to 6 months

Y-axis: Unemployment (000s)

X-axis years: 1993, 1995, 1997, 1999, 2001, 2003, 2005, 2007, 2009, 2011, 2013, 2015

Source: Based on data from *Labour Market Statistics*, series YBWF, YBWG and YBWH (National Statistics)

find a better-qualified person. Likewise, unemployed people may choose not to take the first job they are offered. Instead, they may continue searching, hoping that a better one will turn up.

The problem is that information is imperfect. Employers are not fully informed about what labour is available; workers are not fully informed about what jobs are available and what they entail. Both employers and workers, therefore, have to search: employers searching for the right labour and workers searching for the right jobs.

One obvious remedy for frictional unemployment is for there to be better job information. This could be provided by government Job Centres, by private employment agencies, by local and national newspapers or by the Internet.

Structural unemployment

Structural unemployment is where the structure of the economy changes. Employment in some industries may expand while in others it contracts. There are two main reasons for this.

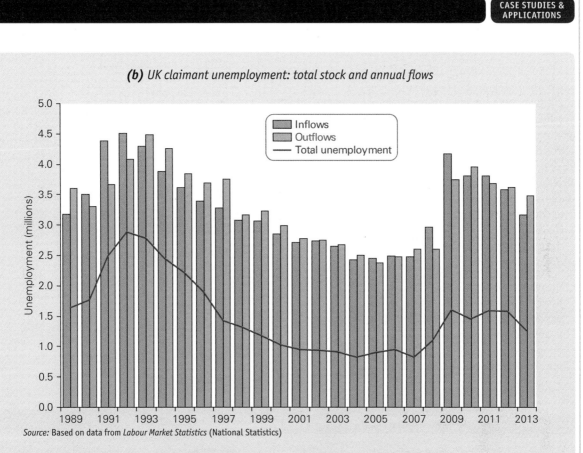

(b) *UK claimant unemployment: total stock and annual flows*

Source: Based on data from *Labour Market Statistics* (National Statistics)

their jobs. They represent an inflow to the stock of unemployment. Other people find jobs and thus represent an outflow from the stock of unemployment. Unemployment is often referred to as 'the pool of unemployment'.

If the inflow of people into the unemployment pool exceeds the outflow, the pool of unemployed people will rise. The duration of unemployment will depend on the rate of inflow and outflow. The rate is expressed as the number of people per period of time. Chart (b) shows the total inflows and outflows in the UK since 1989.

In each of the years, the outflows (and inflows) exceed the total number unemployed. The bigger the flows are relative to the total number unemployed, the less will be the average duration of unemployment. This is because people move into and out of the unemployment pool more quickly, and hence their average stay will be shorter.

The phase of the business cycle
The duration of unemployment will also depend on the phase of the business cycle. At the onset of a recession, unemployment will rise, but as yet the average length of unemployment is likely to have been relatively short. Once a recession has lasted for a period of time, however, people will on average have been out of work longer; and this long-term unemployment is likely to persist even when the economy is pulling out of recession.

1. *If the number unemployed exceeded the total annual outflow, what could we conclude about the average duration of unemployment?*
2. *Make a list of the various inflows to and outflows from employment from and to (a) unemployment; (b) outside the workforce.*

TC 12
p 202

A change in the pattern of demand. Some industries experience declining demand. This may be due to a change in consumer tastes. Certain goods may go out of fashion. Or it may be due to competition from other industries. For example, consumer demand may shift away from coal and to other fuels. This will lead to structural unemployment in mining areas.

A change in the methods of production (technological unemployment). New techniques of production often allow the same level of output to be produced with fewer workers. This is

known as 'labour-saving technical progress'. Unless output expands sufficiently to absorb the surplus labour, people will

Definition

Structural unemployment Unemployment that arises from changes in the pattern of demand or supply in the economy. People made redundant in one part of the economy cannot immediately take up jobs in other parts (even though there are vacancies).

be made redundant. This creates **technological unemployment**. An example is the job losses in the banking industry caused by the increase in the number of cash machines and by the development of telephone and Internet banking.

Structural unemployment is sometimes referred to as 'mismatch unemployment'. Structural changes to an economy will tend to lead to a mismatch between the skills of the workforce and the needs of employers. There are often significant geographical mismatches with structural unemployment focused in particular regions of the country. When it does, it is referred to as **regional unemployment**. This is most likely to occur when particular industries are concentrated in particular areas. For example, the decline in the South Wales coal-mining industry led to high unemployment in the Welsh valleys.

The level of structural unemployment depends on three factors:

■ The degree of regional concentration of industry. The more that industries are concentrated in particular regions, the greater will be the level of structural unemployment if particular industries decline.

■ The speed of change of demand and supply in the economy. The more rapid the rate of technological change or the shift in consumer tastes, the more rapid will be the rate of redundancies.

■ The immobility of labour. Where workers are less able or less willing to move to a new job, the higher will be the level of structural unemployment.

Seasonal unemployment

Seasonal unemployment occurs when the demand for certain types of labour fluctuates with the seasons of the year. This problem is particularly severe in holiday areas, such as Cornwall, where unemployment can reach very high levels in the winter months.

Definitions

Technological unemployment Structural unemployment that occurs as a result of the introduction of labour-saving technology.

Regional unemployment Structural unemployment occurring in specific regions of the country.

Seasonal unemployment Unemployment associated with industries or regions where the demand for labour is lower at certain times of the year.

Recap

1. The two most common measures of unemployment are claimant unemployment (those claiming unemployment-related benefits) and ILO/OECD-defined standardised unemployment (those available for work and actively seeking work or waiting to take up an appointment).

2. Unemployment can be divided into disequilibrium and equilibrium unemployment.

3. Disequilibrium unemployment occurs when the average real wage rate is above the level that will equate the aggregate demand and supply of labour. It can be caused by unions or government pushing up wages (real-wage unemployment), by a fall in aggregate demand (demand-deficient unemployment), or by an increase in the supply of labour.

4. Equilibrium unemployment occurs when there are people unable or unwilling to fill job vacancies. This may be due to poor information in the labour market and hence a time lag before people find suitable jobs (frictional unemployment), to a changing pattern of demand or supply in the economy and hence a mismatching of labour with jobs (structural unemployment – specific types being technological and regional unemployment), or to seasonal fluctuations in the demand for labour.

11.5	THE RELATIONSHIP BETWEEN INFLATION AND UNEMPLOYMENT: THE SHORT RUN

What is the short-run relationship between inflation and unemployment?

Unemployment and inflation at the same time

We saw in Section 11.2 how the extreme Keynesian short-run aggregate supply (AS) curve is horizontal up to the full-employment output level, Y_F. The curve is shown again in Figure 11.14 and is labelled AS_1. Up to Y_F, output and

employment can rise with no rise in prices at all. As this happens, the deflationary gap is closed. At Y_F no further rises in output are possible.[1] Any further rise in aggregate demand is entirely reflected in higher prices. Instead, an inflationary

---

[1] For simplicity, we are ignoring here any temporary rise in output above normal capacity.

gap opens. In other words, this implies that either inflation *or* unemployment can occur, but not both simultaneously.

Some important qualifications need to be made to this analysis to explain the occurrence of both unemployment *and* inflation at the same time.

First, there are *other* types of inflation not caused by an excess of aggregate demand, such as cost-push and expectations-generated inflation. Box 11.5 looks at the actual relationship between the rate of inflation and the amount of excess or deficient demand, as measured by output gaps, in the UK since 1965.

Secondly, there are *other* types of unemployment not caused by a lack of aggregate demand. Examples include frictional and structural unemployment.

Thirdly, not all firms operate with the same degree of slack. A rise in aggregate demand can lead to *both* a reduction in unemployment *and* a rise in prices: some firms responding to the rise in demand by taking up slack and hence increasing output; other firms, having little or no slack, responding by raising prices; others doing both. Similarly, labour markets have different degrees of slack and therefore the rise in demand will lead to various mixes of higher wages and lower unemployment. Thus the short-run *AS* curve will look like AS_2 in Figure 11.15.

Thus, even if a government could manipulate national income so as to achieve a zero output gap, this would not eliminate all inflation and unemployment – only demand-pull inflation and demand-deficient unemployment. Keynesians argue, therefore, that governments should use a whole package of policies, each tailored to the specific type of problem. But certainly one of the most important of these policies will be the management of aggregate demand.

The Phillips curve

The relationship between inflation and unemployment was examined in a famous article by A. W. Phillips back in 1958 (see Case Study 11.10 in MyEconLab). He showed the statistical relationship between wage inflation and

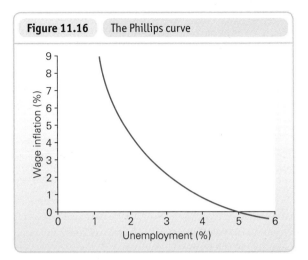

Figure 11.16   The Phillips curve

unemployment in the UK from 1861 to 1957. With wage inflation on the vertical axis and the unemployment rate on the horizontal axis, a scatter of points was obtained. Each point represented the observation for a particular year. The curve that best fitted the scatter has become known as the **Phillips curve**. It is illustrated in Figure 11.16 and shows an inverse relationship between inflation and unemployment.

Given that wage increases over the period were approximately 2 per cent above price increases (made possible because of increases in labour productivity), a similar-shaped, but lower curve could be plotted showing the relationship between *price* inflation and unemployment.

The curve has often been used to illustrate the short-run effects of changes in (real) aggregate demand. When aggregate demand rose (relative to potential output), inflation rose and unemployment fell: there was a movement upwards along the curve. When aggregate demand fell, there was a movement downwards along the curve.

The Phillips curve was bowed in to the origin. The usual explanation for this is that as aggregate demand expanded, at first there would be plenty of surplus labour, which could be employed to meet the extra demand without the need to raise wage rates very much. But as labour became increasingly scarce, firms would find that they had to offer increasingly higher wage rates to obtain the labour they required, and the position of trade unions would be increasingly strengthened.

The *position* of the Phillips curve depended on *non-demand* factors causing inflation and unemployment: frictional and structural unemployment; and cost-push

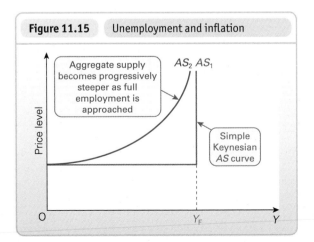

Figure 11.15   Unemployment and inflation

Aggregate supply becomes progressively steeper as full employment is approached

AS_2 AS_1

Simple Keynesian *AS* curve

Price level

O Y_F Y

Definition

Phillips curve A curve showing the relationship between (price) inflation and unemployment. The original Phillips curve plotted wage inflation against unemployment for the years 1861–1957.

KI 29
p 177

Do output gaps explain inflation?

Chapter 9 introduced the concept of output gaps. An output gap measures the difference between an economy's actual level of output and its potential output. A positive output gap shows that the level of actual output is *greater* than the potential level, while a negative output gap shows that the level of output is below the potential level.

The magnitude of the output gap, which is usually expressed as a percentage of potential output, enables us to assess the extent of any demand deficiency (negative output gap) or the extent of excess demand (positive output gap).

The 'moderate view' of the slope of the short-run aggregate supply (see Figure 11.6(c)) is that it is determined by the amount of slack in the economy. As the economy approaches or exceeds its potential output the aggregate supply curve becomes steeper as firms' marginal costs rise faster. Consequently, increases in demand at output levels close to or in excess of an economy's potential output will exert more upward pressure on prices than if the economy has a more significant amount of slack. This suggests that the rate of price inflation is positively related to the size of the output gap.

The chart plots the output gap (as a percentage of potential output) and the annual rate of economy-wide inflation (rate of increase of the GDP deflator) for the UK since 1965.

It would appear that for the period from 1965 to the end of the 1980s there was a positive correlation between output gaps and inflation rates, albeit that turning points in the rates of inflation lag those in the size of output gaps. In other words, it took time for price pressure to work fully through the economy. This reflects, in part, the fact that some prices, such as wage rates, are adjusted relatively infrequently.

Since the 1990s, however, the relationship between output gaps and inflation rates is less clear. Indeed, the period is characterised by relative low rates of inflation regardless of the size of output gaps. This demonstrates that there are several potential influences on inflation rates.

One explanation is a *reduction in global cost-push pressures*. First, labour markets have become more competitive and flexible. Secondly, firms have faced greater competition from across the EU, China and many other countries in an increasingly globalised market. Thirdly, except for the periods from 2007–8 and late 2009–10 (see the chart in Box 11.1), commodity price inflation has been subdued.

Another explanation is *inflation rate expectations*. The adoption of clear and credible inflation targets by central banks, such as the Bank of England, has influenced firms when setting prices and both firms and unions when negotiating wage rates. It has helped to anchor such price and wage setting to the inflation rate target, irrespective of the state of the economy.

1. *What factors may have resulted in the lower inflation rates experienced by the UK from the 1990s?*
2. *Do credible inflation rate targets guarantee low inflation?*

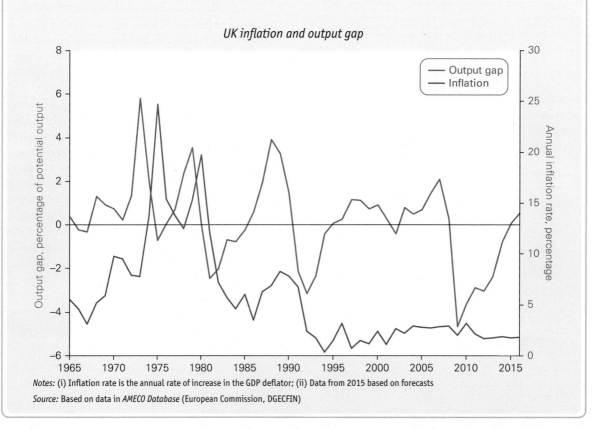

UK inflation and output gap

Notes: (i) Inflation rate is the annual rate of increase in the GDP deflator; (ii) Data from 2015 based on forecasts

Source: Based on data in *AMECO Database* (European Commission, DGECFIN)

and expectations-generated inflation. If any of these non-demand factors changed so as to raise inflation or unemployment, the curve would shift outwards to the right.

KI 29
p 177 The Phillips curve seemed to present governments with a simple policy choice. They could trade off inflation against unemployment. Lower unemployment could be bought at the cost of higher inflation, and vice versa. Unfortunately, the experience since the late 1960s has suggested that no such simple relationship exists beyond the short run.

The breakdown of the Phillips curve

From about 1967 the Phillips curve relationship seemed to break down. The UK, along with many other countries in the western world, began to experience growing unemployment and higher rates of inflation as well.

Figure 11.17 shows price inflation and unemployment in the UK from 1960. From 1960 to 1967 a curve similar to the Phillips curve can be fitted through the data. From 1968 to the early 1990s, however, no simple picture emerges. Certainly the original Phillips curve could no longer fit the data; but whether the curve shifted to the right and then back again somewhat (the dashed lines), or whether the relationship broke down completely, or whether there was some quite different relationship between inflation and unemployment, is not clear by simply looking at the data.

Since 1997 the Bank of England has been targeting consumer price inflation (see Section 11.7). For much of this period, the 'curve' would seem to have become a virtually horizontal straight line!

However, from the late 2000s, against a backdrop of significant economic volatility, the range of inflation rates increased despite inflation rate targeting. Then in the period from late 2013, inflation fell below the target, reflecting lower commodity prices and sluggish demand in the eurozone and elsewhere.

Nonetheless, despite difficulties of keeping inflation to target, many economists continue to argue that expectations concerning future inflation rates are an important influence on the inflation–unemployment relationship and that inflation has become much less volatile since inflation targeting was introduced. We consider this in the next section. TC 9
p 62

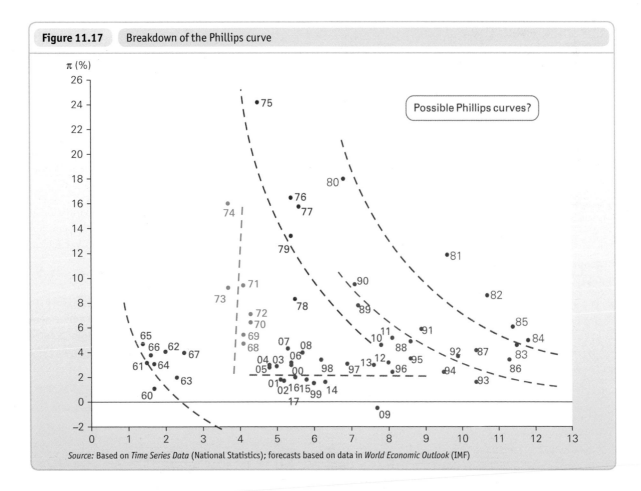

Figure 11.17   Breakdown of the Phillips curve

Source: Based on Time Series Data (National Statistics); forecasts based on data in World Economic Outlook (IMF)

> ### Recap
>
> 1. In the simplest version of this analysis, where output cannot rise above the potential level, the short-run *AS* curve is horizontal up to Y_F and then vertical. To explain how inflation and unemployment can occur simultaneously we need to allow for other types of inflation and unemployment. Consequently, the *AS* curve will be upward sloping but getting steeper as full employment is approached and as bottlenecks increasingly occur.
>
> 2. The Phillips curve showed the trade-off between inflation and unemployment. There seemed to be a simple inverse relationship between the two. After 1967, however, the relationship broke down as inflation and unemployment rose.
>
> 3. Today, many central banks target inflation. In the UK, where the Bank of England has targeted inflation since 1997, the effect has been to make the Phillips curve appear like an almost horizontal straight line.

11.6 THE RELATIONSHIP BETWEEN INFLATION AND UNEMPLOYMENT: INTRODUCING EXPECTATIONS

What happens when people come to expect inflation?

A major contribution to the theory of unemployment and inflation was made by Milton Friedman and others in the late 1960s. They incorporated people's expectations about the future level of prices into the Phillips curve.

This can then be used to derive a *vertical* long-run Phillips curve. In other words, it can be used to explain the contention by many economists that there is *no* trade-off between inflation and unemployment in the long run, and that therefore government policy to reduce unemployment by expanding aggregate demand will be unsuccessful, except perhaps in the very short term. Instead it will simply lead to accelerating inflation.

This theory of the vertical long-run Phillips curve is thus known as the *accelerationist theory*.

The expectations-augmented Phillips curve

In its simplest form, the **expectations-augmented Phillips curve** is given by the following:

$$\pi = f(1/U) + \pi^e$$

What this states is that inflation (π) depends on two things:

■ The inverse of unemployment (1/U). This is simply the normal Phillips curve relationship. The higher the rate of (demand-deficient) unemployment, the lower the rate of inflation.

■ The expected rate of inflation (π^e). The higher the rate of inflation that people expect, the higher will be the level of wage demands and the more willing will firms be to raise prices. Thus the higher will be the actual rate of inflation and thus the vertically higher will be the whole Phillips curve.

Let us assume, for simplicity, that the rate of inflation people expect this year (π_t^e) (where *t* represents the current time period: i.e. this year) is the same rate that inflation actually was last year (π_{t-1}):

$$(\pi_t^e) = (\pi_{t-1})$$

Thus if unemployment is such as to push up prices by 4 per cent ($f(1/U) = 4\%$) and if last year's inflation was 6 per cent, then inflation this year will be 4 per cent + 6 per cent = 10 per cent.

The accelerationist theory

Let us trace the course of inflation and expectations over a number of years in an imaginary economy. To keep the analysis simple, assume there is no growth in the economy.

Year 1

Assume that at the outset, in year 1, there is no inflation at all; that none is expected; that *AD* = *AS*; and that equilibrium unemployment is 8 per cent. The economy will be at point *a* in Figure 11.18 and Table 11.3.

Year 2

Now assume that the government expands aggregate demand in order to reduce unemployment. Unemployment falls to 6 per cent. The economy moves to point *b* along curve I. Inflation has risen to 4 per cent, but people, basing their

> ### Definition
>
> **Expectations-augmented Phillips curve** A (short-run) Phillips curve whose position depends on the expected rate of inflation.

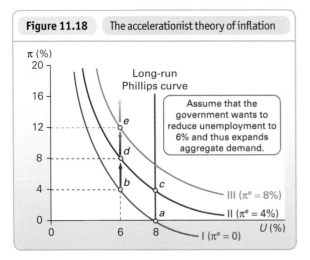

Figure 11.18   The accelerationist theory of inflation

Table 11.3   The accelerationist theory of inflation and inflationary expectations

Year	Point on graph	π	=	$f(1/U)$	+	π^e
1	a	0	=	0	+	0
2	b	4	=	4	+	0
3	c	4	=	0	+	4
4	d	8	=	4	+	4
5	e	12	=	4	+	8

expectations of inflation on year 1, still expect zero inflation. There is therefore no shift as yet in the Phillips curve. Curve I corresponds to an expected rate of inflation of zero.

Year 3

People now revise their expectations of inflation to the level of year 2. The Phillips curve shifts up by 4 percentage points to position II. If *nominal* aggregate demand (i.e. demand purely in money terms, irrespective of the level of prices) continues to rise at the same rate, the whole of the increase will now be absorbed in higher prices. *Real* aggregate demand (i.e. in terms of what it can buy) will fall back to its previous level and the economy will move to point *c*. Unemployment will return to 8 per cent. There is no *demand-pull* inflation now, ($f(1/U) = 0$), but inflation is still 4 per cent due to expectations $\pi^e = 4\%$).

Year 4

Assume now that the government expands *real* aggregate demand again so as to reduce unemployment once more to 6 per cent. This time it must expand *nominal* aggregate demand *more* than it did in year 2, because this time, as well as reducing unemployment, it also has to validate the 4 per cent expected inflation. The economy moves to point *d* along curve II. Inflation is now 8 per cent.

Year 5 onwards

Expected inflation is now 8 per cent (the level of actual inflation in year 4). The Phillips curve shifts up to position III. If at the same time the government tries to keep unemployment at 6 per cent, it must expand nominal aggregate demand 4 per cent faster in order to validate the 8 per cent expected inflation. The economy moves to point *e* along curve III. Inflation is now 12 per cent.

To keep unemployment at 6 per cent, the government must continue to increase nominal aggregate demand by 4 per cent more than the previous year. As the expected inflation rate goes on rising, the Phillips curve will go on shifting up each year.

> **Pause for thought**
>
> *What determines how rapidly the short-run Phillips curves in Figure 11.18 shift upwards?*

Thus in order to keep unemployment below the initial equilibrium rate, inflation must go on *accelerating* each year. For this reason, this theory of the Phillips curve is sometimes known as the **accelerationist theory**.

The more the government reduces unemployment, the greater the rise in inflation that year, and the more the rise in expectations the following year and each subsequent year; and hence the more rapidly will price rises accelerate. Thus the true longer-term trade-off is between unemployment and the rate of *increase* in inflation.

The long-run Phillips curve and the equilibrium rate of unemployment

As long as there are demand-pull pressures ($f(1/U) > 0$), inflation will accelerate as the expected rate of inflation (π^e) rises. In the long run, therefore, the Phillips curve will be vertical at the rate of unemployment where *real* aggregate demand equals *real* aggregate supply. This is the *equilibrium* rate of unemployment. Monetarists refer to it as the **natural rate** (U_n). It is sometimes also known as the **non-accelerating-inflation rate of unemployment (NAIRU)**. In Figure 11.18 the equilibrium rate of unemployment is 8 per cent.

> **Definitions**
>
> **Accelerationist theory** The theory that unemployment can only be reduced below the natural rate at the cost of accelerating inflation.
>
> **Natural rate of unemployment or non-accelerating-inflation rate of unemployment (NAIRU)** The rate of unemployment consistent with a constant rate of inflation: the rate of unemployment at which the vertical long-run Phillips curve cuts the horizontal axis.

The implication for government policy is that expanding aggregate demand can reduce unemployment below the equilibrium rate only in the *short* run. In the long run, the effect will be purely inflationary. On the other hand, a policy of restraining aggregate demand, for example by restraining the growth in the money supply, will *not*, in the long run, lead to higher unemployment: it will simply lead to lower inflation at the equilibrium rate of unemployment. The implication is that governments or central banks should make it a priority to control money supply and thereby nominal aggregate demand and inflation.

Rational expectations

New classical economists go further than the monetarist theory described above. They argue that even the short-run Phillips curve is vertical: that there is *no* trade-off between unemployment and inflation, even in the short run. They base their arguments on the two key assumptions we saw in Section 11.2 (see page 299): *continuous market clearing* and *rational expectations*.

Because prices and wage rates are flexible, markets clear very rapidly. This means that there will be no disequilibrium unemployment. All unemployment will be equilibrium unemployment, or 'voluntary unemployment' as new classical economists prefer to call it.

In the accelerationist theory, expectations are based on *past* information and thus take time to catch up with changes in aggregate demand. Thus for a short time a rise in nominal aggregate demand will raise output, and reduce unemployment below the equilibrium level, while prices and wages are still relatively low.

TC 9
p 62 The new classical analysis is based on rational expectations. Rational expectations are not based on past rates of inflation. Instead they are based on the current state of the economy and the current policies being pursued by the government. Workers and firms look at the information available to them – at the various forecasts that are published, at various economic indicators and the assessments of them by various commentators, at government pronouncements, and so on. From this information they predict the rate of inflation as well as they can. It is in this sense that the expectations are 'rational': people use their reason to assess the future on the basis of current information.

But forecasters frequently get it wrong, and so do economic commentators! And the government does not always do what it says it will. Thus workers and firms will be basing expectations on *imperfect information*. The crucial point about the rational expectations theory, however, is that these errors in prediction are *random*. People's predictions of inflation are just as likely to be too high as too low.

Assume that the government raises aggregate demand and that the increase is expected. People will anticipate that this will lead to higher prices and wages. If both goods

and labour markets clear continuously because of the flexibility of prices and wages, there will be *no* effect on output and employment. If their expectations of higher inflation are correct, this will *fully* absorb the increase in nominal aggregate demand, such that there will have been no increase in *real* aggregate demand at all. Firms will not produce any more output or employ any more people: after all, why should they? If they anticipate that people will spend 10 per cent more money, but that prices will rise by 10 per cent, their *volume* of sales will remain the same.

Output and employment will only rise, therefore, if people make an error in their predictions (i.e. if they under predict the rate of inflation and interpret an increase in money spent as an increase in *real* demand). But they are as likely to *over* predict the rate of inflation, in which case output and employment will fall! Thus there is no systematic trade-off between inflation and unemployment, even in the short run.

The vertical short-run Phillips curve is therefore comparable to the vertical short-run aggregate supply curve we saw in Figure 11.6(c) (see page 298). The vertical *SRAS* curve shows aggregate supply (output) being determined independently of aggregate demand.

Both the vertical short-run Phillips curve and the vertical *SRAS* curve can be used to illustrate how anticipated changes in economic policy, such as changes in government spending, have no effect on output and employment. Instead they remain at their equilibrium levels. This controversial conclusion is known as the **policy ineffectiveness proposition**.

> ### Pause for thought
>
> *For what reasons would a new classical economist support the policy of a central bank publishing its inflation forecasts and the minutes of its deliberations about interest rates?*

Keynesian views

Keynesians criticise the monetarist/new classical approach of focusing exclusively on price expectations. Expectations, argue Keynesians, influence *output* and *employment* decisions, not just pricing decisions. TC 9
p 62

> ### Definition
>
> **Policy ineffectiveness proposition** The conclusion drawn from new classical models that, when economic agents anticipate changes in economic policy, output and employment remain at their equilibrium (or natural) levels.

If there is a gradual but sustained expansion of aggregate demand, firms, seeing the economy expanding and seeing their orders growing, will start to invest more and make longer-term plans for expanding their labour force. People will generally *expect* a higher level of output, and this optimism will cause that higher level of output to be produced, both from existing capacity and from new capacity arising from the increased investment. In other words, expectations will affect output and employment as well as prices, not only in the short term, but over the longer term too.

Graphically, the increased output and employment from the recovery in investment will shift the *AS* curve to the right and the Phillips curve to the left, offsetting (partially, wholly or more than wholly) the upward shift from higher inflationary expectations.

The lesson here for governments is that a sustained, but moderate, increase in aggregate demand can lead to a sustained growth in aggregate supply. What should be avoided is an excessive and unsustainable expansion of aggregate demand. In turn, this raises questions about the role that governments should play in managing economic stability.

Such debates were heightened by the financial crisis of the late 2000s, the subsequent global economic downturn and the fragility of the macroeconomic environment that then characterised the first half of the 2010s. Did the austerity policies pursued in the UK, the eurozone and many other countries affect aggregate supply as well as aggregate demand? Did they reduce *potential* GDP and hence shift the *AS* curve to the left?

Chapter 12 looks at government policy in more detail.

Pause for thought

Why is it important in the Keynesian analysis for there to be a steady expansion of aggregate demand?

Recap

1. Expectations can be incorporated into the analysis of the Phillips curve. The effect is to give a vertical long-run curve at the equilibrium rate of unemployment.

2. The simplest analysis of expectations is that the expected rate of inflation this year is what it actually was last year: $\pi_t^e = \pi_{t-1}$.

3. If there is excess demand in the economy, producing upward pressure on wages and prices, initially unemployment will fall. But as people's expectations adapt upwards to these higher wages and prices, so ever-increasing rises in nominal aggregate demand will be necessary to maintain unemployment below the equilibrium rate. Price and wage rises will accelerate: i.e. inflation will rise.

4. The new classical theory assumes flexible prices and wages in the short run as well as in the long run. It also assumes that people base their expectations of inflation on a rational assessment of the *current* situation.

5. People may predict wrongly, but they are equally likely to under predict or to over predict. On average over the years they will predict correctly.

6. The implication of rational expectations theory and continuous market clearing is that not only the long-run but also the short-run *AS* and Phillips curves will be vertical. If people correctly predict the rate of inflation, they will correctly predict that any increase in nominal aggregate demand will simply be reflected in higher prices. Total output and employment will remain the same: at the equilibrium level.

7. Keynesians argue that if people expect a rise in aggregate demand to be sustained, firms will invest more, thereby increasing potential output (and possibly also reducing unemployment) and not just increasing the rate of inflation. Conversely, austerity policies can reduce potential as well as actual output.

11.7 INFLATION RATE TARGETING AND UNEMPLOYMENT

Does successful inflation rate targeting produce a horizontal Phillips curve?

The Phillips curve appears to have shifted to the right in the 1970s and 1980s and then back to the left in the 1990s. It also seems to have changed its shape. As we saw in Section 11.4, far from being vertical in the long run, in more recent times it appears to have resembled more of a horizontal line. While inflation rates did vary more than they had for some time in the late 2000s and early 2010s, unemployment rates were to fluctuate markedly as aggregate demand collapsed following the financial crisis followed by a gradual recovery in private-sector expenditure. Figure 11.19 traces out the path of inflation and unemployment in the UK since 1967.

What explains the shape of this path? Part of the explanation lies in long-term changes in unemployment. Part lies in the policy of inflation targeting, pursued in the UK since 1992.

Figure 11.19   Phillips loops in the UK

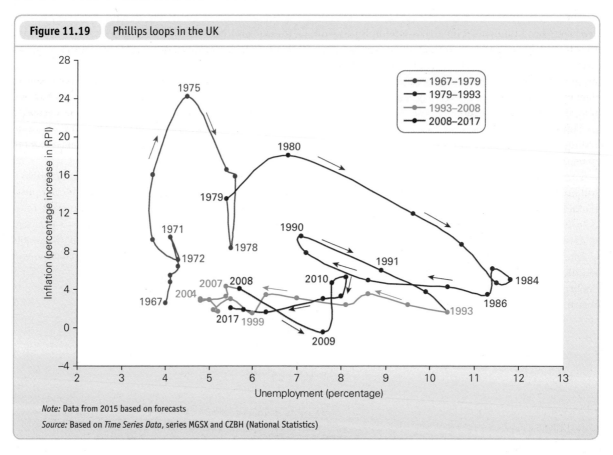

Note: Data from 2015 based on forecasts

Source: Based on *Time Series Data*, series MGSX and CZBH (National Statistics)

Long-term changes in unemployment

Why was there a substantial rise in unemployment from the early 1970s to the mid-1980s? Why, as a result, was there an apparent rightward shift in the Phillips curve? Why was there then a substantial fall in unemployment for over a decade from the mid-1990s? To answer this, we need to look at the labour market and the determinants of the equilibrium level of unemployment (i.e. the natural rate of unemployment or NAIRU).

The 1970s and 1980s were a period of rapid industrial change. The changes included the following:

- Dramatic changes in technology. The microchip revolution, for example, had led to many traditional jobs becoming obsolete.
- Competition from abroad. The introduction of new products from abroad, often of superior quality to domestic goods, or produced at lower costs, had led to the decline of many older industries: e.g. the textile industry.
- Shifts in demand away from the products of older labour-intensive industries to new 'high-tech' capital-intensive products.

The free market simply could not cope with these changes without a large rise in structural/technological unemployment. Labour was not sufficiently mobile – either geographically or occupationally – to move to industries where there were labour shortages or into jobs where there

are skill shortages. A particular problem here was the lack of investment in education and training, with the result that the labour force was not sufficiently flexible to respond to changes in demand for labour.

From the mid-1980s, however, there were increasing signs that the labour market was becoming more flexible. People seemed more willing to accept that they would have to move from job to job throughout their career. At the same time, policies were introduced to improve training (see Section 12.4). Another explanation for first the rise of equilibrium unemployment and later the fall is the phenomenon of 'hysteresis'.

Hysteresis

If a recession causes a rise in unemployment which is not then fully reversed when the economy recovers, there is a problem of **hysteresis**. This term, used in physics, refers to the lagging or persistence of an effect, even when the initial cause has been removed. In our context it refers to the persistence of unemployment even when the initial demand deficiency no longer exists.

KI 28
p 176

Definition

Hysteresis The persistence of an effect even when the initial cause has ceased to operate. In economics it refers to the persistence of unemployment even when the demand deficiency that caused it no longer exists.

The recessions of the early 1980s and early 1990s created a growing number of long-term unemployed who were both deskilled and demotivated. What is more, many firms, in an attempt to cut costs, cut down on training programmes. In these circumstances, a rise in aggregate demand would not simply enable the long-term unemployed to be employed again.

The recessions also caused a lack of investment and a reduction in firms' capacity. When demand recovered, many firms were unable to increase output and instead raised prices. Unemployment thus fell only modestly and inflation rose. The NAIRU had increased: the Phillips curve had shifted to the right.

After 1992, however, the UK, along with most other countries, achieved a protracted period of sustained expansion, with no recession. Equilibrium unemployment began to fall. In other words, the hysteresis was not permanent. As firms increased their investment, the capital stock expanded; firms engaged in more training; the number of long-term unemployed fell.

The financial crisis and its aftermath

UK unemployment rates rose sharply following the financial crisis of the late 2000s. However, the fall from a peak of 8.5 per cent in three months to November 2011 to 6 per cent three years later led some to argue that hysteresis was now less of a problem.

The principal reason, they argue, is the effect of greater labour market flexibility. Consequently, following the economic downturn, firms were able to introduce part-time working or negotiate nominal wage cuts in order to retain workers. Even where there were no wage cuts, many firms introduced nominal wage freezes meaning that real wages fell.

Also, increasing numbers of people have been on 'zero-hour contracts'. This means that workers have no set number of hours per week and hours can be decreased (or increased) according to demand. Thus in a recession, employers can simply cut the number of hours offered to workers on such contracts.

To some extent, therefore, the problem of unemployment has been replaced by a problem of **underemployment** – a situation where people would like to work more hours that are they are able to obtain, either in their current job or in an alternative job or in an additional part-time job. By mid-2014, some 10 per cent of people in employment (3.0 million) in the UK were underemployed. On average,

> **Definition**
>
> **Underemployment** International Labour Organization (ILO) definition: a situation where people currently working less than 'full-time' (40 hours in the UK) would like to work more hours (at current wage rates), either by working more hours in their current job, or by switching to an alternative job with more hours or by taking on an additional part-time job or any combination of the three. Eurostat definition: where people working less than 40 hours per week would like to work more hours in their current job at current wage rates.

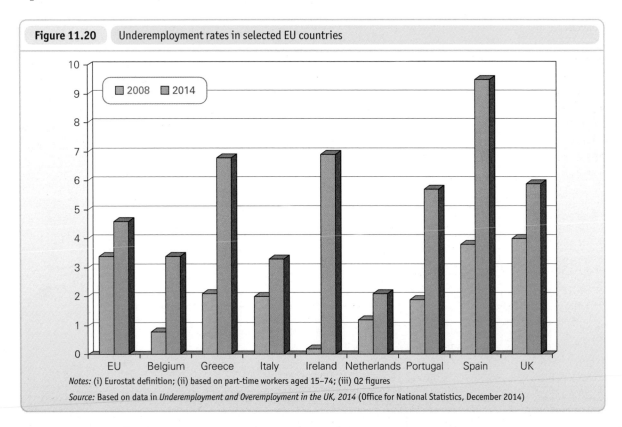

Figure 11.20 Underemployment rates in selected EU countries

Notes: (i) Eurostat definition; (ii) based on part-time workers aged 15–74; (iii) Q2 figures

Source: Based on data in *Underemployment and Overemployment in the UK, 2014* (Office for National Statistics, December 2014)

these underemployed workers wanted to work an additional 11.3 hours per week. If you include just those people who would like to work more in their *current* job, the UK rate in 2014 was 5.9 per cent. This compares with rates of 2.1, 4.1, 6.0, 6.9 and 9.5 per cent respectively in the Netherlands, Germany, France, Ireland and Spain. A comparison with figures before the recession is shown in Figure 11.20.

Nonetheless, the problem of hysteresis remains relevant. Despite the falling aggregate unemployment rate in the UK, 35 per cent of those recorded as unemployed on the claimant count measure at the end of 2014 had been so for a year or more (see Box 11.4). Furthermore, youth unemployment rates remain more than double the aggregate level (see Table 11.2). These factors act as a brake on reductions in unemployment and adversely affect potential output.

Meanwhile, unemployment rates in the first half of the 2010s remained significantly above pre-financial crisis levels in many countries in the eurozone, such as Greece, Portugal and Spain, which have had to seek bailouts because of their high levels of debt. A condition of being granted bailouts has been to reduce public-sector debt. This has ruled out Keynesian expansionary fiscal policy. The very high levels of unemployment in these countries, especially amongst the young (rates of over 50 per cent in Greece and Spain in the 15–24 age group), have resulted in a problem of

entrenchment and hysteresis that will make reductions in unemployment slow and difficult to achieve.

Inflation targeting

As we have seen, a major determinant of the actual rate of inflation is the rate of inflation that people expect. Since 1992, a policy of inflation targeting has been adopted in the UK, and in 1997 the Bank of England was given independence in setting interest rates to achieve the target rate of inflation.

The target was initially set in October 1992 as a range from 1 to 4 per cent for RPIX inflation.[2] With the election of the Labour government in 1997, a single point target of 2.5 per cent was adopted. This was changed to a 2 per cent target for CPI inflation in December 2003.

The public's inflation rate expectations appear to have been affected by inflation rate targeting. Figure 11.21 shows forecast and actual RPI inflation from 1998 to 2016. The forecasts are the average of at least 20 independent forecasts and thus can be taken as an indicator of expectations. As you can see, until the credit crunch of 2008, inflation forecasts were pretty accurate and reflected belief that the Bank of England would be successful in meeting its inflation target (2.5 per cent RPIX inflation up to December 2003 and

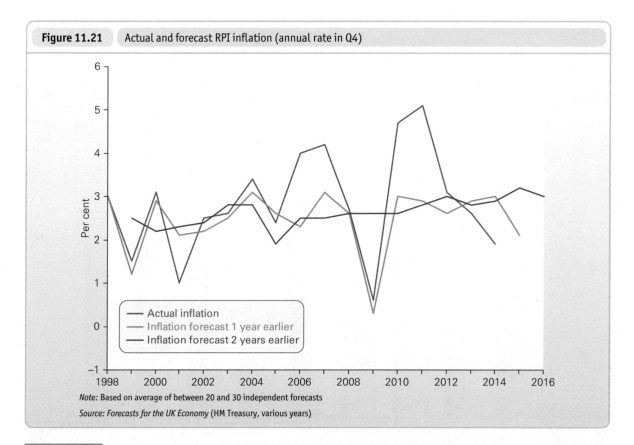

| **Figure 11.21** | Actual and forecast RPI inflation (annual rate in Q4) |

Note: Based on average of between 20 and 30 independent forecasts

Source: Forecasts for the UK Economy (HM Treasury, various years)

---

[2] RPIX is the retail prices index, excluding mortgage interest payments. CPI is the consumer prices index. Differences in how CPI is compiled mean that CPI inflation is typically about 0.5 percentage points below RPIX inflation. Thus the current target of 2 per cent CPI inflation is approximately equivalent to 2.5 per cent RPIX inflation that was used as the target prior to December 2003.

2 per cent CPI inflation thereafter – CPI inflation is typically about 0.5 to 0.8 percentage points below RPIX inflation).

The credit crunch and the onset of recession, however, initially affected the accuracy of 24-month forecasts. Subsequently, the 12-month forecasts became less accurate too as inflation rose as a result of rapid rises in food, oil and other commodity prices.

Implications for the Phillips curve

So, does this mean that the Phillips curve has now become horizontal? The answer is that it depends on policy and, hence, on the central bank's remit. If inflation remains central to this remit, is successfully kept on target and people believe that it will remain so, the path of inflation and unemployment will be a horizontal straight line.

Even if the central bank does succeed in achieving the target rate of inflation, in the short term unemployment will fluctuate with the business cycle. Thus there may be movements left or right along this horizontal line from one year to the next depending on the level of economic activity. Such fluctuations in unemployment are consistent with a stable inflation, provided that the fluctuations are mild and are not enough to alter people's expectations of inflation.

Over the medium term (three to six years), there may a leftward movement if the economy starts in recession and then the output gap is gradually closed through a process of steady economic growth (growth that avoids 'boom and bust'). Demand-deficient unemployment will be gradually eliminated. Thus between 1992 (the trough of the recession) and 1995, the output gap was closed from –3.2 per cent of potential output to zero (see the diagram in Box 11.5 on page 314). Provided the process is gradual, inflation can stay on target.

Over the longer term, movements left (or right) will depend on what happens to equilibrium unemployment. A reduction in equilibrium unemployment will result in a leftward movement. Evidence suggests that between the mid-1980s and the financial crisis of the late 2000s, the equilibrium unemployment rate halved from around 10 per cent to 5 per cent. The precise amount, however, is not certain as it is subject to measurement errors.

What if the central bank's remit changed?

If inflation rate targeting were relaxed, perhaps as a shift to a broader remit, or even abandoned, and if aggregate demand expanded rapidly, the traditionally shaped short-run Phillips curve could re-emerge. A rapid expansion of aggregate demand would both reduce unemployment below the equilibrium rate and raise inflation. There would be a positive output gap. This position could not be sustained, however, as inflationary expectations would rise and the short-run Phillips curve would begin shifting upwards (as in Figure 11.17).

Rising food and commodity prices both before and after the global economic slowdown of the late 2000s (see Box 11.1) provided the Bank of England (and other central

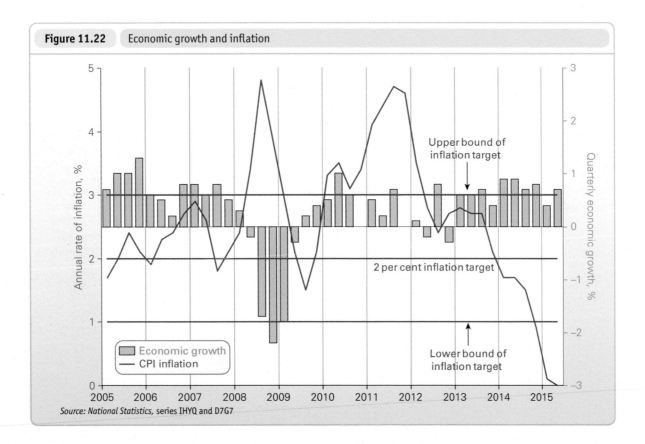

Figure 11.22 Economic growth and inflation

Source: National Statistics, series IHYQ and D7G7

banks) with a dilemma. Inflationary pressure was rising but the economy was weakening (see Figure 11.22). Should it continue rigidly targeting inflation, which would mean raising interest rates, or should it help to boost aggregate demand by cutting or keeping interest rates low?

As it turned out, the Bank of England was able to start cutting interest rates in late 2008 to boost aggregate demand without compromising its inflation target. This is because inflation fell in late 2008 and the output gap rose substantially; inflation was forecast to fall well below the target rate at the 24-month horizon.

The policy dilemma facing the Bank of England was in some ways trickier from 2010 to 2012 as inflation picked up but economic growth remained fragile and unemployment was rising. The increase in the standard rate of VAT from 17.5 per cent to 20 per cent at the start of 2011 further helped to raise the inflation rate (albeit temporarily). Despite inflation consistently exceeding the upper bound of the Bank of England's target, the MPC decided to keep the Bank Rate at 0.5 per cent throughout this period believing that inflation would return to its central target within the 24-month horizon.

Critics argued that the Bank's response compromised the inflation target and meant higher inflationary expectations. The credibility of the inflation target, they maintained, was being compromised. These concerns were further heightened when in 2013 the Bank of England began a policy of *forward guidance*. This is intended to give economic agents a steer as to the direction and level of interest rates.

In August 2013 the Bank announced that it was not minded to raise the policy rate of interest from its historic low of 0.5 per cent at least until the unemployment rate had fallen to 7 per cent or less. However, by February 2014 it had revised its forward guidance. The rate of unemployment was now around 7 per cent and subsequently was to drop further. Despite this, the Bank judged that real national income was still well below its potential level. Therefore, the revised forward guidance detailed how, in setting interest rates, the Bank would be guided not only by the rate of unemployment but by the amount of slack in the economy. Furthermore, it advised that when it did begin to raise rates the process would be a gradual one and that rates would remain 'materially below' the 5 per cent level that was typical prior to the financial crisis.

The hope was that, by providing households and businesses with greater certainty about the path of interest rates, forward guidance would give them the confidence to bring forward expenditure and so boost aggregate demand. Critics argued that the benefits from a straightforward inflation target in securing consistently low expectations of inflation could be lost. We examine these policy issues more closely in the next chapter.

> **Pause for thought**
>
> *How would you explain the apparent re-emergence of a Phillips loop after 2004?*

Recap

1. Data for the UK show its Phillips curve shifting to the right in the 1970s and 1980s. Reasons include a growth in equilibrium unemployment caused by rapid technological changes and a persistence of unemployment beyond the recessions of the early 1980s and early 1990s (hysteresis).

2. In the late 1990s and early 2000s, equilibrium unemployment fell as labour markets became more flexible and as the lagged effects of the recessions of the early 1980s and early 1990s faded.

3. Some argue that the pace with which unemployment fell in the UK in the early 2010s demonstrates that hysteresis is now less of a problem. However, there was a substantial rise in underemployment, which reflected a higher degree of slack in the labour market than that implied by the unemployment statistics. Also rates of youth and long-term unemployment remained high and these would be expected to impact on future unemployment rates.

4. Inflation targeting in the UK has seen the rate of inflation typically very close to the target level. Inflation rate targeting helps to anchor inflationary expectations around the target rate. This has tended to make the time-path of the Phillips curve horizontal at the target rate of inflation.

5. In response to the economic downturn following the financial crisis, the Bank of England introduced a strategy of forward guidance to provide an indication of the likely medium-term path of interest rates. Some economists argue that this could undermine the credibility of inflation rate policy and raise the public's inflationary expectations.

QUESTIONS

1. Do any groups of people gain from inflation?

2. If everyone's incomes rose in line with inflation, would it matter if inflation were 100 per cent or even 1000 per cent per annum?

3. Imagine that you had to determine whether a particular period of inflation was demand-pull, or cost-push, or a combination of the two. What information would you require in order to conduct your analysis?

4. Trace through the effect of a fall in the supply of money on aggregate demand. What will determine the size of the effect?

5. If V is constant, will (a) a £10 million rise in M give a £10 million rise in MV and (b) a 10 per cent rise in M give a 10 per cent rise in MV? (Test your answer by fitting some numbers to the terms.)

6. If both V and Y are constant, will (a) a £10 million rise in M lead to a £10 million rise in P and (b) a 10 per cent rise in M lead to a 10 per cent rise in P? (Again, try fitting some numbers to the terms.)

7. What would be the implications of different assumptions about the V and Y terms in the quantity equation $MV = PY$ for the effectiveness of monetary policy to control inflation?

8. What determines the shape of the long-run aggregate supply curve?

9. Would it be desirable to have zero unemployment?

10. What major structural changes have taken place in the UK economy in the past 10 years that have increased or decreased structural unemployment?

11. What are the causes of unemployment in the area where you live?

12. What would be the benefits and costs of increasing the rate of unemployment benefit?

13. Consider the most appropriate policy for tackling each of the different types of unemployment.

14. Assume that there is a trade-off between unemployment and inflation, traced out by a 'Phillips curve'. What could cause a leftward shift in this curve?

15. Assume that inflation depends on two things: the level of aggregate demand, indicated by the inverse of unemployment ($1/U$), and the expected rate of inflation (π_t^e). Assume that the rate of inflation (π_t) is given by the equation:

$$\pi_t = (48/U - 6) + \pi_t^e$$

Assume initially (year 0) that the actual and expected rate of inflation is zero.

a. Now assume in year 1 that the government wishes to reduce unemployment to 4 per cent and continues to expand aggregate demand by as much as is necessary to achieve this. Fill in the rows for years 0 to 4 in the table below. It is assumed for simplicity that the expected rate of inflation in a given year (π_t^e) is equal to the actual rate of inflation in the previous year (π_{t-1}).

b. Now assume in year 5 that the government, worried about rising inflation, reduces aggregate demand sufficiently to reduce inflation by 3 per cent in that year. What must the rate of unemployment be raised to in that year?

c. Assuming that unemployment stays at this high level, continue the table for years 5 to 7.

Year	U	$48/U - 6$	+	π^e	=	π
0	...	...	+	...	=	...
1	...	...	+	...	=	...
2	...	...	+	...	=	...
3	...	...	+	...	=	...
4	...	...	+	...	=	...
5	...	...	+	...	=	...
6	...	...	+	...	=	...
7	...	...	+	...	=	...

16. In the accelerationist model, if the government tries to maintain unemployment below the natural rate, what will determine the speed at which inflation accelerates?

17. For what reasons may the NAIRU (the equilibrium rate of unemployment) increase?

18. Given the persistence of high levels of unemployment after the recession of the early 1980s, what policies would you advocate to reduce unemployment in such circumstances?

19. Explain each of the following:

    a. Why there were simultaneously higher rates of inflation *and* unemployment in the 1970s and 1980s than in the 1950s and 1960s.

    b. Why there were simultaneously lower rates of inflation *and* unemployment in the late 1990s and early 2000s than in the 1970s and 1980s.

20. In what sense is it true to say that the Phillips curve today is horizontal?

21. Analyse the argument that the strategy of forward guidance compromises the economic gains from inflation rate targeting.

MyEconLab

This book can be supported by MyEconLab, which contains a range of additional resources, including an online homework and tutorial system designed to test and build your understanding.

You need both an access card and a course ID to access MyEconLab:

1. Is your lecturer using MyEconLab? Ask your lecturer for your course ID.

2. Has an access card been included with the book at a reduced cost? Check the inside back cover of the book.

3. If you have a course ID but no access card, go to: http://www.myeconlab.com/ to buy access to this interactive study programme.

ADDITIONAL CASE STUDIES IN THE *ESSENTIALS OF ECONOMICS* MyEconLab (www.pearsoned.co.uk/sloman)

11.1 Cost-push inflation and supply shocks. The distinction between one-off price rises caused by a supply shock, such as an oil price rise or a rise in tax rates, and cost-push inflation.

11.2 Disinflation in Europe and Japan. What happens when there is negative inflation? Is it a case of survival of the fittest?

11.3 Hyperinflation. This looks at the extraordinarily high rates of inflation experienced in Germany in the early 1920s, Serbia and Montenegro in the 1990s and more recently in Zimbabwe.

11.4 The costs of inflation. Is inflation more than a mere inconvenience?

11.5 Money and inflation in ancient Rome. A very early case study of the quantity theory of money: how the minting of extra coins by the Romans caused prices to rise.

11.6 The equation of exchange. This examines two more versions that are commonly used: the Fisher version and the Cambridge version.

11.7 Swimming in the unemployment pool. The composition and duration of unemployment in the EU.

11.8 Classical 'remedies' for unemployment. How the policies advocated by the classical economists to cure unemployment would, according to Keynes, make the problem worse.

11.9 Technology and unemployment. Does technological progress destroy jobs?

11.10 A. W. H. Phillips. A portrait of the shy economist and engineer who invented the famous Phillips curve and Phillips machine.

11.11 Explaining the shape of the short-run Phillips curve. This shows how money illusion on the part of workers can explain why the Phillips curve is downward sloping.

11.12 Milton Friedman (1912–2008). A profile of the most influential of the monetarist economists.

11.13 The political business cycle. This shows how the accelerationist theory and 'clockwise Phillips loops' can be used to analyse the so-called political business cycle.

11.14 The rational expectations revolution. A profile of two of the most famous economists of the new classical rational expectations school.

11.15 A spectrum of views. An overview of the different schools of macroeconomic thought.

11.16 Common ground between economists? A discussion of the 'new consensus' among macroeconomists that is argued to have developed through the 1990s and into the 2000s.

Macroeconomic policy

In this chapter we look at various types of policy the government or central bank can use to tackle the macroeconomic problems of low and fluctuating economic growth, unemployment and inflation.

The first three sections focus on the control of aggregate demand. We start by looking at fiscal policy. This involves altering taxes and/or government spending. Cutting taxes or increasing government expenditure will increase aggregate demand, while increasing taxes or cutting government expenditure will reduce aggregate demand.

We then turn to monetary policy. Monetary policy seeks to control aggregate demand by directly controlling the money supply (narrow money) or by altering the rate of interest and then backing this up by any necessary change in money supply. A reduction in interest rates will encourage more borrowing and hence raise aggregate demand. A rise in interest rates will dampen aggregate demand.

Increasingly attention has focused on the longer-term impact of monetary and fiscal policy. In particular we look at the debate about whether the government should actively intervene to manage demand or whether it should merely set fiscal and monetary rules and then stick to them.

In the final section we turn to the supply side. We will look at various policies that aim to increase *potential* output, and hence shift the aggregate supply curve to the right, and to reduce equilibrium unemployment. As we shall see, some of these policies involve 'freeing up' the market; such policies, not surprisingly, are advocated by the political right. Other supply-side policies involve government investment in training and infrastructure and tend to be more favoured by the political centre and left.

> **After studying this chapter, you should be able to answer the following questions:**
>
> - What are the different types of macroeconomic policy that governments or central banks can use to control the economy?
> - How can fiscal policy be used to alter the level of aggregate demand? What are the strengths and drawbacks of using fiscal policy to (a) stabilise the economy; (b) cure fundamental disequilibria?
> - How is monetary policy operated by the central bank? How does it alter the money supply? How does it control interest rates? What special measures have been introduced since the financial crisis to stimulate the economy?
> - How successful is monetary policy likely to be in controlling (a) aggregate demand and (b) inflation?
> - Should fiscal and monetary policy be frequently adjusted in an attempt to stabilise the economy? Or should the government set fiscal and monetary rules, which are then rigidly followed?
> - What types of supply-side policy are available to governments? What are their strengths and weaknesses?

12.1 FISCAL POLICY

How can government expenditure and taxation be used to affect the level of economic activity?

Fiscal policy involves the government manipulating the level of government expenditure and/or rates of tax. An *expansionary* fiscal policy will involve raising government expenditure (an injection into the circular flow of income) or reducing taxes (a withdrawal from the circular flow). A *deflationary* (i.e. a contractionary) fiscal policy will involve cutting government expenditure and/or raising taxes.

By changing its fiscal stance government can affect the *level* of aggregate demand. Why might it wish to do this?

First, it can try to remove any severe deflationary (recessionary) or inflationary gaps. For instance, an expansionary fiscal policy could be used to try to prevent an economy experiencing a severe or prolonged recession. This was the approach taken around the world from 2008 when substantial tax cuts and increases in government expenditure were undertaken. Likewise, deflationary fiscal policy could be used to prevent rampant inflation, such as that experienced in the 1970s.

Secondly, it can try to smooth out the fluctuations in the economy associated with the business cycle. Stabilisation policies involve the government adjusting the level of aggregate demand so as to prevent the economy's actual output level deviating too far from its potential output level – to keep output gaps to a minimum.

Fiscal policy can also be used to influence aggregate *supply*. For example, government can increase its expenditure on infrastructure, or give tax incentives for investment.

Deficits and surpluses

Central government deficits and surpluses

Since an expansionary fiscal policy involves raising government expenditure and/or lowering taxes, this has the effect of either increasing the budget deficit or reducing the budget surplus. A **budget deficit** in any one year is where central government's expenditure exceeds its revenue from taxation. A **budget surplus** is where tax revenues exceed central government expenditure.

For most of the last 50 years governments around the world have run budget deficits. A deficit in any year adds to the total debt that a government has accumulated over the years. In recent years, however, many countries, the UK included, made substantial efforts to reduce their budget deficits, and some achieved budget surpluses for periods of time. The position changed dramatically in 2008/9, however, as governments around the world increased their expenditure and cut taxes in an attempt to stave off recession. Government deficits, and hence stocks of debt, in many countries soared.

To finance a deficit, the government will have to borrow (e.g. through the issue of bonds (gilts) or Treasury bills). As we saw in Section 10.3, this will lead to an increase in the money supply to the extent that the borrowing is from the banking sector.

General government

'General government' includes central and local government. Table 12.1 shows general government deficits/surpluses and debt for selected countries. They are expressed as a proportion of GDP.

As you can see, in the period from 1995 to 2007, all countries, with the exception of Ireland and Sweden, averaged a deficit. Nevertheless, for most countries these deficits and debts were smaller than in the early 1990s. However, in the period from 2008 to 2016, the average deficit increased for most countries. And the bigger the deficit, the faster debt increased.

The whole public sector

To get a more complete view of public finances, we would need to look at the spending and receipts of the entire public sector: namely, central government, local government and public corporations.

Total public expenditure. First, we need to distinguish between **current** and **capital expenditures**. Current expenditures include items such as wages and salaries of public-sector staff, administration and the payments of welfare benefits. Capital expenditures give rise to a stream of benefits *over time*. Examples include expenditure on roads, hospitals and schools.

Secondly, we must distinguish between **final expenditure** on goods and services, and transfers. This distinction recognises that the public sector directly adds to the economy's aggregate demand through its spending on goods and services, including the wages of public-sector workers, but also that it redistributes incomes between individuals and firms. Transfers include subsidies and benefit payments, such as payments to the unemployed.

Definitions

Fiscal policy Policy to affect aggregate demand by altering government expenditure and/or taxation.

Budget deficit The excess of central government's spending over its tax receipts.

Budget surplus The excess of central government's tax receipts over its spending.

Current expenditure Recurrent spending on goods and factor payments.

Capital expenditure Investment expenditure; expenditure on assets.

Final expenditure Expenditure on goods and services. This is included in GDP and is part of aggregate demand.

| Table 12.1 | General government deficits/surpluses and debt as percentage of GDP |

	General government deficits (−) or surpluses (+)		General government debt	
	Average 1995–2007	Average 2008–2016	Average 1995–2007	Average 2008–2016
Belgium	−1.3	−3.3	108.3	102.3
France	−2.9	−4.7	61.6	87.1
Germany	−2.9	−0.7	61.0	74.1
Greece	−6.4	−8.4	96.8	157.3
Ireland	+1.2	−10.0	41.7	96.5
Italy	−3.5	−3.2	106.4	121.6
Japan	−5.7	−7.4	148.5	230.8
Netherlands	−2.7	−2.6	55.2	63.8
Portugal	−4.3	−5.9	58.6	110.6
Spain	−1.4	−7.2	52.9	77.5
Sweden	0.0	−0.6	55.0	39.7
UK	−2.2	−6.7	42.0	79.8
USA	−2.8	−7.8	61.7	97.2
EU-15	−1.1	−3.9	64.0	84.0

Note: Data from 2015 based on forecasts

Source: Based on data from *AMECO Database*, Tables 16.3 and 18.1 (European Commission, DG ECFIN)

Since 1990 the UK's public expenditure has typically split 93 to 7 per cent between current and capital expenditure, and 62 to 38 per cent between final expenditure and transfers.

Public-sector deficits. If the public sector spends more than it earns, it will have to finance the deficit through borrowing: known as **public-sector net borrowing (PSNB)**. The principal form of borrowing is through the sale of bonds. In the case of central government, these are known as gilt-edged securities (or gilts). Since the 1960s, the UK's public-sector net borrowing has averaged nearly 3 per cent of GDP.

The precise amount of money the public sector requires to borrow in any one year is known as the **public-sector net cash requirement (PSNCR)**. It differs slightly from the PSNB because of time lags in the flows of public-sector incomes and expenditure.

If the public sector runs a surplus (a negative PSNB), it will be able to repay some of the public-sector debts that have accumulated from previous years.

Cyclically adjusted balances

The size of the deficit or surplus is not entirely due to deliberate government policy. It is influenced by the state of the economy.

If the economy is booming with people earning high incomes, the amount paid in taxes will be high. Also, in a booming economy the level of unemployment will be low. Thus the amount paid out in unemployment benefits will be low. The combined effect of increased tax revenues and reduced benefits is to reduce the public-sector deficit (or increase the surplus).

By contrast, if the economy is depressed, tax revenues will be low and the amount paid in benefits will be high.

This will increase the public-sector deficit (or reduce the surplus).

By 'cyclically adjusting' measures of public-sector deficits or surpluses we remove their cyclical component. In other words, we show just the direct effects of government policy, not the effects of the level of economic activity. Figure 12.1 shows both actual and cyclically adjusted public-sector net borrowing as a percentage of GDP since the mid-1970s. Over the long run the economy's output gap is zero (see Box 9.1 on page 236). Hence, over the period shown, both net borrowing measures average the same (around 3 per cent of GDP).

The deficit or surplus that would arise if the economy were producing at the potential level of national income (see Box 9.1) is termed the **structural deficit or surplus**. Remember that the potential level of national income is where there is no excess or deficiency of aggregate demand: where there is a zero output gap.

KI 21 p 148

Definitions

Public-sector net borrowing The difference between the expenditures of the public sector and its receipts from taxation and the revenues from public corporations.

Public-sector net cash requirement (PSNCR) The (annual) deficit of the public sector, and thus the amount that the public sector must borrow. In the UK the principal measure, which takes into account financial transactions by the public sector, is known as the public-sector net cash requirement.

Structural deficit (or surplus) The public-sector deficit (or surplus) that would occur if the economy were operating at the potential level of national income: i.e. one where there is a zero output gap.

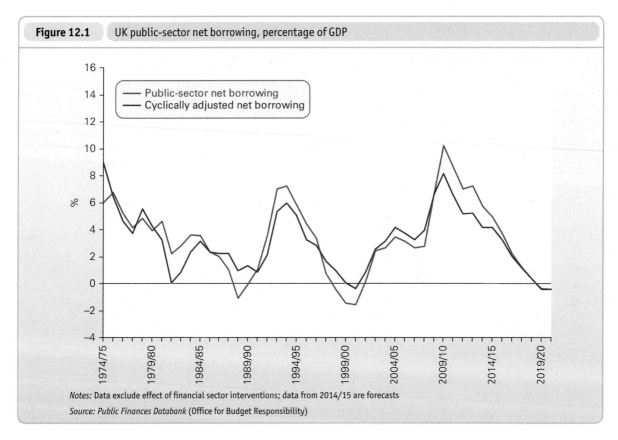

Figure 12.1   UK public-sector net borrowing, percentage of GDP

Notes: Data exclude effect of financial sector interventions; data from 2014/15 are forecasts

Source: Public Finances Databank (Office for Budget Responsibility)

The use of fiscal policy

Automatic fiscal stabilisers

To some extent, government expenditure and taxation will have the effect of *automatically* stabilising the economy. For example, as national income rises, the amount of tax people pay automatically rises. This rise in withdrawals from the circular flow of income helps to dampen down the rise in national income. This effect will be bigger if taxes are progressive (i.e. rise by a bigger percentage than national income). Some government transfers will have a similar effect. For example, the total paid in unemployment benefits will fall, if rises in national income cause a fall in unemployment. This again will have the effect of dampening the rise in national income.

Discretionary fiscal policy

Automatic stabilisers cannot *prevent* fluctuations; they merely reduce their magnitude. If there is a *fundamental* disequilibrium in the economy, or substantial fluctuations in national income, these automatic stabilisers will not be enough. The government may thus choose to *alter* the level of government expenditure or the rates of taxation. This is known as **discretionary fiscal policy**. Box 12.1 looks at discretionary fiscal policy in the UK since the financial crisis of the late 2000s.

If government expenditure on goods and services (roads, health care, education, etc.) is raised, this will create a full multiplied rise in national income. The reason is that all the

money gets spent and thus all of it goes to boosting aggregate demand.

Cutting taxes (or increasing benefits), however, will have a smaller effect on national income than raising government expenditure on goods and services by the same amount. The reason is that cutting taxes increases people's *disposable* incomes, of which only *part* will be spent. Part will be withdrawn into extra saving, imports and other taxes. In other words, not all the tax cuts will be passed on round the circular flow of income as extra expenditure. Thus if one-fifth of a cut in taxes is withdrawn and only four-fifths is spent, the tax multiplier will be only four-fifths as big as the government expenditure multiplier.

Pause for thought

Why will the multiplier effect of government transfer payments, such as child benefit, pensions and social security benefits, be less than the full multiplier effect from government expenditure on goods and services?

Definition

Discretionary fiscal policy Deliberate changes in tax rates or the level of government expenditure in order to influence the level of aggregate demand.

The effectiveness of fiscal policy

There are two main problem areas with discretionary fiscal policy. The first concerns the *magnitude* of the effects of policy measures. If either government expenditure (*G*) or taxation (*T*) is changed, how much will *total* injections and withdrawals change? What will be the size of the resulting multiplier effect? How much will the change in aggregate demand affect output and employment, and how much will it affect prices?

The second concerns the *timing* of the effects. How quickly can policy be changed and how quickly will the changes affect the economy?

Problems of magnitude

Before changing government expenditure or taxation, the government will need to calculate the effect of any such change on national income, employment and inflation. Predicting these effects, however, is often very unreliable for a number of reasons.

Predicting the effect of changes in government expenditure

A rise in government expenditure of £*x* may lead to a rise in total injections (relative to withdrawals) that is smaller than £*x*. This will occur if the rise in government expenditure *replaces* a certain amount of private expenditure. For example, a rise in expenditure on state education may dissuade some parents from sending their children to private schools. Similarly, an improvement in the National Health Service may lead to fewer people paying for private treatment.

Crowding out. Another reason for the total rise in injections being smaller than the rise in government expenditure is a phenomenon known as **crowding out.** If the government relies on **pure fiscal policy** – that is, if it does not finance an increase in the budget deficit by increasing the money supply – it will have to borrow the money from the non-bank private sector. It will thus be competing with the private sector for finance and will have to offer higher interest rates. This will force the private sector too to offer higher interest rates, which may discourage firms from investing and individuals from buying on credit. Thus government borrowing crowds out private borrowing. In the extreme case, the fall in consumption and investment may completely offset the rise in government expenditure, with the result that aggregate demand does not rise at all.

Predicting the effect of changes in taxes

A cut in taxes, by increasing people's real disposable income, increases not only the amount they spend but also the amount they save. The problem is that it is not easy to predict the relative size of these two increases. In part it will depend on whether people feel that the cut in tax is only temporary, in which case they may simply save the extra disposable income, or permanent, in which case they may adjust their consumption upwards. More generally, it may depend on a broader set of variables, including confidence and financial well-being.

Predicting the resulting multiplied effect on national income

Even if the government *could* predict the net *initial* effect on injections and withdrawals, the ultimate effect on national income will still be hard to predict for the following reasons:

- The size of the *multiplier* may be difficult to predict, since it is difficult to predict how much of any rise in income will be withdrawn. In other words, it is difficult to predict the size of the *mpw*. For example, the amount of a rise in income that households save or consume will depend on their expectations about future price and income changes.
- Induced investment through the *accelerator* (see page 241) is also extremely difficult to predict. It may be that a relatively small fiscal stimulus will be all that is necessary to restore business confidence, and that induced investment will rise substantially. Similarly, rising confidence amongst financial institutions could see credit conditions relaxed with the *financial accelerator* (see page 240) resulting in rising levels of investment. In such situations, fiscal policy can be seen as a 'pump primer'. It is used to start the process of recovery, and then the continuation of the recovery is left to the market. But for pump priming to work, people must believe that it will work. Confidence can change very rapidly and in ways that could not have been foreseen a few months earlier.
- Multiplier/accelerator interactions. If the initial multiplier and accelerator effects are difficult to estimate, their interaction will be virtually impossible to estimate. Small divergences in investment from what was initially predicted will become magnified as time progresses.

Random shocks

Forecasts cannot take into account the unpredictable, such as the attack on the World Trade Center in New York in

Definitions

Crowding out Where increased public expenditure diverts money or resources away from the private sector.

Pure fiscal policy Fiscal policy that does not involve any change in money supply.

Pause for thought

Give some other examples of 'random shocks' that could undermine the government's fiscal policy.

BOX 12.1 THE FINANCIAL CRISIS AND THE UK FISCAL POLICY YO-YO

From fiscal expansion to fiscal consolidation

The impact of the financial crisis on economic growth in the UK was stark. The UK economy had expanded by 3.0 per cent in 2006 and by a further 2.6 in 2007. But in 2008 it contracted by 0.3 per cent and then by 4.3 per cent in 2009.

The UK fiscal policy response was initially expansionary as attempts were made to mitigate the worst of the economic slowdown. Then, with a new government in place and with a burgeoning budget deficit, the UK turned rapidly to a policy of fiscal consolidation. Within a short space of time the stance of fiscal policy changed markedly: a fiscal policy yo-yo.

Expansion

The UK economy entered recession in the second quarter of 2008. In the Pre-Budget Report of November 2008, amongst other measures, the Labour government introduced a 13-month cut in VAT from 17.5 per cent to 15 per cent. It also brought forward from 2010/11 £3 billion of capital spending on projects such as motorways, new social housing, schools and energy efficiency.

The effect of the capital spending projects was to increase public-sector gross investment to 5.2 per cent and 5.3 per cent of GDP in 2008/9 and 2009/10 respectively. In the previous 15 years the typical amount of public-sector gross investment spending had been just 3.3 per cent of GDP. Meanwhile, as Chart (a) shows, total government spending (excluding financial interventions) began to rise rapidly, fuelled by rising transfer payments on the back of the faltering economy, peaking at just over 45 per cent in 2009/10.

The UK came out of recession in the third quarter of 2009 after five consecutive quarters of declining output which saw the economy shrink by 6 per cent. Meanwhile, the rate of unemployment which had stood at 5.2 per cent at the start of 2008 peaked at 8 per cent in early 2010 and stood at 7.8 per cent in May when 13 years of Labour government came to an end. Not only did this mark a change of government as a Conservative–Liberal coalition took charge, but it also marked a change in the direction of fiscal policy.

Consolidation

In 2009/10, public-sector net borrowing hit 10.2 per cent of GDP, up from 2.7 per cent in 2007 (see Chart (a)). Consequently, public-sector net debt grew rapidly (see Chart (b)). From £558 billion (37 per cent of GDP) in 2007/8 it rose to £956 billion (62 per cent of GDP) by 2009/10.

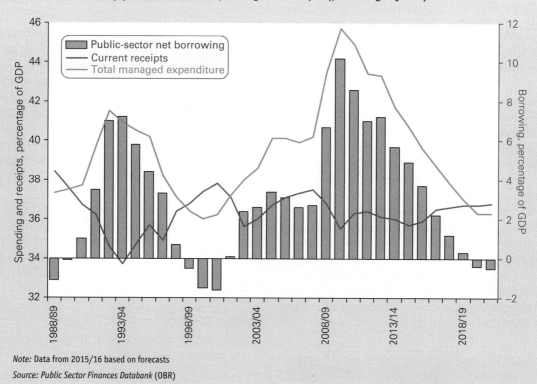

(a) UK public-sector spending and receipts (percentage of GDP)

Note: Data from 2015/16 based on forecasts

Source: Public Sector Finances Databank (OBR)

The response of the new government was to begin a policy of consolidation. The framework for this was to be known as the 'fiscal mandate'. The initial mandate was for a *cyclically adjusted* balanced current budget five years ahead: i.e. after adjusting for the position in the economic cycle. Therefore, at the end of a rolling five-year forecast period public-sector receipts should at least equal public-sector current expenditures, after taking into account the economy's output gap. This mandate was supplemented by a target for public-sector net debt as a percentage of GDP to be falling by 2015/16.

To achieve this, the government embarked on a series of spending cuts and tax rises. This started with a 'discretionary consolidation' of £8.9 billion in 2010/11 comprising spending cuts of £5.3 billion and tax increases worth £3.6 billion. It was announced that the consolidation would continue up to 2015/16. By the end of 2015/16 the government planned to have delivered a discretionary consolidation of £122 billion, with £99 billion coming from discretionary reductions in spending and £23 billion from tax increases. As it turned out, however, in real terms total public-sector spending fell by just 0.7 per cent between 2010/11 and 2014/15.

The principal fiscal target for a cyclically adjusted balanced current budget was therefore not met during the 2010–15 parliamentary period. Nonetheless, the government claimed that 'significant progress' had been made on its fiscal consolidation.

Following the 2015 election, the Conservative government announced an updated fiscal framework. The fiscal mandate now involved the public sector targeting an *actual* buget surplus by 2019/20. Thereafter, it should plan for a budget surplus each year, so long as the annual rate of economic growth does not fall below 1 per cent. The new supplementary target for debt was for net debt to be falling as a percentage of GDP each year from 2015/16. To achieve the revised mandate, the government announced a package of consolidation measures which it said would amount to £37 billion by the end of 2019/20. This consolidation included £12 billion of savings from welfare reform.

Recent UK fiscal frameworks are discussed further in Box 12.3.

 Which is likely to give a bigger boost to aggregate demand: tax cuts of a given amount targeted to (a) the rich or (b) the poor?

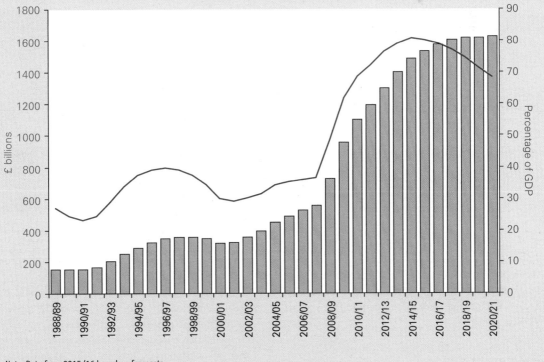

(b) UK public-sector net debt

Note: Data from 2015/16 based on forecasts

Source: Public Sector Finances Databank (OBR) and *Quarterly National Accounts*, series YBHA (ONS)

BOX 12.2   EVOLVING FISCAL FRAMEWORKS, PART I: THE EUROPEAN UNION

Constraining the fiscal discretion of national governments

In this box, we consider the recent turbulent history of the fiscal framework for the member states of the European Union. This framework is intended to ensure sound public finances of member states. This includes an 'Excessive Deficit Procedure' which applies to all EU member states. The UK, however, is not legally bound by this procedure. In Box 12.3 we consider the evolving fiscal framework adopted in the UK.

Preparing for the euro

In signing the Maastricht Treaty in 1992, the EU countries agreed that to be eligible to join the single currency (i.e. the euro), they should have sustainable deficits and debts. This was interpreted as follows: the general government deficit should be no more than 3 per cent of GDP and general government debt should be no more than 60 per cent of GDP, or should at least be falling towards that level at a satisfactory pace.

But in the mid-1990s, several of the countries that were subsequently to join the euro had deficits and debts substantially above these levels (see chart). Getting them down proved a painful business. Government expenditure had to be cut and taxes increased. These fiscal measures, unfortunately, proved to be powerful! Unemployment rose and growth remained low.

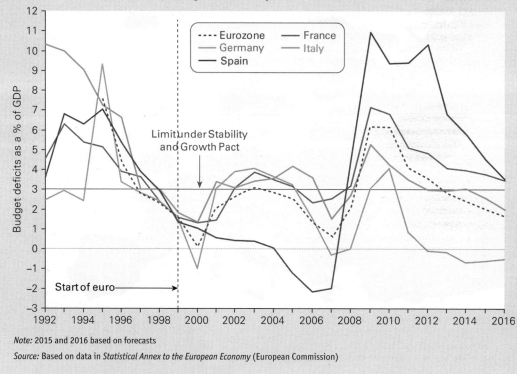

General government deficits in the eurozone

Note: 2015 and 2016 based on forecasts

Source: Based on data in *Statistical Annex to the European Economy* (European Commission)

September 2001. Even events that, with hindsight, should have been predicted, such as the banking crisis of 2007/9, often are not. Unfortunately, unpredictable or unpredicted events do occur and may seriously undermine the government's fiscal policy.

The problem of timing

Fiscal policy can involve considerable time lags. It may take time to recognise the nature of the problem before the government is willing to take action; tax or government expenditure changes take time to plan and implement – changes will have to wait until the next Budget to be announced and may come into effect some time later; the effects of such changes take time to work their way through the economy via the multiplier and accelerator.

If time lags are long enough, fiscal policy could even be *de*stabilising. Expansionary policies taken to cure a recession may not come into effect until the economy has *already* recovered and is experiencing a boom. Under these circumstances, expansionary policies are quite inappropriate: they simply worsen the problems of overheating. Similarly, contractionary policies taken to prevent excessive expansion may not take effect until the economy has already peaked and is plunging into recession. The contractionary policies only deepen the recession.

This problem is illustrated in Figure 12.2. Path (a) shows the course of the business cycle without government

The EU Stability and Growth Pact (SGP)

In June 1997, at the European Council meeting in Amsterdam, the EU countries agreed a Stability and Growth Pact (SGP). Thus stated that member states should seek to balance their budgets (or even aim for a surplus) averaged over the course of the business cycle, and that deficits should not exceed 3 per cent of GDP in any one year. A country's deficit was permitted to exceed 3 per cent only if its GDP had declined by at least 2 per cent (or 0.75 per cent with special permission from the Council of Ministers). Otherwise, countries with deficits exceeding 3 per cent were required to make deposits of money with the European Central Bank. Under the Pact's Excessive Deficit Procedure, these would then become fines if the excessive budget deficit were not eliminated within two years.

There were two main aims of targeting a zero budget deficit over the business cycle. The first was to allow automatic stabilisers to work without 'bumping into' the 3 per cent deficit ceiling in years when economies were slowing. The second was to allow a reduction in government debts as a proportion of GDP (assuming that GDP grew on average at around 2–3 per cent per year).

From 2002, with slowing growth, Germany, France and Italy breached the 3 per cent ceiling (see chart). By 2007, however, after two years of relatively strong growth, deficits had been reduced well below the ceiling.

But then the credit crunch hit. As the EU economies slowed, so deficits rose. To combat the recession, in November 2008 the European Commission announced a €200 billion fiscal stimulus plan, mainly in the form of increased public expenditure. Of this sum, €170 billion would come from member governments and €30 billion from the EU, amounting to a total of 1.2 per cent of EU GDP. The money would be for a range of projects, such as job training, help to small businesses, developing green energy technologies and energy efficiency. Most member governments quickly followed by announcing how their specific plans would accord with the overall plan.

The combination of the recession and the fiscal measures pushed most EU countries' budget deficits well above the 3 per cent ceiling (see chart). The recession in EU countries deepened markedly in 2009, with GDP declining by 4.5 per cent in the eurozone and by 5.4 per cent in Italy, 5.1 per cent in Germany, 3.8 per cent in Spain and 2.9 per cent in France. Consequently, the deficits were not seen to breach SGP rules.

The Fiscal Compact

As the European economy began to recover in 2010, there was tremendous pressure on member countries to begin reining in their deficits. The average eurozone deficit had risen to 6.2 per cent of GDP, and some countries' deficits were very much higher. Indeed, with the Spanish, Greek and Irish deficits being 9.6, 11.0 and 29.3 per cent respectively, reining in deficits would prove to be especially painful for these and several other eurozone countries.

The SGP was no longer seen as a credible vehicle for constraining deficits: it needed reform. The result was an intense period of negotiation that culminated in early 2012 in a new intergovernmental treaty on limiting spending and borrowing. The entire treaty, known as the Fiscal Compact, applies to all eurozone countries. However, non-eurozone member states can choose to be bound by the fiscal rules outlined in the Treaty.

The Fiscal Compact requires that from January 2013 national governments not only abide by the excessive deficit procedure of the SGP but also keep structural deficits no higher than 0.5 per cent of GDP. Structural deficits are that part of a deficit not directly related to the economic cycle and so would exist even if the economy were operating at its potential output. In the cases of countries with a debt-to-GDP ratio significantly below 60 per cent, the structural deficit is permitted to reach 1 per cent of GDP. Finally, where the debt-to-GDP ratio exceeds 60 per cent, countries should, on average, reduce it by one-twentieth per year.

Where a national government is found by the European Court of Justice not to comply with the Fiscal Compact, it has the power to fine that country up to 0.1 per cent of GDP payable to the European Stability Mechanism (ESM). The ESM is a fund from which loans are provided to support a eurozone government in severe financing difficulty or alternatively is used to purchase that country's bonds in the primary market.

What effects will an increase in government investment expenditure have on public-sector debt (a) in the short run; (b) in the long run?

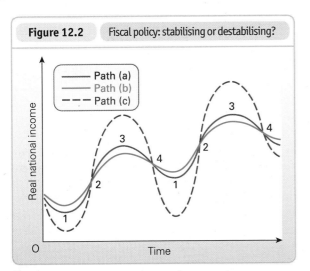

| **Figure 12.2** | Fiscal policy: stabilising or destabilising? |

intervention. Ideally, with no time lags, the economy should be dampened in stage 2 and stimulated in stage 4. This would make the resulting course of the business cycle more like path (b), or even, if the policy were perfectly stabilising, a line that purely reflected the growth in potential output. With time lags, however, contractionary policies taken in stage 2 may not come into effect until stage 4, and expansionary policies taken in stage 4 may not come into effect until stage 2. In this case the resulting course of the business cycle will be more like path (c). Quite obviously, in these circumstances 'stabilising' fiscal policy actually makes the economy *less* stable.

If the fluctuations in aggregate demand can be forecast, and if the lengths of the time lags are known, then all is not lost. At least the fiscal measures can be taken early and their delayed effects can be taken into account.

BOX 12.3   EVOLVING FISCAL FRAMEWORKS, PART II: THE UK

From golden rules to fiscal mandates

Box 12.2 considers the evolving fiscal framework of the European Union. The UK has had specific exemptions from the Excessive Deficit Procedure and is not bound by the recently agreed Fiscal Compact. Nonetheless, the UK adopted a Code for Fiscal Stability back in 1997 with a series of guiding principles resulting in a set of fiscal rules. The turbulence caused by the financial crisis and its economic fallout have resulted in changes to this fiscal framework, as they have to the EU's framework. However, the changes to the framework in the UK also reflect changes in the political environment and, consequently, in the direction of fiscal policy.

The UK Labour government's rules

On being elected in 1997, the Labour government in the UK adopted a similar approach to that of the SGP. It introduced two fiscal rules.

The golden rule. First, under its 'golden rule', the government pledged that over the economic cycle it would borrow only to invest (e.g. in roads, hospitals and schools) and not to fund current spending (e.g. on wages, administration and benefits). In other words, it would seek, over the cycle, to achieve a *current budget balance*, where total receipts equal total current expenditures (i.e. excluding capital expenditures). Investment was exempted from the zero borrowing rule because it contributes towards the growth of GDP.

The chart shows how the cyclically adjusted current budget balanced across the economic cycle from 1997/8 to 2006/7. By cyclically adjusting, we remove the estimated effects of the

---

Definition

Current budget balance The difference between public-sector receipts and those expenditures classified as current rather than capital expenditures.

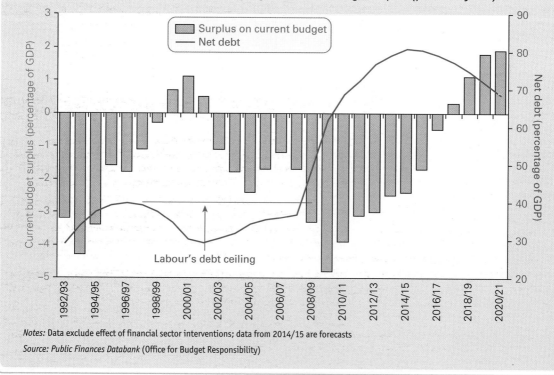

Public-sector net debt and cyclically adjusted current budget surplus (per cent of GDP)

Legend: Surplus on current budget; Net debt

Labour's debt ceiling

Notes: Data exclude effect of financial sector interventions; data from 2014/15 are forecasts

Source: Public Finances Databank (Office for Budget Responsibility)

Fiscal rules

Given the problems of pursuing active fiscal policy, many governments today take a much more passive approach. Instead of the policy being changed as the economy changes, countries apply a set of fiscal rules. These rules typically relate to measures of government deficits and to the stock of accumulated debt. Taxes and government expenditure can then be planned to meet these rules.

But rules cannot cope with severe disruption to the global economy, such as occurred in the credit crunch of 2008. Countries around the world resorted to

economic cycle, such as increased welfare payments and lower tax receipts when output is below its potential.

The sustainable investment rule. Secondly, under its 'sustainable investment rule', the government also set itself the target of maintaining public-sector net debt at no more than 40 per cent of GDP averaged over the economic cycle.

As with the SGP, the argument for the golden rule was that by using an averaging rule over the cycle, automatic stabilisers would be allowed to work. Deficits of receipts over current spending could occur when the economy is in recession or when growth is sluggish (as in 2001–3), helping to stimulate the economy.

The global financial crisis of 2008, however, saw the UK fiscal framework suspended. In the Pre-Budget Report of November 2008, the government argued that its 'immediate priority' was to support the economy by using discretionary fiscal policy. As we saw in Box 12.1, these measures included a 13-month cut in VAT from 17.5 per cent to 15 per cent and bringing forward from 2010/11 £3 billion of capital spending.

However, the deteriorating state of the public finances led the Labour government in late 2009 to introduce through Parliament a Fiscal Responsibility Bill. It required governments to present to Parliament their fiscal plans to deliver sound public finances. The plan of Chancellor Alistair Darling was to halve the size of the deficit over the next Parliament.

Fiscal mandates

May 2010 saw a Conservative–Liberal Democrat Coalition government formed. Its fiscal priority was to get the deficit down. In 2009 public-sector net borrowing (see Figure 12.1 on page 330) had reached 10.4 per cent of GDP, one of the highest percentages in the developed world. The new government set itself a 'fiscal mandate': to achieve a cyclically adjusted current balance by 2015/16. This was, therefore, very similar to the golden rule. The fiscal mandate was supplemented by a target for public-sector debt as a percentage of GDP to be falling by 2015/16.

To achieve its fiscal mandate meant sharp government expenditure cuts and tax rises. As we saw in Box 12.1, the government embarked on a discretionary consolidation that would see reductions in spending of £99 billion by 2015/16 and increases in tax of £23 billion. This meant that expenditure cuts would make up 81 per cent of the total fiscal consolidation.

On its own, the much tighter fiscal policy would substantially dampen aggregate demand. The question was whether the recovery in exports, investment and consumer demand would be sufficient to offset this, which, in turn, would be

heavily dependent on the confidence of people (see Section 12.2). Despite growing by 3 per cent in 2014, the UK economy grew by an average rate of just 1.7 per cent per year from 2010 to 2014 – almost 1 percentage point below its longer-term average (see Section 9.2).

As it turned out, the government failed to meet its fiscal mandate and so was unable to achieve a balanced cyclically adjusted current budget. A Conservative government was elected following the May 2015 election. The government formulated a radical new fiscal mandate and supplementary debt rule. These were contained within a *Charter for Budget Responsibility*[a] which, since 2011, sets out before Parliament the government's objectives for fiscal policy and for managing public-sector debt.

The new fiscal mandate set a target for achieving a surplus on public-sector net borrowing by the end of 2019/20. More controversially, government should then target a surplus in each subsequent year unless real GDP growth falls below 1 per cent on a rolling quarter-on-quarter basis (i.e. if quarterly data show that the annual rate of growth has fallen below 1 per cent). Meanwhile, the revised supplementary target for public-sector debt was for the net debt-to-GDP ratio to fall each year from 2015/16 to 2019/20.

The fiscal mandate of Summer 2015 commits governments to run budget surpluses in normal times, where 'normal times' are defined as when growth does not fall below 1 per cent. The government argues that this is needed to ensure sutainable debt reduction and so bring the country's debt burden down to 'safer' levels. Its opponents argue that the sustainability of the public finances is crucially dependent on economic growth and hence the new mandate does not account sufficiently for economic circumstances and unnecessarily restricts fiscal policy.

The updated Charter for Budget Responsibility signalled further significant fiscal consolidation. The government announced that additional deficit reduction of £37 billion was needed by the end of 2019/20 (see Box 12.1). This would be largely from further spending cuts, but also by cracking down on tax avoidance.

> **?** *If there is danger of recession, should governments loosen the straight-jacket of fiscal policy targets?*

---

[a] http://www.gov.uk/government/publications/
charter-for-budget-responsibility-summer-budget-2015-update
http://budgetresponsibility.org.uk/wordpress/docs/Charter_budget_
responsibility_update_web.pdf

discretionary fiscal policy to boost aggregate demand. They abandoned fiscal rules – at least temporarily. Rules were generally reinstated around the world, however, as the global economy pulled out of recession. In Boxes 12.2 and 12.3 we detail how the fiscal rules in the eurozone and

the UK, respectively, evolved following the events of the late 2000s.

In Section 12.3 we review the debate concerning constraints on a government's discretion over both its fiscal and monetary policies.

Recap

1. Fiscal policy affects the size of government budget deficits or surpluses.

2. The size of these alone, such as public-sector net borrowing, is a poor guide, however, to the government's fiscal stance. A large deficit, for example, may simply be due to the fact that the economy is in recession and therefore tax receipts are low. A better guide is whether the change in the deficit or surplus will be expansionary or contractionary.

3. Automatic fiscal stabilisers are tax revenues that rise, and benefits that fall, as national income rises. They have the effect of reducing the size of the multiplier and thus reducing cyclical upswings and downswings.

4. Automatic stabilisers take effect as soon as aggregate demand fluctuates, but they can never remove fluctuations completely. They also create disincentives and act as a drag on recovery from recession.

5. Discretionary fiscal policy is where the government deliberately changes taxes or government expenditure in order to alter the level of aggregate demand. Changes in government expenditure on goods and services have a full multiplier effect. Changes in taxes and benefits, however, have a smaller multiplier effect as some of the tax/benefit changes will merely affect other withdrawals and thus have a smaller net effect on the consumption of domestic goods.

6. There are problems in predicting the magnitude of the effects of discretionary fiscal policy. Expansionary fiscal policy can act as a pump primer and stimulate increased private expenditure, or it can crowd out private expenditure. The extent to which it acts as a pump primer depends crucially on business confidence – something that is very difficult to predict beyond a few weeks or months. The extent of crowding out depends on monetary conditions and monetary policy.

7. There are various time lags involved with fiscal policy, which make it difficult to use fiscal policy to 'fine-tune' the economy.

8. In recent years many governments around the world preferred a more passive approach towards fiscal policy. Targets were set for one or more measures of the public-sector finances, and then taxes and government expenditure were adjusted so as to keep to the target.

9. Nevertheless, in extreme circumstances, as occurred in 2008/9, governments were prepared to abandon rules and give a fiscal stimulus to their economies.

12.2 MONETARY POLICY

How can the supply of money and interest rates be controlled?

Each month in the UK the Bank of England's Monetary Policy Committee meets to set Bank Rate. The event gets considerable media coverage. Pundits, for two or three days before the meeting, try to predict what the MPC will do and economists give their 'considered' opinions about what the MPC *ought* to do.

The fact is that changes in interest rates have gained a central significance in macroeconomic policy. And it is not just in the UK. Whether it is the European Central Bank setting interest rates for the eurozone countries, or the Federal Reserve Bank setting US interest rates, or any other central bank around the world choosing what the level of interest rates should be, monetary policy is seen as having a major influence on a whole range of macroeconomic indicators.

But is monetary policy simply the setting of interest rates? In reality, it involves the central bank intervening in the money market to ensure that the interest rate that has been announced is also the *equilibrium* interest rate.

The policy setting

In framing its monetary policy, the government must decide on what the goals of the policy are. Is the aim simply to control inflation, or does the government wish also to affect output and employment, or does it want to control the exchange rate?

The government also has to decide the role of the central bank in carrying out monetary policy. There are three possible approaches.

In the first, the government both sets the policy and decides the measures necessary to achieve it. Here the government would set the interest rate, with the central bank simply influencing money markets to achieve this rate. This first approach was used in the UK before 1997.

The second approach is for the government to set the policy *targets*, but for the central bank to be given independence in deciding interest rates. This is the approach adopted in the UK today. The government has set a target rate of inflation of 2 per cent, but then the MPC is free to choose the rate of interest.

The third approach is for the central bank to be given independence not only in carrying out policy, but in setting the policy targets itself. The ECB, within the statutory objective of maintaining price stability over the medium term, has decided on the target of keeping inflation below, but close to, 2 per cent over the medium term.

Finally, there is the question of whether the government or central bank should take a long-term or short-term perspective. Should it adopt a target for inflation or money supply growth and stick to it come what may? Or should it adjust its policy as circumstances change and attempt to 'fine-tune' the economy?

We shall be looking primarily at *short-term* monetary policy – that is, policy used to keep to a set target for inflation or money supply growth, or policy used to smooth out fluctuations in the business cycle.

It is important first, however, to take a longer-term perspective. Governments generally want to prevent an excessive growth in the money supply over the longer term. Likewise they want to ensure that money supply grows enough and that there is not a shortage of credit, such as that during the credit crunch. If money supply grows too rapidly, then inflation is likely to be high; if money supply grows too slowly, or even falls, then recession is likely to result.

Control of the money supply over the medium and long term

In Section 10.3 we identified two major sources of monetary growth: (a) banks choosing to hold a lower liquidity ratio (probably in response to an increase in the demand for loans); (b) public-sector borrowing financed by borrowing from the banking sector. If the government wishes to restrict monetary growth over the longer term, it could attempt to control either or both of these.

Banks' liquidity ratio

The central bank could impose a statutory **minimum reserve ratio** on the banks, above the level that banks would otherwise choose to hold. Such ratios come in various forms. The simplest is where the banks are required to hold a given minimum percentage of deposits in the form of cash or deposits with the central bank.

The effect of a minimum reserve ratio is to prevent banks choosing to reduce their cash or liquidity ratio and creating more credit. This was a popular approach of governments in many countries in the past. Some countries imposed very high ratios indeed in their attempt to slow down the growth in the money supply.

A major problem with imposing restrictions of this kind is that banks may find ways of getting round them. After all, banks would like to lend and customers would like to borrow. It is very difficult to regulate and police every single part of countries' complex financial systems.

Nevertheless, attitudes changed substantially after the excessive lending of the mid-2000s. The expansion of credit had been based on 'liquidity' achieved through secondary marketing between financial institutions and the growth of securitised assets containing sub-prime debt (see Box 10.3). After the credit crunch and the need for central banks or governments to rescue ailing banks, such as Northern Rock and later the Royal Bank of Scotland in the UK and many other banks around the world, there were calls for greater

regulation of banks to ensure that they had sufficient capital and operated with sufficient liquidity and that they were not exposed to excessive risk of default. As we saw earlier (see pages 271–2), a number of measures were taken.

Public-sector deficits

Section 10.3 showed how government borrowing tends to lead to an increase in money supply. To prevent this, public-sector deficits must be financed by selling *bonds* (as opposed to bills, which could well be taken up by the banking sector, thereby increasing money supply). However, to sell extra bonds the government will have to offer higher interest rates. This will have a knock-on effect on private-sector interest rates. The government borrowing will thus crowd out private-sector borrowing and investment. This is known as **financial crowding out.**

If governments wish to reduce monetary growth and yet avoid financial crowding out, they must therefore reduce the size of public-sector deficits.

The less successful a government is in controlling the public-sector deficit, the more it will have to borrow through bond issue, to prevent money supply growing too fast. This will mean high interest rates and the problem of crowding out, and a growing burden of public-sector debt with interest on it that has to be paid from taxation, from further cuts in government expenditure, or from further borrowing.

It is partly for this reason that many governments have constrained fiscal policy choices by applying fiscal rules or agreements, such as the Fiscal Compact in the eurozone (see Box 12.2), or the 'fiscal mandate' in the UK (see Box 12.3).

Short-term monetary measures

Inflation may be off target. Alternatively, the government (or central bank) may wish to alter its monetary policy. What can it do? Various techniques could be used. These can be grouped into three categories: (a) altering the money supply; (b) altering interest rates; (c) rationing credit. These are illustrated in Figure 12.3, which shows the demand for and supply of money. The equilibrium quantity of money is initially Q_1 and the equilibrium interest rate is r_1.

Assume that the central bank wants to tighten monetary policy in order to reduce inflation. It could (a) seek to shift the supply of money curve to the left: e.g. from M_s to M_s'

KI 13
p 66

Definition

Minimum reserve ratio A minimum ratio of cash (or other specified liquid assets) to deposits (either total or selected) that the central bank requires banks to hold.

Financial crowding out Where an increase in government borrowing diverts money away from the private sector.

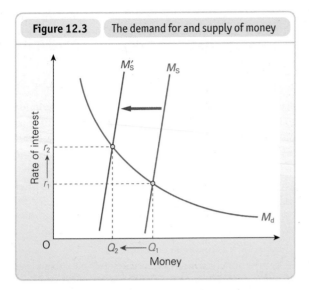

Figure 12.3 The demand for and supply of money

Techniques to control the money supply

There are four possible techniques that a central bank could use to control money supply. They have one major feature in common: they involve manipulating the liquid assets of the banking system. The aim is to influence the total money supply by affecting the amount of credit that banks can create.

Open-market operations. **Open-market operations** are the most widely used of the four techniques around the world. They alter the monetary base (cash and reserves in the central bank). This then affects the amount of credit banks can create and hence the level of broad money (M4 in the UK; M3 in the eurozone).

Open-market operations involve the sale or purchase by the central bank of government securities (bonds or bills) in the open market. These sales or purchases are *not* in response to changes in the public-sector deficit, and are thus best understood in the context of an unchanged deficit.

(resulting in the equilibrium rate of interest rising from r_1 to r_2), (b) raise the interest rate directly from r_1 to r_2, and then manipulate the money supply to reduce it to Q_2, or (c) keep interest rates at r_1, but reduce money supply to Q_2 by rationing the amount of credit granted by banks and other institutions.

Credit rationing was widely used in the past, especially during the 1960s. The aim was to keep interest rates low, so as not to discourage investment, but to restrict credit to more risky business customers and/or to consumers. In the UK, the Bank of England could order banks to abide by such a policy, although in practice it always relied on persuasion. The government also, from time to time, imposed restrictions on hire-purchase credit, by specifying minimum deposits or maximum repayment periods.

Such policies were progressively abandoned around the world from the early 1980s. They were seen as stifling competition and preventing efficient banks from expanding. Hire-purchase controls may badly hit certain industries (e.g. cars and other consumer durables), whose products are bought largely on hire-purchase credit. What is more, with the deregulation and globalisation of financial markets up to 2007, it had become very difficult to ration credit. If one financial institution was controlled, borrowers could simply go elsewhere.

With the excessive lending in sub-prime markets that had triggered the credit crunch of 2007/9, however, there were calls around the world for tighter controls over bank lending. But this was different from credit rationing as we have defined it. In other words, tighter controls, such as applying counter-cyclical buffers of capital to all banks, would be used to prevent reckless behaviour by banks, rather than to achieve a particular level of money at a lower rate of interest.

We thus focus on controlling the money supply and controlling interest rates.

> **Pause for thought**
>
> *Explain how open-market operations could be used to increase the money supply.*

If the central bank wishes to *reduce* the money supply, it will conduct OMOs so as to reduce the reserves of financial institutions. It can do this by borrowing from financial institutions against government securities (reverse repos on banks' balance sheets) or by selling securities outright. The borrowing or sale of these securities reduces banks' balances with the central bank. If this brings bank reserves below their prudent ratio, banks will reduce advances. There will be a multiple contraction of credit and hence of (broad) money supply. (Details of how open-market operations work in the UK are given in Box 12.4.)

Central bank lending to the banks. The central bank in most countries is prepared to provide extra money to banks (through gilt repos, rediscounting bills or straight loans). In some countries, it is the policy of the central bank to keep its interest rate to banks below market rates, thereby encouraging banks to borrow (or sell back securities) whenever such facilities are available. By cutting back the amount it is willing to provide, the central bank can reduce banks' liquid assets and hence the amount of credit they can create.

In other countries, such as the UK and the eurozone countries, it is normally not so much the amount of money made available that is controlled, but rather the rate of interest (or

TC 13
p 219

> **Definitions**
>
> **Open-market operations** The sale (or purchase) by the authorities of government securities in the open market in order to reduce (or increase) money supply.

BOX 12.4 THE DAILY OPERATION OF MONETARY POLICY

What goes on at Threadneedle Street?

The Bank of England (the 'Bank') does not normally attempt to control money supply directly. Instead it seeks to control interest rates by conducting open-market operations (OMOs) through short-term and longer-term repos and through the outright purchase of high-quality bonds. These operations, as we shall see, determine short-term interest rates, which then have a knock-on effect on longer-term rates, as returns on different forms of assets must remain competitive with each other.

Let us assume that the Monetary Policy Committee (MPC) of the Bank of England forecasts that, as a result of a low level of aggregate demand, inflation will fall below target. It thus decides to reduce interest rates. But how does the Bank set about doing this?

The first thing is that it will announce a cut in Bank Rate. It then has to back up the announcement by using OMOs to ensure that its announced interest rate is the equilibrium rate.

Normal operation of the monetary framework

The MPC meets regularly to decide on Bank Rate. From its inception in 1997, it met monthly. However, following an independent report published in December 2014, it announced plans to move to eight meetings a year from 2016.

Changes in the Bank Rate are intended to affect the whole structure of interest rates in the economy, from inter bank rates to bank deposit rates and rates on mortgages and business loans. The monetary framework works to affect the general structure of interest rates, principally by affecting short-term *inter bank rates*.

Central to the process are the reserve accounts of financial institutions at the Bank of England (see Section 10.2, pages 265–71). From the inception of the current system in May 2006, commercial banks have agreed with the Bank of England the average amount of reserve balances they would hold between MPC meetings. So long as the actual average over the period is kept within a small range of the agreed target, the reserves are remunerated at Bank Rate.

In order for individual banks to meet their reserve targets, the Bank of England needs to provide sufficient reserves. To do so, it uses OMOs. In normal circumstances, the Bank of England conducts short-term OMOs every week (on a Thursday) at Bank Rate. The size of the weekly OMO is adjusted to help banks maintain reserves at the target level and to reflect variations in the amount of cash withdrawn or deposited in banks.

To supply reserves the Bank of England will either enter into short-term repo operations lending against collateral ('high-quality' government securities), or buy securities outright. Although there is usually a shortage of liquidity in the banking system, in some weeks there may be a surplus. This would ordinarily drive market interest rates down. In such circumstances the Bank may look to reduce banks' reserves. To do this it can sell government securities on a repo basis, invite bids for Bank of England one-week sterling bills or sell outright some of its portfolio of securities.

At the end of the period between MPC interest rate decisions, the Bank of England conducts a 'fine-tuning' OMO. This is conducted on a Wednesday – the day before the MPC decision on interest rates. The idea is to ensure that banks meet their reserve targets as closely as possible. This OMO could expand or contract liquidity as appropriate.

Longer-term OMOs. Longer-term finance is available through longer-term OMOs. Prior to the financial crisis of the late 2000s, longer-term OMOs would normally be conducted once per month. As well as the outright purchase of gilts, the Bank would conduct repo lending with 3-, 6-, 9- or 12-month maturities.

The rate of interest on the repos is market determined. Banks bid for the money and the funds are offered to the successful bidders. The bigger the demand for these funds by banks and the lower the supply by the Bank of England, the higher will be the interest rate that banks must pay. By adjusting the supply, therefore, the Bank of England can look to influence longer-term interest rates too.

With the aggregate amount of banks' reserves determined by the Bank of England's OMOs, the task now is for individual banks to meet their agreed reserve targets. This requires that they manage their balance sheets and, in particular, their level of liquidity. In doing so, commercial banks can make use either of the *inter bank* market or the 'standing facilities' at the Bank of England. These standing facilities allow individual banks to borrow overnight (secured against high-quality collateral) at a rate *above* Bank Rate if they are short of liquidity; or to deposit reserves with the Bank at a rate *below* Bank Rate if they have surplus liquidity. Consequently, banks will trade reserves with each other if inter bank rates fall within the 'corridor' created by the interest rates of the standing facilities.

The financial crisis and open-market operations

The financial crisis meant that normal OMOs were no longer sufficient to maintain liquidity for purposes of monetary policy. There was a severe liquidity crisis – one which posed grave risks for financial stability.

In response, from January 2009 the Bank of England deliberately injected narrow money in a process known as 'quantitative easing' (see Box 12.6). This involved the Bank of England purchasing assets, largely gilts, from banks. The Bank argued that its asset purchase programme was an important monetary policy tool in meeting its inflation rate target. Between January 2009 and July 2012 the Bank of England injected £375 billion by such means. Quantitative easing thus massively extended the scope of OMOs.

As a result of this significant increase in aggregate reserves, banks were no longer required to set reserve targets. The supply of reserves was now being determined by MPC policy decisions. All reserves were to be remunerated at the Bank Rate.

Furthermore, short-term OMOs were temporarily suspended. Long-term repo operations continued but these were modified to allow financial institutions to sell a wider range of securities.

The Bank also adapted its means of providing liquidity insurance (see Section 10.2, pages 274–5). This included the introduction of the Discount Window Facility (DWF), which enables banks to borrow government bonds (gilts) against a wide range of collateral. Banks can then sell these bonds through repo operations and thereby secure liquidity.

 Assume that the Bank of England wants to raise interest rates. Trace through the process by which it achieves this.

discount). The higher this rate is relative to other market rates, the less will banks be willing to borrow, and the lower, therefore, will be the monetary base. Raising this rate, therefore, has the effect of reducing the money supply.

In response to the credit crunch of the late 2000s, central banks in several countries extended their willingness to lend to banks. The pressure on central banks to act as the 'liquidity backstop' grew as the inter bank market ceased to function effectively in distributing reserves and, hence, liquidity between financial institutions. As a result, inter bank rates rose sharply relative to the policy rate (see Figure 10.3 on page 277). Increasingly, the focus of central banks was on providing the necessary liquidity to ensure the stability of the financial system. Yet, at the same time, by providing more liquidity, central banks were ensuring monetary policy was not being compromised. The additional liquidity was needed to alleviate the upward pressure on market interest rates.

Funding. Rather than focusing on controlling the monetary base (as in the case of the above two techniques), an alternative is for the authorities (the Debt Management Office in the UK) to alter the overall liquidity position of the banks. An example of this approach is a change in the balance of **funding** government debt. To reduce money supply the authorities issue more bonds and fewer bills. Banks' balances with the central bank will be little affected, but to the extent that banks hold fewer bills, there will be a reduction in their liquidity and hence a reduction in the amount of credit created. Funding is thus the conversion of one type of government debt (liquid) into another (illiquid).

One problem with this approach is that bonds are likely to command a higher interest rate than bills. By switching from bills to bonds, the government will be committing itself to these interest rates for the life of the bond.

Variable minimum reserve ratios. In some countries (such as the USA), banks are required to hold a certain proportion of their assets in liquid form. The assets that count as liquid are known as 'reserve assets'. These include assets such as balances in the central bank, bills of exchange, certificates of deposit and money market loans. The ratio of such assets to total liabilities is known as the *minimum reserve ratio*. If the central bank raises this ratio (in other words, requires the banks to hold a higher proportion of liquid assets), then banks will have to reduce the amount of credit they grant. The money supply will fall.

Difficulties in controlling money supply

Targets for the growth in broad money were an important part of UK monetary policy from 1976 to 1985. Money

targets were then abandoned and have not been used since. The European Central Bank targets the growth of M3 (see Box 12.5), but this is a subsidiary policy to that of setting interest rates in order to keep inflation under control. If, however, a central bank did choose to target money supply as its main monetary policy, how would the policy work?

Assume that money supply is above target and that the central bank wishes to reduce it. It would probably use open-market operations: i.e. it would sell more bonds or bills. The purchasers of the bonds or bills would draw liquidity from the banks. Banks would then supposedly be forced to cut down on the credit they create. But is it as simple as this?

The problem is that banks will normally be unwilling to cut down on loans if people want to borrow – after all, borrowing by customers earns profits for the banks. Banks can always 'top up' their liquidity by borrowing from the central bank and then carry on lending. True, they will have to pay the interest rate charged by the central bank, but they can pass on any rise in the rate to their customers.

The point is that as long as people *want* to borrow, banks and other financial institutions will normally try to find ways of meeting the demand. In other words, in the short run at least, the supply of money is to a large extent demand determined. It is for this reason that central banks prefer to control the *demand* for money by controlling interest rates (backed up, normally, by open-market operations).

As we shall see in Box 12.6, there are similar difficulties in *expanding* broad money supply by a desired amount. Following the credit crunch, various central banks around the world engaged in a process of quantitative easing. The process results in an increase in the monetary base (narrow money): banks' liquidity increases. But just how much this results in an increase in broad money depends on the willingness of banks to lend and customers to borrow. In the recessionary climate after 2008, confidence was low. Much of the extra liquidity remained in banks and the money multiplier fell (see Figure 10.4 on page 280). The growth of M4 in the UK fell sharply during 2009, despite quantitative easing, and remained weak throughout the first half of the 2010s (see Figure 10.5 on page 281).

Techniques to control interest rates

The approach to monetary control today in most countries is to focus directly on interest rates. Normally an interest rate change will be announced, and then open-market operations will be conducted by the central bank to ensure that the money supply is adjusted so as to make the announced interest rate the *equilibrium* one. Thus, in Figure 12.3 (on page 340), the central bank might announce a rise in interest rates from r_1 to r_2 and then conduct open-market operations to ensure that the money supply is reduced from Q_1 to Q_2.

Let's assume that the central bank decides to raise interest rates. What does it do? In general, it will seek to keep banks short of liquidity. This will happen automatically on any day when tax payments by banks' customers exceed the money they receive from government expenditure. This

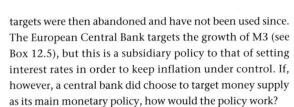

Definitions

Funding Where the authorities alter the balance of bills and bonds for any given level of government borrowing.

BOX 12.5 MONETARY POLICY IN THE EUROZONE

The role of the ECB

The European Central Bank (ECB) is based in Frankfurt and is charged with operating the monetary policy of those EU countries that have adopted the euro. Although the ECB has the overall responsibility for the eurozone's monetary policy, the central banks of the individual countries, such as the Bank of France and Germany's Bundesbank, were not abolished. They are responsible for distributing euros and for carrying out the ECB's policy with respect to institutions in their own countries. The whole system of the ECB and the national central banks is known as the European System of Central Banks (ESCB).

In operating the monetary policy of a 'euro economy' roughly the size of the USA, and in being independent from national governments, the ECB's power is enormous and is equivalent to that of the Fed. So what is the structure of this giant on the European stage, and how does it operate?

The structure of the ECB

The ECB has two major decision-making bodies: the Governing Council and the Executive Board.[a]

The Governing Council consists of the members of the Executive Board and the governors of the central banks of each of the eurozone countries. The Council's role is to set the main targets of monetary policy and to take an oversight of the success (or otherwise) of that policy.

The Executive Board consists of a president, a vice president and four other members. Each serves for an eight-year, non-renewable term. The Executive Board is responsible for implementing the decisions of the Governing Council and for preparing policies for the Council's consideration. Each member of the Executive Board has a responsibility for some particular aspect of monetary policy.

The targets of monetary policy

The overall responsibility of the ECB is to achieve price stability in the eurozone. The target is a rate of inflation below, but close to, 2 per cent over the medium term. It is a weighted average rate for all the members of the eurozone, not a rate that has to be met by every member individually.

Alongside its definition of price stability, the ECB's monetary policy strategy comprises what it calls 'a two-pillar approach to the analysis of the risks to price stability'. These two pillars are an analysis of (a) monetary developments and (b) economic developments. The former includes an analysis of monetary aggregates, including M3. The latter includes an analysis of economic activity, the labour market, cost indicators, fiscal policy and the balance of payments.

The ECB then attempts to 'steer' short-term interest rates to influence economic activity to maintain price stability in the euro area in the medium term. In May 2015, the rates were as follows: 0.05 per cent for the main 'refinancing operations' of the ESCB (i.e. the minimum rate of interest at which liquidity is offered once per week to 'monetary financial institutions' (MFIs) by the ESCB); a 'marginal lending' rate of 0.30 per cent (for providing overnight support to the MFIs); and a 'deposit rate' of −0.20 per cent (the rate paid to MFIs for depositing

overnight surplus liquidity with the ESCB). The negative deposit rate meant that banks were being charged for 'parking' money with the ECB rather than lending it. The hope was that this would encourage banks to lend to each other or to households and businesses and, consequently, stimulate the economy.

Interest rates are set by the Governing Council by simple majority. In the event of a tie, the president has the casting vote.

The operation of monetary policy

The ECB sets a minimum reserve ratio for eurozone banks. The ratio is designed primarily to prevent excessive lending and hence the need for excessive borrowing from the central bank or from other financial institutions. This, in turn, should help to reduce the volatility in interest rates.

The minimum reserve ratio was not designed, however, to be used to make changes in monetary policy. In other words, it was not used as a variable minimum reserves ratio, and for this reason it was set at a low level. From 1 January 1999 to 17 January 2012 the ratio (also known as the reserve coefficient) was 2 per cent of key liquid and relatively liquid liabilities. However, as of 18 January 2012 the ratio was reduced to 1 per cent in an attempt to help stimulate bank lending. In other words, it was now being used for the first time as part of an active monetary policy.

The main instrument for keeping the ECB's desired interest rate as the equilibrium rate is open-market operations in government bonds and other recognised assets, mainly in the form of repos. These repo operations are conducted by the national central banks, which must ensure that the repo rate does not rise above the marginal overnight lending rate or fall below the deposit rate.

The ECB uses four types of open-market operations:

Main refinancing operations. These are short-term repos with a maturity of one week. They take place weekly and are used to maintain liquidity consistent with the chosen ECB interest rate.

Longer-term refinancing operations (LTROs). These take place monthly and normally have a maturity of three months. Longer maturities are available, but such operations are conducted more irregularly. They are to provide additional longer-term liquidity to banks as required at rates determined by the market, not the ECB.

Fine-tuning operations. These can be short-term sales or purchases of short-term assets. They are designed to combat unexpected changes in liquidity and hence to keep money market rates at the ECB's chosen rate.

Structural operations. These are used as necessary to adjust the amount of liquidity in the eurozone. They can involve either the purchase or sale of various assets.

ECB independence

The ECB is one of the most independent central banks in the world. It has very little formal accountability to elected politicians. Although its president can be called before the European Parliament, the Parliament has virtually no powers to influence the ECB's actions.

[a] See http://www.ecb.int/ecb/orga/decisions/govc/html/index.en.html

Until its January 2015 meeting, its deliberations were secret and no minutes of Council meetings were published. Subsequently, an account of meetings is published (usually with a lag of around two weeks) with an explanation of the policy stance. However, the minutes do not include details of how Council members voted or of future policy intentions, unlike the minutes published by the Bank of England which, from 2015, are available at the time of the policy announcement.

Financial crisis

The financial crisis of 2007/8 put incredible strains on commercial banks in the eurozone and, hence, on the ECB's monetary framework. Consequently, monetary operations were gradually modified.

A Securities Market Programme (SMP) began in May 2010 designed to supply liquidity to the ailing banking system. It allowed for ECB purchases of central government debt in the secondary market (i.e. not directly from governments) as well as purchases in both primary and secondary markets of private-sector debt instruments. By June 2012, €214 billion of purchases had been made, largely of government bonds issued by countries experiencing financing difficulties, including Portugal, Ireland, Greece and Spain. This led some to question whether the programme was being implemented to meet fiscal rather than monetary policy objectives.

As we noted earlier, the reserve ratio was reduced in January 2012 from 2 per cent to 1 per cent, so helping to alleviate some of the constraints on the volume of bank lending by banks. This move was preceded in December 2011 by three-year refinancing operations (LTROs) worth €529.5 billion and involving some 800 banks. By the end of February 2012, a further €489.2 billion of three-year loans to 523 banks took place, taking the ECB's repo operations to over €1 trillion. The hope was that the funds would help financially distressed banks pay off maturing debt and again increase their lending.

Then in September 2012, with worries about the continuing difficulties of some eurozone countries, such as Greece, Spain and Italy, to borrow at affordable interest rates and whether this would lead to their being driven from the euro, the ECB announced a replacement for the SMP scheme. This would involve a more extensive programme of purchasing existing government bonds of countries in difficulty. The ECB would purchase bonds with up to three years to maturity in the secondary market. The aim would be to drive down these countries' interest rates and thereby make it cheaper to issue new bonds when old ones matured. These Outright Monetary Transactions (OMTs) were in principle unlimited, with the ECB President, Mario Draghi, saying that the ECB would do 'whatever it takes' to hold the single currency together.

Critics argued that this would still not be enough to stimulate the eurozone economy and help bring countries out of recession. They gave two reasons.

The first is that OMTs differ from the quantitative easing programmes used in the UK and USA. ECB purchases of these bonds would not increase the eurozone money supply as the ECB would sell other assets to compensate. This process is known as *sterilisation*.

The second reason is that OMTs would be conducted only if countries stuck to previously agreed strong austerity measures. Despite the eurozone economy contracting by 0.7 per cent in 2012 and by a further 0.4 per cent in 2013, OMTs had still not been used.

Subsequent measures followed. In June 2014, the ECB announced that it was adopting a negative deposit rate (see above), that it was embarking on a further series of targeted long-term refinancing operations so as to provide long-term loans to commercial banks at cheap rates until September 2018, and that it would stop sterilising its SMP scheme.

Then in September 2014, it announced that it would be commencing the purchase of asset-backed private-sector securities, such as securitised mortgages and commercial loans (see Section 10.2). Nonetheless, concerns remained that the announcements did not go far enough given the problems facing the eurozone economy.

Finally, in January 2015 the ECB launched a large-scale quantitative easing programme. It announced that it would create new money to buy €60 billion of assets every month in the secondary market. Around €10 billion would be private-sector securities that were currently being purchased under September 2014 measures. The remaining €50 billion would be public-sector assets, mainly bonds of governments in the eurozone. This extended programme of asset purchases began in March 2015 and was set to continue until at least September 2016, bringing the total of asset purchases by that time to over €1.1 trillion.

More details of monetary policy in the eurozone and the role of the ECB are given in Case Study 12.9 in MyEconLab.

> *What are the arguments for and against publishing the minutes of the meetings of the ECB'S Governing Council and Executive Board?*

Definition

Sterilisation Actions taken by a central bank to offset the effects of foreign exchange flows or its own bond transactions so as to leave money supply unchanged.

excess is effectively withdrawn from banks and ends up in the government's account at the central bank. Even when this does not occur, issues of government debt will effectively keep the banking system short of liquidity, at least in the short term.

This 'shortage' can then be used as a way of forcing through interest rate changes. Banks will obtain the necessary liquidity from the central bank through repos or by selling it bills. The central bank can *choose the rate of interest to charge* (i.e. the repo rate or the bill price). This will then have a knock-on effect on other interest rates throughout the banking system (see Table 10.5 on page 288). (See Box 12.4 for more details on just how the Bank of England manipulates interest rates on a day-to-day basis.)

The effectiveness of changes in interest rates

Even though central bank adjustment of the repo rate is the current preferred method of monetary control in most countries, it is not without its difficulties. The problems centre on the nature of the demand for loans. If this demand is (a) unresponsive to interest rate changes or (b) unstable because it is significantly affected by other determinants (such as anticipated income or foreign interest rates), then it will be very difficult to control by controlling the rate of interest.

Problem of an inelastic demand for loans. If the demand for loans is inelastic, as in Figure 12.4, any attempt to reduce demand (e.g. from Q_1 to Q_2) will involve large rises in interest rates (r_1 to r_2). The problem will be compounded if the demand shifts to the right, due, say, to a consumer-spending boom. High interest rates lead to the following problems:

- They may discourage investment and hence long-term growth.
- They add to the costs of production, to the costs of house purchase and generally to the cost of living. They are thus cost inflationary.
- They are politically unpopular, since the general public do not like paying higher interest rates on overdrafts, credit cards and mortgages.
- The necessary bond issue to restrain liquidity will commit the government to paying high rates on these bonds for the next 20 years or so.
- High interest rates encourage inflows of money from abroad. This drives up the exchange rate. (We examine this in Chapter 14.) A higher exchange rate makes domestic goods expensive relative to goods made abroad. This can be very damaging for export industries and industries competing with imports. Many firms in the UK suffered badly between 1997 and 2007 from a high exchange rate, caused partly by higher interest rates in the UK than in the eurozone and the USA.

Evidence suggests that the demand for loans may indeed be quite inelastic, especially in the short run. Although investment plans may be curtailed by high interest rates, borrowing to finance current expenditure by many firms cannot easily be curtailed. Similarly, while householders may be discouraged from taking on new mortgages, they may find it difficult to reduce current expenditure as a way of reducing their credit-card debt. What is more, although high interest rates may discourage many firms from taking out long-term fixed-interest loans, some firms may merely switch to shorter-term variable-interest loans.

Problem of an unstable demand. Accurate monetary control requires the authorities to be able to predict the demand curve for money (in Figure 12.4). Only then can they set the appropriate level of interest rates. Unfortunately, the demand curve may shift unpredictably, making control very difficult. The major reason is *speculation*:

- If people think interest rates will rise and bond prices fall, they will in the meantime demand to hold their assets in liquid form. The demand for money will rise.
- If people think exchange rates will rise, they will hold the domestic currency while it is still relatively cheap. The demand for money will rise.
- If people think the rate of inflation will rise, the transactions demand for money may rise. People plan to spend more while prices are still relatively low.
- If people think the economy is going to grow faster, the demand for loans will increase as firms seek to increase their investment.

It is very difficult for the central bank to predict what people's expectations will be. Speculation depends considerably on world political events, rumour and 'random shocks'.

If the demand curve shifts very much, and if it is inelastic, then monetary control will be very difficult. Furthermore, the central bank will have to make frequent and sizeable adjustments to interest rates. These fluctuations can be very damaging to business confidence and may discourage long-term investment thereby reducing long-run economic growth.

Pause for thought

Assume that the central bank announces a rise in interest rates and backs this up with open-market operations. What determines the size of the resulting fall in aggregate demand?

The net result of an inelastic and unstable demand for money is that substantial interest rate changes may be necessary to bring about the required change in aggregate demand. For example, central banks had to cut interest rates to virtually zero in their attempt to tackle the global recession of the late 2000s. Indeed, as we see in Box 12.6, central banks took to other methods as the room for interest rate cuts simply disappeared.

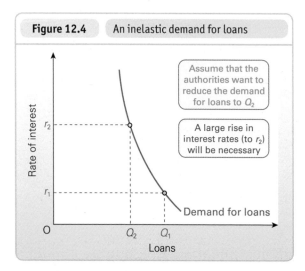

Figure 12.4 An inelastic demand for loans

Assume that the authorities want to reduce the demand for loans to Q_2

A large rise in interest rates (to r_2) will be necessary

BOX 12.6   QUANTITATIVE EASING

Rethinking monetary policy in hard times

As the economies of the world slid into recession in 2008, central banks became more and more worried that the traditional instrument of monetary policy – controlling interest rates – was insufficient to ward off a slump in demand.

Running out of options?

Interest rates had been cut at an unprecedented rate and central banks were reaching the end of the road for further cuts. The Fed was the first to be in this position. By December 2008 the target federal funds rate (the overnight rate at which the Fed lends to banks) had been cut to a range between 0 and 0.25 per cent. Meanwhile in the UK, Bank Rate had fallen to 0.5 per cent by March 2009. But you cannot cut nominal rates below zero – otherwise you would be paying people to borrow money, which would be like giving people free money!

The problem was that there was an acute lack of willingness of banks to lend, and firms and consumers to borrow, as people saw the oncoming recession. Hence the cuts in interest rates were not having enough effect on aggregate demand.

Increasing the money supply

So what were central banks to do? The answer was to increase money supply directly, in a process known as *quantitative easing*. This involves an aggressive version of open-market operations, where the central bank buys up a range of assets, such as securitised mortgage debt and long-term government bonds. The effect is to pump large amounts of additional cash into the economy in the hope of stimulating demand and, through the process of credit creation, to boost broad money too.

In the USA, in December 2008, at the same time as the federal funds rate was cut to a range of 0 to 0.25 per cent, the Fed embarked on large-scale quantitative easing. It began buying hundreds of billions of dollars' worth of mortgage-backed securities on the open market and planned also to buy large quantities of long-term government debt. The Federal Open Market Committee (the interest rate setting body in the USA) said that, 'The focus of the committee's policy going forward will be to support the functioning of financial markets and stimulate the economy through open-market operations and other measures that sustain the size of the Federal Reserve's balance sheet at a high level.'

The result was that considerable quantities of new money were injected into the system.

A similar approach was adopted in the UK. In January 2009, the Bank of England was given powers by the Treasury to buy up to £50 billion of high-quality private-sector assets, such as corporate bonds and commercial paper. In March 2009, this was extended to government bonds (or 'gilts') and quantitative easing started.

Definition

Quantitative easing A deliberate attempt by the central bank to increase the money supply by buying large quantities of securities through open-market operations. These securities could be securitised mortgage and other private-sector debt or government bonds.

Between March and November 2009, the MPC decided to purchase £200 billion of financial assets, mostly 'gilts'. The purchases, largely from private investors, such as insurance companies and pension funds, were with newly created electronic money. When the money found its way back into the banking system, it resulted in an increase in banks' reserve balances in the Bank of England.

With recovery still weak, the MPC sanctioned further asset purchases in October 2011 (£75bn), February 2012 (£50bn) and July 2012 (£50bn), bringing the total to £375 billion, virtually all of which were government bonds.

The transmission mechanism of asset purchases

Quantitative easing involves directly increasing the amount of narrow money. It can also, indirectly, increase broad money. There are two principal ways in which this can happen.

The first is through the effects on asset prices and yields. When non-bank financial companies, including insurance companies and pension funds, sell assets to the central bank, they can use the money to purchase other assets, such as shares. In doing so this will drive up their prices. This, in turn, reduces the yields on these assets (at a higher price there is less dividend or interest per pound spent on them), which should help to reduce interest rates generally and make the cost of borrowing cheaper for households and firms, so boosting aggregate demand.

Also, for those holding these now more expensive assets there is a positive wealth effect. For instance, households with longer-term saving plans involving securities will now have greater financial wealth. Again, this will boost spending.

The second mechanism is through bank lending. Commercial banks will find their reserve balances increase at the central bank as the sellers of assets to the central bank deposit the money in their bank accounts. This will increase the liquidity ratio of banks, which could encourage them to grant more credit.

However, it is all very well increasing the monetary base, but a central bank cannot force banks to lend or people to borrow. That requires confidence. We observed in Box 10.4 the continued weakness of bank lending to the non-bank private sector through the late 2000s and into the early 2010s.

This is not to say that quantitative easing failed in the UK and elsewhere: growth in broad money could have been weaker still. However, it does illustrate the potential danger of this approach if, in the short run, little credit creation takes place. In the equation $MV = PY$, the rise in (narrow) money supply (M) may be largely offset by a fall in the velocity of circulation (V) (see pages 302–3).

On the other hand, there is also the danger that if this policy is conducted for too long, the growth in broad money supply could ultimately prove to be excessive, resulting in inflation rising above the target level. It is therefore important for central banks to foresee this and turn the monetary 'tap' off in time. This would involve 'quantitative tightening' – selling assets that the central bank had purchased, thereby driving down asset prices and driving up interest rates.

? *Would it be appropriate to define the policy of quantitative easing as 'monetarist'?*

Using monetary policy

It is impossible to use monetary policy as a precise means of controlling aggregate demand. It is especially weak when it is pulling against the expectations of firms and consumers, and when it is implemented too late. However, if the authorities operate a tight monetary policy firmly enough and long enough, they should eventually be able to reduce lending and hence aggregate demand, and, with it, inflation. But there will inevitably be time lags and, imprecision in the process.

An expansionary monetary policy is even less reliable. If the economy is in recession, no matter how low interest rates are driven, or however much the monetary base is expanded, people cannot be forced to borrow if they do not wish to. Firms will not borrow to invest if they predict a continuing recession.

A particular difficulty in using interest rate reductions to expand the economy arises if the repo rate is nearly zero but this is still not enough to stimulate the economy. The problem is that (nominal) interest rates cannot be negative, for clearly nobody would be willing to lend in these circumstances. Japan was in such a situation in the early 2000s. It was caught in what is known as the **liquidity trap**. The UK and many eurozone countries were in this position in the early 2010s. Despite record low interest rates and high levels of liquidity, borrowing and lending remained low given worries about fiscal austerity and its dampening effects on economic growth.

Forward guidance. One way in which central banks, like the Federal Reserve, the Bank of England and the ECB, attempted to encourage spending following the financial crisis of the late 2000s was by publicly indicating the expected path of future interest rates. By stating that interest rates were likely to remain low for some time, central banks hoped that this *forward guidance* would give economic agents confidence to bring forward their spending.

Despite these problems, changing interest rates can often be quite effective in the medium term. After all, they can be changed very rapidly. There are not the time lags of implementation that there are with fiscal policy. Indeed, since the early 1990s, most governments or central banks in OECD countries have used interest rate changes as the major means of keeping aggregate demand and inflation under control.

In the UK, the eurozone and many other countries, a target is set for the rate of inflation. As we have seen, in the UK and the eurozone the target is 2 per cent. If forecasts suggest that inflation is going to be above the target rate, the government or central bank raises interest rates. The advantage of this is that it sends a very clear message to people that inflation *will* be kept under control. People will therefore be more likely to adjust their expectations accordingly and keep their borrowing in check.

> ### Definition
>
> **Liquidity trap** When interest rates are at their floor and thus any further increases in money supply will not be spent but merely be held in idle balances as people wait for the economy to recover and/or interest rates to rise.

Recap

1. Control of the growth in the money supply over the longer term will normally involve governments attempting to restrict the size of public-sector deficits.

2. In the short term, the central bank can use monetary policy to restrict/increase the growth in aggregate demand in one of two major ways: (a) reducing/increasing money supply directly, (b) reducing/increasing the demand for money by raising/lowering interest rates.

3. The money supply can be reduced/increased directly by using open-market operations. This involves the central bank selling more government securities and thereby reducing/increasing banks' reserves. Alternatively, the central bank can reduce/increase the amount of lending or rediscounting it is prepared to do (other than as a last-resort measure).

4. Rather than controlling the monetary base in either of these two ways, the authorities could use funding. This involves increasing/reducing the sale of bonds relative to bills, thereby reducing/increasing banks' liquid assets. Finally, it could operate a system of variable minimum reserve ratios. Increasing these would force banks to cut back the amount of credit they create; reducing them would allow banks to create more credit.

5. Controlling either the monetary base or broad liquidity in the short term, however, is difficult given that central banks are always prepared to provide liquidity to the banks on demand. Even if the authorities are successful in controlling the money supply, there then arises the problem of severe fluctuations in interest rates if the demand for money fluctuates and is relatively inelastic.

6. The current method of control in the UK and many other countries involves the central bank influencing interest rates by its operations in the gilt repo and discount markets. The central bank keeps banks short of liquidity and then supplies them with liquidity, largely through gilt repos, at its chosen interest rate (gilt repo rate). This then has a knock-on effect on interest rates throughout the economy.

7. With an inelastic demand for loans, however, changes in interest rates may have to be very large to bring the required changes in monetary growth. High interest rates are politically unpopular and discriminate against those with high borrowing commitments. They also drive up the exchange rate, which can damage exports.

8. Controlling aggregate demand through interest rates is made even more difficult by fluctuations in the demand for money. These fluctuations are made more severe by speculation against changes in interest rates, exchange rates, the rate of inflation, etc.

9. It is impossible to use monetary policy as a precise means of controlling aggregate demand in the short term. Nevertheless, controlling interest rates is a rapid way of responding to changing forecasts, and can be an important signal to markets that inflation will be kept under control, especially when, as in the UK and the eurozone, there is a firm target for the rate of inflation.

10. Faced with a deepening recession after the financial crisis of 2007/8, central banks embarked on programmes of quantitative easing, which involved their creating large amounts of new narrow money. This was used to purchase bonds and other assets from financial institutions, thereby increasing banks' reserves and allowing them to increase lending and hence increase broad money through the process of credit creation.

12.3 DEMAND-SIDE POLICY

What will be the effect of attempts by the government to control the level of spending in the economy?

Attitudes towards demand management

Debates over the control of demand have shifted ground somewhat in recent years. There is now less debate over the relative effectiveness of fiscal and monetary policy in influencing aggregate demand. There is general agreement that a *combination* of fiscal and monetary policies will have a more powerful effect on demand than either used separately.

Economists have become increasingly interested in the environment within which policy is made. Indeed, many countries have, in recent times, been operating economic policy within a framework of rules. This is known as **constrained discretion.** Most commonly we observe this with monetary policy. Many central banks today have prescribed macroeconomic objectives, such as inflation rate targets, which help to determine the monetary policy decisions they make. Similarly, fiscal frameworks, such as the EU's Fiscal Compact (Box 12.2) and the UK's fiscal mandate (Box 12.3), impact on governments' fiscal policy choices.

In this section we analyse debates around the extent to which governments ought to pursue active demand management policies or adhere to a set of policy rules. The financial crisis of the late 2000s, the subsequent global economic downturn and deteriorating public finances have helped to reignite the debate about the merits of constraining the discretion of policy makers over fiscal and monetary policy.

The case for rules and policy frameworks

Why should governments commit to rules or design policy frameworks which may involve their giving up control of economic instruments? There are two key arguments against discretionary policy.

Political behaviour. The first concerns the motivation of government. Politicians may attempt to manipulate the economy for their own political purposes – such as the desire to be re-elected. The government, if not constrained by rules, may over-stimulate the economy some time before an election so that growth is strong at election time. After the election, the government strongly dampens the economy to deal with the higher inflation and rising public-sector debt and to create enough slack for another boost in time for the next election.

When politicians behave in this way, they may lose *credibility* for sound economic management. This can lead to higher inflationary expectations, uncertainty and lower long-term investment.

Time lags with discretionary policy. Both fiscal and monetary policies can involve long and variable time lags, which can make the policy at best ineffective and at worst destabilising. Taking the measures *before* the problem arises, and thus lessening the problem of lags, is not a realistic option since forecasting tends to be unreliable.

In contrast, by setting and sticking to rules, and then not interfering further, the government can provide a sound monetary framework in which there is maximum freedom for individual initiative and enterprise, and in which firms are not cushioned from market forces and are therefore encouraged to be efficient. By the government setting a target for a steady reduction in the growth of money supply, or a target for the rate of inflation, and then resolutely sticking to it, people's expectations of inflation will be reduced, thereby making the target easier to achieve.

Definition
Constrained discretion A set of principles or rules within which economic policy operates. These can be informal or enshrined in law.

This sound and stable monetary environment, with no likelihood of sudden contractionary or expansionary fiscal or monetary policy, will encourage firms to take a longer-term perspective and to plan ahead. This could then lead to increased capital investment and, as we saw in Chapter 9, raise long-term growth rates.

The optimum situation is for all the major countries to adhere to mutually consistent rules, so that their economies do not get out of line. This will create more stable exchange rates and provide the climate for world growth (we explore these issues in Chapters 13 and 14).

Advocates of this point of view in the 1970s and 1980s were monetarists and new classical macroeconomists, but support for the setting of targets was to become widespread. As we have seen, in both the UK and the eurozone countries, targets are set for both inflation and public-sector deficits.

The case for discretion

Keynesians typically reject the argument that rules provide the environment for high and stable growth. Demand, argue Keynesians, is subject to many and sometimes violent shocks: e.g. changes in expectations, domestic political events (such as an impending election), world economic factors (such as the world economic recession of 2008/9) or world political events (such as a war). The resulting shifts in injections or withdrawals cause the economy to deviate from a stable full-employment growth path.

Any change in injections or withdrawals will lead to a cumulative effect on national income via the multiplier and accelerator and via changing expectations. These effects take time and interact with each other, and so a process of expansion or contraction can last many months before a turning point is eventually reached.

Since shocks to demand occur at irregular intervals and are of different magnitudes, the economy is likely to experience cycles of irregular duration and of varying intensity.

Given that the economy is inherently unstable and is buffeted around by various shocks, Keynesians argue that the government needs actively to intervene to stabilise the economy. Otherwise, the uncertainty caused by unpredictable fluctuations will be very damaging to investment and hence to long-term economic growth (quite apart from the short-term effects of recessions on output and employment).

Difficulties with the choice of target

Assume that the government or central bank sets an inflation rate target. Should it then stick to that rate, come what may? Might not an extended period of relatively low inflation rates warrant a lower inflation rate target? The government must at least have the discretion to *change* the rules, even if only occasionally.

Then there is the question of whether success in achieving the target will bring success in achieving other macroeconomic objectives, such as low unemployment and stable economic growth. The problem is that something called **Goodhart's Law** is likely to apply. The law, named after Charles Goodhart of the LSE and formerly of the Bank of England, states that attempts to control an *indicator* of a problem may, as a result, make it cease to be a good indicator of the problem.

> **KEY IDEA 35**
>
> ***Goodhart's Law.*** Controlling a symptom (i.e. an indicator) of a problem will not cure the problem. Instead, the indicator will merely cease to be a good indicator of the problem.

Targeting inflation may make it become a poor indicator of the state of the economy. If people believe that the central bank will be successful in achieving its inflation target, then those expectations will feed into their inflationary expectations, and not surprisingly the target will be met. But that target rate of inflation may now be consistent with both a buoyant and a depressed economy. In other words, the Phillips curve may become *horizontal*. Thus achieving the inflation target may not tackle the much more serious problem of creating stable economic growth and an environment that will therefore encourage long-term investment.

In extreme cases, as occurred in 2008, the economy may slow down rapidly and yet cost-push factors cause inflation to rise. Strictly adhering to an inflation target in these circumstances will demand *higher* interest rates, which could further restrict growth.

Use of a Taylor rule. For this reason, many economists have advocated the use of a **Taylor rule**,[2] rather than a simple inflation target. A Taylor rule takes two objectives into account – (1) inflation and (2) either real national income or unemployment – and seeks to get the optimum degree of stability of the two. The degree of importance attached to each of the two objectives can be decided by

> ### Definitions
>
> **Goodhart's Law** Controlling a symptom of a problem, or only part of the problem, will not cure the problem: it will simply mean that the part that is being controlled now becomes a poor indicator of the problem.
>
> **Taylor rule** A rule adopted by a central bank for setting the rate of interest. It will raise the interest rate if (a) inflation is above target or (b) real national income is above the sustainable level (or unemployment is below the equilibrium rate). The rule states how much interest rates will be changed in each case.

---

[2] Named after John Taylor, from Stanford University, who proposed that for every 1 per cent that GDP rises above sustainable GDP, real interest rates should be raised by 0.5 percentage points, and for every 1 per cent that inflation rises above its target level, real interest rates should be raised by 0.5 percentage points (i.e. nominal rates should be raised by 1.5 percentage points).

the government or central bank. The central bank adjusts interest rates when either the rate of inflation diverges from its target or the level of real national income (or unemployment) diverges from its sustainable (or equilibrium) level.

Take the case where inflation is above its target level. The central bank following a Taylor rule will raise the rate of interest. It knows, however, that this will reduce real national income below the level at which it would otherwise have been. This, therefore, limits the amount that the central bank is prepared to raise the rate of interest. The more weight it attaches to stabilising inflation, the more it will raise the rate of interest. The more weight it attaches to achieving stable growth in real national income, the less it will raise the rate of interest.

Thus the central bank has to trade off inflation stability against stability in economic growth.

> **Pause for thought**
>
> *If people believe that the central bank will be successful in keeping inflation on target, does it matter whether a simple inflation rule or a Taylor rule is used? Explain.*

Difficulties with the target level

When a monetary or an inflation target is first set, the short-term costs of achieving it may be too high. If expectations are slow to adjust downward and inflation remains high, then adherence to a tight monetary or inflation rule may lead to a very deep and unacceptable recession. This was a criticism made by many economists of monetarist policies between 1979 and 1982.

When a target has been in force for some time, it may cease to be the appropriate one. Economic circumstances might change. For example, a faster growth in productivity or a large increase in oil revenues may increase potential growth and thus warrant a faster growth in money supply. Or an extended period of relatively low inflation may warrant a lower inflation target. The government must at least have the discretion to *change* the rules, even if only occasionally.

But if rules should not be stuck to religiously, does this mean that the government can engage in fine-tuning? Keynesians today recognise that fine-tuning may not be possible; nevertheless, significant and persistent excess or deficient demand *can* be corrected by demand management policy. For example, the actions taken by central banks in 2007/8 to cut interest rates substantially, and by governments to increase its expenditure and to cut taxes, helped to stave off even deeper recessions in 2008/9.

Improvements in forecasting, a willingness of governments to act quickly and the use of quick-acting policies can all help to increase the effectiveness of discretionary demand management.

Conclusions

The resolution of this debate will depend on the following factors:

- The confidence of people in the effectiveness of either discretionary policies or rules: the greater the confidence, the more successful is either policy likely to be.
- The degree of self-stabilisation of the economy (in the case of rules), or conversely the degree of inherent instability of the economy (in the case of discretion).
- The size and frequency of exogenous shocks to demand: the greater they are, the greater the case for discretionary policy.
- In the case of rules, the ability and determination of governments to stick to the rules and the belief by the public that they will be effective.
- In the case of discretionary policy, the ability of governments to adopt and execute policies of the correct magnitude, the speed with which such policies can be effected and the accuracy of forecasting.

Case Study 12.19 in MyEconLab looks at the history of fiscal and monetary policies in the UK from the 1950s to the current day. It illustrates the use of both rules and discretion and how the debates about policy shifted with historical events.

> ### Recap
>
> 1. The case against discretionary policy is that it involves unpredictable time lags that can make the policy destabilising. Also, the government may *ignore* the long-run adverse consequences of policies designed for short-run political gain.
> 2. The case in favour of rules is that they help to reduce inflationary expectations and thus create a stable environment for investment and growth.
> 3. The case against sticking to money supply or inflation rules is that they may cause severe fluctuations in interest rates and thus create a less stable economic environment for business planning.
> 4. Although perfect fine-tuning may not be possible, Keynesians argue that the government must have the discretion to change its policy as circumstances demand.

12.4 SUPPLY-SIDE POLICY

How might the government attempt to control the level of output and employment directly?

Supply-side policies, as the name suggests, focus on aggregate supply. If successful, they will shift the aggregate supply curve to the right, thus increasing output for any given level of prices (or reducing the price level for any given level of output).

In Chapter 9 we saw that aggregate supply depends on an economy's factors of production, including labour and capital. Therefore, policies which seek to influence the *quantities* of the factors employed or their *productivity* constitute supply-side policies. If successful they will increase potential output and long-term economic growth. They are also likely to affect employment and unemployment and put downward pressure on prices.

Supply-side policies are commonly grouped under two general types: *market-orientated* and *interventionist*. Market-orientated policies focus on ways of 'freeing up' the market, such as encouraging private enterprise, risk taking and competition: policies that provide incentives for innovation, hard work and productivity. Interventionist policies focus on means of counteracting the deficiencies of the free market and typically involve government expenditure on infrastructure and training and financial support for investment. However, some policies may draw on elements of both types, for instance by providing financial support (interventionist) through the use of tax reliefs (market-orientated).

Market-orientated supply-side policies

Radical market-orientated supply-side policies were first adopted in the early 1980s by the Thatcher government in the UK and the Reagan administration in the USA, but were subsequently copied by other right and centre–right governments around the world. The essence of these policies is to encourage and reward individual enterprise and initiative, and to reduce the role of government; to put more reliance on market forces and competition, and less on government intervention and regulation.

Reducing government expenditure

The desire by many governments to cut government expenditure is not just to reduce public-sector deficits; it is also an essential ingredient of their supply-side strategy.

The public sector is portrayed by some as more bureaucratic and less efficient than the private sector. What is more, it is claimed that a growing proportion of public money has been spent on administration and other 'non-productive' activities, rather than on the direct provision of goods and services.

Two things are needed, it is argued: (a) a more efficient use of resources within the public sector and (b) a reduction in the size of the public sector. This would allow private investment to increase with no overall rise in aggregate demand. Thus the supply-side benefits of higher investment could be achieved without the demand-side costs of higher inflation.

In practice, governments have found it very difficult to cut their expenditure relative to GDP. However, many countries were faced with trying to do this after the financial crisis and global economic slowdown of the late 2000s (see Figure 12.5). Governments found that this means making difficult choices, particularly concerning the levels of services and the provision of infrastructure.

Tax cuts

The imposition of taxation can distort a variety of choices that individuals make. Changes to the rates of taxation can lead individuals to substitute one activity for another. Three examples that are commonly referred to in the context of aggregate supply are:

- taxation of labour income and its impact on labour supply (including hours worked and choice of occupation);
- taxation of interest income earned on financial products (savings) and its impact on the funds available for investment;
- taxation of firms' profits and its impact on capital expenditure by firms.

Over time, many countries have witnessed a decline in the marginal rates of taxation associated with each of these cases. Here we consider the case of the UK.

In 1979, the basic rate of income tax in the UK was 33 per cent, with higher rates rising to 83 per cent. By 1997 the basic rate was only 23 per cent and the top rate was only 40 per cent. The Blair and Brown governments continued with this policy, so that by 2008 the basic rate was 20 per cent. From 2010, an additional 50 per cent tax rate was implemented for those earning in excess of £150 000, largely as a means of plugging the deficit in the public finances. This was subsequently reduced to 45 per cent from 2013.

Similar reductions in rates of tax on business profits have been designed to encourage investment. Reductions in corporation tax (the tax on business profits) have increased after-tax profits, leaving more funds for ploughing back into investment, as well as increasing the after-tax return on investment. In 1983 the main rate of corporation tax in the UK stood at 52 per cent. Further reductions followed. By 2011 the main rate had been halved to 26 per cent and by 2015 there was a single corporation tax rate of 20 per cent. In

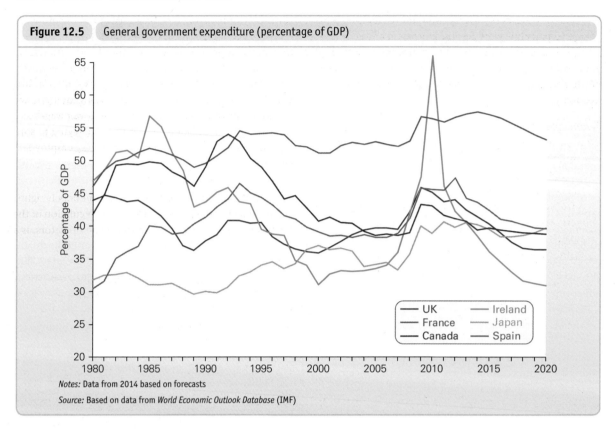

Figure 12.5 General government expenditure (percentage of GDP)

Notes: Data from 2014 based on forecasts

Source: Based on data from *World Economic Outlook Database* (IMF)

the summer Budget of 2015, it was announced that the rate would fall to 19 per cent in 2017 and to 18 per cent in 2020.

Governments have also looked to increase investment allowances. These allow firms to offset the cost of investment against pre-tax profit, thereby reducing their tax liability. Successive governments have used a range of such allowances. For example, in the UK companies can offset a multiple of research and development costs against corporation tax. Since April 2012, the rate of relief for small and medium-sized enterprises (SMEs) has been 225 per cent: i.e. taxable profits are reduced by £225 for every £100 of R&D expenditure. For larger companies the rate of relief is 130 per cent.

Since April 2013, firms have been subject to a lower rate of corporation tax on profits earned from inventions they have patented and certain other innovations. The idea is that firms will be provided with financial support to innovate where this results in their acquiring patents. Patents provide protection for intellectual property rights. From April 2013, firms are liable to corporation tax on the profits attributable to qualifying patents at a reduced rate of 10 per cent. The relief is being phased in, so that by 2017 all profits related to the patent will be subject to the reduced rate.

The argument for reducing tax rates on incomes and profits is that it contributes to higher levels of economic output. Specifically, it contributes to there being more labour hours supplied, more moneys invested with financial institutions and more capital expenditure by firms than would otherwise be the case. In other words, there is a substitution effect (see page 160) inducing more of these beneficial

activities. In the case of labour, people are encouraged to substitute work for leisure.

However, in each case there is a counteracting incentive from the tax cut: an income effect. This is because the higher returns to working, saving and undertaking capital expenditure mean that less of each activity needs to be undertaken to generate the same income flow as before.

Because economic theory offers no firm conclusions as to the benefit of tax cuts, economists and policy makers often look to empirical evidence for guidance. The evidence on whether people will be prepared to work longer hours, for instance, suggests that the substitution and income effects just about cancel each other out. Anyway, for many people there is no such choice in the short run. There is no chance of doing overtime or working a shorter week. In the long run, there may be some flexibility in that people can change jobs.

Reducing the power of labour

The argument here is that, if labour costs to employers are reduced, their profits will probably rise. This could encourage and enable more investment and hence economic growth. If the monopoly power of labour is reduced, then cost-push inflation will also be reduced.

The Thatcher government in the 1980s took a number of measures to curtail the power of unions. These included the right of employees not to join unions, preventing workers taking action other than against their direct employers and enforced secret ballots on strike proposals. It set a lead in resisting strikes in the public sector.

TC 2
p 11

As labour markets have become more flexible, with increased part-time working and short-term and zero-hour contracts, and as the process of globalisation has exposed more companies to international competition, so this has further eroded the power of labour in many sectors of the economy.

Reducing welfare

New classical economists claim that a major cause of unemployment is the small difference between the welfare benefits of the unemployed and the take-home pay of the employed. This causes voluntary unemployment (i.e. frictional unemployment). People are caught in a 'poverty trap': if they take a job, they lose their benefits (see pages 161–3).

A dramatic solution to this problem would be to cut unemployment benefits. A major problem with this approach, however, is that with changing requirements for labour skills, many of the redundant workers from the older industries are simply not qualified for new jobs that are created. What is more, the longer people are unemployed, the more demoralised they become. Employers would probably be prepared to pay only very low wages to such workers. To persuade these unemployed people to take low-paid jobs, the welfare benefits would have to be slashed. A 'market' solution to the problem, therefore, may be a very cruel solution. A fairer one would be an interventionist policy: a policy of retraining labour.

Another alternative is to make the payment of unemployment benefits conditional on the recipient making a concerted effort to find a job. In the Jobseeker's Allowance introduced in the UK in 1996, claimants must be available for and actively seeking work, and must complete a Jobseeker's Agreement, which sets out the types of work the person is willing to do, and the plan to find work. Payment can be refused if the claimant refuses to accept the offer of a job.

Policies to encourage competition

If the government can encourage more competition, this should have the effect of increasing national output and reducing inflation. Five major types of policy have been pursued under this heading.

Privatisation. If privatisation simply involves the transfer of a natural monopoly to private hands (e.g. the water companies), the scope for increased competition is limited. However, where there is genuine scope for increased competition (e.g. in the supply of gas and electricity), privatisation can lead to increased efficiency, more consumer choice and lower prices (pages 184–5). There may still be a problem of oligopolistic collusion, however, and thus privatised industries are monitored and regulated with the aim of making them genuinely competitive.

Alternatively, privatisation can involve the introduction of private services into the public sector (e.g. private contractors providing cleaning services in hospitals, or refuse collection for local authorities). Private contractors may compete against each other for the franchise. This may well lower the cost of provision of these services, but the quality of provision may also suffer unless closely monitored. The effects on unemployment are uncertain. Private contractors may offer lower wages and thus may use more labour. But if they are trying to supply the service at minimum cost, they may employ less labour.

Deregulation. This involves the removal of monopoly rights: again, largely in the public sector. The deregulation of the UK bus industry, opening it up to private operators, is a good example of this initiative.

Introducing market relationships into the public sector. This is where the government tries to get different departments or elements within a particular part of the public sector to 'trade' with each other, so as to encourage competition and efficiency.

One example is in the National Health Service. In 2003, the UK government introduced a system of 'foundation trusts'. Hospitals could apply for foundation trust status. If successful, they would be given much greater financial autonomy in terms of purchasing, employment and investment decisions. By July 2013, there were 147 NHS foundation trusts and 41 mental health NHS foundation trusts. Critics argue that funds were being diverted to foundation hospitals away from the less well-performing hospitals where greater funding could help that performance. In the 2012 Health and Social Care Act the government proposed that in due course all NHS hospitals become foundation trusts.

Primary Care Trusts (PCTs) were abolished in England in April 2013. In their place were Clinical Commissioning Groups (CCGs). These are formed of groups of GP practices. Clinical commissioning groups are responsible for arranging most of the NHS services within their boundaries. They oversee how NHS funds are spent. Therefore, as with GP fundholding, a key principle is to give GPs a choice of 'providers' with the hope of reducing costs and driving up standards.

The Private Finance Initiative (PFI). This is where a private company, after a competitive tender, is contracted by a government department or local authority to finance and build a project, such as a new road or a prison. The government then pays the company to maintain and/or run it, or simply rents the assets from the company. The public sector thus becomes a purchaser of services rather than a direct provider itself.

The aim of these 'public–private partnerships' (PPPs) is to introduce competition (through the tendering process) and private-sector expertise into the provision of public services (see Case Study 12.7 in MyEconLab). By doing so, the objective is to achieve gains in efficiency which outweigh any extra burden to the taxpayer from private-sector profits.

Critics, however, claim that PPPs results in a poorer quality of provision with weak cost control too, resulting in a higher burden for the taxpayer in the long term. Given mounting criticisms of PPPs and general concerns over levels of government borrowing, the Coalition government in November 2011 set up a review of the PFI. The intention was to develop a new model for delivering public investment and services that takes advantage of private-sector expertise, but at a lower cost to the taxpayer. This review coincided with the introduction in 2010 of a National Investment Plan (NIP): a strategic plan to *target* public investment.

In December 2012 the Treasury published its New Approach to Public Private Partnerships. The publication set out the government's new approach: PF2. Changes included the following:

- the public sector taking stakes of up to 49 per cent in individual private finance projects;
- publication of an annual report detailing project and financial information on all projects where the government holds a public-sector equity stake;
- removal of 'soft services', such as cleaning and catering, from PF2 projects;
- the requirement that bidders develop long-term financing plans, in which bank debt does not form the majority of the financing of the project.

Free trade and capital movements. The opening up of international trade and investment is central to a market-orientated supply-side policy. One of the first measures of the Thatcher government (in October 1979) was to remove all controls on the purchase and sale of foreign currencies, thereby permitting the free inflow and outflow of capital, both long term and short term. Most other industrialised countries also removed or relaxed exchange controls during the 1980s and early 1990s.

The Single European Act of 1987, which came into force in 1993, was another example of international liberalisation. As we shall see (in Section 13.6), it created a 'single market' in the EU: a market without barriers to the movement of goods, services, capital and labour.

Interventionist supply-side policies

TC 5
p 23
The basis of the case for government intervention is market failure. In particular, in the context of growth of potential output, the free market is likely to provide too little research and development, training and investment.

KI 26
p 168
There are potentially large external benefits from research and development. Firms investing in developing and improving products, and especially firms engaged in more general scientific research, may produce results that provide benefits to many other firms. Thus the *social* rate of return

on investment may be much higher than the private rate of return. Investment that is privately unprofitable for a firm may therefore still be economically desirable for the nation.

Similarly, investment in training may continue yielding benefits to society that are lost to the firms providing the training when the workers leave.

Investment often involves risks. Firms may be unwilling to take those risks, since the costs of possible failure may be too high. When looked at nationally, however, the benefits of investment might well have substantially outweighed the costs, and thus it would have been socially desirable for firms to have taken the risk. Successes would have outweighed failures.

KI 13
p 66

Even when firms do wish to make such investments, they may find difficulties in raising finance. Banks may be unwilling to lend – a problem that increased after the credit crunch. Alternatively, if firms rely on raising finance by the issue of new shares, this makes them very dependent on the stock market performance of their shares. This depends largely on current profitability and expected profitability in the near future, not on *long-term* profitability. Similarly, the fear of takeovers may make managers over-concerned to keep shareholders happy, further encouraging 'short-termism'.

Types of interventionist supply-side policy

Nationalisation. This is the most extreme form of intervention, and one that most countries had tended to reject, given a worldwide trend for privatisation. Nevertheless, many countries had always stopped short of privatising certain key transport and power industries, such as the railways and electricity generation.

Nationalisation may also be a suitable solution for rescuing vital industries suffering extreme market turbulence. This was the case in 2008 with many banks. With the credit crunch and the over-exposure to risky investments in securitised sub-prime debt, inadequate levels of capital, declining confidence and plummeting share prices, several banks were taken into full or partial public ownership. In the UK, Northern Rock and Bradford & Bingley were fully nationalised, while the government took a majority shareholding in the Royal Bank of Scotland and Lloyds Banking Group.

Direct provision. Improvements in infrastructure, such as a better motorway system, can be of direct benefit to industry. Alternatively, the government could provide factories or equipment to specific firms.

Funding research and development. About one-third of UK R&D is financed by the government, but around half of this has been concentrated in the fields of defence, aerospace and the nuclear power industry. As a result, there has been little government sponsorship of research in the majority of industry. Since the mid-1970s, however, there have been several government initiatives in the field of information

Figure 12.6   Gross expenditure on R&D as a percentage of GDP

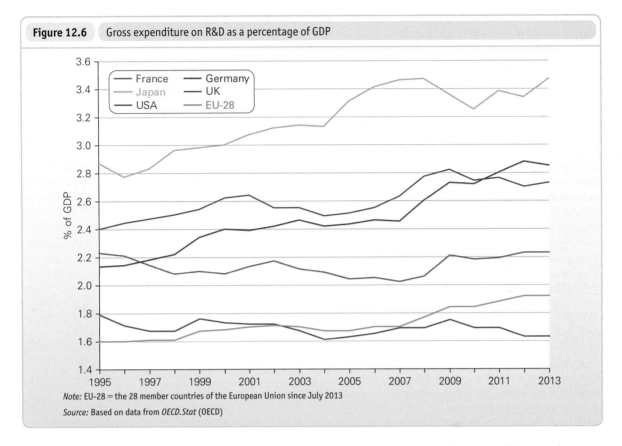

Note: EU-28 = the 28 member countries of the European Union since July 2013

Source: Based on data from *OECD.Stat* (OECD)

technology. Even so, the amount of government support in this field has been very small compared with Japan, France and the USA. What is more, the amount of support declined between the mid-1980s and the late 1990s.

As we saw above, the UK uses the tax system to encourage research and development (R&D). Despite this, as Figure 12.6 demonstrates, UK gross expenditure on research and development as a percentage of GDP has been lower than that of its main economic rivals.

Lower R&D has contributed to a productivity gap between the UK and other G7 countries, although it was gradually narrowing until 2006, but since then has widened (see Chart (a) in Box 9.4 on page 252). The UK's poor R&D record has occurred even though a sizeable number of UK-based companies regularly make a list of the world's largest R&D spending companies. In part, this reflects the limited R&D expenditure by government. But, it also reflects the low R&D intensity across the private sector. In other words, total R&D expenditure by UK firms has often been low *relative* to the income generated by sales.

Training and education. The government may set up training schemes, or encourage educational institutions to make their courses more vocationally relevant, or introduce new vocational qualifications (such as the GNVQs, NVQs and foundation degrees in the UK). Alternatively, the government can provide grants or tax relief to firms which themselves provide training schemes. Alternative approaches to

training in the UK, Germany, France and the USA are examined in Case Study 12.21 in MyEconLab.

Assistance to small firms. UK governments in recent years have recognised the importance of small firms to the economy and have introduced various forms of advisory services, grants and tax concessions. For example, they receive financial support for R&D expenditure through corporation tax relief. This means they can reduce the profits liable for tax by engaging in R&D. As we saw above (page 352), the rate of relief for small and medium-sized enterprises (SMEs) is 225 per cent, compared with 130 per cent for larger companies. In addition, small firms are subject to fewer planning and other bureaucratic controls than large companies. Support to small firms in the UK is examined in Case Study 12.23 in MyEconLab.

Regional and urban policy. Certain parts of a country may suffer from lower economic growth and higher unemployment than others. These regional and urban problems normally result from structural problems – the main one being the decline of certain industries, such as mining or heavy manufacturing industry, which had previously been concentrated in those areas.

A response to this problem is for governments or local authorities to provide support for such areas. This can come in various forms, such as giving grants or subsidies for the creation of jobs; expenditure on infrastructure, such as roads and communications, technical colleges, community

BOX 12.7   MOVES TOWARDS MARKET-BASED POLICIES IN THE UK

Creating the right incentives?

During the early years of the Labour government in the UK from 1997 under Tony Blair, there was much discussion of a 'Third Way' between the unfettered market system advocated by many of those on the right and the interventionist approach advocated by those on the left. The Third Way borrows from the right in advocating incentives, low taxes and free movements of capital. It also borrows from the left in advocating means whereby governments can provide support for individuals in need while improving economic performance by investing in the country's infrastructure, such as its transport and telecommunication systems, and in its social capital, such as schools, libraries and hospitals.

Third Way policies were adopted by many politicians from the centre–left of politics in the late 1990s early 2000s, including Bill Clinton in the USA, Gerhard Schröder in Germany and Wim Kok in The Netherlands. In the UK, although associated primarily with the Blair government, the approach was continued by the Coalition government, which came to office in 2010, albeit with somewhat more emphasis on freeing up the market.

We consider three examples of UK Third Way policies here.

'Welfare to work' and the Work Programme

An example of a 'Third Way' approach to supply-side policy is the 'welfare to work' policy, set up by the UK Labour government elected in 1997 (see Case Study 12.24 in MyEconLab). This provided benefits to people without work in return for their actively seeking employment. In addition, help was provided for the unemployed and people currently outside the workforce in finding jobs. It was interventionist to the extent that it targeted support at particular people, but pro-market to the extent that it provided incentives for people to become more occupationally mobile.

In 2011, the previous system was replaced by the Work Programme. This consists of 18 providers, largely private companies, which seek to place the long-term unemployed in jobs. However, the House of Commons Public Accounts Committee found that the scheme had managed to get only 3.6 per cent of the people on the scheme off benefits and into secure employment in the first 14 months of its operation. This compares with a target of 11.9 per cent set by the Department for Work and Pensions.

Universal Credit

An important aspect of a more market-based approach to welfare is the need to create the 'right incentives' to get people working. This is a central objective of Universal Credit, being rolled out in the UK between 2013 and 2017 to replace various income-related benefits, such as Jobseeker's Allowance, Housing Benefit, Income Support and Tax Credits. The idea is to simplify the system and ensure that people do not lose all their benefit on taking up work and are thus encouraged to seek employment.

However, if benefits taper off too quickly, there may be too little incentive for people to take up work. But if they taper off more slowly, this can make the scheme very expensive. The current withdrawal rate (tapering-off rate) of 65 per cent for Universal Credit gives a marginal effective tax rate for a basic-rate income tax payer of 76.2 per cent (compared with 73 per cent for the former tax credits). This is argued by critics to be too high to create a sufficient incentive for many people to take up part-time work.

There is also the problem of a simplified scheme like this not being able to take sufficient account of people's individual circumstances.

Local Enterprise Partnerships and Enterprise Zones

The introduction by the Coalition government of Local Enterprise Partnerships (LEPs) and Enterprise Zones marked a shift towards a less interventionist industrial strategy. The nine regional development agencies (RDAs) created under the Labour government (1997–2010) were abolished. These had been important drivers in the English regions of the government's regional economic strategy. Indeed, the scope and finances of the RDAs had tended to increase over time. The Coalition government adopted an approach known as *localism*, arguing that the RDAs were unelected bodies detached from local people. More generally, it believed that government needed streamlining.

The LEPs are a natural outcome of localism involving local business and local authorities. However, they receive no direct funding from central government. This has led to concerns about their effectiveness at a time when local authority budgets are stretched.

A further issue is localism itself. LEPs are based on local authority boundaries, while Enterprise Zones typically cover very small geographic areas within the boundaries of an LEP. Some argue that the economic geography of the UK does not correspond straightforwardly to local authority boundaries. Consequently, it is argued by some that there should be mechanisms to ensure that the economic spill overs from one local economic area to another are sufficiently taken into account.

? *What is main thrust of Third Way supply-side policy?*

TC 4 p 20

facilities and housing; the siting of government offices in such areas; the setting up of government agencies to provide advice and support for incoming firms or local community action groups.

An example of such support was the setting up of 21 Enterprise Zones by the Coalition government in 2011. By 2014, there were 24 Enterprise Zones across England and, in July 2015, the new Conservative government announced that it was inviting bids for a new round of Enterprise Zones. These zones are specific geographic locations where firms can benefit from reduced planning restrictions, tax breaks, and access to superfast broadband. Many of the Enterprise Zones encourage clustering: businesses in the same sector grouping together. The hope is that they can mutually benefit from co-operation and/or the sorts of technological spill overs that we came across in the context of endogenous growth theory (see Section 9. 6).

To benefit from clustering effects, the zones typically focus on specific sectors, such as automotive and transport (e.g. the MIRA technology park near Hinckley, Leicestershire) or renewable energy (e.g. Green Port, Hull). The danger of such policies, particularly given the often small geographic area in question, is that they may merely divert investment away from other areas rather than resulting in *additional* investment. (See Box 12.7 for more discussion on enterprise zones and other recent supply-side 'interventions'.)

Advice and persuasion. The government may engage in discussions with private firms in order to find ways to improve efficiency and innovation. It may bring firms together to exchange information, so as to co-ordinate their decisions and create a climate of greater certainty. It may bring firms and unions together to try to create greater industrial harmony.

Information. The government may provide various information services to firms: technical assistance, the results of public research, information on markets, etc.

Pause for thought

How might a new classical economist criticise these various forms of interventionist supply-side policy?

Recap

1. Market-orientated supply-side policies aim to increase the rate of growth of aggregate supply and reduce the rate of unemployment by encouraging private enterprise and the freer play of market forces.

2. Reducing government expenditure as a proportion of GDP is a major element of such policies.

3. Tax cuts can be used to encourage more people to take up jobs, to work longer hours and to work more enthusiastically. The effects of tax cuts will depend on how people respond to incentives.

4. Reducing the power of trade unions and a reduction in welfare benefits, especially those related to unemployment, may force workers to accept jobs at lower wage rates, thereby decreasing equilibrium unemployment.

5. Other examples of market-orientated supply-side policy include privatisation, competitive tendering for public-sector contracts, deregulation, the Private Finance Initiative, free trade and free movement of capital.

6. Interventionist supply-side policy can take the form of nationalisation, grants for investment and research and development, advice and persuasion, the direct provision of infrastructure and the provision, funding or encouragement of various training schemes.

QUESTIONS

1. How does the size of (a) the budget deficit and (b) public-sector debt vary with the course of the business cycle?

2. How would the withdrawals curve shift in each of the following cases? (a) A reduction in the basic rate of tax. (b) An increase in personal allowances.

3. Under what circumstances is a rise in taxes likely to have a disincentive effect?

4. What factors determine the effectiveness of discretionary fiscal policy?

5. Give some examples of changes in one injection or withdrawal that can affect others.

6. Why is it difficult to use fiscal policy to 'fine-tune' the economy?

7. If the government buys back £1 million of maturing bonds from the general public and then, keeping the total amount of its borrowing the same, raises £1 million by selling bills to banks, what will happen to the money supply?

8. Assume that a bank has the simplified balance sheet shown in the following table, and is operating at its desired liquidity ratio. Now assume that the central bank repurchases £5 million of government bonds on the open market. Assume that the people who sell the bonds all have their accounts with this bank.

Liabilities	£m	Assets	£m
Deposits	100	Balances with central bank	10
	—	Advances	90
	100		100

a. Draw up the new balance sheet directly after the purchase of the bonds.

b. Now draw up the eventual balance sheet after all credit creation has taken place.

c. Would there be a similar effect if the central bank rediscounted £5 billion of bills?

d. How would such open-market operations affect the rate of interest?

9. What effect would a substantial increase in the sale of government bonds and bills have on interest rates?

10. Why would it be difficult for a central bank to predict the precise effect on money supply of open-market operations?

11. Imagine you were called in by the government to advise on whether it should adopt a policy of targeting the money supply. What advice would you give and how would you justify the advice?

12. Imagine you were called in by the government to advise on whether it should attempt to prevent cyclical fluctuations by the use of fiscal policy. What advice would you give and how would you justify the advice?

13. What do you understand by the term 'constrained discretion'? Illustrate your answer with reference to the UK and the eurozone.

14. Is there a compromise between purely discretionary policy and adhering to strict targets?

15. Under what circumstances would adherence to inflation targets lead to (a) more stable interest rates and (b) less stable interest rates than pursuing discretionary demand management policy?

16. Why might market-orientated supply-side policies have undesirable side-effects on aggregate demand?

17. If supply-side measures led to a 'shake-out' of labour and a resulting reduction in overstaffing, but also a resulting rightward shift in the Phillips curve, would you judge the policy a success?

18. What types of tax cut are likely to create the greatest (a) incentives and (b) disincentives to effort?

19. In what ways can interventionist supply-side policy work *with* the market, rather than against it? What are the arguments for and against such policy?

MyEconLab

This book can be supported by MyEconLab, which contains a range of additional resources, including an online homework and tutorial system designed to test and build your understanding.

You need both an access card and a course ID to access MyEconLab:

1. Is your lecturer using MyEconLab? Ask your lecturer for your course ID.

2. Has an access card been included with the book at a reduced cost? Check the inside back cover of the book.

3. If you have a course ID but no access card, go to: http://www.myeconlab.com/ to buy access to this interactive study programme.

ADDITIONAL CASE STUDIES IN THE *ESSENTIALS OF ECONOMICS* MyEconLab (www.pearsoned.co.uk/sloman)

12.1 **The national debt.** This explores the question of whether it matters if a country has a high national debt.

12.2 **Fine-tuning in 1959 and 1960.** This looks at two Budgets in the era of Keynesian 'fine-tuning'.

12.3 **Trends in public expenditure.** This case examines attempts to control public expenditure in the UK.

12.4 **The crowding-out effect.** The circumstances in which an increase in public expenditure can replace private expenditure.

12.5 **Injections against the contagion.** The use of discretionary fiscal policy in the late 1990s.

12.6 **Any more G and T?** Did the Code for Fiscal Stability mean that the UK government balanced its books? An examination of the evidence.

12.7 **Assessing PFI.** Has this been the perfect solution to funding investment for the public sector without raising taxes?

12.8 **Discretionary fiscal policy in Japan.** Attempts by successive Japanese governments since 1992 to bring the economy out of recession though expansionary fiscal policy.

12.9 **Monetary policy in the eurozone.** This is a more detailed examination of the role of monetary policy and the ECB than that contained in Box 12.5.

12.10 **The Bank of England's response to the financial crisis.** Focusing on the Bank of England, this case shows the timeline of the responses between 2004 and 2007.

12.11 **Central banking and monetary policy in the USA and its response to the credit crunch.** This case examines how the Fed conducts monetary policy.

12.12 **Goodhart's Law.** An examination of the difficulty of controlling aggregate demand by setting targets for the money supply.

12.13 **Credit and the business cycle.** This case traces cycles in the growth of credit and relates them to the business cycle. It also looks at some of the implications of the growth in credit.

12.14 **Effective monetary policy versus banking efficiency and stability.** This case examines potential conflicts between banking stability, efficiency and the effective operation of monetary policy.

12.15 **Should central banks be independent of government?** An examination of the arguments for and against independent central banks.

12.16 **Managing the macroeconomy.** This considers whether there have been conflicts of objectives in recent UK macroeconomic policy.

12.17 **Interest rate responses and the financial crisis of 2007/8.** A comparison of the policy responses of the Fed, the ECB and the Bank of England to the credit crunch.

12.18 **Monetary targeting: its use around the world.** This examines the types of monetary targets used around the world.

12.19 **Fiscal and monetary policy in the UK.** An historical overview of UK fiscal and monetary policy.

12.20 The supply-side revolution in the USA. 'Reaganomics' and the birth of radical-right supply-side policy in the USA.

12.21 Alternative approaches to training and education. This compares the approaches to training and education – a crucial element in supply-side policy – in the UK, France, Germany and the USA.

12.22 Assistance to small firms in the UK. An examination of current government measures to assist small firms.

12.23 Small-firm policy in the EU. This looks at the range of support available to small and medium-sized firms in the EU.

12.24 Welfare to work. An examination of the policy of the UK Labour government (1997–2010) whereby welfare payments were designed to encourage people into employment.

WEB APPENDIX

12.1 *IS/LM* **analysis of fiscal and monetary policy.** This appendix uses the *IS/LM* model to show the effects of fiscal and monetary policy on national income according to various assumptions about the *IS* and *LM* curves. (For an explanation of *IS/LM* analysis, see Web Appendix 10.2.)

WEBSITES RELEVANT TO PART C

Numbers and sections refer to websites listed in the Web Appendix and hotlinked from this book's website at **www.pearsoned. co.uk/sloman**.

■ For news articles relevant to Part C, follow the 'News' link in MyEconLab or Google 'Sloman Economics News'.

■ For general news on macroeconomic issues and policy see websites in section A, and particularly A1–5, 7–9. See also links to newspapers worldwide in A38, 39, 43 and 44 and the news search feature in Google at A41. See also links to economics news in A42.

■ For general news on money, banking and finance, see websites in section A, and particularly A20–23, 25, 26, 36.

■ For data on economic growth, employment/unemployment, inflation and the business cycle, see links in B1; also see B4, 12 and 35. For UK data, see B2, 3, 5 and 34. For EU data, see B38, 39 and 47. For US data, see B15, 17 and 25. For international data, see B15, 21, 24, 31, 35, 43; H4. For links to data sets, see B1, 4, 28, 35, 46; I14.

■ For national income statistics for the UK, see B2: in *Economic and Fiscal Outlook* and B3: search in *Publications > Books* for *United Kingdom National Accounts – the Blue Book* (annual) and *United Kingdom Economic Accounts* (quarterly).

■ For the Human Development Index, see site H17.

■ For monetary and financial data (including data for money supply and interest rates), see section F and particularly F2. Note that you can link to central banks worldwide from site F17. See also the links in B1.

■ For information on the development of ideas, see C12, 18; see also links under *Methodology and History of Economic Thought* in C14.

■ For a model of the economy (based on the Treasury model), see *The Virtual Chancellor* (site D1). In the model, you can devise your own Budget.

■ For information on UK fiscal policy and government borrowing, see sites E18, 30, 36; F2. See also sites A1–8 at Budget time. For fiscal policy in the eurozone, see G13 and G1.

■ For monetary policy in the UK, see F1 and E30. For monetary policy in the eurozone, see F6 and 5. For monetary policy in the USA, see F8. For monetary policy in other countries, see the respective central bank site in section F.

■ For demand-side policy in the UK, see the latest Budget Report (e.g. section on maintaining macroeconomic stability) at site E30. See also site E18.

■ For inflation targeting in the UK and eurozone see sites F1 and 6.

■ For the current approach to UK supply-side policy, see the latest Budget Report (e.g. sections on productivity and training) at site E30. See also sites E5 and 9. For European policy see sites G5, 7, 9, 12, 14, 19.

■ For support for a market-orientated approach to supply-side policy see C17.

■ For information on training in the UK and Europe, see sites E5, 10; G5, 14.

■ For information on the support for small business in the UK see site E38.

■ For student resources relevant to this Part, see sites C1–7, 9, 10, 12, 19.

International economics

13

Globalisation and international trade

Countries operate in a global economy. In these final two chapters we explore global economic relationships. In particular, we examine the importance of international trade (this chapter) and finance (next chapter) for national economies. We begin this chapter by examining the nature of the interdependencies between countries in the flows of both goods and finance.

We then focus on trade. Trade between nations has the potential to benefit all participating countries (albeit to differing extents). Many people, however, argue strongly for restrictions on trade, seeing unrestrained imports as a threat. But are they justified in fearing international competition, or are they merely trying to protect some vested interest at the expense of everyone else? Section 13.3 examines the arguments for restricting trade.

If there are conflicting views as to whether we should have more or less trade, what has been happening on the world stage? Section 13.4 looks at the various moves towards making trade freer and at the obstacles that have been met.

A step on the road to freer trade is for countries to enter free-trade agreements with just a limited number of other countries. An example is the North American Free Trade Agreement, NAFTA (the USA, Canada and Mexico). We consider such 'preferential trading systems' in Section 13.5. Then, in Section 13.6, we look at probably the world's most famous preferential trading system, the European Union, and, in particular, at the development of a 'single European market'.

Finally we examine the role of trade for developing countries. Does trade with the rich world help them to develop, or does it merely result in their domination by rich countries and giant multinational companies?

After studying this chapter, you should be able to answer the following questions:

- How can economic and financial interdependencies create international business cycles?
- How has international trade grown over the years? Have countries become more or less interdependent?
- What are the benefits from international trade?
- Which goods should a country export and which should it import?
- Why do countries often impose restrictions on trade? Why does the World Trade Organization (WTO) try to get trade restrictions reduced or even eliminated?
- Why do countries form free-trade areas and other types of trading alliance?
- How has the 'single market' in the EU benefited its members?
- What approaches should developing countries adopt towards trade with rich countries?

13.1 GLOBAL INTERDEPENDENCE

How countries are connected through trade and finance

We live in an interdependent world. Countries are affected by the economic health of other countries and by their governments' policies. Problems in one part of the world can spread like a contagion to other parts, with perhaps no country immune. This was clearly illustrated by the credit crunch of 2007/8. A crisis that started in the sub-prime market in the USA soon snowballed into a worldwide recession.

There are two major ways in which this process of 'globalisation' affects individual economies. The first is through trade. The second is through financial markets.

Interdependence through trade

So long as nations trade with one another, the domestic economic actions of one nation will have implications for those which trade with it. For example, if the US administration feels that the US economy is growing too fast, it might adopt various contractionary fiscal and monetary measures, such as higher tax rates or interest rates. US consumers will not only consume fewer domestically produced goods, but also reduce their consumption of imported products. But US imports are other countries' exports. A fall in these other countries' exports will lead to a multiplier effect in these countries. Output and employment will fall.

Changes in aggregate demand in one country thus send ripples throughout the global economy. The process whereby changes in imports into (or exports from) one country affect national income in other countries is known as the **international trade multiplier**.

TC 13
p 219

> **Pause for thought**
>
> *Assume that the US economy expands. What will determine the size of the multiplier effect on other countries?*

The more open an economy, the more vulnerable it will be to changes in the level of economic activity in the rest of the world. This problem will be particularly acute if a nation is heavily dependent on trade with one other nation (e.g. Canada on the USA) or one other region (e.g. Switzerland on the EU).

International trade has been growing as a proportion of countries' national income for many years. This is illustrated in Figure 13.1, which shows the growth in the global volume of exports and in world real GDP. It shows that exports have been growing much more rapidly than GDP. Over the period from 1991 to 2015 world output grew by an average of 3.6 per cent per annum, whereas the volume of exports grew by 5.9 per cent.

> **Definition**
>
> **International trade multiplier** The effect on national income in country B of a change in exports (or imports) of country A.

Figure 13.1 Annual growth in global output and exports of goods

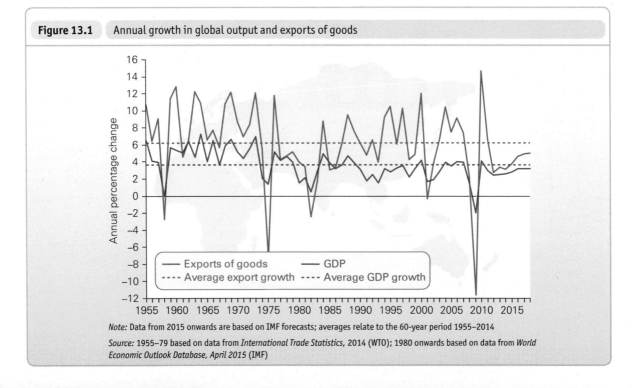

Note: Data from 2015 onwards are based on IMF forecasts; averages relate to the 60-year period 1955–2014

Source: 1955–79 based on data from *International Trade Statistics,* 2014 (WTO); 1980 onwards based on data from *World Economic Outlook Database, April 2015* (IMF)

BOX 13.1   DOCTOR, THE WORLD HAS CAUGHT A COLD!

Global answers to global problems?

We don't have to look far to see how much economic and financial interdependence affects our daily lives. As you walk down the street to the supermarket, many of the passing cars originate overseas or perhaps were built here by foreign-owned companies. You look up and the aircraft flying overhead is taking passengers to some far-flung corner of the world for both business and pleasure. As you enter the supermarket you see an array of goods from all over the world.

Clearly, interdependence through trade connects economies. Box 13.2 looks at trade patterns in more detail. But, the late 2000s demonstrated also just how interdependent financial systems and financial institutions have become. Financial products have a passport to travel and travel they do!

Growth rates across the world have tended to converge in recent decades. The chart shows how we experience an international business cycle, with countries sharing common problems and concerns at the same time. At one time, the most pressing problem may be world inflationary pressures; at another time, such as the late 2000s, it may be a world recession.

Increasing economic and financial interdependence means that problems in one part of the world spread rapidly to other parts. Just look at what happened when the US sub-prime mortgage market collapsed. The USA's illness turned into the world's flu!

But who should dish out the medicine? How potent can the medicine of national governments be in isolation? What role is there for co-ordinated monetary and fiscal policies and does it require stronger international institutions to deal with world problems?

Iceland's cold

The decline in output in Iceland in 2009, at 6.5 per cent, was remarkably stark. The country had been especially badly hit by the global financial crisis.

An aggressive strategy of credit expansion had seen the liabilities of the three largest Icelandic banks rise from 100 per cent of GDP in 2004 to over 1000 per cent by 2008. Some of the funds from this expansion came from the interbank market but also from deposits overseas in subsidiaries of these banks in the Nordic countries and the UK. When the credit crunch hit, they found it increasingly difficult to roll over loans on the interbank market. What is more, the sheer scale of the banks' expansion made it virtually impossible for Iceland's central bank to guarantee repayments of the loans.

The result was that four of its largest banks were nationalised and run by Iceland's Financial Supervisory Authority.

In November 2008, the International Monetary Fund's executive board approved a $2.1 billion loan to Iceland to support an economic recovery programme. An initial payment of $827 million was made with subsequent payments to be spread over time, subject to IMF quarterly reviews of the recovery programme. In August 2011 the bailout support officially ended and in early 2012 Iceland began

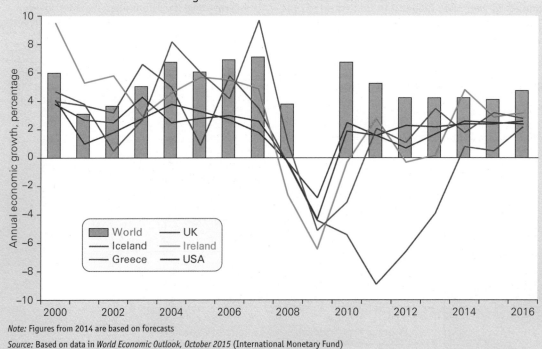

Annual growth in real GDP in selected countries

Legend: World, Iceland, Greece, UK, Ireland, USA

Note: Figures from 2014 are based on forecasts

Source: Based on data in *World Economic Outlook, October 2015* (International Monetary Fund)

repaying the bailout debt. It hoped to complete repayment ahead of schedule in financial year 2015/16.

A Greek tragedy?

Greece has been struggling with the burden of a huge budget deficit for some years and following the credit crunch of 2008 its general government deficit soared. In 2008 it was 9.9 per cent of GDP; by 2009, it was 15.6 per cent – the highest in the EU at the time and over five times higher than EU rules allow. The annual cost to Greece of servicing the debt was running at about 12 per cent of GDP. In early 2010 the government estimated that it would need to borrow €53 billion to cover budget shortfalls. Greece, like many other countries, also experienced rising unemployment. By 2010 the unemployment rate was 12.5 per cent, up from 7.7 per cent in 2008.

Austerity measures, as part of an IMF and EU rescue package, aimed to reduce this deficit to less than 3 per cent of GDP by 2014. This was to be achieved through a variety of spending cuts and tax rises. It was the price that Greece had to pay to receive a bailout package worth €240 billion. This comprised an initial loan of €110 billion agreed in May 2010 and a further €130 billion agreed in October 2011.

However, the costs of the austerity measures in terms of falling disposable income and rising unemployment were incredibly high. The period from 2012 to 2014 saw the unemployment rate consistently around the 25 per cent mark and the country operating with a negative output gap estimated at around 10 per cent of potential GDP. By 2014 real GDP per capita was 22 per cent lower than it had been in 2008. Inevitably, the period saw bouts of social unrest and widespread strikes by public-sector workers. In January 2015, the anti-austerity party Syriza won Greece's general election and was committed to renegotiating the terms of its bailout and to reversing the cuts in public services.

The debt crisis was not just confined to Greece. For instance, in November 2010 Ireland agreed a rescue package of up to €85 billion with the IMF and EU member states. The general government deficit in Ireland in 2010 was estimated at 29 per cent of GDP, up from 13 per cent in 2009. The aim was to reduce to this to 3 per cent of GDP by 2015.

IMF to the rescue?

We have seen how the IMF has been a major player in helping to finance rescue packages for countries like Iceland, Ireland and Greece. But what is the IMF? And what does it do?

The IMF is a 'specialised agency' of the United Nations and is financed by its 188 member countries (as of 2015). The role of the IMF is to ensure macroeconomic stability – as in the cases above – and to foster global growth. It also works with developing nations to alleviate poverty and to achieve economic stability. To do this it provides countries with loans.

The IMF has not been without controversy, however. Conditions attached to loans have often been very harsh, especially for some of the most indebted developing countries.

The global economic and financial crisis provided the IMF with a challenge: which countries to support with a limited budget? Between 2007 and spring 2012, the IMF is estimated to have provided $300 billion of loans to member countries. During this period an increasing amount of assistance was being given to developed economies, especially within the EU.

Following crisis talks with finance ministers in Europe, the IMF agreed to set aside €250 billion to support the eurozone. This would be in addition to €440 billion supplied by eurozone countries under the 'European Financial Stability Facility' and €60 billion from EU funds under the 'European Financial Stabilisation Mechanism'.

In October 2010 the EU agreed to establish a more permanent funding mechanism for eurozone countries in financial difficulties, known as the European Stability Mechanism (see Box 12.2). The mechanism became operational in May 2013. The IMF is a crucial stakeholder in the funding mechanism, both in committing funds but also in assessing, alongside the European Commission and the European Central Banks, the financial position of any country requesting help. This assessment includes possible 'macroeconomic adjustment programmes' for countries in receipt of funds.

Strengthening the IMF

World leaders meeting as part of the G20 in London in April 2009 announced the need to strengthen global financial institutions. They agreed that the resources available to the IMF should be trebled to $750 billion. They also agreed that the IMF would work with a new Financial Stability Board (FSB), made up, among others, of the G20 countries and the European Commission, so as to help in identifying potential economic and financial risks. Essentially, the G20 countries were looking for a better 'early warning system' to meet some of the challenges of an increasingly interdependent world.

However, the ongoing financial problems facing governments, particularly in the eurozone, led the international community in April 2012 to pledge a further increase of $430 billion in resources for the IMF. Further changes in members' subscriptions were expected from 2015 as part of the IMF's 15th periodic review of the 'quota system'. This is the system which helps determine members' subscriptions, their voting power and their access to financing. The intention was to create a credible 'firewall' to contain future financial crises.

Do any problems arise from a strengthening of global economic and financial institutions?

With most nations committed to freer trade, and with the World Trade Organization (see Section 13.4) overseeing the dismantling of trade barriers, so international trade is likely to continue growing as a proportion of world GDP. This will increase countries' interdependence and their vulnerability to world trade fluctuations, such as the global recession of the late 2000s. World output fell by 2.3 per cent in 2009, while worldwide exports fell by 12.0 per cent. This was the biggest contraction in global trade since World War II (see Figure 13.1).

> **Pause for thought**
>
> *Are exports likely to continue growing faster than GDP indefinitely? What will determine the outcome?*

Financial interdependence

International trade has grown rapidly, but international financial flows have grown much more rapidly. It was estimated that, in 2013, around $5.3 trillion of assets were being traded daily across the foreign exchanges. Many of the transactions are short-term financial flows, moving to where interest rates are most favourable or to currencies where the exchange rate is likely to appreciate. This again makes countries interdependent.

Financial interdependency impacts not only on financial institutions in different countries, but also on national economies. It also illustrates how global responses can be needed. As a result of the credit crunch world leaders were seriously worried that the whole world would plunge into deep recession. A co-ordinated policy response from governments and central banks began in earnest in October 2008 when governments in the UK, Europe, North America and other parts of the world injected some $2 trillion of extra capital into banks.

International business cycles

There is an old saying: 'If America sneezes, the rest of the world catches a cold.' Viruses of a similar nature regularly infect the world economy. The credit crunch of the 2007/8 resulting from defaults on US sub-prime debt (see Box 10.2) was a dramatic example of this. As a consequence of both trade and financial interdependence, the world economy, like the economy of any individual country, tends to experience periodic fluctuations in economic activity – an *international* business cycle. The implication of this is that countries will tend to share common problems and concerns at the same time. At one time, the most pressing problem may be world inflationary pressures; at another time, it may be a world recession.

In order to avoid 'beggar-my-neighbour' policies, it is better to seek *common* solutions to these common problems: i.e. solutions that are international in scope and design rather than narrowly based on national self-interest. For example, during a world recession, countries are likely to suffer from rising unemployment. Policies that lead to a depreciation of the exchange rate (such as cutting interest rates) will help to stimulate demand by making exports cheaper and imports more expensive. But this will then only worsen the trade balance of other countries, whose aggregate demand will thus fall. The first country is thus tackling its own unemployment at the expense of rising unemployment in other countries. This was a charge levelled at Japan and then the eurozone in 2014 and 2015, when their programmes of quantitative easing led to depreciation in the yen and the euro and an appreciation in the US dollar. We examine exchange rates in Chapter 14.

However, if other nations (which will also be experiencing higher unemployment) can be convinced to co-ordinate their policy actions, an expansionary *international* economic policy will benefit all. In addition to the resulting rise in their imports, all nations will also experience rising export sales.

Even if national policies are not in the strictest sense co-ordinated, discussions between nations regarding the nature and magnitude of the problems they face may help to improve the policy-making process.

Global policy response

Global economic interdependence and an international business cycle can aid the process of international co-operation between countries. Countries frequently meet in various groupings – from the narrow group of the world's seven richest developed countries (the G7, which includes the USA, Japan, Germany, the UK, France, Italy and Canada) to broader groups such as the G20, which, in addition to the G7 and other rich countries, also includes larger developing countries, such as China, India, Brazil and South Africa.

Global interdependence raises important questions about the role of international organisations like the International Monetary Fund (IMF) and the World Trade Organization (WTO).

The IMF's remit is to promote global growth and stability, to help countries through economic difficulty and to help developing economies achieve macroeconomic stability and reduce poverty. In response to the global economic and financial crisis of the late 2000s, the IMF's budget was substantially increased and it became more actively involved with what were previously defined as 'strong performing economies' (see Box 13.1).

The WTO's role is to encourage freer trade. We consider the WTO in Section 13.4.

13.2 THE ADVANTAGES OF TRADE

Can international trade make all countries better off?

Trading patterns

Patterns in world trade are changing as the dominance of developed economies continues to be challenged. In 2014 developing countries accounted for 43 per cent (by value) of all world merchandise trade; in 2000 they accounted for just 23 per cent. Their share of world trade has tended to rise in recent times as many of the countries with the fastest growth in exports are found in the developing world. One group of developing countries with especially rapid growth in exports has been the 'BRICS'[1] (Brazil, Russia, India, China and South Africa). Between them they accounted for just 5.4 per cent of world exports in 1992. By 2014 this had grown to 18.3 per cent (see Figure 13.2).

Despite this, Africa continues to account for a minute share of world trade. In 2014 only 2.9 per cent of world exports originated from Africa. In contrast, Europe remains an important geographical centre for trade accounting for 35.6 per cent of world exports in 2014.

Globally, 10 nations account for about half of world merchandise exports. In 2014, the three countries with the highest shares were China (12.4 per cent), the USA (8.6 per cent) and Germany (8.0 per cent), while the UK was the 10th largest exporter (2.7 per cent) (see Figure 13.3).

Box 13.2 considers in more detail the observed patterns and trends in world trade. We then go on to consider why countries actually trade with each other.

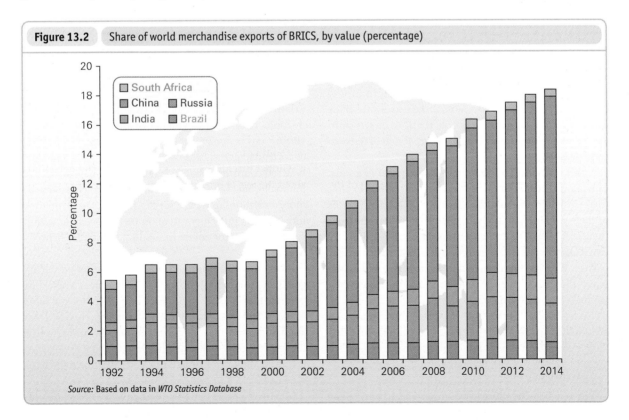

Figure 13.2 Share of world merchandise exports of BRICS, by value (percentage)

Source: Based on data in *WTO Statistics Database*

---

[1] Sometimes the term is used to refer just to the first four countries. When South Africa is excluded, the term is written BRICs rather than BRICS.

Figure 13.3	Share of world merchandise exports by value (2014)

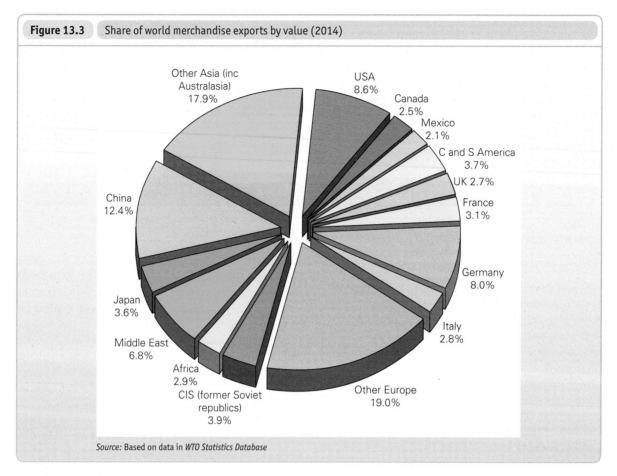

Source: Based on data in *WTO Statistics Database*

Specialisation as the basis for trade

What motivates countries to trade with each other? What do they gain out of it? The reasons for international trade are really only an extension of the reasons for trade *within* a nation. Rather than people trying to be self-sufficient and do everything for themselves, it makes sense to specialise.

Firms specialise in producing certain types of goods. This allows them to gain economies of scale and to exploit their entrepreneurial and management skills and the skills of their labour force. It also allows them to benefit from their particular location and from the ownership of any particular capital equipment or other assets they might possess. With the revenues that firms earn, they buy in the inputs that they need from other firms and the labour they require. Firms thus trade with each other.

Countries also specialise. They produce more than they need of certain goods. What is not consumed domestically is exported. The revenues earned from the exports are used to import goods that are not produced in sufficient amounts at home.

But which goods should a country specialise in? What should it export and what should it import? The answer

is that it should specialise in those goods in which it has a *comparative advantage*. Let us examine what this means.

The law of comparative advantage

Countries have different endowments of factors of production. They differ in population density, labour skills, climate, raw materials, capital equipment, etc. These differences tend to persist because factors are relatively immobile between countries. Obviously land and climate are totally immobile, but even with labour and capital there tend to be more restrictions (physical, social, cultural or legal) on their international movement than on their movement within countries. Thus the ability to supply goods differs between countries.

What this means is that the relative costs of producing goods will vary from country to country. For example, one country may be able to produce one fridge for the same cost as 6 kilos of wheat or three Blu-ray players, whereas another country may be able to produce one fridge for the same cost as only 3 kilos of wheat but four Blu-ray players. It is these differences in relative costs that form the basis of trade.

At this stage we need to distinguish between *absolute advantage* and *comparative advantage*.

Absolute advantage

When one country can produce a good with fewer resources than another country it is said to have an **absolute advantage** in that good. If France can produce wine with fewer resources than the UK, and the UK can produce gin with fewer resources than France, then France has an absolute advantage in wine and the UK an absolute advantage in gin. Production of both wine and gin will be maximised by each country specialising and then trading with the other country. Both will gain.

Comparative advantage

The above seems obvious, but trade between two countries can still be beneficial even if one country could produce all goods with fewer resources than the other, providing the *relative* efficiency with which goods can be produced differs between the two countries.

Take the case of a developed country that is absolutely more efficient than a less developed country at producing both wheat and cloth. Assume that with a given amount of resources (labour, land and capital) the alternatives shown in Table 13.1 can be produced in each country

Despite the developed country having an absolute advantage in both wheat and cloth, the less developed country (LDC) has a **comparative advantage** in wheat, and the developed country has a *comparative* advantage in cloth. This is because wheat is relatively cheaper in terms of cloth in the LDC: only 1 metre of cloth has to be sacrificed to produce 2 kilos of wheat, whereas 8 metres of cloth would have to be sacrificed in the developed country to produce 4 kilos of wheat. In other words, the opportunity cost of wheat is 4 times higher in the developed country (8/4 compared with 1/2).

Pause for thought

Draw up a table similar to Table 13.1, only this time assume that the figures are: LDC 6 wheat or 2 cloth; DC 8 wheat or 20 cloth. What are the opportunity cost ratios now?

On the other hand, cloth is relatively cheaper in the developed country. Here the opportunity cost of producing 8 metres of cloth is only 4 kilos of wheat, whereas in the LDC 1 metre of cloth costs 2 kilos of wheat. Thus the opportunity cost of cloth is 4 times higher in the LDC (2/1 compared with 4/8).

Table 13.1	Production possibilities for two countries			
			Kilos of wheat	Metres of cloth
Less developed country	Either	2	or	1
Developed country	Either	4	or	8

To summarise: countries have a comparative advantage in those goods that can be produced at a lower opportunity cost than in other countries.

If countries are to gain from trade, they should export those goods in which they have a comparative advantage and import those goods in which they have a comparative disadvantage. Given this we can state a **law of comparative advantage**.

> **KEY IDEA 36** *The law of comparative advantage.* Provided opportunity costs of various goods differ in two countries, both of them can gain from mutual trade if they specialise in producing (and exporting) those goods that have relatively low opportunity costs compared with the other country's.

But why do they gain if they specialise according to this law? And just what will that gain be? We consider these questions next.

The gains from trade based on comparative advantage

Before trade, unless markets are very imperfect, the prices of the two goods are likely to reflect their opportunity costs. For example, in Table 13.1, since the less developed country can produce 2 kilos of wheat for 1 metre of cloth, the *price* of 2 kilos of wheat will roughly equal 1 metre of cloth.

Assume, then, that the pre-trade exchange ratios of wheat for cloth are as follows:

LDC: 2 wheat for 1 cloth
Developed country: 1 wheat for 2 cloth (i.e. 4 for 8)

Both countries will now gain from trade, provided the exchange ratio is somewhere between 2:1 and 1:2. Assume, for the sake of argument, that it is 1:1: that 1 wheat trades internationally for 1 cloth. How will each country gain?

The LDC gains by exporting wheat and importing cloth. At an exchange ratio of 1:1, it now has to give up only 1 kilo of wheat to obtain 1 metre of cloth, whereas before trade it had to give up 2 kilos of wheat.

Definitions

Absolute advantage A country has an absolute advantage over another in the production of a good if it can produce it with less resources than the other country can.

Comparative advantage A country has a comparative advantage over another in the production of a good if it can produce it at a lower opportunity cost: i.e. if it has to forgo less of other goods in order to produce it.

Law of comparative advantage Trade can benefit all countries if they specialise in the goods in which they have a comparative advantage.

BOX 13.2 · TRADING PLACES

Patterns and trends in world trade

In 2013 the total *value* of the world's exports of merchandise goods was US$18.8 trillion (with a further $4.7 trillion in the export of services). Back in 1950 the value of exports in merchandise goods was a mere US$62 billion. Therefore, the value of trade in 2013, in nominal terms, was around 300 times larger than in 1950. A more useful figure is that for the *volume* of world merchandise trade (which is measured in constant prices). This grew by a factor of 36 over this period, which is significantly more than world output which was 9.2 times larger in 2013.

The chart illustrates the period from 1950 to 2013. It shows how the growth in the volume of world merchandise

exports has been driven by *manufacturers*, which have increased by a factor of 76, while the export of *fuels and mining* products has increased by a factor of 11 and *agricultural* products by a factor of 9.

Table (a) shows the world's top five merchandise exporters and importers by value. It also shows trade figures for the UK. The four largest exporting nations are also the four largest importers of goods and services.

Trading partners

But who do countries trade with? Table (b) looks at the trading partners of the four largest trading nations and also

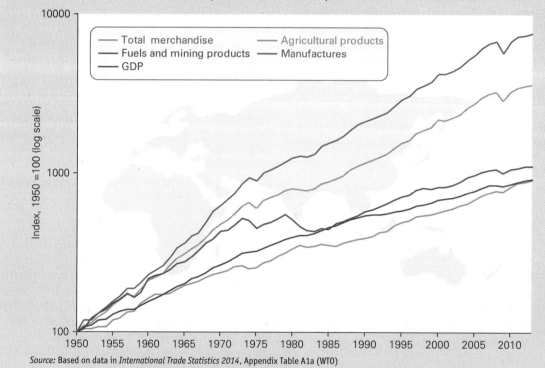

Volume of world merchandise exports and GDP

Legend:
- Total merchandise
- Fuels and mining products
- GDP
- Agricultural products
- Manufactures

Index, 1950 = 100 (log scale)

Source: Based on data in *International Trade Statistics 2014*, Appendix Table A1a (WTO)

The developed country gains by exporting cloth and importing wheat. Again at an exchange ratio of 1:1, it now has to give up only 1 metre of cloth to obtain a kilo of wheat, whereas before it had to give up 2 metres of cloth.

Thus both countries have gained from trade.

The actual exchange ratios will depend on the relative prices of wheat and cloth after trade takes place. These prices will depend on total demand for and supply of the two goods. It may be that the trade exchange ratio is nearer to the pre-trade exchange ratio of one country than the other. Thus the gains to the two countries need not be equal.

The limits to specialisation and trade

Does the law of comparative advantage suggest that countries will completely specialise in just a few products? In practice, countries are likely to experience *increasing* opportunity costs. The reason for this is that, as a country increasingly specialises in one good, it will have to use resources that are less and less suited to its production and which were more suited to other goods. Thus ever-increasing amounts of the other goods will have to be sacrificed. For example, as a country specialises more and more in

those of the UK. The table shows that trading blocs (see Section 13.5) and geography matter. For instance, in the cases of the UK and Germany over one-half of their trade is with other European Union countries. Similarly, one-third of the value of the USA's exports and one-quarter of its imports can be attributed to Canada and Mexico, members of the North American Free Trade Agreement (NAFTA) (see pages 381–2).

 Does the fact that world trade has increased at a much faster rate than world GDP highlight the limitations of trade as a driver of economic growth?

(a) Top trading countries by value and world share, 2013

Rank	Exporters	$ billion	Share	Rank	Importers	$ billion	Share
1	China	2209	11.7	1	USA	2329	12.3
2	USA	1580	8.4	2	China	1950	10.3
3	Germany	1453	7.7	3	Germany	1189	6.3
4	Japan	715	3.8	4	Japan	833	4.4
5	Netherlands	672	3.6	5	France	681	3.6
8	UK	542	2.9	6	UK	655	3.5

Source: From *International Trade Statistics*, 2014 © World Trade Organization (WTO), www.wto.org

(b) Merchandise trade by destination and origin, 2013

	China		USA		Germany		Japan		UK	
	Export destinations	%	Export destinations	%	Export destinations	%	Export destinations	%	Export destinations	%
1	Hong Kong	17.4	Canada	19.0	EU-28	55.7	USA	18.8	EU-28	42.9
2	USA	16.7	EU-28	16.7	USA	8.1	China	18.1	Switzerland	13.0
3	EU-28	15.4	Mexico	14.3	China	6.1	EU-28	10.0	USA	11.5
4	Japan	6.8	China	7.7	Switzerland	4.4	S Korea	7.9	China	3.3
5	S Korea	4.1	Japan	4.1	Russia	3.4	Taiwan	5.8	UAE	2.8
	Import origins	%	Import origins	%	Import origins	%	Import origins	%	Import origins	%
1	EU-28	11.3	China	19.8	EU-28	55.5	China	21.7	EU-28	53.1
2	S Korea	9.4	EU-28	17.0	China	8.3	EU-28	9.4	China	8.8
3	Japan	8.3	Canada	14.5	USA	5.6	USA	8.6	USA	8.3
4	Hong Kong	8.1	Mexico	12.2	Switzerland	4.3	Australia	6.1	Norway	3.9
5	Taiwan	8.0	Japan	6.1	Russia	3.3	Saudi Arabia	6.0	Canada	2.3

Source: From *International Trade Statistics*, 2014, © World Trade Organization (WTO), www.wto.org

grain production, it will have to use land that is less and less suited to growing grain.

These increasing costs as a country becomes more and more specialised will lead to the disappearance of its comparative cost advantage. When this happens, there will be no point in further specialisation. Thus whereas a country like Germany has a comparative advantage in capital-intensive manufactures, it does not produce only manufactures. It would make no sense not to use its fertile lands to produce food or its forests to produce timber. The opportunity costs of diverting all agricultural labour to industry would be very high.

Other reasons for gains from trade

Decreasing costs. Even if there are no initial comparative cost differences between two countries, it will still benefit both to specialise in industries where economies of scale can be gained, and then to trade. Once the economies of scale begin to appear, comparative cost differences will also appear, and thus the countries will have gained a comparative advantage in these industries.

This reason for trade is particularly relevant for small countries where the domestic market is not large enough to support large-scale industries. Thus exports form a much higher percentage of GDP in small countries such as Singapore than in large countries such as the USA.

Differences in demand. Even with no comparative cost differences and no potential economies of scale, trade can benefit both countries if demand conditions differ.

If people in country A like beef more than lamb, and people in country B like lamb more than beef, then rather than A using resources better suited for lamb to produce beef, and B using resources better suited for producing beef to produce lamb, it will benefit both to produce beef *and* lamb and to export the one they like less in return for the one they like more.

Increased competition. If a country trades, the competition from imports may stimulate greater efficiency at home. This extra competition may prevent domestic monopolies/oligopolies from charging high prices. It may stimulate greater research and development and the more rapid adoption of new technology. It may lead to a greater variety of products being made available to consumers.

Trade as an 'engine of growth'. In a growing world economy, the demand for a country's exports is likely to grow over time, especially when these exports have a high income elasticity of demand. This will provide a stimulus to growth in the exporting country.

Non-economic advantages. There may be political, social and cultural advantages to be gained by fostering trading links between countries.

The terms of trade

What price will our exports fetch abroad? What will we have to pay for imports? The answer to these questions is given by the terms of trade. The **terms of trade** are defined as:

$$\frac{\text{The average price of exports}}{\text{The average price of imports}}$$

expressed as an index, where prices are measured against a base year in which the terms of trade are assumed to be 100. Thus if the average price of exports relative to the average price of imports has risen by 20 per cent since the base year, the terms of trade will now be 120. The terms of trade for selected countries are shown in Figure 13.4 (with 2010 as the base year).

Definition

Terms of trade The price index of exports divided by the price index of imports and then expressed as a percentage. This means that the terms of trade will be 100 in the base year.

| Figure 13.4 | Terms of trade for selected countries (2010 = 100) |

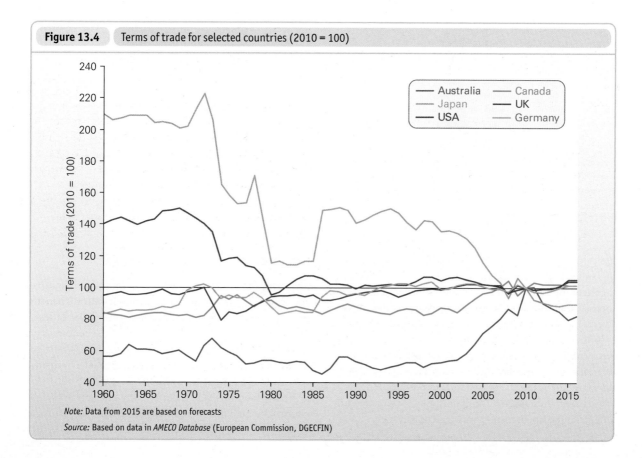

Note: Data from 2015 are based on forecasts

Source: Based on data in *AMECO Database* (European Commission, DGECFIN)

If the terms of trade rise (export prices rising relative to import prices), they are said to have 'improved', since fewer exports now have to be sold to purchase any given quantity of imports. Changes in the terms of trade are caused by changes in the demand and supply of imports and exports and by changes in the exchange rate.

Pause for thought

In Figure 13.4, which countries have seen an improvement in their terms of trade in recent years?

Recap

1. Economies have become increasingly interdependent as a result of the increase in world trade and the interdependencies of countries' financial systems.

2. Countries can gain from trade if they specialise in producing those goods in which they have a comparative advantage: i.e. those goods that can be produced at relatively low opportunity costs. This is merely an extension of the argument that gains can be made from the specialisation and division of labour.

3. If two countries trade, then, provided that the trade price ratio of exports and imports is somewhere between the pre-trade price ratios of these goods in the two countries, both countries can gain.

4. With increasing opportunity costs there will be a limit to specialisation and trade. As a country increasingly specialises, its (marginal) comparative advantage will eventually disappear.

5. The terms of trade give the price of exports relative to the price of imports expressed as an index, where the base year is 100.

6. Gains from trade also arise from decreasing costs (economies of scale), differences in demand between countries, increased competition from trade and the transmission of growth from one country to another. There may also be non-economic advantages from trade.

13.3 ARGUMENTS FOR RESTRICTING TRADE

If trade can benefit everyone, then why do countries attempt to limit trade?

We have seen how trade can bring benefits to all countries. But when we look around the world we often see countries erecting barriers to trade. Their politicians know that trade involves costs as well as benefits.

Possible barriers to imports include the following:

- **tariffs** (i.e. customs duties) on imports;
- *quotas* (i.e. restrictions on the amount of certain goods that can be imported);
- *subsidies on domestic products* to give them a price advantage over imports;
- *administrative regulations* designed to exclude imports, such as customs delays or excessive paperwork;
- *procurement procedures* whereby governments favour domestic producers when purchasing equipment (e.g. defence equipment).

Alternatively, governments may favour domestic producers by subsidising their exports in a process known as **dumping**. The goods are 'dumped' at artificially low prices in the foreign market.

In looking at the costs and benefits of trade, the choice is not the stark one of whether to have free trade or no trade at all. Although countries may sometimes contemplate having completely free trade, typically countries limit their trade. However, they certainly do not ban it altogether.

Arguments in favour of restricting trade

Arguments having some general validity

TC 5
p 23

The infant industry argument. Some industries in a country may be in their infancy but have a potential comparative advantage. This is particularly likely in developing countries. Such industries are too small yet to have gained economies of scale; their workers are inexperienced; there is a lack of back-up facilities – communications networks, specialist research and development, specialist suppliers, etc. – and they may have only limited access to finance for expansion. Without protection, these **infant industries** will not survive competition from abroad.

Definitions

Tariffs Taxes on imported products.

Dumping When exports are sold at prices below marginal cost – often as a result of government subsidy.

Infant industry An industry that has a potential comparative advantage, but which is as yet too underdeveloped to be able to realise this potential.

Protection from foreign competition, however, will allow them to expand and become more efficient. Once they have achieved a comparative advantage, the protection can then be removed to enable them to compete internationally.

To reduce reliance on goods with little dynamic potential. Many developing countries have traditionally exported primaries: foodstuffs and raw materials. The world demand for some of these, however, is fairly income inelastic, and thus grows relatively slowly (see Section 13.7). In such cases, free trade is not an engine of growth. Instead, if it encourages countries' economies to become locked into a pattern of primary production, it may prevent them from expanding in sectors like manufacturing which have a higher income elasticity of demand (see figure in Box 13.2). There may thus be a valid argument for protecting or promoting manufacturing industry. Note, however, that with the rapid growth of China and the other BRICs, the demand for and prices of various raw materials and foodstuffs have increased more rapidly in recent years – at least until 2011 (see Figure 13.6 on page 389).

To prevent 'dumping' and other unfair trade practices. A country may engage in dumping by subsidising its exports. The result is that prices may no longer reflect comparative costs. Thus the world would benefit from tariffs being imposed by importers to counteract the subsidy.

It can also be argued that there is a case for retaliating against countries which impose restrictions on your exports. In the short run, both countries are likely to be made worse off by a contraction in trade. But if the retaliation persuades the other country to remove its restrictions, it may have a longer-term benefit. In some cases, the mere threat of retaliation may be enough to get another country to remove its protection.

To prevent the establishment of a foreign-based monopoly. Competition from abroad could drive domestic producers out of business. The foreign company, now having a monopoly of the market, could charge high prices with a resulting misallocation of resources. The problem could be tackled either by restricting imports or by subsidising the domestic producer(s).

All of the above arguments suggest that governments should adopt a 'strategic' approach to trade. **Strategic trade theory** argues that protecting certain industries allows a net gain in the *long* run from increased competition in the market (see Case Study 13.3 in MyEconLab). This argument has been used to justify the huge financial support given to the aircraft manufacturer Airbus, a consortium based in four European countries. The subsidies have allowed it to compete with Boeing, which would otherwise have a monopoly in many types of passenger aircraft. Airlines and their passengers worldwide, it is argued, have benefited from the increased competition.

To spread the risks of fluctuating markets. A highly specialised economy – Zambia with copper, Cuba with sugar – is highly susceptible to world market fluctuations. Greater diversity and greater self-sufficiency can reduce these risks.

To reduce the influence of trade on consumer tastes. The assumption of fixed consumer tastes dictating the pattern of production through trade is false. Multinational companies through their advertising and other forms of sales promotion may influence consumer tastes. Many developing countries object to the insidious influence of western consumerist values expounded by companies such as Coca-Cola and McDonald's. Thus some restriction on trade may be justified in order to reduce this 'producer sovereignty'.

To prevent the importation of harmful goods. A country may want to ban or severely curtail the importation of things such as drugs, pornographic literature and live animals.

To take account of externalities. Free trade will tend to reflect private costs. Both imports and exports, however, can involve externalities. The mining of many minerals for export may adversely affect the health of miners; the production of chemicals for export may involve pollution; the importation of juggernaut lorries may lead to structural damage to houses; shipping involves large amounts of CO_2 emissions (estimates typically put this at between 3 to 5 per cent of total world emissions).

Arguments having some validity for specific groups or countries

The arguments considered so far are of general validity: restricting trade for such reasons could be of net benefit to the world. There are two other arguments, however, that are used by individual governments for restricting trade, where their country will gain but at the *expense* of other countries, such that there will be a net loss to the world.

The first argument concerns taking advantage of market power in world trade. If a country, or a group of countries, has monopsony power in the purchase of imports (i.e. they are individually or collectively a very large economy, such as the USA or the EU), then they could gain by restricting imports so as to drive down their price. Similarly, if countries have monopoly power in the sale of some export (e.g. OPEC countries with oil [see Box 5.3 on

Definitions

Strategic trade theory The theory that protecting/supporting certain industries can enable them to compete more effectively with large monopolistic rivals abroad. The effect of the protection is to increase long-run competition and may enable the protected firms to exploit a comparative advantage that they could not have done otherwise.

page 120]), then they could gain by restricting exports, thereby forcing up the price (see Web Appendix 13.2 in MyEconLab).

The second argument concerns giving protection to declining industries. The human costs of sudden industrial closures can be very high. In such circumstances, temporary protection may be justified to allow the industry to decline more slowly, thereby avoiding excessive structural unemployment. Such policies will be at the expense of the consumer, however, who will be denied access to cheaper foreign imports.

'Non-economic' arguments for restricting trade. A country may be prepared to forgo the direct economic advantages of free trade in order to achieve objectives that are often described as 'non-economic':

- It may wish to maintain a degree of self-sufficiency in case trade is cut off in times of war. This may apply particularly to the production of food and armaments.
- It may decide not to trade with certain countries with which it disagrees politically.
- It may wish to preserve traditional ways of life. Rural communities or communities built around old traditional industries may be destroyed by foreign competition.
- It may prefer to retain as diverse a society as possible, rather than one too narrowly based on certain industries.

Pursuing such objectives, however, will involve costs. Preserving a traditional way of life, for example, may mean that consumers are denied access to cheaper goods from abroad. Society must therefore weigh up the benefits against the costs of such policies.

Pause for thought

If economics is the study of choices of how to use scarce resources, can these other objectives be legitimately described as 'non-economic'?

Problems with protection

Tariffs and other forms of protection impose a cost on society. This is illustrated in Figure 13.5, which shows the case of a good that is partly home produced and partly imported. Domestic demand and supply are given by D_{dom} and S_{dom}. It is assumed that firms in the country produce under perfect competition and that therefore the supply curve is the sum of the firms' marginal cost curves.

Let us assume that the country is too small to affect world prices: it is a price taker. The world price is given, at

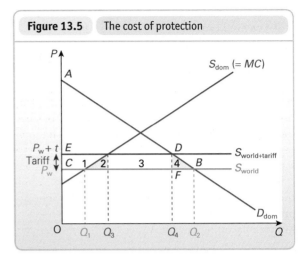

Figure 13.5   The cost of protection

P_w. At P_w, Q_2 is demanded, Q_1 is supplied by domestic suppliers and hence $Q_2 - Q_1$ is imported.

Now a tariff is imposed. This increases the price to consumers by the amount of the tariff. Price rises to $P_w + t$. Domestic production increases to Q_3, consumption falls to Q_4, and hence imports fall to $Q_4 - Q_3$.

What are the costs of this tariff to the country? Consumers are having to pay a higher price, and hence consumer surplus falls from area *ABC* to *ADE* (see pages 33 and 173 if you are unsure about consumer surplus).

The cost to consumers in lost consumer surplus is thus *EDBC* (i.e. areas 1 + 2 + 3 + 4). *Part* of this cost, however, is redistributed as a *benefit* to other sections in society. *Firms* get a higher price, and thus gain extra producer surplus (area 1): where producer surplus is given by the area between the price and the *MC* curve. The *government* receives extra revenue from the tariff payments (area 3): i.e. $Q_4 - Q_3 \times$ tariff. These revenues can be used, for example, to reduce taxes.

But *part* of this cost is not recouped elsewhere. It is a net cost to society (areas 2 and 4).

Area 2 represents the extra costs of producing $Q_3 - Q_1$ at home, rather than importing it. If $Q_3 - Q_1$ were still imported, the country would only be paying P_w. By producing it at home, however, the costs are given by the domestic supply curve (= *MC*). The difference between *MC* and P_w (area 2) is thus the efficiency loss on the production side.

Area 4 represents the loss of consumer surplus by the reduction in consumption from Q_2 to Q_4. Consumers have saved area FBQ_2Q_4 of expenditure, but have sacrificed area DBQ_2Q_4 of utility in so doing – a net loss of area 4.

The government should ideally weigh up such costs against any benefits that are gained from protection.

Pause for thought

In this model, where the country is a price taker and faces a horizontal supply curve (the small-country assumption), is any of the cost of the tariff borne by the overseas suppliers?

Apart from these direct costs to the consumer, there are several other problems with protection. Some are a direct effect of the protection; others follow from the reactions of other nations.

Protection as 'second-best'. Many of the arguments for protection amount merely to arguments for some type of government intervention in the economy. Protection, however, may not be the best way of dealing with the problem, since protection may have undesirable side-effects. There may be a more direct form of intervention that has no side-effects. In such a case, protection will be no more than a *second-best* solution.

Pause for thought

a. *Protection to allow the exploitation of monopoly/monopsony power can be seen as a 'first-best' policy for the country concerned. Similarly, the use of tariffs to counteract externalities directly involved in the trade process (e.g. the environmental costs of an oil tanker disaster) could be seen to be a first-best policy. Explain why.*

b. *All the other arguments for tariffs or other forms of protection that we have considered can really be seen as arguments for intervention, with protection being no more than a second-best form of intervention. Go through each of the arguments and consider what would be a 'first-best' form of intervention.*

For example, using tariffs to protect old inefficient industries from foreign competition may help prevent unemployment in those parts of the economy, but the consumer will suffer from higher prices. A better solution would be to subsidise retraining and investment in those areas of the country in *new efficient industries* – industries with a comparative advantage. In this way, unemployment is avoided, but the consumer does not suffer.

Retaliation. If the USA imposes restrictions on, say, imports from the EU, then the EU may impose restrictions on imports from the USA. Any gain to US firms competing with EU imports is offset by a loss to US exporters. What is more, US consumers suffer, since the benefits from comparative advantage have been lost. (See, for example, Case Study 13.8 in MyEconLab.)

The increased use of tariffs and other restrictions can lead to a trade war, with each country cutting back on imports from other countries. In the end, with such beggar-my-neighbour policies, everyone loses.

Protection may allow firms to remain inefficient. By removing or reducing foreign competition, protection may reduce firms' incentive to reduce costs. Thus if protection is being given to an infant industry, the government must ensure that the lack of competition does not prevent it 'growing up'. Protection should not be excessive and should be removed as soon as possible.

TC 4
p 20

Bureaucracy. If a government is to avoid giving excessive protection to firms, it should examine each case carefully. This can lead to large administrative costs. It could also lead to corrupt officials accepting bribes from importers to give them favourable treatment.

| BOX 13.3 | DO WE EXPLOIT FOREIGN WORKERS BY BUYING CHEAP FOREIGN IMPORTS? | EXPLORING ECONOMICS |

People sometimes question the morality of buying imports from countries where workers are paid 'pittance' wages. 'Is it right', they ask, 'for us to support a system where workers are so exploited?' As is often the case with emotive issues, there is some truth and some misunderstanding in a point of view like this.

First the truth. If a country like the UK trades with a regime that denies human rights and treats its workers very badly, then we may thereby be helping to sustain a corrupt system. We might also be seen to be lending it moral support. In this sense, therefore, trade may not help the cause of the workers in these countries. Arguments like these were used to support the imposition of trade sanctions against South Africa in the days of apartheid.

Now the misunderstanding. If we buy goods from countries that pay low wages, we are *not* as a result contributing to their low-wage problem. Quite the reverse. If countries like Indonesia export textiles to the west, this will help to *increase* the wages of Indonesian workers. If Indonesia has a comparative advantage in labour-intensive goods, these goods will earn a better price by being exported than by being sold entirely in the domestic Indonesian market. Provided *some* of the extra revenues go to the workers (as opposed to their bosses), they will gain from trade.

? *Under what circumstances would a gain in revenues by exporting firms not lead to an increase in wage rates?*

Recap

1. Countries use various methods to restrict trade, including tariffs, quotas, exchange controls, import licensing, export taxes, and legal and administrative barriers. Countries may also promote their own industries by subsidies.

2. Reasons for restricting trade that have some validity in a world context include the infant industry argument, the problems of relying on exporting goods whose market is growing slowly or even declining, dumping and other unfair trade practices, the danger of the establishment of a foreign-based monopoly, the need to spread the risks of fluctuating export prices, and the problems that free trade may adversely affect consumer tastes, that it may allow the importation of harmful goods and not take account of externalities.

3. Countries may also have other objectives in restricting trade, such as remaining self-sufficient in certain strategic products, not trading with certain countries of which it disapproves, protecting traditional ways of life or simply retaining a non-specialised economy.

4. Protection in the form of tariffs results in higher prices. The resulting loss in consumer surplus is not fully offset by the gain in profits to domestic firms and the tariff revenue for the government. Even if government intervention to protect certain parts of the economy is desirable, restricting trade is unlikely to be a first-best solution to the problem, since it involves side-effect costs. What is more, restricting trade may encourage retaliation; it may allow inefficient firms to remain inefficient; it may involve considerable bureaucracy and possibly even corruption.

13.4 THE WORLD TRADING SYSTEM AND THE WTO

Is trade becoming freer or less free?

After the Wall Street crash of 1929 (when prices on the US stock exchange plummeted), the world plunged into the Great Depression. Countries found their exports falling dramatically and many suffered severe balance of payments difficulties. The response of many countries was to restrict imports by the use of tariffs and quotas. Of course, this reduced other countries' exports, which encouraged them to resort to even greater protectionism. The net effect of the Depression and the rise in protectionism was a dramatic fall in world trade. The volume of world trade in manufactures fell by more than a third in the three years following the Wall Street crash. Clearly there was a net economic loss to the world from this decline in trade.

After the Second World War there was a general desire to reduce trade restrictions, so that all countries could gain the maximum benefits from trade. There was no desire to return to the beggar-my-neighbour policies of the 1930s.

In 1947, 23 countries got together and signed the General Agreement on Tariffs and Trade (GATT). By 2015 there were 160 members of its successor organisation, the World Trade Organization, which was formed in 1995. Between them, the members of the WTO account for around 98 per cent of world trade.

The aims of GATT, and now the WTO, have been to liberalise trade. But, whereas GATT focused solely on the trade in goods, the WTO and its agreements also relate to the trade in services and in inventions and designs, sometimes referred to as intellectual property.

WTO rules

The WTO requires its members to operate according to various rules. These include the following:

- **Non-discrimination.** Under the 'most favoured nations clause', any trade concession that a country makes to one member must be granted to *all* signatories. The only exception is with free-trade areas and customs unions (such as the EU). Here countries are permitted to abolish tariffs between themselves while still maintaining them with the rest of the world.
- **Reciprocity.** Any nation benefiting from a tariff reduction made by another country must reciprocate by making similar tariff reductions itself.
- The general prohibition of quotas.
- **Fair competition.** If unfair barriers are erected against a particular country, the WTO can sanction retaliatory action by that country. The country is not allowed, however, to take such action without permission.
- **Binding tariffs.** Countries cannot raise existing tariffs without negotiating with their trading partners.

Unlike GATT, the WTO has the power to impose sanctions on countries breaking trade agreements. If there are disputes between member nations, these will be settled by the WTO, and if an offending country continues to impose trade restrictions, permission will be granted for other countries to retaliate

For example, in March 2002, the Bush administration imposed tariffs on steel imports into the USA in order to protect the ailing US steel industry (see Case Study 13.6 in MyEconLab). The EU and other countries referred the case to the WTO, which in December 2003 ruled that they were illegal. This ruling made it legitimate for the EU and other countries to impose retaliatory tariffs on US products. President Bush consequently announced that the steel tariffs would be abolished.

BOX 13.4 | THE DOHA DEVELOPMENT AGENDA

A new direction for the WTO?

Globalisation, based on the free play of comparative advantage, economies of scale and innovation, has produced a genuinely radical force, in the true sense of the word. It essentially amplifies and reinforces the strengths, but also the weaknesses, of market capitalism: its efficiency, its instability, and its inequality. If we want globalisation not only to be efficiency-boosting but also fair, we need more international rules and stronger multilateral institutions.[2]

In November 1999, the members of the World Trade Organization met in Seattle in the USA. What ensued became known as the 'Battle of Seattle' (see Case Study 13.7 in MyEconLab). Anti-globalisation protesters fought with police; the world's developing economies fell out with the world's developed economies; and the very future of the WTO was called into question. The WTO was accused of being a free traders' charter, in which the objective of free trade was allowed to ride roughshod over anything that might stand in its way. Whatever the issue – the environment, the plight of developing countries, the dominance of trade by multinationals – free trade was king.

As Pascal Lamy, the former EU Trade Commissioner, made clear in the quote above, rules had to be strengthened, and the WTO had to ensure that the gains from trade were fairer and more sustainable.

The rebuilding process of the WTO began in Doha, Qatar, in November 2001. The meeting between the then 142 members of the WTO concluded with the decision to launch a new round of WTO trade talks, to be called the 'Doha Development Agenda' (DDA). As with previous trade rounds, the talks were designed to increase the liberalisation of trade. However, this time such a goal was to be tempered by a policy of strengthening assistance to developing economies.

Other areas identified for discussion included: sustainable development and the environment; greater liberalisation of agriculture; rules to govern foreign direct investment; the co-ordination of countries' competition policies; and the use and abuse of patents on medicines.

The talks were originally scheduled for completion by January 2005, but this deadline was extended several times as new talks were arranged and failed to reach agreement. A particular sticking point was the unwillingness of rich countries, and the USA and the EU in particular, to make sufficient reductions in agricultural protection, given the pressure from their domestic farmers. The USA was unwilling to make substantial cuts in agricultural subsidies and the EU in agricultural tariffs.

There was also unwillingness by large developing countries, such as India and Brazil, to reduce protection to their industrial and service sectors. What is more, there were large divergences in opinion between developing countries on how much they should reduce their own agricultural protection.

Breakdown of the talks

The talks seemed finally to have broken down at a meeting in Geneva in July 2008. Despite the willingness of developing countries to reduce industrial tariffs by more than 50 per cent, and by the USA and the EU to make deep cuts in agricultural subsidies and tariffs, the talks foundered over the question of agricultural protection for developing countries. This was item 18 on a 'to-do' list of 20 items; items 1 to 17 had already been agreed. China and India wanted to protect poor farmers by retaining the ability to impose temporary tariffs on food imports in the event of a drop in food prices or a surge in imports. The USA objected. When neither side would budge, the talks collapsed.

But even 'success' would not have addressed some thorny issues, such as achieving equal access to rich countries' markets by all banana-producing countries (see Case Study 13.8 in MyEconLab) and protecting cotton producers in developing countries from cheap subsidised cotton grown in the USA. And Africa's interests would not have been properly addressed. In fact, no African country was present in the inner circle of talks at the end.

Many commentators, however, argued that failure was no catastrophe. The gain from total liberalisation of trade would have boosted developing countries' GDP by no more than 1 per cent. And anyway, tariffs were generally falling and were already at an all-time low. But, with the global economic downturn of 2008/9, there were worries that protectionism would begin to rise again. This was a classic prisoners' dilemma (see pages 127–9). Policies that seemed to be in the interests of countries separately would be to the overall detriment of the world. The Nash equilibrium of such a 'game', therefore, is one where countries are generally worse off. As it turned out, the worries were largely unfounded.

The Bali Package and the push to agreement

At the WTO's Bali Ministerial Conference in December 2013, an agreement was reached on a package of issues. The result was a streamlining of trade, allowing developing countries more options for providing food security, boosting least developed countries' trade and, more generally, promoting development. The deal was the first substantial agreement since the WTO was formed in 1995.

At the heart of the agreement is the simplifying of customs procedures, making them more transparent, and ensuring that trade is made 'easier, faster and cheaper'. Meanwhile, the deal also permits developing countries to continue subsidising their agriculture in order to promote food security, provided the practice does not distort international trade.

According to the EU's Trade Commissioner Karel De Gucht, about one-quarter of the goals set for the Doha Round have been achieved in this agreement. This, of course, still leaves a long way to go if all the Doha objectives are to be met. World trade, although now likely to be somewhat freer, is still not free; developing countries will still find access restricted for their agricultural products, and manufactures too, to many markets in the rich world; rich countries will still find access restricted for their manufactured products and services to many markets in the developing world.

By the time you read this, a final agreement may have been reached – or perhaps not!

> **?** *Does the process of globalisation mean that the role of the WTO is becoming less and less important?*

---

[2] 'Global policy without democracy', speech by Pascal Lamy, given in 2001 when he was the EU Trade Commissioner. He later became head of the WTO in 2005.

Pause for thought

Could US action to protect its steel industry from foreign competition be justified in terms of the interests of the USA as a whole (as opposed to the steel industry in particular)?

The greater power of the WTO has persuaded many countries to bring their disputes to it. From January 1995 to September 2015, 498 disputes had been brought to the WTO (compared with 300 to GATT over the whole of its 48 years).

Trade rounds

Periodically, member countries have met to negotiate reductions in tariffs and other trade restrictions. There have been eight 'rounds' of such negotiations since the signing of GATT in 1947. The last major round to be completed was the Uruguay Round, which began in Uruguay in 1986, continued at meetings around the world and culminated in a deal being signed in April 1994. By that time, the average tariff on manufactured products was 4 per cent and falling. In 1947 the figure was nearly 40 per cent. The Uruguay Round agreement also involved a programme of phasing in substantial reductions in tariffs and other restrictions up to the year 2002 (see Case Study 13.4 in MyEconLab).

Despite the reduction in tariffs, many countries have still tried to restrict trade by various other means, such as quotas and administrative barriers. Also, barriers have been particularly high on certain non-manufactures.

Agricultural protection in particular has come in for sustained criticism by developing countries. High fixed prices and subsidies given to farmers in the EU, the USA and other advanced countries mean that the industrialised world continues to export food to many developing countries which have a comparative advantage in food production! Farmers in developing countries often find it impossible to compete with subsidised food imports from the rich countries.

The most recent round of trade negotiations began in Doha, Qatar, in 2001 (see Box 13.4). The negotiations have focused on both trade liberalisation and measures to encourage development of poorer countries. In particular, the Doha Development Agenda, as it is called, is concerned with measures to make trade fairer so that its benefits are spread more evenly around the world. This would involve improved access for developing countries to markets in the rich world. The Agenda is also concerned with the environmental impacts of trade and development.

The negotiations were originally due to be completed in 2005, but, as Box 13.4 explains, deadlines continued to be missed. December 2013, however, saw a series of agreements at a WTO ministerial conference in Bali. The so-called Bali Package included commitments to streamline trade, boost trade among least developing countries and provide 'food security' for developing countries. The deal was proclaimed as the first substantial agreement since the WTO was formed in 1995. Nonetheless, considerable work remained in meeting the goals set in Doha.

Recap

1. Most countries of the world are members of the WTO and in theory are in favour of moves towards freer trade.
2. In practice, however, countries have been very unwilling to abandon restrictions if they believe that they can gain from them, even though it might be at the expense of other countries.
3. The WTO is more powerful than its predecessor, GATT. It has a disputes procedure and can enforce its rulings.

13.5 TRADING BLOCS

Why do some countries get together and trade more freely between themselves?

The world economy seems to have been increasingly forming into a series of trade blocs, based upon regional groupings of countries: a European region centred on the European Union, an Asian region on Japan and China, a North American region on the USA and a Latin American region. Such trade blocs are examples of **preferential trading arrangements**. These arrangements involve trade restrictions with the rest of the world, and lower or zero restrictions between the members.

Although trade blocs clearly encourage trade between their members, many countries outside these blocs complain that they benefit the members at the expense of the rest of the world. For many developing economies, in need of access to the most prosperous nations in the world, this represents a significant check on their ability to grow and develop.

Definition

Preferential trading arrangement A trading arrangement whereby trade between the signatories is freer than trade with the rest of the world.

Types of preferential trading arrangement

There are three possible forms of such trading arrangements.

Free-trade areas

A **free-trade area** is where member countries remove tariffs and quotas between themselves, but retain whatever restrictions *each member chooses* with non-member countries. Some provision will have to be made to prevent imports from outside coming into the area via the country with the lowest external tariff.

Customs unions

A **customs union** is like a free-trade area, but in addition members must adopt *common* external tariffs and quotas with non-member countries.

Common markets

A **common market** is where member countries operate as a *single* market. Like a customs union there are no tariffs and quotas between member countries and there are common external tariffs and quotas. But a common market goes further than this. A full common market includes the following features:

- *A common system of taxation.* In the case of a *perfect* common market, this will involve identical rates of tax in all member countries.
- *A common system of laws and regulations governing production, employment and trade.* For example, in a perfect common market there would be a *single* set of laws governing issues such as product specification (e.g. permissible artificial additives to foods, or levels of exhaust emissions from cars), the employment and dismissal of labour, mergers and takeovers, and monopolies and restrictive practices.
- *Free movement of labour, capital and materials, and of goods and services.* In a perfect common market, this will involve a total absence of border controls between member states, the freedom of workers to work in any member country, and the freedom of firms to expand into any member state.
- *The absence of special treatment by member governments of their own domestic industries.* Governments are large purchasers of goods and services. In a perfect common market, they should buy from whichever companies within the market offer the most competitive deal and not show favouritism towards domestic suppliers: they should operate a *common procurement policy*.

The definition of a common market is sometimes extended to include the following two features of *economic and monetary union*:

- *A fixed exchange rate between the member countries' currencies.* In the extreme case, this would involve a single currency for the whole market.
- *Common macroeconomic policies.* To some extent this must follow from a fixed exchange rate, but in the extreme case it will involve a single macroeconomic management of the whole market, and hence the

abolition of separate fiscal or monetary intervention by individual member states.

We will examine European economic and monetary union in Section 14.6.

The direct effects of a customs union: trade creation and trade diversion

By joining a customs union (or free-trade area), a country will find that its trade patterns change. Two such changes can be distinguished: trade creation and trade diversion.

Trade creation

Trade creation is where consumption shifts from a high-cost producer to a low-cost producer. The removal of trade barriers allows greater specialisation according to comparative advantage. Instead of consumers having to pay high prices for domestically produced goods in which the country has a comparative disadvantage, the goods can now be obtained more cheaply from other members of the customs union. In return, the country can export to them goods in which it has a comparative advantage.

Trade diversion

Trade diversion is where consumption shifts from a lower-cost producer outside the customs union to a higher-cost producer within the union.

Assume that the most efficient producer in the world of a particular good is Russia – outside the EU. Assume that before membership, Poland paid a similar tariff on this good from any country, and thus imported the product from Russia rather than from the EU.

After joining the EU, however, the removal of the tariff made the EU product cheaper, since the tariff remained on the Russian product. Consumption thus switched to a higher-cost producer. There was thus a net loss in world efficiency. As far as Poland was concerned, consumers still gained, since they were paying a lower price than before. There was a loss, however, to domestic producers (from the

> **Definitions**
>
> **Free-trade area** A group of countries with no trade barriers between themselves.
>
> **Customs union** A free-trade area with common external tariffs and quotas.
>
> **Common market** A customs union where the member countries act as a single market with free movement of labour and capital, common taxes and common trade laws.
>
> **Trade creation** Where a customs union leads to greater specialisation according to comparative advantage and thus a shift in production from higher-cost to lower-cost sources.
>
> **Trade diversion** Where a customs union diverts consumption from goods produced at a lower cost outside the union to goods produced at a higher cost (but tariff free) within the union.

KI 36
p 369

TC 1
p 7

reduction in protection, and hence reduced prices and profits) and to the government (from reduced tariff revenue). These losses may have been smaller or larger than the gain to consumers: in other words, there may still have been a net gain to Poland, but there could have been a net loss, depending on the circumstances. See Web Appendix 12.3 in MyEconLab for a graphical analysis of these arguments.

> ### Pause for thought
>
> *Is joining a customs union more likely to lead to trade creation or trade diversion in each of the following cases? (a) The union has a very high external tariff. (b) Cost differences are very great between the country and members of the union.*

Longer-term effects of a customs union

Over the longer term, there may be other gains and losses from being a member of a customs union.

Longer-term advantages

- Increased market size may allow a country's firms to exploit (*internal*) *economies of scale*. This argument is more important for small countries, which have therefore more to gain from an enlargement of their markets.

KI 26
p 168
- *External economies of scale.* Increased trade may lead to improvements in the infrastructure of the members of the customs union (better roads, railways, financial services, etc.). This in turn could bring bigger long-term benefits from trade between members, and from external trade too, by making the transport and handling of imports and exports cheaper.

KI 17
p 101
- The bargaining power of the whole customs union with the rest of the world may allow member countries to gain *better terms of trade.* This, of course, will necessarily involve a degree of political co-operation between the members.

- *Increased competition* between member countries may stimulate efficiency, encourage investment and reduce monopoly power. Of course, a similar advantage could be gained by the simple removal of tariffs with any competing country.

- Integration may encourage a *more rapid spread of technology*.

Longer-term disadvantages

- *Resources may flow from the country* to more efficient members of the customs union, or to the geographical centre of the union (so as to minimise transport costs). This can be a major problem for a *common market* (where there is free movement of labour and capital). The country could become a depressed 'region' of the community.

- If integration encourages greater co-operation between firms in member countries, it may also encourage *greater oligopolistic collusion*, thus keeping prices higher to the consumer. It may also encourage mergers and

takeovers that would increase monopoly power. The extent to which this takes place will depend on whether the customs union has a joint competition policy and how effective it is.

- *Diseconomies of scale*. If the union leads to the development of very large companies, they may become bureaucratic and inefficient.

- The *costs of administering* the customs union may be high. This problem is likely to be worse the more intervention there is in the affairs of individual members.

Preferential trading in practice

Preferential trading has the greatest potential to benefit countries whose domestic market is too small, taken on its own, to enable them to benefit from economies of scale, and where they face substantial barriers to their exports. Most developing countries fall into this category and as a result many have attempted to form preferential trading arrangements.

Examples in Latin America and the Caribbean include the Latin American Integration Association (LAIA), the Andean Community, the Central American Integration System (SICA) and the Caribbean Community (CARICOM). A Southern Common Market (MerCoSur) was formed in 1991, consisting of Argentina, Brazil, Paraguay and Uruguay. It has a common external tariff and most of its internal trade is free of tariffs.

In 1993, the six original ASEAN nations (Brunei, Indonesia, Malaysia, the Philippines, Singapore and Thailand) agreed to work towards an ASEAN Free Trade Area (AFTA). ASEAN (the Association of South-East Asian Nations) now has 10 members (the new ones being Laos, Myanmar, Vietnam and Cambodia) and is dedicated to increased economic co-operation within the region. What progress has been made in achieving AFTA? Virtually all tariffs between the six original members were eliminated by 2010 and there were plans to eliminate them for the remaining countries by 2015. ASEAN hoped to announce the establishment of a common market known as the ASEAN Economic Community (AEC) by the end of 2015.

In Africa, the Economic Community of West African States (ECOWAS) has been attempting to create a common market between its 15 members. The West African franc is used in eight of the countries by a population of over 100 million people. A further six countries plan to introduce a common currency, as part of the West African Monetary Zone (WAMZ). However, the start date for the eco, as the currency is to be known, has had to be put back several times as countries struggle to meet a series of convergence criteria. The ultimate goal is to combine the two currency areas and adopt a single currency for all member states.

North American Free Trade Agreement (NAFTA)

NAFTA is one of the two most powerful trading blocs in the world (the other being the EU). It came into force in 1994 and consists of the USA, Canada and Mexico. These three countries have agreed to abolish tariffs between themselves in the hope that increased trade and co-operation will follow. Tariffs between the USA and Canada were phased out by 1999, and tariffs between all three countries were eliminated as of 1 January 2008. New non-tariff restrictions will not be permitted either, but many existing ones can remain in force, thus preventing the development of true free trade between the members. Indeed, some industries, such as textiles and agriculture, will continue to have major non-tariff restrictions.

NAFTA members hope that, with a market similar in size to the EU, they will be able to rival the EU's economic power in world trade. Other countries may join in the future, so NAFTA may eventually develop into a western hemisphere free-trade association.

NAFTA is principally a free-trade area and not a common market. Unlike the EU, it does not seek to harmonise laws and regulations, except in very specific areas such as environmental management and labour standards. Member countries are permitted total legal independence, subject to the one proviso that they must treat firms of other member countries equally with their own firms – the principle of 'fair competition'. Nevertheless, NAFTA has encouraged a growth in trade between its members, most of which is trade creation rather than trade diversion.

Case Study 13.9 in MyEconLab looks at the costs and benefits of NAFTA membership to the three countries involved.

Asia–Pacific Economic Cooperation Forum (APEC)

The most significant move towards establishing a more widespread regional economic organisation in east Asia appeared with the creation of the Asia–Pacific Economic Cooperation Forum in 1989 (APEC). APEC links 21 economies of the Pacific rim, including Asian, Australasian and North and South American countries (19 countries, plus Hong Kong and Taiwan). These countries account for around 57 per cent of the world's total output and 46 per cent of world merchandise trade. At the 1994 meeting of APEC leaders, it was resolved to create a free-trade area across the Pacific by 2010 for the developed industrial countries, and by 2020 for the rest.

Unlike the EU and NAFTA, APEC is likely to remain solely a free-trade area and not to develop into a customs union, let alone a common market. Within the region there exists a wide disparity in GDP per capita, ranging in 2015 from $56 400 in the USA, $52 400 in Australia and $33 200 in Japan to a mere $2600 in Papua New Guinea and $2200 in Vietnam. Such disparities create a wide range of national interests and goals. Countries are unlikely to share common economic problems or concerns. In addition, political differences and conflicts within the region are widespread, reducing the likelihood that any organisational agreement beyond a simple economic one would succeed. However, the economic benefits from free trade, and the resulting closer regional ties, could be immense.

In the next section we consider the longest established and most comprehensive preferential trading arrangement: the European Union.

Recap

1. Countries may make a partial movement towards free trade by the adoption of a preferential trading system. This involves free trade between the members, but restrictions on trade with the rest of the world. Such a system can be either a simple free-trade area, or a customs union (where there are common restrictions with the rest of the world) or a common market (where in addition there is free movement of capital and labour, and common taxes and trade laws).

2. A preferential trading area can lead to trade creation, where production shifts to low-cost producers within the area, or to trade diversion, where trade shifts away from lower-cost producers outside the area to higher-cost producers within the area.

3. Preferential trading may bring longer-term advantages of increased economies of scale (both internal and external), improved terms of trade from increased bargaining power with the rest of the world, increased efficiency from greater competition between member countries and a more rapid spread of technology. On the other hand, it can lead to increased regional problems for members, greater oligopolistic collusion and various diseconomies of scale. There may also be large costs of administering the system.

4. There have been several attempts around the world to form preferential trading systems.

13.6 THE EUROPEAN UNION

What have been the effects of the creation of a 'single market' in the EU?

The European Economic Community (EEC) was formed by the signing of the Treaty of Rome in 1957 and came into operation on 1 January 1958.

The original six member countries of the EEC (Belgium, France, Italy, Luxembourg, Netherlands and West Germany) had already made a move towards integration with the formation of the European Coal and Steel Community in 1952. This had removed all restrictions on trade in coal, steel and iron ore between the six countries. The aim had been to gain economies of scale and allow more effective competition with the USA and other foreign producers.

The EEC extended this principle and aimed eventually to be a full common market with completely free trade between members in all products, and with completely free movement of labour, enterprise and capital.

All internal tariffs between the six members had been abolished and common external tariffs established by 1968. But this still only made the EEC a *customs union*, since a number of restrictions on internal trade remained (legal, administrative, fiscal, etc.). Nevertheless the aim was eventually to create a full common market.

In 1973 the UK, Denmark and Ireland became members. Greece joined in 1981, Spain and Portugal in 1986, and Sweden, Austria and Finland in 1995, Then in May 2004 a further 10 countries joined: Cyprus, the Czech Republic, Estonia, Hungary, Latvia, Lithuania, Malta, Poland, Slovakia and Slovenia. Bulgaria and Romania joined in 2007. With the accession of Croatia in July 2013, the European Union now has 28 members.

From customs union to common market

The EU is clearly a customs union. It has common external tariffs and no internal tariffs. But is it also a common market? For many years there have been *certain* common economic policies.

Common Agricultural Policy (CAP). The Union has traditionally set common high prices for farm products. This has involved charging variable import duties to bring foreign food imports up to EU prices and intervention to buy up surpluses of food produced within the EU at these above-equilibrium prices (see Box 3.5 on page 70). Although the main method of support has shifted to providing subsidies (or 'income support') unrelated to current output, this still represents a common economic policy of agricultural support.

Regional policy. EU regional policy provides grants to firms and local authorities in relatively deprived regions of the Union.

Competition policy. EU policy here has applied primarily to companies operating in more than one member state. For example, Article 101 of the Lisbon Treaty prohibits agreements between firms operating in more than one EU country (e.g. over pricing or sharing out markets) which adversely affect competition (see Case Studies 5.16 and 5.18 in MyEconLab).

Harmonisation of taxation. VAT is the standard form of indirect tax throughout the EU. There are, however, substantial differences in VAT rates between member states, as there are with other tax rates (see Box 13.5).

Social policy. In 1989 the European Commission presented a *Social Charter* to the EU heads of state. This spelt out a series of worker and social rights that should apply in all member states (see Case Study 13.11 in MyEconLab). These rights were grouped under 12 headings covering areas such as the guarantee of decent levels of income for both the employed and the non-employed, freedom of movement of labour between EU countries, freedom to belong to a trade union and equal treatment of women and men in the labour market. The Social Charter was only a recommendation and each element had to be approved separately by the European Council of Ministers.

The Social Chapter of the Maastricht Treaty (1991) attempted to move the Community forward in implementing the details of the Social Charter in areas such as maximum hours, minimum working conditions, health and safety protection, information and consultation of workers, and equal opportunities.

The UK Conservative government refused to sign this part of the Maastricht Treaty. It maintained that such measures would increase costs of production and would, therefore, make EU goods less competitive in world trade and increase unemployment. Critics of the UK position argued that the refusal to adopt minimum working conditions (and also a minimum wage rate) would help to make the UK the 'cheap labour sweat-shop' of Europe. One of the first acts of the incoming Labour government in 1997 was to sign up to the Social Chapter.

Despite these various common policies, in other respects the Community of the 1970s and 1980s was far from a true common market: there were all sorts of non-tariff barriers such as high taxes on wine by non-wine-producing countries, special regulations designed to favour domestic producers, governments giving contracts to domestic producers (e.g. for defence equipment), and so on. The Single European Act of 1986, however, sought to remove these barriers and to form a genuine common market by the end of 1992 (see Box 13.5).

The benefits and costs of the single market

It is difficult to quantify the benefits and costs of the single market, given that many occur over a long period, and that it is difficult to know to what extent the changes that are taking place are the direct result of the single market.

In 2012, the European Commission published *20 Years of the European Single Market*. This stated that, 'EU27 GDP in 2008 was 2.13 per cent or €233 billion higher than it would have been if the Single Market had not been launched in 1992. In 2008 alone, this amounted to an average of €500 extra in income per person in the EU27. The gains come from the Single Market programme, liberalisation in network industries such as energy and telecommunication, and the enlargement of the EU to 27 member countries.'

Even though the precise magnitude of the benefits is difficult to estimate, it is possible to identify the *types* of benefit that have resulted, many of which have been substantial.

BOX 13.5   **FEATURES OF THE SINGLE MARKET**

Since 1 January 1993 trade within the EU has operated very much like trade within a country. In theory, there should be no more difficulty for a firm in Birmingham to sell its goods in Paris than in London. At the same time, the single market allows free movement of labour and involves the use of common technical standards.

The features of the single market are summed up in two European Commission publications:[3]

- Elimination of border controls on goods within the EU: no more long waits.
- Free movement of people across borders.
- Common security arrangements.
- No import taxes on goods bought in other member states for personal use.
- The right for everyone to live in another member state.
- Recognition of vocational qualifications in other member states: engineers, accountants, medical practitioners, teachers and other professionals able to practise throughout Europe.
- Technical standards brought into line, and product tests and certification agreed across the whole EU.
- Common commercial laws – making it attractive to form Europe-wide companies and to start joint ventures.
- Public contracts to supply equipment and services to state organisations now open to tenders across the EU.

So what does the single market mean for individuals and for businesses?

Individuals

Before 1993, if you were travelling in Europe, you had a 'duty-free allowance'. This meant that you could only take goods up to the value of €600 across borders within the EU without having to pay VAT in the country into which you were importing them. Now you can take as many goods as you like from one EU country to another, provided they are for your own consumption. But to prevent fraud, member states may ask for evidence that the goods have been purchased for the traveller's own consumption if they exceed specified amounts.

Individuals have the right to live and work in any other member state. Qualifications obtained in one member state must be recognised by other member states.

Firms

Before 1993 all goods traded in the EU were subject to VAT at every internal border. This involved some 60 million customs clearance documents resulting in a cost of some €70 per consignment.[4]

This has all now disappeared. Goods can cross from one member state to another without any border controls: in fact, the concepts of 'importing' and 'exporting' within the EU no longer officially exist. All goods sent from one EU country to another will be charged VAT only in the country of destination. They are exempt from VAT in the country where they are produced.

One of the important requirements for fair competition in the single market is the convergence of tax rates. Although income tax rates, corporate tax rates and excise duties still differ between member states, there has been some narrowing in the range of VAT rates. Higher rates of VAT on luxury goods were abolished and countries are allowed to have no more than two lower rates of at least 5 per cent on 'socially necessary' goods, such as food and water supply.

There is now a lower limit of 15 per cent on the standard rate of VAT. Standard rates in January 2015 nonetheless varied from 17 per cent in Luxembourg to 27 per cent in Hungary. During the early 2010s several countries, including the UK, Ireland, Greece, Italy, Hungary and Portugal, increased their standard rate of VAT as a means of reducing their budget deficits (see Section 12.1). One effect of this has been that the vast majority of EU countries now have a standard rate of VAT between 19 and 25 per cent.

 In what ways would competition be 'unfair' if VAT rates differed widely between member states?

---

[3] *A Single Market for Goods* (Commission of the European Communities, 1993); *10 Key Points about the Single European Market* (Commission of the European Communities, 1992).

[4] See *A Single Market for Goods* (Commission of the European Communities, 1993).

KI 36
p 369

Trade creation. Costs and prices have fallen as a result of a greater exploitation of comparative advantage. Member countries can now specialise further in those goods and services that they can produce at a comparatively low opportunity cost.

Reduction in the direct costs of barriers. This category includes administrative costs, border delays and technical regulations. Their abolition or harmonisation has led to substantial cost savings.

Economies of scale. With industries based on a Europe-wide scale, many firms can now be large enough, and their plants large enough, to gain the full potential economies of scale (see Box 4.5 on page 88). Yet the whole European market

is large enough for there still to be adequate competition. Such gains have varied from industry to industry, depending on the minimum efficient scale of a plant or firm. Economies of scale have also been gained from mergers and other forms of industrial restructuring.

Greater competition. Increased competition between firms has led to lower costs, lower prices and a wider range of products available to consumers. This has been particularly so in newly liberalised service sectors such as transport, financial services, telecommunications and broadcasting. In the long run, greater competition can stimulate greater innovation, the greater flow of technical information and the rationalisation of production.

KI 18
p 108

Despite these gains, the single market has not received a universal welcome within the EU. Its critics argue that, in a Europe of oligopolies, unequal ownership of resources, rapidly changing technologies and industrial practices, and factor immobility, the removal of internal barriers to trade has merely exaggerated the problems of inequality and economic power. More specifically, the following criticisms are made.

Radical economic change is costly. Substantial economic change is necessary to achieve the full economies of scale and efficiency gains from a single European market. These changes necessarily involve redundancies – from bankruptcies, takeovers, rationalisation and the introduction of new technology. The severity of this 'structural' and 'technological' unemployment (see Section 11.3) depends on (a) the pace of economic change and (b) the mobility of labour – both occupational and geographical. Clearly, the more integrated markets become across the EU, the less the costs of future change.

Adverse regional effects. Firms are likely to locate as near as possible to the 'centre of gravity' of their markets and sources of supply. If, before barriers are removed, a firm's prime market was the UK, it might well have located in the Midlands or the north of England. If, however, with barriers now removed, its market has become Europe as a whole, it may choose to locate in the south of England or in France, Germany or the Benelux countries instead. The creation of a single European market thus tends to attract capital and jobs away from the edges of the Union and towards its geographical centre.

In an ideal market situation, areas like Cornwall, the south of Italy or Portugal should attract resources from other parts of the Union. Being relatively depressed areas, wage rates and land prices are lower. The resulting lower industrial costs should encourage firms to move into the areas. In practice, however, as capital and labour (and especially young and skilled workers) leave the extremities of the Union, so these regions are likely to become more depressed. If, as a result, their infrastructure is neglected, they then become even less attractive to new investment.

The development of monopoly/oligopoly power. The free movement of capital can encourage the development of giant 'Euro-firms' with substantial economic power. Indeed, recent years have seen some very large European mergers (see Case Study 5.19 in MyEconLab). This can lead to higher, not lower prices, and less choice for the consumer. It all depends on just how effective competition is, and how effective EU competition policy is in preventing monopolistic and collusive practices.

Trade diversion. Just as increased trade creation has been a potential advantage of completing the internal market, so trade diversion has been a possibility too. This is more likely if *external* barriers remain high (or are even increased) and internal barriers are *completely* abolished.

Perhaps the biggest objection raised against the single European market is a political one: the loss of national sovereignty. Governments find it much more difficult to intervene at a microeconomic level in their own economies.

Completing the internal market

Despite the reduction in barriers in the 1990s, the internal market is still not 'complete'. In other words, various barriers to trade between member states still remain.

To monitor progress an 'Internal Market Scoreboard' was established in 1997. This is published every six months and shows progress towards the total abandonment of any forms of internal trade restrictions (Case Study 13.13 in MyEconLab). It shows the percentage of EU Single Market Directives still to be transposed into national law. In addition to giving each country's 'transposition deficit', the Scoreboard identifies the number of infringements of the internal market that have taken place. The hope is that the 'naming and shaming' of countries will encourage them to make more rapid progress towards totally free trade within the EU.

In 1997, the average transposition deficit of member countries was 6.3 per cent. By 1999, this had fallen to 3.5 per cent. An average deficit target of 1 per cent was set in 2007 and this was reached by 2008. Data for 2014 show the average transposition deficit at just 0.7 per cent.

Nevertheless, national governments have continued to introduce *new* technical standards, several of which have had the effect of erecting new barriers to trade. Also, infringements of single market rules by governments have not always been dealt with. The net result is that, although trade is much freer today than in the early 1990s, especially given the transparency of pricing with the euro, there still exist various barriers, especially to the free movement of goods.

To counteract new barriers, the EU periodically issues new Directives. If this process is more rapid than that of the transposition of existing Directives into national law, the transposition deficit increases.

The effect of the new member states

Given the very different nature of the economies of many of the new entrants to the EU, and their lower levels of GDP per head, the potential for gain from membership has been substantial. The gains come through trade creation, increased competition, technological transfer and inward investment, both from other EU countries and from outside the EU.

A study in 2004[5] concluded that Poland's GDP would rise by 3.4 per cent and Hungary's by almost 7 per cent.

---

[5] M. Maliszewska, *Benefits of the Single Market expansion for current and new member states* (Centrum Analiz Społeczno-Ekonomicznych, 2004).

Real wages would rise, with those of unskilled workers rising faster than those of skilled workers, in accordance with these countries' comparative advantage. There would also

> **Pause for thought**
>
> *Why may the new members of the EU have the most to gain from the single market, but also the most to lose?*

be benefits for the 15 pre-2004 members from increased trade and investment, but these would be relatively minor in comparison to the gains to the new members.

In future years, now that the euro is used by at least 19 of the member states, with the possibility of others joining at some time, trade within the EU is likely to continue to grow as a proportion of GDP. We examine the benefits and costs of the single currency and the whole process of economic and monetary union in the EU in Section 14.6.

Recap

1. The European Union is a customs union, in that it has common external tariffs and no internal ones. But virtually from the outset it has also had elements of a common market, particularly in the areas of agricultural policy, regional policy, competition policy, and to some extent in the areas of tax harmonisation and social policy.

2. Nevertheless, there were substantial non-tariff barriers to trade within the EU. The Single European Act of 1986 sought to sweep away these restrictions and to establish a genuine free market within the EU: to establish a full common market. Benefits from completing the internal market have included trade creation, cost savings from no longer having to administer barriers, economies of scale for firms now able to operate on a Europe-wide scale, and greater competition leading to reduced costs and prices, greater flows of technical information and more innovation.

3. Critics of the single market point to the costs of radical changes in industrial structure, the attraction of capital away from the periphery of the EU to its geographical centre, possible problems of market power with the development of giant 'Euro-firms', and the possibilities of trade diversion.

4. The actual costs and benefits of EU membership to the various countries vary with their particular economic circumstances. These costs and benefits in the future will depend on just how completely the barriers to trade are removed, on the extent of monetary union and on the effects of enlarging the Union.

13.7 TRADE AND DEVELOPING COUNTRIES

The importance of international trade to developing countries

The role of international trade is one of the most contentious for developing countries. Should they adopt an open trading policy with few if any barriers to imports? Should they go further and actively promote trade by subsidising their export sector? Or should they restrict trade and pursue a policy of greater self-sufficiency? These are issues we shall be examining in this section.

Whether it is desirable that developing countries should adopt policies of more trade or less, trade is still vital. Certain raw materials, capital equipment and intermediate products that are necessary for development can be obtained only from abroad. Others *could* be produced domestically but only at much higher cost.

The relationship between trade and development

What makes the issue of trade so contentious is the absence of a simple relationship between trade and development. Instead, the relationship is complex and determined by a series of interactions between variables affecting both trade

and development. Furthermore, while some countries have managed to use trade as an engine for economic growth and wider human development, others, despite trade liberalisation, have seen relatively little improvement in either their export performance or human development.

In constructing a trade and development index, the UN[6] identified three broad groups of influences or dimensions which interact and affect a country's trade and development performance. Within these broad groups are various indicators which themselves interact. We consider briefly these three dimensions and some of the indicators within each dimension.

Structural and institutional dimension

Human capital. This relates to the skills and expertise of the workforce which affect a country's performance and its productivity (see Section 9.6). Education and health are key

---

[6] *Developing countries in international trade 2005: Trade and development index* (United Nations, 2005).

influences here. As well as affecting the economic growth of a country, higher educational attainment and better health conditions positively impact on social and human development.

Physical infrastructure. Infrastructure affects a country's productive capacity and so its potential output. Poor transport infrastructure, for example, is thought to be a major impediment on a country's export performance.

Financial environment. Credit is important to producers and consumers alike in helping to finance both short-term and longer-term commitments. For instance, it enables firms to finance day-to-day operational purchases but also longer-term investments in fixed assets such as buildings and machinery.

Institutional quality. This relates to issues of governance not just of firms themselves, but also of institutions, largely governmental.

Environment sustainability. The argument here is that excessive activity, particularly at the early stages of development, can result in environmental degradation. This can adversely affect human development and, in turn, economic development.

Trade policies and process dimension

Openness to trade. In the absence of market failures and externalities, trade liberalisation is argued to be a driver of development. However, there can be significant human costs in the transition process.

Effective access to foreign markets. The success of a country's export performance is crucially dependent on its access to markets. Barriers to access include tariffs and non-tariff barriers, such as regulatory standards in the markets of recipient countries. A wider definition of 'effective' access recognises other factors too. These might include the size of foreign markets, transport links, the characteristics of the goods being exported – for example, how differentiated they are – as well as the cost of the exported goods.

Levels of development dimension

The third series of factors affecting both trade and human development relate to existing levels of development. We can think of the relevant development issues here as encompassing three components: economic development, social development and gender development.

Trade strategies

Despite the complexity of the relationship between trade and development, countries' policies towards trade typically go through various stages as they develop.

Primary outward-looking stage. Traditionally, developing countries have exported primaries – minerals such as copper, cash crops such as coffee, and non-foodstuffs such as cotton – in exchange for manufactured consumer goods. Having little in the way of an industrial base, if they want to consume manufactured goods, they have to import them.

Secondary inward-looking stage. In seeking rapid economic development, most developing countries drew lessons from the experience of the advanced countries. The main conclusion was that industrialisation was the key to economic success.

But industrialisation required foreign exchange to purchase capital equipment. This led to a policy of **import-substituting industrialisation**, which involved cutting back on non-essential imports and thereby releasing foreign exchange. Tariffs and other restrictions were imposed on those imports for which a domestic substitute existed or which were regarded as unimportant.

Secondary outward-looking stage. Once an industry had satisfied domestic demand, it had to seek markets abroad if expansion was to continue. What is more, as we shall see, import substitution brought a number of serious problems for developing countries. The answer seemed to be to look outward again, this time to the export of manufactured goods. Many of the most economically successful developing countries (especially Hong Kong, Singapore, South Korea, Taiwan and, more recently, China, India and Indonesia) have owed their high growth rates to a rapid expansion of manufactured exports.

We will now examine the three stages in more detail.

Approach 1: Exporting primaries – exploiting comparative advantage

The justification for exporting primaries

Despite moves towards import substitution and secondary export promotion, many developing countries still rely heavily on primary exports. Three major arguments have traditionally been used for pursuing a policy of exporting primaries. In each case the arguments have also been used to justify a policy of free or virtually free trade.

Exporting primaries exploits comparative advantage. Traditional trade theory implies that countries should specialise in producing those items in which they have a comparative advantage: i.e. those goods that can be produced

KI 36
p 369

> ### Definition
>
> **Import-substituting industrialisation (ISI)** A strategy of restricting imports of manufactured goods and using the foreign exchange saved to build up domestic industries.

at relatively low opportunity costs. For most developing countries this means that a large proportion of their exports should be primaries.

Exporting primaries provides a 'vent for surplus'. Trade offers a vent for surplus: i.e. a means of putting to use resources that would otherwise not be used. These surpluses occur where the domestic market is simply not big enough to consume all the available output of a particular good. There is far too little demand within Zambia to consume its potential output of copper. The same applies to Namibian uranium and Peruvian tin.

Exporting primaries provides an 'engine for economic growth'. According to this argument, developing countries benefit from the growth of the economies of the developed world. As industrial expansion takes place in the rich North, this creates additional demand for primaries from the poor South. In more recent years, the rapid growth in China, India and other industrialising developing countries has seen a rapid growth in demand for commodities, many produced in the least developed countries. This has driven up commodity prices and benefited primary exporters (see Figure 13.6).

Traditional trade theory in the context of development

There are several reasons for questioning whether the above arguments justify a policy of relying on primary exports as the means to development.

Comparative costs change over time. Over time, with the acquisition of new skills and an increase in the capital stock, a developing country that once had a comparative advantage in primaries may find that it now has a comparative advantage in certain *manufactured* products, especially those which are more labour intensive and use raw materials of which the country has a plentiful supply. The market, however, cannot necessarily be relied upon to bring about a smooth transition to producing such products.

Concentrating on primary production may hinder growth. A country may gain in the short run by exporting primaries and using the money earned to buy imports. But the production of certain primaries may have little potential for expansion and thus growth may be slower.

The benefits from trade may not accrue to the nationals of the country. If a mine or plantation is owned by a foreign company, it will be the foreign shareholders who get the profits from the sale of exports. In addition, these companies may bring in their own capital and skilled labour from abroad. The benefits gained by the local people will probably be confined to the additional wages they earn. With these companies being in a position of monopsony power, these wages are often very low.

Trade may lead to greater inequality. Trade shifts income distribution in favour of those factors of production employed intensively in the export sector. If exports are labour-intensive, greater equality will tend to result. But if they are land- or raw-material-intensive then trade will redistribute income in favour of large landowners or mine owners.

Exporting primary exports may involve external costs. Mining can lead to huge external costs, such as the despoiling of the countryside and damage to the health of miners. Mines and plantations can lead to the destruction of traditional communities and their values.

These arguments cast doubt on whether a policy of relying on free trade in primary exports is the best way of achieving economic development. Various trends in the international economy have also worked against primary exporters.

Problems for primary exporters: long term

Long-term trends in international trade have caused problems for primary exporting countries in a number of ways.

Low income elasticity of demand for certain primary products. As world incomes grow, so a smaller proportion of these incomes is spent on primaries. But why? Since food is a necessity of life, consumers, especially in rich countries, already consume virtually all they require. A rise in incomes, therefore, tends to be spent more on luxury goods and services, and only slightly more on basic foodstuffs.

Agricultural protection in advanced countries. Faced with the problem of a slowly growing demand for food produced by their own farmers, advanced countries increasingly imposed restrictions on imported food. Reducing these restrictions has been one of the main aims of the Doha Development Agenda (the latest round of WTO trade negotiations: see Box 13.4).

Technological developments. Synthetic substitutes have in many cases replaced primaries in the making of consumer durables (such as furniture and household appliances), clothing and industrial equipment. Also, the process of miniaturisation, as microchips have replaced machines, has meant that less and less raw material has been required to produce any given amount of output.

Rapid growth in imports. There tends to be a high income elasticity of demand for imported manufactures. This is the result partly of the better-off in developing countries increasingly being able to afford luxury goods, and partly of the development of new tastes as people are exposed to the products of the developed world – products such as Coca-Cola, Levi jeans, mobile phones and iPods. In fact, the whole process has been dubbed 'Coca-Colanisation'.

The terms of trade. Between 1980 and 2000 the prices of many primary products declined. For instance, the nominal price index in 2000 for beverages (coffee and tea) was only one-third of its level in the late 1970s – and even less than that in real terms. This reflected the slow growth in demand for primaries and led to a decline in the terms of trade for primary exporters. This is because they were having to export more and more in order to buy any given quantity of imports, such as manufactured goods.

As Figure 13.6 shows, a quite different picture emerged in the 2000s. As the demand for food and raw materials grew rapidly, reflecting the rapid growth of China and various other emerging economies, so primary commodity prices rose sharply.

This was to come to an abrupt halt with the world recession of 2008/9, when primary product prices fell sharply. But the resumption of global growth saw primary commodity prices climb once more and in the case of many agricultural commodities to levels considerably higher than before the world recession. But then, with a slowing in global growth, commodity prices fell, so that by January 2015 the aggregate commodity price index had returned to the level before the financial crisis. Nevertheless, it was more than 120 per cent higher than in January 2000 (in nominal terms).

Approach 2: Import-substituting industrialisation (ISI)

Dissatisfaction with relying on primary exporting led most developing countries to embark on a process of

industrialisation. The newly industrialised countries (NICs), such as China, Malaysia, Brazil and India, are already well advanced along the industrialisation road. Other developing countries have not yet progressed very far, especially the poorest African countries.

The most obvious way for countries to industrialise was to cut back on the import of manufactures and substitute them with home-produced manufactures. This could not be done overnight: it had to be done in stages, beginning with assembly, then making some of the components, and finally making all, or nearly all, of the inputs into production. Most developing countries have at least started on the first stage. Several of the more advanced developing countries have component manufacturing industries. Only a few of the larger NICs, such as China, India and Brazil, have built extensive capital goods industries.

The method most favoured by policy makers was **tariff escalation**. Here tariff rates (or other restrictions) increased as one moves from the raw materials to the

Definition

Tariff escalation The system whereby tariff rates increase the closer a product is to the finished stage of production.

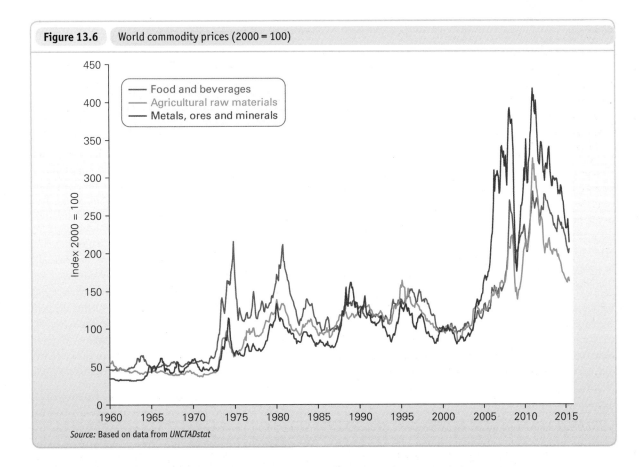

Figure 13.6 World commodity prices (2000 = 100)

Source: Based on data from *UNCTADstat*

intermediate product to the finished product stage. Thus finished goods had higher tariffs than intermediate products. This encouraged assembly plants, which were protected by high tariffs from imported finished products, and were able to obtain components at a lower tariff rate.

One of the problems with ISI was that countries were desperately short of resources to invest in industry. As a result, a policy of ISI usually involved encouraging investment by multinational companies. But even without specific 'perks' (e.g. tax concessions, cheap sites, the cutting of red tape), multinationals would still probably be attracted by the protection afforded by the tariffs or quotas.

Adverse effects of import substitution

Some countries, such as South Korea and Taiwan, pursued an inward-looking ISI policy for only a few years. For them it was merely a stage in development, rapidly to be followed by a secondary outward-looking policy. Infant industries were initially given protection, but when they had achieved sufficient economies of scale, the barriers to imports were gradually removed.

The countries that continued to pursue protectionist ISI policies generally had a poorer growth record. They also tended to suffer from other problems, such as a deepening of inequality. The development of the modern industrial sector was often to the detriment of the traditional sectors and also of the export sector.

The criticisms of ISI are numerous, and include the following.

KI 36 **p 369** *It ran directly counter to the principle of comparative advantage.* Rather than confining ISI to genuine infant industries and then gradually removing the protection, ISI was applied indiscriminately to a whole range of industries. Countries found themselves producing goods in which they had a comparative *disadvantage*.

KI 17 **p 101** *It cushioned inefficient practices and encouraged the establishment of monopolies.* Without the competition from imports, many of the industries were highly inefficient and wasteful of resources. What is more, in all but the largest or most developed of the developing countries the domestic market for manufactures is small. If a newly established industry is to be large enough to gain the full potential economies of scale, it must be large relative to the market. This means that it will have considerable monopoly power.

It involved artificially low real interest rates. In order to encourage capital investment in the import-substituting industries, governments often intervened to keep interest rates low. This encouraged the use of capital-intensive technology with a consequent lack of jobs. It also starved other sectors (such as agriculture) of much needed finance, and discouraged saving.

It led to urban wages above the market-clearing level. Wage rates in the industrial sector, although still low compared with advanced countries, are often considerably higher than in the traditional sectors.

- They are pushed up by firms seeking to retain labour in which they have invested training.
- Governments, seeking to appease the politically powerful urban industrial working class, have often passed minimum wage laws.
- Trade unions, although less widespread in developing than in advanced countries, are mainly confined to the new industries.

Higher industrial wages again encourage firms to use capital-intensive techniques.

It involved overvalued exchange rates. Restricting imports tends to lead to an appreciation of the exchange rate. This makes non-restricted imports cheaper, which then discourages the production of domestic goods, such as food and component parts, which compete with those imports. Also, a higher exchange rate discourages exports. Exports tend to be priced in dollars. If the exchange rate appreciates, domestic currency will buy more dollars; or put another way, a dollar will exchange for less domestic currency. Thus exporters will earn less domestic currency as the exchange rate appreciates.

It did not necessarily save on foreign exchange. Many of the new industries were highly dependent on the importation of raw materials, capital equipment and component parts. These imported inputs, unlike foreign finished goods, were often supplied by a single firm, which could thus charge monopoly prices. What is more, a large proportion of the extra incomes generated by these industries tended to be spent on imports by the new urban elites.

Protection was not applied evenly. Many different tariff rates were used in one country: in fact, a policy of tariff escalation demands this. In addition, governments often used a whole range of other protectionist instruments – such as the licensing of importers, physical and value quotas and foreign exchange rationing. These were often applied in a haphazard way. The result was that protection was highly uneven.

Income distribution was made less equal. Additional incomes generated by the modern sector tended to be spent on modern-sector goods and imported goods. Thus there was a multiplier effect *within* the modern sector, but virtually none between the modern sector and the traditional sectors. Also, as we saw above, an overvalued exchange rate leads to a bias against agriculture and thus further deepens the divide between rich and poor. Finally, the relatively high wages of the modern sector encourage workers to migrate to the towns, where many, failing to get a job, live in dire poverty. **KI 22** **p 159**

Social, cultural and environmental problems. A policy of ISI often involves imposing an alien set of values. Urban life can be harsh, competitive and materialistic. Moreover, the drive for industrialisation may involve major costs to the **KI 26** **p 168** environment, as a result of waste products from new industries, often with low environmental standards.

Finally, import substitution is necessarily limited by the size of the domestic market. Once that is saturated, ISI can come to an abrupt halt. At that stage, further expansion can only come from exporting; but if these industries have been overprotected, they are less able to compete successfully in world markets.

Approach 3: Exporting manufactures – a possible way forward?

In Box 13.2 we observed the significant expansion of global exports in manufactures, with the annual rate of growth in export volumes since 1950 being just under 7.5 per cent. The countries with the highest rates of economic growth have been those that have successfully made the transition to being exporters of manufactures. Table 13.2 gives some examples.

The transition from inward-looking to outward-looking industrialisation

How is a country to move from import substituting to being outward looking? One approach is to take it industry by industry. When an industry has saturated the home market and there is no further scope for import substitution, it should then be encouraged to seek markets overseas. The trouble with this approach is that if the country is still protecting other industries, there will probably still be an overvalued exchange rate. Thus specific subsidies, tax concessions or other 'perks' would have to be given to this industry to enable it to compete. The country would still be

highly interventionist, with all the distortions and misallocation of resources this tends to bring.

The alternative is to wean the whole economy off protection. Three major things will need doing:

- A devaluation of the currency (see Section 14.4) in order to restore the potential profitability of the export sector.
- A dismantling of the various protective measures that had biased production towards the home market.
- A removal, or at least a relaxing, of price controls.

But these are things that cannot be done 'at a stroke'. Firms may have to be introduced gradually to the greater forces of competition that an outward-looking trade policy brings. Otherwise there may be massive bankruptcies and a corresponding massive rise in unemployment.

The benefits from a secondary outward-looking policy

The advocates of outward-looking industrialisation make a number of points in its favour.

It conforms more closely to comparative advantage. Countries pursuing an open trade regime will be able to export only those goods in which they have a comparative advantage. The resources used in earning a unit of foreign exchange from exports will be less than those used in saving a unit of foreign exchange by replacing imports with home-produced goods. In other words, resources will be used more efficiently.

Economies of scale. If the home market is too small to allow a firm to gain all the potential economies of scale, these can be gained by expanding into the export market.

Table 13.2	Growth rates and export performance of selected secondary outward-looking countries			
	Average 1985–2013			2013
	Annual growth in real GDP (%)	Annual growth in real GNY per capita (%)	Annual growth rate of exports (%)	Share of manufactures in merchandise exports (%)
Brazil	3.0	1.6	6.0	49.8
China	9.9	8.9	14.0	81.1
Hong Kong	4.5	3.5	7.7	90.5
India	6.3	4.5	11.8	70.1
Malaysia	5.8	3.4	8.3	65.3
Singapore	6.4	4.0	9.7	76.2
South Korea	6.2	5.4	11.8	90.9
Low- and middle-income economies	4.8	3.1	7.4	61.4
High-income economies	2.4	1.8	5.3	73.7
World	2.9	1.4	5.8	70.9

Source: Data drawn from *World Development Indicators* (World Bank, 2015)

BOX 13.6 THE CHINESE 'ECONOMIC MIRACLE'

Riding the dragon

'China is amazing. It is capitalism, but at an unprecedented speed.' 'The talent of Chinese software engineers is unbelievable. I can't believe how effective they are.' (Bill Gates, Chairman, Microsoft)

'If your business isn't making money in China, it probably wouldn't make money anywhere else.' (Carlos Ghosn, President, Nissan Motor Company)[7]

On the basis of several indicators, China's economic performance is extraordinary. From 1990 to 2015 annual economic growth averaged 9.7 per cent. Its exports grew by an average of 15.9 per cent (see chart). In 2009 it overtook Germany to become the world's largest exporter.

Then in 2014 China overtook the USA to become the world's largest economy when measured in purchasing power parity (PPP) terms (i.e. after adjusting for differences in the average price of goods between countries, which are not accurately reflected in exchange rates). China is still a developing country, however. In terms of *per capita* GDP, China was only the 85th richest economy in 2014.

As China's economy and exports have boomed, so foreign investment has flooded into the country. In 1990 annual foreign direct investment (FDI) into China was $3.5 billion. By 2013 the figure had risen to $123.9 billion or 8.5 per cent of global FDI flows.

Chinese export-orientated growth has been based on three key factors: specialising in goods in which it has a comparative advantage; having an economy that is favourable to both domestic and inward investment; and having an exchange rate that is undervalued in PPP terms.

Specialisation

China has been industrialising rapidly. With the huge size of the domestic market and with an open policy towards exporting, China has specialised in goods that exploit its diverse but relatively well-trained labour force. Huge industrial complexes have sprung up along the coast, from where it is easy to export.

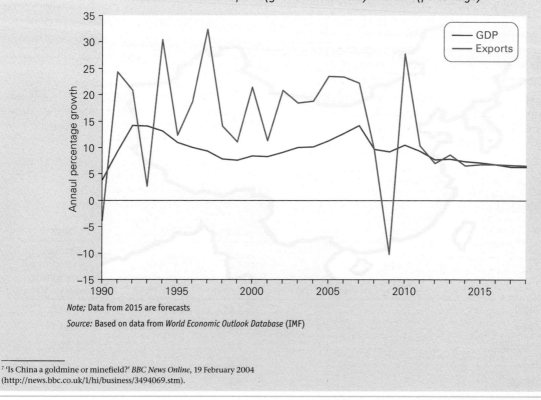

Growth in Chinese exports (goods and services) and GDP (percentage)

Note; Data from 2015 are forecasts

Source: Based on data from *World Economic Outlook Database* (IMF)

---

[7] 'Is China a goldmine or minefield?' *BBC News Online*, 19 February 2004 (http://news.bbc.co.uk/1/hi/business/3494069.stm).

KI 18 p 108 *Increased competition.* By having to compete with foreign companies, exporters will be under a greater competitive pressure than industries sheltering behind protective barriers. This will encourage (a) resource saving in the short run through reductions in inefficiency, and (b) innovation and investment, as firms attempt to adopt the latest technology, often obtained from developed countries.

Increased investment. To the extent that outward-looking policies lead to a greater potential for economic growth,

Chinese firms have adapted to changing world markets and to their own changing comparative advantage. Twenty years ago, textiles and clothing were China's main export industries. These relatively labour-intensive industries were ideally suited to exploit the abilities of China's abundant labour. Today textiles and clothing account for a sixth of China's exports. Electronic goods, by contrast, account for more than a third and are growing at a rate three times as fast as textiles. Electronic goods exploit China's increasingly well-trained and well-educated workforce.

Investment

But why are foreign investors attracted to China? Is it simply that the economy is growing rapidly? Clearly that is part of the attraction, but it is more than that. For a start, the Chinese economy is huge. With a population of 1.4 billion and a GDP close to $11.3 trillion in 2015 (which, in real terms, is expected to have risen to around $16 trillion by the end of the 2010s), China represents a massive potential market. The government has also invested heavily in improving the country's transport, power and communications infrastructure.

What is more, much of the growth in income in the Chinese economy is concentrated in the hands of the middle class, which now constitutes over 20 per cent of the population and 50 per cent of the urban population. The demand for consumer goods by these middle-class Chinese is very income elastic. As a result, sales of electrical goods, furniture, cars and fashion clothing are growing rapidly. Not only foreign manufacturers, but foreign retailers too are taking advantage of this. For example, Wal-Mart entered China in 1996 and by 2014 had over 400 stores, largely sourcing its merchandise from local suppliers. Carrefour, the French supermarket chain, entered China in 1995 and by 2014 had 230 stores.

But foreign investors are attracted not only by the growing domestic Chinese market. They are also attracted by the opportunity to manufacture high-tech products with a highly skilled workforce.

More and more companies become cutting edge and leapfrog foreign rivals. Whether games consoles, DVD recorders or flat-screen monitors, Chinese factories are grabbing high-tech market share.

'Ten years ago, China was about low cost,' says Infineon's Ulrich Schumacher. 'Now it is at the forefront of technical development. Infineon can develop twice as fast in China as anywhere else.'

'Engineers are working in three shifts, seven days a week,' enthuses Mr Schumacher. 'In Germany that would not be possible: there, engineers don't work on weekends.'

Bill Gates is similarly impressed after his latest visit to Microsoft's research lab in Beijing, one of four in China

and Hong Kong. 'The talent of the people there is unbelievable, I can't believe how effective they are,' he says.

All this is worrying news for high-tech workers in industrialised countries, who hoped their skills would give them a competitive advantage in the globalised economy.[8]

An undervalued exchange rate

Despite the booming economy and export sector, and a massive current account surplus against the USA ($162 billion in 2004), the Chinese yuan remained pegged to the US dollar at $1 = 8.28 yuan from 1995 to 2005. This undervaluation of the yuan against the dollar was a major contributing factor in the growth in Chinese exports.

The situation had become even more extreme with other countries. With the fall in the dollar in 2003–4 against the euro, yen and sterling, the dollar-pegged yuan thus also fell against these currencies. This made Chinese exports even cheaper in Europe and east Asia, further fuelling the trade imbalance.

The USA for some time had been pressing for a revaluation of the yuan or a floating of the yuan so that it could appreciate. Indeed, in 2005 the US Senate was pushing the Bush administration to adopt a 27.5 per cent tariff on all Chinese imports unless China revalued its currency.

In 2005 China eventually moved to a pegged exchange rate with a basket of 11 currencies, each currency being weighted in the basket by the amount of trade with China. It also revalued the yuan by 2.1 per cent.

By January 2015 the yuan–dollar exchange rate was $1 = 6.25 yuan, while the yuan's effective exchange rate was nearly 40 per cent higher than in July 2005. Nonetheless, it was still considerably undervalued in PPP terms, giving China a strong competitive edge against other developing countries seeking export-led growth. The effect has been a huge current account surplus, which peaked at 10.1 per cent of GDP in 2007. Since then it has fallen and during the first half of the 2010s averaged close to 2.4 per cent of GDP.

The surplus has resulted in massive Chinese purchases of dollars and other currencies. By the middle of 2014 China had amassed nearly $4 trillion in foreign exchange reserves. The inflows have also allowed China to purchase stakes in many American and European companies and to make substantial investments in various developing countries.

1. *In what ways does a booming Chinese economy benefit the rest of the world?*
2. *Why may the Chinese be reluctant to adopt a freely floating exchange rate?*

[8] Ibid.

they may attract more foreign capital. To the extent that they involve an increase in interest rates, they will tend to encourage saving. To the extent that they lead to increased incomes, additional saving will be generated, especially given that the *marginal* propensity to save may be quite

high. The extra savings can be used to finance extra investment.

It can lead to more employment and a more equal distribution of income. The manufactured goods in which a country has a comparative advantage will be those produced by labour-intensive techniques (since wage rates are comparatively low in developing countries). Export expansion will thus increase the demand for labour relative to capital and thus create more employment. The increased demand for labour will tend to lead to a rise in wages relative to profits.

It removes many of the costs associated with ISI. Under a policy of ISI, managers may spend a lot of their time lobbying politicians and officials, seeking licences (and sometimes paying bribes to obtain them), adhering to norms and regulations or trying to find ways around them. If an outward-looking policy involves removing all this, managers can turn their attention to producing goods more efficiently.

Drawbacks of an export-orientated industrialisation strategy

The export of manufactures is seen by many developed countries as very threatening to their own industries. Their response has often been to erect trade barriers. These barriers have tended to be highest in the very industries (such as textiles, footwear and processed food) where developing countries have the greatest comparative advantage. Even if the barriers are *currently* low, developing countries may feel that it is too risky to expand their exports of these products for fear of a future rise in barriers. Recognising this problem, the WTO is very keen to ensure fair access for developing countries to the markets of the rich world (see Box 13.4).

The successes of developing countries such as China, India and Malaysia in exporting manufactures do not imply that other developing countries will have similar success. As additional developing countries attempt to export their manufactures, they will be facing more and more competition from each other.

Another problem is that, if a more open trade policy involves removing or reducing exchange and capital controls, the country may become more vulnerable to speculative attack. This was one of the major factors contributing to the east Asian crisis of the late 1990s. Gripped by currency and stock market speculation, and by banking and company insolvency, many countries of the region found that economic growth had turned into a major recession. The 'miracle' seemed to be over. Nevertheless, the countries with the least distortions fared the best during the crisis. Thus Singapore and Taiwan, which are open and relatively flexible, experienced only a slowdown, rather than a recession.

Exporting manufactures can be a very risky strategy for developing countries. Perhaps the best hope for the future lies in a growth in manufacturing trade *between* developing countries. That way they can gain the benefits of specialisation and economies of scale that trade brings, while at the same time producing for a growing market. The feasibility of this approach depends on whether developing countries can agree to free-trade areas or even customs unions (see Section 13.5). There does, however, seem to be a strong movement in this direction.

Pause for thought

Why may small developing countries have more to gain than large ones from a policy of becoming exporters of manufactured products?

Recap

1. Trade is of vital importance for the vast majority of developing countries, and yet most developing countries suffer from chronic balance of trade deficits.

2. Developing countries have traditionally been primary exporters. This has allowed them to exploit their comparative advantage in labour-intensive goods and has provided a market for certain goods that would otherwise have no market at home.

3. There are reasons for questioning the wisdom of relying on traditional primary exports, however. With a low world income elasticity of demand for many primary products, with the development of synthetic substitutes for minerals and with the protection of agriculture in developed countries, the demand for primary exports from the developing world has grown only slowly. At the same time, the demand for manufactured imports into developing countries has grown rapidly. Until recently, the result was a decline in the terms of trade. The rapid growth in demand for primary products from China and India has, to some extent, reversed this trend and the terms of trade have improved for many primary exporters.

4. Import-substituting industrialisation (ISI) was seen to be the answer to the problems of primary exporting. ISI was normally achieved in stages, beginning with the finished goods stage and then working back towards the capital goods stage. ISI, it was hoped, would allow countries to benefit from the various long-term advantages associated with manufacturing.

5. For many countries, however, ISI brought as many problems, if not more, than it solved. It often led to the establishment of inefficient industries, protected from foreign competition and facing little or no competition at home either. It led to considerable market distortions, with tariffs and other forms of protection haphazardly applied; to overvalued exchange rates, with a resulting bias against exports and the agricultural sector generally; to a deepening of inequalities and to large-scale social problems as the cities expanded, as poverty and unemployment grew and as traditional values were undermined; to increased dependency on imported inputs; and to growing environmental problems.

6. The most rapidly growing of the developing countries are those that have pursued a policy of export-orientated industrialisation. This has allowed them to achieve the benefits of economies of scale and foreign competition, and to specialise in goods in which they have a comparative advantage (i.e. labour-intensive goods) and yet which have a relatively high income

elasticity of demand. Whether countries that have pursued ISI can successfully turn to an open, export-orientated approach will depend to a large extent on the degree of competition they face not only from advanced countries but also from other developing countries.

QUESTIONS

1. How might the interdependence of economies through trade affect an economy's business cycle? Could other forms of interdependence also affect an economy's business cycle?

2. Referring to Table 13.1 (page 369), show how each country could gain from trade if the LDC could produce (before trade) 3 wheat for 1 cloth and the developed country could produce (before trade) 2 wheat for 5 cloth, and if the exchange ratio (with trade) was 1 wheat for 2 cloth. Would they both still gain if the exchange ratio was (a) 1 wheat for 1 cloth and (b) 1 wheat for 3 cloth?

3. Imagine that two countries, Richland and Poorland, can produce just two goods, computers and coal. Assume that for a given amount of land and capital, the output of these two products requires the following constant amounts of labour:

	Richland	Poorland
1 computer	2	4
100 tonnes of coal	4	5

Assume that each country has 20 million workers.

a. If there is no trade, and in each country 12 million workers produce computers and 8 million workers produce coal, how many computers and tonnes of coal will each country produce? What will be the total production of each product?

b. What is the opportunity cost of a computer in (i) Richland; (ii) Poorland?

c. What is the opportunity cost of 100 tonnes of coal in (i) Richland; (ii) Poorland?

d. Which country has a comparative advantage in which product?

e. Assuming that price equals marginal cost, which of the following would represent possible exchange ratios: (i) 1 computer for 40 tonnes of coal; (ii) 2 computers for 140 tonnes of coal; (iii) 1 computer for 100 tonnes of coal; (iv) 1 computer for 60 tonnes of coal; (v) 4 computers for 360 tonnes of coal?

f. Assume that trade now takes place and that 1 computer exchanges for 65 tonnes of coal. Both countries specialise completely in the product in which they have a comparative advantage. How much does each country produce of its respective product?

g. The country producing computers sells 6 million domestically. How many does it export to the other country?

h. How much coal does the other country consume?

4. Why doesn't the USA specialise as much as General Motors or Texaco? Why doesn't the UK specialise as much as Unilever? Is the answer to these questions similar to the answer to the questions, 'Why doesn't the USA specialise as much as Luxembourg?' and 'Why doesn't Unilever specialise as much as the local florist?'

5. To what extent are the arguments for countries specialising and then trading with each other the same as those for individuals specialising in doing the jobs to which they are relatively well suited?

6. The following are four items that are traded internationally: wheat; computers; textiles; insurance. In which one of the four is each of the following most likely to have a comparative advantage: India; the UK; Canada; Japan? Give reasons for your answer.

7. Would it be possible for a country with a comparative disadvantage in a given product at *pre*-trade levels of output to obtain a comparative advantage in it by specialising in its production and exporting it?

8. Go through each of the arguments for restricting trade and provide a counter-argument for not restricting trade.

9. It is often argued that if the market fails to develop infant industries, then this is an argument for government intervention, but not necessarily in the form of restricting imports. What *other* ways could infant industries be given government support?

10. How would you set about judging whether an industry had a genuine case for infant industry protection?

11. Does the consumer in the importing country gain or lose from dumping? (Consider both the short run and the long run.)

12. What is fallacious about the following two arguments? Is there any truth in either?

a. 'Imports should be reduced because money is going abroad which would be better spent at home.'

b. 'We should protect our industries from being undercut by imports produced using cheap labour.'

13. Make out a case for restricting trade between the UK and Japan. Are there any arguments here that could not equally apply to a case for restricting trade between Scotland and England or between Liverpool and Manchester?

14. In what ways may free trade result in harmful environmental effects? Is the best solution to these problems to impose restrictions on trade?

15. If countries are so keen to reduce the barriers to trade, why do many countries frequently attempt to erect barriers?

16. What factors will determine whether a country's joining a customs union will lead to trade creation or trade diversion?

17. How would you set about assessing whether or not a country had made a net dynamic gain by joining a customs union? What sort of evidence would you look for?

18. What would be the economic effects of (a) different rates of VAT; (b) different rates of personal income tax; (c) different rates of company taxation between member states, if in all other respects there were no barriers to trade or factor movements between the members of a customs union?

19. Is trade diversion in the EU more likely or less likely in the following cases?

a. European producers gain monopoly power in world trade.

b. Modern developments in technology and communications reduce the differences in production costs associated with different locations.

c. The development of the internal market produces substantial economies of scale in many industries.

20. Why is it difficult to estimate the magnitude of the benefits of completing the internal market of the EU?

21. Look through the costs and benefits that we identified from the single European market. Do the same costs and benefits arise from a substantially enlarged EU?

22. If there have been clear benefits from the single market programme, why do individual member governments still try to erect barriers, such as new technical standards?

23. If a developing country has a comparative advantage in primary products, should the government allow market forces to dictate the pattern of trade?

24. Why will a high exchange rate harm the agricultural sector in a developing country?

25. In what ways may free trade have harmful cultural effects on a developing country?

26. If a developing country has a comparative advantage in the production of wheat, should it specialise as much as possible in the production of wheat and export what is not consumed domestically?

27. What are the advantages and disadvantages for a developing country of pursuing a policy of ISI?

28. Will the production of labour-intensive manufactures for export lead to more or less inequality in a developing country?

29. Would the use of import controls help or hinder a policy of export-orientated industrialisation?

30. Should all developing countries aim over the long term to become *exporters* of manufactured products?

MyEconLab

This book can be supported by MyEconLab, which contains a range of additional resources, including an online homework and tutorial system designed to test and build your understanding.

You need both an access card and a course ID to access MyEconLab:

1. Is your lecturer using MyEconLab? Ask your lecturer for your course ID.

2. Has an access card been included with the book at a reduced cost? Check the inside back cover of the book.

3. If you have a course ID but no access card, go to: http://www.myeconlab.com/ to buy access to this interactive study programme.

ADDITIONAL CASE STUDIES IN THE *ESSENTIALS OF ECONOMICS* MyEconLab (www.pearsoned.co.uk/sloman)

13.1 David Ricardo and the law of comparative advantage. The first clear statement of the law of comparative advantage (in 1817).

13.2 Fallacious arguments for restricting trade. Some of the more common mistaken arguments for protection.

13.3 Strategic trade theory. The case of Airbus is used to illustrate the arguments that trade restrictions can be to the strategic advantage of countries in developing certain industries and preventing the establishment of foreign monopolies.

13.4 The Uruguay Round. An examination of the negotiations that led to substantial cuts in trade barriers.

13.5 The World Trade Organization. This looks at the various opportunities and threats posed by this major international organisation.

13.6 Steel barriers. This case considers the US administration's imposition of tariffs on imported steel in 2002, and the reactions of other countries to these tariffs.

13.7 The Battle of Seattle. This looks at the protests against the WTO at Seattle in November 1999 and considers the arguments for and against the free-trade policies of the WTO.

13.8 Banana, banana. The dispute between the USA and the EU over banana imports.

13.9 Assessing NAFTA. Who are the winners and losers from NAFTA?

13.10 Free trade and the environment. Do whales, the rainforests and the atmosphere gain from free-trade?

13.11 The social dimension of the EU. The principles of the Social Charter.

13.12 The benefits of the single market. Evidence of achievements and the Single Market Action Plan of 1997.

13.13 The Internal Market Scoreboard. Keeping a tally on progress to a true single market.

13.14 Multinational corporations and developing economies. Do MNCs benefit developing economies?

WEB APPENDICES

13.1 The gains from trade. This appendix uses general equilibrium analysis (see Web Appendix 7.1) to analyse the gains from trade and the limits to specialisation under increasing opportunity costs.

13.2 Exploiting market power in world trade. A graphical analysis of the effects of a country having monopoly power in the export market or monopsony power in the import market.

13.3 Trade creation and trade diversion. A graphical analysis of the welfare gains and losses from joining a customs union.

day's rates   We buy   We sel

	We buy	We sel
EURO	1.28__	1.__04
USA	1.77__	__920
AUSTRALIA	2.00__	1.7892
TURKEY	3.65__	3.1968
THAILAND	59.5440	47.8915
HONG KONG	14.2542	11.7390
DENMARK	9.8041	8.4503
CANADA	1.9061	1.6867

14 Chapter

Balance of payments and exchange rates

In this chapter we will first explain what is meant by the balance of payments. In doing so we will see just how the various monetary transactions between the domestic economy and the rest of the world are recorded.

Then (in Sections 14.2 and 14.3) we will examine how rates of exchange are determined, and how they are related to the balance of payments. We will see what causes exchange rate fluctuations, and how the government can attempt to prevent these fluctuations.

A government could decide to leave its country's exchange rates entirely to market forces (a free-floating exchange rate). Alternatively, it could attempt to fix its currency's exchange rate to some other currency (e.g. the US dollar). Or it could simply try to reduce the degree to which its currency fluctuates. In Section 14.4, we look at the relative merits of different degrees of government intervention in the foreign exchange market: of different 'exchange rate regimes'.

We then turn to look at attempts to achieve greater currency stability between the members of the EU. Section 14.5 looks at the European exchange rate mechanism, which sought in the 1980s and 1990s to limit the amount that member currencies were allowed to fluctuate against each other. Then Section 14.6 examines the euro. Has the adoption of a single currency by 17 EU countries been of benefit to them? How have members sought to tackle the debt problems of some of the member states?

Finally, as with Chapter 13, we look at the position of developing countries, and this time focus on the issue of debt. Why are so many developing countries facing severe debt problems and what can be done about it?

After studying this chapter, you should be able to answer the following questions:

- What is meant by 'the balance of payments' and how do trade and financial movements affect it?
- How are exchange rates determined and what effects do changes in the exchange rate have on the economy?
- How do governments and/or central banks seek to influence the exchange rate and what are the advantages and disadvantages of such intervention?
- What are the advantages and disadvantages of the euro for member countries? What threats to the stability of the euro arise from the debt and deficit problems of some member states? What can be done to achieve economic growth while tackling these debt problems?
- What are the origins of the severe debt problem faced by many developing countries? What has been done about the problem and what more needs to be done?

14.1 THE BALANCE OF PAYMENTS ACCOUNT

What is meant by a balance of payments deficit or surplus?

In Chapter 8 we identified balance of payments deficits as one of the main macroeconomic problems that governments face. But what precisely do we mean by 'balance of payments deficits' (or surpluses), and what is their significance?

A country's balance of payments account records all the flows of money between residents of that country and the rest of the world. *Receipts* of money from abroad are regarded as credits and are entered in the accounts with a positive sign. *Outflows* of money from the country are regarded as debits and are entered with a negative sign.

There are three main parts of the balance of payments account: the *current account*, the *capital account* and the *financial account*. Each part is then subdivided. We shall look at each part in turn, and take the UK as an example. Table 14.1 gives a summary of the UK balance of payments for 2014, while also providing an historical perspective.

The current account

The **current account** records payments for imports and exports of goods and services, plus incomes flowing into

and out of the country, plus net transfers of money into and out of the country. It is normally divided into four subdivisions.

The trade in goods account. This records imports and exports of physical goods (previously known as 'visibles'). Exports result in an inflow of money and are therefore a credit item. Imports result in an outflow of money and are therefore a debit item. The balance of these is called the **balance on trade in goods or balance of visible trade or merchandise balance**. A *surplus* is when exports exceed imports. A deficit is when imports exceed exports.

The trade in services account. This records imports and exports of services (such as transport, tourism and insurance). Thus the purchase of a foreign holiday would be a debit, since it represents an outflow of money, whereas the purchase by an overseas resident of a UK insurance policy would be a credit to the UK services account. The balance of these is called the **services balance**.

The balance of both the goods and services accounts together is known as the **balance on trade in goods and services** or simply the **balance of trade**.

We can relate the balance of trade to our circular flow of income model in Chapter 8. A balance of trade deficit, which as Table 14.1 shows has been the norm in the UK for some time, represents a net leakage from the circular flow because imports (a withdrawal) are greater than exports (an injection). Conversely, a balance of trade surplus is a net injection for an economy.

In equilibrium, injections must equal withdrawals. Thus a net withdrawal on the balance of trade must be offset by a net injection elsewhere: either investment exceeding saving and/or government expenditure exceeding tax revenue. This is why we often see countries with trade deficits

Table 14.1	UK balance of payments		
	2014		**Average 1987–2014 as % of GDP**
	£m	**% of GDP**	
CURRENT ACCOUNT			
Balance on trade in goods	−119 605	−6.7	−4.1
Balance on trade in services	85 863	4.8	2.5
Balance of trade	**−33 742**	**−1.9**	**−1.6**
Income balance	−38 754	−2.2	0.2
Net current transfers	−25 421	−1.4	−0.9
Current account balance	**−97 920**	**−5.5**	**−2.3**
CAPITAL ACCOUNT			
Capital account balance	**625**	**0.0**	**0.0**
FINANCIAL ACCOUNT			
Net direct investment	80 143	4.5	−0.9
Portfolio investment balance	102 363	5.7	1.7
Other investment balance	−96 828	−5.4	1.4
Balance of financial derivatives	14 890	0.8	−0.1
Reserve assets	−7 113	−0.4	−0.2
Financial account balance	**93 455**	**5.2**	**1.9**
Net errors and omissions	**3 840**	**0.2**	**0.3**
Balance	*0*	*0*	*0*

Source: Balance of Payments, Quarter 4 and Annual 2014, (Office for National Statistics, 2015)

Definitions

Current account of the balance of payments The record of a country's imports and exports of goods and services, plus incomes and transfers of money to and from abroad.

Balance on trade in goods or balance of visible trade or merchandise balance Exports of goods minus imports of goods.

Services balance Exports of services minus imports of services.

Balance on trade in goods and services or balance of trade Exports of goods and services minus imports of goods and services.

running government budget deficits. The USA and the UK are two notable examples.

Countries which run both trade deficits and government budget deficits are said to experience *twin deficits*. A notable exception, however, is Japan which, since the early 1990s, has consistently seen budget deficits accompanied by trade surpluses. Case Study 14.1 in MyEconLab considers further the evidence for twin deficits (and surpluses).

> ### Pause for thought
>
> *Can countries run twin surpluses with both a budget surplus and a balance of trade surplus?*

Income flows. These consist of wages, interest and profits flowing into and out of the country. For example, dividends earned by a foreign resident from shares in a UK company would be an outflow of money (a debit item).

Current transfers of money. These include government contributions to and receipts from the EU and international organisations, and international transfers of money by private individuals and firms. Transfers out of the country are debits. Transfers into the country (e.g. money sent from Greece to a Greek student studying in the UK) would be a credit item.

The **current account balance** is the overall balance of all the above four subdivisions. A *current account surplus* is where credits exceed debits. A *current account deficit* is where debits exceed credits. Figure 14.1 shows the current account balance expressed as a percentage of GDP for a sample of countries. Since 1984, the UK has consistently experienced a current account deficit.

The capital account

The **capital account** records the flows of funds, into the country (credits) and out of the country (debits), associated with the acquisition or disposal of fixed assets (e.g. land or intangibles, such as patents and trademarks), the transfer of funds by migrants, the payment of grants by the government for overseas projects, debt forgiveness by the government and the receipt of money for capital projects (e.g. from the EU's Agricultural Guidance Fund).

> ### Definitions
>
> **Balance of payments on current account** The balance on trade in goods and services plus net income flows and current transfers.
>
> **Capital account of the balance of payments** The record of transfers of capital to and from abroad.

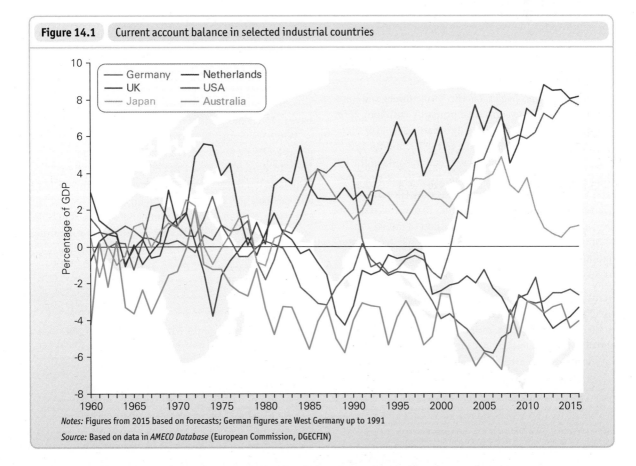

Figure 14.1 Current account balance in selected industrial countries

Notes: Figures from 2015 based on forecasts; German figures are West Germany up to 1991

Source: Based on data in *AMECO Database* (European Commission, DGECFIN)

As Table 14.1 shows, the balance on the capital account is small in comparison to that on the current and financial accounts.

The financial account[1]

The **financial account** of the balance of payments records cross-border changes in the holding of shares, property, bank deposits and loans, government securities, etc. In other words, unlike the current account, which is concerned with money incomes, the financial account is concerned with the purchase and sale of assets. Case Study 14.2 in MyEconLab considers some of the statistics behind the UK's financial account.

Direct investment. This involves a significant and lasting interest in a business in another country. If a foreign company invests money from abroad in one of its branches or associated companies in the UK, this represents an inflow of money when the investment is made and is thus a credit item. (Any subsequent profit from this investment that flows abroad will be recorded as an investment income outflow on the current account.) Investment abroad by UK companies represents an outflow of money when the investment is made. It is thus a debit item.

Note that what we are talking about here is the acquisition or sale of assets: e.g. a factory or farm, or the takeover of a whole firm, not the imports or exports of equipment.

Portfolio investment. This relates to transactions in debt and equity securities which do not result in the investor having any significant influence on the operations of a particular business. If a UK resident buys shares (equity securities) in an overseas company, this is an outflow of funds and is hence a debit item.

Other investment and financial flows. While direct and portfolio investments are concerned primarily with long-term investment, these consist primarily of various types of short-term monetary movement between the UK and the rest of the world. Deposits by overseas residents in banks in the UK and loans to the UK from abroad are credit items, since they represent an inflow of money. Deposits by UK residents in overseas banks and loans by UK banks to overseas residents are debit items. They represent an outflow of money.

Short-term monetary flows are common between international financial centres to take advantage of differences in countries' interest rates and changes in exchange rates.

In the financial account, credits and debits are recorded *net*. For example, UK investment abroad consists of the *net* acquisition of assets abroad: i.e. the purchase less the sale of assets abroad. Similarly, foreign investment in the UK consists of the purchase less the sale of UK assets by foreign residents. By

recording financial account items net, the flows seem misleadingly modest. For example, if UK residents deposited an extra £100bn in banks abroad but drew out £99bn, this would be recorded as a mere £1bn net outflow on the other investment and financial flows account. In fact, *total* financial account flows vastly exceed current plus capital account flows.

Pause for thought

Where would interest payments on short-term foreign deposits in UK banks be entered on the balance of payments account?

Flows to and from the reserves. The UK, like all other countries, holds reserves of gold and foreign currencies. From time to time the Bank of England (acting as the government's agent) will sell some of these reserves to purchase sterling on the foreign exchange market. It does this normally as a means of supporting the rate of exchange (see below). Drawing on reserves represents a *credit* item in the balance of payments accounts: money drawn from the reserves represents an *inflow* to the balance of payments (albeit an outflow from the reserves account). The reserves can thus be used to support a deficit elsewhere in the balance of payments.

Conversely, if there is a surplus elsewhere in the balance of payments, the Bank of England can use it to build up the reserves. Building up the reserves counts as a debit item in the balance of payments, since it represents an outflow from it (to the reserves).

When all the components of the balance of payments account are taken together, the balance of payments should exactly balance: credits should equal debits. As we shall see below, if they were not equal, the rate of exchange would have to adjust until they were, or the government would have to intervene to make them equal.

When the statistics are compiled, however, a number of errors are likely to occur. As a result there will not be a balance. To 'correct' for this, a **net errors and omissions item** is included in the accounts. This ensures that there will be an exact balance. The main reason for the errors is that the statistics are obtained from a number of sources, and there are often delays before items are recorded and sometimes omissions too.

Definitions

Financial account of the balance of payments The record of the flows of money into and out of the country for the purpose of investment or as deposits in banks and other financial institutions.

Net errors and omissions item A statistical adjustment to ensure that the two sides of the balance of payments account balance. It is necessary because of errors in compiling the statistics.

---

[1] Prior to October 1998 this account was called the 'capital account'. The account that is *now* called the capital account used to be included in the transfers section of the current account. This potentially confusing change of names was adopted in order to bring the UK accounts in line with the system used by the International Monetary Fund (IMF), the EU and most individual countries.

Figure 14.2 UK balance of payments as a percentage of GDP

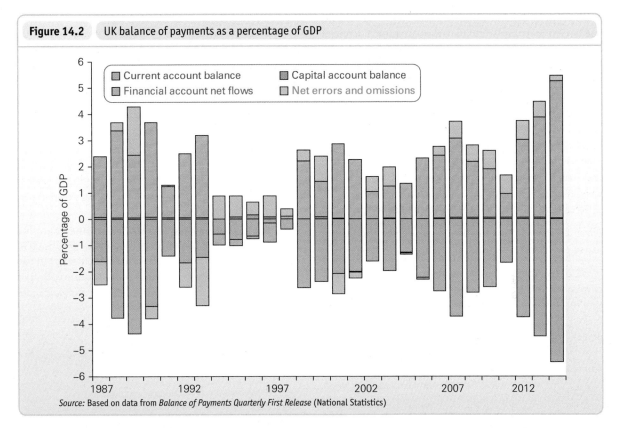

Source: Based on data from *Balance of Payments Quarterly First Release* (National Statistics)

Figure 14.2 graphically summarises the main accounts of the UK's balance payments: current, capital and financial accounts. It presents each as a percentage of national income (see also right-hand column of Table 14.1). In conjunction with the net errors and omissions item, which averages close to zero over the long run, we can see how the accounts combine to give a zero overall balance. For much of the period since the late 1980s, current account deficits have been offset by surpluses on the financial account. The persistence of the UK's current account deficit is discussed further in Case Study 14.3 in MyEconLab.

Recap

1. The balance of payments account records all payments to and receipts from foreign countries.
2. The current account records payments for the imports and exports of goods and services, plus incomes and transfers of money to and from abroad.
3. The capital account records all transfers of capital to and from abroad.
4. The financial account records inflows and outflows of money for investment and as deposits in banks and other financial institutions. These flows represent a transfer of assets rather than income earned. The financial account also includes dealings in the country's foreign exchange reserves.
5. The whole account must balance, but surpluses or deficits can be recorded on any specific part of the account. Thus the current account could be in deficit, but it would have to be matched by an equal and opposite capital plus financial account surplus.

14.2 EXCHANGE RATES

What causes exchange rates to change?

An exchange rate is the rate at which one currency trades for another on the foreign exchange market.

If you want to go abroad, you will need to exchange your pounds into euros, dollars, Swiss francs or whatever.

To do this you may go to a bank. The bank will quote you that day's exchange rates: for example, €1.35 to the pound, or $1.50 to the pound. It is similar for firms. If an importer wants to buy, say, some machinery from Japan, it will require yen to pay the Japanese supplier. It will thus ask the foreign exchange section of a bank to quote it a rate of exchange of the pound into yen. Similarly, if you want to buy some foreign stocks and shares, or if companies based in the UK want to invest abroad, sterling will have to be exchanged into the appropriate foreign currency.

Likewise, if Americans want to come on holiday to the UK or to buy UK assets, or American firms want to import UK goods or to invest in the UK, they will require sterling. They will be quoted an exchange rate for the pound in the USA: say, £1 = $1.50. This means that they will have to pay $1.50 to obtain £1 worth of UK goods or assets.

Exchange rates are quoted between each of the major currencies of the world. These exchange rates are constantly changing. Minute by minute, dealers in the foreign exchange dealing rooms of the banks are adjusting the rates of exchange. They charge commission when they exchange currencies. It is important for them, therefore, to ensure that they are not left with a large amount of any currency unsold. What they need to do is to balance the supply and demand of each currency: to balance the amount they purchase to the amount they sell. To do this they will need to adjust the price of each currency – namely, the exchange rate – in line with changes in supply and demand.

Not only are there day-to-day fluctuations in exchange rates, but also there are long-term changes in them. Figure 14.3 shows the average quarterly exchange rates between the pound and various currencies for selected years from 1985.

> **Pause for thought**
>
> *How did the pound 'fare' compared with the US dollar, Australian dollar and the yen from 1985 to 2009? What conclusions can be drawn about the relative movements of these three currencies?*

One of the problems in assessing what is happening to a particular currency is that its rate of exchange may rise against some currencies (weak currencies) and fall against others (strong currencies). In order to gain an overall picture of its fluctuations, therefore, it is best to look at a weighted average exchange rate against all other currencies. This is known as the **exchange rate index** or the **effective exchange rate**. The weight given to each currency in the index depends on the proportion of trade done with that country. Figure 14.3 also shows the sterling exchange rate index based on January 2005 = 100.

> **Definition**
>
> **Exchange rate index or effective exchange rate** A weighted average exchange rate expressed as an index, where the value of the index is 100 in a given base year. The weights of the different currencies in the index add up to 1.

Figure 14.3 Sterling exchange rates against selected currencies

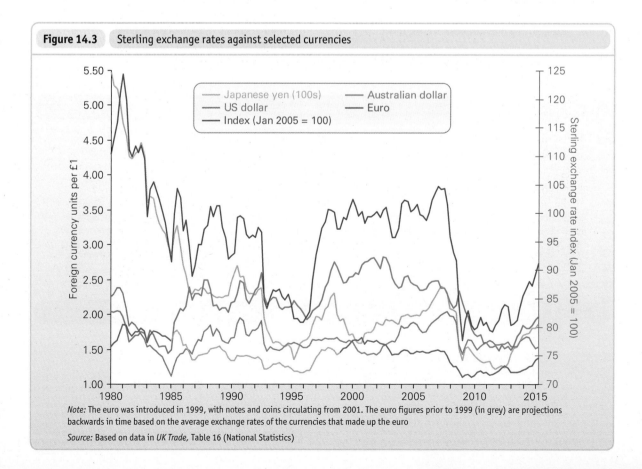

Note: The euro was introduced in 1999, with notes and coins circulating from 2001. The euro figures prior to 1999 (in grey) are projections backwards in time based on the average exchange rates of the currencies that made up the euro

Source: Based on data in *UK Trade*, Table 16 (National Statistics)

BOX 14.1 **NOMINAL AND REAL EXCHANGE RATES**   EXPLORING ECONOMICS

Searching for a real advantage

TC 14
p 227

We have seen on several occasions just how important the distinction between nominal and real is. But, what does this distinction mean when applied to exchange rates? A *nominal* bilateral exchange rate is simply the rate at which one currency exchanges for another. All exchange rates that you see quoted in the newspapers, on television or the Internet, or at travel agents, banks or airports, are nominal rates. Up to this point we have solely considered nominal rates.

The *real* exchange rate is the exchange rate index adjusted for changes in the prices of imports (measured in foreign currencies) and exports (measured in domestic prices): in other words, adjusted for the terms of trade. Thus if a country has a higher rate of inflation for its exports than the weighted average inflation of the imports it buys from other countries, its real exchange rate index (RERI) will rise relative to its nominal exchange rate index (NERI).

The real exchange rate index can be defined as:

$$\text{RERI} = \text{NERI} \times P_X/P_M$$

where P_X is the domestic currency price index of exports and P_M is the foreign currencies weighted price index of imports. Thus if (a) a country's inflation is 5 per cent higher than the trade-weighted average of its trading partners (P_X/P_M rises by 5 per cent per year) and (b) its nominal exchange rate depreciates by 5 per cent per year (NERI falls by 5 per cent per year), its real exchange rate index will stay the same.

Take another example: if a country's export prices rise faster than the foreign currency prices of its imports

(P_X/P_M rises), its real exchange rate will appreciate relative to its nominal exchange rate.

The real exchange rate thus gives us a better idea of the *quantity* of imports a country can obtain from selling a given quantity of exports. If the real exchange rate rises, the country can get more imports for a given volume of exports.

The chart shows the nominal and real exchange rate indices of sterling. As you can see, the real exchange rate has tended to rise over time relative to the nominal exchange rate. This is because the UK has typically had a higher rate of inflation than the weighted average of its trading partners.

The real exchange rate also gives a better idea than the nominal exchange rate of how competitive a country is. The lower the real exchange rate, the more competitive will the country's exports be. From the chart we can see that the UK became less competitive between 1996 and 2001, and remained at similarly uncompetitive levels until 2008, thanks not only to a rise in the nominal exchange rate index, but also to higher inflation than its trading partners. However, as the financial crisis of the late 2000s unfolded, sterling depreciated sharply. Between July 2007 and October 2009 the nominal and real exchange rate indices fell by 26 per cent and 23 per cent respectively.

?   *If differences in inflation rates were to be reflected in longer-term changes in real exchange rates, what pattern should we observe in real exchange rates? Is this supported by the data in the chart?*

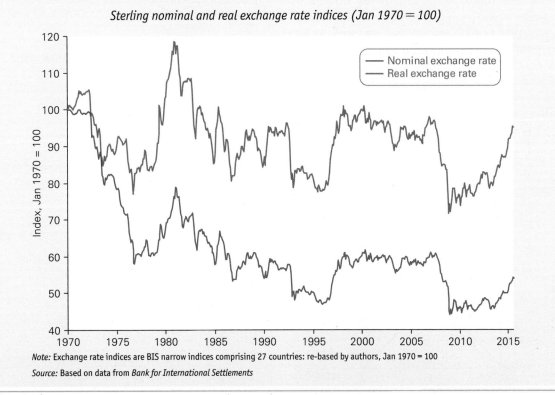

Sterling nominal and real exchange rate indices (Jan 1970 = 100)

Note: Exchange rate indices are BIS narrow indices comprising 27 countries: re-based by authors, Jan 1970 = 100

Source: Based on data from *Bank for International Settlements*

Determination of the rate of exchange in a free market

In a free foreign exchange market, the rate of exchange is determined by demand and supply. This is known as a **floating exchange rate**, and is illustrated in Figure 14.4.

For simplicity, assume that there are just two countries: the UK and the USA. When UK importers wish to buy goods from the USA, or when UK residents wish to invest in the USA, they *supply* pounds on the foreign exchange market in order to obtain dollars. In other words, they go to banks or other foreign exchange dealers to buy dollars in exchange for pounds. The higher the exchange rate, the more dollars they obtain for their pounds. This effectively makes US goods cheaper to buy, and investment more profitable. Thus the *higher* the exchange rate, the *more* pounds are supplied. The supply curve of pounds therefore typically slopes upwards.

When US residents wish to purchase UK goods or to invest in the UK, they *require* pounds. They *demand* pounds by selling dollars on the foreign exchange market. In other words, they go to banks or other foreign exchange dealers to buy pounds in exchange for dollars. The lower the dollar price of the pound (the exchange rate), the cheaper it is for them to obtain UK goods and assets, and hence the more pounds they are likely to demand. The demand curve for pounds, therefore, typically slopes downwards.

The equilibrium exchange rate is where the demand for pounds equals the supply. In Figure 14.4 this is at an exchange rate of £1 = $1.60. But what is the mechanism that equates demand and supply?

If the current exchange rate were above the equilibrium, the supply of pounds being offered to the banks would exceed the demand. For example, in Figure 14.4 if the exchange rate were $1.80, there would be an excess supply of pounds of $a - b$. Banks would not have enough dollars to exchange for all these pounds. But the banks make money by *exchanging* currency, not by holding on to it. They would thus lower the exchange rate in order to encourage a greater demand for

pounds and reduce the excessive supply. They would continue lowering the rate until demand equalled supply.

Similarly, if the rate were below the equilibrium, say at $1.40, there would be a shortage of pounds of $c - d$. The banks would find themselves with too few pounds to meet all the demand. At the same time they would have an excess supply of dollars. The banks would thus raise the exchange rate until demand equalled supply.

In practice, the process of reaching equilibrium is extremely rapid. The foreign exchange dealers in the banks are continually adjusting the rate as new customers make new demands for currencies. What is more, the banks have to watch closely what each other is doing. They are constantly in competition with each other and thus have to keep their rates in line. The dealers receive minute-by-minute updates on their computer screens of the rates being offered around the world.

Shifts in the currency demand and supply curves

Any shift in the currency demand or supply curves will cause the exchange rate to change. This is illustrated in Figure 14.5, but this time by considering the number of euros per £1. If the demand and supply curves shift from D_1 and S_1 to D_2 and S_2 respectively, the exchange rate will fall from €1.30 to €1.20. A fall in the exchange rate is called a **depreciation**. A rise in the exchange rate is called an **appreciation**.

> ### Definitions
>
> **Floating exchange rate** When the government does not intervene in the foreign exchange markets, but simply allows the exchange rate to be freely determined by demand and supply.
>
> **Depreciation** A fall in the free-market exchange rate of the domestic currency with foreign currencies.
>
> **Appreciation** A rise in the free-market exchange rate of the domestic currency with foreign currencies.

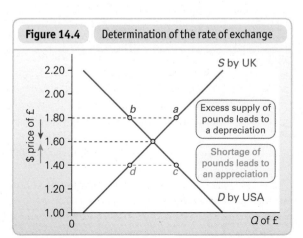

Figure 14.4 Determination of the rate of exchange

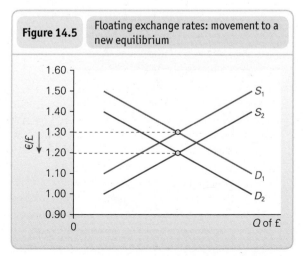

Figure 14.5 Floating exchange rates: movement to a new equilibrium

But why should the demand and supply curves shift? The following are the major possible causes of a depreciation:

■ *A fall in domestic interest rates.* UK rates would now be less competitive for savers and other depositors. More UK residents would be likely to deposit their money abroad (the supply of sterling would rise), and fewer people abroad would deposit their money in the UK (the demand for sterling would fall).

■ *Higher rates of inflation in the domestic economy than abroad.* UK exports will become less competitive. The demand for sterling will fall. At the same time, imports will become relatively cheaper for UK consumers. The supply of sterling will rise.

■ *A rise in domestic incomes relative to incomes abroad.* If UK incomes rise, the demand for imports, and hence the supply of sterling, will rise. If incomes in other countries fall, the demand for UK exports, and hence the demand for sterling, will fall.

■ *Relative investment prospects improving abroad.* If investment prospects become brighter abroad than in the UK, perhaps because of better incentives abroad, or because of worries about an impending recession in the UK, again the demand for sterling will fall and the supply of sterling will rise.

■ *Speculation that the exchange rate will fall.* If businesses involved in importing and exporting, and also banks and other foreign exchange dealers, think that the exchange rate is about to fall, they will sell pounds now before the rate does fall. The supply of sterling will thus rise.

> ### Pause for thought
>
> *Go through each of the above reasons for shifts in the demand for and supply of sterling and consider what would cause an appreciation of the pound.*

> ### Recap
>
> 1. The rate of exchange is the rate at which one currency exchanges for another. Rates of exchange are determined by demand and supply in the foreign exchange market. Demand for the domestic currency consists of all the credit items in the balance of payments account. Supply consists of all the debit items.
>
> 2. The exchange rate will depreciate (fall) if the demand for the domestic currency falls or the supply increases. These shifts can be caused by a fall in the domestic interest rates, higher inflation in the domestic economy than abroad, a rise in domestic incomes relative to incomes abroad, relative investment prospects improving abroad or the belief by speculators that the exchange rate will fall.
>
> 3. The opposite in each case would cause an appreciation (rise).

14.3 EXCHANGE RATES AND THE BALANCE OF PAYMENTS

How does the balance of payments affect the exchange rate?

Exchange rates and the balance of payments: no government or central bank intervention

KI 6
p 20

In a free foreign exchange market, the balance of payments will *automatically* balance. But why?

The credit side of the balance of payments constitutes the demand for sterling. For example, when people abroad buy UK exports or assets they demand sterling in order to pay for them. The debit side constitutes the supply of sterling. For example, when UK residents buy foreign goods or assets, the importers of them require foreign currency to pay for them. They thus supply pounds. A floating exchange rate ensures that the demand for pounds is equal to the supply. It thus also ensures that the credits on the balance of payments are equal to the debits: that the balance of payments balances.

This does not mean that each part of the balance of payments account separately balances, but simply that any current account deficit must be matched by a capital plus financial account surplus and vice versa.

For example, suppose initially that each part of the balance of payments *did* separately balance. Then let's assume that interest rates rise. This encourages larger short-term financial inflows as people abroad are attracted to deposit money in the UK: the demand for sterling would shift to the right (e.g. from D_2 to D_1 in Figure 14.5). It will also cause smaller short-term financial outflows as UK residents keep more of their money in the country: the supply of sterling shifts to the left (e.g. from S_2 to S_1 in Figure 14.5). The financial account will go into surplus. The exchange rate will appreciate.

As the exchange rate rises, this will cause imports to be cheaper and exports to be more expensive. The current account will move into deficit. There is a movement up along the new demand and supply curves until a new equilibrium

TC 6
p 37

BOX 14.2 | **DEALING IN FOREIGN CURRENCIES**

A daily juggling act

Imagine that a large car importer in the UK wants to import 5000 cars from Japan costing ¥15 billion. What does it do?

It will probably contact a number of banks' foreign exchange dealing rooms in London and ask them for exchange rate quotes. It thus puts all the banks in competition with each other. Each bank will want to get the business and thereby obtain the commission on the deal. To do this it must offer a higher rate than the other banks, since the higher the ¥/£ exchange rate, the more yen the firm will get for its money. (For an importer a rate of, say, ¥180 to £1 is better than a rate of, say, ¥150.)

Now it is highly unlikely that any of the banks will have a spare ¥15 billion. But a bank cannot say to the importer 'Sorry, you will have to wait before we can agree to sell them to you.' Instead the bank will offer a deal and then, if the firm agrees, the bank will have to set about obtaining the ¥15 billion. To do this it must offer the Japanese who are supplying yen the chance to obtain pounds at a sufficiently *low* ¥/£ exchange rate. (The lower the ¥/£

exchange rate, the fewer yen the Japanese will have to pay to obtain pounds.)

The banks' dealers thus find themselves in the delicate position of wanting to offer a *high* enough exchange rate to the car importer in order to gain its business, but a *low* enough exchange rate in order to obtain the required amount of yen. The dealers are thus constantly having to adjust the rates of exchange in order to balance the demand and supply of each currency.

In general, the more of any foreign currency that dealers are asked to supply (by being offered sterling), the lower will be the exchange rate they will offer. In other words, a higher supply of sterling pushes down the foreign currency price of sterling.

? *Assume that an American firm wants to import Scotch whisky from the UK. Describe how foreign exchange dealers will respond.*

---

is reached. At this point, any financial account surplus is matched by an equal current (plus capital) account deficit.

Exchange rates and the balance of payments: with government or central bank intervention

TC 5
p 23 The government or central bank may be unwilling to let the country's currency float freely. Frequent shifts in the demand and supply curves would cause frequent changes in the exchange rate. This, in turn, might cause uncertainty for businesses, which might curtail their trade and investment.

The central bank may thus intervene in the foreign exchange market. But what can it do? The answer to this depends on its objectives. It may simply want to reduce the day-to-day fluctuations in the exchange rate, or it may want to prevent longer-term, more fundamental shifts in the rate.

Reducing short-term fluctuations

Assume that the UK government believes that an exchange rate of €1.20 to the pound is approximately the long-term equilibrium rate. Short-term leftward shifts in the demand for sterling and rightward shifts in the supply, however, are causing the exchange rate to fall below this level (see Figure 14.5). What can the government do to keep the rate at €1.20?

Using reserves. The Bank of England can sell gold and foreign currencies from the reserves to buy pounds. This will shift the demand for sterling back to the right. However, with the growth of short-term international financial flows it is in practice very difficult for individual central banks to influence exchange rates significantly by buying and selling currencies. The combined actions of central banks might, however, be more successful.

Borrowing from abroad. In extreme circumstances, the government could negotiate a foreign currency loan from other countries or from an international agency such as the International Monetary Fund. It can then use these moneys to buy pounds on the foreign exchange market, thus again shifting the demand for sterling back to the right.

Raising interest rates. If the Bank of England raises interest rates, it will encourage people to deposit money in the UK and encourage UK residents to keep their money in the country. The demand for sterling will increase and the supply of sterling will decrease. However, the changes in interest rates necessary to manage the exchange rate may come into conflict with other economic objectives, such as keeping the rate of inflation on target.

Maintaining a fixed rate of exchange over the longer term

Governments may choose to maintain a fixed rate over a number of months or even years. The following are possible methods it can use to achieve this (we are assuming that there are downward pressures on the exchange rate: e.g. as a result of higher aggregate demand and higher inflation).

Contractionary policies. This is where the government deliberately curtails aggregate demand by either *fiscal policy* or *monetary policy* or both.

Contractionary fiscal policy involves raising taxes and/or reducing government expenditure. Contractionary monetary policy involves raising interest rates. Note that in this case we are talking about not just the temporary raising of interest rates to prevent a short-term outflow of money from the country, but the use of higher interest rates to reduce borrowing and hence dampen aggregate demand.

A reduction in aggregate demand works in two ways:

- It reduces the level of consumer spending. This directly cuts imports, since there will be reduced spending on Japanese electronics, German cars, Spanish holidays, and so on. The supply of sterling coming onto the foreign exchange market thus decreases.
- It reduces the rate of inflation. If inflation falls below that of other countries, this makes UK goods more competitive abroad, thus increasing the demand for sterling. It will also cut back on imports as UK consumers switch to the now more competitive home-produced goods. The supply of sterling falls.

Supply-side policies. This is where the government attempts to increase the long-term competitiveness of UK goods by encouraging reductions in the costs of production and/ or improvements in the quality of UK goods. For example,

the government may attempt to improve the quantity and quality of training and research and development (see Section 12.4).

Controls on imports and/or foreign exchange dealing. This is where the government restricts the outflow of money, either by restricting people's access to foreign exchange, or by the use of tariffs (customs duties) and quotas. For instance, the Icelandic government put in place controls on foreign currency exchanges in the aftermath of the collapse of its largest banks (see Box 13.1) in order to bolster the krona and to build up foreign reserves.

> ### Pause for thought
>
> *What problems might arise if the government were to adopt this third method of maintaining a fixed exchange rate?*

Recap

1. In a free foreign exchange market, the balance of payments will automatically balance, since changes in the exchange rate will balance the demand for the currency (credits on the balance of payments) with the supply (debits on the balance of payments).

2. There is no guarantee, however, that there will be a balance on each of the separate parts of the balance of payments account.

3. The government can attempt to prevent the rate of exchange falling by central bank purchases of the domestic currency in the foreign exchange market, either by selling foreign currency reserves or by using foreign loans. Alternatively, the government can raise interest rates. The reverse actions can be taken if it wants to prevent the rate from rising.

4. In the longer term, it can attempt to prevent the rate from falling by pursuing contractionary policies, protectionist policies or supply-side policies to increase the competitiveness of the country's exports.

14.4 FIXED VERSUS FLOATING EXCHANGE RATES

Should exchange rates be 'left to the market'?

Are exchange rates best left free to fluctuate and be determined purely by market forces, or should the government or central bank intervene to fix exchange rates, either rigidly or within bands? Unfortunately, the answer is not clear-cut. Both floating and fixed exchange rates have their advantages and disadvantages.

Advantages of fixed exchange rates

Surveys reveal that most businesspeople prefer relatively rigid exchange rates: if not totally fixed, then pegged for periods of time, or at least where fluctuations are kept to a minimum. The following arguments are used to justify this preference.

Certainty. With fixed exchange rates, international trade and investment become much less risky, since profits are not affected by movements in the exchange rate.

Assume that a firm correctly forecasts that its product will sell in the USA for $1.50. It costs 80p to produce. If the rate of exchange is fixed at £1 = $1.50, each unit will earn £1 and hence make a 20p profit. If, however, the rate of exchange were not fixed, exchange fluctuations could wipe out this profit. If, say, the rate appreciated to £1 = $2, and if units continued to sell for $1.50, they would now earn only 75p each, and hence make a 5p loss.

Little or no speculation. Provided the rate is *absolutely* fixed – and people believe that it will remain so – there is no point in speculating. For example, between 1999 and 2001, when the old currencies of the eurozone countries were still used, but were totally fixed to the euro, there was no speculation that the German mark, say, would change in value against the French franc or the Dutch guilder.

Prevents governments pursuing 'irresponsible' macroeconomic policies. If a government deliberately and excessively expands aggregate demand – perhaps in an attempt to gain short-term popularity with the electorate – the resulting balance of payments deficit will force it to constrain demand again (unless it resorts to import controls).

Governments cannot allow their economies to have a persistently higher inflation rate than competitor countries without running into balance of payments crises, and hence a depletion of reserves. Fixed rates thus force governments (in the absence of trade restrictions) to keep the domestic rate of inflation close to the world rate.

Disadvantages of fixed exchange rates

KI 29
p 177

Exchange rate policy may conflict with the interests of domestic business and the economy as a whole. A balance of payments deficit can occur even if the economy is not 'overheating'. For example, there can be a fall in the demand for the country's exports as a result of an external shock (such as a recession in other countries) or because of increased foreign competition. If protectionism is to be avoided, and if supply-side policies work only over the long run, the government will be forced to raise interest rates. This is likely to have two adverse effects on the domestic economy:

TC 15
p 248

■ Higher interest rates may discourage long-term business investment. This in turn will lower firms' profits in the long term and reduce the country's long-term rate of economic growth. The country's capacity to produce will be restricted and businesses are likely to fall behind in the competitive race with their international rivals to develop new products and improve existing ones.

■ Higher interest rates will have a dampening effect on the economy by making borrowing more expensive and thereby cutting back on both consumer demand and investment. This can result in a recession with rising unemployment.

The problem is that, with fixed exchange rates, domestic policy is entirely constrained by the balance of payments. Any attempt to reflate and cure unemployment will simply lead to a balance of payments deficit and thus force governments to deflate again.

TC 13
p 219

Competitive contractionary policies leading to world recession. If deficit countries pursued contractionary policies, but surplus countries pursued expansionary policies, there would be no overall world contraction or expansion. Countries may be quite happy, however, to run a balance of payments surplus and build up reserves. Countries may thus competitively deflate – all trying to achieve a balance of payments surplus. But this is beggar-my-neighbour policy. Not all countries can have a surplus! Overall the world must be in balance. The result of these policies is to lead to a general world recession and a restriction in growth.

Problems of international liquidity. If trade is to expand, there must be an expansion in the supply of currencies acceptable for world trade (dollars, euros, gold, etc.): there must be adequate **international liquidity**. Countries' reserves of these currencies must grow if they are to be sufficient to maintain a fixed rate at times of balance of payments disequilibrium. Conversely, there must not be excessive international liquidity, otherwise the extra demand that would result would lead to world inflation. It is important under fixed exchange rates, therefore, to avoid too much or too little international liquidity.

The problem is how to maintain adequate control of international liquidity. The supply of dollars, for example, depends largely on US policy, which may be dominated by its internal economic situation rather than by any concern for the well-being of the international community. Similarly, the supply of euros depends on the policy of the European Central Bank, which is governed by the internal situation in the eurozone countries.

Inability to adjust to shocks. With sticky prices and wage rates, there is no swift mechanism for dealing with sudden balance of payments crises – like that caused by a sudden increase in oil prices. In the short run, countries will need huge reserves or loan facilities to support their currencies. There may be insufficient international liquidity to permit this. In the longer run, countries may be forced into a depression by having to deflate. The alternative may be to resort to protectionism, or to abandon the fixed rate and **devalue**.

TC 12
p 202

Speculation. If speculators believe that a fixed rate simply cannot be maintained, speculation is likely to be massive. If, for example, there is a large balance of payments deficit, speculative selling will worsen the deficit and may itself force a devaluation. Speculation of this sort had disastrous effects on some south-east Asian currencies in 1997 (see Case Study 14.9 in MyEconLab) and on the Argentinean peso in 2002 (see Case Study 14.10).

TC 9
p 62

Advantages of a free-floating exchange rate

The advantages and disadvantages of free-floating rates are to a large extent the opposite of fixed rates.

Automatic correction. The government simply lets the exchange rate move freely to the equilibrium. In this way, balance of payments disequilibria are automatically and

KI 6
p 20

Definitions

International liquidity The supply of currencies in the world acceptable for financing international trade and investment.

Devaluation Where the government refixes the exchange rate at a lower level.

BOX 14.3 | **THE IMPORTANCE OF INTERNATIONAL FINANCIAL MOVEMENTS** | EXPLORING ECONOMICS

How a current account deficit can coincide with an appreciating exchange rate

Since the early 1970s most of the major economies of the world have operated with floating exchange rates. The opportunities that this gives for speculative gain have led to a huge increase in short-term international financial movements. Vast amounts of moneys transfer from country to country in search of higher interest rates or a currency that is likely to appreciate. This can have a bizarre effect on exchange rates.

If a country pursues an expansionary fiscal policy, the current account will tend to go into deficit as extra imports are 'sucked in'. What effect will this have on exchange rates? You might think that the answer is obvious: the higher demand for imports will create an extra supply of domestic currency on the foreign exchange market and hence drive down the exchange rate.

In fact the opposite is likely. The higher interest rates resulting from the higher domestic demand can lead to a massive inflow of short-term finance. The financial account can thus move sharply into surplus. This is likely to out-weigh the current account deficit and cause an *appreciation* of the exchange rate.

Exchange rate movements, especially in the short term, are largely brought about by changes on the financial rather than the current account.

? *Why do high international financial mobility and an absence of exchange controls severely limit a country's ability to choose its interest rate?*

---

instantaneously corrected without the need for specific government policies.

No problem of international liquidity and reserves. Since there is no central bank intervention in the foreign exchange market, there is no need to hold reserves. A currency is automatically convertible at the current market exchange rate.

Insulation from external economic events. A country is not tied to a possibly unacceptably high world inflation rate, as it could be under a fixed exchange rate. It is also to some extent protected against world economic fluctuations and shocks.

Governments are free to choose their domestic policy. Under a floating rate the government can choose whatever level of domestic demand it considers appropriate, and simply leave exchange rate movements to take care of any balance of payments effect. Similarly, the central bank can choose whatever rate of interest is necessary to meet domestic objectives, such as achieving a target rate of inflation. The exchange rate will simply adjust to the new rate of interest – a rise in interest rates causing an appreciation, a fall causing a depreciation. This freedom for the government and central bank is a major advantage, especially when the effectiveness of contractionary policies under fixed exchange rates is reduced by downward wage and price rigidity, and when competitive contractionary policies between countries may end up causing a world recession.

Disadvantages of a free-floating exchange rate

Despite these advantages there are still some potentially serious problems with free-floating exchange rates.

Unstable exchange rates. The less elastic are the demand and supply curves for the currency in Figure 14.5, the greater the change in exchange rate that will be necessary to restore

equilibrium following a shift in either demand or supply. In the long run, in a competitive world with domestic substitutes for imports and foreign substitutes for exports, demand and supply curves are relatively elastic. Nevertheless, in the short run, given that many firms have contracts with specific overseas suppliers or distributors, the demands for imports and exports are less elastic.

Speculation. Short-run instability can be lessened by stabilising speculation, thus making speculation advantageous. If, due to short-run inelasticity of demand, a deficit causes a very large depreciation, speculators will *buy* pounds, knowing that in the long run the exchange rate will appreciate again. Their action therefore helps to lessen the short-run fall in the exchange rate.

Nevertheless, in an uncertain world where there are few restrictions on currency speculation, where the fortunes and policies of governments can change rapidly, and where large amounts of short-term deposits are internationally 'footloose', speculation can be highly destabilising in the short run. Considerable exchange rate overshooting can occur.

An example of such overshooting occurred between July 2008 and March 2009 when the pound depreciated 14 per cent against the euro, 29 per cent against the US dollar, 35 per cent against the yen and the exchange rate index fell 17 per cent (see Figure 14.6). Speculators were predicting that interest rates in the UK would fall further than in other countries and stay lower for longer. This was because recession was likely to be deeper in the UK, with inflation undershooting the Bank of England's 2 per cent target and perhaps even becoming negative. But the fall in the exchange rate represented considerable overshooting and the exchange rate index rose 9 per cent between March and June 2009.

This is just one example of the violent swings in exchange rates that have occurred in recent years. They

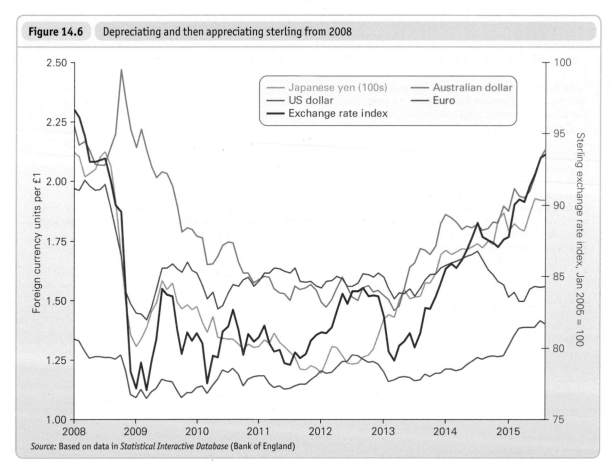

Figure 14.6 Depreciating and then appreciating sterling from 2008

Source: Based on data in *Statistical Interactive Database* (Bank of England)

even occur under managed floating exchange rate systems where governments have attempted to dampen such fluctuations!

The continuance of exchange rate fluctuations over a number of years is likely to encourage the growth of speculative holdings of currency. This can then cause even larger and more rapid swings in exchange rates.

Pause for thought

If speculators on average gain from their speculation, who loses?

KI 13
p 66 *Uncertainty for traders and investors.* The uncertainty caused by currency fluctuations can discourage international trade and investment. To some extent the problem can be overcome by using the **forward exchange**

Definition

Forward exchange market Where contracts are made today for the price at which a currency will be exchanged at some specified future date.

market. Here traders agree with a bank *today* the rate of exchange for some point in the future (say, six months' time). This allows traders to plan future purchases of imports or sales of exports at a known rate of exchange. Of course, banks charge for this service, since they are taking on the risks themselves of adverse exchange rate fluctuations.

But dealing in the futures market only takes care of short-run uncertainty. Banks will not be prepared to take on the risks of offering forward contracts for several years hence. Thus firms simply have to live with the uncertainty over exchange rates in future years. This may discourage long-term investment. For example, the possibility of exchange rate appreciation may well discourage firms from investing abroad, since a higher exchange rate means that foreign exchange earnings will be worth less in the domestic currency.

As Figure 14.3 showed (see page 402) there have been large changes in exchange rates. Such changes make it difficult not only for exporters. Importers too will be hesitant about making long-term deals. For example, a UK manufacturing firm signing a contract to buy US components in March 2008, when $2.00 worth of components could be purchased for £1, would find it a struggle to make a profit some four years later when less than $1.60 worth of US components could be purchased for £1!

BOX 14.4 | **THE EURO/DOLLAR SEE-SAW** |

Ups and downs in the currency market

For periods of time, world currency markets can be quite peaceful, with only modest changes in exchange rates. But with the ability to move vast sums of money very rapidly from one part of the world to another and from one currency to another, speculators can suddenly turn this relatively peaceful world into one of extreme turmoil.

In this box we examine the huge swings of the euro against the dollar since the euro's launch in 1999. In Case Studies 14.7 and 14.8 in MyEconLab we examine other examples of currency turmoil.

First the down...

On 1 January 1999, the euro was launched and exchanged for $1.16. By October 2000 the euro had fallen to $0.85.

What was the cause of this 27 per cent depreciation? The main cause was the growing fear that inflationary pressures were increasing in the USA and that, therefore, the Federal Reserve Bank would have to raise interest rates. At the same time, the eurozone economy was growing only slowly and inflation was well below the 2 per cent ceiling set by the ECB. There was thus pressure on the ECB to cut interest rates.

The speculators were not wrong. As the diagram shows, US interest rates rose, and ECB interest rates initially fell, and when eventually they did rise (in October 1999), the gap between US and ECB interest rates soon widened again.

In addition to the differences in interest rates, a lack of confidence in the recovery of the eurozone economy and a continuing confidence in the US economy encouraged investment to flow to the USA. This inflow of finance (and lack of inflow to the eurozone) further pushed up the dollar relative to the euro.

The low value of the euro against the dollar meant a high value of other currencies, including the pound, relative to the euro. This made it very difficult for companies outside the eurozone to export to eurozone countries and also for those competing with imports from the eurozone (which had been made cheaper by the fall in the euro).

In October 2000, with the euro trading at around 85¢, the ECB plus the US Federal Reserve Bank, the Bank of England and the Japanese central bank all intervened on the foreign exchange market to buy euros. This arrested the fall, and helped to restore confidence in the currency. People were more willing to hold euros, knowing that central banks would support it.

... then the up

The position changed completely in 2001. With the US economy slowing rapidly and fears of an impending recession, the Federal Reserve Bank reduced interest rates 11 times during the year: from 6.5 per cent at the beginning of the year to 1.75 per cent at the end (see the chart). Although the ECB also cut

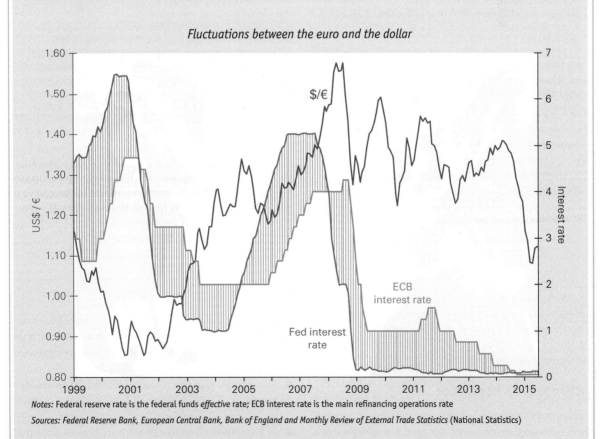

Fluctuations between the euro and the dollar

Notes: Federal reserve rate is the federal funds *effective* rate; ECB interest rate is the main refinancing operations rate

Sources: Federal Reserve Bank, European Central Bank, Bank of England and Monthly Review of External Trade Statistics (National Statistics)

interest rates, the cuts were relatively modest: from 4.75 at the beginning of the year to 3.25 at the end. With eurozone interest rates now considerably above US rates, the euro began to rise.

In addition, a massive deficit on the US current account, and a budget deficit nearing 4 per cent of GDP, made foreign investors reluctant to invest in the US economy. In fact, investors were pulling out of the USA. One estimate suggests that European investors alone sold $70 billion of US assets during 2002. The result of all this was a massive depreciation of the dollar and appreciation of the euro, so that by December 2004 the euro had risen to $1.36: a 60 per cent appreciation since July 2001!

In 2004–5, the US economy began to experience strong economic growth once more (an annual average of 3.4 per cent) and consequently the Fed raised interest rates several times, from 1 per cent in early 2004 to 5.25 by June 2006. With growth in the eurozone averaging just 1.8 per cent in 2004–5, the ECB kept interest rates constant at 2 per cent until early 2006. The result was that the euro depreciated against the dollar in 2005. But then the rise of the euro began again as the US growth slowed and eurozone growth rose and people anticipated a narrowing of the gap between US and eurozone interest rates.

In 2007 and 2008 worries about the credit crunch in the USA led the Fed to make substantial cuts in interest rates to stave off recession. In August 2007 the US federal funds rate was 5.25 per cent. It was then reduced on several occasions to stand at between 0 and 0.25 per cent by December 2008. The ECB, in contrast, kept the eurozone rate constant at 4 per cent for the first part of this period and even raised it to 4.25 temporarily in the face of rapidly rising commodity prices. As a result, short-term finance flooded into the eurozone and the euro appreciated again, from $1.37 in mid-2007 to $1.58 in mid-2008.

Eventually, in September 2008, with the eurozone on the edge of recession and predictions that the ECB would cut interest rates, the euro at last began to fall. It continued to do so as the ECB cut rates. However, with monetary policy in the eurozone remaining tighter than in the USA, the euro began to rise again, only falling once more at the end of 2009 and into 2010 as US growth accelerated and speculators anticipated a tightening of US monetary policy.

... then see-sawing on the back of economic and fiscal fragility

The first half of the 2010s was characterised by concerns over the weakness of the eurozone economy and the public finances of several eurozone economies. Growth in the eurozone was often illusive, averaging just 0.8 per cent per year from 2010 to 2015. Meanwhile gross public-sector debt across the eurozone countries rose to 96 per cent of GDP by 2015 compared to 66 per cent in 2007. These concerns contributed to the volatility of the euro.

In particular, the euro would tend to weaken at times when there were growing fears of debt default as investors became increasingly reluctant to hold the currency. For instance, in early 2010 fear of a Greek default and growing worries about contagion to other highly indebted eurozone countries, such as Portugal, Ireland, Italy and Spain, led to speculation against the euro. In January 2010, the euro stood at $1.44; by early June, it had fallen to $1.19. This represented a 17 per cent depreciation. But by the end of October 2010 the euro was trading at $1.39 as efforts were made to strengthen the funding mechanisms for eurozone countries in financial distress.

In January 2015 on the back of continuing economic fragility, the ECB finally announced what many had being expected: full-scale quantitative easing (see Boxes 12.5 and 12.6). This marked a crucial stage in monetary easing within the eurozone. Monetary easing creates an increased demand for foreign currencies and drives down the exchange rate. With the ECB reducing interest rates and people increasingly predicting QE, the euro depreciated during 2014. Between March and December 2014 the euro depreciated by 11 per cent against the dollar, while the euro exchange rate index depreciated by 4 per cent. With the announced programme of QE being somewhat larger than markets expected, in the week following the announcement the euro fell a further 2.3 per cent against the dollar, and the euro exchange rate index also fell by 2.3 per cent. The result was that the euro was trading at its lowest level against the US dollar since April 2003.

The path of the euro against the US dollar shows how interest rate volatility and the relative level of interest rates between countries are a major contributory factor to exchange rate volatility. However, more recently concerns over the economic and fiscal health of national eurozone governments have played a particularly important role in explaining fluctuations in the euro.

> **?** *Find out what has happened to the euro/dollar exchange rate over the past 12 months. (You can find the data from the Bank of England's Statistical Interactive Database at www.bankofengland.co.uk/statistics.) Explain why the exchange rate has moved the way it has.*

Lack of discipline on the domestic economy. Governments may pursue irresponsibly inflationary policies (for short-term political gain, say). This will have adverse effects over the longer term as the government will at some point have to deflate the economy again, with a resulting fall in output and rise in unemployment.

Exchange rates in practice

Exchange rates have become extremely volatile. Currencies can gain or lose several percentage points in the space of a few days. These changes can then make all the difference between profit and loss for trading companies. There are a number of reasons for this volatility:

- Inflation or money supply targets. Central banks may have to make considerable changes to interest rates in order to keep to their targets. These in turn cause exchange rate fluctuations.
- A huge growth in international financial markets, with around $5.3 trillion worth of foreign exchange traded each day in 2014.
- The abolition of exchange controls in most industrialised countries.

- The growth in information technology. The simple use of a computer can transfer capital and finance internationally in a matter of seconds.
- The preference for liquidity. With the danger of currency fluctuations, companies prefer to keep their financial capital as liquid as possible. They do not want to be locked into assets denominated in a declining currency.
- The growing speculative activities of trading companies. Many large companies have a team of dealers to help manage their liquid assets: to switch them from currency to currency in order to take advantage of market movements.
- The growing speculative activities of banks and other financial institutions.

- The growing belief that rumour and 'jumping on the bandwagon' are more important determinants of currency buying or selling than cool long-term appraisal. If people believe that speculation is likely to be destabilising, their actions will ensure that it is. Many companies involved in international trade and finance have developed a 'speculative mentality'.
- The growing belief that governments are powerless to prevent currency movements. As short-term capital (or 'hot money') grows relative to official reserves, it is increasingly difficult for central banks to stabilise currencies through exchange market intervention.

Recap

1. Completely fixed exchange rates bring the advantage of certainty for the business community, which encourages trade and foreign investment. They also help to prevent governments from pursuing irresponsible macroeconomic policies.

2. However, with fixed rates domestic policy is entirely constrained by the balance of payments. What is more, they can lead to competitive contractionary policies worldwide; there may be problems of excessive or insufficient international liquidity; there may be difficulty in adjusting to external shocks; and speculation could be very severe if people came to believe that a fixed rate was about to break down.

3. The advantages of free-floating exchange rates are that they automatically correct balance of payments disequilibria; they eliminate the need for reserves; and they give governments a greater independence to pursue their chosen domestic policy.

4. On the other hand, a completely free exchange rate can be highly unstable, especially when the elasticities of demand for imports and exports are low and there are shifts in currency demand and supply; in addition, speculation may be destabilising. This may discourage firms from trading and investing abroad. What is more, a flexible exchange rate, by removing the balance of payments constraint on domestic policy, may encourage governments to pursue irresponsible domestic policies for short-term political gain.

14.5 THE ORIGINS OF THE EURO

How did the majority of the EU countries arrive at a single currency?

There have been many attempts to regulate exchange rates since 1945. By far the most successful was the Bretton Woods system, which was adopted worldwide from the end of the Second World War until 1971. This was a form of **adjustable peg** exchange rate, where countries pegged (i.e. fixed) their exchange rate to the US dollar, but could re-peg it at a lower or higher level ('devalue' or 'revalue' their exchange rate) if there was a persistent and substantial balance of payments deficit or surplus.

With growing world inflation and instability from the mid-1960s, it became more and more difficult to maintain fixed exchange rates, and the growing likelihood of devaluations and revaluations fuelled speculation. The system was abandoned in the early 1970s. What followed

was a period of exchange rate management known as **managed floating**. Under this system, exchange rates

---

Definitions

Adjustable peg A system whereby exchange rates are fixed for a period of time, but may be devalued (or revalued) if a deficit (or surplus) becomes substantial.

Managed floating A system of flexible exchange rates, but where the government intervenes to prevent excessive fluctuations or even to achieve an unofficial target exchange rate.

TC 9
p 62

were not pegged but allowed to float. However, central banks intervened from time to time to prevent excessive exchange rate fluctuations. This system largely continues to this day.

However, on a regional basis, especially within Europe, there were attempts to create greater exchange rate stability. The European system involved establishing exchange rate bands: upper and lower limits within which exchange rates were allowed to fluctuate. The name given to the EU ystem was the **exchange rate mechanism (ERM)**.

The ERM

The ERM came into existence in March 1979 and the majority of the EU countries were members. The UK, however, chose not to join. Spain joined in 1989, the UK in 1990 and Portugal in April 1992. Then in September 1992, the UK and Italy indefinitely suspended their membership of the ERM, but Italy rejoined in November 1996 as part of its bid to join the single European currency (see Section 14.6). Austria joined in 1995, Finland in 1996 and Greece in 1998. By the time the ERM was replaced by the single currency in 1999, only Sweden and the UK were outside the ERM.

Features of the ERM

Under the system, each currency was given a central exchange rate with each of the other ERM currencies in a grid. However, fluctuations were allowed from the central rate within specified bands. For most countries these bands were set at ±2.25 per cent. The central rates could be adjusted from time to time by agreement, thus making the ERM an 'adjustable peg' system. All the currencies floated jointly with currencies outside the ERM.

If a currency approached the upper or lower limit against *any* other ERM currency, intervention would take place to maintain the currencies within the band. This would take the form of central banks in the ERM selling the strong currency and buying the weak one. It could also involve the weak currency countries raising interest rates and the strong currency countries lowering them.

The ERM in practice. In a system of pegged exchange rates, countries should harmonise their policies to avoid excessive currency misalignments and hence the need for large

devaluations or revaluations. There should be a convergence of their economies: they should be at a similar point on the business cycle and have similar inflation rates and interest rates.

The ERM in the 1980s. In the early 1980s, however, French and Italian inflation rates were persistently higher than German rates. This meant that there had to be several realignments (devaluations and revaluations). After 1983 realignments became less frequent, and then from 1987 to 1992 they ceased altogether. This was due to a growing convergence of members' internal policies.

By the time the UK joined the ERM in 1990, it was generally seen by its existing members as being a great success. It had created a zone of currency stability in a world of highly unstable exchange rates, and had provided the necessary environment for the establishment of a truly common market by the end of 1992.

Crisis in the ERM. Shortly after the UK joined the ERM, however, strains began to show. The reunification of Germany involved considerable reconstruction in the eastern part of the country. Financing this reconstruction was causing a growing budget deficit. The Bundesbank (the German central bank) thus felt obliged to maintain high interest rates in order to keep inflation in check. At the same time, the UK was experiencing a massive current account deficit (partly the result of entering the ERM at what many commentators argued was too high an exchange rate). It was thus obliged to raise interest rates in order to protect the pound, despite the fact that the economy was sliding rapidly into recession. The French franc and Italian lira were also perceived to be overvalued, and there were the first signs of worries as to whether their exchange rates within the ERM could be retained.

At the same time, the US economy was moving into recession and, as a result, US interest rates were cut. This led to a large outflow of capital from the USA. With high German interest rates, much of this capital flowed to Germany. This pushed up the value of the German mark and with it the other ERM currencies.

In September 1992, things reached crisis point. First the lira was devalued. Then two days later, on 'Black Wednesday' (16 September), the UK and Italy were forced to suspend their membership of the ERM: the pound and the lira were floated. At the same time, the Spanish peseta was devalued by 5 per cent.

Definition

Exchange rate mechanism (ERM) A semi-fixed system whereby participating EU countries allow fluctuations against each other's currencies only within agreed bands. Collectively they float freely against all other currencies.

Pause for thought

Under what circumstances may a currency bloc like the ERM (a) help to prevent speculation; (b) aggravate the problem of speculation?

Turmoil returned in the summer of 1993. The French economy was moving into recession and there were calls for cuts in French interest rates. But this was only possible if Germany was prepared to cut its rates too, and it was not. Speculators began to sell francs and it became obvious that the existing franc/mark parity could not be maintained. In an attempt to rescue the ERM, the EU finance ministers agreed to adopt very wide ±15 per cent bands. The result was that the franc and the Danish krone depreciated against the mark.

A return of calm. The old ERM appeared to be at an end. The new ±15 per cent bands hardly seemed like a 'pegged' system at all. However, the ERM did not die. Within months, the members were again managing to keep fluctuations within a very narrow range (for most of the time, within ±2.25 per cent!). The scene was being set for the abandonment of separate currencies and the adoption of a single currency: the euro.

The Maastricht Treaty and the road to the single currency

The ERM was conceived as a stage on the road to complete economic and monetary union (EMU) of member states. Details of the path towards EMU were finalised in the Maastricht Treaty, which was signed in February 1992. The timetable for EMU involved the adoption of a single currency by 1999 at the latest.

Before they could join the single currency, member states were obliged to achieve convergence of their economies. Each country had to meet five convergence criteria:

- Inflation: should be no more than 1.5 per cent above the average inflation rate of the three countries in the EU with the lowest inflation.
- Interest rates: the rate on long-term government bonds should be no more than 2 per cent above the average of the three countries with the lowest inflation.
- Budget deficit: should be no more than 3 per cent of GDP.
- National debt: should be no more than 60 per cent of GDP.
- Exchange rates: the currency should have been within the normal ERM bands for at least two years with no realignments or excessive intervention.

Before the launch of the single currency, the Council of Ministers had to decide which countries had met the convergence criteria and would thus be eligible to form a **currency union** by fixing their currencies permanently to the euro. Their national currencies would effectively disappear.

At the same time a European System of Central Banks (ESCB) would be created, consisting of a European Central Bank (ECB) and the central banks of the participating member states. The ECB would be independent, both from governments and from EU political institutions. It would operate the monetary policy on behalf of the countries that had adopted the single currency.

Definition

Currency union A group of countries (or regions) using a common currency.

Recap

1. One means of achieving greater currency stability is for a group of countries to peg their internal exchange rates and yet float jointly with the rest of the world. The exchange rate mechanism of the EU (ERM) was an example. Members' currencies were allowed to fluctuate against other member currencies within a band. The band was ±2.25 per cent for the majority of the ERM countries until 1993.

2. The need for realignments seemed to have diminished in the late 1980s as greater convergence was achieved between the members' economies. However, growing strains in the system in the early 1990s led to a crisis in September 1992. The UK and Italy left the ERM. There was a further crisis in July 1993 and the bands were widened to ±15 per cent.

3. Thereafter, as convergence of the economies of ERM members increased, fluctuations decreased and remained largely within ±2.25 per cent.

4. The ERM was seen as an important first stage on the road to complete economic and monetary union (EMU) in the EU.

5. The Maastricht Treaty set out a timetable for achieving EMU. This would culminate in the creation of a currency union: a single European currency with a common monetary policy operated by an independent European Central Bank.

14.6 ECONOMIC AND MONETARY UNION (EMU) IN EUROPE

Do countries benefit from using the euro?

Birth of the euro

In March 1998, the European Commission ruled that 11 of the 15 member states were eligible to proceed to EMU in January 1999. The UK and Denmark were to exercise an opt-out negotiated at Maastricht, and Sweden and Greece failed to meet one or more of the convergence criteria. (Greece joined the euro in 2001.)

The euro came into being on 1 January 1999, but euro banknotes and coins were not introduced until 1 January 2002. In the meantime, national currencies continued to exist alongside the euro, but at irrevocably fixed rates. The old notes and coins were withdrawn a few weeks after the introduction of euro notes and coins.

In May 2004, ten new members joined the EU and in January 2007 another two. Under the Maastricht Treaty, they should all make preparations for joining the euro by meeting the convergence criteria and being in a new version of the exchange rate mechanism with a wide exchange rate band. Under ERM II, euro candidate countries must keep their exchange rates within ±15 per cent of a central rate against the euro. Estonia, Lithuania and Slovenia were the first to join ERM II in June 2004 with Latvia, Cyprus, Malta and Slovakia following in 2005. Slovenia adopted the euro in 2007, Malta and Cyprus in 2008, Slovakia in 2009, Estonia in 2011, Latvia in 2014 and Lithuania in 2015, making a total of 19 countries using the euro.

How desirable is EMU?

Advantages of the single currency

Elimination of the costs of converting currencies. With separate currencies in each of the EU countries, costs were incurred each time one currency was exchanged into another. The elimination of these costs, however, was probably the least important benefit from the single currency. The European Commission estimated that the effect was to increase the GDP of the countries concerned by an average of only 0.4 per cent. The gains to countries like the UK, which have well-developed financial markets, would be even smaller.

Increased competition and efficiency. Despite the advent of the single market, large price differences remained between member states. Not only has the single currency eliminated the need to convert one currency into another (a barrier to competition), but it has brought more transparency in pricing, and has put greater downward pressure on prices in high-cost firms and countries.

Elimination of exchange rate uncertainty (between the members). Removal of exchange rate uncertainty has helped to encourage trade between the eurozone countries. Perhaps more importantly, it has encouraged investment by firms that trade between these countries, given the greater certainty in calculating costs and revenues from such trade.

In times of economic uncertainty, exchange rate volatility between currencies can be high, as the experience of sterling showed during the credit crunch of 2008. The associated uncertainty for the UK in its trade with eurozone countries would have been eliminated had it adopted the euro.

Increased inward investment. Investment from the rest of the world is attracted to a eurozone of around 340 million inhabitants, where there is no fear of internal currency movements. By contrast, the UK, by not joining, has typically found that inward investment has been diverted away to those countries within the eurozone.

From 1990 to 1998, the UK's share of inward investment to EU countries (including from other EU countries) was 20.6 per cent. From 1999 to 2003, it was 12.9 per cent (see Figure 14.7). From 2003 to 2005, as the UK economy grew more strongly than other major economies in the EU, its share increased to 36.1 per cent. This proved to be relatively short-lived, with the volatility of sterling acting as a deterrent to investment. By 2011, the UK's share of inward investment to EU countries had fallen to 9.4 per cent. The share then rose as the UK experienced stronger growth than in most other EU countries. By 2014, its share had risen to 28.1 per cent.

Lower inflation and interest rates. A single monetary policy forces convergence in inflation rates (just as inflation rates are very similar between the different regions within a country). With the ECB being independent from short-term political manipulation, this has resulted in a low average inflation rate in the eurozone countries. This, in turn, has helped to convince markets that the euro will be strong relative to other currencies. The result is lower long-term rates of interest. This, in turn, further encourages investment in the eurozone countries, both by member states and by the rest of the world.

Opposition to EMU

European monetary union has, however, attracted considerable criticism. 'Eurosceptics' see within it a surrender of national political and economic sovereignty. Others, including those more sympathetic to monetary union in principle, raise concerns about the design of the monetary and financial systems within which monetary union operates – a design that, in principle, can be amended (see Boxes 12.2 and 12.4). We begin with those arguments against EMU in principle.

KI 13
p 66

Figure 14.7   Inward investment to selected EU countries, percentage of total EU inward investment

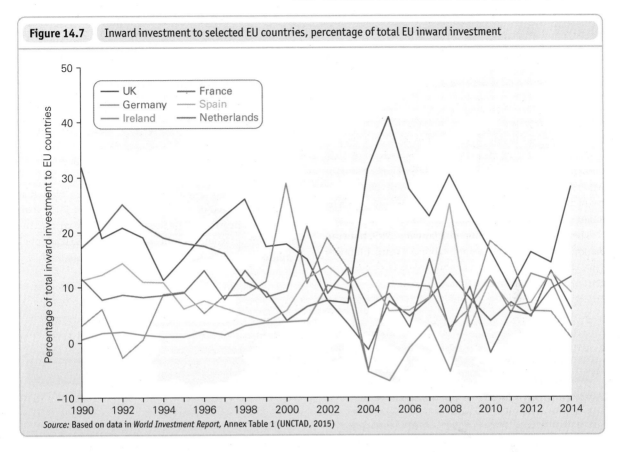

Source: Based on data in *World Investment Report,* Annex Table 1 (UNCTAD, 2015)

The lack of national currencies. This can be a serious problem if an economy is at all out of harmony with the rest of the eurozone. For example, if countries such as Greece and Spain have lower productivity or higher rates of inflation (due, say, to greater cost-push pressures), then how are they to make their goods competitive with the rest of the Union? With separate currencies these countries could allow their currencies to depreciate. With a single currency, however, they could become depressed 'regions' of Europe, with rising unemployment and all the other regional problems of depressed regions *within* a country.

> **Pause for thought**
>
> *How might multiplier effects (the principle of cumulative causation) lead to prosperous regions becoming more prosperous and less prosperous regions falling even further behind?*

This problem was made worse following the financial crisis of 2007/8 and subsequent recession. Weaker countries in the eurozone, which included Greece, Ireland, Portugal and Cyprus, faced increasing government debt and problems in servicing that debt. They were forced to seek additional loans from the so-called Troika of the IMF, the European Commission (now through its European Stability Mechanism (ESF)) and the European Central Bank. But such loans were conditional on the countries pursuing policies of government expenditure cuts to reduce their budget deficits (dubbed 'austericty policies') and structural reforms to cut down on bureaucracy, corruption, ineffectiveness in collecting taxes and impediments to the functioning of markets.

Unable to devalue, such countries faced massive reductions in aggregate demand and a severe recession. By 2015, Greek real GDP had shrunk by 26 per cent since 2008 and unemployment had reached 27 per cent, with unemployment for 18–24-year-olds exceeding 60 per cent.

Proponents of EMU argue that it is better to tackle the problem of high inflation or low productivity in such countries by the disciplines of competition from other EU countries, than merely to feed that inflation by keeping separate currencies and allowing periodic depreciations, with all the uncertainty that they bring.

What is more, the high-inflation countries tend to be the poorer ones with lower wage levels (albeit faster wage *increases*). With higher mobility of labour and capital as the single market develops, resources are likely to be attracted to such countries. This could help to narrow the gap between the richer and poorer member states.

TC 15
p 248

The critics of EMU counter this by arguing that labour is relatively immobile, given cultural and language barriers. Thus an unemployed worker in Dublin could not easily move to a job in Turin or Helsinki. What the critics are arguing here is that the EU is not an **optimal currency area** (see Box 14.5).

Loss of separate monetary policies. Perhaps the most significant criticism is that the same central bank rate of interest must apply to all eurozone countries: the 'one-size-fits-all' problem. The trouble is that while some countries might require a lower rate of interest in order to ward off recession (such as Portugal, Ireland and Greece in 2010–11), others might require a higher one to prevent inflation. The greater the divergence between economies within the eurozone, the greater this problem becomes. It was hoped, however, that, with common fiscal rules and free trade, these divergences would diminish over time.

Asymmetric shocks. A third and related problem for members of a single currency occurs in adjusting to a shock when that shock affects members to different degrees. These are known as **asymmetric shocks**. For example, the banking crisis affected the UK more severely than other countries, given that

---

Definitions

Optimal currency area The optimal size of a currency area is one that maximises the benefits from having a single currency relative to the costs. If the area were to be increased or decreased in size, the costs would rise relative to the benefits.

Asymmetric shocks Shocks (such as an oil price increase or a recession in another part of the world) that have different-sized effects on different industries, regions or countries.

BOX 14.5 OPTIMAL CURRENCY AREAS

EXPLORING ECONOMICS

When it pays to pay in the same currency

Imagine that each town and village used a different currency. Think how inconvenient it would be having to keep exchanging one currency into another, and how difficult it would be working out the relative value of items in different parts of the country.

Clearly there are benefits of using a common currency, not only within a country but across different countries. The benefits include greater transparency in pricing, more open competition, greater certainty for investors and the avoidance of having to pay commission when you change one currency into another. There are also the benefits from having a single monetary policy if that is delivered in a more consistent and effective way than by individual countries.

So why not have a single currency for the whole world? The problem is that the bigger a single-currency area gets, the more likely the conditions are to diverge in the different parts of the area. Some parts may have high unemployment and require expansionary policies. Others may have low unemployment and suffer from inflationary pressures. They may require *contractionary* policies.

What is more, different members of the currency area may experience quite different shocks to their economies, whether from outside the union (e.g. a fall in the price of one of their major exports) or from inside (e.g. a prolonged strike). These 'asymmetric shocks' would imply that different parts of the currency area should adopt different policies. But with a common monetary policy and hence common interest rates, and with no possibility of devaluation/revaluation of the currency of individual members, the scope for separate economic policies is reduced.

The costs of asymmetric shocks (and hence the costs of a single-currency area) will be greater, the less the mobility of labour and capital, the less the flexibility of prices and wage rates, and the fewer the alternative policies there are that can be turned to (such as fiscal and regional policies).

So is the eurozone an optimal currency area? Certainly strong doubts have been raised by many economists:

- Labour is relatively immobile.
- There are structural differences between the member states.
- The transmission effects of interest rate changes are different between the member countries. This arises partly because countries have both different proportions of debt relative to GDP and different proportions of debt at variable interest rates.
- Exports to countries outside the eurozone account for different proportions of the members' GDP and thus their economies are affected differently by a change in the rate of exchange of the euro against other currencies.
- Wage rates are relatively inflexible.
- Under the Stability and Growth Pact and the Fiscal Compact (see Box 12.2), the scope for using discretionary fiscal policy is curtailed, except in times of severe economic difficulty (as in 2009).

This does not necessarily mean, however, that the costs of having a single European currency outweigh the benefits. Also, the problems outlined above should decline over time as the single market develops. Finally, the problem of asymmetric shocks can be exaggerated. European economies are highly diversified; there are often more differences *within* economies than between them. Thus shocks are more likely to affect different industries or localities than whole countries. Changing the exchange rate, if that were still possible, would hardly be an appropriate policy in these circumstances.

Why is a single-currency area likely to move towards becoming an optimal currency area over time?

London is a global financial centre. This problem is more serious, the less the factor mobility between member countries and the less the price flexibility within member countries.

Even when shocks are uniformly felt in the member states, however, there is still the problem that policies adopted centrally will have different impacts on each country. This is because the transmission mechanisms of economic policy (i.e. the way in which policy changes impact on economic variables like growth and inflation) vary across countries.

There are others who are critical of the design of EMU but who argue that, with appropriate changes, the problems could be significantly reduced.

Monetary policy. In the case of monetary policy, it is argued that the ECB was not proactive in tackling the recession that followed the aftermath of the financial crisis. Large-scale programmes of quantitative easing were quickly adopted by the US Federal Reserve and the Bank of England (see Box 12.5).

The ECB, by contrast, was seen as more cautious in its response. Between December 2011 and March the ECB provided liquidity to the banking system by undertaking large-scale, long-term repo operations. As a result, over €1 trillion of long-term (three-year) repo loans were provided. Meanwhile, between May 2010 and June 2012 it purchased €214 billion of assets, largely government bonds under the Securities Market Programme (see Box 12.5). However, the effects on the money supply were sterilised by ECB sales of other assets. In other words, monetary operations were undertaken to offset the injected liquidity.

However, the eurozone economy remained weak, with low growth and increasing fears of a deflationary spiral. Gradually, announcements of further monetary easing were made which saw reductions to the ECB's main interest rates and, in doing so, the adoption of a negative deposit rate for overnight deposits by financial institutions. Yet by the start of 2015 the annual rate of consumer price inflation had fallen to −0.6 per cent.

Then in late January a large-scale programme of quantitative easing was announced, to begin in March 2015, which would see asset purchases of €60 billion per month until at least September 2016, by which time the total would be €1.1 trillion. The assets were to be mainly government bonds issued by countries not still in bail out programmes.

Critics point to the underlying weakness of a single currency operating alongside separate *national* government debt issues. The greater the divergence of the eurozone countries, in terms of growth, inflation, deficits, debt and the proportions of debt securities maturing in the short term, the greater this problem becomes.

Fiscal policy. Under the Stability and Growth Pact (SGP), countries were supposed to keep public-sector deficits below 3 per cent of GDP and their stocks of debt below 60 per cent of GDP (see Box 12.2). However, the Pact was not rigidly enforced. Furthermore, because the rules allowed for discretion in times of recession, deficits and debt rose sharply in the late 2000s (see Table 12.1 on page 329).

Subsequently, efforts have been made to change the framework within which national governments make their fiscal choices. The result is the Fiscal Compact, signed in March 2012 (see Box 12.2). This reaffirmed the SGP's excessive deficit rules, but added other requirements. For example, eurozone countries would now be required to keep *structural deficits* (i.e. budget deficits that would exist even if economies were operating at their potential output level) at or below 0.5 per cent of GDP. Furthermore, tougher penalties would be imposed on countries breaking the rules.

There are those who argue that for eurozone members to benefit fully from monetary union, tighter fiscal rules alone are insufficient. Instead, they advocate greater fiscal harmonisation. In other words, the problem, they say, is one of incomplete integration. This would probably require greater fiscal transfers to weaker eurozone countries, such as Greece and Portugal – something that stronger countries, such as Germany and The Netherlands, have resisted.

Future of the euro

When Lithuania adopted the euro on 1 January 2015 it became the nineteenth country to do so. Yet debates around the future of the euro intensified during 2015 as the Greek debt crisis raised the prospect of Greece's exit from the euro (Grexit).

The Greek crisis

The perilous state of Greece's public finances had already seen two international bailouts agreed. These involved the IMF, the European Commission and the ECB – the so-called 'Troika' – and were worth €240 billion. However, these loans were contingent on the Greek government undertaking a series of economic measures, including significant fiscal tightening. However, the fiscal austerity measures contributed to a deterioration of the macroeconomic environment (see Box 13.1). Matters came to a head at the end of 2014 when the final tranches of the Greek bailout programme were suspended by the Troika. This followed the formation in December 2014 of a Syriza-led Greek government which had fought the election on an anti-austerity platform.

What followed was a drawn-out set of negotiations between Greece and its international creditors. With no agreement on further aid to Greece yet reached, Greece was unable to meet a €1.55 billion repayment to the IMF on 30 June 2015. This made Greece the first developed country to have defaulted on a loan from the IMF.

Meanwhile conditions for Greek citizens continued to deteriorate. In July the ECB announced that it would maintain its emergency liquidity assurance for the Greek financial system at levels agreed at the end of June. Without further credit for an already financially-distressed banking system, capital controls were imposed with strict limits on withdrawals from bank accounts.

KI 31
p 205

In August 2015 the Greek government and its international creditors reached an agreement on the terms of a third bailout worth €85 billion over three years. Despite winning a referendum to resist the austerity measures demanded by the Troika, the Syriza government felt forced to adopt a large proportion of such measures in order to secure the bailout. For the time being at least, Grexit had been avoided. Nonetheless, fundamental questions remained about the future of the euro and the conditions under which it would be beneficial for other EU member states to join or for existing members to exit.

The single currency and gains from trade

The benefits from a country being a member of a single currency are greater the more it leads to trade creation with other members of the single currency. Table 14.2 shows for a sample of member states of the European Union the proportion of their exports and imports to and from other member states. From the table we can see that about two-thirds of trade in the European Union is between member states. However, there are considerable differences in the importance of intra-EU trade for member states.

On the basis of intra-industry trade, it might be argued that countries like Greece and Malta (and the UK should it have chosen to join) have least to gain from being part of a single currency with other EU nations. But, we need to consider other factors too. The theory of optimal currency areas (see Box 14.5) suggests, for example, that the degree of convergence between economies and the flexibility of labour markets are important considerations for countries considering the costs of relinquishing their national currency.

Table 14.2	Intra-European Union exports and imports, % of total exports or imports			
	Exports		**Imports**	
	2002–8	2009–15	2002–8	2009–15
Belgium	76.6	71.8	71.9	67.4
France	65.3	60.5	69.0	67.9
Germany	64.4	58.9	64.9	64.4
Greece	64.9	50.3	59.8	50.3
Ireland	63.6	58.5	67.3	68.9
Italy	61.8	55.8	60.1	56.0
Lithuania	64.9	59.2	60.7	60.0
Malta	47.8	43.2	72.4	70.2
Portugal	79.0	72.6	77.5	74.4
Spain	72.7	65.7	65.0	57.4
UK	58.9	49.6	55.3	50.2
Eurozone (19 countries)	68.8	64.2	65.3	62.4
EU-28	68.4	64.0	64.9	62.2

Source: AMECO database (European Commission, DGECFIN).

Convergence or divergence?

The more similar economies are, the more likely it is that they will face similar or symmetric shocks which can be accommodated by a common monetary policy. Furthermore, greater wage flexibility and mobility of labour provide mechanisms for countries within a single currency to remain internationally competitive.

Table 14.3 shows a series of macroeconomic indicators for a sample of countries within the eurozone. From it we can see

Table 14.3	Macroeconomic indicators for eurozone, 2002–15											
	2002–8						**2009–15**					
	Eurozone	France	Germany	Greece	Italy	Spain	Eurozone	France	Germany	Greece	Italy	Spain
Economic growth, % p.a.	1.8	1.6	1.3	3.5	0.8	3.1	0.0	0.5	0.9	−4.0	−1.1	−0.5
Output gap, % of potential output	0.9	1.9	−0.3	1.5	1.0	2.5	−2.4	−1.6	−1.1	−7.6	−3.3	−5.6
Unemployment rate, %	8.5	8.4	9.4	9.4	7.5	10.2	10.9	9.8	5.8	20.6	10.3	22.4
Current account, % of GDP	0.3	−0.1	4.5	−12.0	−1.2	−7.0	1.7	−1.8	6.8	−6.5	−0.5	−1.2
Growth in output per hour worked, % p.a.	0.9	1.2	1.2	1.8	−0.1	0.5	0.8	0.6	0.5	−0.7	0.0	1.9
Growth in unit labour costs, % p.a.	2.0	2.0	0.1	4.0	3.1	3.8	1.3	1.3	2.2	−0.6	1.5	−0.7
Economy-wide inflation rate, %	2.1	2.1	1.0	3.3	2.5	3.6	1.0	0.9	1.5	−0.3	1.1	0.2

Notes: 1) Unit labour costs are the ratio of compensation per employee to real GDP per person employed; 2) The economy-wide inflation rate is the annual rate of change of the GDP deflator; 3) Output per hour worked - data up to 2014 and euro area average excludes Lithuania.

Sources: Output per hour worked based on data from OECDstat, (OECD); other figures based on data from *AMECO* database, (European Commission, DGECFIN)

that there remain considerable differences in the macroeconomic performance of these countries. These were exacerbated by the financial crisis of the late 2000s and the subsequent deterioration of the macroeconomic environment.

Among the differences captured by Table 14.3 are the contrasting trade positions of eurozone economies. In the period 2002–8 Greece and Spain ran large current account deficits averaging 12 and 7 per cent of GDP respectively. In contrast, Germany ran a current account surplus of around 4.5 per cent of its GDP.

In the absence of nominal exchange rate adjustments, countries like Greece and Spain, looking to a fall in the *real* exchange rate to boost competitiveness, need to have relatively lower rates of price inflation (see Box 14.1). Therefore, in a single currency productivity growth and wage inflation take on even greater importance in determining a country's competitiveness.

In Table 14.3 labour productivity is captured by the growth in output per hour worked. Again significant variations exist. Where labour productivity growth is lower, it needs lower nominal wage growth to help prevent countries losing their competitiveness. Even in countries where labour productivity is higher, as is often observed in countries with lower levels of income, their competitive position will deteriorate if wage growth exceeds productivity growth. In this scenario unit labour costs (labour costs per unit of output) will increase. In the period from 2002 to 2008, Table 14.3 shows unit labour costs increasing at between 3 and 4 per cent per annum in Greece, Spain and Italy compared with close to zero in Germany. This, other things being equal, puts these countries at a growing competitive disadvantage.

The fiscal framework

The discussion so far highlights the importance of economic convergence in affecting the benefits and costs of being a member of the euro. Fiscal policy can provide some buffer against asymmetric shocks by enabling transfers of income to those areas experiencing lower rates of economic growth. Therefore, the fiscal framework within which the euro operates is important when considering the future of the euro.

To date, the eurozone has resisted a centralisation of national budgets. In a more centralised (or federal) system we would see automatic income transfers between different regions and countries. A country, say Greece, affected by a negative economic shock would pay less tax revenues and receive more expenditures from a central eurozone budget, while in a country, say Germany, experiencing a positive shock the opposite would be the case.

Since national budgets in the eurozone remain largely decentralised, fiscal transfers are principally determined by national fiscal frameworks. But the ability of these to offset the effects of negative economic shocks is constrained by the sustainability of national budgets. This is important because it places limits on the ability of national governments to use fiscal policy to offset the effects of negative economic shocks.

When analysing the sustainability of national budgets economists look at the balance needed between spending and revenues necessary to prevent the ratio of the stock of public-sector debt to annual GDP from rising. The key here is the flow of receipts compared to those expenditures other than the interest payments on servicing the existing public-sector debt. If receipts are greater than expenditures excluding interest payments then a **primary surplus** occurs. A primary surplus is needed to maintain

KI 22
p 159

> **Definitions**
>
> **Primary surplus** The situation when the sum of public-sector expenditures excluding interest payments on public-sector debt is less than public-sector receipts.

Table 14.4	Public-sector debt relative to GDP and some of its determinants in selected eurozone economies				
	Public sector debt-to-GDP, %		2010-14 averages		
	2010	2014	Primary surplus-to-GDP, %	Real short-term interest rates, %	Economic growth, % p.a.
Eurozone	83.9	94.2	−1.0	−0.4	0.8
Belgium	99.5	106.5	−0.4	−1.1	1.1
France	81.7	95.0	−2.5	−0.4	1.0
Germany	80.5	74.7	1.4	−0.8	1.9
Greece	146.0	177.1	−4.0	1.3	−3.9
Ireland	87.4	109.7	−8.9	0.1	1.8
Italy	115.3	132.1	1.4	−0.4	−0.3
Lithuania	36.2	40.9	−2.7	−1.4	3.4
Malta	67.6	68.0	0.2	−1.7	3.0
Portugal	96.2	130.2	−2.3	0.0	−0.5
Spain	60.1	97.7	−5.6	0.5	0.0

Source: *AMECO database* (European Commission, DGECFIN).

the debt-to-GDP ratio if the effective real rate of interest payable on public-sector debt (the nominal interest rate *less* the inflation rate) is greater than the economy's economic growth rate. Furthermore, the required size of the primary surplus-to-GDP ratio rises the lower the rate of economic growth relative to the real interest rate and the larger the existing debt-to-GDP ratio.[1]

Table 14.4 shows the public-sector debt-to-GDP ratios in a sample of eurozone economies in 2010 and 2014 alongside the factors that affect the path of the ratio. The

table illustrates considerable differences between countries in the state of their public finances. Therefore, in a decentralised fiscal environment, countries with an already high debt-to-GDP ratio, such as Greece, Italy and Portugal, will find it considerably more difficult to use fiscal policy to mitigate the impact of future adverse economic shocks. Consequently, the sustainability of the current decentralised approach to fiscal policy in the eurozone is likely to be crucial in determining the future for the euro and those countries using the euro.

KI 31 p 205

Recap

1. The euro was born on 1 January 1999. Twelve countries adopted it, having at least nominally met the Maastricht convergence criteria. Euro notes and coins were introduced on 1 January 2002, with the notes and coins of the old currencies withdrawn a few weeks later.

2. The advantages claimed for EMU are that it eliminates the costs of converting currencies and the uncertainties associated with possible changes in inter-EU exchange rates. This encourages more investment, both inward and by domestic firms. What is more, a common central bank, independent from domestic governments, provides the stable monetary environment necessary for a convergence of the EU economies and the encouragement of investment and inter-Union trade.

3. Critics claim, however, that it might make adjustment to domestic economic problems more difficult. The loss of independence in policy making is seen by such people to be a major issue, not only because of the loss of political sovereignty, but also because domestic economic concerns may be at variance with those of the Union as a whole. A single monetary policy is claimed to be inappropriate for dealing with asymmetric shocks. What is more, countries and regions at the periphery of the Union may become depressed unless there is an effective regional policy.

14.7 DEBT AND DEVELOPING COUNTRIES

Can their debt burden be lifted?

Perhaps the most serious of all balance of payments problems in the world today is that faced by some of the poorest developing countries. Many of them experience massive financial outflows year after year as a result of having to 'service' debt (i.e. pay interest and make the necessary repayments). Much of this debt has been incurred in their attempts to finance development. Figure 14.8 shows the growth of external debt (as a proportion of national income) that began in the early 1970s.

KI 13 p 66

The oil shocks of the 1970s

In 1973–4 oil prices quadrupled and the world went into recession. Oil imports cost more and export demand was sluggish. The current account deficit of oil-importing developing countries rose from 1.1 per cent of GDP in 1973 to 4.3 per cent in 1975.

It was not difficult to finance these deficits, however. The oil surpluses deposited in commercial banks in the industrialised world provided an important additional source of finance. The banks, flush with money and faced with slack demand in the industrialised world, were very willing to lend to developing countries to help them finance continued expansion. The world recession was short-lived, and with a recovery in the demand for their exports and with their debts being eroded by high world inflation, developing countries found it relatively easy to service these increased debts.

In 1979–80 world oil prices rose again (from $15 to $38 per barrel). This second oil shock, like the first one, caused a large increase in the import bills of developing countries. But the full effects on their economies this time were very much worse, given the debts that had been accumulated in the 1970s and given the policies adopted by the industrialised world after 1979. But why were things so much worse this time?

■ The world recession was deeper and lasted longer (1980–3) and, when recovery came, it came very slowly. Developing countries' current account balance of payments

---

[1] As a rule-of-thumb, the primary surplus-to-GDP ratio required to maintain a given public-sector debt to GDP ratio can be calculated by multiplying the existing debt-to-GDP ratio by the sum of the real rate of interest minus the rate of economic growth.

| Figure 14.8 | External debt as a percentage of gross national income |

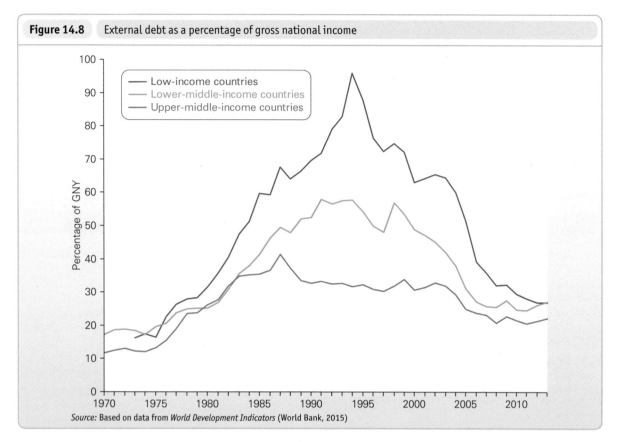

Source: Based on data from *World Development Indicators* (World Bank, 2015)

deteriorated sharply. This was due both to a marked slowing down in the growth of their exports and to a fall in their export prices.

- The tight monetary policies pursued by the industrialised countries led to a sharp increase in interest rates. This greatly increased developing countries' costs of servicing their debts as can be seen in Figure 14.8. It also led to a sharp fall in inflation, which meant that the debts were not being eroded so rapidly.

- The problem was made worse by the growing proportion of debt that was at variable interest rates. This was largely due to the increasing proportion of debt that was in the form of loans from commercial banks.

Figure 14.9 shows how after 1979 debt servicing costs as a proportion of national income rose across developing countries, making it increasingly difficult for them to service their debts. Then in 1982 Mexico, followed by several other countries such as Brazil, Bolivia, Zaire and Sudan, declared that it would have to suspend payments. There was now a debt crisis, which threatened not only the debtor countries, but also the world banking system.

There have been two dimensions to tackling debt problems of developing countries. The first is coping with difficulties in servicing their debt. This usually involves some form of rescheduling of the repayments. The second dimension is dealing with the underlying causes of the problem. Here we will focus on rescheduling.

Rescheduling official loans

Official loans are renegotiated through the 'Paris Club'. Industrialised countries are members of the club, which arranges terms for the rescheduling of their loans to developing countries. Agreements normally involve delaying the date for repayment of loans currently maturing, or spreading the repayments over a longer period of time. Paris Club agreements are often made in consultation with the International Monetary Fund (IMF), which works out a programme for the debtor country to tackle its underlying economic problems.

Several attempts have been made since the mid-1980s to make rescheduling terms more generous, with longer periods before repayments start, longer to repay when they do start, and lower interest rates. In return, the developing countries have had to undertake various 'structural adjustment programmes' supervised by the IMF (see below).

But despite apparent advances made by the Paris Club in making its terms more generous, the majority of low-income countries failed to meet the required IMF conditions, and thus failed to have their debts reduced. What is more, individual Paris Club members were often reluctant to reduce debts unless they were first convinced that other members were 'paying their share'. Nevertheless, some creditor countries unilaterally introduced more generous terms and even cancelled some debts.

The net effect of rescheduling, but only very modest debt forgiveness, can be seen in Figure 14.8 and Figure 14.9.

Figure 14.9 Debt servicing costs as a percentage of gross national income (GNY)

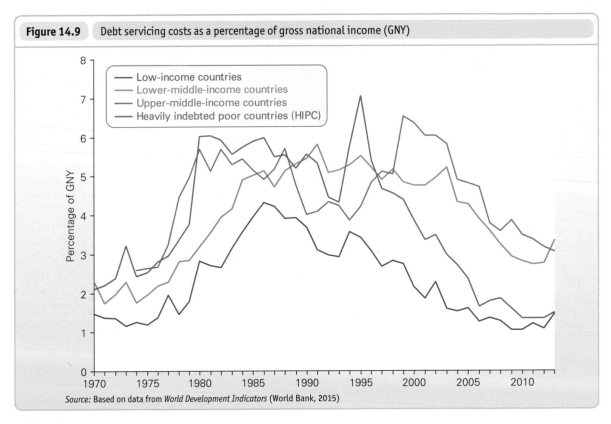

Source: Based on data from *World Development Indicators* (World Bank, 2015)

By the mid-1990s average debt service ratios had fallen from the levels of the mid-1980s and yet the ratio of total debt to GNY was higher. There were thus growing calls for the cancellation of debts (see below).

Rescheduling commercial bank loans

After the declarations by Mexico and other countries of their inability to service their debts, there was fear of an imminent collapse of the world banking system. Banks realised that disaster could only be averted by collective action of the banks to reschedule debts. Banks were prepared to reschedule some of the debts and to provide some additional loans in return for debtor countries undertaking structural adjustment (as described below). Additional loans, however, fell well short of the amount that was needed. Nevertheless, banks were increasingly setting aside funds to cover bad debt, and thus the crisis for the banks began to recede.

As banks felt less exposed to default, so they became less worried about it and less concerned to negotiate deals with debtor countries. Many of the more severely indebted countries, however, found their position still deteriorating rapidly. What is more, many of them were finding that the IMF adjustment programmes were too painful (often involving deep cuts in government expenditure) and were therefore abandoning them. Thus in 1989 US Treasury Secretary Nicholas Brady proposed measures to *reduce* debt.

> **Pause for thought**
>
> *What are the relative advantages and disadvantages to a developing country of rescheduling its debts compared with simply defaulting on them (either temporarily or permanently)?*

The *Brady Plan* involved the IMF and the World Bank lending funds to debtor countries to enable them to repay debts to banks. In return for this instant source of liquidity, the banks would have to be prepared to accept repayment of less than the full sum (i.e. they would sell the debt back to the country at a discount). To benefit from such deals, the debtor countries would have to agree to structural adjustment programmes. Several such agreements were negotiated; much of the debt reduction has involved 'debt swaps' of one sort or another (see Case Study 14.17 in MyEconLab).

Dealing with the debt

Structural reforms

The IMF has typically demanded that debtor countries pursue severe structural adjustment programmes before it has been prepared to sanction the rescheduling of debts. Such programmes have included:

- Tight fiscal and monetary policies to reduce government deficits, reduce interest rates and reduce inflation.

- Supply-side reforms to encourage greater use of the market mechanism and greater incentives for investment.
- A more open trade policy and devaluation of the currency in order to encourage more exports and more competition.

These policies, however, often brought extreme hardship as countries were forced to deflate. Unemployment and poverty increased and growth slowed or even became negative. Even though in the long run some developing countries emerged as more efficient and better able to compete in international trade, in the short run the suffering for many was too great to bear. Popular unrest and resentment against the IMF and the country's government led to riots in many countries and a breakdown of law and order.

A more 'complete' structural adjustment would extend beyond simple market liberalisation and tough monetary policies to much more open access to the markets of the rich countries (the subject of much of the Doha Round negotiations: see Box 13.4 (on page 378)), to more aid and debt relief being channelled into health and education, and to greater research and development in areas that would benefit the poor (e.g. into efficient labour-intensive technology and into new strains of crops that are suitable for countries' specific climate and soil conditions and which do not require large amounts of chemicals).

Debt forgiveness

By the end of the 1990s, the debt burden of many of the poorest countries had become intolerable. Despite portions of their debt being written off under Paris Club terms, the debts of many countries were still rising. Between 1980 and 2000, the debt of sub-Saharan Africa had increased some 3½ times, from $61 billion to $212 billion. Some countries, such as Ethiopia and Mozambique, were spending nearly half their export earnings on merely servicing their debt.

Even with substantial debt rescheduling and some debt cancellation, highly indebted countries were being forced to make savage cuts in government expenditure, much of it on health, education and transport. The consequence was a growth in poverty, hunger, disease and illiteracy. African countries on average were paying four times more to rich countries in debt servicing than they were spending on health and education: it was like a patient giving a blood transfusion to a doctor! The majority of these countries had no chance of 'growing their way out of debt'. The only solution for them was for a more substantial proportion of their debt to be written off.

The heavily indebted poor countries (HIPC) initiative. In 1996 the World Bank and the IMF launched the HIPC initiative. A total of 42 countries, mainly in Africa, were identified as being in need of substantial debt relief. This number was subsequently reduced to 39, most of them in sub-Saharan Africa. The object of the initiative was to reduce the debts of such countries to 'sustainable' levels by cancelling debts above 200–250 per cent of GDP (this was reduced to 150 per cent in 1999 and to a lower level for five countries).

The HIPC process involves countries passing through two stages. In the first stage, eligible countries must demonstrate a track record of 'good performance'. This means that they must satisfy the IMF, World Bank and Paris Club that they are undertaking adjustment measures, such as cutting government expenditure and liberalising their markets. It also involves the countries preparing a Poverty Reduction Strategy Paper (PRSP) to show how they will use debt relief to tackle poverty, and especially how they will improve health and education. Once the IMF and World Bank are satisfied that the country is making sufficient progress, the 'decision point' is reached and the country enters the second stage.

During this second stage, some interim debt relief is provided. Meanwhile the country must establish a 'sound track record' by implementing policies established at the decision point and based on the PRSP. The length of this stage depends on how long it takes the country to implement the policies. At the end of the second stage, the country reaches the 'completion point' and debts are cancelled by the various creditors, on a pro rata basis, to bring the debt to the sustainable threshold.

In 2006, debt relief for the HIPCs that have reached the completion point was extended under the Multilateral Debt Relief Initiative (MDRI). This involves cancelling multilateral debt incurred before 2004. By 2013, it is estimated that in present value terms $75.0 billion had been cancelled under the HIPC programme and a further $41.1 billion under MDRI. The debt stocks of the 36 post-decision-point HIPCs had been reduced by over 95 per cent while poverty-reducing expenditure as a share of government revenue had increased from 42 per cent in 1999 to 49 per cent in 2013. The effect on various debt indicators is shown in Table 14.5. As you can see, the improvement has been dramatic.

Despite this substantial relief, the programme has been heavily criticised for taking too long and imposing excessively harsh conditions on the HIPC countries. According to many charities, such as Oxfam, a much better approach would be to target debt relief directly at poverty reduction, with the resources released being used for investment in fields such as health, education, rural development and

Table 14.5	Debt indicators of 36 post-decision-point HIPCs	
	1999 (%)	2013 (%)
Present value of debt to exports	457	78
Present value of debt to GDP	114	20
Debt service to exports	18	5
Present value of debt to government revenue	552	111
Debt service to government revenue	22	7

Source: From www.imf.org, *HIPC At-A-Glance Guide* (IMF, Autumn 2014)

426 CHAPTER 14 BALANCE OF PAYMENTS AND EXCHANGE RATES

basic infrastructure. The focus, they argue, should be on what countries can afford to pay *after* essential spending on poverty relief and human development.

Should all debt be cancelled and aid increased?

In recent years there have been growing calls for the cancellation of debts and a significant increase in aid, especially for the poorest developing countries, many ravaged by war, drought or AIDS. The United Nations has for many years called on wealthy countries to give 0.7 per cent of their GDP in aid. In 2013 the net flow of aid ('official development assistance' (ODA)) from the 29 donor countries which are members of the OECD's Development Assistance Committee (DAC) amounted to $134.5 billion, a mere 0.3 per cent of gross national income (GNY).

As we have seen, the HIPC and MDRI relief has reduced such countries' debt dramatically. However, low-income countries' debt still amounts to $147 billion and developing countries as a whole owe some $5.5 trillion. Then there is the plight of many non-HIPC countries, such as Kenya, which could be argued to be in greater need of debt relief than some HIPCs.

The argument against debt cancellation and a substantial increase in aid is that this could represent a 'moral hazard'. Once the burden of debt had been lifted and aid had been increased, countries might be tempted to squander the money. It might also encourage them to seek further loans, which might again be squandered.

If, however, moneys were paid into national 'Poverty Funds', which could be monitored by civil society, the parliaments of the individual countries and possibly multilateral agencies, this might help to ensure that the money would be used to fund key poverty-reducing projects, such as health, education, clean water and other basic infrastructure projects. (Case Study 14.18 in MyEconLab examines some of the issues surrounding aid and provides further detail on aid statistics.)

> **Pause for thought**
>
> *Should rich countries cancel all debts owed to them by developing countries?*

Recap

1. After the 1973 oil crisis many developing countries borrowed heavily in order to finance their balance of trade deficits and to maintain a programme of investment. After the 1979 oil price rises the debt problem became much more serious. There was a world recession and real interest rates were much higher. Debt increased dramatically, and much of it at variable interest rates.

2. Rescheduling can help developing countries cope with increased debt in the short run and various schemes have been adopted by creditor countries and the banks.

3. If the problem is to be tackled, however, then either debts have to be written off – something that banks have been increasingly forced to do – or the developing countries themselves must take harsh corrective measures. The IMF has traditionally favoured 'structural adjustment' policies of deflation and market-orientated supply-side policies. An alternative is to use debt relief and aid to invest in health, education, roads and other infrastructure.

4. In 1996 the World Bank and the IMF launched the HIPC initiative to help reduce the debts of heavily indebted poor countries to sustainable levels. HIPC relief has been criticised, however, for being made conditional on the debtor countries pursuing excessively tough IMF adjustment programmes, for having an excessively long qualifying period and for delays in its implementation. A better approach might be to target debt relief directly at programmes to help the poor.

QUESTIONS

1. Which of the following items are credits on the UK balance of payments and which are debits?
   a. The expenditure by UK tourists on holidays in Greece.
   b. The payment of dividends by foreign companies to investors resident in the UK.
   c. Foreign residents taking out insurance policies with UK companies.
   d. Drawing on reserves.
   e. Investment by UK companies overseas.

2. The table below shows the items in the UK's 2007 balance of payments.
   a. Fill in the missing totals for (a) the balance of trade, (b) the current account balance, (c) the portfolio investment balance, and (d) net errors and omissions.
   b. UK GDP in 2007 was estimated at £1 480 956 million. Calculate each item on the balance of payments as a percentage of GDP.
   c. Compare the value of each item in £ millions and as percentages of GDP with those for 2014 in Table 14.1.

	£ millions
Current account:	
Balance on trade in goods	−93 926
Balance on trade in services	52 602
Balance of trade	
Income balance	14 065
Net current transfers	−13 996
Current account balance	
Capital account:	
Capital account balance	310
Financial account:	
Net direct investment	−8 722
Portfolio investment balance	
Other investment balance	−24 411
Balance of financial derivatives	−26 989
Reserve assets	−1 191
Financial account net flows	35 592
Net errors and omissions	

3. What is the relationship between the balance of trade and the circular flow model?

4. Explain how the current account of the balance of payments is likely to vary with the course of the business cycle.

5. Is it a 'bad thing' to have a deficit on the direct and portfolio investment part of the financial account?

6. Why may credits on a country's short-term financial account create problems for its economy in the future?

7. List some factors that could cause an increase in the credit items of the balance of payments and a decrease in the debit items. What would be the effect on the exchange rate (assuming that it is freely floating)? What effect would these exchange rate movements have on the balance of payments?

8. What policy measures could the government adopt to prevent the exchange rate movements in question 7?

9. What are the major advantages and disadvantages of fixing the exchange rate with a majority currency such as the US dollar?

10. What adverse effects on the domestic economy may follow from (a) a depreciation of the exchange rate and (b) an appreciation of the exchange rate?

11. What will be the effects on the domestic economy under free-floating exchange rates if there is a rapid expansion in world economic activity? What will determine the size of these effects?

12. Why would banks not be prepared to offer a forward exchange rate to a firm for, say, five years' time?

13. Under what circumstances would the demand for imports be likely to be inelastic? How would an inelastic demand for imports affect the magnitude of fluctuations in the exchange rate?

14. Why are the price elasticities of demand for imports and exports likely to be lower in the short run than in the long run?

15. Assume that the government pursued an expansionary fiscal policy and that the resulting budget deficit led to higher interest rates. What would happen to (a) the current account and (b) the financial account of the balance of payments? What would be the likely effect on the exchange rate, given a high degree of international financial mobility?

16. Consider the argument that in the modern world of large-scale short-term international financial movements the ability of individual countries to affect their exchange rate is very limited.

17. Why does high international financial mobility and an absence of exchange controls severely limit a country's ability to choose its interest rate?

18. What practical problems are there in achieving a general harmonisation of economic policies between (a) EU countries; (b) the major industrialised countries?

19. What are the causes of exchange rate volatility? Have these problems become greater or lesser in the past 10 years? Explain why.

20. Why did the ERM with narrow bands collapse in 1993? Could this have been avoided?

21. Did the exchange rate difficulties experienced by countries under the ERM strengthen or weaken the arguments for progressing to a single European currency?

22. Under what circumstances may a pegged exchange rate system like the ERM (a) help to prevent speculation; (b) aggravate the problem of speculation?

23. By what means would a depressed country in an economic union with a single currency be able to recover? Would the market provide a satisfactory solution or would (union) government intervention be necessary, and, if so, what form would the intervention take?

24. Assume that just some of the members of a common market like the EU adopt full economic and monetary union, including a common currency. What are the advantages and disadvantages to those members joining the full EMU and to those not joining?

25. Is the eurozone likely to be an optimal currency area? Is it more or less likely to be so over time? Explain your answer.

26. It is often argued that international convergence of economic indicators is a desirable objective. Does this mean that countries should seek to achieve the same rate of economic growth, monetary growth, interest rates, budget deficits as a percentage of their GDP, etc.?

27. Why is it difficult to achieve international harmonisation of economic policies?

28. To what extent was the debt crisis of the early 1980s caused by inappropriate policies that had been pursued by the debtor countries?

29. Imagine that you are an ambassador of a developing country at an international conference. What would you try to persuade the rich countries to do in order to help you and other poor countries overcome the debt problem? How would you set about persuading them that it was in their own interests to help you?

30. Has increased globalisation been a good thing for national economies?

MyEconLab

This book can be supported by MyEconLab, which contains a range of additional resources, including an online homework and tutorial system designed to test and build your understanding.

You need both an access card and a course ID to access MyEconLab:

1. Is your lecturer using MyEconLab? Ask your lecturer for your course ID.

2. Has an access card been included with the book at a reduced cost? Check the inside back cover of the book.

3. If you have a course ID but no access card, go to: http://www.myeconlab.com/ to buy access to this interactive study programme.

ADDITIONAL CASE STUDIES IN THE *ESSENTIALS OF ECONOMICS* MyEconLab (www.pearsoned.co.uk/sloman)

14.1 **Balance of trade and the public finances.** An examination of countries' budget and balance of trade balances.

14.2 **Making sense of the financial balances on the balance of payments.** An examination of the three main components of the financial account.

14.3 **The UK's balance of payments deficit.** An examination of the UK's persistent trade and current account deficits.

14.4 **Does PPP hold in the long run?** This considers the relationship between inflation rate differentials and movements in sterling.

14.5 **The Gold Standard.** A historical example of fixed exchange rates.

14.6 **A high exchange rate.** This case looks at whether a high exchange rate is necessarily bad news for exporters.

14.7 **The sterling crisis of early 1985.** When the pound fell almost to $1.00.

14.8 **Currency turmoil in the 1990s.** A crisis in Mexico; a rising yen and German mark; a falling US dollar – why did this all happen?

14.9 **The 1997/8 crisis in Asia.** The role played by the IMF.

14.10 **Argentina in crisis.** An examination of the collapse of the Argentinean economy in 2001–2.

14.11 **The Tobin tax.** An examination of the possible use of small taxes on foreign exchange transactions. The purpose is to reduce currency fluctuations.

14.12 **The euro, the US dollar and world currency markets.** An analysis of the relationship between the euro and the dollar.

14.13 **Using interest rates to control both aggregate demand and the exchange rate.** A problem of one instrument and two targets.

14.14 **The UK Labour government's convergence criteria for euro membership.** An examination of the five tests set by the UK government that would have to be passed before the question of euro membership would be put to the electorate in a referendum.

14.15 **Debt and the environment.** How high levels of debt can encourage developing countries to damage their environment in an attempt to increase export earnings.

14.16 **The great escape.** This case examines the problem of capital flight from developing countries to rich countries.

14.17 **Swapping debt.** Schemes to convert a developing country's debt into other forms, such as shares in its industries.

14.18 **Economic aid.** Does aid provide a solution to the debt problem?

WEB APPENDIX

14.1 The effectiveness of fiscal and monetary policies. A comparison of the effectiveness of fiscal and monetary policies under fixed and floating exchange rates.

WEBSITES RELEVANT TO PART D

Numbers and sections refer to websites listed in the Web Appendix and hotlinked from this book's website at **www.pearsoned. co.uk/sloman.**

- For news articles relevant to Part D, follow the *News* link in MyEconLab or Google the Sloman Economics News site.

- For general news on countries' trade, balance of payments and exchange rates, see websites in section A, and particularly A1–5, 7–9, 20, 26, 31, 35, 36. For articles on various aspects of economic development, see A27, 28; I9. See also links to newspapers worldwide in A38, 39, 43, 44, and the news search feature in Google at A41.

- For international data on imports and exports, see section B in site B1. See also H16 > *Documents, data and Resources* > *Statistics*. See also trade data in B31 and 35. See also the trade topic in I14.

- For international data on balance of payments and exchange rates, see B1, B31 and OECD Economic Outlook in B21 (also in section 7 of B1). See also the trade topic in I14.

- For UK data on balance of payments, see B3: search in *Publications* > *Books* for *United Kingdom Balance of Payments – the Pink Book* (annual) and *United Kingdom Economic Accounts* (quarterly). See also B34. For EU data, see B38 and 47.

- For exchange rates, see A1, 3; B34, 45; F2, 6, 8.

- For data on debt and development, see B24 (Global Development Finance) and B31. Also see the debt section in I14.

- For discussion papers on international trade, the balance of payments and exchange rates, see H4 and 7.

- For trade disputes, see H16.

- For information on various preferential trading arrangements, see H20–23.

- For various pressure groups critical of the effects of free trade and globalisation, see H11, 13, 14.

- For EU sites, see G1, 3, 7–14, 16–19.

- For information on trade, debt and developing countries, see H4, 7, 9, 10, 13, 14, 16–21. See also links to development sites in I9.

- For student resources relevant to Part D, see sites C1–7, 9, 10, 19.

Web appendix

All the following websites can be accessed from this book's own website (www.pearsoned.co.uk/sloman). When you enter the site, click on **Hotlinks**. You will find all the following sites listed. Click on the one you want and the 'hot link' will take you straight to it.

The sections and numbers below refer to the ones used in the websites listed at the end of each chapter. Thus if the list contained the number A21, this would refer to the Moneyextra site.

A General news sources

As the title of this section implies, the websites here can be used for finding material on current news issues or tapping into news archives. Most archives are offered free of charge. However, some do require you to register. As well as key UK and US news sources, you will also notice some slightly different places from where you can get your news, such as the *Moscow Times* and *Kyodo News* (from Japan). Check out site numbers 38. *Refdesk,* 43. *Guardian World News Guide* and 44. *Online newspapers* for links to newspapers across the world. Try searching for an article on a particular topic by using site number 41. *Google News Search.*

1. BBC News
2. The Economist
3. The Financial Times
4. The Guardian
5. The Independent
6. ITN
7. The Observer
8. The Telegraph
9. Aljazeera
10. The New York Times
11. Fortune
12. Time Magazine
13. The Washington Post
14. Moscow Times (English)
15. Pravda (English)
16. Straits Times (Singapore)
17. New Straits Times (Malaysia)
18. The Scotsman
19. The Herald
20. Euromoney
21. Moneyextra
22. Market News International (MNI)
23. Bloomberg Businessweek
24. International Business Times
25. CNN Money
26. Vox (economic analysis and commentary)
27. Asia News Network
28. allAfrica.com
29. Greek News Sources (English)
30. Kyodo News: Japan (English)
31. Euronews
32. Australian Financial Review
33. Sydney Morning Herald
34. Japan Times
35. Reuters
36. Bloomberg
37. David Smith's Economics UK.com
38. Refdesk (links to a whole range of news sources)
39. Newspapers and Magazines on World Wide Web
40. Yahoo News Search
41. Google News Search
42. ABYZ news links
43. Guardian World News Guide
44. Online newspapers

B Sources of economic and business data

Using websites to find up-to-date data is of immense value to the economist. The data sources below offer you a range of specialist and non-specialist data information. Universities have free access to the *UK Data Service* site (site 35 in this set), which is a huge database of statistics. Site 34, the *Treasury Pocket Data Bank*, is a very useful source of key UK and world statistics, and is updated monthly; it downloads as an Excel file. The Economics Network's *Economic data freely available online* (site 1) gives links to various sections in 40 UK and international sites.

1. Economics Network gateway to economic data
2. Office for Budget Responsibility
3. National Statistics
4. Data Archive (Essex)
5. Bank of England Statistical Database
6. Economic Resources (About)
7. Nationwide House Prices Site
8. House Web (data on housing market)

9. Economist global house price data
10. Halifax House Price Index
11. House prices indices from ONS
12. Penn World Table
13. Economist economic and financial indicators
14. FT market data
15. Economagic
16. Groningen Growth and Development Centre
17. AEAweb: Resources for economists on the Internet (RFE): data
18. Joseph Rowntree Foundation
19. Intute: Social Sciences (Economics) (archive site)
20. Energy Information Administration
21. OECD.Stat
22. CIA world statistics site (World Factbook)
23. Millennium Development Goal Indicators Database
24. World Bank Data
25. Federal Reserve Bank of St Louis, US Economic Datasets (FRED)
26. Ministry of Economy, Trade and Industry (Japan)
27. Financial data from Yahoo
28. DataMarket
29. Index Mundi
30. Oanda Currency Converter
31. World Economic Outlook Database (IMF)
32. Telegraph shares and markets
33. OFFSTATS links to data sets
34. Treasury Pocket Data Bank (source of UK and world economic data)
35. UK Data Service (incorporating ESDS)
36. BBC News, market data
37. NationMaster
38. Statistical Annex of the European Economy
39. Business and Consumer Surveys (all EU countries)
40. Gapminder
41. WebEc Economics Data
42. WTO International Trade Statistics database
43. UNCTAD trade, investment and development statistics (UNCTADstat)
44. London Metal Exchange
45. Bank for International Settlements, global nominal and real effective exchange rate indices
46. EconStats from EconomyWatch
47. AMECO database

C Sites for students and teachers of economics

The following websites offer useful ideas and resources to those who are studying or teaching economics. It is worth browsing through some just to see what is on offer. Try out the first four sites, for starters. The *Internet for Economics* (site 8) is a very helpful tutorial for economics students on using the Internet.

1. The Economics Network
2. Teaching Resources for Undergraduate Economics (TRUE)
3. Ecedweb
4. Studying Economics
5. Economics and Business Education Association
6. Tutor2U
7. Council for Economic Education
8. Internet for Economics (tutorial on using the Web)
9. Econoclass: Resources for economics teachers
10. Teaching resources for economists (RFE)
11. METAL – Mathematics for Economics: enhancing Teaching And Learning
12. Federal Reserve Bank of San Francisco: Economics Education
13. Excel in Economics Teaching (from the Economics Network)
14. WebEc resources
15. Dr. T's EconLinks: Teaching Resources
16. Online Opinion (Economics)
17. The Idea Channel
18. History of Economic Thought
19. Resources For Economists on the Internet (RFE)
20. Classroom Expernomics
21. Bank of England education resources
22. Why Study Economics?
23. Economic Classroom Experiments
24. Veconlab: Charles Holt's classroom experiments
25. Embedding Threshold Concepts
26. MIT Open Courseware in Economics
27. EconPort

D Economic models, simulations and classroom experiments

Economic modelling is an important aspect of economic analysis. There are several sites that offer access to a model or simulation for you to use: e.g. *Virtual Chancellor* (where you can play being Chancellor of the Exchequer). Using such models can be a useful way of finding out how economic theory works within a specific environment. Other sites link to games and experiments, where you can play a particular role, perhaps competing with other students.

1. Virtual Chancellor
2. Virtual Factory
3. Interactive simulation models (Economics Web Institute)
4. About.com Economics
5. Classic Economic Models
6. Economics Network Handbook, Chapter on Simulations, Games and Role-play
7. Classroom Experiments, Internet Experiments, and Internet Simulations
8. Simulations
9. Experimental economics: Wikipedia

10. Software available on the Economics Network site
11. RFE Software
12. Virtual Worlds
13. Veconlab: Charles Holt's classroom experiments
14. EconPort Experiments
15. Denise Hazlett's Classroom Experiments in Macroeconomics
16. Games Economists Play
17. Finance and Economics Experimental Laboratory at Exeter (FEELE)
18. Classroom Expernomics
19. The Economics Network's Guide to Classroom Experiments and Games
20. Economic Classroom Experiments (Wikiversity)

E UK government and UK organisations' sites

If you want to see what a government department is up to, then look no further than the list below. Government departments' websites are an excellent source of information and data. They are particularly good at offering information on current legislation and policy initiatives.

1. Gateway site (GOV.UK)
2. Department for Communities and Local Government
3. Prime Minister's Office
4. Competition & Markets Authority
5. Department for Education
6. Department for International Development
7. Department for Transport
8. Department of Health
9. Department for Work and Pensions
10. Department for Business, Innovation and Skills
11. Environment Agency
12. Department of Energy and Climate Change
13. Low Pay Commission
14. Department for Environment, Food and Rural Affairs
15. Office of Communications (Ofcom)
16. Office of Gas and Electricity Markets (Ofgem)
17. Official Documents OnLine
18. Office for Budget Responsibility
19. Office of Rail and Road (ORR)
20. The Takeover Panel
21. Sustainable Development Commission
22. OFWAT
23. National Statistics (ONS)
24. List of ONS releases from UK Data Explorer
25. HM Revenue and Customs
26. UK Intellectual Property Office
27. Parliament website
28. Scottish Government
29. Scottish Environment Protection Agency
30. Treasury
31. Equality and Human Rights Commission
32. Trades Union Congress (TUC)
33. Confederation of British Industry
34. Adam Smith Institute
35. Chatham House
36. Institute for Fiscal Studies
37. Advertising Standards Authority
38. Businesses and Self-employed
39. Campaign for Better Transport
40. New Economics Foundation
41. Financial Conduct Authority
42. Prudential Regulation Authority

F Sources of monetary and financial data

As the title suggests, here are listed useful websites for finding information on financial matters. You will see that the list comprises mainly central banks, both within Europe and further afield. The links will take you to English language versions of non-English-speaking countries' sites.

1. Bank of England
2. Bank of England Monetary and Financial Statistics
3. Banque de France
4. Bundesbank (German central bank)
5. Central Bank of Ireland
6. European Central Bank
7. Eurostat
8. US Federal Reserve Bank
9. Netherlands Central Bank
10. Bank of Japan
11. Reserve Bank of Australia
12. Bank Negara Malaysia
13. Monetary Authority of Singapore
14. Bank of Canada
15. National Bank of Denmark
16. Reserve Bank of India
17. Links to central bank websites from the Bank for International Settlements
18. The London Stock Exchange

G European Union and related sources

For information on European issues, the following is a wide range of useful sites. The sites maintained by the European Union are an excellent source of information and are provided free of charge.

1. Economic and Financial Affairs: (EC DG)
2. European Central Bank
3. EU official Web site
4. Eurostat
5. Employment, Social Affairs and Inclusion: (EC DG)
6. Booklets on the EU
7. Internal Market, Industry, Entrepreneurship and SMEs: (EC DG)

8. Competition: (EC DG)
9. Agriculture and Rural Development: (EC DG)
10. Energy: (EC DG)
11. Environment: (EC DG)
12. Regional Policy: (EC DG)
13. Taxation and Customs Union: (EC DG)
14. Education and Culture: (EC DG)
15. European Patent Office
16. European Commission
17. European Parliament
18. European Council
19. Mobility and Transport: (EC DG)
20. Trade: (EC DG)
21. Internal Market and Services: (EC DG)
22. International Cooperation and Development: (EC DG)
23. Banking and Finance (EC DG)

H International organisations

This section casts its net beyond Europe and lists the Web addresses of the main international organisations in the global economy. You will notice that some sites are run by charities, such as Oxfam, while others represent organisations set up to manage international affairs, such as the International Monetary Fund and the United Nations.

1. Food and Agriculture Organization (FAO)
2. United Nations Conference on Trade and Development (UNCTAD)
3. International Labour Organization (ILO)
4. International Monetary Fund (IMF)
5. Organization for Economic Co-operation and Development (OECD)
6. OPEC
7. World Bank
8. World Health Organization (WHO)
9. United Nations (UN)
10. United Nations Industrial Development Organization (UNIDO)
11. Friends of the Earth
12. Institute of International Finance
13. Oxfam
14. Christian Aid (reports on development issues)
15. European Bank for Reconstruction and Development (EBRD)
16. World Trade Organization (WTO)
17. United Nations Development Programme
18. UNICEF
19. EURODAD – European Network on Debt and Development
20. NAFTA
21. South American Free Trade Areas
22. ASEAN
23. APEC

I Economics search and link sites

If you are having difficulty finding what you want from the list of sites above, the following sites offer links to other sites and are a very useful resource when you are looking for something a little bit more specialist. Once again, it is worth having a look at what these sites have to offer in order to judge their usefulness.

1. Gateway for UK official sites
2. Alta Plana
3. Data Archive Search
4. Inomics (search engine for economics information)
5. RePEc bibliographic database
6. Estima: Links to economics resources sites
7. Portal sites with links to other sites (Economics Network)
8. WebEc
9. One World (link to economic development sites)
10. Economic development sites (list) from OneWorld.net
11. DMOZ Open Directory: Economics
12. Web links for economists from the Economics Network
13. EconData.Net
14. OFFSTATS links to data sets
15. Excite Economics Links
16. Internet Resources for Economists
17. National Association for Business Economics links
18. Resources for Economists on the Internet
19. UK University Economics Departments
20. Economics education links
21. Development Gateway
22. Find the Data

J Internet search engines

The following search engines have been found to be useful.

1. Google
2. Bing
3. Whoosh UK
4. Excite
5. Zanran (search engine for data and statistics)
6. Search.com
7. MSN
8. Economics search engine (from RFE)
9. Yahoo
10. Ask
11. Kartoo
12. Blinkx (for videos and audio podcasts)

Key ideas and glossary

KEY IDEAS

1. **Scarcity** is the excess of human wants over what can actually be produced. Because of scarcity, various choices have to be made between alternatives **(page 5)**.
2. **Opportunity cost.** The cost of something measured in terms of what you give up to get it/do it. The best alternative forgone **(page 7)**. **(Threshold Concept 1)**
3. **Rational decision making** involves weighing up the marginal benefit and marginal cost of any activity. If the marginal benefit exceeds the marginal cost, it is rational to do the activity (or to do more of it). If the marginal cost exceeds the marginal benefit, it is rational not to do it (or to do less of it) **(page 11)**. **(Threshold Concept 2)**
4. **Modelling in economics** involves specifying how one variable (the 'dependent variable') depends on one or more other variables ('independent variables'). It involves 'holding constant' all other variables that might influence the outcome (the *ceteris paribus* assumption). A model can be expressed in words, as a graph, or mathematically in terms of one or more equations. In this book we use mainly verbal descriptions and graphs **(page 12)**. **(Threshold Concept 3)**
5. **People respond to incentives**. It is important, therefore, that incentives are appropriate and have the desired effect **(page 20)**. **(Threshold Concept 4)**
6. **Changes in demand or supply cause markets to adjust.** Whenever such changes occur, the resulting 'disequilibrium' will bring an automatic change in prices, thereby restoring equilibrium (i.e. a balance of demand and supply) **(page 20)**.
7. **Government intervention may be able to rectify various failings of the market.** Government intervention in the market can be used to achieve various economic objectives that may not be best achieved by the market. Governments, however, are not perfect and their actions may bring adverse as well as beneficial consequences **(page 23)**. **(Threshold Concept 5)**
8. **The principle of diminishing marginal utility.** The more of a product a person consumes over a given period of time, the less will be the additional utility gained from one more unit **(page 31)**.

9. **Equilibrium is the point where conflicting interests are balanced.** Only at this point is the amount that demanders are willing to purchase the same as the amount that suppliers are willing to supply. It is a point that will be automatically reached in a free market through the operation of the price mechanism **(page 37)**. **(Threshold Concept 6)**
10. **People gain from voluntary interaction**. When people buy from or sell to other people, or when they are employed by or employ other people, both parties will gain from the interaction **(page 46)**. **(Threshold Concept 7)**
11. **Elasticity.** The responsiveness of one variable (e.g. demand) to a change in another (e.g. price). This concept is fundamental to understanding how markets work. The more elastic variables are, the more responsive is the market to changing circumstances **(page 59)**. **(Threshold Concept 8)**
12. **People's actions are influenced by their expectations.** People respond not just to what is happening now (such as a change in price), but to what they anticipate will happen in the future **(page 62)**. **(Threshold Concept 9)**
13. **People's actions are influenced by their attitudes towards risk**. Many decisions are taken under conditions of risk or uncertainty. Generally, the lower the probability of (or the more uncertain) the desired outcome of an action, the less likely it is that people will undertake the action **(page 66)**.
14. **Output depends on the amount of resources and how they are used**. Different amounts and combinations of inputs will lead to different amounts of output. If output is to be produced efficiently, then inputs should be combined in the optimum proportions **(page 76)**.
15. **The law of diminishing marginal returns**. When increasing amounts of a variable factor are used with a given amount of a fixed factor, there will come a point when each extra unit of the variable factor will produce less extra output than the previous unit **(page 76)**.

16. **The principal–agent problem**. Where people (principals), as a result of a lack of knowledge, cannot ensure that their best interests are served by their agents. Agents may take advantage of this situation to the disadvantage of the principals **(page 97)**.

17. **Market power benefits the powerful at the expense of others**. When firms have market power over prices, they can use this to raise prices and profits above the perfectly competitive level. Other things being equal, the firm will gain at the expense of the consumer. Similarly, if consumers or workers have market power, they can use this to their own benefit **(page 101)**.

18. **Economic efficiency** is achieved when each good is produced at the minimum cost and where consumers get maximum benefit from their income **(page 108)**.

19. **People often think and behave strategically**. How you think others will respond to your actions is likely to influence your own behaviour. Firms, for example, when considering a price or product change will often take into account the likely reactions of their rivals **(page 118)**.

20. **The fallacy of composition**. What applies in one case will not necessarily apply when repeated in all cases **(page 129)**.

21. **Stocks and flows**. A stock is a quantity of something at a given point in time. A flow is an increase or decrease in something over a specified period of time. This is an important distinction and a common cause of confusion **(page 148)**.

22. **Equity** is where income is distributed in a way that is considered to be fair or just. Note that an equitable distribution is not the same as a totally equal distribution and that different people have different views on what is equitable **(page 159)**.

23. **Allocative efficiency in any activity is achieved where any reallocation would lead to a decline in net benefit**. It is achieved where marginal benefit equals marginal cost. Private efficiency is achieved where marginal private benefit equals marginal private cost ($MB = MC$). Social efficiency is achieved where marginal social benefit equals marginal social cost ($MSB = MSC$) **(page 167)**. **(Threshold Concept 10)**

24. **Markets generally fail to achieve social efficiency**. There are various types of market failure. Market failures provide one of the major justifications for government intervention in the economy **(page 167)**.

25. **General equilibrium**. A situation where all markets are in equilibrium. This situation can be assessed as to whether or not allocative efficiency is achieved. This will depend on whether or not markets are perfect **(page 168)**. **(Threshold Concept 11)**

26. **Externalities are spillover costs or benefits**. Where these exist, even an otherwise perfect market will fail to achieve social efficiency **(page 168)**.

27. **The free-rider problem**. People are often unwilling to pay for things if they can make use of things other people have bought. This problem can lead to people not purchasing things which would be to the benefit of themselves and other members of society to have **(page 172)**.

28. **The problem of time lags**. Many economic actions can take a long time to take effect. This can cause problems of instability and an inability of the economy to achieve social efficiency **(page 176)**.

29. **Societies face trade-offs between economic objectives**. For example, the goal of faster growth may conflict with that of greater equality; the goal of lower unemployment may conflict with that of lower inflation (at least in the short run). This is an example of opportunity cost: the cost of achieving more of one objective may be achieving less of another. The existence of trade-offs means that policy makers must make choices **(page 177)**.

30. **Economies suffer from inherent instability**. As a result, economic growth and other macroeconomic indicators tend to fluctuate **(page 202)**. **(Threshold Concept 12)**

31. **Balance sheets affect people's behaviour**. The size and structureof governments', institutions' and individuals' liabilities (and assets too) affect economic well-being and can have significant effects on behaviour and economic activity **(page 205)**.

32. **The principle of cumulative causation**. An initial event can cause an ultimate effect that is much larger **(page 219)**. **(Threshold Concept 13)**

33. **The distinction between nominal and real figures**. Nominal figures are those using current prices, interest rates, etc. Real figures are figures corrected for inflation **(page 227)**. **(Threshold Concept 14)**

34. **Long-term growth in a country's output depends on growth in the quantity and/or productivity of its resources**. Potential economic growth depends on the country's resources, technology and productivity. This is crucial to understanding what underlies the wealth of nations and why some countries have faster growth rates than others **(page 248)**. **(Threshold Concept 15)**

35. **Goodhart's Law**. Controlling a symptom (i.e. an indicator) of a problem will not cure the problem. Instead, the indicator will merely cease to be a good indicator of the problem **(page 349)**.

36. **The law of comparative advantage**. Provided opportunity costs of various goods differ in two countries, both of them can gain from mutual trade if they specialise in producing (and exporting) those goods that have relatively low opportunity costs compared with the other country's **(page 369)**.

GLOSSARY

Absolute advantage   A country has an absolute advantage over another in the production of a good if it can produce it with less resources than the other country can.

Accelerationist theory   The theory that unemployment can only be reduced below the natural level at the cost of accelerating inflation.

Accelerator theory   The *level* of investment depends on the *rate of change* of national income, and as a result tends to be subject to substantial fluctuations.

Active balances   Money held for transactions and precautionary purposes.

Actual growth   The percentage annual increase in national output actually produced.

Ad valorem tariffs   Tariffs levied as a percentage of the price of the import.

Ad valorem tax   A tax on a good levied as a percentage of its value. It can be a single-stage tax or a multi-stage tax (such as VAT).

Adaptive expectations hypothesis   The theory that people base their expectations of inflation on past inflation rates.

Adjustable peg   A system whereby exchange rates are fixed for a period of time, but may be devalued (or revalued) if a deficit (or surplus) becomes substantial.

Adverse selection   The tendency of those at greatest risk to take out insurance.

Aggregate demand   Total spending on goods and services made in the economy. It consists of four elements, consumer spending (C), investment (I), government spending (G) and the expenditure on exports (X), less any expenditure on imports of goods and services (M): $AD = C + I + G + X - M$.

Aggregate demand for labour curve   A curve showing the total demand for labour in the economy at different levels of real wage rates.

Aggregate supply   The total amount of output in the economy.

Aggregate supply of labour curve   A curve showing the total number of people willing and able to work at different average real wage rates.

Allocative efficiency   A situation where the current combination of goods produced and sold gives the maximum satisfaction for each consumer at their current levels of income. Note that a redistribution of income would lead to a different combination of goods that was allocatively efficient.

Allocative role for government intervention   Interventions by government to affect the allocation of resources in consumption and/or production.

Appreciation   A rise in the free-market exchange rate of the domestic currency with foreign currencies.

Arc elasticity   The measurement of elasticity between two points on a curve.

Assets   Possessions, or claims held on others.

Asymmetric information   Where one party in an economic relationship (e.g. an agent) has more information than another (e.g. the principal).

Asymmetric shocks   Shocks (such as an oil price increase or a recession in another part of the world) that have different-sized effects on different industries, regions or countries.

Automatic fiscal stabilisers   Tax revenues that rise and government expenditure that falls as national income rises. The more they change with income, the bigger the stabilising effect on national income.

Average cost pricing or mark-up pricing   Where firms set the price by adding a profit mark-up to average cost.

Average fixed cost   Total fixed cost per unit of output: $AFC = TFC/Q$.

Average (or 'mid-point') formula for price elasticity of demand ΔQ_D/average $Q_D \div \Delta P$/average P.

Average physical product   Total output (TPP) per unit of the variable factor in question: $APP = TPP/Q_v$.

Average rate of income tax   Income taxes as a proportion of a person's total (gross) income: T/Y.

Average revenue   Total revenue per unit of output. When all output is sold at the same price, average revenue will be the same as price: $AR = TR/Q = P$.

Average (total) cost   Total cost (fixed plus variable) per unit of output: $AC = TC/Q = AFC + AVC$.

Average variable cost   Total variable cost per unit of output: $AVC = TVC/Q$.

Balance of payments account   A record of the country's transactions with the rest of the world. It shows the country's payments to or deposits in other countries (debits) and its receipts or deposits from other countries (credits). It also shows the balance between these debits and credits under various headings.

Balance of payments on current account   The balance on trade in goods and services plus net investment income and current transfers.

Balance on trade in goods   Exports of goods minus imports of goods.

Balance on trade in goods and services (or balance of trade)   Exports of goods and services minus imports of goods and services.

Balance on trade in services   Exports of services minus imports of services.

Balance sheet recession   An economic slowdown or recession caused by private-sector agents looking to improve their financial well-being by increasing their saving and/or paying down debt.

Balancing item (in the balance of payments)   A statistical adjustment to ensure that the two sides of the balance of payments account balance. It is necessary because of errors in compiling the statistics.

Bank bills   Bills that have been accepted by another institution and hence insured against default.

Bank (or deposits) multiplier   The number of times greater the expansion of bank deposits is than the additional liquidity in banks that causes it: $1/L$ (the inverse of the liquidity ratio).

Barometric firm price leadership   Where the price leader is the one whose prices are believed to reflect market conditions in the most satisfactory way.

Barriers to entry   Anything that prevents or impedes the entry of firms into an industry and thereby limits the amount of competition faced by existing firms.

Barter economy   An economy where people exchange goods and services directly with one another without any payment of money. Workers would be paid with bundles of goods.

Base year (for index numbers)   The year whose index number is set at 100.

Basic rate of tax   The main marginal rate of tax, applying to most people's incomes.

Benefits in kind   Goods or services which the state provides directly to the recipient at no charge or at a subsidised price. Alternatively, the state can subsidise the private sector to provide them.

Bilateral monopoly   Where a monopsony buyer faces a monopoly seller.

Bill of exchange   A certificate promising to repay a stated amount on a certain date, typically three months from the issue of the bill. Bills pay no interest as such, but are sold at a discount and redeemed at face value, thereby earning a rate of discount for the purchaser.

Bounded rationality   When the ability to make rational decisions is limited by lack of information or the time necessary to obtain such information.

Bretton Woods system   An adjustable peg system whereby currencies were pegged to the US dollar. The USA maintained convertibility of the dollar into gold at the rate of $35 to an ounce.

Broad definitions of money   Items in narrow definitions plus other items that can be readily converted into cash.

Broad money in UK (M4)   Cash in circulation plus retail and wholesale bank and building society deposits.

Budget deficit   The excess of central government's spending over its tax receipts.

Budget surplus   The excess of central government's tax receipts over its spending.

Business cycle or trade cycle   The periodic fluctuations of national output round its long-term trend.

Capital   All inputs into production that have themselves been produced: e.g. factories, machines and tools.

Capital account of the balance of payments   The record of the transfers of capital to and from abroad.

Capital adequacy ratio (CAR)   The ratio of a bank's capital (reserves and shares) to its risk-weighted assets.

Capital expenditure   Investment expenditure; expenditure on assets.

Cartel   A formal collusive agreement.

Central bank   Banker to the banks and the government.

Centrally planned or command economy   An economy where all economic decisions are taken by the central authorities.

Certificates of deposit (CDs)   Certificates issued by banks for fixed-term interest-bearing deposits. They can be resold by the owner to another party.

Ceteris paribus   Latin for 'other things being equal'. This assumption has to be made when making deductions from theories.

Change in demand   This is the term used for a shift in the demand curve. It occurs when a determinant of demand *other* than price changes.

Change in supply   The term used for a shift in the supply curve. It occurs when a determinant *other* than price changes.

Change in the quantity demanded   The term used for a movement along the demand curve to a new point. It occurs when there is a change in price.

Change in the quantity supplied   The term used for a movement along the supply curve to a new point. It occurs when there is a change in price.

Claimant unemployment   Those in receipt of unemployment-related benefits.

Clearing system   A system whereby inter bank debts are settled.

Closed shop   Where a firm agrees to employ only union members.

Coase theorem   By sufferers from externalities doing deals with perpetrators (by levying charges or offering payments), the externality will be 'internalised' and the socially efficient level of output will be achieved.

Collateralised debt obligations (CDOs)   These are a type of security consisting of a bundle of fixed-income assets, such as corporate bonds, mortgage debt and credit-card debt.

Collusive oligopoly   Where oligopolists agree (formally or informally) to limit competition between themselves. They may set output quotas, fix prices, limit product promotion or development, or agree not to 'poach' each other's markets.

Collusive tendering   Where two or more firms secretly agree on the prices they will tender for a contract. These prices will be above those which would be put in under a genuinely competitive tendering process.

Command-and-control (CAC) systems   The use of laws or regulations backed up by inspections and penalties (such as fines) for non-compliance.

Commercial bills   Bills of exchange issued by firms.

Common market   A customs union where the member countries act as a single market with free movement of labour and capital, common taxes and common trade laws.

Comparative advantage   A country has a comparative advantage over another in the production of a good if it can produce it at a lower opportunity cost: i.e. if it has to forgo less of other goods in order to produce it.

Competition for corporate control The competition for the control of companies through takeovers.

Complementary goods A pair of goods consumed together. As the price of one goes up, the demand for both goods will fall.

Compounding The process of adding interest each year to an initial capital sum.

Compromise strategy One whose worst outcome is better than the maximax strategy and whose best outcome is better than the maximin strategy.

Conglomerate merger When two firms in different industries merge.

Constrained discretion A set of principles or rules within which economic policy operates. These can be informal or enshrined in law.

Consumer durable A consumer good that lasts a period of time, during which the consumer can continue gaining utility from it.

Consumer sovereignty A situation where firms respond to changes in consumer demand without being in a position in the long run to charge a price above average cost.

Consumer surplus The excess of what a person would have been prepared to pay for a good (i.e. the utility) over what that person actually pays.

Consumption The act of using goods and services to satisfy wants. This will normally involve purchasing the goods and services.

Consumption function The relationship between consumption and national income. It can be expressed algebraically or graphically.

Consumption of domestically produced goods and services (C_d) The direct flow of money payments from households to firms.

Consumption smoothing The act by households of smoothing their levels of consumption over time despite facing volatile incomes.

Continuous market clearing The assumption that all markets in the economy continuously clear so that the economy is permanently in equilibrium.

Convergence of economies When countries achieve similar levels of growth, inflation, budget deficits as a percentage of GDP, balance of payments, etc.

Core workers Workers, normally with specific skills, who are employed on a permanent or long-term basis.

Cost–benefit analysis The identification, measurement and weighing up of the costs and benefits of a project in order to decide whether or not it should go ahead.

Cost-plus pricing (full-cost pricing) When firms price their product by adding a certain profit 'mark-up' to average cost.

Cost-push inflation Inflation caused by persistent rises in costs of production (independently of demand).

Countervailing power When the power of a monopolistic/oligopolistic seller is offset by powerful buyers who can prevent the price from being pushed up.

Cournot model A model of duopoly where each firm makes its price and output decisions on the assumption that its rival will produce a particular quantity.

Credible threat (or promise) One that is believable to rivals because it is in the threatener's interests to carry it out.

Cross-price elasticity of demand The percentage (or proportionate) change in quantity demanded of one good divided by the percentage (or proportionate) change in the price of another.

Cross-price elasticity of demand (arc formula) ΔQ_{Da}/average $Q_{Da} \div \Delta P_b$/average P_b.

Cross-subsidise To use profits in one market to subsidise prices in another.

Crowding out Where increased public expenditure diverts money or resources away from the private sector.

Currency union A group of countries (or regions) using a common currency.

Current account balance of payments Exports of goods and services minus imports of goods and services plus net incomes and current transfers from abroad. If inflows of money (from the sale of exports, etc.) exceed outflows of money (from the purchase of imports, etc.), there is a 'current account surplus' (a positive figure). If outflows exceed inflows, there is a 'current account deficit' (a negative figure).

Current budget balance The difference between public-sector receipts and those expenditures classified as current rather than capital expenditures.

Current expenditure Recurrent spending on goods and factor payments.

Customs union A free-trade area with common external tariffs and quotas.

Cyclical or demand-deficient unemployment Disequilibrium unemployment caused by a fall in aggregate demand with no corresponding fall in the real wage rate.

Deadweight loss of an indirect tax The loss of consumer plus producer surplus from the imposition of an indirect tax.

Deadweight welfare loss The loss of consumer plus producer surplus in imperfect markets (when compared with perfect competition).

Debit card A card that has the same use as a cheque. Its use directly debits the person's current account.

Debt-servicing costs The costs incurred when repaying debt, including debt interest payments.

Decision tree (or game tree) A diagram showing the sequence of possible decisions by competitor firms and the outcome of each combination of decisions.

Deflationary gap The shortfall of national expenditure below national income (and injections below withdrawals) at the full-employment level of national income.

Deflationary policy Fiscal or monetary policy designed to reduce the rate of growth of aggregate demand.

Demand curve A graph showing the relationship between the price of a good and the quantity of the good demanded over a given time period. Price is measured on the vertical axis; quantity demanded is measured on the horizontal axis. A demand curve can be for an individual consumer or group of consumers, or more usually for the whole market.

Demand-deficient or cyclical unemployment Disequilibrium unemployment caused by a fall in aggregate demand with no corresponding fall in the real wage rate.

Demand management policies Demand-side policies (fiscal and/or monetary) designed to smooth out the fluctuations in the business cycle.

Demand-pull inflation Inflation caused by persistent rises in aggregate demand.

Demand schedule for an individual A table showing the different quantities of a good that a person is willing and able to buy at various prices over a given period of time.

Demand schedule (market) A table showing the different total quantities of a good that consumers are willing and able to buy at various prices over a given period of time.

Demand-side policies Policies designed to affect aggregate demand: fiscal policy and monetary policy.

Dependency Where the development of a developing country is hampered by its relationships with the industrialised world.

Depreciation (of a currency) A fall in the free-market exchange rate of the domestic currency with foreign currencies.

Depreciation (of capital) The decline in value of capital equipment due to age, or wear and tear.

Deregulation Where the government removes official barriers to competition (e.g. licences and minimum quality standards).

Derived demand The demand for a factor of production depends on the demand for the good that uses it.

Destabilising speculation Where the actions of speculators tend to make price movements larger.

Devaluation Where the government re-pegs the exchange rate at a lower level.

Diminishing marginal utility As more units of a good are consumed, additional units will provide less additional satisfaction than previous units.

Diminishing marginal utility of income Where each additional unit of income earned yields less additional utility than the previous unit.

Direct taxes Taxes on income and wealth. Paid directly to the tax authorities on that income or wealth.

Discount market A money market in which new or existing bills of exchange are bought and sold.

Discounting The process of reducing the value of future flows to give them a present valuation.

Discretionary fiscal policy Deliberate changes in tax rates or the level of government expenditure in order to influence the level of aggregate demand.

Diseconomies of scale Where costs per unit of output increase as the scale of production increases.

Disequilibrium unemployment Unemployment resulting from real wage rates in the economy being above the equilibrium level.

Disguised unemployment Where the same work could be done by fewer people.

Disposable income Original income plus cash benefits and minus direct taxes and other deductions.

Distribution of income by class of recipient Measurement of the distribution of income between the classes of person who receive it (e.g. homeowners and non-homeowners or those in the north and those in the south).

Distribution of income: functional distribution Measurement of the distribution of income according to the source of income (e.g. from employment, from profit, from rent, etc.).

Distribution of income: size distribution Measurement of the distribution of income according to the levels of income received by individuals (irrespective of source).

Distributive role for government intervention Interventions by government to affect the distribution of resources such as the distribution of incomes.

Diversification Where a firm expands into new types of business.

Dominant firm price leadership When firms (the followers) choose the same price as that set by a dominant firm in the industry (the leader).

Dominant strategy game Where the *same* policy is suggested by different strategies.

Dumping When exports are sold at prices below marginal cost – often as a result of government subsidy.

Duopoly An oligopoly where there are just two firms in the market.

Economic efficiency A situation where each good is produced at the minimum cost and where individual people and firms get the maximum benefit from their resources.

Economic model The representation, either graphically, mathematically or in words, of the relationship between two or more variables. A model is a simplification of reality designed to explain just part of a complex process of economic relationships. It is thus based on various simplifying assumptions.

Economies of scale When increasing the scale of production leads to a lower cost per unit of output.

Economies of scope When increasing the range of products produced by a firm reduces the cost of producing each one.

ECU (European Currency Unit) The predecessor to the euro: a weighted average of EU currencies. It was used as a reserve currency and for the operation of the exchange rate mechanism (ERM).

Efficiency (allocative) A situation where the current combination of goods produced and sold gives the maximum satisfaction for each consumer at their current levels of income. Note that a redistribution of income would lead to a different combination of goods that was allocatively efficient.

Efficiency (productive) A situation where firms are producing the maximum output for a given amount of inputs, or producing a given output at the least cost.

Efficiency wage hypothesis The hypothesis that the productivity of workers is affected by the wage rate that they receive.

Efficiency wage rate The profit-maximising wage rate for the firm after taking into account the effects of wage rates on worker motivation, turnover and recruitment.

Elastic demand (with respect to price) Where quantity demanded changes by a larger percentage than price. Ignoring the negative sign, it will have a value greater than 1.

Elasticity A measure of the responsiveness of a variable (e.g. quantity demanded or quantity supplied) to a change in one of its determinants (e.g. price or income).

Endogenous growth theory A theory that the rate of economic growth depends on the rate of technological progress and diffusion, both of which depend on size of the capital stock and the capital goods industries, and also on institutions, incentives and the role of government.

Endogenous money supply Money supply that is determined (at least in part) by the demand for money.

Entrepreneurship The initiating and organising of the production of new goods, or the introduction of new techniques, and the risk taking associated with it.

Envelope curve A long-run average cost curve drawn as the tangency points of a series of short-run average cost curves.

Environmental charges Charges for using natural resources (e.g. water or national parks), or for using the environment as a dump for waste (e.g. factory emissions or sewage).

Equation of exchange $MV = PY$. The total level of spending on GDP (MV) equals the total value of goods and services produced (PY) that go to make up GDP.

Equilibrium A position of balance. A position from which there is no inherent tendency to move away.

Equilibrium ('natural') unemployment The difference between those who would like employment at the current wage rate and those willing and able to take a job.

Equilibrium price The price where the quantity demanded equals the quantity supplied: the price where there is no shortage or surplus.

Equities Company shares. Holders of equities are owners of the company and share in its profits by receiving dividends.

Equity A distribution of income that is considered to be fair or just. Note that an equitable distribution is not the same as an equal distribution and that different people have different views on what is equitable.

ERM (the exchange rate mechanism) A system of semi-fixed exchange rates used by most of the EU countries prior to adoption of the euro. Members' currencies were allowed to fluctuate against each other only within agreed bands. Collectively they floated against all other currencies.

Excess capacity (under monopolistic competition) In the long run, firms under monopolistic competition will produce at an output below their minimum-cost point.

Exchange equalisation account The gold and foreign exchange reserves account in the Bank of England.

Exchange rate The rate at which one national currency exchanges for another. The rate is expressed as the amount of one currency that is necessary to purchase *one unit* of another currency (e.g. $1.60 = £1).

Exchange rate band Where a currency is allowed to float between an upper and lower exchange rate, but is not allowed to move outside this band.

Exchange rate index or effective exchange rate A weighted average exchange rate expressed as an index where the value of the index is 100 in a given base year. The weights of the different currencies in the index add up to 1.

Exchange rate overshooting Where a fall (or rise) in the long-run equilibrium exchange rate causes the actual exchange rate to fall (or rise) by a greater amount before eventually moving back to the new long-run equilibrium level.

Exchange rate regime The system under which the government allows the exchange rate to be determined.

Exchange rate transmission mechanism How a change in money supply affects aggregate demand via a change in exchange rates.

Exogenous money supply Money supply that does not depend on the demand for money but is set by the authorities.

Exogenous variable A variable whose value is determined independently of the model of which it is part.

Expectations-augmented Phillips curve A (short-run) Phillips curve whose position depends on the expected rate of inflation.

Expected value The predicted or average value of an outcome over a number of occurrences, calculated by taking each of the possible outcomes and multiplying it by its probability of occurrence and then adding each of these values.

Explicit costs The payments to outside suppliers of inputs.

External benefits Benefits from production (or consumption) experienced by people *other* than the producer (or consumer).

External costs Costs of production (or consumption) borne by people *other* than the producer (or consumer).

External diseconomies of scale Where a firm's costs per unit of output increase as the size of the whole industry increases.

External economies of scale Where a firm's costs per unit of output decrease as the size of the whole *industry* grows.

Externalities Costs or benefits of production or consumption experienced by society but not by the producers or consumers themselves. Sometimes referred to as 'spillover' or 'third-party' costs or benefits.

Factors of production (or resources) The inputs into the production of goods and services: labour, land and raw materials, and capital.

Final expenditure Expenditure on goods and services. This is included in GDP and is part of aggregate demand.

Final income Original income plus the addition of all benefits (cash and in kind) and the deduction of all taxes (direct and indirect).

Financial account of the balance of payments The record of the flows of money into and out of the country for the purposes of investment or as deposits in banks and other financial institutions.

Financial crowding out When an increase in government borrowing diverts money away from the private sector.

Financial deregulation The removal of or reduction in legal rules and regulations governing the activities of financial institutions.

Financial flexibility Where employers can vary their wage costs by changing the composition of their workforce or the terms on which workers are employed.

Financial instruments Financial products resulting in a financial claim by one party over another.

Financial intermediaries The general name for financial institutions (banks, building societies, etc.) which act as a means of channelling funds from depositors to borrowers.

Financialisation A term describing the significance of the financial system in our everyday lives and in influencing economic activity.

Fine-tuning The use of demand management policy (fiscal or monetary) to smooth out cyclical fluctuations in the economy.

First-degree price discrimination Where a firm charges each consumer for each unit the maximum price they are willing to pay for that unit.

First-mover advantage When a firm gains from being the first one to take action.

Fiscal drag The tendency of automatic fiscal stabilisers to reduce the recovery of an economy from recession.

Fiscal policy Policy to affect aggregate demand by altering the balance between government expenditure and taxation.

Fiscal stance How deflationary or reflationary the Budget is.

Fixed costs Total costs that do not vary with the amount of output produced.

Fixed exchange rate (totally) Where the government takes whatever measures are necessary to maintain the exchange rate at some stated level.

Fixed factor An input that cannot be increased in supply within a given time period.

Flexible firm A firm that has the flexibility to respond to changing market conditions by changing the composition of its workforce.

Floating exchange rate When the government does not intervene in the foreign exchange markets, but simply allows the exchange rate to be freely determined by demand and supply.

Forward exchange market Where contracts are made today for the price at which currency will be exchanged at some specified future date.

Franchising Where a firm is gramted the licence to operate a given part of an industry for a specified length of time.

Free-market economy An economy where all economic decisions are taken by individual households and firms and with no government intervention.

Free-rider problem When it is not possible to exclude other people from consuming a good that someone has bought.

Free-trade area A group of countries with no trade barriers between them.

Freely floating exchange rate Where the exchange rate is determined entirely by the forces of demand and supply in the foreign exchange market with no government intervention whatsoever.

Frictional (search) unemployment Unemployment that occurs as a result of imperfect information in the labour market. It often takes time for workers to find jobs (even though there are vacancies) and in the meantime they are unemployed.

Full-employment level of national income The level of national income at which there is no deficiency of demand.

Functional distribution of income Measurement of the distribution of income according to the source of income (e.g. from employment, from profit, from rent, etc.).

Functional flexibility Where employers can switch workers from job to job as requirements change.

Funding Where the authorities alter the balance of bills and bonds for any given level of government borrowing.

Future price A price agreed today at which an item (e.g. commodities) will be exchanged at some set date in the future.

Futures or forward market A market in which contracts are made to buy or sell at some future date at a price agreed today.

Gaia philosophy The respect for the rights of the environment to remain unharmed by human activity. Humans should live in harmony with the planet and other species. We have a duty to be stewards of the natural environment, so that it can continue to be a self-maintaining and self-regulating system.

Game theory (or the theory of games) The study of alternative strategies oligopolists may choose to adopt, depending on their assumptions about their rivals' behaviour.

GDP (gross domestic product at market prices) The value of output (or income or expenditure) in terms of the prices actually paid. GDP = GVA + taxes on products − subsidies on products.

GDP deflator The price index of all final domestically produced goods and services: i.e. all items that contribute towards GDP.

General equilibrium A situation where all the millions of markets throughout the economy are in a simultaneous state of equilibrium.

General government debt The combined accumulated debt of central and local government.

General government deficit (or surplus) The combined deficit (or surplus) of central and local government.

Geographical immobility The lack of ability or willingness of people to move to jobs in other parts of the country.

Gini coefficient The area between the Lorenz curve and the 45° line divided by the total area under the 45° line.

GNI (see GNY)

GNY (gross national income) GDP plus net income from abroad.

Goodhart's Law Controlling a symptom of a problem, or only part of the problem, will not cure the problem: it will simply mean that the part that is being controlled now becomes a poor indicator of the problem.

Government bonds or 'gilt-edged securities' A government security paying a fixed sum of money each year. It is redeemed by the government on its maturity date at its face value.

Government surplus (from a tax on a good) The total tax revenue earned by the government from sales of a good.

Green tax A tax on output designed to charge for the adverse effects of production on the environment. The socially efficient level of a green tax is equal to the marginal environmental cost of production.

Gross domestic final expenditure Total expenditure by a country's residents on final goods and services. It thus includes expenditure on imports and excludes expenditure on exports.

Gross domestic product (GDP) The value of output produced within the country over a 12-month period.

Gross income Original income plus cash benefits.

Gross national income (GNY) GDP plus net income from abroad.

Gross value added at basic prices (GVA) The sum of all the values added by all industries in the economy over a year. The figures exclude taxes on products (such as VAT) and include subsidies on products.

Heuristics People's use of strategies that draw on simple lessons from past experience when they are faced with similar, although not identical, choices.

Historic costs The original amount a firm paid for factors it now owns.

Hit-and-run competition When a firm enters an industry to take advantage of temporarily high profits and then leaves again as soon as the high profits have been exhausted.

Horizontal integration A business growth strategy that involves expanding within an existing market at the same stage of production by moving into allied products. An example would be an electricity supplier moving into gas supply or a car manufacturer moving into the production of coaches or heavy goods vehicles.

Horizontal merger When two firms in the same industry at the same stage in the production process merge.

Households' disposable income The income available for households to spend: i.e. personal incomes after deducting taxes on incomes and adding benefits.

Human capital The qualifications, skills and expertise that contribute to a worker's productivity.

Human Development Index (HDI) A composite index made up of three elements: an index for life expectancy, an index for school enrolment and adult literacy, and an index for GDP per capita (in PPP$).

Hysteresis The persistence of an effect even when the initial cause has ceased to operate. In economics, it refers to the persistence of unemployment even when the demand deficiency that caused it no longer exists.

Idle balances Money held for speculative purposes: money held in anticipation of a fall in asset prices.

Imperfect competition The collective name for monopolistic competition and oligopoly.

Implicit costs Costs that do not involve a direct payment of money to a third party, but which nevertheless involve a sacrifice of some alternative.

Import-substituting industrialisation (ISI) A strategy of restricting imports of manufactured goods and using the foreign exchange saved to build up domestic substitute industries.

Income effect (of a price change) The effect of a change in price on quantity demanded arising from the consumer becoming better or worse off as a result of the price change.

Income effect of a rise in wage rates Workers get a higher income for a given number of hours worked and may thus feel they need to work *fewer* hours as wage rates rise.

Income effect of a tax rise Tax increases reduce people's incomes and thus encourage people to work more.

Income elasticity of demand The percentage (or proportionate) change in quantity demanded divided by the percentage (or proportionate) change in income.

Income elasticity of demand (arc formula) ΔQ_D/average $Q_D \div \Delta Y$/average Y.

Increasing opportunity costs of production When additional production of one good involves ever-increasing sacrifices of another.

Independence (of firms in a market) Where the decisions of one firm in a market will not have any significant effect on the demand curves of its rivals.

Independent risks Where two risky events are unconnected. The occurrence of one will not affect the likelihood of the occurrence of the other.

Index number The value of a variable expressed as 100 plus or minus its percentage deviation from a base year.

Indirect taxes   Taxes on expenditure (e.g. VAT). Paid to the tax authorities, not by the consumer, but indirectly by the suppliers of the goods or services.

Indivisibilities   The impossibility of dividing a factor into smaller units.

Induced investment   Investment that firms make to enable them to meet extra consumer demand.

Industrial policies   Policies to encourage industrial investment and greater industrial efficiency.

Industry's infrastructure   The network of supply agents, communications, skills, training facilities, distribution channels, specialised financial services, etc., that supports a particular industry.

Inelastic demand   Where quantity demanded changes by a smaller percentage than price. Ignoring the negative sign, it will have a value less than 1.

Infant industry   An industry that has a potential comparative advantage, but which is as yet too underdeveloped to be able to realise this potential.

Inferior goods   Goods whose demand *decreases* as consumer incomes increase. Such goods have a negative income elasticity of demand.

Inflation rate (annual)   The percentage increase in prices over a 12-month period.

Inflationary gap   The excess of national expenditure over income (and injections over withdrawals) at the full-employment level of national income.

Infrastructure (industry's)   The network of supply agents, communications, skills, training facilities, distribution channels, specialised financial services, etc., that supports a particular industry.

Injections (J)   Expenditure on the production of domestic firms coming from outside the inner flow of the circular flow of income. Injections equal investment (I_d) plus government expenditure (G_d) plus expenditure on exports (X).

Input–output analysis   This involves dividing the economy into sectors where each sector is a user of inputs from and a supplier of outputs to other sectors. The technique examines how these inputs and outputs can be matched to the total resources available in the economy.

Insiders   Those in employment who can use their privileged position (either as members of unions or because of specific skills) to secure pay rises despite an excess supply of labour (unemployment).

Integration: horizontal   A business growth strategy that involves expanding within an existing market at the same stage of production by moving into allied products. An example would be an electricity supplier moving into gas supply or a car manufacturer moving into the production of coaches or heavy goods vehicles.

Integration: vertical   A business growth strategy that involves expanding within an existing market, but at a different stage of production. Vertical integration can be 'forward', such as moving into distribution or retail, or 'backward', such as expanding into extracting raw materials or producing components.

Interdependence (under oligopoly)   One of the two key features of oligopoly. Each firm will be affected by its rivals' decisions. Likewise its decisions will affect its rivals'. Firms recognise this interdependence. This recognition will affect their decisions.

Interest rate transmission mechanism   How a change in money supply affects aggregate demand via a change in interest rates.

International business cycle   The cyclical nature of economic growth in the international economy, which both reflects the synchrony in national business cycles and impacts on individual economies' cycles.

International harmonisation of economic policies   Where countries attempt to co-ordinate their macroeconomic policies so as to achieve common goals.

International liquidity   The supply of currencies in the world acceptable for financing international trade and investment.

International substitution effect   As prices rise, people at home and abroad buy less of this country's products and more of products from abroad.

International trade multiplier   The effect on national income in country B of a change in exports (or imports) of country A.

Inter-temporal substitution effect   Higher prices may lead to higher interest rates and thus less borrowing and more saving.

Intervention price (in the CAP)   The price at which the EU is prepared to buy a foodstuff if the market price were to be below it.

Interventionist supply-side policies   Policies to increase aggregate supply by government intervention to counteract the deficiencies of the market.

Investment   The production of items that are not for immediate consumption.

Joint float   Where a group of currencies pegged to each other jointly float against other currencies.

Joint supply   Where the production of more of one good leads to the production of more of another.

Kinked demand theory   The theory that oligopolists face a demand curve that is kinked at the current price, demand being significantly more elastic above the current price than below. The effect of this is to create a situation of price stability.

Labour   All forms of human input, both physical and mental, into current production.

Labour force   The number employed plus the number unemployed.

Land (and raw materials)   Inputs into production that are provided by nature: e.g. unimproved land and mineral deposits in the ground.

Law of comparative advantage   Trade can benefit all countries if they specialise in the goods in which they have a comparative advantage.

Law of demand The quantity of a good demanded per period of time will fall as price rises and will rise as price falls, other things being equal (*ceteris paribus*).

Law of diminishing (marginal) returns When one or more factors are held fixed, there will come a point beyond which the extra output from additional units of the variable factor will diminish.

Law of large numbers The larger the number of events of a particular type, the more predictable will be their average outcome.

Lender of last resort The role of the Bank of England as the guarantor of sufficient liquidity in the monetary system.

Liabilities All legal claims for payment that outsiders have on an institution.

Liquidity The ease with which an asset can be converted into cash without loss.

Liquidity preference The demand for holding assets in the form of money.

Liquidity ratio The proportion of a bank's total assets held in liquid form.

Liquidity trap When interest rates are at their floor and thus any further increases in money supply will not be spent but merely be held in idle balances as people wait for the economy to recover and/or interest rates to rise.

Lock-outs Union members are temporarily laid off until they are prepared to agree to the firm's conditions.

Long run The period of time long enough for *all* factors to be varied.

Long-run average cost curve A curve that shows how average cost varies with output on the assumption that *all* factors are variable. (It is assumed that the least-cost method of production will be chosen for each output.)

Long-run marginal cost The extra cost of producing one more unit of output assuming that all factors are variable. (It is assumed that the least-cost method of production will be chosen for this extra output.)

Long-run profit maximisation An alternative theory of the firm which assumes that managers aim to shift cost and revenue curves so as to maximise profits over some longer time period.

Long-run shut-down point This is where the *AR* curve is tangential to the *LRAC* curve. The firm can just make normal profits. Any fall in revenue below this level will cause a profit-maximising firm to shut down once all costs have become variable.

Long run under perfect competition The period of time that is long enough for new firms to enter the industry.

Lorenz curve A curve showing the proportion of national income earned by any given percentage of the population (measured from the poorest upwards).

Macroeconomic role for government intervention Interventions by government either to stabilise the economy in the short term or to promote longer-term economic growth.

Macroeconomics The branch of economics that studies economic aggregates (grand totals): e.g. the overall level of prices, output and employment in the economy.

Macro-prudential regulation Regulation which focuses on the financial system as a whole and which monitors its impact on the wider economy.

Managed floating A system of flexible exchange rates but where the government intervenes to prevent excessive fluctuations or even to achieve an unofficial target exchange rate.

Marginal benefit The additional benefit of doing a little bit more (or 1 unit more if a unit can be measured) of an activity.

Marginal consumer surplus The excess of utility from the consumption of one more unit of a good (MU) over the price paid: $MCS = MU - P$.

Marginal cost (of an activity) The additional cost of doing a little bit more (or 1 unit more if a unit can be measured) of an activity.

Marginal cost (of production) The cost of producing one more unit of output: $MC = \Delta TC/\Delta Q$.

Marginal disutility of work The extra sacrifice/hardship to a worker of working an extra unit of time in any given time period (e.g. an extra hour per day).

Marginal physical product The extra output gained by the employment of one more unit of the variable factor: $MPP = \Delta TPP/\Delta Q_v$.

Marginal productivity theory The theory that the demand for a factor depends on its marginal revenue product.

Marginal propensity to consume The proportion of a rise in national income that goes on consumption: $mpc = \Delta C/\Delta Y$.

Marginal propensity to consume domestically produced goods (mpc_d) The proportion of a rise in national income that is spent on goods and services produced within the country.

Marginal propensity to import The proportion of an increase in national income that is spent on imports: $mpm = \Delta M/\Delta Y$.

Marginal propensity to save The proportion of an increase in national income saved: $mps = \Delta S/\Delta Y$.

Marginal propensity to withdraw The proportion of an increase in national income that is withdrawn from the circular flow: $mpw = \Delta W/\Delta Y$, where $mpw = mps + mpt + mpm$.

Marginal rate of income tax The income tax rate. The rate paid on each *additional* pound earned: $\Delta T/\Delta Y$.

Marginal revenue The extra revenue gained by selling one more unit per time period: $MR = \Delta TR/\Delta Q$.

Marginal revenue product (of a factor) The extra revenue a firm earns from employing one more unit of a variable factor: $MRP_{factor} = MPP_{factor} + MR_{good}$.

Marginal tax propensity The proportion of an increase in national income paid in tax: $mpt = \Delta T/\Delta Y$.

Marginal utility The extra satisfaction gained from consuming one extra unit of a good within a given time period.

Market The interaction between buyers and sellers.

Market clearing A market clears when supply matches demand, leaving no shortage or surplus.

Market for loanable funds The market for loans from and deposits into the banking system.

Market loans Short-term loans (e.g. money at call and short notice).

Market-orientated supply-side policies Policies to increase aggregate supply by freeing up the market.

Mark-up A profit margin added to average cost to arrive at price.

Mark-up pricing (or Average cost pricing) Where firms set the price by adding a profit mark-up to average cost.

Maturity gap The difference in the average maturity of loans and deposits.

Maturity transformation The transformation of deposits into loans of a longer maturity.

Maximum price A price ceiling set by the government or some other agency. The price is not allowed to rise above this level (although it is allowed to fall below it).

Mean (or arithmetic mean) The sum of the values of each of the members of the sample divided by the total number in the sample.

Means-tested benefits Benefits whose amount depends on the recipient's income or assets.

Median The value of the middle member of the sample.

Medium of exchange Something that is acceptable in exchange for goods and services.

Menu costs of inflation The costs associated with having to adjust price lists or labels.

Merit goods Goods which the government feels that people will under consume and which therefore ought to be subsidised or provided free.

Microeconomics The branch of economics that studies individual units: e.g. households, firms and industries. It studies the interrelationships between these units in determining the pattern of production and distribution of goods and services.

Minimum price A price floor set by the government or some other agency. The price is not allowed to fall below this level (although it is allowed to rise above it).

Minimum reserve ratio A minimum ratio of cash (or other specified liquid assets) to deposits (either total or selected) that the central bank requires banks to hold.

Mixed economy An economy where economic decisions are made partly by the government and partly through the market.

Mixed market economy A market economy where there is some government intervention.

Mobility of labour The willingness and ability of labour to move to another job.

Monetarists Those who attribute inflation solely to rises in money supply.

Monetary base Notes and coin outside the central bank.

Monetary financial institutions (MFIs) Deposit-taking financial institutions including banks, building societies and central banks.

Monetary policy Policy to affect aggregate demand by altering the supply or cost of money (rate of interest).

Money illusion When people believe that a money wage or price increase (i.e. a nominal increase) represents a *real* increase: in other words, they ignore or underestimate inflation.

Money market The market for short-term loans and deposits.

Money multiplier The number of times greater the expansion of money supply (M_s) is than the expansion of the monetary base (M_b) that caused it: $\Delta M_s/\Delta M_b$.

Monopolistic competition A market structure where, like perfect competition, there are many firms and freedom of entry into the industry, but where each firm produces a differentiated product and thus has some control over its price.

Monopoly A market structure where there is only one firm in the industry.

Monopsony A market with a single buyer or employer.

Moral hazard The temptation to take more risk when you know that other people (e.g. insurers) will cover the risks.

Multiplier (injections multiplier) The number of times a rise in income exceeds the rise in injections that caused it: $k = \Delta Y/\Delta J$.

Multiplier effect An initial increase in aggregate demand of £xm leads to an eventual rise in national income that is greater than £xm.

Multiplier formula (injections multiplier) The formula for the multiplier is $k = 1/mpw$ or $1/(1 - mpc_d)$.

Narrow definitions of money Items of money that can be spent directly (cash and money in cheque-book/debit-card accounts).

Nash equilibrium The position resulting from everyone making their optimal decision based on their assumptions about their rivals' decisions. Without collusion, there is no incentive for any firm to move from this position.

National debt The accumulated budget deficits (less surpluses) over the years: the total amount of government borrowing.

National expenditure on domestic product (E) Aggregate demand in the Keynesian model: i.e. $C_d + J$.

Nationalised industries State-owned industries that produce goods or services that are sold in the market.

Natural level of output The level of output in monetarist analysis where the vertical long-run aggregate supply curve cuts the horizontal axis.

Natural level of unemployment The level of equilibrium unemployment in monetarist analysis measured as the difference between the (vertical) long-run gross labour supply curve (N) and the (vertical) long-run effective labour supply curve (AS_L).

Natural monopoly A situation where long-run average costs would be lower if an industry were under monopoly than if it were shared between two or more competitors.

Natural rate of unemployment The rate of unemployment at which there is no excess or deficiency of demand for labour.

Natural wastage When a firm wishing to reduce its workforce does so by not replacing those who leave or retire.

Near money Highly liquid assets (other than cash).

Negative income tax A combined system of tax and benefits. As people earn more, they gradually lose their benefits until beyond a certain level they begin paying taxes.

Neoclassical analysis The analysis of market economies where it is assumed that individuals and firms are self-interested rational maximisers.

Net errors and omissions A statistical adjustment to ensure that the two sides of the balance of payments account balance. It is necessary because of errors in compiling the statistics.

Net investment Total investment minus depreciation.

Net national product (NNY) GNY minus depreciation.

Network economies The benefits to consumers of having a network of other people using the same product or service.

New classical school The school of economists which believes that markets clear virtually instantaneously and that expectations are formed 'rationally'.

New Keynesians Economists who seek to explain the downward stickiness of real wages and the resulting persistence of unemployment.

Nominal GDP GDP measured in current prices. These figures take no account of inflation.

Nominal values Money values measured at *current* prices.

Non-accelerating-inflation rate of unemployment (NAIRU) The rate of unemployment consistent with a constant rate of inflation. (In monetarist analysis, this is the same as the natural rate of unemployment: the rate of unemployment at which the vertical long-run Phillips curve cuts the horizontal axis.)

Non-bank private sector Households and non-bank firms. In other words, everyone in the country other than banks and the government (central and local).

Non-collusive oligopoly Where oligopolists have no agreement between themselves, either formal, informal or tacit.

Non-excludability Where it is not possible to provide a good or service to one person without it thereby being available for others to enjoy.

Non-price competition Competition in terms of product promotion (advertising, packaging, etc.) or product development.

Non-rivalry Where the consumption of a good or service by one person will not prevent others from enjoying it.

Normal goods Goods whose demand increases as consumer incomes increase. They have a positive income elasticity of demand. Luxury goods will have a higher income elasticity of demand than more basic goods.

Normal profit The opportunity cost of being in business: the profit that could have been earned in the next best alternative business. It is counted as a cost of production.

Normal rate of return The rate of return (after taking risks into account) that could be earned elsewhere.

Normative statement A value judgement.

Numerical flexibility Where employers can change the size of their workforce as their labour requirements change.

Occupational immobility The lack of ability or willingness of people to move to other jobs irrespective of location.

Oligopoly A market structure where there are few enough firms to enable barriers to be erected against the entry of new firms.

Oligopsony A market with just a few buyers or employers.

Open economy One that trades with and has financial dealings with other countries.

Open-market operations The sale (or purchase) by the authorities of government securities in the open market in order to reduce (or increase) money supply or influence interest rates.

Opportunity cost Cost measured in terms of the best alternative forgone.

Optimal currency area The optimal size of a currency area is the one that maximises the benefits from having a single currency relative to the costs. If the area were increased or decreased in size, the costs would rise relative to the benefits.

Original income Income before taxes and benefits.

Output gap The difference between actual and potential output. When actual output exceeds potential output, the gap is positive. When actual output is less than potential output, the gap is negative.

Outsiders Those out of work or employed on a casual, part-time or short-term basis, who have little or no power to influence wages or employment.

Overheads Costs arising from the general running of an organisation, and only indirectly related to the level of output.

Participation rate The percentage of the working-age population that is part of the workforce.

Perfect competition A market structure where there are many firms; where there is freedom of entry into the industry; where all firms produce an identical product; and where all firms are price takers.

Perfectly contestable market A market where there is free and costless entry and exit.

Phillips curve A curve showing the relationship between (price) inflation and unemployment. The original Phillips curve plotted *wage* inflation against unemployment for the years 1861–1957.

Picketing When people on strike gather at the entrance to the firm and attempt to dissuade workers or delivery vehicles from entering.

Plant economies of scale Economies of scale that arise because of the large size of the factory.

Policy ineffectiveness proposition The conclusion drawn from new classical models that, when economic agents anticipate changes in economic policy, output and employment remain at their equilibrium (or natural) levels.

Poll tax A lump-sum tax per head of the population. Since it is a fixed *amount*, it has a marginal rate of zero with respect to both income and wealth.

Pooling risks (for an insurance company) The more policies an insurance company issues and the more independent the risks from these policies are, the more predictable will be the number of claims.

Portfolio balance The balance of assets, according to their liquidity, that people choose to hold in their portfolios.

Positive statement A value-free statement that can be tested by an appeal to the facts.

Post-tax income Disposable income minus indirect taxes.

Potential growth The percentage annual increase in the capacity of the economy to produce.

Potential output The economically sustainable level output that could be produced in the economy: i.e. one that involves a 'normal' level of capacity utilisation and does not result in rising inflation.

Poverty trap Where poor people are discouraged from working or getting a better job because any extra income they earn will be largely taken away in taxes and lost benefits.

Predatory pricing Where a firm sets its prices below average cost in order to drive competitors out of business.

Preferential trading arrangements A trade agreement whereby trade between the signatories is freer than trade with the rest of the world.

Price benchmark A price that is typically used. Firms, when raising prices, will usually raise them from one benchmark to another.

Price discrimination Where a firm sells the same or similar product at different prices and the difference in price cannot be fully accounted for by any differences in the costs of supply.

Price discrimination: first degree Where a firm charges each consumer for each unit the maximum price they are willing to pay for that unit.

Price discrimination: second degree Where a firm charges customers different prices for the same (or similar) product depending on the amount or time purchased.

Price discrimination: third degree Where a firm divides consumers into different groups based on some characteristic that is relatively easy to observe and acceptable to the consumer. The firm then charges a different price to consumers in different groups, but the same price to all the consumers within a group.

Price elasticity of demand ($P\varepsilon_D$) The percentage (or proportionate) change in quantity demanded divided by the percentage (or proportionate) change in price: $\%\Delta Q_D \div \%\Delta P$.

Price elasticity of demand (arc formula) ΔQ/average $Q \div \Delta P$/average P. The average in each case is the average between the two points being measured.

Price elasticity of supply The percentage (or proportionate) change in quantity supplied divided by the percentage (or proportionate) change in price: $\%\Delta Q_S \div \%\Delta P$.

Price elasticity of supply (arc formula) ΔQ_S/average $Q_S \div \Delta P$/average P.

Price maker A firm that can choose the price it charges; it faces a downward-sloping demand curve. If, however, it alters its price, this will affect the quantity sold: a fall in price will lead to more being sold; a higher price will lead to less.

Price mechanism The system in a market economy whereby changes in price in response to changes in demand and supply have the effect of making demand equal to supply.

Price taker A person or firm with no power to be able to influence the market price.

Primary labour market The market for permanent full-time core workers.

Principal–agent problem Where people (principals), as a result of lack of knowledge, cannot ensure that their best interests are served by their agents.

Principle of diminishing marginal utility As more units of a good are consumed, additional units will provide less additional satisfaction than previous units.

Prisoners' dilemma Where two or more firms (or people), by attempting independently to choose the best strategy for whatever the other(s) are likely to do, end up in a worse position than if they had co-operated in the first place.

Private efficiency Where a person's marginal benefit from a given activity equals the marginal cost.

Private limited company A company owned by its shareholders. Shareholders' liability is limited to the value of their shares. Shares can only be bought and sold privately.

Producer surplus The excess of total revenue over total cost: i.e. profit.

Product differentiation When one firm's product is sufficiently different from its rivals' to allow it to raise the price of the product without customers all switching to the rivals' products. A situation where a firm faces a downward-sloping demand curve.

Production The transformation of inputs into outputs by firms in order to earn profit (or meet some other objective).

Production possibility curve A curve showing all the possible combinations of two goods that a country can produce within a specified time period with all its resources fully and efficiently employed.

Productive efficiency A situation where firms are producing the maximum output for a given amount of inputs, or producing a given output at the least cost.

Productivity deal   When, in return for a wage increase, a union agrees to changes in working practices that will increase output per worker.

Profit (rate of)   Total profit ($T\Pi$) as a proportion of the total capital employed (K): $r = T\Pi/K$.

Profit-maximising rule   Profit is maximised where marginal revenue equals marginal cost.

Profit satisficing   Where decision makers in a firm aim for a target level of profit rather than the absolute maximum level.

Progressive tax   A tax whose average rate with respect to income rises as income rises.

Proportional tax   A tax whose average rate with respect to income stays the same as income rises.

Prudential control   The insistence by the Bank of England that banks maintain adequate liquidity.

Public good   A good or service that has the features of non-rivalry and non-excludability and as a result would not be provided by the free market.

Public limited company   A company owned by its shareholders. Shareholders' liability is limited to the value of their shares. Shares may be bought and sold publicly – on the stock exchange.

Public-sector borrowing requirement   The old name for the public-sector net cash requirement.

Public-sector debt repayment (PSDR) or Public-sector surplus   The old name for a negative public-sector net cash requirement. The (annual) surplus of the public sector, and thus the amount of debt that can be repaid.

Public-sector net borrowing   The difference between the expenditures of the public sector and its receipts from taxation and the revenues from public corporations.

Public-sector net cash requirement   The (annual) deficit of the public sector, and thus the amount that the public sector must borrow. In the UK the principal measure, which takes into account financial transactions by the public sector, is known as the public-sector net cash requirement (PSNCR).

Purchasing-power parity exchange rate   The rate of exchange of a country's currency into the US dollar that would allow a given amount of that currency to buy the same amount of goods in the USA as within the country concerned.

Pure fiscal policy   Fiscal policy that does not involve any change in money supply.

Quantitative easing   A deliberate attempt by the central bank to increase the money supply by buying large quantities of securities through open-market operations. These securities could be securitised mortgage and other private-sector debt or government bonds. It uses electronic money (reserve liabilities) created specifically for this purpose.

Quantity demanded   The amount of a good a consumer is willing and able to buy at a given price over a given period of time.

Quantity theory of money   The price level (P) is directly related to the quantity of money in the economy (M).

Quota (set by a cartel)   The output that a given member of a cartel is allowed to produce (production quota) or sell (sales quota).

Rate of economic growth   The percentage increase in output between two moments of time, typically over a 12-month period.

Rate of profit   Total profit ($T\Pi$) as a proportion of the capital employed (K): $r = T\Pi/K$.

Rational choices   Choices that involve weighing up the benefit of any activity against its opportunity cost.

Rational consumer   A person who weighs up the costs and benefits to him or her of each additional unit of a good purchased.

Rational consumer behaviour   The attempt to maximise total consumer surplus: i.e. the attempt to get as much value as possible from your money when purchasing a good. If $MU > P$, you will buy more; if $MU < P$, you will buy less (or not buy at all); if $MU = P$, you will maintain your current level of consumption.

Rational economic behaviour   Doing more of activities whose marginal benefit exceeds their marginal cost and doing less of those activities whose marginal cost exceeds their marginal benefit.

Rational expectations   Expectations based on the *current* situation. These expectations are based on the information people have to hand. Whilst this information may be imperfect and therefore people will make errors, these errors will be random.

Rational producer behaviour   When a firm weighs up the costs and benefits of alternative courses of action and then seeks to maximise its net benefit.

Rationalisation   The reorganising of production (often after a merger) so as to cut out waste and duplication and generally to reduce costs.

Rationing   Where the government restricts the amount of a good that people are allowed to buy.

Real balance effect   As the price level rises, the value of people's money assets falls. They therefore spend less in their attempt to protect the real value of their savings.

Real business cycle theory   The new classical theory that explains cyclical fluctuations in terms of shifts in aggregate supply, rather than aggregate demand.

Real GDP   GDP measured in constant prices that ruled in a chosen base year, such as 2000 or 2005. These figures *do* take account of inflation. When inflation is positive, real GDP figures will grow more slowly than nominal GDP figures.

Real growth values   Values of the rate of growth of GDP or any other variable after taking inflation into account. The real value of the growth in a variable equals its growth in money (or 'nominal') value minus the rate of inflation.

Real income   Income measured in terms of how much it can buy. If your *money* income rises by 10 per cent, but prices rise by 8 per cent, you can only buy 2 per cent more goods than before. Your *real* income has risen by 2 per cent.

Real values Money values corrected for inflation.

Real-wage unemployment Disequilibrium unemployment caused by real wages being driven up above the market-clearing level.

Recession A period where national output falls for six months or more.

Recognised banks Banks licensed by the Bank of England. All financial institutions using the word 'bank' in their title have to be recognised by the Bank of England. This requires them to have paid-up capital of at least £5 million and to meet other requirements about their asset structure and range of services.

Rediscounting bills of exchange Buying bills before they reach maturity.

Reflationary policy Fiscal or monetary policy designed to increase the rate of growth of aggregate demand.

Regional multiplier effects When a change in injections into or withdrawals from a particular region causes a multiplied change in income in that region.

Regional unemployment Structural unemployment occurring in specific regions of the country.

Regressive tax A tax whose average rate with respect to income falls as income rises.

Regulatory capture Where the regulator is persuaded to operate in the industry's interests rather than those of the consumer.

Regulatory role for government intervention Interventions by government to regulate economic activity through legally enforceable rules or actions.

Relative price The price of one good compared with another (e.g. good X is twice the price of good Y).

Repos Sale and repurchase agreements. An agreement between two financial institutions whereby one in effect borrows from another by selling it assets, agreeing to buy them back (repurchase them) at a fixed price and on a fixed date.

Restrictive practice Where two or more firms agree to adopt common practices to restrict competition.

Retail banking Branch, telephone, postal and Internet banking for individuals and businesses at published rates of interest and charges. Retail banking involves the operation of extensive branch networks.

Retail deposits and loans Deposits and loans made through bank/building society branches at published interest rates.

Retail prices index (RPI) An index of the prices of goods bought by a typical household.

Revaluation Where the government re-pegs the exchange rate at a higher level.

Reverse repos When gilts or other assets are *purchased* under a sale and repurchase agreement. They become an asset to the purchaser.

Rights issue An issue of additional shares confined to existing shareholders who have the right to buy them at a predetermined price.

Risk When an outcome may or may not occur, but its probability of occurring is known.

Risk averse A person not prepared to take a gamble even if the odds are favourable.

Risk transformation The ability of financial institutions to spread risks by having a large number of clients.

Sale and repurchase agreement (repos) An agreement between two financial institutions whereby one in effect borrows from another by selling it assets, agreeing to buy them back (repurchase them) at a fixed price and on a fixed date.

Sales revenue maximisation An alternative theory which assumes that managers aim to maximise the firm's short-run total revenue.

Scarcity The excess of human wants over what can actually be produced to fulfil these wants.

Search theory This examines people's behaviour under conditions of ignorance where it takes time to search for information.

Seasonal unemployment Unemployment associated with industries or regions where the demand for labour is lower at certain times of the year.

Second-degree price discrimination Where a firm charges customers different prices for the same (or similar) product depending on the amount or time purchased.

Secondary action Industrial action taken against a company not directly involved in a dispute (e.g. a supplier of raw materials to a firm whose employees are on strike).

Secondary labour market The market for peripheral workers, usually employed on a temporary or part-time basis, or a less secure 'permanent' basis.

Secondary marketing Where assets are sold before maturity to another institution or individual.

Securitisation Where future cash flows (e.g. from interest rate or mortgage payments) are turned into marketable securities, such as bonds.

Self-fulfilling speculation The actions of speculators tend to cause the very effect that they had anticipated.

Set-aside A system in the EU of paying farmers not to use a certain proportion of their land.

Short run (in production) The period of time over which at least one factor is fixed.

Short-run shut-down point This is where the AR curve is tangential to the AVC curve. The firm can only just cover its variable costs. Any fall in revenue below this level will cause a profit-maximising firm to shut down immediately.

Short run under perfect competition The period during which there is too little time for new firms to enter the industry.

Short selling (or shorting) Where investors borrow an asset, such as shares or foreign currency; sell the asset, hoping the price will soon fall; then buy it back later and return it to the lender. Assuming the price has fallen, the short seller will make a profit of the difference (minus any fees).

Sight deposits Deposits that can be withdrawn on demand without penalty.

Size distribution of income Measurement of the distribution of income according to the levels of income received by individuals (irrespective of source).

Social benefit Private benefit plus externalities in consumption.

Social cost Private cost plus externalities in production.

Social efficiency Production and consumption at the point where marginal social benefit equals marginal social cost ($MSB = MSC$).

Solow growth model A model which explains economic growth in terms of the effects on the capital stock and output of a change in investment.

Special deposits A system used up to 1980. Deposits that the banks could be required to make in the Bank of England. They remained frozen there until the Bank of England chose to release them.

Special purpose vehicle (SPV) Legal entities created by financial institutions for conducting specific financial functions, such as bundling assets together into fixed-interest bonds and selling them.

Specialisation and division of labour Where production is broken down into a number of simpler, more specialised tasks, thus allowing workers to acquire a high degree of efficiency.

Specific tax A tax on a good levied at a fixed amount per unit of the good, irrespective of the price of that unit.

Speculation Where people make buying or selling decisions based on their anticipations of future prices.

Speculators People who buy (or sell) commodities or financial assets with the intention of profiting by selling them (or buying them back) at a later date at a higher (lower) price.

Spot price The current market price.

Stabilising speculation Where the actions of speculators tend to reduce price fluctuations.

Stakeholders (in a company) People who are affected by a company's activities and/or performance (customers, employees, owners, creditors, people living in the neighbourhood, etc.). They may or may not be in a position to take decisions, or influence decision taking, in the firm.

Standardised unemployment rate The measure of the unemployment rate used by the ILO and OECD. The unemployed are defined as persons of working age who are without work, available to start work within two weeks and either have actively looked for work in the last four weeks or are waiting to take up an appointment.

Steady-state national income The long-run equilibrium level of national income. The level at which all investment is used to maintain the existing capital stock at its current level.

Strategic trade theory The theory that protecting/supporting certain industries can enable them to compete more effectively with large monopolistic rivals abroad.

The effect of the protection is to increase long-run competition and may enable the protected firms to exploit a comparative advantage that they could not have done otherwise.

Structural deficit (or surplus) The public-sector deficit (or surplus) that would occur if the economy were operating at the potential level of national income: i.e. one where there is a zero output gap.

Structural unemployment Unemployment that arises from changes in the pattern of demand or supply in the economy. People made redundant in one part of the economy cannot immediately take up jobs in other parts (even though there are vacancies).

Sub-prime debt Debt where there is a high risk of default by the borrower (e.g. mortgage holders who are on low incomes facing higher interest rates and falling house prices).

Substitute goods A pair of goods that are considered by consumers to be alternatives to each other. As the price of one goes up, the demand for the other rises.

Substitutes in supply These are two goods where an increased production of one means diverting resources away from producing the other.

Substitution effect of a price change The effect of a change in price on quantity demanded arising from the consumer switching to or from alternative (substitute) products.

Substitution effect of a rise in wage rates Workers will tend to substitute income for leisure as leisure now has a higher opportunity cost. This effect leads to *more* hours being worked as wage rates rise.

Substitution effect of a tax rise Tax increases reduce the opportunity cost of leisure and thus encourage people to work less.

Sunk costs Costs that cannot be recouped (e.g. by transferring assets to other uses).

Supernormal profit (also known as **pure profit**, **economic profit**, **abnormal profit**, or simply **profit**) The excess of total profit above normal profit.

Supply curve A graph showing the relationship between the price of a good and the quantity of the good supplied over a given period of time.

Supply schedule A table showing the different quantities of a good that producers are willing and able to supply at various prices over a given time period. A supply schedule can be for an individual producer or group of producers, or for all producers (the market supply schedule).

Supply-side economics An approach that focuses directly on aggregate supply and how to shift the aggregate supply curve outwards.

Supply-side policy Government policy that attempts to alter the level of aggregate supply directly (rather than through changes in aggregate demand).

Sustainability (environmental) The ability of the environment to survive its use for economic activity.

Sustainable output The level of national output corresponding to no excess or deficiency of aggregate demand.

Tacit collusion Where oligopolists take care not to engage in price cutting, excessive advertising or other forms of competition. There may be unwritten 'rules' of collusive behaviour such as price leadership.

Takeover bid Where one firm attempts to purchase another by offering to buy the shares of that company from its shareholders.

Tariff escalation The system whereby tariff rates increase the closer a product is to the finished stage of production.

Tariffs (or import levies) Taxes on imported products: i.e. customs duties.

Tax allowance An amount of income that can be earned tax-free. Tax allowances vary according to a person's circumstances.

Taylor rule A rule adopted by a central bank for setting the rate of interest. It will raise the interest rate if (a) inflation is above target or (b) real national income is above the sustainable level (or unemployment is below the equilibrium rate). The rule states how much interest rates will be changed in each case.

Technological unemployment Structural unemployment that occurs as a result of the introduction of labour-saving technology.

Terms of trade The price index of exports divided by the price index of imports and then expressed as a percentage. This means that the terms of trade will be 100 in the base year.

Third-degree price discrimination Where a firm divides consumers into different groups based on some characteristic that is relatively easy to observe and acceptable to the consumer. The firm then charges a different price to consumers in different groups, but the same price to all the consumers within a group.

Time deposits Deposits that require notice of withdrawal or where a penalty is charged for withdrawals on demand.

Total consumer expenditure on a product (TE) (per period of time) The price of the product multiplied by the quantity purchased: $TE = P \times Q$.

Total consumer surplus The excess of a person's total utility from the consumption of a good (TU) over the amount that person spends on it (TE): $TCS = TU - TE$.

Total cost The sum of total fixed costs and total variable costs: $TC = TFC + TVC$.

Total physical product The total output of a product per period of time that is obtained from a given amount of inputs.

Total (private) surplus Total consumer surplus ($TU - TE$) plus total producer surplus ($TR - TVC$).

Total producer surplus (TPS) Total revenue minus total variable cost ($TR - TVC$): in other words, total profit plus total fixed cost ($T\Pi + TFC$).

Total revenue (TR) (per period of time) The total amount received by firms from the sale of a product, before the deduction of taxes or any other costs. The price multiplied by the quantity sold: $TR = P + Q$.

Total social surplus Total benefits to society from consuming a good minus total costs to society from producing it. In the absence of externalities, total social surplus is the same as total (private) surplus.

Total utility The total satisfaction a consumer gets from the consumption of all the units of a good consumed within a given time period.

Tradable permits Each firm is given a permit to produce a given level of pollution. If less than the permitted amount is produced, the firm is given a credit. This can then be sold to another firm, allowing it to exceed its original limit.

Trade creation Where a customs union leads to greater specialisation according to comparative advantage and thus a shift in production from higher-cost to lower-cost sources.

Trade cycle or business cycle The periodic fluctuations of national output round its long-term trend.

Trade diversion Where a customs union diverts consumption from goods produced at a lower cost outside the union to goods produced at a higher cost (but tariff free) within the union.

Traditional theory of the firm The analysis of pricing and output decisions of the firm under various market conditions, assuming that the firm wishes to maximise profit.

Transfer payments Moneys transferred from one person or group to another (e.g. from the government to individuals) without production taking place.

Transmission mechanism The process by which a change in a policy instrument (such as interest rates or taxation) affects economic outcomes (such as inflation or unemployment).

Treasury bills Bills of exchange issued by the Bank of England on behalf of the government. They are a means whereby the government raises short-term finance.

Uncertainty When an outcome may or may not occur and its probability of occurring is not known.

Underemployment When people work fewer hours than they would like at their current wage rate. *International Labour Organization (ILO) definition*: a situation where people currently working less than 'full-time' (40 hours in the UK) would like to work more hours (at current wage rates), either by working more hours in their current job, or by switching to an alternative job with more hours or by taking on an additional part-time job or any combination of the three. *Eurostat definition*: where people working less than 40 hours per week would like to work more hours in their current job at current wage rates.

Underground markets Where people ignore the government's price and/or quantity controls and sell illegally at whatever price equates illegal demand and supply.

Unemployed (economist's definition) Those of working age who are without work, but who are available for work at current wage rates.

Unemployment rate The number unemployed expressed as a percentage of the labour force.

Unit elastic demand   Where quantity demanded changes by the same percentage as price. Ignoring the negative sign, it will have a value equal to 1.

Universal benefits   Benefits paid to everyone in a certain category irrespective of their income or assets.

Value added tax (VAT)   A tax on goods and services, charged at each stage of production as a percentage of the value added at that stage.

Variable costs   Total costs that vary with the amount of output produced.

Variable factor   An input that can be increased in supply within a given time period.

Velocity of circulation   The number of times annually that money on average is spent on goods and services that make up GDP.

Vent for surplus   When international trade enables a country to exploit resources that would otherwise be unused.

Vertical integration   A business growth strategy that involves expanding within an existing market, but at a different stage of production. Vertical integration can be 'forward', such as moving into distribution or retail, or 'backward', such as expanding into extracting raw materials or producing components.

Wage–price spiral   Wages and prices chasing each other as the aggregate demand curve continually shifts to the right and the aggregate supply curve continually shifts upwards.

Wage taker   An employer (or employee) who is unable to influence the wage rate.

Weighted average   The average of several items, where each item is ascribed a weight according to its importance. The weights must add up to 1.

Wholesale banks   Banks specialising in large-scale deposits and loans and dealing mainly with companies. Interest rates and charges may be negotiable.

Wholesale deposits and loans   Large-scale deposits and loans made by and to firms at negotiated interest rates.

Wide monetary base (M0)   Notes and coin outside the central bank plus banks' operational deposits with the central bank.

Withdrawals (W) (or leakages)   Incomes of households or firms that are not passed on round the inner flow. Withdrawals equal net saving (S) plus net taxes (T) plus expenditure on imports (M): $W = S + T + M$.

Working to rule   Workers do the bare minimum they have to, as set out in their job descriptions.

Index